K

3 x 22 (09)

A dirty, trifling, piece of business

VOLUME I:
THE REVOLUTIONARY WAR AS WAGED FROM CANADA IN 1781

Canada Indians hunting waterfowl from a canoe.

A dirty, trifling, piece of business

VOLUME I:
THE REVOLUTIONARY WAR AS WAGED FROM CANADA IN 1781

Gavin K. Watt

with the research assistance of James F. Morrison and William A. Smy

DUNDURN PRESS
TORONTO

Editor: Shannon Whibbs
Designer: Courtney Horner
Printer: Friesens

Library and Archives Canada Cataloguing in Publication

Watt, Gavin K
     A dirty, trifling piece of business / written by Gavin
K. Watt ; research assistance by James F. Morrison and
William A. Smy.

 Includes bibliographical references and index.
Contents: v. 1. The revolutionary war as waged in
Canada in 1781.

     1. Canada--History--1775-1783. 2. United States--History--
Revolution, 1775-1783. 3. Haldimand, Frederick, Sir, 1718-1791.
I. Morrison, James F. II. Smy, William A. III. Title.

FC420.W38 2009   971.02'4   C2009-900010-5

1   2   3   4   5   13   12   11   10   09

Conseil des Arts du Canada   Canada Council for the Arts   Canadä   ONTARIO ARTS COUNCIL CONSEIL DES ARTS DE L'ONTARIO

We acknowledge the support of the **Canada Council for the Arts** and the **Ontario Arts Council** for our publishing program. We also acknowledge the financial support of the **Government of Canada** through the **Book Publishing Industry Development Program** and **The Association for the Export of Canadian Books**, and the **Government of Ontario** through the **Ontario Book Publishers Tax Credit** program and the **Ontario Media Development Corporation**.

Care has been taken to trace the ownership of copyright material used in this book. The author and the publisher welcome any information enabling them to rectify any references or credits in subsequent editions.

J. Kirk Howard, President

Printed and bound in Canada   MAY 1 4 2009

www.dundurn.com

Dundurn Press
3 Church Street, Suite 500
Toronto, Ontario, Canada
M5E 1M2

Gazelle Book Services Limited
White Cross Mills
High Town, Lancaster, England
LA1 4XS

Dundurn Press
2250 Military Road
Tonawanda, NY U.S.A.
14150

For Nancy E. Watt

My silent editor and greatest supporter

CONTENTS

List of Maps and Plans | *9*

Introduction and Acknowledgements | *11*

List of Abbreviations | *14*

A Cast of the More Important Persons | *16*

The Flood of Raids, Scouts, and Abduction Attempts of 1781 | *19*

1. The Governor of a Strategic Backwater | *21*

2. The Background to the 1781 Campaign | *38*
   A Plan of Attack Upon Quebec

3. Winter Turmoil on the Western Frontier | *68*
   Driven to the Last Extremity

4. Spring: The Calamities of the Country | *94*
   Ravages of a Barbarous & Ruthless Savage Enemy

5. A Bloody Early Summer on the Frontiers | *165*
    A Long Train of Horrid Villainy

6. Constantly Infested with Parties of the Enemy | *238*
    I Shou'd Hope to Give a Good Account of Him

7. The Hammers Fall | *307*
    Comparative Chronology: Ross and St. Leger
    They Broke and Fled with Precipitation
    They Cannot Have the Least Hope of Success

    Appendices | *403*
    Notes | *410*
    Bibliography | *471*
    Index | *494*

LIST OF MAPS AND PLANS

Haldimand's Responsibilities 31

The Republic of Vermont and Unions of 1781 41

Montreal and St. John's Military Districts 63

Plan of Fort St. John's 74

Settlements in Vermont's Western Union and Along the
    Hudson River south to Kingston 79

Plan of Schenectady 141

The Schoharie Valley and Adjacent Settlements 148

Mid-Mohawk Valley Showing Tryon's Four Districts and
    the Edge of Albany County 172

Plan of the Fort and Settlment of Kahnawake (a.k.a.
    Caghnawaga or Sault St. Louis) 217

The Raid Deep into Ulster County 253

Plan of Fort Haldimand, Carleton Island 263

Scenes of Action: Fall 1781 301

Ross's Inbound and Outbound Routes 325

Ticonderoga and Environs 381

*T*his book is intended to appeal to students of the American Revolution in Canada and the northern United States. The text will be enjoyed by those with a good knowledge of the reasons for, and the progress of, the war, as well as the primary personalities involved and the various organizations that fought in the conflict. Only a few of the participants receive personality development, on the assumption that readers will already know of such personages as Molly and Joseph Brant, Philip Schuyler, John Butler, and Sir John Johnson.

One of the more serious criticisms of my book, *Burning of the Valleys*, which told the tales of the four raids mounted from Canada against New York's frontiers in 1780, was my failure to describe what occurred the following year. It was implied that I was hiding something; that I had failed to admit that the Crown Forces had enjoyed their "last hurrah" in the fall of 1780 and that, when the defence of the Mohawk region was placed under Marinus Willett's command in 1781, the loyal Natives, Tories, and Regulars were thwarted in all of their designs and raiding virtually ceased. There was no more destruction of farms, crops, and livestock; there were no more captures or killings and life almost returned to normal, indicating that by 1781, the United States had won the war in the north. Another suggestion was that just maybe I had remained mum about 1781 because I had plans for a second book that would reveal all. This was correct.

This volume is a departure from my earlier works, as it is significantly wider in scope and covers a full campaign season.

Once again, Jim Morrison of Gloversville, New York, has freely provided immense amounts of research material in packages sent north through the mail, his pensions website and in his many published works.

Butler's Rangers expert, Bill Smy of St. Catharines, Ontario, has assembled a superb collection of archival transcripts and provided me with copies that have proven invaluable, as have his several publications.

Just as I was finishing the text, I was in touch with Ken Johnson of Fort Plain, New York, and stumbled into the contentious issue of the forts' names and locations. After much back-and-forth dialogue, Ken convinced me that by 1781 Fort Plank had been renamed Fort Plain and that Fort Rensselaer lay three miles to the east. Ken also helped me by locating the many smaller forts and other key features in the Mohawk Valley.

Drew Smith first brought the Hanau Jägers's papers to my attention. Justin Boggess expanded the search in various archives and provided wonderful details of St. Leger's 1781 adventure on Lake Champlain.

Jeff O'Connor, the Schoharie Valley historian, again provided me with details of events, personalities, and forts.

Neil Goodwin, a Vermont historian, assisted with the perambulations of the Haldimand negotiations.

My friend, John A. Houlding, far off in Germany, traced the careers of many of the Regular officers in this account.

Christopher Fox of Fort Ticonderoga provided a superb map of that installation. Hugh McMillan gave me copies of a wonderful study of the intrepid Walter Sutherland's career as a British intelligence agent. Margaret Gordon sent details of that naughty fellow, Jacob Klock Jr., and Wilson Brown revealed William Marsh's Secret Service role.

Chris Armstrong provided yeoman service in the design and research of the book cover and assisting with many of the illustrations.

My thanks to Christian Cameron, who suggested the path that this book should follow.

Lastly, to my daughter Nancy, who corrected my syntax and massaged my narrative.

Of course, all misinterpretations or errors may be laid at the feet of the author.

Gavin. K. Watt, Museum of Applied Military History
King City, Ontario, Canada, 2008

LIST OF ABBREVIATIONS

1/84RHE	1st Battalion, 84th Royal Highland Emigrants
1CDN	1st Canadian Regiment, Continental Line
1KRR	1st Battalion, King's Royal Regiment of New York
2KRR	2nd Battalion, King's Royal Regiment of New York
1NH	1st New Hampshire Continental Line
1NY	1st New York Continental Line
2/60RA	2nd Battalion, 60th Regiment, Royal Americans
2-I-C	Second-in-Command
2KR	2nd, King's Rangers
6NID	Six Nations' Indian Department
ACM	Albany County Militia
2ACM	2nd Albany County Militia Regiment
13ACM	13th Albany County Militia Regiment
16ACM	16th Albany County Militia Regiment
AR	Adams's Rangers
AV	American Volunteers
BR	Butler's Rangers
BV	Brant's Volunteers
C-in-C	Commander-in-Chief
CO	Commanding officer
DQMG	Deputy Quartermaster General
GO	General Orders
HQ	Headquarters

KLA	King's Loyal Americans
LID	Leake's Independent Company
LV	Loyal Volunteers
OC	Officer Commanding
Pdr	Pounder (weight of solid shot capable of being fired from a gun)
QID	Quebec Indian Department
QLR	Queen's Loyal Rangers
QM	Quartermaster
QMG	Quartermaster General
RA	Royal Americans
RHE	Royal Highland Emigrants
RO	Regimental Orders
RN	Royal Navy
TCM	Tryon County Militia
2TCM	Second Tryon County Militia Regiment
3TCM	Third Tryon County Militia Regiment
UCM	Ulster County Militia
WL	Willett's Levies

A CAST OF THE MORE IMPORTANT PERSONS

Loyalist

Anderson, Joseph	Captain, 1KRR
Bettys, Joseph	Notorious Loyalist Secret Service agent
Brant, Joseph	Mohawk war captain, BV/captain 6NID
Butler, John	Deputy superintendent, 6NID; lieutenant-colonel, BR
Butler, Walter	Captain, 2-I-C, BR/killed on Ross raid
Caldwell, William	Captain, BR/led raid to Monbackers
Campbell, John	Lieutenant-Colonel, QID
Carleton, Guy	General/past governor, Quebec
Chambers, William	RN commodore, Lake Champlain
Claus, Daniel	Senior deputy superintendent, 6NID
Clinton, Sir Henry	General, C-in-C British Forces America
Clossen, Caleb	Daring Secret Service agent
Crawford, William Redford	Captain 2KRR/formerly with QID
Crysler, Adam Valley	Lieutenant, 6NID/scourge of Schoharie
Deserontyon, John	Senior Fort Hunter Mohawk war captain
Docksteder, John	Lieutenant, 6NID/led raid on Currytown
Gray, James	Major-Commandant, 1KRR
Haldimand, Frederick	Governor of Canada
Hill, David Karaghgunty	Fort Hunter Mohawk war captain
Jessup, Edward	Major, KLA
Johnson, Guy	Colonel/superintendent, 6NID
Johnson, Sir John	Lieutenant-Colonel, KRR NY/previous OC, Secret Service

Maclean, Allan	Brigadier-General, Montreal Military District
Mathews, Robert	Captain, 8th/Haldimand's military secretary
Meyers, John/Johan Walden	Captain/Secret Service agent
Munro, John	Second senior captain, 1KRR
Peters, John	Lieutenant-Colonel, QLR
Powell, Henry Watson	Brigadier-General/OC Niagara District
Pritchard, Azariah	Captain, 2KR/active Secret Service agent
Robertson, Daniel	Captain, 84RHE/OC Oswegatchie
Rogers, James	Major-Commandant, 2KR
Ross, John	Major-Commandant, 2KRR
St. Leger, Barry	Lieutenant-Colonel, 34th/OC St. John's Military District
Sherwood, Justus	Captain, QLR/later OC Secret Service
Smyth, Dr. George	Spy in Albany/deputy OC, Secret Service
Sommer, William	Renegade Tory from New Dorlach
Stuart, John	Anglican priest/agent in Schenectady
Von Kreutzbourg, Carl	Lieutenant-Colonel, Hanau Jägers

Rebel

Allen, Ethan	Founder, Green Mountain Boys/key member, Vermont Council
Allen, Ira	Ethan's brother/colonel/key member, Vermont Council
Bayley, Jacob	Militia Brigadier-General, Cöos/opposes Allens
Chittenden, Thomas	Governor, Vermont
Clinton, George	Governor, New York State
Clinton, James	Brigadier-General, NY Continental Line
Cochran, Robert	Lieutenant-Colonel, 2-I-C, Second New York Continental Line
Colonel Louis Atayataghronghta	Kahnawake/lieutenant-colonel/war chief of the rebel Natives
Dunham, Holtham	Captain, WL/traitor
Fay, Joseph	Major, negotiator, VT talks
Finck, Andrew	Brigade Major, WL/Tryon Conspiracy commissioner

Gansevoort, Peter	Brigadier-General, 1st Brigade, ACM
Gros, Johann Daniel	Chaplain, WL/from Tryon County
Gros, Lawrence	Captain, WL/from Tryon County/Johann's brother
Heath, William	Continental major-general/replaced Washington in the North mid-1781
Johnson, Thomas	Militia lieutenant-colonel, Cöos/later double agent
Klock, Jacob	Colonel, 2TCM; OC Tryon Militia Brigade
Klock, Jacob J.	Son of Colonel Klock/ex-ensign, 1NY/traitor
Moodie, Andrew	Captain, Lamb's Artillery/served with WL in Mohawk Valley
Paine, Brinton	Former lieutenant-colonel, Dubois's Levies 1780/13ACM, Saratoga District
Sammons, Jacob	Very active lieutenant of Gros's Coy, WL
Schuyler, Philip	Major-General, Indian Affairs commissioner, Northern Department
Stark, John	Major-General/OC Northern Frontiers
Stirling, Lord (William Alexander)	Major-General/Washington's confidant
Van Cortlandt, Philip	Colonel, 2nd NY
Van Rensselaer, Robert	Brigadier-General, OC, 2ACM
Vrooman, Peter	Colonel, 15ACM/OC Schoharie Valley
Washington, George	General, C-in-C Allied Forces
Weissenfels, Frederick	Lieutenant-Colonel, Weissenfels's Levies
Willett, Marinus	Lieutenant-Colonel, WL/OC Northwest Frontiers
Woodworth, Solomon	Captain, WL Rangers
Younglove, John	Second Major, 16ACM/Committee of Sequestration, Albany County

THE FLOOD OF RAIDS, SCOUTS, AND ABDUCTION ATTEMPTS OF 1781

This list contains only the more noteworthy events.

Early February	Raid at Fort Davis, NY.
March 2	Raid at Fort Stanwix, NY.
March 6	Abduction in Cöos District, NY.
Early April	Abductions at Coxsackie, NY.
April 24	Raid along Bowman's Creek and Cherry Valley, NY.
Mid-May	Raid at Fort Clyde, NY.
May 26	Raid at Walradt's ferry.
Late May	Raid on Fort House, NY.
Early June	Raid in Schoharie Valley, NY.
June 5	Raid at Johnstown, NY.
June 13	Abductions at Ballstown, NY.
June 24	Raid near Fort Dayton, NY.
June 26	Raids at Forts Timmerman and Windecker, NY.
Early July	Raid along Connecticut River, NH.
Early July	Raid near Canajoharie, NY.
July 6	Raid at Steele's Creek, NY.
July 9	Raid at Currytown, NY.
July 10	New Dorlach Swamp Battle, NY.
July 18	Raid near Upper Indian Castle, NY.
Mid-July	Raid near Fort Paris, NY.
July 26	Raid in Palatine District, NY.

July 28	Bettys's abduction attempt aborted.
July 29	Skirmish at Lampman's Farm, NY.
July 30	Abduction attempt aborted near Saratoga, NY.
End July	British scouts captured near Saratoga, NY.
August 5	Raid near Fort Walradt, NY.
August 6	Howard's abduction attempt fails.
August 7	Meyers's abduction attempt fails.
August 12	Raid strikes Warwarsink, Nipenack, Monbackers.
August 14	Raid at Fort Timmerman, NY.
August 26	Raid on Bowman's Creek and in Cobleskill, NY.
September 1	Raid at Beaver Dam.
September 6	Raid destroys Willett's ranging company.
Mid-September	Raid along Hazen Road, VT.
Mid-September	Raid at German Flatts, NY.
End September	Raids at Fort Plain, Fall Hill, and in Palatine District, NY.
End September	Raid destroys crops in VT.
Early October	Raids at Forts Stanwix, Timmerman, and Rensselaer, NY.
October 7	Scouts alarm Fort Johnstown, NY.

*See Chapter 7 for a comparative chronology
of the Ross and St. Leger expeditions.*

1

THE GOVERNOR OF A STRATEGIC BACKWATER

*A*s 1780 drew to a close, Captain-General Frederick Haldimand, the civil and military governor of Quebec, had no illusions about his province's role in the American rebellion. Britain's current focus was to hold tight to New York City and pacify the southern colonies, which made Quebec a strategic backwater. Britain's ancient enemies, France and Spain, were in full and active support of the American rebels and sought every chance to profit from British distress. The Dutch had aided the rebels since 1777, and by this sixth year of the war the conflict had spread around the world, even to Britain's shores. The Empire's assets were stretched so thin that Haldimand could scarcely expect the means to maintain his position. Yet, Quebec was the newest American colony, rich in natural resources and providing a critical base for military operations with water routes that led deep into the continent. Haldimand's primary task was to defend the province and, secondarily, to assist the armies below by alarming the northern frontiers, drawing off and tying down rebel troops, and raiding their food production. Any measure that diverted rebel attention from the southern theatre would assist the British cause.[1]

How did Frederick Haldimand rise to such a critical responsibility? Born the second of four Franco-Swiss sons in 1718, he was only fifteen when he chose a military career. Details of his education are unknown, but judging from his superbly written, voluminous correspondence, he had been well educated. His earliest service was with the States General of Holland and then with the king of Sardinia. By 1740, he was in Prussia serving under

Captain-General Frederick Haldimand (1718–1791).

Frederick the Great, in whose service he saw action in three major battles and most likely when he became proficient in German. By 1748, he was a first lieutenant in a corps of Swiss Guards in Holland and, by the early 1750s, he was a Guards' captain-commandant, a rank equivalent to an army lieutenant-colonel.

In 1755, Britain established the Royal Americans, a regiment intended for colonial defence. Many foreign officers were recruited under the restriction of only holding command in America and forty of them landed at New York City in 1756, amongst them, Frederick Haldimand.

Haldimand had been unaware of the British xenophobia and had not foreseen the obstacles he and his fellows would confront in their early duties, but his positive personality overcame these problems, although his doubts lingered. He had only a slight use of English, which continued during his service, yet he thrived and advanced rapidly in an army where everyone of note spoke and wrote in French. His record of achievement indicates tremendous energy, an agile mind, and a superior intellect.

Lieutenant-Colonel Haldimand's battalion was sent to Philadelphia, where he observed first-hand the colonists' independent spirit. He was thoroughly unimpressed with their complaints and thought the taxes levied for defence were "so trifling that they do not deserve the name." After experiencing little success recruiting in Pennsylvania, he went to New York, Georgia, and the Carolinas, where he found widespread shock over the failure of Braddock's expedition. Now the frontiers were demanding protection from the very army they had recently spurned. His travels exposed him to America's vastness, its limited road network, and its reliance on waterways for communication. Campaigning in America would be unlike Europe and he readily absorbed these lessons and exhibited a great aptitude for adaptation. His biographer, Jean McIlwraith, wrote:

[He was] already highly esteemed by [his] seniors, as
well as the juniors … and never wanted for warm friends
in [his] own profession. [He] had the thorough German
genius for details, and it ere long became known that
any programme entrusted to [him] would be faithfully
carried out.

Haldimand was a tall, spare man. His portrait in middle age emphasizes
a high, square forehead, swept-back natural hair and quietly intense,
intelligent eyes under heavy, dark eyebrows. His mouth is set in a quiet,
friendly smile, which seems often reflected in the humour of his lively,
thoughtful correspondence with his many friends. Although he never
married, his courtly demeanour and social affability made him popular
with the ladies, whose company he appreciated and with whom he enjoyed
exchanging gifts of seeds, plants, preserves, and fruit. He took an intense
interest in his nephews, bringing them to America for a solid grounding in
the military and making financial provisions for their later life.[2]

In January 1758, he was promoted to colonel and, when Abercrombie
arrived as the new C-in-C America, he asked Haldimand to join the
Lake Champlain expedition. By June, he was at Saratoga organizing the
movement of provisions and directing Provincials to build a blockhouse,
which was perhaps his first command of colonial troops. Haldimand was
given the honour of commanding the massed grenadier battalion for the
failed Ticonderoga attack. Over the following winter, he commanded
Fort Edward, an isolated post on the edge of New York's frontier, where
he settled disputes between his Regulars and Provincial rangers. He
found colonials "as touchy as Indians" and, as there were too few of them
to perform scouting duties, he had 200 Regulars learn ranging skills. At
this time, he developed a close, personal relationship with his superior,
General Thomas Gage, who was stationed nearby at Albany.

In 1759, Haldimand's battalion joined a 5,000-man expedition of
Regulars and Provincials to reduce Fort Niagara. As the expedition's
second-in-command (2-I-C), he was detached with 600 men to
rebuild Oswego, while the rest of the army laid siege to Niagara. With
due caution, he barricaded his camp with barrels of provisions in case

of French attack. Consequently, his men were prepared when 1,000 Regulars, Canadiens, and Indians struck, and, although badly dispersed, they stood firm. When the French assaulted next morning, his cleverly concealed guns and brisk musketry drove them off. Upon hearing of the army commander's death, he went to Niagara to take command as senior Regular officer, but the fort had already fallen and Sir William Johnson, the superintendent general of Northern Indians, had assumed the role. Unwilling to make a fuss, Haldimand returned to Oswego. For the final thrust, Jeffery Amherst, C-in-C America, chose to attack down the St. Lawrence River, supported by forces from Quebec City and on Lake Champlain. Upon his arrival at Oswego, Amherst praised Haldimand's expert reconstruction of Fort Ontario and gave him command of the massed Grenadiers and Light Infantry and a battalion of Highlanders. His brigade participated in the reduction of Fort de Lévis and, a few days later, the army entered Montreal. After surrender terms were agreed upon, Amherst demonstrated his confidence in Haldimand's judgment and tact by giving him several delicate tasks. He was to take possession of the city's main gate and receive the formal surrender of Quebec's governor; then march the Grenadiers, Lights, and a twelve-pounder (12-pdr) into the city and, according to custom, demand the restoration of all British colours taken during the war and the surrender of the French standards. Finally, he was to oversee the embarkation of the French officers for their return to France.

After the peace, Haldimand remained in Montreal under Gage's command. For the first four years, Quebec was governed by martial law; however, the three regional governors at Montreal, Quebec, and Three Rivers, were conciliatory men who prevented abuse of the Canadiens by the soldiery or by the anglophone adventurers who had filled the vacuum left by the departed civil and commercial administrators. In 1762, he was promoted to colonel in the army and, when Parliament passed an act to naturalize all foreign officers who had served faithfully during the Seven Years' War, he became a British citizen.

He gained invaluable civil administration experience when he was appointed governor of Three Rivers (Trois-Rivières] District, which was populated by 6,600 Canadiens and 500 Abenakis at Bécancour and

St. Francis (Saint-François). He divided his government into four sub-districts in which Canadien militia captains officiated over civil cases according to the long-established laws of the country. Serious crimes, such as theft and murder, were tried by court martial. He initiated a great many long-overdue improvements such as fire prevention, the widening, ditching, and crowning of the highways between Quebec and Montreal, and the rebuilding of the St. Maurice iron mines, smelters, and forges — one of the province's few industries. He was at his energetic best when there were challenging tasks to perform and he saw the iron mines as an important supplier to the Royal Navy. By his fourth month of management, the works had a large inventory of pig iron bars. This feat required a personal investment, puzzling the Canadiens, who had a narrow perspective regarding commerce and a strongly parochial outlook. They were also extremely litigious and he encouraged them to settle issues by arbitration. The most difficult citizens were the holders of the Croix de St. Louis medal, some of whom had returned from exile in France because of their indifferent treatment there. Frequently poor, these proud men tended to live on their past glories in the *petit guerre*. Of course, an understanding and considerate British officer who spoke French as his first language was up to this challenge.[3] Although Haldimand's eye was on iron and timber for naval supplies, he saw that the fur trade involved the majority of the inhabitants and was the most important local industry. He stopped greedy traders from intercepting the Natives carrying their peltry to Three Rivers and organized a market where townsfolk and Indians received fair treatment and a proper distribution of ammunition and liquor. When the Pontiac Uprising broke out in the far west, there was unrest amongst the Abenakis and he visited their villages to calm them. The revolt spread and several posts fell and the governor raised Canadien troops to send west with a body of Regulars to convince the western nations that the French regime had ended. Only Haldimand was successful in meeting and exceeding his quota of troops. As predicted, when the Indians saw Canadiens in the company of British troops, they accepted that France had been defeated and the rebellion sputtered out. When martial law ended in Quebec, British government and laws were imposed, much to the Canadiens' displeasure, as they saw immigrants gaining control of commerce and government. Just as the first disturbances broke out, the newly promoted Brigadier Haldimand was sent to England in poor health.

In 1767, Haldimand was appointed governor of southern Florida, although he would have preferred a more northern clime. In characteristic fashion, he thoroughly researched his new posting prior to sailing. The colony's population was more diverse than Quebec's with a mixture of Spanish, American, French, Acadian, and Native peoples. It stretched from the Atlantic west to the Mississippi and bordered on Louisiana, where Spain governed a restive French population. His civil counterpart was a difficult, temperamental individual who acted as if he commanded the troops, which made his task much more difficult. The main fortification was in terrible condition and the garrison very sickly. Haldimand took immediate action; sinking new wells; building a hospital; draining swamp water; changing the troops' diet from salt provisions to poultry and fish and planting herbs, vegetables, and grains. Within the year, his men were as healthy as any garrison on the continent. He had earlier initiated gardens at Niagara and Oswego and continued this practice in all his later assignments; perhaps his grasp of the nutritional and medicinal value of plants had been a product of his Swiss upbringing.

After spending six frustrating years in Florida, he was promoted to major-general and appointed colonel-commandant of 2/60RA, which helped his chronic financial prob-lems. When Thomas Gage, C-in-C America, was allowed a leave of absence to England, he recommended Haldimand as his successor. After a debate about giving a foreign-born officer such a critical role, the king and ministry approved and, in June 1773, the fifty-five-year-old Haldimand came ashore at New York City to a salute of seventeen guns. He had thought Florida difficult, but soon found New York more complex and dangerous. That Americans could be in such an uproar over an insignificant tea tax was beyond his understanding. In his opinion, their standard of living was well above Europeans and, once again, he was appalled that, like spoiled, ignorant children, they ignored their responsibility to fund their own security. Six months after taking supreme command, a Boston mob seized three East India Company vessels and destroyed an immense quantity of tea. Many New York officials and businessmen prompted him to take action, but he prudently chose not to employ the army to enforce an act of parliament and waited for a call from the civil power. Crown officials debated various punishments for this vandalism. Haldimand recommended against the most draconian of these, the closure of the port of Boston; however other views prevailed. As he had foreseen, colonies that had originally deplored the incident were drawn into sympathy with Massachusetts and unrest deepened.

Although there had been no strong feelings against tea importation in New York City, the ministry's overreaction stimulated resistance. Haldimand went about his business in his usual calm, elegant, self-assured manner while quietly arranging for military stores and artillery to be moved to more secure locations; however, when the much-delayed tea arrived at New York, the citizens prevented its landing.

Haldimand had witnessed strife between military and civil authorities in Quebec and personally suffered poor relations with civil governors in Florida, so he took special care to develop a rapport with William Tryon, New York's vain and stubborn royal governor. An issue that came close to causing a serious breech was his refusal to send troops against the "rioters" in the New Hampshire Grants of northeast New York. He wrote:

> [I]t appears to me of a dangerous tendency to employ Regular Troops where there are Militia Laws and where the Civil Magistrate can at any time call upon its trained inhabitants to aid and assist them ... the idea that a few lawless Vagabonds can prevail in such a Government as New York, as to oblige its governor to have recourse to the Regular troops ... appears to carry with it such [a] reflection of weakness ... and render the authority of the Civil Magistrate, when not supported by troops, contemptible to the Inhabitants.

The king later supported his approach. It was wondrously ironic that, in just a few years, Haldimand would invest so much time and energy negotiating with these same Vermont "ruffians."

With rebellion threatening, the Crown decided that a native-born Briton should be in supreme command, so Gage returned to Boston in April 1774 in the midst of great turmoil. Initially, Haldimand remained at New York, where he had conducted himself "with so much discretion," but by mid-September, affairs had deteriorated, and he and his troops transferred to Boston. In November he was appointed the city's army commander. Then, the tense situation was exacerbated by Parliament's passage of the Quebec Act, which guaranteed the Canadiens' use of the French language and civil law and the practice of Roman Catholicism. The act enraged New Englanders, who saw it as a threat to the Protestant religion and the liberties of America. Gage and Haldimand spent a stressful winter trying to keep the citizenry calm and controlling the troops, who were being insulted on every hand. Meanwhile, the province's legislature passed seditious resolutions and its militia drilled for war. Pennsylvania and Maryland called out 100,000 militia in opposition to the royal government. Haldimand became concerned about his possessions and house in New York City and soon word came that all had been confiscated and the Virginian, George Washington, had taken up residence in his home.

Despite initial reports that Haldimand had been killed in the Lexington skirmish, he first heard of the event from his barber, which suggests that Gage had bypassed his army commander, perhaps over disagreements of strategy. With open conflict initiated, Haldimand's letters to the government took on an unyielding tone; after all, he had been tutored in firm Prussian methods. As Britain's manpower pool was small, he suggested using Russians to quell the unrest and the abolishment of New England's provincial governments and the closure of all ports from Halifax to Florida to halt commerce and set up the interior towns against the coastal.

The ministry decided to recall Gage because of his despairing reports and as a result of the debacle at Lexington and Concord. Haldimand was the obvious replacement both in seniority and experience, but the bugaboo of foreign birth was again a stumbling block and it was decided to recall him as well. Three junior generals, William Howe, Henry Clinton, and John Burgoyne, were sent out to serve as Gage's assistants with the understanding that one of them would rise to supreme command. Tactlessly, word of Haldimand's recall came on the same ship as the three generals, none of whom had his depth of knowledge of America. With his worst fears confirmed, he chose to leave immediately. His quick exit the day before the bloodbath at Bunker Hill led to rumours that he was leaving the service, which caused a subordinate to write: "The regret and good wishes of ye whole army follow him, his experience, his great abilities, his integrity and disinterestedness will never be forgot by them." Haldimand arrived in London in August and was warmly received by the king and the prime minister, Lord North, as much in embarrassment over his abrupt recall, as to hear his advice about American affairs. A month later he was given the sinecure of inspector general of the West Indies' forces; however, for a man of his energy and temperament, the sudden inactivity weighed heavily. In January 1776, he was appointed a lieutenant-general in the army and, in September, was relieved to receive £3000 in much-needed compensation for his expenses as C-in-C at New York. Later that year, he visited his family in Switzerland where he invested in a large property and reduced his modest fortune by making improvements.

In June 1778, when Haldimand stepped ashore in Quebec City's lower town to assume the governorship, he was met by a very impatient predecessor, Guy Carleton. The previous spring, Carleton had been supplanted as the 1777 campaign commander. Acutely affronted, he demanded a recall and when his notice reached London, the American colonial secretary, Lord George Germain, just as promptly accepted it as — to put it mildly — the two men did not care for each other. Germain had already considered Haldimand as Carleton's replacement. The king accepted the proposal and a summons was sent to Switzerland. Haldimand had so much to recommend him: substantial colonial experience; proven skill and valour as a soldier; competence as a military and civil administrator; an ability to adapt to the colonies' social, racial, and cultural diversity; and an appreciation for the vast spaces involved. Yet, for all his pertinent qualifications, his foreign birth continued to haunt him and Germain stressed that he owed the appointment to the king, tacitly suggesting that the administration and army were uncertain. Haldimand returned to London, unaware that Carleton had requested a recall and, upon hearing rumours that Guy had been unjustly treated, asked for an annulment of his employment in sympathy for his fellow officer. Lord North thought this "most handsome."When it became clear that Carleton yearned for the recall, Haldimand was satisfied. During his briefing, he was pleased to hear that he had been granted the same powers Carleton had enjoyed. When Haldimand took ship in October, he was driven back by atrocious weather. He made an attempt to sail early in the spring, but was again disappointed and through all these delays, Carleton soldiered on as Canada's C-in-C in mounting frustration. When Haldimand's vessel returned to Britain, Carleton was aboard.

So much had happened in Canada since Haldimand had left in 1765. He discovered that the Quebec Act had been proclaimed too late. Soon after the "conquest," the British governor recommended the continuation of the Quebeckers' "ancient customs," a radical proposal for the treatment of a conquered people in an era of monolithic empires. The idea was supported by Lieutenant-Governor Hector Cramahé, a Franco-Irish protestant, and, much to the disgust of the Anglo migrants, the second governor, the Scots-Irish protestant, Guy Carleton, also agreed. Further, it was recommended to restore Quebec's pre-conquest borders. These issues were debated in Parliament through several sessions and administrations till all points passed into law at the brink of the rebellion. New Englanders, already in turmoil over British attempts to raise taxes, were instantly threatened by the new act. Restoration of Quebec's former boundaries limited their participation in the lucrative fur trade in the upper country and sealed off western migration. Agitators raised the spectre of a British-supported army of Canadiens and "praying Indians" attacking their frontiers as in the last war.[4] In Philadelphia, the Continental Congress adopted a Massachusetts resolution of September 1774 without a single dissenting voice. It read in part: "The late Act of Parliament for establishing the Roman Catholic religion and French laws in that extensive country now called Canada is dangerous in an extreme degree to the Protestant religion and to the civil rights and liberties of all America; and therefore, as men and Protestant Christians, we are indispensably obliged to take all proper measures to protect our safety." A month later, Congress declared the Quebec Act "impolitic, unjust, and cruel ... unconstitutional

and most danger-
ous and destructive
of American rights.
[It] abolish[ed] the
equitable system of
English laws to the
great danger from so
total a dissimilarity
of religion, law and
government of the
neighbouring Brit-
ish colonies." New
Englanders and New

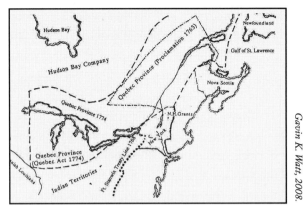

Gavin K. Watt, 2008.

The map illustrates the boundary expansion of Quebec Province as a result of the Quebec Act of 1774.

Yorkers immediately poured a propaganda deluge over an unwitting Canadien rural population and met with substantial success, particularly as the act's provisions had yet to be translated into French. In contrast, the townfolk, who were more directly influenced by the administration and its supporters and who were more discerning and better informed, seemed quite unaffected by the flood of half-truths.

Not long after Haldimand left Boston for England in 1775, the rebels had invaded Quebec and captured all the cities and towns except the capital. Many Anglos openly favoured the invaders and, although the Canadien clergy and gentry supported the British, numerous rural folk assisted the rebels as scouts, boatmen, labourers, and food suppliers. Several hundred took up arms. When the invasion stalled under the frozen walls of Quebec City and the rebels' shaky finances faltered, Canadien support collapsed, as their devotion to "liberty" rested more on financial gain than grand theories. In the spring, a British fleet raised the siege and brought substantial reinforcements to assist in driving the rebels from Canada. Although many of Carleton's peers thought he had been too soft on the Canadiens prior to the invasion, when rebellion came home to roost, he took a tough stand. Once the rebels had been expelled, he ferreted out and punished those who had assisted them. It was in this strained, tense atmosphere that Frederick Haldimand assumed his post in 1778.

The province of Quebec, most often called Canada by its neighbours, was the Empire's largest colony in America and for the moment was firmly back under British control. Its boundaries stretched from Hudson Bay in the north, to the Atlantic shore in the east, to the St. Lawrence River and the Great Lakes in the south, and in the far southwest touched the Mississippi River. Although huge in area, Quebec had only 100,000 inhabitants, concentrated primarily in the Laurentian Mountain region. By comparison, tiny Rhode Island had almost 53,000 citizens. West of the Ottawa River, there were only three settlements of any size. About 800 souls clustered in farms on the south shore of the Detroit River opposite the fort and supplied the garrison with fresh foods. South in the Illinois country were small Canadien settlements at Vincennes and Kaskaskia, which were soon fought over and lost to the rebels.[5]

The vast majority of Canadiens, known in Britain as "new subjects," were passively reluctant citizens of the Empire. They spoke French, were papists, had a vibrant, distinct culture, and were governed by French civil law. People in the other American colonies, despite richly diverse immigration and varied methods of founding and systems of governance, officially spoke English, were predominantly Catholic-intolerant Protestants, and lived under English common law. As another cultural distinction, most Canadiens were farmers, known as *habitants*. Although hardy and industrious, the fruits of their labours were consumed locally. The flourishing export trade of the lower provinces — seafood, grains, meats, timber — was not a major factor of Quebec life, with one notable exception — fur. The peltry trade was managed by Montreal trading houses supported by an army of workers. Furs were collected in the north and west where the Natives' hunting grounds criss-crossed the province's vast land mass and beyond. Access to Native villages and the companies' trading posts was by waterways that penetrated thousands of miles into the interior. During the war, one of Haldimand's most demanding duties was to maintain this crucial export industry.

While the surprisingly liberal Quebec Act guaranteed Quebeckers their "ancient customs," most Canadiens knew little of these benefits. Nevertheless, when the British were driving the rebels out of Quebec, Canadiens eagerly assisted, yet once they were over the border, disinterest in the "Englishmen's war" quickly set in. In 1777, it was difficult to raise just three companies of young men for active service and equally troublesome to man *corvées* to move troops, baggage, and stores. This reluctance took a substantial turn for the worse in 1778 when France declared war on Britain. A new barrage of inflammatory French and rebel propaganda was smuggled across the border and revived many Canadiens' hopes for a restored French Canada. Haldimand inherited this apathy and unrest.[6]

As each new campaign approached, Canada was threatened anew with invasion. Haldimand reasoned that, if an attack occurred, the enemy would not be a cobbled-together force of amateurs as in 1775, but a powerful combination of French and American armies and navies. To prevent surprise, he expanded his Secret Service and collected a constant flow of intelligence from New York, Vermont, New Hampshire, Massachusetts, Pennsylvania, and Virginia. For reliable information about French plans and preparations, he relied on Britain's European spy network, but the flow across the ocean was often interrupted by bad weather, in particular during the late winter planning of the next campaign.

The governor's anxiety was entirely justified. His provincial navy of small ships, galleys, and gunboats dominated the Great Lakes and Lake Champlain, but he had no control over the St. Lawrence estuary. The few small ships that patrolled that vital gateway into his domain were suited to scaring off privateers and warning of an invading fleet, but incapable of challenging even small warships. If an invading fleet slipped past the thin screen of Royal Navy ships patrolling from Halifax and St. John's, a horde could be on his doorstep in a trice.

His land force was small and spread far and wide. He had inherited Carleton's army of 1777 — sixteen line companies of the 29th and 31st Regiments; ten of the 8th and six of the 34th totalling 1,700 all ranks. Added to these were Burgoyne's castoffs, 920 British and 650 German soldiers, sick and weary, whom Carleton colourfully described as men "the Regiments usually disburthen themselves of on like occasions." Several hundred of Burgoyne's Regulars made it back to Canada — Ticonderoga's garrison of 100 of the 53rd and five 100-man companies of Prinz Friedrich's Regiment and, from Lake George, 100 of the 47th. As well, he had 130 of

Detail of the siege by W. Faden, circa 1776. Digitales Archiv Marburg, Document 9.

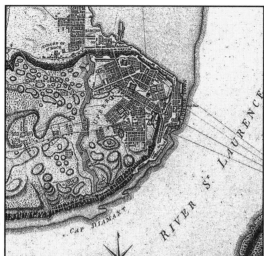

Haldimand's Headquarters, the Fortress City of Quebec.

St. Leger's 34th and 340 Hanau Jägers.

As for artillery, after Burgoyne filled his requirements, there was only a tiny contingent of five NCOs and thirty-seven men left at Quebec City's fortress, so Carleton had a large supply of field and garrison guns, but few men to serve them. The number doubled when the artillerists from Ticonderoga returned after Burgoyne's surrender, but British reinforcements remained so scarce that Haldimand had to form a second company by blending in Hanau artillerymen who in 1777 had been left behind in Canada as sick.[7]

Carleton had retained only one Provincial unit — the 1st Battalion, Royal Highland Emigrants, which had been elevated to the British Regular establishment and numbered the 84th in 1778. By 1781 1/84RHE had grown to 525 all ranks.

The largest regiment to serve under St. Leger against Fort Stanwix (a.k.a. Fort Schuyler) was Lieutenant-Colonel Sir John Johnson's Provincials, the King's Royal Regiment of New York. Unlike the rest of the army, the Royal Yorkers returned to Canada stronger than when it left, with 390 all ranks. The regiment grew at a remarkable rate and by 1781 had one battalion (1KRR) complete, with a second underway and a total strength of 955.

At the close of the 1777 campaign, Major John Butler of the Six Nations' Indian Department (6NID) was given a beating order for a battalion. The growth of Butler's Rangers (BR) to ten companies in 1781 is a key part of this story.

The beaten-up remnants of Burgoyne's several loyalist units had returned to Canada and the attempts to rebuild their strength are dealt with herein, as is the acceptance of James Rogers's 200 men of the 2nd Battalion, King's Rangers (KR) into the Canadian Department.

As for the Quebec Militia — it was believed that no reliance could be placed on them if Frenchmen were even a small proportion of an invading force. In this case, Canadiens might not take up arms against the British, nor would they offer support. On the other hand, if the rebels came without the French, there was a good chance that Quebeckers would rally in numbers, as their earlier experiences with "liberty" had not been entirely positive. Militia strength was 18,600 officers and men, including 400 Anglos. Of the three companies raised for active service in 1777, two had been shattered and struck off at the campaign's close and one was kept. In the face of such ambiguity, no further attempt was made to employ lower Quebec's militia on active duty.

In the years following Haldimand's arrival, his Regular army grew modestly. The badly mauled 44th, which had seen much action in the Central Department, was his sole British reinforcement, arriving in June 1780 with 355 men.

The major increase was in German infantry. In 1778, the Princess of Anhalt's Regiment arrived with 615 men. Two battalions were created from remnants of several Brunswick regiments and the sick left behind in Canada; soldiers from Prinz Ludwig's Dragoon Regiment, von Breymann's Grenadier Battalion, and the Musketeer regiments von Rhetz, von Riedesel and von Specht were put into a single battalion of 585 all ranks known as von Ehrenkrook's. Their light infantry were combined with the Brunswick light infantry and some newly arrived recruits to form the Regiment von Barner of 610 men. In 1779, a fifth company of Hanau Jägers arrived, bringing that regiment up to 495. Next year, remnants of two Hesse-Cassel regiments arrived from New York City — 295 men from von Lossberg's and 170 men from von Knyphausen's.

Haldimand's army had just over 9,500 men, giving him eight reliable men per linear mile and a handful of small ships and boats to defend a 1,200-mile border. Although his army was small compared to a total of 30,000 men in the Central and Southern Departments, he had a second asset — a large number of Indians who were excellent military auxiliaries. On his return in 1778, he found two organizations managing the Indians where formerly there had been one. He had been familiar with Sir William Johnson's department, which had been organized in two sections led by deputy superintendents — the Six Nations in one and the Seven Nations of Canada in the other. Carleton decided the management of Quebec's Indian affairs should be under his personal control and, in 1775, established a Quebec Indian Department (QID) for the Canada, Lakes, and Ohio nations with Major John Campbell at its head. As it transpired, the administration of the Ohio and Lakes nations was beyond sensible control from lower Quebec and civil and military officers at Detroit assumed that responsibility, assisted by resident Canadiens and a few of Johnson's old appointees. Sir William's much-reduced department was headed by his nephew and son-in-law, Colonel Guy Johnson, and two deputies. By 1779, Guy had joined Deputy-Superintendent Major John Butler at Fort Niagara, which, due to the fortunes of war, had come under control of the governor of Canada. The Mississaugas from the north shore of Lake Ontario lay between the two departments and their management was in some manner shared. They were the first Natives to support the Crown and stayed true through to the end, without the constant coaxing required by the Iroquois. Haldimand found the 6NID badly fragmented. Lieutenant-Colonel Daniel Claus, Guy's senior deputy and elder brother-in-law, had formerly been Sir William's deputy in Canada. He had managed the Natives during St. Leger's expedition, but when that effort failed, he took residence at Montreal to care for the Fort Hunter Mohawks who had abandoned their village in the Mohawk Valley to support Burgoyne and then settled at Lachine. Initially, co-operation between the two departments was awkward, but latterly a degree of goodwill was in evidence, although the astonishing expenses of two departments distressed Haldimand.

The Sullivan-Clinton expedition of 1779 resulted in a disastrous diaspora of the central and western Six Nations and their allies. The rebels ravaged their settlements, destroying every house, crop, and orchard lying in their path. As a result, over 7,000 dispossessed Indians moved to Fort Niagara where they relied upon the British to provide food and the tools of war. Not only had the rebels ruined their highly developed vegetable and fruit crops, but the British demand that the warriors constantly wage war prevented them from hunting to supply their families' needs for meat. The Indian Department's costs escalated and the pressures on the fragile supply line from Britain were so excessive that failures were common and the superintendents turned to local traders to make up shortages, a measure that increased costs and led to fraud.

The 680 warriors of the Canada Indians posed different problems. The largest village, Kahnawake, near Montreal, had been early influenced by rebel propaganda and, as the war progressed, its men were rarely relied upon for scouting or raids. Similarly, the Abenakis of St. Francis and Bécancour near Three Rivers and the Hurons at Lorette, outside Quebec City, were indifferent and suspected of helping rebel provocateurs. Warriors from Akwesasne and Oswegatchie on the St. Lawrence and the three Lake of the Two Mountains' towns were more reliable and often used, but all had relations at Kahnawake, which led to intelligence leaks.

Haldimand's early days in America paint a picture of a highly competent, studious, industrious individual with a sense of humour and a light heart, but, by 1781, he had become grave and overly meticulous. He managed his slim resources with great care and skill and was intolerant of sharp practices and malingering, to which many of his chastised subordinates could attest. Although a good friend to the Canadiens, many found him harsh. General von Riedesel, one his closest confidants, found Frederick Haldimand to be a morose character who kept to himself.[8]

In 1781, Haldimand cleverly employed his sparse resources to constantly raid the rebels' frontiers and cause their high command the maximum of anxiety, dislocation, and depravation. Throughout the campaign, his Secret Service undermined rebel morale with rumours of invasion and threatened their Union by negotiating with Vermont to return to the British fold.

In order to address in detail the myriad events impacting both sides during Haldimand's complex campaign, only scant attention has been paid to two significant elements of the Canadian war, namely, the many raids from Niagara against Pennsylvania and from Detroit against the Midwest regions later known as Ohio, Indiana, and Kentucky.

2

*O*ne of the war's strangest dialogues began on March 30, 1780, with a highly secret letter written by Lieutenant-Colonel Beverly Robinson, head of the British Secret Service in New York City, to General Ethan Allen, the primary leader in the breakaway government of the republic of Vermont.

> I have often been informed that you & most of the Inhabitants of Vermont, are opposed to ye wild & chimerical Skeme of ye Americans, in attempt'g to separate this Continent from Great Britain & to establish an Independ't State of their own: & that you would willingly assist in uniting America again to Great Britain, & restoring that happy Constitution we have so wantonly & inadvisadly Destroyed ... I think upon yr taking an active part and imbod[y]ing ye Inhabitants of Vermont in favour of ye Crown of England, to act as the Comd in Chief shall direct that you may obtain a separate Government under the King & Constitution of England ...

This letter heralded the Vermont negotiations, a protracted series of clandestine conferences and proposals that dominated the activities of the Canadian Secret Service until the end of the war and beyond. Lord George

Germain, the American colonial secretary, revealed the motives behind the effort in a letter to Haldimand: "[It] appears a Matter of such vast Importance for the safety of Canada & as affording the Means of annoying the Northern revolted Provinces ... No pains on my Part shall be wanting towards effecting His Majesty's wishes in reclaiming the inhabitants of Vermont, altho' I fear there is little Hope of Success. They are ... a profligate Banditti totally without Principle, and now become desperate."

Allen shared Robinson's secret proposal with his brother Ira, Vermont's governor, Thomas Chittenden, and five confidential persons. The group visualized using the British to lever Vermont into full statehood. When responsibility for the talks shifted to Canada, Haldimand saw the possibility of collateral benefits, such as a halt to hostilities between Britain and Vermont, which would greatly stress the Continental Congress and, in particular, New York State. As the game unfolded, this, and much more, was achieved. Haldimand "played" as though Vermont's return to the British fold was a genuine possibility and, at times, it appeared so. Of course, historians wanting to portray Vermont as utterly committed to independence and her support for the war as continuous and unstinting, deride Haldimand's successes.

How did this situation evolve? After decades of strife between New York and New Hampshire over the settlement of land between Lake Champlain and the Connecticut River, the Crown intervened in 1764 and gave control to New York, but failed to address the conflicting land grants previously issued by both provinces. When New York exerted authority in the region (the New Hampshire Grants), Ethan Allen, his several brothers, Seth Warner, and many other influential locals organized a band of armed men who held land under New Hampshire titles. Known as the Green Mountain Boys, the "rioters" defied New York's authority, often flirting with open warfare. New York's royal governor, William Tryon, was outraged and, ignoring his provincial council, called for intervention by the British Army, but was refused by the C-in-C America, Frederick Haldimand. When open rebellion broke out in Massachusetts in 1775, Allen already had an organized force. Ever the opportunists, the Allen brothers saw the British army post at Ticonderoga as a ripe plum to their ambition, reasoning that, by seizing the fort and

(left) Colonel Ira Allen (1751–1814). The most subtle and clever of the Allen brothers, Ira shared Ethan's concerns for Vermont.
(right) General Ethan Allen (1737–1789). A dynamic, colourful personality. Some viewed his willingness to negotiate with Haldimand as treason, but there is every reason to believe his concerns for Vermont were genuine.
(bottom) The Great Seal of Vermont created by Ira Allen in 1778.

its armament, they would ingratiate themselves and their cause with New York and the Continental Congress. As an opening ploy, they visited the fort and convinced the commandant of their good will, even arranging a truce between the post and The Grants, then, a day or two later, took the tiny garrison in a surprise attack. Soon after, Seth Warner led the Boys north to take Crown Point in an equally bloodless adventure; however, these two successes failed to soften New York's stance. Undaunted, the Boys served as a Continental regiment during the invasion of Canada. Although Ethan Allen was captured at Montreal and taken to England in chains, the Vermonters fought on right up to Quebec City's walls. Huddled in the frozen siege lines, they were angered that their sacrifices in the cause of liberty had failed to gain redress for their grievances and they plotted for independence from New York.

A convention held in the Grants resulted in an open declaration of intent to separate, which was followed by a year of rioting and reactionary assemblies, not only in the core Grants, but also in adjacent localities, which had their own complaints against New York. When the United States declared independence from Britain, the Grants followed suit, fully expecting their brother states in arms to embrace them, but New York's influence was far too strong and they were again disappointed. Of course, not everyone in the Grants and abutting areas favoured independence from New York, or from Britain for that matter. Many loyalists had gone to Canada in 1776 and many more joined Burgoyne's army the next year. Other large numbers of activists had no objection to abandoning Britain, but wanted to hold firm to New York — a complex situa-

The Background to the 1781 Campaign | **41**

The Republic of Vermont of 1777 and the two "Unions" of 1781. Illustrates the region known as the New Hampshire Grants that in 1777 were declared independent of Britain and New York State. The boundaries of three of New York's counties that were involved are shown.

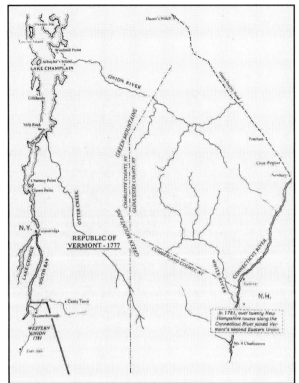

Gavin K. Watt, 2008.

tion in the extreme. In the midst of this confusion, the new republic's assembly took the name Vermont in June 1777. New York's northeastern frontiers had been carved away. In March 1778, Thomas Chittenden, a Connecticut militia colonel who had come to the Grants in 1774, was elected Vermont's governor. Rather than using Ethan Allen's methods of civil disobedience, Chittenden chose politics to fight New York. He was the first president of Bennington's Committee of Safety and a delegate at the 1776 convention investigating independence. The next year, he assisted in drafting Vermont's declaration and constitution and he and several others visited the Continental Congress to ask how the republic might be useful to the cause.

Handsome Ira Allen, Ethan's youngest brother, was elected secretary of state. Ira shared his brother's cunning and determination, but had a much more sophisticated touch on the reins. As the family's smallest male, he was nicknamed "Stub" and was early recognized in the Grants for his keen intellect. It was Ira's adroit mind that devised the plan to finance Vermont's war effort by selling Tory properties, which avoided taxes and endeared the new government to a great many Vermonters. Yet, like so many Allen inspirations, the confiscation had the taint of impropriety when family and friends unduly benefited from the scheme.[1]

An example of Allen intimidation tactics occurred in May 1779, when a pro-Yorker committee met at Brattleborough. Ethan, who had returned the year before, descended on the meeting supported by several "well arm'd & Equipp't" Green Mountain Boys. Shouting in typical profane, violent language, Ethan laid about him ferociously with his sword, wounding several and smothering resistance. Yet, for all their calculated violence, keen vision, and manipulative powers, the Allens' grip on Vermont depended on their membership in a small cabinet council. While the republic's assembly convened infrequently for short sessions, the council met almost every day. Although the constitution vested legislative power entirely in the assembly, political decisions had to be made and the council often found reasons to circumvent that restriction. Despite their autocratic approach, many Vermonters were grateful to the Allen faction for defying New York and avoiding taxes, but not everyone shared this admiration. The humbling of the Allen cabal became the ambition of Jacob Bayley, the most energetic leader east of the Green Mountains and west of the Connecticut River. Bayley had agreed to Vermont's independence only as a last resort and there was little love between his supporters and those of the Allens' "Bennington mob." A method to undermine the power of the Allen faction was to increase representation in the Vermont Assembly by incorporating New Hampshire's towns on the Connecticut's east bank into a so-called Eastern Union. In June 1778, at a moment when the Allens' attention was diverted, the assembly outraged New Hampshire by voting to admit sixteen of her towns. Ethan rushed to Congress to disingenuously inquire if New Hampshire's dismemberment was favoured. Having received the expected answer, he returned to the assembly to warn that the total wrath of the United States would fall on Vermont if the Eastern Union was not dissolved. Despite the threat, it was a year before the Allens were able to shed the towns. Before that, Vermont sent a commission to Congress to negotiate entry into the union, but their encroachments on New York and New Hampshire killed the attempt. The commissioners were so disillusioned by their reception there that they took the incredible step of writing to the British secretary, Lord George Germain, lamenting that entry into the union would only come through force or by negotiations "with separate Bodies of men and Individuals," which opened some routes for Germain to pursue.

The war surged on during all these machinations. Although the British 1777 northern campaign was a staggering failure, they had managed to retain control of the Champlain Valley water corridor. In late 1778, Haldimand reported his troops had destroyed the equivalent of four months' provisions for 12,000 men along the Champlain Valley and had driven Vermonters off the lakeshore and destroyed settlements along Otter Creek. This raid brought terror and misery to Vermonters, which was quite the opposite of what they had expected after Burgoyne's defeat. In the face of constant British patrols, New Yorkers were unable to re-inhabit the west shores of Lakes Champlain and George. The Ticonderoga fortifications, which had been so significant in 1776 and 1777, lay in stark ruins. By 1781, Forts Ann and George were burned-out shells and the state's farthest north, regularly manned post was Saratoga.

From his headquarters (HQ) in New York City, Britain's C-in-C America, Sir Henry Clinton, kept a sharp eye on Vermont's quarrel with New York and New Hampshire. In January 1779, he reported that Allen's troops "continue to give umbrage to … the New York Government." Two months later, Germain suggested that Vermont might be discreetly lured away from the revolutionary cause if promised recognition as a separate province under the Crown. Soon after, Beverly Robinson wrote his secret letter to Ethan Allen. The Allen cabal chose not to answer directly, but opened a second avenue by approaching Governor Haldimand to suggest a prisoner exchange. As Congress had not recognized the surrender terms agreed to at The Cedars in 1776 and Saratoga in 1777, Haldimand had refused such requests from other states; however, he was inclined to treat with Vermont, as the republic had not been party to either event and, more importantly, an exchange would open opportunities to exploit Robinson's secret offers. Haldimand chose Queen's Loyal Ranger captain, Justus Sherwood, a prominent Vermonter and former Green Mountain Boy, to lead the talks. Sherwood had proven himself a competent combat officer,

Unattributed engraver. (Washington Irving. The Life of George Washington. 4 vols. Boston: Dana Estes & Company, 1855.)

(left) General Sir Henry Clinton, British commander-in-chief, America.
(right) George Clinton, governor of New York and Militia General.

leading his company in the Bennington bloodbath. Burgoyne wrote of Sherwood: "[he] was forward in every service of danger to the end of the campaign."[2]

After the annual threat of invasion had passed, Sir John Johnson led a large force to Johnstown in May 1780. His primary mission was to relieve local loyalists from persecution. The rebels were unprepared. New York had passed a regulation in March to raise levies for frontier defence, but the law had not yet taken effect. The raiders burned many farms, incapacitated several militia officers and raised 150 recruits, which substantially increased the Royal Yorkers, one of Haldimand's most useful regiments. Local militia companies assembled, but chose not to engage in fear of being overwhelmed and the rest of the county's militia was slow to react. Their performance came as no surprise to George Clinton, as the Tryon officer corps had been harshly criticized as being inefficient the previous year. After the raid, he promoted Robert Van Rensselaer to brigadier to command in a second Albany County militia brigade that would incorporate Tryon's regiments.

An articulate man of great energy and determination, the ambitious George Clinton was born in modest circumstances in Ulster County, New York, in 1739. His military exposure came early as a lieutenant in his father's regiment during the 1758 attack on Fort Frontenac. After the Seven Years' War, he practised law, but politics were his first interest. As a member of the provincial assembly, he was a proponent of independence from Britain. In 1774, he sat in the Second Continental Congress and, in 1776, voted for independence, but was unable to sign the declaration as he had been called away to perform his duties as a militia brigadier. He fought at White Plains and Fort Montgomery and at Esopus in 1777. That same year, he was chosen state governor, a post he held for all the war. A big bear of a man with lowering, bushy eyebrows, he was immensely popular with rebel Yorkers.[3]

As Haldimand lacked British reinforcements and had little confidence in his Germans, refugees became a vital source of manpower. Although his three largest loyalist regiments, the Royal Highland Emigrants (RHE), the King's Royal Regiment of New York (KRR), and Butler's Rangers (BR) are best known, he also had fragments of several small corps that had survived the Burgoyne debacle.

Each had arrived in Canada with a different story. When Lieutenant-Colonel John Peters and his Queen's Loyal Rangers (QLR) planned to break out from the cordon around Burgoyne's army, Peters foresaw that Governor Carleton would doubt the loyalty of anyone who had left the army before the surrender and obtained Burgoyne's written permission to withdraw. His surmise was correct, but once he displayed Burgoyne's consent, his men were welcomed with open arms. Captain-Commandant Samuel Mackay was not as perceptive as Peters. His battalion of Loyal Volunteers (LV) was cut off while guarding a bridge being repaired and Mackay chose not to return to the main army; Carleton removed him from command. When Lieutenant-Colonel Eben Jessup returned with a small rump of his King's Loyal Americans (KLA), he escaped even the momentary wrath of the governor, as his corps had stayed to the bitter end. As a result, most of his men had given their parole not to fight again, including Jessup and his brothers, Major Edward and Captain

Joseph. Dr. Samuel Adams's company of rangers also remained with Burgoyne until the end and he limped back to Canada with half his men under the Convention parole. Captain-Commandant Daniel McAlpin escaped reprimand, as part of his small battalion of American Volunteers (AV) was sent back to Canada as the guard for Burgoyne's military chest and the rest were in a bateaux company that was permitted to break out, which a few men did three days before the end.

Haldimand felt bound not to use the "Convention men" for military duties until it became clear in mid-1778 that the rebels were defaulting on two surrender agreements.[4] The fragmented units were placed under Sir John Johnson's management, who suggested they be organized into a Royal Yorker second battalion. The governor approved, but the plan was aborted as the smaller units' field officers hoped to retain their unconfirmed ranks. So, the little corps languished for the next two years — at times providing men for raids, or working in the Secret Service or with the Engineers. Their colonels and majors repeatedly importuned Haldimand for permission to re-recruit their strength, but were quietly ignored in favour of Allan Maclean, John Johnson, and John Butler. Because Johnson was fully occupied running the Secret Service and recruiting the Royal Yorkers, he was relieved from responsibility for the small corps in 1779 and replaced by Captain Daniel McAlpin, who was promoted to major. One might imagine how this sat with Lieutenant-Colonels Jessup and Peters. It is likely that Haldimand was influenced by McAlpin having served under him in the Royal Americans.

Captain Robert Leake, who had been given command of the LV, escaped this general malaise when he was ordered to form Leake's Independent Company (LIC) of "seventy to eighty men with four or five good officers." Leake's was attached to 1KRR to serve as its de facto eleventh company. As Maclean, Johnson, and Butler had been unable to take full advantage of their recruiting monopoly, Haldimand relented and allowed Jessup and Peters to recruit in the colonies. Anticipating a demand for arms, he indented for 2,000–3,000 stand of Light muskets with bayonets and cartridge boxes and 2000 suits of brown and green clothing.[5]

Sir John had completed his first battalion and Haldimand authorized a second in a new beating order dated July 13. Johnson reported on the

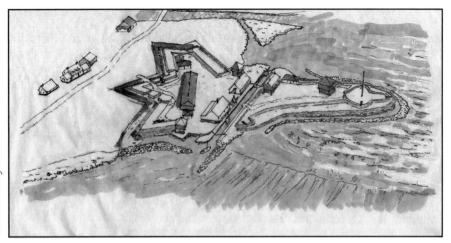

The post at Coteau-du-Lac. This post guarded the locks built by Royal Yorker labour to ease the movement of supplies to the Upper Posts and to guard the rebel prisoners housed on an offshore island.

July 20 that the regiment would canton at Lachine magazine so he could form the supernumeraries into companies. None of the 1KRR captains wished to transfer to the second, so there was nothing to prevent the promotion of the recommended subalterns, yet the appointments were repeatedly delayed. Captain-Lieutenant Thomas Gumersall was put in charge of the recruits until a major was appointed, while he retained responsibility for 1KRR's Colonel's Company. On July 21, Grenadier Captain John Ross, 34th, was appointed a Provincial major to command 2KRR. He brought with him Ensign Humphrey Arden, 34th, as his adjutant. Ross asked that Gumersall continue with the new battalion and permission was granted.

Ross had been born in Scotland in 1744 and first appeared on the Army List as a 34th lieutenant in 1762. He performed noteworthy service in America in 1765 when he drew the first British map of the lower Mississippi. He was captain-lieutenant in 1771 and the next year a captain, in which rank he arrived in Quebec with a line company. On the January 1777 return, he was captain of the 34th's Grenadiers and went with Burgoyne, serving in the Advance Guard. Badly wounded at Hubbardton, he returned to Quebec to convalesce and, after returning to duty, led a mixed raid of Natives, Indian Department rangers, and troops to the Mohawk Valley in

June 1778 and rescued several Mohawks held hostage near Fort Hunter. Ross's varied and noteworthy service recommended him to Haldimand.[6]

In the late summer of 1780, all of Burgoyne's Provincials were heartened to hear that the King was "anxious to reward their faithful and spirited conduct" and had given them some "Marks of His Royal favour." The officers would rank as junior when serving with Regulars of the same grade and gratuities were provided for men who had lost a limb or were otherwise maimed on service. Most important, they would have permanent rank in America and half-pay upon disbandment, if they were able to recruit their companies to fifty-six rank and file, including three contingent men. Other provisions were made for NCOs and privates.

As the RHE had been elevated to the British Establishment and Butler's Rangers held an odd status due to its association with the Indian Department, the Royal Yorkers was Haldimand's only recognized Provincial regiment. In May 1779, the governor had damned the Yorkers with faint praise, noting it "a usefull Corps with the Ax," but "not altogether to be Depended on with the Firelock." Yet by September, he ranked the KRR amongst his "best and most active." How much of his favourable impression was due to Sir John's influence, energy, and competence is unclear. By mid-1780, the two-battalion KRR was the largest corps in Haldimand's department, and he invariably favoured it in recruiting disputes with smaller corps. By mid-August, 2KRR was at Coteau-du-Lac, improving the works and building canal locks to bypass the rapids. Gummersall was appointed quartermaster (QM) on October 14 and, a day later, went to Montreal to draw Indian fusils from Campbell's QID, as military arms were being held for another purpose. Clothing was drawn from the quartermaster general's (QMG) stores, as there was insufficient regimental clothing remaining from the spring shipment from Britain, which likely put the second battalion's men in the same pattern of green coats earlier worn by 1KRR.

On September 6, Haldimand advised Eben Jessup and John Peters that he was anxious to have their corps completed and, when effected, they would be confirmed as lieutenant-colonels, as would their captains when their companies were complete. He also promised that clothing would be available for all recruits.

Unattributed (author's collection).

CWM 19800027-001.1 © Canadian War Museum.

(left) Major John Nairne, 84th RHE. Nairne had settled in Quebec after the Seven Years' War and joined the Highland Emigrants in 1775. He served with distinction during the defence of Canada and, in 1780, was given responsibility for the remnants of Burgoyne's Provincials. (right) Major Nairne's Highland dirk. One of the very few extant military items attributed to Provincial soldiers. This is an excellent example of a sidearm carried by Highland officers and men.

After Major McAlpin's death from overwork in July 1780, Major John Nairne, 84th, took direction of the smaller corps that December. Nairne was a veteran of the Seven Years' War who had settled in Canada after 1760. As a Highland Emigrant captain, he had been prominent in the defence of Quebec City in 1775.

In the fall of 1780, General Haldimand sent a number of raids into upstate New York. Simultaneously, Captain Sherwood made the initial effort to bring Vermont back into the British fold under the cover of settling a prisoner exchange. After some minor indignities and a hostile examination by a council of officers, he found some private time with his old friend, Ethan Allen:

> I walked out with him, & after much conversation Inform'd him that I had some business of Importance, but before I communicated it must request his honour as a Gentleman, that should it not please him he would take no advantage of me nor Ever mention it while I remained in the Country. He said he would if it was

no Dam'd Arnold Plan to sell his Country & his own
honour by Betraying the trust repos'd in him.

Over a few tots of rum, he advised Allen that Haldimand was aware
of Vermont's unsuccessful attempts to gain statehood and suggested that
the time had come for the republic to shake loose from its shackles and
return to Britain. Sherwood said it was his fondest wish for the people
of Vermont to accept this proposal. He was risking much and placing
great trust in Allen, as Sherwood had earlier been publicly flogged
for loyalism and sentenced to imprisonment. In typical fashion, Allen
pontificated. No offer was of any interest to him personally, but only the
will of the people of Vermont could sway him. To allay any suspicion, the
pair returned to the council to discuss the public business of a prisoner
exchange. At another quiet time, Sherwood mentioned the written
proposals he was secretly carrying. Over more rum, Ethan suggested a
meeting in a more secure location with his brother Ira and Joseph Fay.
While encouraging, it became obvious that a neutrality pact was of more
interest to Allen than changing allegiance. During a long drinking bout,
he revealed the republic's desire to absorb more of New York, which,
although unexpected, was welcome for the disruption it would cause. It
also became obvious the Allen faction was anything but universally loved
across the republic.

This encouraging session was followed by an extremely unpleasant
experience with Allen's cousin, Major Ebenezer Allen, who led a party
that wanted no truck with the British. He marched Sherwood back
and forth under guard through heavy snowstorms, forbidding him to
speak to a soul, claiming he had definite knowledge that the British were
violating the flag. At last, Sherwood was saved by a letter from Governor
Chittenden, ordering he should be treated as "an officer of a Flag had
a right to expect." After five more miserable days, he was sent through
another snowstorm to meet with Ira Allen and Fay. They decided to go
to Canada to continue talks in safety, but found the lake frozen over.
Sherwood's cutter crew hacked through the ice trying to reach open
water, but after two days, it was decided that Allen and Fay should come
to St. John's over the ice later.

As a first effort, the talks had mixed, but promising, results. On the positive side, contact had been made with some of Vermont's key leaders. With his knowledge of the violent passions of the people, Sherwood had expected open hostility from some, but not such deep enmity from Eben Allen, a former acquaintance. Such was the life of a Tory; he had faced extreme personal danger and knew it was only the beginning.

While Sherwood was undergoing his ordeal, four raids shook upstate New York. Major Christopher Carleton, 29th, led 775 Regulars, Provincials, and Canada Indians against the upper Hudson River. After reducing Fort Ann, homes and farms were burned in Queensbury and Kingsbury districts and parties of Jessup's KLA and Rogers's KR destroyed riverbank farms almost as far south as Saratoga. This was followed by a sharp action at Bloody Pond near Fort George fought by KR and Indians. Many prisoners were taken there and at the reduction of Fort George, including Warner's badly depleted Green Mountain Boys, who were serving as a poorly supported, unenthusiastic, "Additional Continental" regiment accredited to New York. Simultaneously, Captain John Munro led two 1KRR companies with Fraser's Independent company, Claus's Indian Department rangers, and the Fort Hunter Mohawks on a raid to Ballstown. A militia colonel and thirty men were taken and farms destroyed. Sir John led the biggest raid, setting out from Oswego with 940 troops and warriors from Montreal and Niagara. A massive destruction of grain, livestock, and farms resulted. Massachussetts and New York Levies and Albany and Tryon militia pursued his column and were defeated at Stone Arabia and fought to a stalemate at Klock's Field. Johnson extracted his raiders with minimal losses and captured a company of New York Levies while withdrawing. Angry Tryon citizens accused Brigadier Van Rensselaer of misconduct. Yet another raid struck over the Green Mountains almost to the Connecticut River. Led by a QID officer, 200 Canada Indians ravaged settlements and carried off many prisoners. As the Continental Army had been suffering a supply crisis, these raids were truly dreadful blows. Washington's aide said the general fell into catatonic shock when told of the news.

Haldimand had a reputation for meticulous financial management and was extremely uneasy about the Indian Department's heavy

Colonel Guy Johnson (Uraghquadirha), superintendent of the Six Nations' Indian Department.

expenditures. This was perfectly understandable, as Colonel Guy Johnson's requisition for 1781 listed 12,500 blankets, 8,000 brass kettles, 16,000 silver ornaments, 25,500 yards of cloth, 10,000 needles, 75 dozen razors, 1,000 hats — including 100 white beaver hats for women — and 20 gross of Jew's harps. The previous campaign, Johnson had issued his charges every month with 350 gallons of rum, 35,180 pounds of pork, and 1,710 pounds of butter. This consumption rate could not be maintained from government stores. On such occasions, he turned to merchants to supplement his needs, despite the governor's strictures against the practice. The governor's patience was wearing thin. He had little faith in Guy's competence and wrote to Germain:

> He is not possessed of either abilities, Temper, or the necessary Talents to conduct a department of such Importance…. [I]f His Majesty should think proper to annex a high Rank to that Employment, Mr. Johnson is, in every Respect, but particularly as an Officer, a very unfit Person to be entrusted with the Power it will give Him — I find He takes to Himself a great Share of the Merit of the Conduct which has been observed by the Five Nations in the present Contest which, in fact, He has not the smallest Claim to any part of, having left his Duty in 75 (When the Province was invaded) instead of remaining in the Indian Country, where His Presence was, at that Period, indispensably necessary, by which His Department was thrown into the last Confusion,

from which, it was rescued by the unwearied attention, application, & judicious Conduct of Major Butler, his Deputy, who returned from Quebec to Niagara for that Purpose, and who, so far from being in any shape assisted by Colonel Johnson, never heard from Him until July 1777 so that to Major Butler ... together with the Activity of Joseph Brant, whatever has been accomplished with, and by the Five Nations, is entirely due.

Obviously, Guy Johnson's time was short.[7]

On October 25, intelligence was received from Sir Henry Clinton that temporarily drove thoughts of economy from the governor's mind. A "Plan of an Attack upon Quebec" had been captured from Henry Laurens, former president of the Continental Congress and the present delegate to the French Court. First, 1,500 Virginia and Pennsylvania troops were to collect at Fort Pitt with 100 light dragoons, one half armed with lances. On June 1, they would march to attack Detroit and destroy all the towns of Indians "inimicable to the United States." Second, 500 men were to winter at or near Wyoming to cover the Pennsylvania and New Jersey frontiers. By May 1 they would be reinforced by 1,000 men from each state who were to march against Oquaga, and then against Fort Niagara. Third, in addition to the garrison of Fort Stanwix, 1,500 men would winter on the Mohawk River. Preparations would be made to build "Vessels of Force" on Lake Ontario early next spring, and to take post at or near Oswego. In the spring, 2,500 militia from New York and the western counties of Connecticut and Massachusetts would be raised. Five hundred Continentals and 1,000 militia were to march from Schenectady to join those from Oquaga, plus "all the warriors which can be collected from the Friendly Tribes" to destroy the Seneca and other hostile Indians. Fourth, 2,500 men would march from Fort Stanwix to Oswego as early as possible after mid-May and take post there, or in the neighbourhood. Five hundred would defend the Oswego works; the balance would forward "the Vessels to be built for securing the Navigation of Lake Ontario, & in making excursions towards Niagara ... to keep the Indian Country in

Alarm & facilitate the Operations in that Quarter." Fifth, a body of 5,000 Regulars was to be recruited and stationed "along the Upper Posts of the Connecticut River," presumably in New Hampshire. Every preparation would be made to penetrate into Canada along the St. Francis River. The timing would depend on circumstances. When at the St. Lawrence, the force would build a post at the mouth of the St. Francis River and take St. John's and Montreal. As the operations farther west would start before the St. Francis venture, much of Haldimand's army would have been drawn off. The force would protect its rear facing Quebec City while up to 2,000 men, with as many Canadiens as would join, would go up the St. Lawrence to assist the western expeditions in securing Lake Ontario. That detachment would take post at Cataraqui and build works and man them with 300 men. The rest would join those at Oswego and move west against Fort Niagara. This combination would unite with the troops that attacked Detroit, whether or not they had been successful.

Should these operations succeed, it would still be necessary to mount a new campaign next season to capture Quebec City. American troops wintering over in Canada would need warm clothing and provisions, all of which would prove ruinously expensive and impractical and would allow the British to reinforce Quebec from Britain and Halifax. The text rather enigmatically continued, "considering these circumstances, it is perhaps more prudent to make incursions with cavalry, light infantry and Chasseurs to harass and alarm the enemy & thereby prevent them desolating our frontiers." Then came Congress's main thrust: "But if the Reduction of Halifax & Quebec are objects of the highest Importance to the Allies, they must be attempted." Benefits for France were seen as: control of Newfoundland and its fishery. For the United States: peace on her frontiers, a rearrangement of her finances, addition of two states to the Union, security to American commerce, and to allow the states to "bend their whole Attention & Resources to the Creation of a Marine [that] will at once serve them and Assist their Allies." As long as Britain held Nova Scotia and Newfoundland, it could "infest the Coasts of America with small ships" and cripple allied commerce. Aid from France was a necessity. A body of 4,000–5,000 French troops was required to reduce Halifax and Quebec with four ships of the line and four frigates.

They were to disguise their purpose by showing clothing suitable for the West Indies, but each soldier would have a large blanket to convert into a coat for cold weather. Winter clothing was to be forwarded in August to be available in Quebec City. The expedition would occupy the city and leave the capital ships with the Marines and a small number of troops and Canadians supplied from the arms provided for them, which would be disguised as being intended for a West Indies' militia. The frigates and transports would proceed up the St. Lawrence and subdue Montreal, if not already taken. The troops were to be supplied with salt rations, as it was known that the British Army had exhausted the Quebec countryside of grain and livestock. By the end of July or middle of August, the reduction of Canada could be so far completed that the ships could move against Halifax. A large portion of the French troops, with a large number of American Regulars and Massachusetts and New Hampshire militia, would attack that place, and, if it fell by mid-October, they could move on Newfoundland, or remain in garrison until next spring and complete the conquest then. Or, if the island could not be taken, the squadron and troops would still be in time to operate against the West Indies. Enclosed with the letter was a proclamation from the well-known young French adventurer, the Marquis de Lafayette, calling upon the Canadiens to rise in revolt. Haldimand already possessed a handbill from le Comte de Rochambeau, the commander of a large French army at Rhode Island, which had been given to some Canada Indians' headmen, who had visited his HQ in August. He had urged them to take up arms in support of France and her ally, the United States.

Haldimand wrote to Sir Henry on October 26, acknowledging receipt of the letter and Lafayette's handbill and advising him of Rochambeau's. He saw these as indicative of "a real design upon this Province," although, he had a bit of good news. "You will hear of the Alarm upon the Frontiers, I wish it may serve you. Forts Ann & George are destroyed."

Frederick Haldimand was no fool. He recognized these ambitious plans were beyond American resources; however, in 1779, his attention had been concentrated on internal disorders, invasion rumours and a severe lack of provisions and he had been caught napping while the rebels amassed a surprisingly large army, invaded Indian Territory and destroyed their villages. He would not underestimate them again. He also wrote to Germain, enclosing Henry Laurens's letter and Lafayette's proclamation:

> Our Signal Successes in Carolina will probably render the Rebels incapable of undertaking such formidable Expeditions against Detroit and Niagara as are proposed in [the Laurens letter]. A small new Fort has been constructed at the former, and the works at the latter have been considerably improved, besides both are tolerably well provided with artillery, & the Garrisons, altho' few, composed of the best Troops.... Nor does the Enemy seem fully apprised of the Difficulties He has to surmount before he renders Himself Master of the Navigation of Lakes Erie & Ontario. The former is Navigated by Six Armed Vessels.... On Lake Ontario we have three Vessels of 16 guns and two smaller ones, besides a new Post which I established in 1778 [Carleton Island]. The Operations proposed by the enemy at Oswego, are more formidable and much better calculated to ensure them Success than any other Part of their Plan, not only from its favorable Situation for building, but the awe it must create thro'out the whole Six Nation Indians. I have, in former Letters, Expressed ... how much I wish to establish a Post there, and the advantages it would afford us. I am now more than ever convinced of its necessity, & early in the Spring I mean to take Possession.

Not one of the provision ships that had left Britain in August had arrived and he stressed the necessity to stock the Upper Posts with twelve months' rations before the close of navigation. As the local harvest had been very good, he expected he could collect a "tolerable supply of Grain" by applying martial law. The engineering and artillery stores had not arrived either, which left every post in the province short. In particular, Quebec City was in need of gunpowder. No doubt, most of the fortress's

Knife and neck sheath, late eighteenth century. Mohawk type — iron blade in wooden handle wrapped with tanned skin and dyed quills. Sheath, which would have hung around the neck suspended by a fibre cord, is tanned and smoked skin edged in white beads and quills with tassels of red-dyed hair.

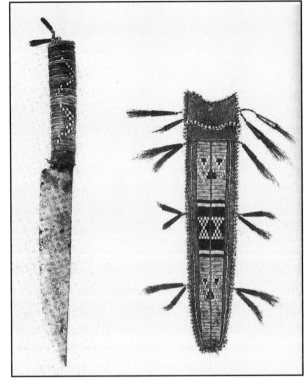

stock had been shipped west in expectation of an imminent resupply from Britain. He continued with cogent comments about the conduct of offensive operations from Canada:

> To Attempt any serious attack, or the Establishment of a formidable Post in the midst of an Enemy's Country intersected with Woods, strong Passes &c thro' which your Artillery, your Provisions &c must be conveyed, is too imaginary an Object even to occupy for a moment Your Lordship's Attention, and I am convinced no Post at, or near Albany can be taken or supplied except by the Navigation of the Hudson River — yet I am persuaded, was it practicable to occupy & support such a Post from New York, it would be scarce possible for the enemy to prevent me from giving or receiving the assistance of

Troops from that Quarter, but they must always move totally unprovided with Artillery, Provisions, or Baggage, & every man, from the Commanding Officer [down] must Carry his own Knapsack — It is true that with a considerable Force and Great Exertion, Fort Stanwix might be invested from this Province, but when we are distressed about supplying and maintaining our present distant out Posts, I am of opinion the same Force might be employed elsewhere to much greater advantage — these considerations induced me to conclude that the Troops from hence to be employed elsewhere must be transported by Sea — At the same time I conceive considerable Detachments from this Province, moving on the Enemy's Frontiers & sometimes even penetrating to a considerable distance, but always so formed as to be ready to make quick movements, may be done with great Security, and are, and will be of great detriment to the Enemy, my Opinion on this Point is supported by the Success of Sir John Johnson last May on the Mohawk River, as well as that of Major Carleton in the taking of Fort Ann and Fort George ... Having frequently mentioned the difficulty of transporting Provisions to the Upper Posts ... we have used our Endeavours to lessen them as much as possible, particularly at Coteau-du-Lac, where new Store Houses are erected, & a very Compleat Canal finished, by which loaded Bateaux Pass thro' three Locks & avoid a most tedious & laborious Passage up a Violent Rapid.

In late summer, loyal Indians had coerced 200 Oneidas to move to Niagara. This had given great relief, as they and their friends had proven to be the rebels' most effective irregulars in the north. Now, grim news was received that many of them had abandoned Niagara and returned to the Mohawk Valley where they were guarding a plentiful harvest on lands usurped from their Mohawk brothers.

Following acceptance of Sir John's request that 2KRR be sent to Carleton Island to experience some real soldiering, Major Ross selected 100 of the better-trained men along with Leake's Independent Company to act as a stiffener. Gumersall was left behind to care for the remaining 160, who were attached to 1KRR for further training.

Major Gray had recruited twenty men from the prisoners taken in October who claimed a connection with his troops and Sir John proposed recruiting from the rebel prisoners who had been paroled to work around Montreal. Haldimand cautioned that, unless they were known as true loyalists, it would be "unsafe to trust arms in their hands" and, after some more words of caution, reluctantly approved. As it transpired, the governor's fears were fully justified.[8]

———————————

———————————

Following the fall orgy of destruction, Continentals were sent to winter over in the Mohawk Valley. As a detachment of 4NY marched upriver along the nine-mile stretch of devastation from Tribes Hill to the Noses, they found only a parsonage and the house of George Adam Docksteder had been spared. To men who had passed so many burned-out shells, the Docksteder place reeked of Tory and they were in a grim mood as they fell out along the road. While First Major John Davis questioned the family, a search revealed a locked upstairs room. Davis demanded the key and was told it was lost, but, when he shouted for an axe, the key magically appeared. The room was stuffed full of smoked meats whose different hues indicated they had been collected from far and wide. These spoils were shared amongst the troops. Davis may have been a novice in the valley, as he exhibited a humanity not often displayed along the river when he left the Tory family a year's supply. On the 18th, Davis's detachment was welcomed at Fort Herkimer by a three-gun salute, which was returned with three cheers. The 4NY arrived at Fort Stanwix on November 20.

On November 6, the Albany city Commission for Detecting and Defeating Conspiracies examined a letter from Dr. George Smyth. He claimed that being confined to his home put his family in distress, as he was unable to earn a living and asked to enter under a recognizance to remain within Albany's limits so that he might move about on professional business. After £500 bail was posted, he got his wish.

Three days later the commission heard a report from Colonel Van Bergen, 11th, Albany County Militia (ACM), that disaffected persons had collected back of Coxsackie on the pretence of religious worship and some would join the British in the spring. Another informant advised that, when the notorious Tory courier, Hans Walden Meyers, a former farmer from Cooeyman's, south of Albany, passed through the country, he crossed the river at Kinderhook. On November 20, the board was told that Simeon Garret, who lived on Meyers's farm, had sheltered the courier and they summoned him to appear.

Just fifteen days after gaining release from confinement, Dr. Smyth told the board it was impossible to maintain his family in Albany and he had sold his effects in anticipation of being allowed to go to Canada. He requested to stay on a farm in Rensselaer Manor and this was permitted after his brother Patrick, an Albany merchant, posted another £100.

The truth was, George Smyth was a viper in their midst. He was a committed loyalist and he and his sons, Terrence and Thomas, had been active spies since early in the rebellion. Although repeatedly under suspicion and at times jailed, George Smyth somehow escaped the more serious penalties meted out to incorrigible Tories — lengthy prison terms, physical abuse, or worse, the hanging tree. His first significant act of espionage had been a report sent to Carleton in April 1777 that gave critical information about Ticonderoga. It was signed "Hudibras," a codename that became well known to the British high command. The choice reflected Smyth's dry Irish wit, as "Hudibras" was the title of a seventeenth-century mock-heroic poem. The Smyths were jailed after the fall of Ticonderoga, but George later boasted that, even from his cell in Albany's city hall, he was able to correspond with New York and Canada over the eighteen months. In the winter of 1780, he was paroled home. His two sons, who had been released earlier, acted as his couriers, travelling to Canada with intelligence gathered from his widespread contacts. George knew he was living on borrowed time and, in March 1780, wrote to Governor Clinton asking for a pass to take his family to Canada, deceitfully claiming he wanted to collect funds owed by some "absconding Tories" and return to Ireland. The request was ignored and, in April, he sent Haldimand reports about rebel strength at Stanwix and Savannah, the fighting and prices of wheat in New Jersey, rum in Washington's camp, and beef and flour at Philadelphia. The governor came to rely on such varied and reliable information and urged Sir John to have him boost the flow. When George warned he would have to escape to Canada, Haldimand told Johnson to have him establish a firm network in and about Albany before he left. When the board discovered George had gone to Fort Edward in breach of his agreement, he and Terrence were placed under house arrest. George immediately asked to be sent within British Lines or exchanged. Amazingly, the board failed to recognize that this well-spoken, mild-mannered medical doctor was the mastermind of a wide network of informants and agreed that he, his wife, son, and a black servant could go to Canada, if he gave security and sent two named prisoners in exchange. Getting permission and getting away proved to be quite different issues and, after disposing of his house, he found the commissioners lacked the authority to grant passes and again had to apply to Governor Clinton.

At the end of November, unrest burst out in New York's Continental Line over a rumoured reduction in the number of regiments. Colonel Philip Van Cortlandt, OC 2NY, was told by officers of the 3rd that "Colonel Gansevoort is oblig'd to retire from the Army through the Perseverance of Col Van Schaick, and that you are to command the [new] 2nd Regt." Van Schaick had never been close to his brother-in-law, Peter Gansevoort, but it is unclear what prompted these intrigues, other than a scramble to keep command.[9]

Haldimand had earlier jailed a handful of notably rebellious Canadiens and censured many others; however, he realized the roots of insurrection lay far deeper and devised an interesting plan to smoke out these agents of rebellion. On November 16, he wrote Sir Henry to ask General Benedict Arnold (a main player in the rebels' 1775 invasion and a recent convert to loyalism) to name Quebec's traitors.

On military matters, Sir John requested a supply of carbines from the 500 held in stores in exchange for the Indian fusils issued to 2KRR. He noted the latter were very unfit for service and added that carbines would be better for woods' service than muskets. His request was denied.

On November 28, the governor took the last opportunity to write Germain before the close of navigation on the St. Lawrence: "Every day gives me more and more reason to think that an Invasion is intended early in the Summer. The more the affairs of the Enemy are desperate in the Sou-thern Colonies, the more they will find it necessary to use every effort to make themselves Masters of Canada, it is their last resource & if their efforts should succeed, they would soon recover their losses to the Southward." He was concerned that:

> The large Body of Indians which we have employed against them & which has prevented thousands of their best men from joining Washington's Army [might be diverted] by ... Intrigues of their French Allies, which I see daily increasing ... [I]f Carleton Island should fall into the Enemy's Hands, Niagara & Detroit would infallibly be lost, for with all the Industry & Attention, which I have employed to that object, I have not been able to furnish these Posts with Provisions for more than the Commencement of next Spring. On the other hand if the Enemy should penetrate into the Province by a road which they have been some time making and which is now greatly advanced from the Cohoes to the Bay of [Missisquoi,] I must have a Body of Troops to oppose their further progress, otherwise Montreal, which is totally indefensible, would fall into their Hands & would be attended with the same fatal consequences to the Upper Posts as the loss of Carleton Island.

He trusted the report and attachments would ensure the granting of his earlier request for reinforcements, "which I hope will consist of British Regiments." He detailed plans to guard the Richelieu River posts and the Missisquoi Bay route and described how he would secure the harvest to prevent grain from falling into the hands of the invaders:

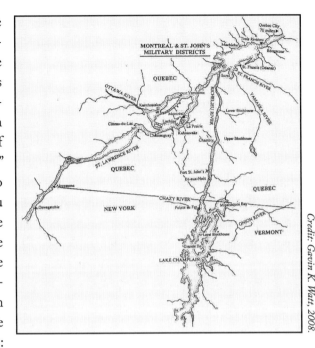

Credit: Gavin K. Watt, 2008.

> I have no confidence in being able to collect many [of the militia]. I am certain there is frequent intercourse by letter or message between the French or Rebel Generals in Rhode Island and some of the Priests & Jesuits, assisted by some disaffected old subjects [anglos] whom with all my industry I could not discover. And tho' the Noblesse will probably behave well, I make no doubt there are many Inhabitants, in each Parish, who would swerve from their Allegiance upon the Approach of a French Army. Severity & rigor will be necessary and in Proportion my Conduct has hitherto been mild & forbearing, it will be the reverse if I find no other means can preserve the province.

Haldimand was unaware that the French were discouraging their American allies from this very venture, reasoning that as long as the British occupied or contested any one of the American states, all efforts should be concentrated on ejecting them.[10]

Remnants of Burgoyne's Provincials were quartered at Verchères on the south shore of the St. Lawrence, a short distance below Montreal Island. Two lieutenant-colonels, two majors, eighteen captains, twenty-four lieutenants, and thirteen ensigns jealously hoarded about 400 men while they strove to recruit their units up to strength in order to have their commissions confirmed by a governor who was growing very impatient. With the threat of invasion, Haldimand recognized the potential of these disparate groups if they could just be moulded into an operational battalion. The first move was made on December 5, when Adams's Rangers was drafted into the AV. Then, orders were issued that the several corps were to be managed as a single battalion under the command of Major Nairne, RHE with Neil Robertson, AV as Adjutant and Titus Simons, QLR as QM. Nairne quickly took action, ordering the men to assemble at his quarters on November 12 with their arms and accoutrements in order to assess shortages. He vowed, "Every step shall be taken ... to form them into a respectable well disaplind corps ... Recruiting young able bodied men shall be encouraged and ... [he would] form them into companeys and ... procure commissions for the officers." Two independent companies were formed, with officers chosen from the AV; one under Peter Drummond with Neil Robertson and James McAlpin as subalterns, the second under William Fraser, his brother, Thomas, and Gideon Adams.

Haldimand addressed Sir John's questions about the appointment of officers to 2KRR, cautioning that the first battalion's officers who had been recommended for promotion would risk their half pay if the new battalion did not complete. Rather than chance this, Johnson could have officers appointed to companies as each completed, or wait until the battalion was two-thirds complete and appoint a full complement. He recommended incorporating Fraser's Independent Company into 2KRR, noting the Fraser brothers were most deserving and their merits as recruiters were undeniable. William would rank as the 2KRR's youngest captain and his company would continue on the Yamaska frontier, as he was so well acquainted with the region. As to the contentious matter of whether casuals (killed, discharged, prisoners, missing) would be credited when battalion strengths were assessed, the governor noted that Peters claimed 210 Rangers had been killed at Bennington and thirty captured and other loyalist corps had suffered similarly, so if casuals were credited, very little additional strength could be expected from the "New Levies."

Johnson chose not to absorb Fraser's company, not over any objection to the brothers, as he held both in high regard, but because he already had officers chosen and was confident he could fill the battalion without them. He wrote to the governor on December 14 advising he wished to appoint officers to 2KRR as companies completed, but Haldimand wrote back that the findings of the Board of Officers examining the claims of the several corps must be heard before appointments could take place.

Another loyalist corps in Quebec had an entirely different lineage. In late 1778, Lieutenant-Colonel Robert Rogers, of Seven Years' War fame, asked Haldimand for a warrant to raise two battalions on the northern frontiers. This was denied, but the bold Rogers was undeterred and persuaded Sir Henry Clinton to give him a beating order for a two-battalion regiment to be known as the King's Rangers. When Sir Henry recommended him to Haldimand's protection, Rogers had an excuse to send officers to Quebec to receive recruits. A short time later, Rogers asked the governor to assist his brother, Major James Rogers, a veteran company commander of rangers in the previous war, who was coming to Quebec to command the second battalion. Haldimand found it uncomfortable to have a unit raised under Clinton's warrant taking up residence in his jurisdiction, reasoning it might be recalled south at any moment.

When James Rogers arrived in Montreal, he found recruiting parties from several loyalist corps chasing a tiny number of recruits and soon came to grief with the other commanders. This conflict led the governor to stress that the King's Rangers were not to recruit inside Canada's borders. Then, personal disaster struck James. His brother Robert was deeply in debt, and worse, he had lied about the number of recruits in his first battalion in Nova Scotia. James confessed to the governor that his brother's conduct had almost unmanned him and, rather surprisingly, found a sympathetic ear. The King's Rangers were employed in Secret Service duties, allowing them to combine recruiting with this duty. The Rangers grew slowly, but steadily, and in 1780, gave excellent service on Carleton's raid.

————————————————————
————————————————————

At Fort Stanwix in the Mohawk Valley, a twenty-five-man 4NY patrol with a brass 3-pdr from Moodie's Continental Artillery Company set off in the snow aboard five sleighs to search the abandoned Old Oneida Castle where a cache of corn was rumoured to be hidden. The patrol returned a day later with corn and potatoes, two salvaged swivel guns and news that 1,000 bushels of corn remained, which would be very useful to the garrison and, of course, to British raiders.

An official report from Tryon County reported that 1,200 farms had been abandoned and 354 families had left their habitations, which was only a partial count, as in places like Cherry Valley, Springfield, and Harpersfield, there was no one left to enumerate. Once-thriving settlements were abandoned and Schenectady had become virtually the outermost limit of civilization.

————————————————————
————————————————————

On November 9, Sir Henry Clinton sent Haldimand further word of the enemy's plans in a ciphered dispatch that took only twenty days to arrive: "[A]n Attempt against Canada is probably intended as soon as the Winter is so far set in as to render Naval transactions on the Coast improbable, as the French under Rochambault will Compose the Principal Part of the Armament. I am inclined to credit the Accounts." As the invaders would rely upon the country for food, he recommended removing all but family supplies.

Haldimand increased Captain Sherwood's responsibilities. He was to act not only as the commissioner of prisoners and refugees, a role that gave ideal cover for his talks with Vermont, but was sent to Isle aux Noix to take charge of all scouting parties in the Lake Champlain region, leaving Sir John in charge of northern New York. Sherwood was to confer with the island's commandant, Major Alexander Dundas, 34th, the only Regular officer who would have knowledge of the Vermont negotiations.

Major Ross observed that Carleton Island's Fort Haldimand was in need of improvements, as the parapets were "only Six feet thick [and] Partially filled with Rubbish and Stones." He set his men to work. Wary Gonwatsijayenni (Molly Brant), the Mohawk Wolf clan matron and widow of Sir William Johnson, and her children were happily ensconced in a new house that had been built for them on the bulbous peninsula below the fort.

At Niagara, Molly's brother, the ever-enterprising Captain Joseph, had developed his own plan. Although less grand than the rebels' strategies, the significance for the Six Nations was no less imposing. During the summer, he had helped persuade many Oneidas, Tuscaroras, and ambivalent Onondagas to leave their towns and move to Niagara. With them gone, the early-warning screen that had lain between the stubborn whites clinging to their farms in the Mohawk and the swarms of raiders coming from Niagara and Carleton Island was gone. Of course, many rebel Indians had previously relocated in the lower Valley and they continued to assist the rebels, but the removal of so many enemies from Indian Territory had been a major triumph. Now, many of these Oneida converts had left Niagara and Brant fumed at their treachery. He wrote Fort Hunter war captain, John Deserontyon, to secretly propose combining forces in the early spring and take revenge. Brant had a litany of grievances against the Oneidas: they had spurned his early call to join the British; had joined the rebels under arms at Oriskany; had insulted his sister and her family, had occupied her home and looted her property; had assisted the rebels to destroy their brothers' towns in Indian Territory, and had repeatedly opposed him in the following years (as recently as last October.) If Brant had known that these Oneidas were on Mohawk land at Canajoharie guarding a harvest for the rebels, he would have been enraged. Deserontyon agreed to be at Carleton Island about mid-March. As neither knew the Oneidas' present location, much scouting would be required before a strike could be mounted.[11]

3

WINTER TURMOIL ON THE WESTERN FRONTIER
Driven to the Last Extremity

*O*n New Year's Day 1781, the rearrangement of the U.S. Army came into effect. Congress wanted all the states' regiments completed with 612 rank and file each and in the field that day. New York's five undermanned infantry regiments were reduced to two. The 2nd, 4th, and 5th were combined as a new 2NY under the command of Colonel Van Cortlandt. The 3rd was rolled into the new 1NY, under Colonel Van Schaick. Officers for the new regiments were chosen by seniority, and, because the five regiments had been heavy in officers, a great many were retired. A few positions came open as some men took the opportunity to resign, in some cases to take higher ranks in the militia. Even so, a number of good men were lost and, one supposes, a few duds retained, as length of service did not always measure competence.

At Stanwix, when the 4NY was told that the regiment would become a "Detachment of the 2nd N. York ... [and that] Gentlemen Who are or who may be Deranged [retired] are to keep post till further Orders," the news was not well received. This led to a strongly worded order:

> [I]t appears by sundry Reports that Elibaral Intentions are freely published with Respect to the Command in this Garrison After the first day of January Next which May have a tendancy to Subvert Order and disapline, the Command't Publishes Again, that he has Received Orders from Gen'l Clinton to wait for further

Orders and that the Officers by no means Leave the Garrison till Released, he therefore forwarns Every one Concerned not to persist in any Mutiness [mutinies] or unmilitary Designs, as they will Answer at their Perill for the Consequence."

On the actual day, an order was issued prohibiting all firing in the garrison, but whether to curb a celebration or a further outbreak of displeasure is unclear.

On January 1, the ten Pennsylvania Line regiments mutinied at Morristown, New Jersey. Rioters killed and wounded several men and seized field pieces. There was fear that the men intended to desert to the British; however, it was soon apparent that their grievances were over lack of food, pay, clothing, and spirits — all long-standing disorders. Mutiny spread to the New England and New Jersey regiments. The riots were quelled with little loss of life, but these were tense times for the United States, following the previous year of disasters. Efforts to stabilize the union's exhausted credit by issuing paper money had failed. There was no hard specie to pay troops, and with 6,000 French troops lying inactive in Rhode Island, recruiting had slowed to a trickle.

Back at Stanwix on January 5, Lieutenant-Colonel Robert Cochran, 2NY relieved Colonel Frederick Weissenfels, former CO of the 4th. The next day, the colonel and other deranged officers left for home and, on January 7, the

Colonel Philip Van Cortlandt, 2nd New York Continental Line.

companies were reorganized along the lines of the new establishment.

One of the first events to rattle the Champlain region in 1781 occurred on January 6 when six Vermonters were captured while scavenging Ticonderoga's ruins and taken to Canada.

Colonel Samuel Clyde, OC of Tryon County's 1st Regiment (1TCM) wrote a heartrending letter to the governor on January 6 about the problems of raising men for the Continentals. Last spring, he had sent twelve for the seven-months' levy, one for every class in his regiment. When Sir John struck in May, a great many moved out of his district, yet he still managed to supply eighteen more for the three-months' levy. In all, his "Littcl Rej'mt" had given thirty. Those left were almost constantly on duty, often providing their own provisions and acting without pay. These hardships had been endured for the past two years. Of his regiment's ten companies in 1777, only two were left and one of them had apparently been saved last fall by joining Sir John. Clyde pled for pay for his men to relieve their distress and to encourage them to continue to do their duty. He asked when the governor would visit Albany so he could discuss what to do about the company that had assisted Sir John.

Colonel Klock's 2TCM was in considerably better shape with 354 all ranks including exempts. Of eight original captains, three were missing and their companies struck off. Thirty-five men had joined the enemy, forty-eight had been killed, twenty-seven were prisoners, and ninety-seven families had moved away. In the 6th Company, Captain Richter had left and there were only seven privates remaining, whom the two lieutenants recommended dispersing to other companies. An undated return of Bellinger's 4TCM listed six captains, seven lieutenants, four ensigns, fifteen serjeants, eleven corporals, one drummer, but only 103 privates.[1]

Albany HQ recognized the extreme plight of the posts along the Mohawk River where the snow was heavy and the roads blocked or badly torn up. On January 16, Brigadier-General James Clinton, Northern Department OC, advised Van Cortlandt that ninety barrels of flour would be ready for Stanwix in a few days and ordered a 2NY company as escort. Twelve barrels of beef were also to go to Fort Dayton in German Flatts for the use of the posts in that quarter. The next day, Clinton instructed the colonel to command the escort and take his Light Company to reinforce

Stanwix. The second escort company would march back with the sleighs to Forts Herkimer and Dayton and remain there in garrison.

On January 16, three men voluntarily appeared before the Albany Commission and promised to advise the board whenever "John Waltymier" appeared again. A man from Livingston's Manor was charged with drinking the King's health and dissuading men from entering the nine-months' levies. He was released on £100 bail and charged to appear before the next Supreme Court.

At Charlestown, New Hampshire, various political factions from forty-three towns on both sides of the Connecticut River met to hammer out a solution to the hostility felt toward western Vermont on one hand and New Hampshire's seaboard on the other. At first, it was resolved to unite the towns on both sides of the river with New Hampshire, in the thought that this would increase the power of the back country people; but the very next day, a second resolution joined all the towns to Vermont, a decision that revived the first Eastern Union of 1778 on a much larger scale. The kettle was again on the boil between Vermont and New Hampshire.

On January 17, the 1NY reported a strength of 509 all ranks with 43 men absent and 10 in hospital. Four companies were posted at Saratoga under Lieutenant-Colonel Van Dyck, one at Fort Edward and three at Albany. Next day, General Philip Schuyler, the union's senior Indian Affairs' commissioner in the Northern Department, wrote a third letter of complaint to Congress about the Native allies. Four hundred Oneida, Tuscarora, and Kahnawake Indians were barely surviving in miserable bark huts outside Schenectady. He had emptied his personal stores of supplies to assist these people, as had local militia colonel, Abraham Wemple:

> Yesterday a deputation from the Oneida Indians waited on me, they assured me that they were driven to the last Extremity for want of provisions, that they were not only perishing with famine, but also with cold haveing not where with all to cover their nakedness and entreated me in the most pathetic terms, to administer to their relief, I had but to open my eyes, to be convinced of the

truth of the one and the other, but alas, It was not in my power to afford them the relief I wished. I borrowed to supply their present necessity of provision, my private stock is expended and the public magazines have litterally nothing In them, but Impelled by gratitude to a people who have sacrificed all for us, and Influenced by duty I shall make every effort on my private credit to supply them with provisions beyond that It cannot go as no Cloathing is to be procured here, and I hope that will be sent.… The enemy in small parties have already re-appeared in Tryon County and If the Oneidas should be driven to desperation by the hardship they endured and Join the enemy all beyond this place will be one dreadful Scene of desolation and Slaughter, no endeavours on my part shall be wanting to avert so dreadful a Calamity.

These Natives suffered these hardships at the hands of the very people with whom they had thrown in their lot at the sacrifice of their own liberties. Yet, most folk in Albany and Tryon counties ignored their plight, standing aside and expecting Congress to take action. Why? The Natives had repeatedly proven their value as military auxiliaries. Frontier security depended on their assistance, yet they lacked clothing, provisions, and medical care. Surely, these Indians knew they would fare significantly better at Niagara![2]

A series of war parties set out from Niagara in January. Early in the month, the Mahican chief, Philip Hough, led fourteen Delawares to the Hudson River followed by Mohawk David Hill Karaghgunty, and his party, and, two days later, Captain Shenop and nine Nanticokes went to raid their homelands along the Susquehanna.

Haldimand was anxious about the Canadiens. He had been unable to identify the principal agitators amongst them and was worried the

Lieutenant-Colonel Sir John Johnson, King's Royal Regiment of New York (1741–1830). The most significant northern New York loyalist of the Revolution in middle age.

Unknown artist, watercolour on ivory (Library and Archives Canada, 1938-34-1).

clergy was involved, which would defy detection. He was also concerned that leaving the grain with the *habitants* would allow the gathering of supplies to feed an invading army and decided to pass an ordnance to enforce threshing. His lieutenant governor opposed this measure, arguing that purchasing the wheat for hard cash would be more in "the spirit of British Government [and] no men in the world are more governed by the love of gain than the Canadian peasantry." Haldimand seldom agreed with his deputy and dismissed his proposal. Buying wheat would be too time consuming and an order to thresh simply followed British home precedent when under threat of invasion.

Military life marched on. Lieutenant Fraser's Independent Company was issued new clothing and sent to garrison the Yamaska Blockhouse on the south shore of the St. Lawrence, a few miles east of Sorel and patrol the area's approach routes often used by enemy agents to infiltrate the province. Fraser marched fifty rank and file, picking up a serjeant, corporal, and twelve men of the 29th Regiment en route to share the duty. On January 11, Captain Robert Mathews, 8th, Haldimand's accomplished military secretary, instructed Sir John to have a Royal Yorker scout determine whether French and American troops were assembling at Albany and, if so, were they intending to invade Quebec or "reduce

Detail from James Peachey, 1784, after Hunter. (Library and Archives Canada, negative C-2003.)

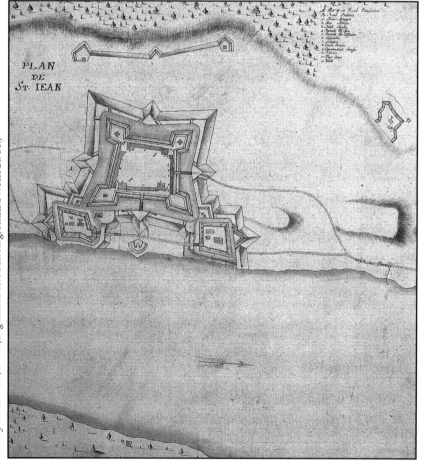

Detail from Du Fais, 1777. (Digitales Archiv Marburg, HstAM WHK 28/36.)

The headquarters of St. John's military district and home of the King's Rangers. Design assistance, Christopher Armstrong 2008.

Vermont"? Claus was to send two or three Mohawks separately for the same purpose. Johnson sent four men with orders to split into two parties and take different routes, avoiding all rebel posts until reaching the settlements. Captain Daniel Robertson, 84th, who commanded Oswegatchie on the St. Lawrence, proposed a strike against Ellice's Mills at Little Falls, one of the Mohawk Valley's last operational gristmills. He reported that local Indians, probably Akwesasnes and Oswegatchies, would conduct a large scout in February to "amuse the people on the Mohawk River" — an indelicate euphemism for *terrorize*.[3]

Captain Sherwood's new role had been ill-defined by HQ, which caused friction to develop with Colonel St. Leger, the OC of St. John's district. On January 18, he ordered Sherwood to take six men and the chief engineer along Lake Champlain. Sherwood declined, as he was waiting for Joseph Fay and Ira Allen, both of whom had been delayed by the Eastern Union business, but he could hardly explain this to St. Leger. The colonel was furious. It would be some weeks before this fracas was resolved. Also on the 18th, the *Quebec Gazette* published the governor's ordnance:

> Whereas the safety of the property of his Majesty's liege Subjects, and the necessary defence of this province, may speedily require that all Grain, Cattle and Provisions, which might in any degree favor or afford succour to an Invasion in the Province by the King's subjects in Rebellion, should be deposited in Places of Security, for Protection and Defence by the King's Troops under my Command; Therefore, with the advice of his Majesty's Council, I have published this Proclamation, requiring all of his Majesty's faithful subjects, to prepare without Delay … by diligently causing their Grain of what kind soever, to be forth-with threshed and prepared, ready to be transported.

In response, the townsmen of Quebec City and Montreal sent addresses "full of sentiments of Loyalty to the King and of Attachment to the Constitutional Government." Unimpressed, Haldimand wrote

Germain, these "are of no great Consequence but as the Inhabitants of the Towns give the Ton [fashion] to the Traders in the Country, who have but too often been the Instruments of retailing sedition & rebellion to the ignorant Inhabitants, I gave my consent to have the addresses … published in the *Quebec Gazette*."

Mathews advised Sir John that, to improve control of his limited resources, the governor had instructed the board of officers examining loyalist claims to look into reducing the allowances of the dependents whom, he thought, were getting "much Superior to what they before enjoyed."

On January 24, St. Leger reported from Fort St. John's about the patrols on the frontiers. He had men guarding the exit of the Chazy River and others in constant rotation from St. John's and the Yamaska blockhouse scouring Missisquoi Bay, Lake Memphremagog, and the paths leading to and from St. Francis.

Colonel Guy Johnson, 6NID, had sought to better his personal status by being put on the Provincial establishment and applied directly to the home government for permission to expand his tiny corps of Foresters to operate alongside the Indians in the same fashion as Butler's Rangers. This would require massive recruiting and Haldimand showed great restraint when he wrote to Germain that there was a great need for troops in the Indian country and that nothing could be better than to raise "a respectable body of woodsmen"; however, surely Johnson recognized that Butler would not obtain the rank of lieutenant-colonel nor would his son be promoted to major until they completed eight companies and the Butlers had not been able to do so over the past two years. Haldimand continued, "I can assure Your Lordship, that I should find no difficulty in raising officers for any number of battalions who would all promise to find their complement of men. Rank is the idol worship by all on this continent." Guy's circumlocution of proper procedures did nothing to improve the governor's opinion of him.

On February 1, Joseph Brant and Volunteer John Bradt set out from Niagara on snowshoes with 150 Indians and thirty Butler's Rangers to intercept Fort Stanwix's supplies. Perhaps Brant hoped to return in time to meet Deserontyon at Carleton Island; perhaps he was impatient for action or, more probably, Guy Johnson had ordered the mission.

The Vermont situation continued to heat up. Not having received a direct reply to his first letter, Colonel Robinson wrote a second to Ethan Allen on February 2: "The frequent accounts we have had for three months past … confirms me in the opinion that I had of your inclination to join the King's cause…. This induces me to make another trial; especially as I can now write with more authority, and assure you, that you may obtain the terms mentioned … provided you and the people of Vermont take a decisive and active part with us." Whether or not Allen chose to answer was of little moment. Most important was keeping the issue foremost in the mind of that very disgruntled Vermonter.[4]

On January 29, yet another politician entered the fray on the behalf of the suffering Native allies. The president of the state senate, wrote to the state's congressional delegates, "The Oneida's [are] naked and precariously subsisted and threatening to go over to the Enemy; the Effects of which will be severaly felt by the frontier Inhabitants." Still, no action was taken. Governor Clinton wrote a wrenching letter to Congress on February 5:

> We are now arrived at the year 1781, deprived of a great Portion of our most valuable and well inhabited Territory, numbers of our Citizens have been barbarously butchered by ruthless Hand of the Savages, many are carried away into Captivity, vast numbers entirely ruined, and these with their Families become a heavy Burthen to the distressed Remainder; the frequent Calls on the Militia has capitally diminished our Agriculture in every Part of the State….We are not in a Condition to raise Troops for the Defence of our Frontier, and if we were, our Exertions for the common cause have so effectually drained and exhausted us, that we should not have it in our Power to pay and subsist them. [W]ithout

correspondent Exertions in other States and without Aid from those for whom we have not hesitated to sacrifice all, we shall soon approach to the Verge of Ruin.

Colonel Jacob Klock and Peter S. Deygart, past chairman of Tryon's Committee, wrote to the governor on February 6 from their winter homes in Albany to suggest that, with the county lying open to the enemy, the state should raise a company of rangers officered and manned by the Valley's citizens. It is difficult not to conclude that Klock was seeking employment for his son Jacob, who had resigned from the 1NY; later attempts were more blatant.

Colonel Van Cortlandt arrived at Stanwix after "Various and many Difficulties." He found there was only fourteen days of beef on hand and wrote to the QM at Schenectady to request that another convoy be sent soon. Discrepancies must have occurred with previous convoys, as he recommended assigning a conductor to make a roll of the teamsters' names and be responsible for their performance. Due to bad roads, the guns he had been forwarding had been left at Fort Herkimer and there were only three sheets of paper in the garrison — an item in chronic short supply in the north.

Random, constant incursions struck the frontier. A war party fell on Little Fort Davis, the home of the Davis family in German Flatts, which was one of twenty similar little forts spread across the Mohawk region. In a typical terror raid; three of Peter Davis's daughters were wounded; one stabbed three times and cut with a hatchet. Elsewhere, a second Indian party fired on a sleigh and wounded the horse. The animal ran a half-mile before dropping dead, which allowed the occupants to escape. Despite the danger lurking about Stanwix, unarmed troops persisted in going out to search for firewood. The colonel ordered them to sling their muskets across their backs and stay near the patrols.

On February 8, a British deserter, who was employed as a tailor in Livingston Manor and had been recently jailed for disaffection, was released by the Albany commission after giving £100 bail. On the 15th and 16th, four Tories, one from Argyle Township, Charlotte County, two from Cambridge District, Albany County, and one from Fort Edward

Settlements in Vermont's Western Union and along the Hudson River south to Kingston.

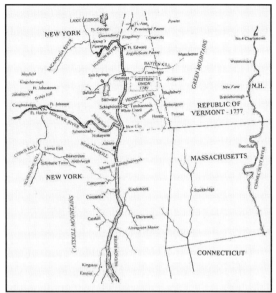

Gavin K. Watt, 2008.

were released after paying £100 bail. As the latter lived on the frontiers and might aid and comfort the enemy, he was ordered to "remove into the Interior Parts of this State."

At Stanwix, a private was sentenced to fifty lashes for using abusive language with his superior. Van Cortlandt stressed there was far too great a familiarity between the NCOs and the men, which destroyed subordination and led to impertinence. Any NCO who failed to respect his rank would be reduced. The colonel was disturbed about poor guard procedures and gave orders about challenging strangers who approached the fort by day or night, setting what guards were to turn out and when to give alarms. Bedding was so scarce that a drummer was awarded fifty lashes for "cutting his Blanket without Liberty," but the penalty was forgiven when it was discovered he owned it.

Amos Ansley, one of Sir John's spies, had a close call while resting at a friend's place near Johnstown. He was shocked when his old employer, who had been Sir William Johnson's house architect and carpenter, drove up in a sleigh. When Ansley had run off with Sir John in 1776, he had been the man's apprentice and now the fellow was a justice of peace. Nervous about discovery, Ansley hid in his friend's hay barrack, but the man had come to fetch hay and strode up to the barrack to pitch a load onto his sled. Ansley cringed as each fork strike hit inches from his body, but his luck held.

On February 14, Vermont planned a Western Union, by confiscating a huge area of New York lying west of the Connecticut River and north of Massachusetts up to Quebec. The success of this manoeuvre would remain to be seen. Needless to say, bankrupt New York, fighting the British and threatened by internal unrest — would be shocked and resentful. Ironically, a number of committeemen and citizens from eight communities in the original Grants area petitioned Vermont's Assembly to "Protest, against setting up, at present, a government independent of New York." This had little effect, other than to mark them as malcontents.[5]

───────────────
───────────────

The board of officers chosen to examine issues relating to the loyalist corps assembled at St. John's on February 8. Its members were many of the leading lights of the British army in Canada: Lieutenant-Colonels Barry St. Leger, 34th, and Forbes Macbean, RA; Majors Robert Hoyes, 34th, and John Adolphus Harris, 84th; Captains Alexander Fraser, 34th/QID and Thomas Scott, 53rd. Most had extensive exposure to provincial troops. The same day, Colonel Campbell, QID, reported that he had completed clothing his Natives and found them in the best disposition possible and ready to take to the field should the rebels attempt invasion. Word had been sent to the Mississaugas to "Be Ready to come Down Shall they be Called for" and a scout had been sent via Fort George down the North [Hudson] River to loop back through Skenesborough. Another had gone up Otter Creek and a third to Hazen's Road. "[T]his and the party down the North River are Conducted by two Serjeants of Sir John Johnson's[,] intelligent men thoroughly acquainted in the Country and very Capable for the trust."

One of St. Leger's scouts returned to Isle aux Noix with a detailed account of the Continental Line mutiny and news that the thirty-man garrison at Fort Edward was ripe for revolt. Mathews asked Major Jessup to estimate the size of a force required to bring off the discontents, but later advised that Haldimand had rejected the idea.

Because of the great need to move goods and troops to the Upper Posts more efficiently, a Provincial bateaux company under Captain

Johan (Hon) Jost Herkimer had been established at Coteau-du-Lac. As his boatmen were poorly armed, Colonel Campbell was instructed to deliver thirty stand of arms and ammunition from QID stores and to issue scalping knives to be made into plug bayonets.

Niagara's commandant, Brigadier Henry Watson Powell, had a great deal of experience in America before the rebellion. He had commanded brigades under Carleton and Burgoyne and the Montreal district under Haldimand. On February 19, Powell advised the governor of Brant's departure and that many small scouts of Rangers were "on the communication." At John Butler's request, he again sought a first lieutenantcy for the colonel's second son, Thomas, which had been refused six months before on the grounds of his lack of experience. The Rangers had completed an eighth company and he given Butler granted permission for another two. He advised that Butler had complained bitterly about the appointment of an unknown captain named McKinnon to command the new company, as his nephew, Andrew Bradt, the senior lieutenant, had been given hopes of this post. Enclosed was Guy Johnson's report that the Indians' needs were "so alarming that I am really at a loss what to do to relieve them." While housekeeping activities occupied the British, the rebels had their own concerns.[6]

On February 16, Brigadier-General James Clinton ordered six 1NY companies to march to West Point and Colonel Van Schaick set out immediately with four. On February 19, Washington answered Governor Clinton's request that the 1 and 2NY be left on New York's frontiers by explaining that he required all of his Regulars for vigorous offensive measures and he was concerned that, even after January's reorganization, many regiments would be far from complete, which made it imperative that everyone be with the army. In answer to the governor's request for ammunition, he showed his confidence in Clinton by sharing a secret: "Our stock of ammunition is more scanty than your Excellency can have any idea of, but … small as it is, I shall order a part to be deposited at Albany." As to the request for artillery, he thought some guns could be sent and registered surprise that Stanwix was short of provisions. Inventories were frightfully low, but he would forward supplies. Washington's letter had not arrived when the governor sent another plea, repeating his earlier comment about the distressed frontiers and the danger of the inhabitants abandoning their habitations. Albany's fears had increased since the 1NY companies had been sent south and he again asked for the two regiments to remain on the frontiers. It was all to no avail.

On February 24, a letter from Schuyler and his fellow Indian commissioner, Volkert Douw, was read in the State Legislature addressing yet again the miserable condition of the Native allies. As Schuyler had offered a loan of $1000, it was resolved to buy 200 blankets and forward them to Douw, yet only 185 were provided and not until March 8, after the worst of the weather had passed.

At Stanwix on February 25, a luckless private was tried for sleeping at his post and awarded 100 lashes, a moderate penalty considering the Articles of War dictated the death penalty. And, as if Tryon County needed another grim warning, the very next day, two militiamen from Little Falls were captured and run off to Canada. On the February 28, Van Cortlandt announced the victory at Cowpens in South Carolina. Most news from the south had been discouraging, so word of so many enemy casualties gave the men a huge morale boost.

After twenty days on short rations, a convoy arrived and a full issue of bread and beef was made, but not before some soldiers had stolen three barrels. As the troops refused to expose the thieves, the colonel held back another three barrels as a just punishment for everyone.

In expectation that Schenectady would be a target for attack in the coming campaign, the magistrates and field officers of the city's militia, the 2nd Albany regiment, wrote to the governor asking that seven blockhouses be added to the city's perimeter. An engineer would be required for the construction and a detachment with guns and ammunition.

The Albany commission heard from Lieutenant-Colonel Henry K. Van Rensselaer that there had recently been a meeting in the East District of Rensselaerwyck at which a man, in open violation of state law, read a proclamation from Sir Henry Clinton. A warrant was sworn out for the reader and all disaffected persons present at the meeting.[7]

Captain Crawford, 2KRR and adjutant Arden, arrived back at Carleton Island from the Mohawk Valley with a prisoner in tow. As the locals had been shut up in forts, Crawford, with typical sangfroid, had entered one, spoken to some women and concluded there was no threat to the island that winter. Ross assured the governor that the fort was too strong to be stormed in any event.

Campbell was very upset to report the accidental death of an Abenaki headman at St. Francis at the hands of the resident agent, Lieutenant Wills Crofts, 34th. The Abenakis had never been warm to the British and, although Americans had destroyed their town in the previous war, the rebels had much influence and this killing could result in serious repercussions. Campbell empathized with Crofts, as he knew he had only taken the difficult post in hopes of promotion. He had developed a "thorough knowledge of the Characters of the different Indians ... and that Local Knowledge of the Country Necessary for the person employed there." He had been most efficient in gathering intelligence and managed the village with utmost economy. Nonetheless, he had to be replaced by Luc Schmid, a Canadien militia officer from Yamaska. There was good reason to worry about the Abenakis, for under Washington's orders, Lieutenant-Colonel Bayley of Cöos had supported fifty, "as rangers to keep an eye on movements from Canada and assist agitators to infiltrate into Quebec." Of course, their ease of movement in and out of Canada made detection difficult.

Campbell's bad news continued, this time with a note of humour. The scout sent to Otter Creek had found a cache of rum and "Drank so much off, That they forgot the Business they went upon" and had to return. Another party would be sent out and Campbell hoped there would be "no more rum to Barr up the Path." On the February 26, he reported, "The party of Indians sent to the north river conducted by Serjeant Murchison of Sir John Johnson's Regt, returned here on Friday last" and reported the Oneidas were quartered in a blockhouse at Palmerstown just west of Saratoga. The patrol had met a Jessup's serjeant who had been at the Scots Patent and then pursued some sleighs, but failed to catch them because of bad ice and deep snow.[8]

Haldimand wrote a secret dispatch to Dr. Smyth on February 28, repeating the concept he had shared earlier with Sir John. Smyth was to "establish a system of intercourse with trustworthy loyalists before he left the country. Each man should know as little as possible of the instructions given to others so that the various accounts might be compared and the value assessed at Headquarters." He was to use a depository like a hollow tree in a remote situation to hide his packets of intelligence. A long list of critical military and political topics was provided, three of which were of special interest. Two related to the state of public opinion in Vermont. Was it "possible to open the Eyes of the deluded People, and recall them to Allegiance?" Would it be "possible to seize and carry off some of their Leaders, in order more readily to engage the People to Submission?" If an expedition against Albany was undertaken, what force might be

After an oil painting by George Romney. (National Gallery of Canada.)

needed and what were the prospects of success? That same day, Haldimand sent a ciphered letter to Sir Henry Clinton reporting that the province was quiet and that his preparations to meet an invasion had been made with little stir. It was said the enemies' plans had failed because the rebels could not fulfill their part. Some guns had

The Mohawk War Captain, Joseph Brant, 1776. One of the many effective Native leaders, Brant's skill and dedication was recognized by an appointment as a Six Nations' Indian Department captain.

been sent to Stanwix and "dissentions prevail in the Rebel Troops thro'out the Provinces & those at Philadelphia have quitted their Army. I have been put upon my Guard by an Intelligent & staunch friend at Albany against the People of Vermont … who seek to deceive both the Congress & the Royal Army. I shall spare no Pains to work upon those People & if I succeed I shall not fail to tell you of it, but I have great doubts."

Brant had just missed intercepting the provisions convoy and lurked outside Stanwix waiting for another opportunity. The convoy's escort left on March 1, but the sleighs were kept back to draw firewood and next day Brant's scout watched an eight-man woodcutting party with a serjeant's guard of seven leave the fort. He noted their direction of travel, then ran to advise his captain. The detail went a half mile and stopped to cut. At about ten o'clock, a huge volley crashed out of the woods, immediately followed by a swarm of hallooing Indians and Rangers who rushed to take prisoners. The guard serjeant ran off in a hail of bullets. One shot broke a soldier's thigh; another punctured a man's cheek. As the man with the broken leg was unable to march, he was tomahawked and scalped, then the raiders set off with sixteen prisoners in tow. At the road leading to Fort Dayton, Brant halted and ordered the latchets and buckles cut off the prisoners' shoes and carefully displayed on the heavily crusted snow where the pursuit would find them and know that the men were alive and how many were being taken to Niagara. After the captives secured their shoes with deerskin straps, the party crossed the Mohawk and disappeared into the woods. When the escaped serjeant arrived at the fort, a gun was fired to signal to the prisoners that he was safe. He then led a strong sortie to the ambush site where they found the scalped man just as he expired. Pushing on, they came across the latchets and buckles, but, with night falling, they turned back in fear of ambush.

Exactly when Brant knew that one of his men had slipped away is unknown, but Daniel Hewson deserted to the garrison and at 3:00 a.m. an express was sent to warn the Valley below of the raid. Despite the previous day's excitement, the garrison slipped back into its routine. Two men were tried for clothing offences and Hewson was sent to Albany. At Oneida Castle, Brant drew corn, then set off for Niagara, leaving the Valley unaware he had left.

First Major Nicholas Fish, 2NY, forwarded the colonel's report about the attack to Brigadier Clinton from Schenectady, noting the town was alarmed over the news. He planned to impress twenty sleighs for another provisions run to Stanwix and asked advice about what size of guard to send and from where to draw it. His own company had only forty effectives, as did those upriver. He did not want to increase local anxiety by lessening the number of men at any post and wondered if a militia call-out might not be in order. Clinton reckoned the new escort would not run so great a risk as the last and, as Fish's company had recently been upriver, it should be transferred to Johnstown and the company there, plus twenty men from each of the other two companies, would form the escort. Schenectady's townsmen would just have to turn out in their own defence. Fish led the convoy through snow so deep that the road was almost impassable. No path had been cleared past Canajoharie and he could only manage two or three miles a day.

On the way to Niagara, Brant called a noon halt one day. With an Indian's penchant for games, he gave the rebel corporal unloaded firelocks and had him drill the men in Steuben's manual exercise. The Rangers mocked the Continentals, but Brant silenced them with a dark look, saying they drilled a damned sight better than the Rangers and besides, he enjoyed seeing the exercise well done, even by rebels. The party arrived at the fort on March 17.

Infiltration into rebel country was relentless. In March, a pair of Delawares left Niagara and Lieutenant Joseph Ferris of Butler's headed for the Catskills.

Sherwood examined letters that had been intercepted and forwarded by Dr. Smyth. One told of the desire of citizens in two New Hampshire counties to unite with Vermont, as they were envious of the republic's freedom from the concerns of war. Another warned Congress that deserters, malcontents, and Tories were migrating to Vermont. The republic should be admitted without delay lest other states follow her example and collapse the war effort.

On March 1, Haldimand proposed sending a KLA party to cut off the Oneidas at Palmerstown. The same day, he instructed Robertson "to furnish Joseph Brant with such men as he may require for an expedition" and to make fifty pair of snowshoes. Then, he ordered Ross to send sixty men with Brant to Saratoga. Was the governor hedging his bets or planning a two-prong strike or simply keeping all his posts on their toes?

On March 4, the Board of Officers sat at Fort St. John's to examine charges leveled against Major Rogers by Lieutenant-Colonel Peters. The complaints were a mixture of confusion, misrepresentation, and resentment; particularly damning was an allegation that Rogers's recruiters were luring men previously engaged for other corps by making outrageous claims, such as, "if they Joined the Loyalists, their Officers would sell them to General McLean or Sir John for one Guinea Pr. Man." And, should they join "the Loyalists, they would be obliged to go into the works like Slaves and be removed into the back Settlements with the Canadians. That Major Rogers Regiment is to Continue at St Johns during the War for the sole purpose of Ranging at half a dollar Pr. Day; That they will have three Guineas Bounty; That the Royalists will have none; That the Families belonging to Major Rogers get full Rations." Recruiters traditionally used white lies to paint their corps in an alluring light, but there was a danger that such fabrications would damage every unit's chances of recruiting. Rogers denied the charges, noting that seventy of his men were on fatigue duty and others guarding Fort St. John's barracks. Nonetheless, the board recommended that all recruits arriving in the province be examined before assignment to any corps and this was duly implemented.

On the 7th, the enterprising Captain Robertson wrote Haldimand from Oswegatchie for approval to lead a raid against Fort Dayton in German Flatts. Though always pleased to hear bold, imaginative plans from his officers, in this instance, the governor declined.[9]

On the fifth of March, the Albany Conspiracy Committee received alarming news from Lieutenant-Colonel Henry K. Van Rensselaer, 6ACM, about a platoon-sized group of citizens on the Hoosic road who, in an "outrageous, intolerable disregard of the law," rescued two men who had been jailed for refusing to do militia duty. A party from Colonel Cuyler's 1ACM took some of the men and brought them before the board, but for all the uproar, the affair came to nothing.

A rather repugnant strategy that had emerged over the years of the war was the abduction of prominent persons. This could yield several benefits such as creating fear and alarm; disrupting political or military planning; providing critical intelligence and offering the potential to exchange the victim for a key individual of one's own. Such a target was Lieutenant-Colonel Thomas Johnson, a Massachusetts man who was a resident of Newbury in the Cöos country of Vermont. Thomas had migrated to the area in the service of Jacob Bayley and settled beside his mentor on the Great Oxbow of the Ammonoosic River. An innkeeper, church deacon, millwright, merchant, and farmer, he was one of the region's most prosperous and had been an ardent rebel since early in the conflict. As a captain in 1776, Johnson, four men, and Native guide blazed a ninety-two-mile trail over the mountains from Newbury to Fort St. John's. This inland route was seventy-three miles shorter from Boston than the traditional one up Lake Champlain and, on snowshoes, reinforcements for the rebel army in Canada saved ten days' travel. The trail later became the basis of the Hazen-Bayley road. Like Bayley, Johnson was in virulent opposition to Allen's "Bennington mob." Although Haldimand was at pains not to upset Vermont, he thought the removal of Allen's rivals might hasten the secret talks.

The man chosen to scoop Johnson was Captain Azariah Pritchard, a Connecticut man from a divided family whose "Father and Brother were both violent friends to the Rebel cause." A bold adventurous fellow, it was said he had rescued the loyalist mayor of New York City in 1776. In 1777, he had been taken carrying dispatches, but bribed his way free and escaped to Canada where he acted as a guide along the east shore of Lake Champlain until he had recruited sufficient men to join the King's Rangers as a captain in 1780. Pritchard selected ten men, including Levi Sylvester, a

Newbury man, who had been captured while hunting the year before and persuaded to serve as a British express. Oddly enough, his corporal, Abner Barlow, and Ranger John Gibson had also been taken while hunting.

On March 5, Johnson was at Deacon Elkins's house on the Hazen-Bayley road. In the dead of night, the Rangers struck like lightning catching the occupants in their beds. Hearing the furor, Johnson tried to escape out a window, but two Tories pounced on him, brandishing their guns. Later, he dubiously claimed to not being the least afraid, because he recognized his captors as old acquaintances. Pritchard warned the captives not to attempt escape, as 500 Indians were coming to destroy Newbury, a quite plausible threat given the raid on Royalton the year before. Johnson, Jon Elkins Jr., his brother, and a teamster donned snowshoes, hoisted a supply of provisions and were hustled off. The Tories were dressed like Indians in blanket coats, leggings, and pointed snowshoes. They marched through four feet of snow and met up with more of Pritchard's men, who carried the packs along Hazen's road to the notch in the mountains where they sheltered in a hut built the previous winter. Next morning, Elkins's brother looked peaked and, after Thomas explained he had almost drowned as a boy and never been robust, he was sent back. Elkins was amazed by how Johnson chastised Pritchard as a mean, cowardly character who crawled into people's houses to take them in their sleep, but the Tory took it in good grace, agreeing it was a dirty business, but orders were orders. Johnson was allowed to fix a letter to a tree for a passerby to find, a method often used to advise captives' families they were alive. The party followed a river to its mouth, "mushed" fifteen miles up the lake, and crossed the Grande Isle portage. After another ten miles, they came to Pointe au Fer and dined with the commandant.

On March 8, changes were made to Tryon Militia's officers, replacing men who had moved, declined to serve, deserted, or been captured. Captain Andrew Wemple, a relative of John Butler's wife, had deserted 3TCM, gone to Niagara and was now a second lieutenant of the Rangers; he was replaced by the popular John Littel of Johnstown. The company's first lieutenant, William Lord, had been captured in May 1780, joined the enemy and returned as a King's Rangers' recruiter in September. Once apprehended, he was released after agreeing to serve in the nine-months' Levies and tough, popular Solomon Woodworth took his place as first lieutenant. Henry H. Vrooman became second lieutenant vice the disabled Henry B. Vrooman. Days later, second lieutenant Myndert W. Quackenboss of the same company and 3TCM adjutant, Peter Conyne, were suspended for disaffected practices. In a single company, three officers had to be replaced and the rot had seemingly spread to the regimental staff.

When the New York Line was deranged, Colonel Peter Gansevoort, the hero of Fort Stanwix, faced the prospect of unemployment. Fortunately for him, Abraham Ten Broeck, who had commanded Albany County's first brigade for several years, had been elected Albany's mayor in 1779 and was finding the two roles too demanding. He chose to retire to politics and Gansevoort became a militia brigadier.

The Albany board received word that Peter Ball of Beaver Dam, a BR first lieutenant, was at home recruiting. Means were to be found to take him. Two days later, the commissioners permitted Dr. George Smyth to come to the city to settle private business. They also examined a list of wives of men who were with the enemy and had been warned to leave the state or remove to its interior. When two trusted men certified that several had always behaved well, they were allowed to remain at their homes.[10]

At Carleton Island, Major Ross, 2KRR, wrote to HQ to reinforce Sir John's complaint that the Indian fusils were improper for training, as without bayonets, the men could not be indoctrinated in the key British tactic — the charge with cold steel. The governor replied that Indian arms would have to continue in use until the following summer, but gave no explanation. There was no lack of arms, as the previous October, there were 595 stand of "fuzees" at Sorel and 410 "fuzees" at St. John's. As well, a very large stock of Canadian Provincial clothing was at Sorel and Quebec. The governor was prepared to arm and clothe Quebeckers in case of invasion, but chose not to alarm Ross by saying so.

On March 9, Ethan Allen sent copies of Lieutenant-Colonel Robinson's secret letters to the Continental Congress, hoping to promote so much concern that the United States would admit Vermont as a separate state rather than risk her defection to the British. In his usual blustering fashion, he wrote, "I am resolutely determined to defend the independence of Vermont … and rather than fail, will retire with the hardy Green Mountain Boys into the desolate caverns of the mountains and wage war with Human nature at large."

That day, Colonel Johannes Snyder, 1UCM, wrote to the governor about the treasonous activities of his captain whose company beat was in the mountains on Albany County's border. The fellow proposed to not pay taxes, or obey military orders, or comply with assessments for grain or forage, and, when some Whigs protested, cursed them and swore he would kill the collector that laid hands on his goods. A few days later, he and some supporters signed a "Protection" from Sir Henry Clinton. Since then, local Tories had been in high spirits and the Whigs entirely cowed. Snyder was frozen into indecision about how to address the situation. In frustration, the governor wrote, "I am surprised that you should be in Doubt how to proceed … they are guilty of Treason, or at least sedition; & you can as a Civil Magistrate by your warrant commit them to goal."

On March 12, the long-awaited court of inquiry into the conduct of militia brigadier, Robert Van Rensselaer, met in Albany to examine his conduct during Sir John's fall raid. The finding was unanimous and unequivocal: "The whole of General Rensselaer's Conduct both before and after, as well as in the action of the 19th of October last, was not only unexceptionable, but such as became a good, active, faithful, prudent & spirited officer and that the public Clamore raised to his Prejudice … are without the least Foundation"; however, Tryon residents remained unpersuaded and his role as CO of their militia was not renewed.

On March 13, the Albany commission was told that the notorious Tory spy, Joseph Bettys, had been seen sleighing in Rensselaerwyck Manor. Next day, word came about his exact whereabouts, but he managed to slip away. On the March 15, Lieutenant Jacob Snyder brought two men from Schoharie who were said to have assisted Sir John the previous fall. One was a Beaver Dam farmer and Snyder produced a list of the many other disaffected persons from there. Both men were jailed and later released under bail. The commission was simply overwhelmed by the disaffected. A few could be confined for brief periods, but the sheer volume prevented long jail terms. In any event, goods from Tory farms could always be confiscated later. Only the most fervent and outrageous were sent away for long prison terms; from which, many did not return.

When the Albany commission examined Brant's deserter, Daniel Hewson, he coughed up a flood of information including specific details of Haldimand's spy network and the identity of its chief coordinator — Dr. George Smyth. The doctor's very successful run was almost at an end. How he managed to escape the rope is a mystery.

———————————————

At Isle aux Noix, Thomas Johnson was joined by Pritchard and Sherwood over a dinner, bottle of wine, and conversation. Sherwood stayed with Johnson overnight. This special treatment was leading somewhere and, either Thomas was too naïve to recognize it, or he welcomed it.

Sir John reported that 1KRR Light Infanteer, John Parker, one of his favourite agents, had brought newspapers from Schenectady that his father had obtained at some risk from Reverend Stuart. As the Parkers were so useful, Johnson pled for a pardon for John's brother, who had been sentenced to death for theft while he was "greatly disguised in liquor." This was granted.

Claus reported:

> Captain John with twenty-two of his Tribe had set off from la Chine to be at Carleton Island by the 25th Inst., the Day Appointed between him & Joseph, and yesterday I heard of his arrival at St. Regis [Akwesasne], and that the Six Nations Indians settled there (chiefly

Onondagas) asked Leave to join him with about 20 men, to which he consented, upon which they dispatched an Express to Colo. Campbell and an Order for their Necessaries for the March ... they may easily get to Carleton Island about the day appointed ... But I hope ... John will proceed at any rate should Joseph delay coming, having fixed his Rout before leaving this.

———————————————
———————————————

On March 21, with a treasury devoid of funds, New York State passed an act "for Raising Two Regiments on Bounties of Unappropriated Lands."[11]

4

*T*he new season at Stanwix was marked by another ugly event when a private abused Captain Moodie's wife and daughter and abandoned his post. He was given fifty lashes, but unrest deepened when two men deserted their guard posts and refused to return. The ringleader was awarded 100 lashes, his mate, fifty.

Governor Clinton was in Schenectady on March 24 to discuss the town's defence. He approved building new perimeter works and recommended Major Fish to oversee construction, as no engineer was available. As he was unable to provide guns, he suggested gathering up the small pieces and swivels scattered along the river, but at the same time cautioned it would be prudent to rely primarily on musketry for defence. Two blockhouses were named Forts Squash and Volunteer, each garrisoned by twenty-three locals raised for the duty along with a fifteen-man artillery company.

On March 27, the governor wrote to Haldimand:

> Sir, While I entertain too high an opinion of your character as a gentleman to suppose you inclined to add to the miseries of war by involving in it the Captivity of helpless women and Children, permit me to assure you it has always been my Desire from motives of humanity, to afford them whether connected with friends or enemies, any relief that their situation required and circumstances

would admit. Influenced by these considerations I directed Coll: Gansevoort last fall to forward to Major Carleton, who was then in the vicinity of Crown Point, upwards of one hundred women & Children whose husbands and parents were then in Canada.

I now inclose your Excellency a list of the names of sundry women & Children, who at different periods have been taken by parties in the British service in the ravaging incursions on the frontiers … and have to request, that your Excellency will order them to be liberated, and furnished with the necessary means to return to their families.

His next sentences must have struck a raw nerve:

It becomes at the same time my duty to inform your Excellency that unless the inhuman & unmilitary practice of capturing women & Children ceases, I shall be reduced to the disagreeable necessity of detaining & treating the remaining families of those who have gone into the British Lines as objects of Exchange, and thus involuntarily increase the Distresses of many whom the Fate of War have separated from their nearest Connections.

The mournfully long list was organized by place of capture and date. Particularly revealing were those taken at Fort Plank in August 1780. None were males of militia age; thirteen were women, twenty-five or under, and one thirty-seven. Thirty-seven were children, sixteen male, twenty-one female, fifteen of which were five or younger, seven only one year old. The bitterness barely hidden in Clinton's letter is easily understood by imagining the terror of being captured, driven through the wilderness and thrust into the harsh, unfamiliar and, at times, vengeful life of the Native villages.

On August 29, Brigadier-General Clinton complained to his brother about his troops' lack of provisions. He had had to remove the

Fort Edward detachment and other posts may have to be abandoned unless means were found to furnish subsistence. The governor wrote to Washington explaining that, although the state agent was empowered to draw funds to buy beef, the treasury was destitute and there would be none until new currency was printed. He requested a supply of provisions from Continental stores, adding, if the troops left the frontiers, the inhabitants would surely follow.

John Stuart, the Tory Anglican minister, wrote to Governor Clinton on August 30 to say he had been a paroled prisoner of the conspiracy commission for two years and confined to Schenectady and his farm lay empty, unused and unprotected. His family wished to be exchanged for some citizen of the state held in Canada and asked permission to proceed under the protection of the first public flag. The same day, the commission confiscated the properties of five men serving in the Royal Yorkers.[1]

Washington knew that when the Continentals were gone from the north, the defence would rely on militiamen. He had earlier written, "no Militia will ever acquire the habits necessary to resist a regular force. Even those nearest the seat of War are only valuable as light Troops to be scattered in the woods and plague rather than do serious injury to the Enemy. The firmness requisite for the real business of fighting is only to be attained by a constant course of discipline and service." He had noted his deep concern about short-term enlistments in the army to Governor Clinton, warning that the British were sending reinforcements for the 1781 campaign and that their last hope "is built upon our inability to raise a new army, and they are probably preparing to push us in our enfeebled State." His fond wish was to raise "men whose services are permanent," but this hope was not met and short-terms persisted, as men shied away from serving for the length of the war.

In prior years when the Continentals had been withdrawn for duty elsewhere, the problem of militia ineffectiveness was addressed by levying men from the militia to serve in state regiments for terms ranging from three to nine months. When a company's term was up, another arrived to replace it, which kept the regiment at full strength through to December 1. This same method was employed to fill the States' quotas for Continental service with the difference that recruits for the Levies knew they would serve only in a defined region, like the frontiers, not across the union. For 1781, New York ultimately raised four regiments of Levies, two specifically to defend the northern frontiers. As in 1780, Massachusetts provided a third for the same purpose. In April, Governor Clinton approached Marinus Willett to command the regiment slated for northwest defence.

Willett was a New York native and former lieutenant-colonel commandant of the deranged 5NY. The youngest of six sons, his schoolteacher father ensured his sound education, which was later obvious from his excellent writing skills and rich vocabulary. His father left school-teaching to keep a tavern in New York City, where the active and daring Willett grew up to be a tall, hawk-nosed, politically active young man. In 1758, he was a second lieutenant of the NY Provincials and fought in the disastrous Ticonderoga battle, and later, at the reduction of Fort Frontenac. The joy of his second action ended on a low note when he caught dysentery. Ironically, he lay close to death for over two months in the camp outside the construction site of Fort Stanwix, where he later made such a name for himself. Despite the long convalescence, his martial ardour remained, displaying a physical toughness that was to be of such importance to his Revolutionary War career. Willett yearned to re-enter the regiment, but his father dissuaded him and he joined a cabinet factory. Two years later, he married the proprietor's daughter and the couple started a family.

Willett might have settled into a quiet routine had it not been for the tumult in the city over British attempts to raise revenue to offset the costs of the Seven Years' War. He soon found himself at odds with his pro-British father when he joined the Sons of Liberty, a secret cell of extremists, and participated in several acts of open defiance. In 1775, he made a bold stroke when the city's small garrison of Regulars was leaving to reinforce Boston. He was at a tavern with some of the Sons when word came that soldiers were removing wagons full of military stores. The activists dispersed through the city to see what was afoot and Willett came across the small convoy. Recognizing a need for bold, decisive action, he stopped the lead wagon. When a major came to find the reason for the halt, Willett claimed the troops had no right to remove weapons from the city other than personal arms. This was pure bluff, as

Detail of oil painting by Ralph Earl, circa 1790. (Metropolitan Museum of Art, Bequest of George Willett Van Nest, 1917. [17.87.1])

Lieutenant-Colonel Marinus Willett (1740–1830). An officer of conduct and ability.

the army had every right to remove the King's arms, but there had been so many earlier disorders, the officer was befuddled. The city's Tory mayor and some leading Whigs arrived and a debate ensued. Willett closed the matter by simply ordering the drivers to follow him and headed the lead horse down a side lane. These weapons later equipped the 1NY (in which Willett commanded a company for the 1775 invasion of Canada). After some time commanding Fort St. John's, his company fell under strength and he was sent home where, in recognition of his services and fervent, early support of the rebellion, he received a major promotion to lieutenant-colonel of the 3NY. In 1777, the regiment was in the Mohawk Valley at Fort Stanwix, where he burnished to legendary proportions his reputation for decisive and daring action.

Clinton saw him as the ideal candidate, not only to command the Levies, but to manage the overall defence of the northwest frontier. Thanks to his daring deeds during the Stanwix siege and his common sense, inspirational style of command, he had the confidence of the Tryon and Albany militias; however, the opportunity was not overly attractive to a man of Willett's ambitions, as the frontiers were a career backwater, offering no chance for advancement in the Line. He knew that Tryon's militia had been shattered at Oriskany and that the Mohawk region was an open target for raiding. He was also aware of the people's anger over the ruinous raids of last fall and recognized that once the Regulars left, the commander could only count on the new Levies and a dispirited militia. With Brigadier-General Van Rensselaer discredited, command of the militia rested with the senior colonel, Jacob Klock, who, while a Valley man, was ill regarded. Yet, Clinton was persuasive, stroking Willett's ego and appealing to his strong sense of duty. The task was a major challenge, and Willett, who revelled in tests, accepted.[2]

At Stanwix on April 1, more orders were issued warning of severe punishments for leaving the fort without consent. Next day, the garrison's baker, an artillery serjeant, was reduced to matross for stealing flour and bread and half his pay was stopped until the losses were made good. Then, some infantry NCOs were found guilty of calling in sentinels from their posts rather than collecting them. The very next day, three matrosses were found guilty of "strolling from the fort without permission" and awarded fifty lashes each. One was excused when he pled that his captain had given approval, which prompted the commandant to publicly chastise the officer for defying his orders.

Congress resolved that the two regiments of Levies to be embodied by New York until December 1 would be paid, clothed, and subsisted at public expense like Continentals. There were two conditions: 1) the State must complete the First and Second New York and 2) the Levies must be led by reduced, half-pay officers in proportion to the number of men in service. Their employment would result in savings and their experience would be of value.

Dr. Smyth was examined on the April 3 to hear why he was in Albany without the commission's permission. He said he had been ordered to the city by General Clinton to prepare for removal to Canada and was given eight days to complete his business. He was to post a bond of £500, one-fifth of which allowed him to remove a black man who was judged capable of bearing arms. Smyth promised to arrange an exchange for one of four significant rebels held in Canada; should he fail to do so, he and his slave were to return to Albany or lose the £500. His real estate was forfeit, although he could sell or carry off personal goods. With understandable bitterness, he chose to leave nothing behind that would require him to return after the war. As soon as it was safe and convenient, the family would travel under a flag by wagons to Fort Ann and from there in bateaux. With both Smyth and Stuart under close watch, Haldimand's Secret Service network was becoming fragile. On April 17, Brigadier-General Clinton permitted the Smyth family to remove to New City to await exchange.

On April 6, Washington wrote a secret letter about Vermont to his confidant, Lord Stirling, enclosing copies of the official letters and laws on the matter and details of the republic's claim. Ira Allen had represented to Congress that the "Northern and Western Frontier could only be protected from the Ravages of a barbarous & Ruthless Savage Enemy by the Numbers & Military Prowess of the State of Vermont" and that the price of its assistance was independence as a state. There were daily reports, probably emanating from Vermont, promoting fear in Albany and Schenectady of a British invasion once the lakes froze over. There was even news that raiders were on the way. Washington had heard that Vermont's proposition had been prepared early last fall and that some "monied Gentlemen" were speculating in Vermont land in anticipation of its independence from New York. They had become "warmly interested" in the outcome and were swaying the Senate toward acceptance. Immediately prior to the Senate's sitting, Vermont had extended its claim west "to the deepest Channel of Hudson's River," i.e. the Western Union. This certainly altered affairs. Washington also mentioned the two New Hampshire counties on the east bank of the Connecticut that were involved in Vermont's machinations and thought Stirling would be able to see the danger of these various expansions which were so far beyond the original claim to the "old" Grants.

Despite his many reasons for distress, Governor Clinton wrote a remarkably buoyant letter to the United States' representative in Paris, undoubtedly for the edification of the French ally. When he mentioned the destruction of Tryon and Schoharie the year before, he reported how the inhabitants had remained in those districts and hutted themselves, continuing to work their farms and assist in the defence. Of militiamen, he wrote, "Every Man, indeed every Boy, has become a Soldier, and I do not believe a superior Spirit of Bravery & Enterprize ever possessed a People." He acknowledged the union's faltering finances, but noted that resources remained great and provisions, whose prices in hard coin had not inflated since the start of the war, abounded (the fact that specie had nearly vanished went unstated). Further, last fall, the British impatiently waited for Continental enlistment terms to expire, hoping that new recruiting would fail; however, men had "as ready a Disposition to enter into the Service as at any Time since the Beginning, with this advantage, every Recruit we now engage has the Experience & habit of a veteran Soldier." The grief with Vermont was dismissed with a simple statement of his hopes for a speedy and just decision.

In view of what was actually occurring with shortages of provisions and halting enlistments, this letter was a tour de force in fantasy. In contrast, that very same day, he wrote to James Duane, a NY congressional delegate, saying the conduct of "the People on the Grants" became more serious daily and Congress should have stepped in long before now. He had no positive proof of "a criminal Communication between them & the Enemy," but there was much reason for suspicion. He knew of the Haldimand correspondence, ostensibly over a prisoner exchange, but doubted Vermont had a single British prisoner. He was aware that Joseph Fay had set out for Canada in sleighs, but had been foiled by bad ice. He reminded Duane that the British had been unmolested when they passed Vermont the previous fall to destroy posts and farms in New York and mentioned his yearning for a settlement as long as it did not exceed the original Grants.

Killings and captures on the frontiers continued through the spring. In April, a man was taken on the Delaware River perhaps by Captain Shenop's Nanticokes on their return from Wyoming. Near Fort Plain, the family of a former soldier of the Levies was attacked. A son was killed and the father escaped, but his wife, daughter, and two other sons were taken. The two women and one son were released, but the other was killed in a skirmish between the war party and the pursuit. On April 9 at Stanwix, two men of the 2NY's Light Company were killed and one taken.[3]

At Fort Niagara, 8th Regiment surgeon Dr. James Causeland reported that over the two previous years and part of a third, he had under his care the sick of the various corps at the post, listing the 34th, 47th, 84th, KRR and Brant's volunteers, oddly ignoring the major and constant elements of the garrison, his own regiment and BR. "[T]he sick at the fort had amounted to more than 100 each year" for the last five. Yet, Niagara was no more prone to illness than any British post where severe weather and poor diet took a toll over the winter. Nor could health have been much better at the rebel posts on the Mohawk River. As the winter wore on, Butler had found himself with a "naked store." He was constantly equipping parties for the frontiers and often had to send away Native families seeking subsistence with promises that their needs would be met when the first vessels made it through in the spring. He shared his concerns with Ross and, when the navigation of Lake Ontario opened on April 2, the major dispatched provisions' ships.

In lower Quebec, attempts to fill up the small loyalist corps continued. On April 3, Rogers reported the completion of three companies and his hopes to have a battalion by the fall if he was allowed to recruit from New England and in Quebec from men who had declined other regiments. He sought permission to amalgamate his companies with Peters's QLR, "first to Compleat one Battalion and afterwards a Second" and offered assurances that his brother Robert had no objection to him being commissioned in Canada. In a second letter, they suggested their ranks in the new unit; Rogers would be lieutenant-colonel and

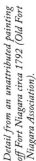

Detail from an unattributed painting of Fort Niagara circa 1792 (Old Fort Niagara Association).

The French castle predominates the skyline with two heavy redoubts and a garrison flag to the right. The outbuildings housed naval and Six Nations' Indian Department stores.

Peters the major. This accommodation indicated they had resolved their earlier disagreements and, by being willing to accept a lower rank, Peters acknowledged his diminished reputation with the governor; however, the proposal went nowhere.

Powell reported on April 7 that he had mustered Butler's Rangers and the men looked fine in their new clothing. Butler believed he could raise two more companies and he had given him permission to send out recruiting parties. He broached a significant and revealing issue:

> [T]he Rangers, when ... out upon scouts, are frequently obliged to sell their necessaries to supply ... provisions, which is seldom reimbursed, I send the account of expense incurred by ... Lieut Turney's last party ... the things mentioned in it were sold to supply the whole party and as they received no provisions from Government ... would [it] not be right upon such occasions, either to reimburse them the money laid out for provisions, or to make their provisions up to them for the time they received none from the garrison?[4]

Haldimand's need for fresh intelligence was insatiable. On April 9, Robertson reported details of Forts Dayton and Herkimer gleaned from prisoners brought to Oswegatchie. Two days later, the captain was instructed to send out "an intelligent party," presumably of Indians and Highlanders, to intercept a convoy of seventy sleighs going from Schenectady to Stanwix. They were to take prisoners, but no scalps, and bring any news of the guns being sent upriver.

Brant's earlier plan to punish the Oneidas at Palmerston had gone awry. A disappointed Deserontyon wrote to Claus on April that Brant was not at Carleton Island. Nonetheless, John would leave in three days with forty warriors and be back in twenty days. Just after this letter was sent to Claus, news came to the island of Brant's injury in a drunken brawl with a departmental officer at Niagara. Deserontyon again wrote to Claus instructing him to tell General Assaregowa (Haldimand) about the incident so he would "preserve mutual peace and welfare." John's reaction was mild compared to Brant's sister, Mary. In her view, he was "almost murdered by Colo. Johnsons people. [W]hat adds to my Grief and Vexation is that [he] being scarce returned safe from the Rebel Country, he must be thus treated by those of the Kings people who always stay quietly at home & in the Fort, while my Brother continually exposes his Life in going against the Enemy." Realizing the harm that might arise, Guy Johnson sent Brant to Detroit with belts for the Lakes' Nations the day after the fracas. He was to visit their villages and engage them to defend Detroit against Clark's rumoured attack. The fight's cause was never discussed.

When Joseph Brant wrote Claus from Fort Erie on April 11 that he was upset at having failed Captain John and blamed Guy Johnson, whose mind he found incomprehensible. On April 17, Ross reported that Deserontyon had set off and that two new scouts would soon be sent to the Mohawk.

Mathews sent Butler approval for the promotion of his son Thomas to first lieutenant and for the raising of two new companies. In the interest of reducing Niagara's dependence on British rations, ten bushels of spring wheat seed and four each of buckwheat, oats, and peas, with some smaller seeds, had been sent to Coteau-du-Lac with instructions they be in the first bateau to start upriver.

A second blockhouse was being erected on the Yamaska River and a twenty-two-man detachment from the loyalist corps was sent to assist under Lieutenant John Dulmage's command.

Haldimand advised Sir John that Dr. Smyth had fled to Major Fay's in Vermont after the deserter Hewson testified at Albany. He bemoaned the loss of his best source and hoped Reverend Stuart would replace him. He added that he required men to make regular ventures for information, but cautioned that they must agree not to visit their families, as so many had been taken while doing so. Always one to offer practical ideas, he suggested a drop box such as a hollow tree as a safe depository for packets.

On April 9, five 2NY men were attacked outside Stanwix. Three were killed, two taken prisoner, and one wounded. As the snow melted, Tryon's roads became quagmires. Peter Walradt was called out with his team to carry provisions from Fort Plain to Stanwix, a distance of sixty miles. The mud was so deep he could only move two or three miles a day. When he arrived at Stanwix, he was kept to draw wood for several days and was away from home for five weeks.

A mixed party of fifteen Indians and Butler's Rangers "broke out" at Coxsackie and took prisoner Captain David Abeel, 11ACM, and his son, Lieutenant Anthony. The Natives who brought the Abeels to Niagara said the Rangers stayed behind to organize thirty recruits they had enlisted over the winter. Obviously, in order to winter over in the Catskills, they had been assisted by the locals and it may have been this incident that prompted the governor to write his brother about persons who had come last fall from the enemy and were at the Hellebergh and nearby places. The brigadier was to consult with Gansevoort about how to proceed and to send parties from Catskill, Coxsackie, Schoharie, and Albany to apprehend them. Detachments were sent, but, apparently, to no avail.

On April 11, the commissioners heard that Philip Lansingh, who had run off to Canada the year before, was in the area carrying dispatches destined for New York City and a plan was made to take him. They then heard that a Tory suspect, previously warned to appear before the Supreme Court, had instead enlisted in the nine-months' service.

At Stanwix, it was Cochran's turn to find irregularities with the guards. He ordered, "Sentinals on their posts after Tattoo beating are to call all is well once in a quarter of an Hour, but not till ordered, which order is to be Given by the officer of the Guard, to the Sergeant Who is to order Number one at the Guard house to call all is well, which call is to be answered distinctley in Rotation, as they are Numbered except the Sentinal at the Commanding officers door, who is not to answer, he is in case of an alarme to call the Commanding officer." Eminently sensible, but why did Regulars need so much reminding?[5]

Unrest at Niagara took a different form. The governor wrote Powell about the implications of a General Court Martial ordered by Butler to punish men who had been stirring up dissension prejudicial to the Service and the corps. This was to play out later. Haldimand was irritated that Butler had taken exception to McKinnon being appointed to company command and wrote, "[he] ought not, to think extraordinary what is every day unavoidably practiced in established regiments." The governor was at a loss to see how Butler could consider the appointment of a long-service captain a hardship to the Rangers, as he had so recently sought the same rank for his son Thomas, who had never served at all. As to disappointing men he had appointed, he should not put them in orders until they were approved at HQ. The new companies were to be raised one at a time, swiftly, and without hindrance to the service and, to lessen the blow of so much censure, Andrew Bradt was approved as captain for the first company completed.

———————————————

———————————————

Washington advised Brigadier-General Clinton on April 12 of measures taken to "throw" salt provisions into Albany. He understood that the U.S. armoury in Albany had badly declined, but there were insufficient funds to correct the problem.

Once again, Cochran observed irregularities in guard mounting at Stanwix and repeated his February orders, adding, "the officer of the Guard is ... to remain at all times with his Guard paraded, when the gates are opened or when a party is marching in. The Sentinals after Nine Oclock are to Chalenge every person and not suffer them to pass unless they give the Countersign except those who are going to the Necesary House who are not to pass or Repass without giving their Names." Two days later, he ordered the troops to exercise from ten in the morning till twelve and from three in the afternoon till five, weather permitting. Perhaps it was hoped to address the many disorders amongst the troops with some positive activity.

On the April 14, Brigadier-General Gansevoort sent the governor a sorry report. Eight barrels of powder had arrived from the main army, but he had no ball, lead, twine, thread, cartridge paper, or flints. Many militiamen were without arms. On occasion, they had been supplied from the Continental armoury, but he understood the C-in-C had stopped such issues and ordered a recall of those Continental arms now in militia hands. Yet, those who had received arms were so poor they could not purchase their own. Clinton held out little hope of making up these supplies or for arming the poor, as the state's and Continental stores were empty.

On April 15, letters were sent by the New York legislature to Marinus Willett and Frederick Weissenfels to formally inquire of their willingness to command the Levies. The same day, the conspiracy commission heard about a suspicious person who had stopped for a few days at a house near Cooeyman's Patent. An officer went to take the fellow and next day reported success, but when his party arrived at Albany, the man escaped. A second party retook him and, a day later, he was brought before the board with the householder, a known disaffected person.

On April 16, Governor Clinton received intelligence that Moses Harris Jr. of Kingsbury was to take a packet to Albany for the Tory Secret Service

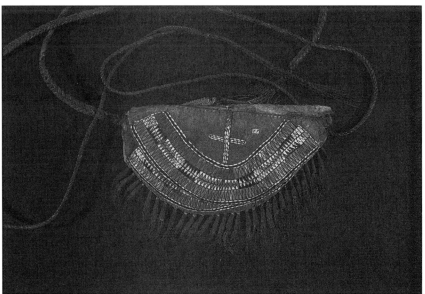

McCord Museum, ME984X.59.

Eastern Woodlands' Native Pouch, late eighteenth, early nineteenth century. Smoke-tanned deer hide decorated with dyed quills in white, orange, and black slung by a finger-woven and braided strap of natural vegetable fibre.

agent, Thomas Smyth, and to carry another back to him. Washington suggested that Schuyler could open the letters without breaking the seals and make copies, then allow the packet to continue on its way and the British would be none the wiser. On similar business, Washington sent the governor an anonymous report from a man who had been near Skenesborough and, when he fell in with an enemy party from Canada, pretended he was a Tory. The party's leader was the same Ensign Thomas Smyth, 1KRR, late of Albany, and his men were Caleb Clossen, Andrew Rikely, and one other. The pretend Tory was told that the Grants had privately agreed to lay down their arms on the approach of the British early in the spring. Also, the British had boats and shipping at St. John's to put into Lake George and many other preparations, even pickets for fortification, and 8,000 Regulars and Tories. Schuyler was immediately informed.[6]

Brinton Paine, lieutenant-colonel of Dubois's Levies in 1780, reported to Governor Clinton that folk on the east side of the Hudson River were restless after Ethan Allen had visited and promised them security if they joined Vermont. Paine had some success in dissuading them from the idea and in urging them to raise men for the Levies, but people moved away daily, regardless of arguments to keep them on their farms. Personally, he was unable to serve in the new Levies, but recommended Captain Holtham Dunham, 13ACM. He believed Albany County's five northern regiments would supply enough men for two companies, but noted that the locals were concerned about the large quantities of flour being sent to Albany from their local mill, as none would be left for their own troops. Days later, Clinton wrote that Dunham had been appointed a Levies' captain and instructed Paine to warn the people of the "fatal Consequences that must result to them should they swerve from their allegiance by encouraging & uniting with the People of the Grants."

Sir John shared Haldimand's concerns about Hewson's betrayal of Smyth and, unaware that Reverend Stuart was planning to take his family to

Canada, predicted that the priest and other Schenectady men could fill the gap. He reported that he had many men willing to act as agents, "whose fidelity, Secrecy and Knowledge of the Country he [could] vouch for." He would use two of Claus's Mohawks and send Lieutenant Mathew Howard, QLR, and Volunteer Philip Lansingh, KRR, to locate drop points near Johnstown and west of Fort Edward. Tin cases would be provided to protect the documents. His most recent scout had been delayed due to a lack of salt provisions. They had been ordered to go to Gilliland's, a well-known rendezvous on Champlain, and remain there to intercept "Indian Emissaries" coming to Kahnawake, but St. Leger had stopped them at Fort St. John's, as they were without orders from the governor. As well, Brigadier-General Maclean, OC Montreal District, had quibbled over supplying scouts with salt provisions. Three days later, Haldimand wrote to advise Johnson that he had clarified both officers' instructions. The flow of information from New York was now firmly in the baronet's hands.

Thomas Johnson, Pritchard's Cöos prisoner, continued to bask in British hospitality. Later, he claimed to have gained his keepers' confidence by convincing them he favoured a reunion of Britain and Vermont, yet the treatment of fellow Cöos prisoner, Jon Elkins, was in such marked contrast, other reasons must be suspected. Elkins suffered terrible deprivation before being sent to prison in England. As a norm, prisoners were kept in Canada and exchanged from there, so it seems Elkins's removal was an artifice to keep secret Johnson's agreement to aid the British. Lieutenant-Colonel Peters warned Sherwood: "Don't think I take too much on myself when I tell you, he is very subtle, will not stick at 50 guineas ... to give intelligence to his rebel friend Bailey ... at the same time will speak light ... to you. I am not prejudiced against ... [him] as an Individual, but a Rebel he is."

Colonel Klock of Tryon's Palatine District advised the governor that he had formed his district's males of age sixteen and up into classes of twenty. Some classes were manning Forts Walrath and Nelles where the only gristmills in his district were located. He worried that if the mills were destroyed, a general evacuation would result. Klock recommended his son, Jacob Jr., (who had resigned the year before as a 1NY ensign), as the captain to receive Levies' recruits. He also recommended two others as his lieutenants, one of whom might have been seen as more qualified to command a company — but blood was thicker than water. As it transpired, none of them were appointed by the state, which perhaps said more about the colonel than the men in question. Klock sought a solution to a problem that must have plagued all militia regiments. Four returned prisoners of war had been classed, but refused to pay toward the recruiting of a man until their exchange was officially recognized. The governor's advice has not been found.

On April 18, a former conspiracy commissioner reported being at a Charlotte County court where Vermont's agents circulated petitions urging the inhabitants to abandon New York and come under the republic's jurisdiction. "Granville and Skenesborough have almost to a man signed it, and so has Cambridge. White Creek are in general against it." He had heard that Ethan Allen had received secret letters from the British about making the Grants' folk "a distinct People not under the authority of Congress." Major John Younglove of Cambridge sent a similar report. Ira Allen and others had taken pains to throw local people into great disorder and held meetings to get them to join Vermont. Of great concern, the major noted that Colonel John Blair, 16ACM, was in favour of the idea, as were a hundred others.

Next day, the Albany commission ordered a man seized for distributing counterfeit Continental bills, which was a severe threat against an already devalued currency. On April 20, the board got word that the Tory fugitive, John Ruiter of Hoosic, was hiding there. A veteran Provincial lieutenant, John had been passed over when Leake's Company was formed and was likely recruiting to reestablish his rank.[7]

Also on April 20, Mathews sent confidential advice to Powell about the "Lauren's plan" to attack Canada. The rebels' most threatening goal for the Upper Country was to occupy Oswego, which would endanger Niagara and Detroit. Powell was to take every precaution to secure his post; plan how to oppose a rebel advance on Oswego and regularly to send out scouts to determine enemy activity. He was advised that the rebels had forwarded extra provisions and guns to Stanwix and that Washington had been at Albany, ostensibly to improve affairs with Vermont. As Smyth had been exposed, Powell was to ask Butler about using Rangers to collect intelligence, possibly by posing as deserters.

As for Vermont affairs, there was William Marsh, a rather shadowy figure who had been a pre-war colonel of Grants' militia, a Green Mountain Boy, and friend of the Allens and Chittenden. He had served under Burgoyne as an advisor and, after the surrender, became a useful member of the Secret Service. On April 21, he suggested to Haldimand that he make a peaceable offer to the Vermonters to stir up dissension amongst them and, if they spurned the proposal, he recommended harassing their frontiers. On a related issue, he opined that no man in Canada knew Cumberland and Gloucester counties better than James Rogers. He could raise more men than any other, as he was known as one of the region's best soldiers in the previous war.

On April 21, Colonel Guy Johnson submitted a return of 6NID's activities for year-to-date 1781. Five hundred men had been out on service. War parties had burned 4 forts, 102 houses, 60 granaries, and 10 mills and killed 44 men, released 44, and taken 143 males prisoner — a grim record indeed for so early in the campaign. Of course, this report excluded QID's activities.

———————————————

———————————————

By chance, War Captains John Deserontyon and Aaron Hill and their forty-four-man party of Fort Hunters and Tuscaroras met up with Lieutenant William Ryer Bowen's (6NID) party out of Niagara, probably at a secret supply depot. Bowen had earlier suffered a long captivity and his family had been harshly used by Tryon's committee, so he had little sympathy for rebels. In the afternoon of April 24, the two parties struck Bowman's Creek near Canajoharie, destroying a house and gristmill. They then went to Cherry Valley and divided into three groups: thirty men

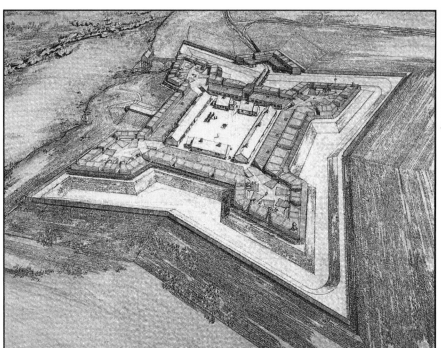

Orvill W. Carroll, artist. (Casemates and Cannonballs, Archeological Investigations at Fort Stanwix National Monument. Washington: U.S. Department of the Interior, National Park Service, 1975.)

Fort Stanwix (Fort Schuyler) — an isolated, unpopular posting on the far western frontier. Great attention was paid to holding this post "to the last extremity," yet when rain and fire rendered it untenable, it was remarkable to observe how readily it was abandoned.

destroyed the local fort, another bunch killed and mutilated four people and carried off sixteen, and the rest went to a farm, killed five, took a prisoner or two, and burned the buildings. At the latter, Moses Nelson watched his mother's killer tear off her scalp. There was no firm reaction to these attacks in Canajoharie District; no attempt to catch and punish the raiders; no attempt to recover the captives. A serjeant and twenty 1TCM men came to bury the dead and met up with an escaped man who warned that the war party was eighty strong, all but two painted like Indians. The detail wisely turned back. When the raiders withdrew, they divided into small groups for ease of collecting food. Two Stockbridge brothers took Nelson down Cherry Valley creek to Otsego Lake where they built a basswood bark canoe to paddle the Susquehanna to Tioga. Their share of the hogs and sheep was roasted in the Native manner by burning off hair or wool. When the war party reassembled at the

Genesee flats villages, the captives were made to run the gauntlet. An older fellow ran with a heavy pack on his back and was almost killed. One of the brothers took Nelson's pack and stood at a wigwam door to watch him. He was fast and agile and was little hurt. His captor remarked, "You did run well." When the other brother decided to kill Nelson, he was cynically told, "You must first kill me, then you will have two scalps and be a big man." This tale was typical of the capriciousness of captives' ordeals. Captain Butler's report dispassionately itemized the parties' successes: six rebels killed, ten captured, twenty-four houses and barns and a gristmill destroyed, thirty cattle and seven horses taken.[8]

———————————————————

———————————————————

Despite the many warnings, on about April 24, two Continentals wandered outside Stanwix and were captured. Next day, a soldier who had been punished for sleeping on duty in February, was found guilty of using firewood for his personal use. In the belief that a good dose of public humiliation might improve the fellow, he was sentenced to have a large block of wood chained to his leg for six days while he performed the noxious duties of colourman, removing waste from the fort's streets and buildings. Another soldier was found guilty of leaving his post to urinate. After he pled that many did the same, Cochran forgave his penalty with a warning that those who followed such "corrupt" practices could expect the full penalty for their crimes.

On April 26, Smyth managed to secretly report to Haldimand that, if a force large enough to protect local loyalists could come from Canada, he had an excellent plan to "reduce" Albany and vicinity. Rumours of this were assiduously spread about and shook Albanian confidence; however, the governor had neither the resources for nor interest in such a venture, as he was convinced that a force would fail without ample support from New York City.

On April 27, Governor Clinton took firm action against Vermont's machinations, issuing instructions to five Charlotte County Justices of the Peace. He was loath to believe that any of the state's citizens had given "countenance or encouragement" to proposals that obstructed the "Peace & good government of this State." The Justices were to investigate these matters and encourage people to persevere in their allegiance to New York and report on all disruptive meetings and use every lawful means to defeat them.

On April 28, he issued orders to Willett:

> The Regiment of Levies ... is to be ... raised in the Counties of Albany, Tryon, Charlotte and Part of Dutchess ... to give the best Security to the Frontier Settlements of the three first above mentioned Counties. In making the Distribution for this Purpose, you are to have Regard to the Aid to be derived from the Continental Troops & Militia, and as your Regiment is subject to the order of the Commander in Chief of the army, you are to be governed by the advice of the Commanding Officer of the Northern Department. You will immediately dispatch Officers to the different Militia Regiments to receive their respective Levies & march them to such Places of Rendevouz as you shall appoint. The Officers for this Service must be instructed not to receive any but able bodied Men fit for active Service, completely armed & Provided agreable to Law, & to reject deserters from the British Service ... [and] To obtain from the Commanding Officers of Regiments Returns of the number of Men to be furnished by them respectively, that you may be able to determine when they have delivered their full Quota. If any shoud be rejected as unfit for Service either on account of Innability or not being properly armed &c., Report ... the Names of the Persons rejected & of the Persons at the Heads of the Classes delivering them ... to the Commanding Officer of the Militia Regt. that he may cause others to be detached agreable to Law to supply the Deficiency. The Levies of Dutchess will rendevouz at Fishkill and

the Proportion of them intended for your Regiment will be dispatched from thence to Albany under such of your Officers as reside in that County. You will make Regular Returns to me of your Regiment, noting the Distribution you shall from Time to Time make of it.

Lieut. Colo. Pawling Regt. is stationed on the Frontiers of Ulster, Orange & West Chester Counties, himself in Ulster, & it will be necessary that a constant Correspondence shou'd be maint[ain]ed between you & him & the earliest advice of the movements of the Enemy, reciprocally communicated. For a variety of Reasons, I conceive it will conduce most to the good of the service, that you shoud take Post yourself in Tryon County, & that Major Mc[Ki]nstry be with that Part of the Regt. stationed to [t]he Northward & I will give such orders to the Militia in that County as will enable you to avail yourself of their Aid. When you have taken the necessary Measures for drawing out & mustering the Levies ... & made the proper Distribution of them, you must then return to this Place & settle your Private affairs & provide yourself for the Campaign, when you will also be able to report to me what further arrangements will be proper to make of the Militia to enable them to render the most effectual assistance.

That evening, the governor wrote to Levies' lieutenant-colonel, Albert Pawling, about an enemy party reported near Minisink. As Brant had raided there in 1779, Clinton reacted strongly, ordering out the Ulster and Orange Counties' counties' militia. Pawling was to take command and secure the area.

On April 29, Brigadier-General Clinton sent his brother his brigade's returns. He grimly noted 2NY's losses at Stanwix, adding, "the absolute Scarcity of Provision not only retards the recruiting service of the Levies but has excited a spirit of Desertion among the regular Troops — but I have preached this Doctrine so long that I am perfectly sick of it."

In the atmosphere of insecurity that hung over Albany, the commissioners met on April 30 and ordered disaffected families on the north side of the Hudson around Jessup's Patent to move to interior parts of the state without delay. Watercraft on both sides of the river were to be destroyed and all males sixteen and older from those families, were to appear on or before May 20. Tory wives (of men with the enemy) who were residing at Saratoga were to be sent south and remain there.[9]

––––––––––––––––––––––––––
––––––––––––––––––––––––––

At month end, Ross sent Serjeant John Service, 2KRR, on an extremely hazardous mission. Service had been captured just the previous year while serving the rebels. Now he was to turn himself in as a deserter, gain trust and find a way to enter the forts along the Mohawk to determine the state of their defences, armament, and morale.

Quebec's chief engineer had recommended constructing a ditch and bomb-proof at Fort Haldimand and Ross indented for thirty barrels of powder and six-dozen portfires.

Sir John sent five men to Johnstown. Two were to return immediately with current information and three were to stay a fortnight before bringing further accounts.

Along Buffalo Creek at Niagara, crops had been planted to feed 1,540 Indians. The Indian Department provided hoes and seed corn from Detroit. As only a few barrels had arrived in time for spring planting, other types of seeds were liberally distributed. The Senecas' fall crop was larger than the other nations and Guy Johnson gave presents to those who shared their harvest with distressed families.

Early in May, a prisoner from Stanwix gave Ross details of the strength, distribution, and morale of the garrisons in the Valley. Three scouting parties brought news that provisions were scarce at Stanwix. Only a few troops were at Albany and the Valley people were in misery. It was said that fifty recruits, who had gathered at Stone Arabia to come off to Sir John, had been intercepted.

On May 3, Sir John informed HQ that in seven days he would send off Volunteer Philip Lansingh, 1KRR, with twelve soldiers and four Mohawks. Philip was to abduct General Schuyler and destroy mills and buildings at Saratoga. Although the kidnapping of Schuyler had often been contemplated, this would have been the first real attempt; however, something went awry and the venture was postponed.

On May 10, Captain Robertson, 84th, reported the return of four Oswegatchies from a six-week hunting trip. As their hunting grounds were only three days from Stanwix, he had asked them to look in at the fort and take a prisoner. They came across two armed soldiers and took them easily. When the men were questioned separately, both claimed to be deserters. Their reports about Stanwix were quite accurate: Lieutenant-Colonel "Cochlin" had a 150-man garrison with a captain and eleven subalterns; for guns, he had one 9-pdr, eight 6-pdrs, and two 3-pdrs; only four Oneidas, two men, and two women were in the fort. As food was scarce and the duty hard, the men were "Much inclined to Desertion." About eighty sleds of beef and flour had arrived from Albany, but each had contained only three barrels due to the poor road conditions. One of the captives had been at Albany during the winter and made rather misleading reports about conditions. He said only the sick and lame from the Hudson and Mohawk Rivers were in the city's garrison. There were no bateaux, nor any being built and that the same was true at Schenectady where Major Fish had eight men. Timber was stockpiled there to build three small blockhouses and a stockade. He claimed the 2NY had some 400 men spread amongst the small forts on the Mohawk. Two 12-pdrs meant for Stanwix had been left at Fort Herkimer due to bad roads. Both men promptly enlisted in 2KRR.

At Fort St. John's, Colonel St. Leger bolstered the Lake Champlain naval squadron with men from the Regulars and Rogers's corps. In the absence of a Regular officer, he sent Captain Henry Ruiter, KR, to command at Pointe au Fer. This important outpost about twenty miles south of Isle aux Noix had been retaken from the rebels in 1776 after they had strengthened an existing stone house and built barracks and guns. The British then added a blockhouse.[10]

On May 1, the Albany commission examined four German prisoners of war who were later bailed out by farmers at Hellebergh and Beaver Dam due to the shortage of labour.

The next day, another 1NY company left for West Point; only three remained in the north. On the May 3, while a 2NY ensign waited at Fort Plain to escort a provision convoy to Stanwix, Indians were seen on the east side of the Mohawk. They burned buildings, killed several people, and captured two privates of Keyser's Company, 2TCM. Then, a man and woman were taken at Herkimer, perhaps part of this same war party's yield. That day at Stanwix, two matrosses, one of whom was the serjeant who had been reduced to the ranks for theft, were found guilty of strolling out of the fort. They said that Moodie had given them permission. In his defence, the captain said they had gone further than he expected. Once again, the CO's orders had been flouted and his frustration was apparent, but his resolve was weak and he gave in to this blatantly foolish breach of discipline.

At Albany, the commission heard that the notorious Tory agent, Joseph Bettys, was at the Hellebergh to take a party of recruits to Canada. On May 4, a second cause for alarm was revealed; the recruits were black! Any sign of armed resistance by blacks, enslaved or free, sent shock waves across the country. A patrol was sent from Coxsackie to Peeksink to stop Bettys's escape by that route. Worse news — word came that several blacks in two other communities were ready to bolt and a pair of militia captains were sent to apprehend six of them. The men confessed and were committed, but there was no sign of the bold Bettys. In the midst of this ferment, approval was received to release Hazelton Spencer, a Tory agent taken in 1780. He gave £500 surety and was allowed the freedom of the city's confines. Spencer was a 1KRR ensign and one of Sir John's favourite agents.

General Schuyler mused philosophically about the Grants to Governor Clinton:

> When I reflect that the people of the Grants are chiefly
> emigrants from the eastern states, that they have left
> behind them, their Fathers, Brothers, sons, and other

relations, who must in common with others feel the consequences of the defection from the common cause, I do not know how to believe that they are in league with the enemy. On the Contrary, when I daily learn that the Tories are removing from all quarters to reside with them, where report says they are well received, when I learn with certainty that more families are now actually settled at Skenesborough, and these are all from the Grants, than ever were there before, and that place may be fairly considered within the enemies lines, that Ethan Allen openly invites the inhabitants on the east side of Hudson's river down to its banks to annex themselves with the Grants and gives explicit assurances that they will not in that case be molested by the British, that the report is general that the inhabitants of Granville who were on the point of moving into the interior part of the state, have since their junction with the Grants determined to remain, I say when all these circumstances are added to that of the negociation last fall, and the recent intelligence of Harris, I confess my faith in the political virtue of these people is staggered, as to be only supported by the hope that the bulk of the people are artfully misled by some of their leaders, who may make them believe that all their measures only tend to secure them against the claims of this state to Jurisdiction and soil. It is, however, a business of much too serious a nature to be slighted, and I shall spare neither pains nor expence to sift it to the bottom.

Plotting raids was by no means the sole preserve of the British. Lieutenant-Colonel Cochran sent a proposal to the governor to attack Carleton Island. He would need 200–300 of the best Regulars and they should be sent to Stanwix with a number of boats, each with a scaling ladder. The raid would cross the Oneida Carry, proceed down Wood Creek and across Lake Oneida. Provisions would be pre-cooked, so no fires would be lit. He had concern about passing Oswego Falls in daylight, but thought there was one chance in ten of being discovered. They would approach the island with their oars muffled with green hides or old clothes and easily surprise and carry the weak garrison; however, as the Continentals were about to be withdrawn, the proposal was rejected.

Washington confessed his concerns about foodstuffs to Brigadier-General Clinton: "[H]ow far Congress will be able to devise ways and means for immediate relief, or induce the States to comply with their former requisitions, I cannot determine, but … every possible exertion should be used, to obtain Bread from this State, and Meat from the Counties of Massachusetts most contiguous to you." Where pleas and requisitions fail, military coercion must be used. Rather than see Stanwix fall and the frontiers laid waste, he believed the state would make a great effort to supply flour for the troops. A day later, he again expressed alarm over the critical situation at Stanwix. He had ordered fifty barrels of meat from "the small pittance in our Magazines" and the same of flour to be "instantly thrown into the Garrison," but the commissary reported there were only thirty-four barrels of meat and he sent it all. The shortfall would be made up from fish lately barreled on the river. The brigadier wrote to Van Cortlandt reporting a sloop had docked at Albany with twenty-six barrels of pork, eight of beef, sixteen of Shad, and a load of flour for Stanwix. It was of the utmost import that these supplies get through and that none be diverted en route. He was to personally command their movement. If there was room, the new guns and their stores were to go.

On May 5, Washington told Congress that Stanwix might have to be abandoned due to a lack of provisions. To stress the urgency, he mentioned sending 100 barrels of flour, which left only thirty-one in army stores. Then, he instructed Brigadier-General Clinton: "Fort [Stanwix] should hold out to the last extremity; and I have no doubt of your still continuing to use your unremitting exertions, thro' every possible difficulty, and embarrassment, to succour that Garrison, and to avert the disasters and calamities we have but too much reason to apprehend, from the present temper of the Troops, and complexion of our affairs in that quarter."[11]

Intelligence had been received at Whitehall, the seat of the British government's major ministries in London, that the French Court was dissuading the Continental Congress from making an attack on Canada until after the British armies were driven out of the "Thirteen States." Of course, Haldimand would not receive this information until many weeks later when Germain's May 4 dispatch landed at Quebec. The secretary wrote, "As … you will have nothing to apprehend for the safety of your own Government, you will have it more in your power to co-operate with Sir Henry Clinton. [T]he most efficient means you Can employ for that purpose is by sending up to Vermont so considerable a Force as to encourage Ethan Allen and the people of Vermont to declare for His Majesty's Government and cut off all Communication between Albany and the Mohawk River and prevent Washington … receiving … Supplies down the Hudson's River."

On more routine matters, Captain Butler wrote to Adjutant General Lernoult on May 6 about a critical financial issue, which revealed a great deal about the woes of a Provincial regimental commander. His father had ordered, on his private credit, a complete stand of arms, accoutrements, and clothing for the Rangers. These supplies were to be on the first ship setting out for Quebec and the suppliers' bills were promised payment on landing. Like other loyalist leaders, Butler's substantial wealth was tied up in real property held in enemy hands and his personal credit was limited, so the administration's ponderously slow remittance had the potential to cause him great personal embarrassment. Not content to simply agitate over his father's problems, Walter Butler complained that the governor had promised him the purchase of a company in an established regiment six months ago and had advised him to have the funds ready. He had done so, but the purchase never materialized and he was forced to dispose of the funds, as the interest was nearly half his pay. Such impertinences, such as his blatant effort to push the system and his moaning about his promotion, though often justified, tarnished his reputation at HQ.

Major Alex Dundas, 34th, commandant at Isle aux Noix, reported that Colonel Ira Allen, a lieutenant, and fourteen privates had arrived with a Vermont flag to settle a prisoner exchange cartel. Sherwood had grown tired of waiting for them and had retired to St. John's where he found a secret note advising that Major Lernoult would be his assistant for the Vermont talks. Dundas was to be kept from all details except the prisoner exchange, but, strangely, would see all correspondence before it left the island.

When word came of Ira's arrival, Sherwood found Lernoult too ill to travel and returned to Isle aux Noix alone. The talks over a prisoner cartel proved awkward and were complicated by the escort lieutenant, an "Illiterate Zealous-pated Yankee … [with] just breeding enough to listen and look over a man's shoulder when he is writing." Although the lieutenant was unaware of the broader base of the talks, he was very suspicious, causing Sherwood to wonder if he had been sent to spy. The fellow was quartered in the same room as Allen and Sherwood, so there was scarce a moment when issues, other than prisoners, could be discussed. Sherwood also thought that the devious, tight-lipped Allen encouraged him to hang about to prevent expansion of the talks, but he finally found the private opportunity to outline Haldimand's proposals: First, Vermont would be considered a separate province and 3,000 troops would be sent up Lake Champlain to protect her territory; and, second, if she were accepted into the United States, the negotiations would be kept secret. Allen was annoyed that Vermont's right to elect its own governor had been left out of the terms. He inquired about Haldimand's powers and whether Parliament had passed a law to admit Vermont into the empire. He spoke of the republic's concern that reunion would prompt an attack by the United States and craved to know the outcome of the war, as he doubted the propriety of rejoining the Empire while the success of British arms remained so uncertain.

The talks dragged on interminably and Dundas, in his ignorance of the real purpose, found many reasons to give Sherwood sidelong glances when the captain made cryptic suggestions to Allen. The situation was ludicrous. Even if Dundas was absent during some discussions, he read all the reports before they left the island, which gave rise to questions that

Sherwood could not answer. This was only part of Sherwood's frustration, as he found Allen at times "induces contempt and always suspicion." He thought Vermont's leaders were playing off Congress, New York, and Britain against one another. To put it mildly, the talks were not going well, yet the fact that Ira had come was, in itself, a useful victory.

On May 8, George Smyth made many strong recommendations to Haldimand. Considering his vulnerability, he must have worded his letter for prying eyes, as the very actions he counseled were soon rumoured all over Albany.

> Now is the season to strike a blow at this place when multitudes will join, provided considerable force comes down. The sooner the attempt is made, the better; Let it be Rapid & Intrepid; carefully avoiding to Sour the Inhabitants' tempers by savage cruelties on their defenceless Families. If a few Hand Bills, Intimating Pardon, Protection &c &c were sent Down and Distributed about this part of the Country, they would effect wonders. And shuld your Excellency think proper to send an Army against this Den of Persecutors, notice ought to be given ten days before, by some careful intelligent person, to a certain Mr. McPherson in Ball's Town, who will immediately convey the intention to the well-affected of New Scotland, Norman's Kill, [Hellebergh], Neskayuna, &c, all in the vicinity of Albany. The Plan is already fixt and should a formidable Force appear, I make no doubt provisions & other succours will immediately take place. A few lines of comfort, in print, from Your Excellency to those people, would make them more eager in prose-cuting their Designs; and if the Vermonters lie still … there is no fear of success. No troops are yet raised.

An important agreement was being negotiated at Niagara on May 9 by Guy Johnson and the chiefs of the Chippewa and Mississauga nations concerning the ceding of a tract of land on the west bank of the Niagara River, from the mouth of Lake Erie to its egress at Lake Ontario, for a depth of four miles. The Senecas had ceded a similar tract to the Crown on the east bank in 1764. A single chief signed for the Chippewas and three for the Mississaugas, including senior War Captain Wabakinine. Johnson signed as "His Majesty's Sole Agent" with two captains of the 8th and two Deputy Agents. The treaty formalized the settlement of discharged Rangers opposite Fort Niagara and marked the first ceding of Indian lands for American loyalists in western Quebec.[12]

Along the Mohawk, constant raids kept the inhabitants and troops on edge, as their relentless enemy punished the slightest breach of vigilance. Between May 10 and 12, three more Tryon militiamen were snatched, but not every attack favoured the raiders. Provisions convoys working upriver were favourite enemy targets. Corporal Jacob Shew recalled on one occasion that guards were ashore ahead of the boats with eyes peeled for an ambush, when Indians and Tories opened fire. One guard was wounded, but so were several raiders and one Indian was killed and left behind.

Schuyler was at his large country estate at Saratoga. Although he had no responsibility for local military matters, he was unable to see problems without taking action. On May 11, he sent the governor a distressing report: "The Garrison here has now been ten days without any meat, except what they procure by maroding; every eatable animal in this part of the Country is already expended, not a single scout can be kept out, and I fear … that a great majority of the troops here will go off to the enemy … unless provision is instantly procured for them." He had bought 100 barrels of flour on his own account and prevailed on the Schaghticoke people to give forty to fifty barrels as an advance on their 1781 quota. Once again, he had delved into his own pocket to correct his country's fumbling.

That same day, Cochran reported that more than two-thirds of Stanwix's sod-covered works had eroded away in heavy rains and predicted the other third would crumble in a few days. Only the pickets on the glacis were intact. There were not enough men to effect repairs and he estimated that 500–600 men with artificers, wagons, and tools would be required to accomplish the work over the summer.

On May 12, Volunteer Ebenezer Allen, 6NID, and a party of Tuscaroras returned to Niagara after an epic, three-month scout to New Jersey. Next day, Powell reported he had five scouting parties on the Mohawk. Two serjeants and three Rangers had left in March to collect intelligence in and around Schenectady and were expected on May 25. Others had been in that part of the country since last December with orders to stay until something of note occurred. He hoped to send out three new parties including one led by 6NID captain, John Johnston, who would head for the area of Fort Pitt. Niagara's pace of activity was frenetic.

Deserontyon brought a prisoner to Carleton Island who confirmed there was only one Continental regiment along the river with four companies posted at Stanwix and one each at Stone Arabia, Johnstown, and Schenectady.[13]

Of all of Governor Clinton's many problems — supplies, manpower, traitors, finances — perhaps the most aggravating was Vermont. He wrote to Schuyler on May 13, "I am left without a Doubt that the Leaders of the Faction on the Grants, maintain a Criminal Intercourse with the Enemy both in Canada & New York; how far the Bulk of the People are privy to it is hard to determine, I ... believe that few among them[,] the disaffected excepted[,] are let into the secret[;] that the disaffected are is natural to believe & it is confirmed by the Sentiments & Conduct of the Tories in different Quarters of the Country." He said that 100 Levies would march to Albany during the week. There had been difficulty in raising them and he thought want of provisions was the major reason they had not appeared earlier. Consequently, he had employed the "odious measure" of issuing impress warrants to Brigadier-General Clinton. The same day, Schuyler wrote to the brigadier from Saratoga noting that the lack of provisions was alarming, observing it "was the natural consequence of such a system as was adopted for supplying the army." He trusted that, if the war continued, "our rulers will learn to conduct it with propriety and economy; at present they are certainly ignoramuses ... Not a barrel of meat or fish is to be had in this quarter if any equal weight of silver was to be offered for it, and as there is not above a quarter of the flour or wheat sufficient for the use of the inhabitants, it would be needless to appoint persons here to impress the articles." He mentioned the likelihood of flour at Schaghticoke and emphasized, "*I am certain* that a very considerable quantity of both wheat and flour is lodged in Albany," which might be impressed "*without much trouble.*" A small amount of meat had been found for the troops at Stillwater, but was already consumed. There was equal distress at Fort Stanwix. Cochran reported to Van Cortlandt that the garrison was on a half allowance of beef and had no rum. "We live exceeding poor and no hopes of liveing batter — the late heavy rains has almost Demolished our garrisons[;] the works are all tumbling into the ditch and cannot be repaired without more men."

Washington instructed Brigadier-General Clinton not to allow the issuing of the ammunition sent to Albany to any troops, on any occasion, or under any pretext unless by his personal express order. He was to immediately assemble all the Levies so that the Regulars, particularly the 1NY, could depart at a moment's warning.

Between 11 o'clock and noon on May 13, a major fire broke out at Fort Stanwix. Cochran reported that the fire, "consumed every Barrack, notwithstanding every exertion was made to extinguish the flames. I still remain in possession of the works, and have saved the magazine, with a small part of the provisions, tho' at the risque of our lives." Private Samuel Pettit recalled that the pickets escaped burning, but the fort was consumed except the bomb-proof, which was saved by throwing dirt on it. When the alarm sounded, he and some mates were not far off playing ball and

Colonel Louis. The Kahnawake, Louis Atayataghronghta was the highest-ranking and possibly most effective Native in the rebel service. The "of Louis" noted by Trumbull may refer to "Sault St. Louis," the French designation for Kahnawake.

rushed into the fort to assist. A barrack was afire and a lieutenant offered a guinea to any man who would rescue his sword that was hanging near a window out of which flames were bursting. Pettit was scorched while retrieving the sidearm and got his well-earned reward. He believed the fire began accidentally, as charcoal had been brought into the armoury to repair arms and some live coals ignited. An artillerist agreed and made the dubious observation that two months' provisions for 300 men had been consumed. If so, why were the troops under so much stress for food? He recalled that flames spread to the laboratory, which was well supplied with powder. The officers' investigation was clear-cut without any hint of misdeed or cover-up; however, headquarters, knowing the unpopularity of Stanwix, had other thoughts.

Van Cortlandt arrived at Fort Plain with the provisions' convoy on May 14 and next day was met on the road by an express with the news of the fire. Unsure of what action to take, the convoy continued till near Little Falls and laid up for the night.[14]

Schuyler reported to Brigadier Clinton that the Kahnawake, Colonel Louis Atayataghronghta, a noted rebel partisan, said that he and his men had been hunting on the west side of the upper Hudson when they heard gunfire. Investigating, they fell in with the enemy and one of his Oneidas was killed. From the volume of fire, Louis thought the enemy was in force and that they might strike at Saratoga or along the Mohawk, a vagueness that suggested he had stumbled into an ambush. Schuyler urged sending scouts from Schenectady and reported that Lieutenant-Colonel Van Dyck, 1NY, had sent a party toward Palmerstown from Albany.

Vermont further distressed New York by holding a convention at Cambridge led by John Rodgers, a Yorker with a history of troubled relations with the royal province, and recently, the state. Rodgers's faction preached that, if New York towns like Cambridge, Granville, and Saratoga joined Vermont, they would be out of the war and protected from British raids. And, they would gain the township form of governance previously denied to them, but guaranteed in Vermont's constitution. The Allen cabal was eager for the Western Union, as it would strengthen them against the increased influence of easterners brought about by the second Eastern Union.

Two days after the fire, there was more unrest at Stanwix when three guards were tried for allowing the theft of provisions. Not content with the findings, Cochran warned his men that, if anything of this nature happened in the future, no further evidence would be required other than proof that items were missing. The corporal would be reduced to the ranks and he and his sentinels would receive 100 lashes without benefit of court martial if they failed to name the guilty parties.

Upon hearing of the fire, Brigadier-General Clinton wrote to ask his brother George to advise Washington that Stanwix could not be held without major repairs, which would be impossible to make without more men. Then, he made an astounding suggestion in the face of all the blood, sweat, and treasure that had been expended since 1776 (in particular the recent intense efforts); in other words: "[W]ould it not be best to remove the stores and take post at the German Flatts?" He said such a move had the support of Tryon's leading men, as the primary reason for keeping Stanwix was gone once the Oneidas had moved to Schenectady. How incredible that this conclusion had only been reached after the fire!

The brigadier's letter to Cochran was nothing short of accusatory: "I cannot find words to express my surprise at the unexpected accident, or how a fire should break out in the middle of noon day, in a Garrison where the Troops could not possibly be absent, after a most violent and incessant rain of several days and be permited to do so much damage. I am sorry to say that the several Circumstances which accompanied this melancholy affair, affords plausible ground for suspicion that it was not the effect of meer accident. I hope when it comes to be examined in a Clearer point of view such lights may be thrown upon it as will remove the suspicion for which there appears too much reason." Cochran was to hold the post until Washington's advice was received. The troops were to be sheltered "in the best manner possible" and work at recovering all nails, hinges, and other useful material. The women and children were to be sent down in the boats, which was done a few days later. He wrote to Van Cortlandt the same day recommending he leave the mortar, cannon, and stores at Fort Herkimer until Washington's orders were known. The colonel was to march to Stanwix with the provisions and assist the garrison and, when done, return with the boats. If Willett ordered his Levies to take post in the interim, a 2NY company was to man the boats and return them to Schenectady, as another escort would have to go up in a short time. Clinton warned, "Be very cautious as you march … there is a Body of Enemy out." Two days later, Cochran ordered all the salvaged iron put in one place under guard, likely fearing the soldiers would steal it to trade for liquor.

General Washington wrote a remarkably mild letter to Brigadier Clinton, expressing his sorrow over the loss of Stanwix. The business of relocation was left entirely in his and his brother's hands. Washington's amazing ability to deal with severe reversals of fortune with such calm decisiveness endeared him to all his subordinates.

In concern over enemy plans and rising internal unrest, the state passed a law to forcibly remove the disaffected from the frontiers and Gansevoort was ordered to evacuate all suspects in his jurisdiction. On

May 17, James Clinton sent his brother a description of the damage at Stanwix and reiterated his earlier point that the people at German Flatts thought it proper, even necessary, to remove the garrison to near Fort Herkimer. They promised to assist in erecting a new work and were confident it would give more protection, not just to their district, but also the whole frontier. He added, "I must confess that this has long been my opinion." In a second letter, he warned that the enemy intended something serious against the frontiers. As the 2NY and part of the new Levies were fully occupied with Stanwix's evacuation, there were few men available and he wished he had the 1NY's six companies from West Point, but lacked confidence in his ability to feed them.

Captain Elsworth, Willett's Levies [WL], wrote a worrying report to the governor about recruiting in Livingston Manor, a notorious Tory enclave. Forty-seven classes had provided only thirty-two men; the remaining twenty-eight classes produced a single, fully-equipped, able-bodied man each, as required in General Orders, which gave him sixty. He told the men they would march next morning and cautioned them not to be absent, but when the time came, forty-four had absconded. He sent the remaining sixteen to Albany with his lieutenant and, en route, four deserted. Although he received five more on May 16, he forewarned that if he did not get more from the Manor, his company would be no larger than twenty, including NCOs. Probably half would desert, as they were "a pack of villains without regard for their country." Ten classes were delinquent and he had no hope of getting a man from any one of them. Class members dared the officers to take them or to assess any goods or chattels. Not a single officer was willing to make the attempt unless one of the regiment's majors intervened.[15]

Brigadier Powell sent a disturbing report to HQ on May 15 about Joseph Brant, which in part explained his sudden departure for Detroit. The Mohawk had fallen into very low spirits and wanted to resign his 6NID company, a significant responsibility that gave him the rank and wages of a captain. As he was the only Native so favoured, he thought he would have more influence with his people if he was without it. Had the fight brought on his melancholy? Whatever the case, Brant kept his rank.

On May 17, Lieutenant Ball of Butler's was sent with six Rangers and some Delawares to the Delaware River. War Captain Cansopi was sent to Virginia with twenty-two Senecas. The reach of Niagara's operations, ranging across New York, south to New Jersey, Pennsylvania, Virginia, and west to Detroit, was nothing short of incredible.

St. Leger reported to Haldimand that his choice of commander for Pointe au Fer had been injudicious. This was obviously a jab at Henry Ruiter's competence, but what had earned the colonel's all too frequent wrath was unstated.

———————————————

———————————————

Although Haldimand had no plans to invade New York, his Secret Service fed rebel paranoia. A rumour was abroad that 400–500 loyalists and Indians were marching to southwest of Albany to begin burning, and 1,500 were at Ticonderoga intending to destroy Albany and Schenectady. On May 19, Albany's commission sent Governor Clinton copies of the articles agreed upon by the recent Cambridge convention and a note about Vermont's negotiations with the enemy. The board seemed to believe the talks were simply a treaty about exchanging prisoners, suggesting that the subterfuge was proving effective. An informant said that the Grants' people were against Ethan Allen's influence, as the Assembly had found a letter from him to Sir Henry Clinton, and had vowed he should not hold a command. That same day, Governor Clinton received a letter from Cambridge. The writer had spoken with convention attendees who said that several districts outside the Grants had joined Vermont as a means of defence. Amongst his acquaintances, very few stood against this step and he learned that "many great ones" favoured it.

To hasten the decision about whether or not to abandon the Stanwix site, Governor Clinton asked militia brigadier Robert Van Rensselaer to meet with Brigadier-General Clinton at Albany and discuss relocating the far western garrison at German Flatts. Willett was in the city assembling his regiment when he wrote to the governor to introduce his officers and describe methods he would use for regional defence:

> I have sent officers to the regiments of militia, in the counties of Albany, Tryon and Charlotte, and find that the County of Tryon, furnishes about sixty men, and … Albany rather better than 400, exclusive of the regiment commanded by John Blair [16ACM (Cambridge),] which refuses to send any at present, having formed an alliance with Vermont. This is likewise the case with Charlotte County, so that the whole of the levies, (besides those [from] Dutchess County) will amount to about four hundred & sixty or seventy, and some of those deserted. A very small number to be posted so as to range the frontiers, from Saratoga to Catskill, including Ballstown, Schohare, and the extensive settlements along the Mohawk River, where alone there are upwards of twenty fortifications, of one sort or another, which I have been requested to place troops in. The levies in this quarter are mostly rec'd, and I have been forming them into companies, and disposing of them at different posts upon the frontiers as they arrived. I have had a meeting with some of the Field officers of the County of Tryon, the particulars of which I shall report to your Excellency in a few days … Since the arrival of warrants for impress, the prospect of a supply of flower brightens. But our expectations of beef are exceeding slender.

After listing all his officers by company, he advised:

> The officers are to take rank agreeable to their former Commissions. The officers will take post … in the manner following: Major McKinster [McKinstry] with the companies of Captains Gray, Dunham & Whelp at

Saratoga; Captain White with his company at Ballstown; Captain Marshall's company at Johnstown; Captain Elsworth's at the German Flats; Captain Gross at Conojoharie; Captain Putnam at Ft Hunter; Captain Dubois at Schoharia; and Captain Conine at Cats-Kill[.] Captains Gray & Dunham's companies are to be composed of the levies that are already assembling at Saratoga together with such as are yet to be rec'd from the regiments of militia commanded by Colo. Whiting [17ACM (King's District)], Colo. Van Ness [9ACM (2nd Claverack)], Colo. Blair [16ACM (Cambridge)], Colo. Van Veghten [13ACM (Saratoga)], Colonel Peter Yates [14ACM (Hoosic/Schaghticoke)] and such as may be furnished by Charlotte County, which Major McKinster … will dispatch officers to receive without delay. Captain Marshall's company is to be formed of the troops already assembled at Johnstown under the charge of Capt McKain. Captain Elsworth's company will be made up of the troops he has already rec'd from the [Manor] of Livingston [10ACM] and those ordered to be haulted with Lieutenant Bloodgood at the German Flats. [In an afterthought, levies from Colonel Bellinger's (4TCM) at the German Flatts to be included in Elsworth's.]

Captain White's Company is to consist of those he has already in charge and such as are yet to be rec'd from Major Taylor's regiment [12ACM (Half Moon/ Ballstown)] and Colo. Philip Schuyler [3ACM (1st Rensselaerwyck)] for which he will dispatch one of his subalterns without delay. Captain Putnam's Company will consist of levies from Col Fisher's [3TCM (Mohawk)] regiment only, untill a more equal distribution can be made. Capt Conine will form his company of the levies from Colo. Van Bergen's regt [11ACM (Coxsackie/Groote Imbocht)] and those that are yet to be received from Colo. Henry Livingston [10ACM (Livingston Manor)], Col Van Alstine [7ACM (Kinderhook)], Col Van Rensselaer of Claverack [8ACM (1st Claverack)], and Colonel Henry K. Van Rensselaer [6ACM (4th Rensselaerwyck)] to which places he will immediately dispatch officers to receive them. Captain Grosses company composed of levies from Colonel Wemple's [2ACM (Schenectady)] regiment, those already ordered to him from Colo. Van Ness['s] [9ACM (2nd Claverack)] regiment and those from Colonel Klock['s] [2TCM (Palatine)] and Colonel Cloide's [Clyde's 1TCM (Canajoharie)] regiment, with such as are yet to be furnished by Col Kilian Van Rensselaer [4ACM (2nd Rensselaerwyck),] to which last place Lieutenant Hutten will repair to receive them and march them to [Canajoharie] with as much expedition as possible. Capt Dubois is to take charge of the levies from Colonel Vrooman's regt. [15ACM (Schoharie/Duanesburgh)] and all those that may arrive from Dutchess County, except a sufficient number to form a moderate company for Captain Whelp.

The greenness of the troops, and the importance of the service they are called to, most powerfully point out the necessity of the greatest assiduity, vigilance and perseverance. The disstresses of the inhabitants we are called to protect, demand every possible effort for their security. A cruel and barbarous enemy, that cant be too severely chastised, ought to stimulate every officer & soldier to employ every possible exertion for their chastisement. The thought of receiving any other treatment to such as fall into their hands but what is consistent with the most hellish barbarism should establish in every breast a determination never to be disarmed by them, but with our latest breath. The enemy we have to deal, are artful as well as cruel, and require all our invention as well as alacrity. The officers commanding at the different posts, will keep out proper scouts on all the trails leading to their respective posts, and observe a regular intercourse with each other in order to regulate the ground they are severally to range. They are to pay particular attention to the disciplane & health of their troops, and by no means suffer them to straggle from their main body. Officers commanding companies, will make returns of the strength of their companies, particularizing the numbers they have rec'd from the different militia regiments, including officers. That the exact deficiencies of the several Classes of Militia may be known, deserters are to be included in this return.

Due to the sad state of Tryon's militia, its contribution was small; however, the county provided two of Willett's best and most active company commanders. First, was Captain Lawrence Gross, 1TCM. An ardent rebel, Gross was the brother of the firebrand, Johann Daniel Gross, the Reformed Lutheran minister in the Upper Valley who was chaplain of the Levies. As a lieutenant of a ranging company in 1776, Gross had a very good knowledge of the county's byways. He had fought as a supernumerary officer at Oriskany and been given a company after the battle. Second was Captain Garrett Putman, who had commanded a 3TCM company for most of 1778 and in November, a ranging company. The following year, he resumed command of a line company and in 1779 was captain of volunteers under Colonel John Harper on the Sullivan-Clinton expedition. In 1780, he was a captain in Harper's NY Levies.

To improve his chronic lack of timely intelligence, Willett took the Tryon ranger, William Nellis, from Gros's company to act as a spy. Nellis often scouted for a week of more, watching for signs of enemy infiltration and sniffing out Tories who were or could be supplying raiders.

Way off in northern Vermont on the east side of the Green Mountains, General Jacob Bayley sent Washington a roll of seventeen Abenaki rangers from St. Francis. A much larger number had been with him at times, but they were unsteady, while those listed were serviceable scouts.[16]

Watercolour and gouache by George Heriot (Library and Archives Canada, C-011062).

Canada Indians' hunting camp.

At Fort St. John's, Bayley's friend Thomas Johnson, whom Captain Pritchard had taken at Cöos, met Major Lernoult and correctly concluded he was one of Haldimand's principal confidants. William Marsh was involved in enticing Johnson to become an agent, which led Sherwood to write, "Mr. Marsh has always till lately had much greater Expectations from Mr. Johnson's Loyalty than I could ever see any grounds for. But I believe he is now fully persuaded that he has been rather too sanguine."

Ira Allen arrived at the post in the role of Vermont's "sole commissioner Plenipotentiary," but when he presented his commission, it was signed only by Chittenden, not over the authority of the Vermont Council or Assembly. Consequently, the British thought it would be incorrect to proceed further, but that did not stop them from making a proposal that would truly test Vermont's intentions. To wit — the republic was to raise a standing army of 600 Regulars and man a twenty-gun ship to patrol Lake Champlain commanded by her own officers under a King's commission and she would raise another 2,000 men in case of emergency.

In keeping with his broader Secret Service role, Sherwood reported some noteworthy news. Edward Carscallen, a Grants settler who had served in 1777 as a lieutenant in his company, had been with Carleton's expedition the previous October and had been left behind to gather recruits and intelligence. He had spent the winter in concealment at Camden and recruited twenty-five men. When he was about to come away, the men were dissuaded from leaving by rumours that Vermont would rejoin the British. Carscallen and Sherwood's brother-in-law, Ensign Elijah Bothum, QLR, who had just come in from a scout to Arlington, both offered the opinion that half the people were "in favour of Government and would, if any army was to lie at Tyconderoga, come in, by hundreds." People said Vermont refused to assist the United States against Britain. Bothum had gathered forty men at Arlington, but Ethan Allen, correctly suspecting they were about to go off to Canada, told them that "a Flag had gone to make Peace … and if there was not a settlement soon, he would raise a party and come to the King's Army himself."

At Fort Niagara, John Butler filed a detailed report on May 20 about the various parties that had been on the frontiers. The first had captured the two 11ACM officers, David and Anthony Abeel. The Indians from three other mixed parties had returned. One had been at the Hellebergh, another at Norman's Kill, and a third a little below Albany. Butler had high expectations that the Rangers who remained behind would return with recruits and intelligence, and he was about to send out a new party of three Rangers and two Indians to the Mohawk.

Even while Butler was reporting his successes, a war party struck Fort Clyde, a fortified home on the Cherry Valley road. The attackers surprised sentinel John Balsly and gave him thirteen wounds to remember them by. Incredibly, he survived. Fort Clyde fifer, George H. Nellis, recalled playing signals at times when the garrison was weak to deceive lurking Indians into thinking troops were present.

Colonel Van Cortlandt arrived at Stanwix with the provisions convoy on May 19. A note was made in the orderly book that the enemy was frequently seen lurking about the fort, which is of no surprise considering the number of parties sent out from Niagara, Montreal, Oswegatchie, and Carleton Island. Two days later, a soldier pled guilty to stealing rations from a mate and was awarded 100 lashes.

Willett prepared a very informative return of his companies confirming their strength and postings. Apparently, men with the same enlistment terms (three, six, or nine months) were grouped into companies. Present were the lieutenant-colonel, seven captains, twenty lieutenants and a surgeon. Absent collecting recruits were a major, three captains and six lieutenants. Major McKinstry was stationed at Saratoga.

Posting	Captains	Subalterns	NCOs and Privates
Saratoga (Captains Gray, Dunham & Whelp) [three named, only two returned]	2	4	70
Ballstown (Captain White)	1	2	15
German Flatts (Captain Elsworth)	1	3	69
Canajoharie (Captain Gross)	1	2	53
Fort Hunter (Captain Putman)	1	2	29
Catskill (Captain Conine)	1	2	22
Albany		1	9
Johnstown		3	61
Schohary (Captain Dubois)		1	11
Total	7	20	339

Willett noted two days later that the regiment had received 326 NCOs and privates, but nineteen had deserted and two were jailed for debt. Surely the state's leadership was thoroughly dissatisfied, for how could Willett be expected to defend such a vast area with this tiny regiment? Brigadier-General Clinton advised Van Cortlandt on the May 22 that orders had been sent to Cochran to evacuate Stanwix. Not realizing that the colonel had arrived at Stanwix, he ordered, "I believe The Ginn from Ft [Stanwix] … brought Down last winter to weigh the Cannon … was left at Ft Herkimer which you will take up with you … I have ordered Some of the Ammunition with the most valuable Artillery to Schenectady until the works near Ft Herkimer can be made Tenable; as I have reason to believe the Enemy mean to Carry on something Capital perhaps from both the North & West." On May 23, the Stanwix garrison set an unsuccessful ambush in the pouring rain. When Cochran found that the fort's spears for repelling assaults had been thrown about, he ordered them gathered and properly restored.

Captain Conine, WL, at his Catskill post, found the locals had failed to provide his troops with provisions. Some of his men went without for two days and, when he sent them to collect, they came back with only enough for a few days, so he had men spending half their time bringing in food. He expected to have a full company soon, but had no idea how they would be fed. He wrote to the local militia colonel in hopes the district would make a victualling plan and that militia officers would be given responsibility to collect the food, as his men were supposed to be gathering recruits.[17]

On May 21, Haldimand ordered Sherwood to suspend all talks about prisoner exchanges until Vermont stopped stalling on the subject of reunion.

Claus wrote to Mathews to advise that the Lachine Mohawks were still eager to raid the Oneidas; undoubtedly, Colonel Louis's recent activities had whetted their appetite for revenge. At Smyth's suggestion, a handbill written over Sir John's name came off the press in Montreal on May 22:

PROCLAMATION BY SIR JOHN JOHNSON TO
PEOPLE ON MOHAWK RIVER
The Officers & Soldiers of Sir John Johnson's Regt.
present their affectionate and loving wishes to their
Friends & Relations on the Mohawk River & earnestly
entreat them to assemble themselves & come into Canada
or the upper Posts, where under that Gallant leader, they
may assist their Countrymen to quell & put an end to
the present unnatural Rebellion, in hopes soon to return
to their native homes, there to enjoy the happiness they
were formerly blessed with under the best of Kings, who
is willing to do every thing for his subjects.
May 22nd, 1781

The handbill would give support to loyalists living under threats
in the Valley, but the primary goal was to influence rebels who were
wavering. Over the following months, a steady trickle of recruits came
to Niagara, St. John's, and Carleton Island, but whether as a result of the
proclamation or not is unknown.

At Niagara, six Brant's volunteers, led by one of the Huffs, marched
for Coxsackie. Hendrick Huff and his son, John, joined Joseph Brant
early in the war and became notorious to the rebels, so much so that when
Hendrick and another volunteer were captured in 1780, Brant feared for
their lives. He employed one of his tricks and wrote a threatening letter
to the rebel authorities, passing it through the hands of a local woman.
This had the desired effect and both men returned to Niagara in the
spring of 1781 and served till the end.

On May 26, a serious incursion occurred at Walradt's Ferry, which
crossed the Mohawk near Fort Plain. A small party of Indians attacked
a guard mounted by House's Company, 2TCM, wounding a serjeant in
the arm and capturing four privates.

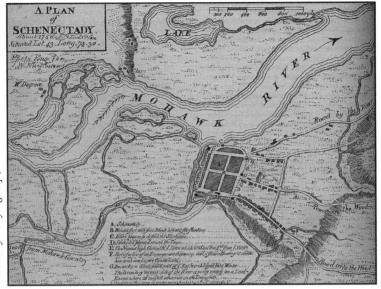

A Plan of Schenectady. The source dates this plan circa 1770, but the ring of palisades and blockhouses indicates it was prepared after the major improvements were made to the city's defences in the spring of 1781.

An obviously leaked British Secret Service dispatch was intercepted on May 27, which reinforced prevalent fears. It detailed the force coming to attack Albany and said handbills would be dispersed ahead of time pardoning anyone who assisted the raiders. Schenectady was described as "strongly picketed all round, six pieces of Ordinance, 6 pounders, Block Houses preparing … it is to be defended by the Inhabitants who except about a Dozen, are for Government." In British parlance, to be "for Government" was a phrase meaning to be loyal. Whether "except about a Dozen" was true or not, it must have raised much mistrust.

Washington wrote to Congress about the necessity to abandon Stanwix and remove the garrison and stores to German Flatts. Surely heads shook in that august assembly over the amount of funds and anxiety showered on Stanwix, only to have its utility dismissed so perfunctorily.

A soldier of Willett's Levies marched up the Mohawk to Fort Plain, where he found several scalped children he had helped to rescue the year before during Johnson's fall raid. They were apparently happily readjusting to life. Such sad sights were a jolting reminder of the terrors that were part of everyday life on the Mohawk frontier.

On May 28, the Albany commission decided that Dr. Smyth and his son Terrence were "persons detrimental to the safety of the State," and ordered them confined. Later that day, the constable reported he had taken Terrence, but his father could not be found. There was discussion about the persons relocated from Jessup's Patent who had been given permission to fetch the rest of their possessions. As they had not returned by the agreed time, Lieutenant-Colonel Van Dyck, 1NY, was requested to round them up.

General Washington requested that the French officer commanding the Continental Engineers appoint one of his men to oversee the new German Flatts fortification. Then, in response to the concern being shown by Generals Clinton and Schuyler about an enemy invasion from the north, he reluctantly put the 1NY companies at West Point under marching orders for an instant movement.

On May 28, a Fort Herkimer patrol found two bloody local men, one scalped twice, the other shot through the chest. Both survived. When the Albany commission met two days later, they read a letter from Colonel Whiting, 17ACM, that illustrated the distrust that was rampant. He claimed a number of Shaking Quakers had purchased arms and ammunition for the enemy. As less likely agitators could scarcely be found, he was asked to gather evidence. Brigadier-General Clinton visited the board to emphasize the importance of removing the disaffected from the Ballstown area. It was thought a better solution would be to send the miscreants to Canada, where they would be unable to cause more mischief or soak up provisions.

A man reported to the board that he met Dr. Smyth and four men on the road between Hoosic and Albany. He thought the doctor was on his way to Bennington. Without realizing they were contacting one of Vermont's secret negotiators, the board wrote a letter to Joseph Fay, asking him to apprehend Smyth.

During the doctor's escape from the clutches of the commissioners, he travelled to Bennington in a wagon with two close friends; however, instead of finding political asylum, they fell into the hands of some men who favoured New York and sent them back to Albany under escort. En route, the ever-resourceful Smyth escaped, but his friends were not so fortunate. Yet, when examined, they claimed to have fallen in with Smyth purely by chance and, without proof to the contrary, were released. Smyth seems to have returned to Bennington, where he was jailed. Secret Service Agent Lieutenant Mathew Howard, QLR, had been recruiting and gathering intelligence in his home area of Hoosic when he heard of Smyth's plight and went to rescue him. Somehow, he accomplished the feat and set off for Canada with the doctor and three other men.

Governor Clinton appointed Andrew Finck as a conspiracy commissioner for Tryon County. Finck had served as a 1NY captain since the start of the war and was commanding the Light Infantry at the time of derangement, after which he returned home to his parents in Stone Arabia. On April 5, he had been appointed a Palatine District Justice of the Peace. By an odd quirk of fate, Jacob J. Klock, son of Colonel Jacob, had served for four years as Finck's ensign. His father's attempt to obtain him a new posting had failed. Frustrated, young Jacob would soon run off to Canada and re-emerge as a Tory partisan right on Finck's doorstep.[18]

On May 27, Captain Robertson reported sending a scout of eight Indians to the Mohawk. Another war party had come back the day before with a prisoner taken near Little Falls from Van Cortlandt's convoy. "[H]e … belong[ed] to a Brigade of Sixteen Batteaux Guarded by about three hundred Men and Loaded with Provisions from Schenectady to Fort Stanwix, as likewise One eight inch Howitzer." This was the convoy that halted at Fort Herkimer when hearing of the fire at Stanwix. In another incident, "Indians killed Two men so near a Stockaded House that they could not scalp them."

On May 29, a Secret Service report was received from Ensign Thomas Sherwood, QLR, advising there were 250 1NY men building a blockhouse at Saratoga:

They have no Provision but what they take from the Inhabitants — A Lieutenant & 30 men was sent out last week ... to take cattle from the Inhabitants. He demanded a Pair of Oxen from a man who was ploughing with them. The poor Farmer pleaded that he had no other Oxen & if he must part with them it would ruin him — The Lieut. said he would have them — the man asked whether young cattle would not do as well, he said Yes if he could have them within Two hours. The Ploughman promised he should & run'd off to look for them, but ... returned with 50 Inhabitants armed. The Lieut. asked where the young Cattle ware, the man pointed to the armed Posse & told him there the[y] ware, they then took the Lieutenant rung his nose, kicked & beat him Severely & forced him to Return without any Cattle.

Thomas had organized Moses Harris Jr. of Kingsbury to carry Haldimand's dispatches to a sympathizer in Fishkill, who went to New York City once a fortnight. Now, urgent messages could be forwarded to the city expeditiously. Of course, he was unaware that Harris was a double agent.

Despite Haldimand's insistence on the strictest secrecy, Walter Butler made an offer to Mathews that showed how pervasive were the rumours of the Vermont talks: "Should Allen and his Green Mountain lads return to their duty, I would wish ... a few companies of Rangers were sent to join them. I should like the service, as being convinced we could be of very essential service in that quarter and I have now given over all those prejudices against serving with people who were formerly our enemies. The good of the Service requires we should give up sentiments of this kind." He continued, "We have had no account yet of the success of our recruiting parties, though in daily expectation of hearing from them. Lieutenant Bradt is gone to the New Jerseys. If no misfortune befalls him, he must get a number of men." More indications of his ambitions and resentments were revealed, leading one to wonder if his father was aware of his dissatisfaction: "I don't mean to apply again to His Excellency … for the purchase of a company. For on considering everything, it would not be to my advantage. If he ever thinks me worthy of promoting me to an established regiment, it will be an act of his own, without my application. And therefore I must be solely obliged to him. But I can't help being surprised, between you and me, that officers employed in the Indian Department in Canada, who receive double pay and do no duty with their regiment, and … have not done more than others … having talk of being in the first promotions and in fact one has succeeded. But doubtless they merit it. For my part, I think so. But not before many others I could name. Excuse this liberty."

On May 30, Guy Johnson reported that 101 men led by Captain John McDonell, BR, including his own company and a war party of Natives directed by the sexagenarian 6NID captain, John Johnston, had set off for Schoharie.

On the last day of May, Brigadier-General Maclean was overcome by a fit of righteous indignation over the behaviour of several Royal Yorker officers. In a letter to Captain John Munro, 1KRR, he noted that the battalion's captain-lieutenant, Thomas Gumersall, had come down from Coteau-du-Lac and reported to his fellow captain, Joseph Anderson, without first reporting to himself as district brigadier. As Gumersall was from a frontier post and Anderson had been on a leave of absence for the

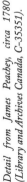

Detail from James Peachey, circa 1780 (Library and Archives Canada, C-35351).

Scene of the Mutiny, the post at Coteau-du-Lac. In the mid foreground are the outbuildings, stockade, and defensive works that were home to the garrison and Herkimer's bateaux company. The trees rising behind are on Prison Island.

past six months, Maclean had at first assumed that the visit had nothing to do with regimental duties, yet the battalion's commander, Major Gray, who was also absent from the regiment, had chosen to report a certain event to his lieutenant-colonel, Sir John Johnson, who was also absent in Quebec City, but had not seen fit to inform Maclean or his brigade-major. In consequence, the first news Maclean had of a conspiracy at one of his district's posts was the announcement of a General Court Martial. Outraged, the irascible Maclean advised Munro that Gumersall had neglected his duty and that Anderson was even more culpable in not having reported the true reason for the visit to the brigade-major, prior to going to Gray. It was obvious to Maclean that there was a cover-up going on at his expense, which was not the first instance of a breach of military protocol by the KRR in its dealings with him. During the previous fall's preparations for Johnson's expedition, Haldimand, in the interests of maintaining security, had colluded with Sir John to explain why a large 1KRR detachment from Montreal district was being sent to Carleton Island. This subterfuge blew apart when a British officer told Maclean the true reason for the movement and the incensed Scotsman rounded on Johnson and then fumed when Haldimand censured him for his public outburst, which had risked a security leak. Now, here was a second incident and his ready temper was aflame, which led to his brigade-major issuing a harsh district order concerning protocol, citing the Royal Yorkers as an improper example. Once again, the governor interceded with a note of censure, which could hardly have stanched Maclean's wrath.[19]

While the officers in Canada were occupied with internal squabbles, Captain John Walden Meyers, one of the governor's favourite secret couriers, was returning from delivering dispatches to New York City with eight recruits in tow. Near Kinderhook, he was warned that his presence was known. With his usual caution, he made his way to Simeon Garett's at Cooeyman's Landing, where he had found refuge before, but once there, his friend told him that he was personally under suspicion. Before leaving, Meyers picked up two French deserters who had been hiding nearby. Splitting into small parties, he placed a trusted man in charge of the Frenchmen and instructed everyone to gather at a tavern run by a sympathizer outside Schenectady. Meyers travelled the Kinderhook Road and, about eight miles from Albany, took a prisoner, then questioned and released him. On June 2, the commission examined this fellow and sent his information to Generals Clinton and Gansevoort so that a plan could be made to capture the bold agent.

By June 3, Meyers's band was reunited at the tavern near Schenectady, where he found one of Burgoyne's Regulars of the 62nd who had escaped from Virginia, fled north, and was in hiding, waiting for an opportunity to continue his trek. Meyers now had a tidy little group and his next move was wondrously audacious. That same day, the commission sent a detachment to the Kinderhook Road so Meyers's prisoner could show them exactly where he had been taken. The hunt for the slippery Tory was not going too well. Next day, the Albany commission got firm word that Meyers was lurking on the east side of the Hudson. Garett was again examined and reported being abducted and held for some time in the woods by the spy. One can see Meyers's clever hand at work to throw the rebels off the scent and simultaneously remove suspicion from his friend. When Garett was again examined on June 5, he said that the captain had slept several nights a barn at Cooeyman's Patent; however, when the owner was questioned, he denied any knowledge of it — yet another incidence of nominally co-operative behaviour that yielded no useful information.

The rebels were on full alert against raids or expeditions. Detachments of Schenectady's 2ACM were called out for duties in the Mohawk region. Serjeant Gerrit De Spitzer of Van Slyck's company, who, from previous scouts, was familiar with the Sacandaga area north of Johnstown, was sent there with a detail to search for Indians. Captain Banker's Company spent about ten days at Fort Plank and then a week at Stone Arabia before returning home.

Sometime during the month, Christopher Reddick from the Tory enclave of New Dorlach sent a message through the secret loyalist network to Joseph Brant, asking him to fetch away several families who had sons with the British. Although Reddick was unaware that Brant was at Detroit, his appeal may have prompted what was soon to follow.

Early in the month, agents from Canada seized Moses Harris at his home and took him to a secret island rendezvous in the big swamp northeast of Fort Edward. It was a close call for Harris, as his captors accused him of treachery, but he had a glib tongue and gained release to continue his career as a double agent.

On June 1, a convoy, including men of Gros's Company, WL, arrived at Stanwix with orders to evacuate the post and remove the artillery to Fort Herkimer. By the June 3, the troops and bateaux brigade set off downriver. At Caughnawaga, six men of Putman's under newly promoted Serjeant Jacob Tanner went to guard John Veeder's gristmill.

At West Point, the six 1NY companies and Colonel Moses Hazen's Congress's Own Canadian regiment were ordered to board vessels for the trip north. The latter regiment was a product of the January 1 reorganization, combining Livingston's 1st Canadian with Hazen's 2nd into a four battalion configuration, which incorporated all the Canadien volunteers left from the 1775 invasion. Hazen's had been in the Hudson Highlands' Department and, on June 5, transferred to the Northern.

Schoharie's defences were improved when Stubrach's company, 15ACM, built a picketed

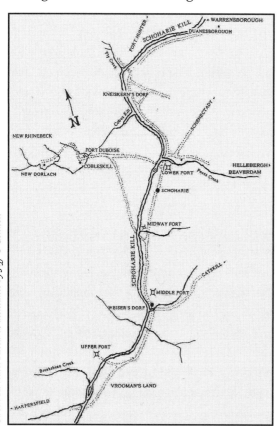

Gavin K. Watt. Research assistance by Jeff O'Connor.

The Schoharie Valley and adjacent settlements.

blockhouse in Kneiskern's Dorf, five miles north of the Lower Fort on the river's east side. Another blockhouse, called Midway Fort, was erected on high ground beside a ravine between the Middle and Lower Forts. At Beaver Dam, two houses were fortified and became known as Forts Weidman and Switz Kill. Schoharie society had been riddled with deep distrust from the beginning of the rebellion, as a cryptic, damning letter from Colonel Vrooman, 15ACM, to his brigadier illustrated: "Some of the Inhabitants of this place have Erected two forts or Blockhouses in this Settlement and one more Erecting within Sight of [the Upper Fort], which gives great uneasiness to the well affected here, as most of those that have and are Erecting as above have not Excerted Themselves as they Should in the Caus of American Liberty, But to the Contrary Some of them have Remained in their houses when Sir John Johnson was here Last fall, and thro that means ... Savd their Buildings and others took to the woods altho the[y] had Timly notice to Repair to the fort, and Assist to Defend it ... Lieut. Johannes Dietz ... will more particularly inform you thereof."

Just prior to Stanwix's evacuation, three Oneidas arrived at the fort after a month-long hunt in Indian Territory and told a tale that revealed aspects of Native behaviour often considered by their white allies as proof of their ambivalence toward the war. The trio had left Schenectady and travelled to Onondaga Falls where they built a hut and set out beaver traps. Returning to camp, they found two white boys taken at Stone Arabia in the care of five Mohawks, who had been on the trail for thirty-three days. They were politely invited to travel with the warriors, an invitation they distrusted, as many of their two nations were at war; however, the hunters complied and soon the Mohawks split away and went on alone. The Oneidas returned to their hut and one went fishing at the Falls, but soon returned after spotting five Indians in a canoe. The trio climbed to a height and saw this new party seated around a fire. Then, hearing four gunshots, they ran to discover the cause and were seen by another four Indians who hallooed them and landed on the opposite shore. These four spoke a "back nations" tongue that the Oneidas had difficulty understanding and signed they had come from Oswegatchie and that their headman, who spoke Oneida, was behind them and would arrive soon with thirty Mohawks and others of their nation. Soon after those four left, some thirty Kahnawakes arrived. Two came forward and told the Oneidas that their headman wanted to talk. They were to take all their possessions with them, but they said they had traps out and could not. On arrival, a ring was formed; the Oneidas were led into the middle and all sat down to smoke. That formality over, they were taken by canoe to meet a number of other canoes filled with twenty-four Tories who wanted to take them prisoner. Everyone went ashore, formed another ring and the hunters were again set in the middle. The Kahnawake headman rose and said the commander's orders were that any Oneidas who were discovered were to be held prisoner until the war party completed its business. The trio protested they were not out for war, but only to hunt; however, they were held for four days before their guards left. They again started to hunt and came across the tracks of three horses and met another two "back nations" Indians who made signs that there were ten others in their party. After those two were gone, the Oneidas spotted smoke near the falls and supposed it was the camp of the "back nations." The hunters lifted their traps and left, no doubt feeling their luck might finally run out. Their story showed that Native courtesy was extended to all visitors on the trail, regardless of nation and also illustrated a basic reality of native life — the need to hunt for subsistence or to take peltry for trade. All Indians accepted this fact.[20]

On June 1, Robertson reported from Oswegatchie the return of his large scout from the Mohawk River. They had taken seven prisoners along East Canada Creek near Fort House, had been fired at from the fort and had one Indian killed and another slightly wounded. Two rebels were killed and another wounded, although not taken. Four houses and barns had been burned and 100 milk cows and a number of horses killed. Once again, the captain sensibly questioned the prisoners separately and found one "intelligent and cooperative." Examination yielded the following: "The Barracks of Fort Stanwix were burned about three weeks ago,

Camp colour of the Royal Highland Emigrants. Likely made before the regiment was raised to the British Establishment as the 84th of Foot.

some say by accident, others on purpose by the Soldiers, And that the Fort was to be abandoned. Colonel Willet with one thousand six hundred men were to occupy the different Posts on the Mohawk river, and now on their March from Albany for that purpose, with all the Oneida and Stockbridge Indians. A Large Fort to be built near the little falls, and to be the Frontier, and Head Quarters. A Captn Ailsworth with seventy men have taken post there." Considering that Willett had his companies spread all over upstate New York and less than 400 enlisted men, these "intelligent," "cooperative" facts were grossly misleading.

Guy Johnson sent a detailed report to HQ on June 1. In the first half of the year, Niagara alone had dispatched thirty-six war parties (totalling 1,095 warriors); twenty-six of which had returned (as warriors sortied repeatedly, the number did not represent the sum of available manpower). Rebel losses were two officers killed, one captured, forty-two men killed, sixty-five taken, ten women released; of livestock, eighteen horses taken, sixteen cattle killed; of buildings, two forts, thirty-two houses, and six mills destroyed. Contrasting this mournful toll, he claimed the loss of only one warrior.

The next day, Sherwood reported Vermont's plan to annex lands for the Western Union. Schuyler was said to half-heartedly agree to the idea simply to prevent a wholesale migration of Tories and war-weary rebels from that part of New York into neutral Vermont. Thomas Sherwood and Elijah Bothum, both QLR, reported that Schuyler had all the boats along the Hudson burned to check a possible exodus. Of course, the measure was intended to remove craft from the path of invaders, but the story made good telling.

On June 3, it was reported that eight St. Francis Abenakis led by Chief Joseph Louis Gill had captured the notorious rebel partisan, Benjamin Whitcomb, who had become a wanted man after his 1776 sniping of a British general. In the more refined days of the early war, this act had been considered murder. Making the situation worse, Whitcomb had proven a very capable leader and a thorn in the side of Burgoyne's army, yet Gill released him after extracting a promise that St. Francis would not be destroyed if the United States won the war. How pragmatic, and how distresssing for the British!

On June 4, Sir John sent newspapers to HQ that had been brought in by the two men sent to Johnstown. They also had fetched twelve recruits and reported that the other three scouts, who remained behind, had hopes of another thirty. Less pleasing, Johnson wrote that Brigadier-General Maclean's actions had "cast injurious and malicious reflections upon the Regiment in General for the mistake of one or two officers" and asked to be removed from under his command.

Sherwood received some welcome news from Mathews on June 5. He would no longer be subordinate to the commandants at Fort St. John's, Isle au Noix, or Pointe au Fer and was to head the Secret Service reporting directly to the governor and commanding all scouting and intelligence gathering, except at the western posts. He responded to his new freedom by asking permission to establish a private headquarters free of the gossip of the posts and recommended a secluded bay on Long Isle as an ideal site.

On June 5, Washington advised James Clinton that the 1NY companies had sailed for Albany. He recommended that the troops on the Hudson and Mohawk not be as widely scattered as previously in attempts to protect every inch of ground, as efficiency was "dissipated and lost, and the several Posts are so weakened as to invite the Enemy to enterprise … concentrate your strength as much as possible at the Points you may judge most expedient; to form a plan of defence for the frontier; and to transmit to me the result."

The troops and boats from Stanwix arrived at Fort Herkimer on June 4. Next day, Major Peter S. Dygert, 1TCM, reported to Colonels Klock and Waggoner, 2TCM, that a party of 60–70 men had struck Johnstown, burned a few buildings, and taken several prisoners and was believed heading for Stone Arabia or elsewhere upriver. He suggested giving notice to all the posts without a moment's delay.

At White Creek on June 5, Colonel John Williams of Charlotte County's militia reported to Governor Clinton that Vermont's Flag of Truce to Canada had returned. The Vermonters had been told that no prisoners would be provided until they produced an equal number for exchange and he understood that Washington would be asked to release some candidates. He had been told that the enemy's best troops were in Quebec and that the same troops that "harassed us last fall" were at Isle aux Noix and could "be expected on our frontier in a few days." He had repeatedly asked "the Grants people" for assistance if the enemy attacked, but received no firm answer and thought it unlikely they would comply: "I make no doubt but that you have been informed of our difficulties here; nothing but, Yorkers & Vermonters is talked of and even the boys and youngsters, are fighting almost dailey on the subject, and I can assure you that only a cool and calm disposition of some, hath prevented its being a general quarrell. I believe this is the only district which hath voted for New York, and I expect that Vermont will Exercise Jurisdiction over it in a few days." It was rumoured that two of the Allens were going to pursue New York military commissions, which he thought should be granted. He opined that if just 100 men had been at Fort Edward in early May, the unrest in Charlotte County and the success enjoyed by pro-Vermont agitators could have been prevented. Now, all the locals could talk about was the legislature's ineptitude — no troops on the frontiers, no provisions, no money, and no ammunition, even though an alarm was daily expected. The week before, Vermont had given ammunition to the Charlotte County militia at Cambridge and some of his own regiment had been similarly supplied.

On June 5, Colonel Van Cortlandt wrote to Brigadier Clinton from Fort Herkimer, advising that the first boats were set to return to Stanwix the next morning to take off the rest of the garrison. He sought directions about the number and size of guns and quantity of ammunition to be sent down to Schenectady and recommended that the powder go by land. Nearby Franks Hill was suggested as the site for a new fortification and he asked what size of garrison was intended, pointing out that a great many artificers would be required, with sufficient provisions and adequate stores, as well as a quartermaster and engineer. He sent a well-conceived proposal for lodging 100 men in a work commanding the river and billeting in whatever houses the locals would build nearby. If a large installation were in mind, he advised that 1,000 men would be required for the whole summer.

He had heard an unwelcome rumour and pled, "I hope it will not fall my Lott to have my Regt in Fatigue this Summer and Colo Willets Levies to form a flying Camp as is Reported[.] I Rely more on your better Judgement than to suppose a thing of the kind." That his Regulars might take a back seat to Levies was an anathema.

Early in the month, a prisoner was brought to Fort Haldimand who reported that Stanwix had been burned and abandoned and that troops in the Valley's other forts were greatly dispirited and ill-supplied with ammunition. Supposedly, seventy men had deserted to join Sir John and only two had been retaken. Ross reported that Captain Crawford had been sent to confirm Stanwix's abandonment and begged to send a strong 2KRR party to harass the enemy, as his troops were young, active, eager, and well-disciplined.

On June 6, John McKinnon, who had yet to take post at Niagara, wrote to Haldimand to offer his "warmest and most sincere thanks" for his appointment to Butler's. He created considerable doubt about his professed sincerity by making the qualifying comment that he was "fully convinced that if there was a vacancy in an older Corps, Your

Excellency would grant me the preference on account of my long services joined with that recommendation which Your Excellency received of me from Lord George Germain, to whom I shall embrace the earliest opportunity of acquainting him with Your Excellency's friendly adherence to his recommendation."

On June 7, Haldimand advised Sir John that the Royal Yorkers would be removed from Maclean's command, but not immediately. He then reminded Maclean of the inexperience of young corps. It would seem this deft handling of the situation restored a measure of calm in Montreal district while everyone awaited the sitting of the General Court Martial that had sparked Maclean's outrage.

At Niagara, Powell reported the arrival of a Ranger party with fifteen recruits and an "old" Ranger who had escaped after being captured the previous fall. They brought newspapers and tales of the "calamities of the country" and the general dissatisfaction of the inhabitants. A court martial was avoided over some sort of dispute between two Ranger officers (Captain George Dame and Lieutenant John Turney) when Powell asked two Regular officers to join him in an enquiry. Happily, the hearing concluded that the affair could be settled without dishonour to either man and that Turney's conduct had been fully justified.

Guy Johnson sent Lieutenant Adam Crysler to the Schoharie with a party of Oquagas. Adam was a former resident who had become the particular scourge of his homeland. He later reported scrimmaging with the rebels, taking five scalps, two prisoners, and eighteen horses. Some houses and barns were burned and one Indian killed, another wounded. A soldier of Duboise's Company, WL, was at the Middle Fort when the irruption occurred and recalled a fight near the Upper Fort against Indians led by Crysler.[21]

On June 9, a war party appeared in Canajoharie district and took two men of Gros's Company. The same day, the Albany commission apprehended William, Isabel, and James Parker, relatives of Sir John's agent John, and

John and Jane Wait. They were accused of harbouring and feeding Tory parties. William Parker and John Wait were jailed and Isabel, her son James, and Jane Wait were released to fetch the rest of their families and their effects. These were precisely the type of people the commissioners wanted removed to less vulnerable places.

Lieutenant-Colonel Brinton Paine wrote Governor Clinton from Saratoga, enclosing a letter he had just received from Vermont's Governor Chittenden. With some success, Paine had worked at stopping the revolt of the people in his district, but the "evil had grown again." His regiment's recruits refused to join Captain Dunham, saying they would not abandon their own places just to guard Schuyler's farm; however, they agreed to march to Fort Edward or Lake Champlain if they were guaranteed provisions. Paine was very upset over these events and requested directions about how to deal with Chittenden's challenging letter:

> Arlington, June 9th 1781.
> I am informed you are about to move of a number of familys from your Quarter by force who have been peaceable inhabitants more than two years past. If this … be true I am satisfied, sir, you mistake your policy. The way to Disuade a people from the pursuit of the sweats of Liberty is not … to Exercise the most notorious acts of Tyariny; you may rely on it, sir, it is not viewed in this part of the State to be a small thing you are practicing. Pray, sir, Reflect a moment, and as you value your own peace and the peace and safety of this whole District from such Conduct — such arbitary proceedings have a Direct tendency to Drive people … to Disperation.

On June 10, the bateaux brigade left Stanwix with all the remaining stores and the rest of the troops marched for Fort Herkimer. The dismantlement and evacuation of Stanwix was now complete, marking the end of an era.

By the morning of June 13, the Tory courier and spy, John Meyers, had evaded all the rebels' searches and his thirteen-man band lay under cover near Ballstown. He knew of the town's reputation for the harsh treatment of loyalists. After a careful scout, he developed his plan and when night fell, the party struck the jail, capturing two sentries and releasing twelve political prisoners. Continuing at speed, the band rushed a house where several militia officers were billeted, catching them totally off guard and taking 12ACM's adjutant, Captain David Ramsey, and three subalterns of White's company. Meyers left several captives behind, after forcing them to take an oath for the King. This bold, well-executed stroke followed an equally slick victory of the year before when Munro's raid took 12ACM's lieutenant-colonel, a captain, an ensign, three serjeants and twelve privates. Like Munro's, Meyers's band escaped unimpeded and without casualties.

That day, Schenectady's conspiracy commissioners advised their Albany counterparts of a number of persons at the Hellebergh who had at times harboured Meyers and Bettys. It was resolved that Schenectady commissioners Hugh Mitchell and a colleague should send a party to apprehend Bettys who was said to be there at that very moment. Such a convoluted manner of conducting the business!

The Canadian Regiment arrived at Albany and the QMG was directed to supply its detachments that were about to go upriver with "Every Necessary Assistance in his power."

Serjeant John Coon, BR, arrived at Niagara on June 12 and reported he had been near Albany a month earlier and sent a trusty man into the city for news where he heard that Stanwix had caught fire by accident and only six barrels of provisions were saved. Adam Vrooman, another Ranger serjeant, reported hearing the fire was no accident and that the rebels were planning to fortify Fort Herkimer.

On June 14, Sir John sent newspapers and a document to HQ which Secret Service agent, Oliver Church, QLR, had been given by two prominent loyalist sympathizers from New Fane in the Grants. Dr. Smyth wrote Haldimand from Fort St. John's, "Yesterday I arrived at this post, much indisposed. The Climbing of Mountains & Rocks, & traveling thro' Swamps & Thickets renders me incapable, at present to pay my personal respects to your Excellency, but when my Health is restor'd [I]will.... Inform you of the Cause of my flight." Unaware of Hewson's betrayal, Smyth thought he had been exposed by Sir Henry Clinton's domestics.[22]

The discontent that infected the 2NY at Stanwix had transferred to Fort Herkimer. On June 14, a soldier was convicted of stealing a calf from Captain Moodie and plotting to desert to the enemy. He was sentenced to run the "Gantloop" twice through the ranks and pay for the calf. Van Cortlandt apologized to the men for being "under the absolute necessity of making so many capital examples for that most enormas crime of desertion, but ... he is determined to... punish every offence of that nature." The next day, another man was convicted of plotting to desert with several others and was sentenced to "run the gantloop three times through the regiment with a file of men with fixed bayonets at his breast." Obviously, the man would not be "running."

Certain that local Tories had assisted Meyers, the Albany commission ordered Major Ezekiel Taylor to compile a list of 12ACM detailing each man's "Political Character."

Next day, Brigadier-General Clinton sent a message to Hazen's: "It is with pain ... that the Services of the troops has not been so punctually rewarded as he could wish. He assures the Troops that he will make an immediate Representation of their distresses to the Commander in Chief and the moment cash arrives it shall be transmitted to them ... in the meantime he hopes that invincible Fortitude Uniformity, Regularity of Conduct which has hither to characterized American soldiers may still be punctually observed." One wonders if his Canadiens were so understanding.

On June 16, the brigadier informed his brother that small parties of the enemy "frequently make their appearance on the frontier, and take off some of the Inhabitants, and it appeared evident that their parties are not only harboured by the disaffected families, but assisted with every necessary while they commit their Depredation. I have, therefore ... ordered parties out to scour the settlements ... known to be notoriously disaffected, to remove their families into the Country, and seize all the provisions which may be more than sufficient to support them, and apprehend those who are suspicious characters." It is quite amazing how often similar orders to this were issued, which raises the obvious question — were they obeyed or not?

He enclosed a horrific report from Lieutenant Cannon of Marshall's Company, WL, at Johnstown:

> [T]he Enemy Yesterday morning entered the house of Johannes Awl about six in the morning. Made him and his son and a servant boy Prisoners, and abused the women and plundered the house of Clothing and furniture. The Party (by the nearest Guess the Women could make) Consisted of Seventy or Eighty men, among which were only one white man; the rest were all Indians; they said they would carry them to Buck Island. They behaved in a Barbarous Manner to the Prisoners. Dragged them out of Door by the hair, and would not allow them as much as their cloathing; they threatned the women if they should go out of the house to Alarm the Neighbors before two Days had Expired, which has hindred me from getting Intelligence before this Day, upon which I immediately sent an express to Stone Arabia for fear they should break out in that Place. We are almost out of ammunition. Please to order some this Way. Parker and the other Prisoners will be sent down to Morrow... Inclosed you have a handbill left at the house where the Prisoners were taken from. N.B. The Man that was taken Prisoner has two sons in Canada.

The handbill was from Sir John to his friends on the Mohawk. If Awl did have two sons serving in Canada, he and his family had received anything but friendly treatment, but such mistakes were common fare on the frontier.

The commissary of Continental Stores at Albany wrote to Governor Clinton about his attempts to obtain 100 barrels of tar from a local producer. "The Dogs were deceiving us — and selling or secreting of it. I have now taken possession of their kilns and shall get a sufficient." He closed his report with an understated report of Meyers's raid on Ballstown. A man examined by the Albany commission vociferously denied accusations that he had harboured enemy agents and was released in the hopes he would collect news of Joseph Bettys. Major Taylor's list of the political pretensions of 12ACM men was forwarded to the Schenectady commission for action.

———————————————
———————————————

Powell reported that Lieutenant Frederick Docksteder, BR, left Niagara for the Philadelphia Road on June 16 with fifty-four Rangers and Senecas. As to Hewson's betrayal of Dr. Smyth, he advised that intelligence collection might be accomplished from Niagara and reported that forty-seven men had already been recruited for Butler's 9th Company. It is remarkable that forty-seven men travelled through enemy territory and the wilderness of Indian Territory to enlist at Fort Niagara for what would clearly be hazardous duties, particularly when compared to Willett's recruiting experiences.

On June 19, Lieutenant Robert Nelles, 6NID, reported on a raid led by Old Smoke (Sayenqueraghta), one of the Confederacy's two principal war chiefs, whose war party was deep in Pennsylvania on June 3, when they attacked a thirty-three-man unit, took eight soldiers prisoner, and eleven scalps for the loss of one man and two wounded. They were told that rebel colonel, George Rogers Clark, and 700 men were at Fort Pitt two months earlier with the intent of investing Detroit.

Sherwood received permission on June 18 to establish a forward headquarters. Haldimand told St. Leger that Sherwood and Lieutenant Parrot, QLR, were to take a party of loyalists to Dutchman's Point and establish the post.[23]

On June 18, Brigadier-General Clinton wrote to Van Cortlandt about the new works to be built at German Flatts. Major Villefranche, a French engineer, would oversee the construction. "[T]he major has the reputation of being eminent in his Profession I shall forbare to give any Directions, but leave the Matter entirely with him, with this Observation that I could wish it to be effected with as much Expedition, as may be, & that it may contain 250 men inclusive" of artillery. Willett would provide all possible assistance and Rev. Gros and Dr. Petrie had agreed to find local teams and carpenters. As no boatmen were available, 2NY detachments would act as crews. "[K]eep a Small Guard at the Mills near the Carrying place [Little Falls], as it is of the last Importance to secure that Pass, and preserve the Mills. I am informed there is a Sawmill about four Miles from the Rear near Stone Rapia, where I would have Coll Willet keep a Guard, and have Plank sawed for the Barracks."

The rebels' need for timely, accurate news was as critical as their enemy's. During the month, a 2NY detachment led by Colonel Louis with twenty-eight Indians and two men of White's Company, WL, investigated enemy activity at Crown Point and captured Claus's ranger, Randall Hewitt, and William Empey, 1KRR. A Tory youngster named Stevens witnessed the captives' arrival at Schenectady and said the Indians treated them well and did not surrender them for three days. Their examination by the Albany commission began on June 18 and lasted many days. Hewitt was eventually released after his father gave bail of £100.

On June 19, the commission reviewed a list, similar to Major Taylor's, of the political dispositions of militiamen from four companies in the Hellebergh. Their findings were forwarded to Brigadier-General Clinton for action. The board also interviewed Robert Tripp on a charge of assisting Meyers, then released him on bail of £100. He soon fled to Canada and joined Meyers's company.

On June 20, Second Major Younglove, 16ACM, reported that he had warned the inhabitants of their danger on the first day of the

Cambridge convention and told them to disperse and hold no further meetings. When they persisted, he went to the committeemen from Vermont and told them to stop the disturbances. For all his efforts, the men attending the convention threw off allegiance to New York and a majority voted for union with Vermont and elected members to sit in the Assembly. Younglove said people were about equally divided pro and con and almost "at swords-points." It will be recalled that Colonel John Blair had earlier declared for Vermont and ignored orders from New York. Before he made this decision, he had ordered his captains to "class" their men in preparation for raising men for the levies and then later told them to disregard that instruction, as the district would soon join Vermont. When some captains ignored his equivocation and raised recruits, he refused to send them. In reaction, Younglove called for the first major to take command, but he refused, making several excuses. The district was in much confusion; those who adhered to New York were resolved to never submit to Vermont unless it was the order of Congress.

On the last day of spring, Willett sent a detailed report to Governor Clinton from Fort Rensselaer:

> I have visited most of the parts in this County and find a pretty general disposition of the Inhabitants to exert themselves for their defence ... [I]n every place w[h]ere there are a few settlers[,] the people have erected stockades and Blockhouses or both, for their security ... But this scheme of the peoples for their own immediate safty against parties of the enemy ... [,] however proper it may be for the[ir] protection...while they are cultivating their farms ... runs counter to the plan which I could wish to execute in event of the appearance of the enemy with anything of force.
>
> In such a situation it would undoubtedly be best to have the force of the County collected to a point that a joint opposition may be made ... This appears to me one of the greatest difficultties I have to surmount. In

times of alarm the Inhabitants fly to their fortrice ... with their women looking as much to the men as to the fortifications to save them. How then to draw the men from these places ... and their families is a difficulty I fear I shall not be able to get over.

A force ought to be collecting sooner then we can expect it from below on account of our perilously remote situation from the Body of the Inhabitants this certainly is a propriety in continuing as much force as possible upon the Fort, let us have the force and I think I may venter to promise that should the enemy appear in this parts they shall not return altogether unpunished ...

A promising harvist presents itself ... in this country, a very great Quantity of Grane more then will be required for the use of the Inhabitants may be expected. Should we be so fortunite as to have it all preserved and its preservation is an object of publick importance. This ... ought to serve as an Indusment not to leave the Country without sufficient aid[.]

[A]mong other articles of provision I am much misstakenifaquantityofPorkmightnot[be]packedinthis country, an article tho of great use in a army appears difficult to be procured by our Commissioners. But Grane in large quantities may still be furnished from these parts[.] Dryed Clams would be a very useful article. I wish if there are any to be had application might be made to the Commander in Chief through every proper Channel to have some ordered this way. I am anxious to learn whether there is a prospect of succeeding in the raising the troops for 3 yrs., But as I should not trouble you upon this _____ I shall try to learn from Major Throop, But shall be obliged to your excellency to let me know whether I am like to come in for a share in the Clothing.

_____

_____

The long memory of military justice was at work in lower Quebec on June 19 when a court martial met to try two Hanau Jägers who had deserted at Ticonderoga in the fall of 1777. They had been found three years later serving with the rebels at Fort George. At Lieutenant-Colonel von Kreutzbourg's request, the felons were turned over to him, with the governor's insistence that they be hanged ringing in his ears.

As spring ended, Captain Crawford returned to Fort Haldimand to report he had scouted the ruins of Fort Stanwix and fires were still burning when he left.[24]

5

Brigadier Clinton sent the final word about the disposition of the Continental troops in the north in a secret letter to his brother George on June 21. He quoted Washington's instructions: "[O]perations ... concerted between ... Count de Rochambeau, and myself against New York, will probably compel me to withdraw, not only these [Hazen's] Troops, but also the remainder of V Schaick's Reg't, and the whole of Courtlandt's." Early notice was being given to avoid alarming the inhabitants and to allow the maximum number of Levies to be sent to relieve the Regulars. The C-in-C added that "nothing but absolute necessity" would cause him to order the troops away, but warned, "when the measure becomes indispensably necessary, there is not anything which can divert me from it." James said it was necessary to expedite the raising of levies, noting they only numbered 400 men, as he worried an immediate incursion by the enemy once the troops were removed. Although work had begun on the new fort at German Flatts and Van Cortlandt had selected a site and put the 2NY and Elsworth's Levies to work on clearing off trees and brush, the C-in-C altered the plan, instructing Villefranche to concentrate on the current installations, noting that improvements could be made when time and circumstances allowed.

At Albany, Willett issued a regimental order on June 21. The recruits from Dutchess County were to be equally divided between Duboise's company at Schoharie and Conine's at Catskill. Both captains were to send an officer to Fishkill to receive their men. Whelp's company was to march from Saratoga to Johnstown and await further orders. Willett then left the city to begin a tour of his new responsibility, riding to Schenectady, and the following day to Johnstown.

Washington sent a report to the Board of War that included his best estimate of the volume of rations consumed daily by the northern Continental army. One figure stood out boldly; in the area of Albany, the Regulars, friendly Indians, and those displaced Canadien families, who had fled Quebec in 1776, drew 2,000 rations per day. Congress would soon reduce this astonishing expenditure.

On June 22, Lieutenant-Colonel Edward Antill of Hazen's sent an ensign and some troops to Johnstown to relieve the Levies. The ensign was to instruct the commissary to transfer with all his provisions and stores to Caughnawaga. He was told to seek out a knowledgeable man, such as Solomon Woodward, to learn about the routes leading into town and to post scouts, in particular at Sacandaga, a common access route. Flour was to be drawn from the commissary to bake hard bread for his scouts. A report was to be made about the grain and fattened cattle amongst the disaffected.

Willett continued his tour on June 23, riding to Canajoharie and next day visiting George Herkimer, a brother of Tryon's dead brigadier. On June 24, the Schell family was working in their fields four miles north of Fort Dayton. Frederick and his brother Marks were standing guard when Indians stole up to within range and mortally wounded their father, John Christian, and their brother, Demas, who kept the Indians at bay with musket fire and saved his father from being scalped. Frederick was shot through the thigh, but escaped with Marks, who kept up a brisk fire. The Indians withdrew through the standing wheat, leaving behind signs of having dragged off their casualties. On an earlier occasion, the family had vigorously defended their blockhouse and mortally wounded one of the Valley's Tory McDonells, which may explain the second attack.

Willett continued his tour on June 25 by travelling to German Flatts. That day, a detachment of Hazen's took post at Caughnawaga to regulate movement by road and river and to guard the relocated commissary.[1]

Major General John Stark was sent to Albany to replace James Clinton as Northern Department commander. Energetic, capable, charismatic, and irascible, Stark had been a Rogers's Rangers captain in the Seven Years' War. When rebellion broke out in 1775, he quickly became involved and vigorously commanded the beach defences at Bunker's Hill. He resigned in a fit of pique at being passed over for promotion and retired to New Hampshire, but soon accepted the rank of brigadier of state militia. Still miffed with Congress, he refused to join Schuyler in 1777 at Ticonderoga, but when Burgoyne sent a raid toward Bennington, Stark rallied the New Hampshire

Detail from an engraving after a painting attributed to Forest (New York Public Library Digital Gallery, No.424988).

Major-General John Stark of New Hampshire. The sensitive, irascible hero of Bennington.

and Vermont militia and soundly defeated the enemy. For this signal victory, he was awarded a Continental brigadier's commission and later a promotion to major-general. With his solid reputation in New York and the New England States, Washington saw him as the ideal man to coordinate forces after the Regulars left:

> Upon finding it necessary ... to recall the Continental Troops from the Northward, I have ordered 600 militia from the Counties of Berkshire and Hampshire to that quarter, in addition to the Militia and State Troops of New York; and I have now to request that you will assume the general Command of all the troops in that Department ... I am induced to appoint you to this Command on account of your knowledge of, and influence among the Inhabitants of that Country ... You will be pleased, therefore, to repair to Saratoga, and establish your Head Quarters at that place, retaining with you 400 of the troops from Massachusetts, and sending the other 200 to Colonel Willet, who will remain in command on the

Mohawk River, as his popularity in that Country will enable him to render essential services there.

In case of an incursion from the Enemy, you will make such dispositions, as you shall judge most advantageous (not withdrawing the troops from the Mowhawk River) … [Y]ou will use your utmost exertions to draw forth the force of the Country from the Green Mountains and all the contiguous territory; and I doubt not your requisitions will be attended with success, as your personal influence must be unlimited among those people, at whose head, you have formerly fought and conquered with so much reputation and glory.

While Willett was visiting German Flatts, Indians struck a party from Gros's company that was collecting provisions at Fort Timmerman and three were taken.[2]

––––––––––––––––––––––––––––––––
––––––––––––––––––––––––––––––––

In concern for the security of the Vermont talks, Haldimand inquired of Sir John whether Secret Service agent Oliver Church had read the papers he had brought in. Johnson advised that the document had been open when handed to Church and that he was fully aware of the contents. Further, he had discussed with an informant that, if loyalist properties were part of an agreement, all uneasiness could be removed by a gift of equivalent lands in another quarter. The baronet strongly recommended Church as the best man to continue this secret correspondence.

On June 24, Haldimand instructed Powell not to send any more troops to Detroit. He was to keep his Regulars and Rangers "in perfect readiness for any service they may be called upon." As to supplies and Native presents, he hoped the Cork fleet would soon arrive as well as the one that had wintered at Halifax. In another letter, he approved Powell's settlement of the contentious Dame and Turney affair, as the latter was an active, useful partisan who would have been a loss to the

Rangers. This same day, Guy Johnson reported that 500 Natives were on the frontiers.

A June 24 KRR subsistence return listed: 1 lieutenant-colonel; 1 major; 8 captains; 12 lieutenants, including a captain-lieutenant; 3 ensigns; a chaplain; an adjutant; a quartermaster; a surgeon, and a mate. In 1KRR, there were: 30 serjeants; 30 corporals; 20 drummers; 575 privates; 30 contingent men and 2 recruits; in 2KRR, 277 recruits. Sir John's regiment was now the largest in the Northern Department.

In Quebec City, the sentences of the General Court Martial examining the treasonous plot that had so aroused Maclean's ire were announced on June 25. Nine 2KRR soldiers who had been training with 1KRR at Coteau-du-Lac had "formed & agreed upon a Conspiracy to kill the Commanding Officer, and all other Officers and Soldiers ... who should oppose their proceedings ... to lay that Post in Ashes, desert the Service, and join the enemy." The men bribed a local Indian to guide them over the Adirondacks after the deed was done, but rather than take any risk, he revealed the plot and received a reward. Six mutineers were sentenced to 1,000 lashes each, a seventh to 500. They were to be sent to Quebec "in Irons in a Batteau as soon as they can undertake the Journey after ... their Corporal Punishments," presumably to be sent to Africa or the West Indies. Another man who had been awarded 500 lashes had his sentence forgiven, probably for providing evidence. All of the mutineers had been captured the year before: five in October while serving in Harper's NY Levies; one, a MA Levy, at Stone Arabia on October 19; another a Tryon man at Remensnyder's Bush in April 1780. A rebel prisoner who had been on Prison Island recalled, "Only one of the guards escaped whipping, he appearing to be such a simpleton as to be incapable of devising any mischief." One man missed the flogging when it was found that he was a German who had deserted at Ticonderoga in 1777. Lieutenant-Colonel Ernst Von Speth claimed him, so he could be punished according to German law. Oddly enough, a tenth fellow had been taken under arms in the 4TCM and enlisted in the Royal Yorkers on the same date as the men from Harper's Levies and, although not listed in the court martial, was also given 1,000 lashes for desertion. A rebel witness recalled, "The skin was entirely gone and the flesh over their whole backs was … torn and hanging in shreds and strings as though a pack of hungry dogs had gnawed and mangled them, the naked bones protruding through the flesh in many places." He thought the victims were banished to Prison Island, which, if true, did not fit with their sentence. He failed to mention that one mutineer and the deserter died under the lash. One victim's son, who was also a captive in Quebec, was allowed to visit his father. Sadly, he arrived too late to speak to his parent and, when witnessing the flogging, found it necessary to avert his eyes.[3]

A report of June 26 noted that twenty-eight St. Francis Abenakis were on a scouting party. Their task was unstated, yet just the fact that they were active was a bonus.

On June 27, a return was prepared for Colonel John Lamb's 2nd Regiment of Continental Artillery. Moodie's company at German Flatts was listed as: a captain; a captain-lieutenant; first lieutenant; second lieutenant; three serjeants; three corporals; two gunners; and fourteen matrosses.

Lieutenant-Colonel Antill reported from Caughnawaga that there were only fifteen useable bateaux on the river. Obviously, those being built at Schenectady were not ready. Brigadier-General Clinton concluded that a large number were with Van Cortlandt at German Flatts and ordered him to retain only two "large six-handed boats" and send the balance downriver crewed by the Levies. He also ordered deputy quartermaster general (DQMG) Henry Glen at Schenectady to go to Fort Herkimer and assist Van Cortlandt to put the works in a state of defence before the Regulars left. Next day, a Regimental Order was issued to Hazen's "to hold themselves in readiness to march at a minutes notice. [A]ll the heavy baggage … (blacksmith tools excepted) the soldiers and womens useless baggage will be packed up and ready to be put into boats that will pass tomorrow for Schenectady where they will be safely stowed under the care of an officer, verry few wagons will move with the regiment, the surplus baggage [will] not just be left on the ground when the regiment moves." This order proved quite premature.

Washington urged Stark to seek Schuyler's advice about troop distribution when he arrived in the north, noting his excellent knowledge of the country. Thus, he could be of great assistance in locating local means of subsistence if the public stores were exhausted. It is difficult to imagine how Stark, that quintessential New Englander, received this instruction. In 1777, he had blatantly ignored Schuyler's call for assistance when Burgoyne threatened to overwhelm the Northern Army and it had been New Englanders who had wangled Schuyler's removal shortly thereafter.

On June 28, Willett reported to Brigadier-General Clinton from Fort Rensselaer:

> I have visited the German flatts and returned to this place yesterday. Nothing new had occurred except the loss of two men of the Levies who were missing two days ago from Fort Windecker. They were seen at a distance from the fort without their arms and are supposed to be taken by the enemy as some Indians were discovered the day before. We are Intirely without Amunition at this place except the triffel the men have possible. As the mens Firelocks differ in their Callibers it will be necessary to order Cartridges of diferent sizes. I hope this Vicinity will not be forgot in the Beef way as we are put to no small shifts in furnishing the troops with provisions ... I am very desirous of sending out as many and as large [scouts] as possible. To ... accomplish this I must heartily wish to have Salt provisions & hard bread. Could we not be furnished with dried Clams?

The Albany conspiracy board examined Jellis Legrange on suspicion of assisting Joseph Bettys. His fate was sealed when a second man testified Joseph had taken him to see Bettys in order to enlist for the King. Legrange chose to talk to save his hide and two days later eight men answered charges about assisting Bettys.

A busy, conscientious Willett continued his tour, visiting Forts Willett and Plain in Canajoharie District.[4]

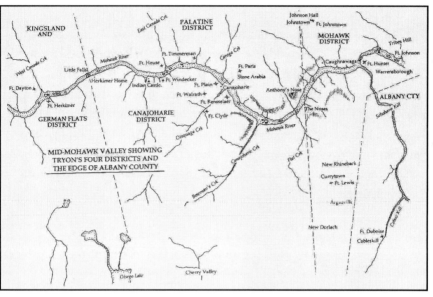

Gavin K. Watt. Research assistance by Ken D. Johnson, after Charles Wintersmith (Carl Winterschmidt) 1777.

Mid-Mohawk Valley Showing Tryon's four districts and the edge of Albany County.

On June 28, Guy Johnson reported the return of Captain Hendrick Nelles. His ninety-five-man Six Nations' and Mississauga party had gone to the Mohawk, killed thirteen, and brought in seven prisoners. Year-to-date, war parties had killed or taken 150 persons. Several small and two large parties were on the frontiers as he wrote and others in Indian Territory.

On the first of July, Willett was still at Canajoharie village consulting with militia officers and prominent citizens when Colonel Klock's son, Jacob Jr., allowed his resentment at being passed over for company command in the Levies to get the best of him and ran off to Oswegatchie with a number of Tory sympathizers.

Hazen's Regimental Orders at Caughnawaga illustrated the keen sense of patriotism growing across rebel America:

> Tomorrow will be celebrated the anniversary of the great and glorious Independency of the Rising Empire of America, when she will enter into the sixth year of that Establishment that will be the envy of Europe, the scourge of Britain, and the Surprise of future Nations; the patience, sufferings; and firmness of the Soldery in persuit of this End, will adorn the page of History and generations yet to come will mention them with Gratitude Respect and Love, from the best Inteligence the period is not far distant when we shall Retire to our Homes, amply Repaid for all our Services, and the heart felt satisfaction of having Saved our Country from Tirrany and Oppression, The Regiment will parade Clean dressed with their Arms in good Order at half after Eleven, to give a fuea de Joiy on the Occasion, the Quarter master will furnish Cartridges…. The Gentlemen officers and staff are Requested to Honor Lt Col Antill with their Company at dinner at two oclock, a Gill of Spirits will be Issued to Each man after Parade is over, from Lt Col Antill. [O]n this Occasion it is Expected that decency and good Order will be preserved; those on duty will have their liquor sent to them.

However, Hazen's Canadians were unable to enjoy their patriotic festival, as orders arrived the morning of July 4 to march to Schenectady. They arrived there in late afternoon and, two days later, left Albany for West Point. The first of the Regular units had left the north.

Although it was primarily Continentals and Levies on duty on the northern frontiers in July, detachments of the various militia regiments were also employed. 2ACM had men garrisoning Forts Hunter and Plain, the Schoharie forts and a palisaded log house at Claas Viele's Rifts on the Mohawk fourteen miles above Schenectady.

One of the goals of Willett's extended tour was to list the buildings, crops, and livestock of the disaffected. Expropriation to fund the war and feed troops had been employed throughout Tryon County from the earliest days of the rebellion and, with more and more inhabitants gone to the enemy or exposed as Tories, there was a great deal of property and goods to be seized. For example, the Fort Edward homes of Dr. Smyth and his brother Patrick were occupied by the state, fortified, and picketed. The doctor was incensed and asked Haldimand to send a party to destroy both buildings, but the governor declined.

On July 4, Captain Mathews wrote to Sherwood from HQ about Smyth's list of "the most obnoxious" rebels in and about Albany who might be carried off by small parties. Haldimand requested a similar list from Sherwood for New England and Vermont. After urging profound secrecy, the governor left the matter solely in the hands of Sherwood and Smyth. Small parties led by the most experienced men were to be selected from the Fort St. John's garrison.

Haldimand, who was still in the dark about Germain's May 4 dispatch, wrote a "Most Secret" report to Sir Henry Clinton in New York City:

> Tho' it is scarce possible the following Report (just rec'd from an approved Loyalist in Albany) should not have reached Your Excellency yet the extreme difficulty our Messengers find in escaping the Vigilance of the Enemy induces me to mention it.
>
> The Troops upon the Hudson & Mohawk Rivers are ordered immediately to Peekskill where a Body of French Troops are arrived — it is supposed an Attack upon New York [City] is intended — General Schuyler came up in a great Hurry & has ordered 1000 Boats to be got ready by August, the Workmen to be

paid in hard cash — The Frontiers to be guarded by the nine months men — a Draft of 800 men to be made from the Militia — All the Tories near the Frontiers are ordered to move to the East side of Hudson's River and are by order plundered at Discretion.

Uninformed as I am of what is passing in any & all Quarters it is impossible to judge from the Above what is the Enemy's real design or to give that Assistance by well-timed Diversion which I otherwise might — tho' a want of Provisions would render it less Effectual, it would still be in my power to Alarm & to Diminish the Enemy's Force, should the Attack expected be their Object — I hope this will arrive safe and procure me the pleasure of hearing fully from Your Excellency your opinion of what is likely to happen & if in Your Quarter what you wish done from this to favor you — The cipher is a very Tedious one but impossible to be discovered. We therefore can run no Risk in communicating our Ideas to each other — Should their Intention be against this Province, I can only say that every measure in my Power to adopt for its defence is in active forwardness — My situation in regard to Provisions is very alarming, we are now living from Hand to Mouth in Expectation of the Fleet. Should any misfortune befall it[,] the Consequences must be very distressing, this Country being threatened by Famine owing to Caterpillars which have destroyed almost all the Hay & a great part of the Grain.

The Cöos prisoner, Lieutenant-Colonel Thomas Johnson, recalled details of his stay at Fort St. John's during July:

At this time provisions were so scarce that they were obliged to distribute what little they had in very small quantities, by the barrel &c to every quarter. Wheat was now four dollars or upwards per bushel, Beef twenty coppers per pound, Butter, and Veal double that sum. The Officers often said that all the Prisoners must be sent out of the Province. One third part of their cattle died in the spring for want of forage; the worms devoured almost every green thing so that there was no prospect of wintering more than one third part of what cattle the winter had spared. During the carrying on the aforesaid expeditions it was agreed by the Allens &c on the part of Vermont that they would lay still and give them no trouble as the Officers had often told me. Thus Ethan Allen did at Castleton in the fall of the year 1780, when the British destroyed Fort George, Fort Ann and many of the Inhabitants in that quarter, and came round within one day's march of the place where Allen lay with near a thousand men and suffered them all to pass on unmolested, when at the same time I heard many of the officers often say that Allen might easily have cut them off if he would but he had agreed to the contrary. The rehearsal of these actions of the infernal villains is enough to make my blood run cold in every vein. Now I was reduced to straight quarters and offered a commission of major on swearing allegiance to the King and taking part with them; otherwise they told me that I must be sent away with other prisoners and take my fate with them. Now I was obliged to deal on punctilios. I told them I had rather lay in gaol five years than lift my finger to shed the blood of my countrymen. But that everything in my power for peace I would invariably pursue. Notwithstanding all the plausible pretences of the Vermonters, the spirit of jealousy was high. They constantly kept Spies amongst them to watch their motions some of whom came in and said that some of the Inhabitants of the Grants were for fighting, but generally they were for neutrality or submission.[5]

In July, the community of Katzeburgh near Canajoharie was destroyed by a war party. Lieutenant-Colonel Willett detailed his plans for defence to Brigadier-General Clinton:

> I find the business this way in rather a perplexed situation and am as far as my Command extends endeavoring to put it into a regular Train. By the withdrawing of the regular Troops, the Command will I expect rest wholly in me. The method I had already entered upon with such forts as I was to have in charge was to relieve the Guards at the different forts every few days by detachments[,] As the method of leaving the same men at one place anytime is obviously a bad one and unmilitary when it can be avoided. This plan I purpose to pursue at every place as far as my command may extend. Except in cases were it may be very clear that it will be for the good of the servise to leave the same troops fixed at any one fort. Which by the by I think will seldom be the case. I should be very glad to know from you before you leave this department what troops I may expect to have in charge and how far those troops are expected to Guard or protect the Country. I heartily desire to pursue such measures as may be most beneficial to the service the better to do this I wish to have matters so formed as to have it in my power to from time to time [see] every officer & Soldier that I may have in charge that so I may have oppertunities of rectifying mistakes and preventing abuses personally. The system of doing business by detachments will be the likeliest way to afford me such opportunities. But I mean not to rely upon this altogether I shall endeavor from time to time to visit every part of my Command. I shall take it as a particular favour in you to let me have your sentiments

upon every part of this business. You know the whole of our situation. I wrote to you two days ago respecting tents for the troops ... at the German Flats ... I should be glad to have as many as you think necessary against the time the regular troops are relieved without tents[,] I don't see how those works can be prosecuted.

Willett wrote to Colonels Wemple, 2ACM, and Beeckman, 4ACM, about recruiting for a new form of service. Each able-bodied recruit would receive a bounty of 500 acres of unappropriated state land, excepting land located in the Oneida and Tuscarora territories. The men were to serve three years, unless discharged earlier, and were intended for the defence of the state. Congress was to pay, subsist, and clothe these men similar to Continentals. As short-term Levies had been difficult to recruit, it remained to be seen if land bounties would lure men into longer terms.

Sherwood reported from Dutchman's Point, "I arriv'd here yesterday with

Artist thought to be William Berczy. (John Ross Robertson Collection, Baldwin Room, Metropolitan Toronto Reference Library, No.4395.)

twenty-three men including old men, Boys and unincorporated Loyalists. I am now Building an Oven & Hutting the men, shall tomorrow begin felling timber for the blockhouse.

Dr. Robert Kerr, surgeon of the 2nd Battalion, Royal Yorkers. While stationed at Fort Haldimand, Kerr treated sick and wounded Natives as well as the garrison. He attended the Ross Expedition. Postwar, he married Elizabeth Brant Johnson, eldest daughter of Mary Brant. In 1788, he was appointed surgeon to the Indian Department.

Timber is not so plentiful here as I expect'd & we must draw it a mile at least." He added that the assistant engineer had advised it was the wrong season "to cut oak, hickory and cherry or birch timber as it will be too open and brittle for any fine work or for duration."

Haldimand was clearly in a tough mood when he issued a July 1 order. He was well informed that there were many able, young male loyalists at St. John's, Machiche, and other quarters who had previously earned their keep by labour and now were idly passing their time. This was an abuse of the King's bounty, and he ordered them to be struck off the provisions list by August 1. This notice was being given so they could find employment for their own maintenance.

John Butler advised Lernoult that his 9th company was complete and asked for a commission certificate for his son Thomas as its first lieutenant. He noted that Lieutenant Bradt had returned with five men; one was a Ranger who had been left behind last fall, another a rebel who had declared for the Crown, plus three black recruits. Bradt had heard that a great many loyalists were daily joining Ethan Allen. Butler also had seven men for his 10th company and expected to complete it in a few weeks as Bradt had left three men to pilot forty recruits to Niagara and other parties would yield more.

On a different tack, Butler reported that a General Court Martial had absolved him and Walter of any wrongdoing. In this nasty, divisive affair, Lieutenant Jacob Ball and, to a lesser extent, his son Lieutenant Peter Ball, with Second Lieutenant Joseph Ferris and Serjeant Benjamin Freylick, had stirred up mutiny and sedition. An anonymous letter had been sent to Brigadier-General Powell charging Lieutenant-Colonel Butler and other officers "with Capital Crimes" and ungentlemanly behaviour. The two Balls had been honorably acquitted, but the court found Ferris's involvement of a serjeant in the affair to be reprehensible, as were his expressions in the letter. He was found guilty of a breach of the 3rd Article of the 20th Section of the Articles of War and sentenced to publicly ask Lieutenant-Colonel Butler's pardon and to be reprimanded by the governor. Freylick was acquitted of two charges, but found guilty of speaking disrespectfully of his commanding officer and reduced to corporal. Haldimand approved the sentences and credited Ferris's involvement to inexperience.

There was a second nasty trial of the disruptive lieutenant, Peter Ball. In this instance, he was charged with refusing to join Captain McDonell when ordered into action near Fort Herkimer the previous fall. Allegedly, he told the men it was too dangerous and not to go. It was bruited about that "the Corps w[ould]not do duty with him till he clear this up." Ball was ultimately acquitted.

Powell reported on July 1 that Butler's new company was "a very good one." Bradt had attributed his relative lack of recruiting success to having been "discovered and obliged to fly" as well as the loss of so many loyalists to Allen. More Ranger business arose when two wives of the regiment, Elizabeth Phillips and Dorothy Windecker, who had been sent with a number of women and invalid Rangers to lower Quebec to reduce the burden at the fort, petitioned for permission to rejoin their husbands at Niagara with their children. "As for provisions, we can have no complaint of, as there is no more allowed; but the water and firewood is the only reason we have to complain on, and at this place there is nothing to be had the whole year through." Of her son in the KRR, Phillips wrote, "[I] should be glad to have him back as all the other sons and my husband is in the Rangers."

Sir John reported to HQ on July 2 that his two scouts sent out in late April had returned from Johnstown with the sad news that the Parker family had been taken and were closely confined in Fort Johnstown awaiting removal to Albany. He noted that they had for several years harboured scouts and gathered intelligence. His men had been unable to get any news other than a report of the loss of Hewitt and Empey. Johnson said that no parties would be safe while the Oneidas patrolled the pathways and suggested sending a force of 150–200 picked men with 10–15 Mohawks to cut them off and take any rebel couriers going to Canada. Haldimand did not favour this idea, as the rebels were fortifying at Saratoga and Ballstown and a small patrol from either place could baffle an attempt by 200 men. Anything useful would require a larger force. Meanwhile, scouts and couriers would have to take every precaution to avoid interception. Although unwilling to commit, he asked Johnson to suggest a route that a detachment might employ and to recommend the supplies required and make note of any unusual problems.

Lieutenant-Colonel Claus reported that the Lachine Mohawks were very upset by the capture of Ranger Randall Hewitt, a particular favourite of theirs. In 1776, the sixteen-year-old had been taken from the rebels and when Claus passed through Oswegatchie on his way to Stanwix in 1777, he had forced himself on the colonel. Ever since, he had served faithfully and become a keen, active woodsman, acquiring the Iroquois language and taking part on every important service. The Mohawks thought the threat to the communications' routes "too great an Insult to put up with from a Banditti of Indians, who were the Scum & Refuse of 6 Nations & Canada Indians." They were willing to take on the task themselves, or would happily join "with a Body of active white Men in order to do the Thing more effectually." The Schenectady youngster, Stevens, reported that the chief of the rebel Kahnawakes had recently been in Canada with messages for the Seven Nations and he had heard that the rebel Natives were to continue their interdiction of the routes to and from Canada as far north as Split Rock for the whole summer.

In response to Smyth's list of noxious rebels, Haldimand told St. Leger he would send several scouts to the Albany area for intelligence and, if possible, to carry off some of the most inveterate and active leaders. St. Leger was to supply thirty-six men for these missions. He advised Sherwood that he would "leave to your discretion the sending out Parties as you shall think expedient without the tedious necessity of previous communication with me, having often seen the best imagin'd plans fail by being too long delayed."[6]

———————————————

———————————————

The 1NY companies at Albany had received no pay in quite some time and were particularly agitated by a rumour that a quantity of specie was in the city. When no pay materialized, the situation rapidly escalated, fueled by the men's liberal consumption of rum. Brigadier-General Clinton commented that the most dangerous consequences could be expected from "minds … poisoned by such Ideas as this, and whose heads were inflamed by liquor." The troops became rowdy, then rebellious, then violent. Coercive measures were resorted to and order was restored after a brief conflict in which two mutineers were badly wounded and twelve principals confined. To set an example, several were punished. The night following the punishment parade, thirteen deserted, including three serjeants. Clinton promised to pardon those who returned to duty and many came in, but others ran to Vermont. It was a sour 1NY that left for West Point.

While Willett was at Fort Herkimer on July 5, Indians captured an artillerist. Next day, the colonel reported to Washington, providing in a few succinct paragraphs the strategies he would employ in the coming campaign. At the same time, he revealed why he was so effective as a leader, openly admiring the people he was to protect, their stubborn courage and stamina in the face of unrelenting raids. He also painted an excellent picture of Tryon County's value to the Union:

> It is a country of the most luxuriant soil. Not only the lands along the river are exceedingly rich, but the back lands are also of the first quality.... Most of the settlements lie along, or not far back from the Mohawk river. At the commencement of the present war, both sides of the river, from Schenectady to Germantown, [German Flatts] which is seventy miles, the settlements were considerably thick; and every thing had the appearance of ease and plenty. There were besides several valuable farms, extending fifteen miles higher up the river than Germantown [which was] the last place where any number of families had fixed themselves together.
>
> At the beginning of the war the militia of the county did not amount to less than two thousand five hundred men. In such a country, blessed with so fine a soil, lying along a delightful river, which affords an easy transportation of the produce to valuable market, with a climate exceeded by none, one would have expected a consequent increase of population. But this

was retarded by means which you are undoubtedly acquainted with...

The place from which I now write ... is ... the advance settlement up the river, and lies sixty-three miles from Schenectady. This strip, sixty miles in length, is liable to Indian incursions, on both sides of the river. This the inhabitants have frequently experienced; and so severe has been their experience, that, out of two thousand five hundred upon the militia rolls ... at present the whole number of classable inhabitants, (this is, of those who are liable to be assessed to pay taxes, in order to raise the men for public service), there not being twelve hundred, the number liable to be called upon to do military duty, will hardly exceed eight hundred; so that there is a reduction in the county of at least two thirds, since the commencement of the war.

I do not think I am wild in my calculations, when I say, that one third of them have been killed, or carried captive by the enemy; one third have removed into the interior parts of the country; and one third have deserted to the enemy. The present distressed situation of the inhabitants, is such, as to demand sympathy, from the most unfeeling heart. Each neighbourhood has erected for itself a fortification.... Each fort contains from ten to upwards of fifty families. There are twenty-four of these fortifications within the county. [N]otwithstanding their deplorable situation, should they be fortunate enough to preserve the grain they at present have in the ground, they will have an immense quantity more than will be sufficient for their own consumption.

... By withdrawing the regular troops, the county is, undoubtedly, much weakened. At this time, I have not, in the whole county, more than two hundred and fifty men, exclusive of the militia. Some reinforcements, Governor Clinton writes me word, are coming from the eastward. Part of these, we may hope, will come this way; and, by others being sent to the northward, I flatter myself, I shall be able to withdraw those levies, which have been placed under my command, which are, at present, that way. [i.e. at Saratoga].

I heartily wish to have as much force as possible, to assist in the preservation of a people, whose sufferings have, already, been so exceeding great. But, be the force larger or smaller, I can only promise to do everything in my power, for the relief of a people, of whom I had some knowledge in their more prosperous days; and am now acquainted with in the time of their distress: a people, whose case I must sincerely commiserate. At the same time, I think it my duty to inform your Excellency, that, after withdrawing the two regular regiments from these parts, I expect to have the command of all the troops that may be ordered into this county for its common defence. This is what Governor Clinton told me would be the case. Should the legislature make such further provision, for the defence of the county, as I have requested, notwithstanding its present deplorable situation, I shall hope to have the state of things much more respectable than hitherto it has been. Nor shall I exceed my hopes, if, in the course of less than twelve months, I shall be able to convince the enemy, that they are not without their vulnerable quarters, in these parts.

Since I have been in this part of the country, I have been endeavoring to put matters in some kind of regulation. With the approbation of the governor I have fixed my quarters at Canajoharie, on account of its central position. And my intention is to manage business so as to have an opportunity of acquainting myself as well as possible with every officer and soldier I may have in my charge. In order the better to do this, I propose … to guard the different posts by detachments, to be relieved as the nature of the case will admit. And as the relieved troops will always return to Fort Rensselaer, where my quarters will be, I shall have an opportunity of seeing them all in turn. Having troops constantly marching backwards and forwards through the country, and frequently changing their route, will answer several purposes, such as will be easily perceived by you, sir, without my mentioning them. This not the only way by which I expect to become particularly acquainted with the troops and their situation. I intend occasionally to visit every part of the country, as well to rectify such mistakes as are common among the kind of troops I have at present in charge, as to enable me to observe the condition of the militia, upon whose aid I shall be under the necessity of placing considerable reliance.

In order to shew that I have some reason to place dependence upon the militia, I shall first mention a transaction that took place a few nights ago at Canajoharie. An account was sent me at one o'clock in the morning that about fifty Indians and tories were in the neighbourhood of a place six miles off. Having with me at the fort no more regular troops than were sufficient to guard it, I sent for a captain of the militia; and in less than an hour he was out with seventy men in search of the enemy. In short, they are a people, who, having experienced no inconsiderable portion of British barbarism, are become keen for revenge, and appear properly determined.

… I am desirous of giving you as good a sketch as I can of the situation of this country… the strength we now have this way is inadequate to the fortress intended to be erected at this place … Nor did I see the great necessity of such works… some small improvements to the works we already have, will answer our present purpose …

If it should meet with your approbation, I should be glad to make such a disposition of the cannon and other ordnance stores, as may appear most secure, and best calculated to protect the country, for to me it is clear, that the way to protect these parts is ... to collect all the strength we can get to a point, and endeavour to beat them in the field, and not attempt to defend any one particular spot: for such is the exposed state of the country, that the enemy can make incursions in almost any quarter. Beside this, it is not their policy or custom to halt to invest any particular place. It is therefor my opinion, that by joining our whole force together, and not be defending any one post, we are to endeavour to protect these frontiers: whilst these small stockade forts, and block houses, which the inhabitants themselves have built, are in general sufficient to cover them against such parties of Indians and tories as usually make this way. I should count myself happy in having your sentiments upon this subject. At present I have at this place about one hundred men: nor is it possible without calling on the inhabitants below, to afford this place more men until I receive some reinforcements. I need not say to you, sir that nothing can be done erecting [a] new fort, with the men I now have. I shall, therefore, only endeavour to repair the works already at this place, until I shall receive further orders.[7][end block quote]

On July 6, Colonel Van Cortlandt was ordered to call in all of his officers and men from their different postings and repair to Albany leaving Captain Moodie and Levies' Captain Elsworth behind at Fort Herkimer. The last of the Continental infantry was leaving the frontier.

On the same day that Willett sent his detailed report to the C-in-C, he also wrote to his political master, Governor Clinton. As Willett was less than happy with the state's support, it is not surprising the letter was rather testy.

At present I am at this place, with 120 of the levies, including officers; and captain Moody's company of artillery, which is but 20 strong. The total of all the levies in this county besides is 96. A very insufficient number indeed to perform such business as is expected ... I am crowded with applications for guards, and have nothing to guard with. I will, however, do my best, and have no doubt, you will pay as much attention to our situation as you can. That part of my regiment of levies not with me at this place is stationed as follows. At Schoharie I have placed a little over 20 men: Kaatskill about the same number, unless they have rec'd recruits from Dutchess County, where I ordered them to send officers for that purpose. Captain White has his company still at Ballstown, except a few left with the commissioners of Albany, which I have ordered to join him. This whole company consists of about 30 men. Captain Whelp's coy is ordered this way from Saratoga, where the companies of Captains Gray and Dunham still remain. I shall endeavour to make some alterations, but am at a loss, with the very few men we have, to know how. I shall be glad to have your sentiments on this matter as soon as possible. I confess myself not a little disappointed in having such a trifling force for such extensive business as I have upon my hands; and also that nothing is done to enable me to avail myself of the aid of the militia. The prospect of a suffering country hurts me. Upon my own account I am not uneasy. Every thing I can do shall be done; and more cannot be looked for. If it is, a reflection that I have done my duty, must fix my own tranquility.

The governor responded to Colonel Brinton Paine's letter of June 10 about those Yorkers who were favouring Vermont. He had advised the legislature and delayed replying while awaiting their thoughts; however, the politicians had found no time to deal with the issue. Clinton instructed Paine to be steady and firm in his duty, avoiding controversy or strife that would weaken the state's ability to battle the British, "at least until the close of the present Campaign." As to Chittenden's letter, it was simply beneath Paine's notice. He advised that, to compensate for the removal of the Regulars, the legislature had ordered "a second levy of Troops equal to the former" to be embodied without delay.

In contrast to Willett's difficulties, Colonel Albert Pawling's five-company regiment of Levies raised for the defence of Ulster's and Orange's frontiers submitted an almost complete roster of officers and serjeants and an average of sixty enlisted men per company. This total matched Willett's and he had twice as many companies to fill.

On this topic, a State Commissary irascibly wrote from Albany to Major McKinstry about men recruited by Lieutenant Pliny Moore. If he "pays Attention to his Warrant, he will find that my Residence is fixd at this place to Muster & Receive all the Recruits for that Service, for the Legislature have made no provisions for my traveling Expenses. [He] may for this time have the men Sworn agreeable to the form herewith Delivered [figure 1] & send me their Respective oaths I shall then send them their several Certificates."

I A.B do swear to be true to the United States of America to serve them honestly & faithfully Against all their Enemies or Opposers Whatever to Observe & Obey the Orders of the Continental Congress Generals & Officers set over me by them so help me God.

Sworn before me this July 1781

Willett lost his first company commander when Captain Peter Elsworth's twenty-five-man detachment was at the burned-out ruins of the Steele's Creek hamlet about three miles upriver from Fort Herkimer on July 6. Some sources say they were fishing; others, scouting; of course, they could have been doing both. Twelve Mississaugas, led by principal warrior David van der Heyden, attacked the Levies as they crossed an open field. Elsworth, a serjeant and a private were killed outright. A second private took a rifle ball in the side, but eluded capture, as did two others who were wounded in their limbs. George Herkimer, who was carrying important papers, and another man were taken prisoner.

When Ross reported this action, he noted that van der Heyden was a "zealous partisan … of essential service to this post," though only a "mere Indian." Ross later had trouble over his frequent tactless, pejorative comments concerning Natives. (van der Heyden said all the Levies would have been dead if his party had known they were unsupported.)

That same day, Henry Maracle of Butler's Rangers slipped into New Dorlach to advise that Brant was on his way with a strong party to destroy Currytown.

A Secret Service report of July 6 advised Haldimand of the Continentals' transfer south to Peekskill for a likely attack on New York City and that Schuyler had contracted for the building of 1,000 boats for the French.

Detail of watercolour by James Peachey, 1785. (Library and Archives Canada, C-045559.)

The Canadien Habitant, Thomas Johnson's "curse to their king." Independent, tough and wily, the Canadien was anything but a curse when he was motivated to fight; however, the King's cause was a confusing issue, as the French were supporting the rebels. Seen here, a "cursed" habitant and boy with two "fair and delicate" ladies.

The Cöos prisoner, Thomas Johnson, was allowed the freedom of Trois-Rivières. He wrote, "I think it is a curse to the land and a curse to their king to have such a miserable set of inhabitants as these Canadians." Yet while he despised the males, this was not the case for Canadien ladies. "The women in this Town are much fairer and much more delicate than in any town that I have seen in this Province. They are very polite. There are six young Women … to one young man." He also noted it was "[a]bout ten days since the worms began to be bad in this Province [and] have increased till they have done great damage."[8]

On July 8, the Albany commission heard from a Coxsackie man that a party of Tories led by Serjeant Joseph Smith, a former servant of John Walden Meyers, entered his house, stole several items, and wounded him in the arm.

The war party presaged by Ranger Henry Maracle arrived at Otsego Lake, near Cherry Valley, just after the wheat harvest. One hundred and fifty strong, it was led by thirty-two-year-old Lieutenant John Docksteder, 6NID, and a Canajoharie principal warrior, Quahyocko Brant Johnson, son of Sir William. Many of the Indians were Oquagas. The war party followed fresh tracks and overtook two riflemen, killing one and capturing James Butterfield who claimed to be a captain of Willett's in the three-years' service recruiting in the area before joining the regiment. The party moved on to New Dorlach and camped in a thick cedar swamp where William Sommer and other New Dorlach people arrived with provisions, as arranged by Maracle.[9]

Also that day, a party of Levies retrieved the remains of Elsworth and his men from Steele's Creek and buried them in the cemetery at the Old Stone Church near Fort Herkimer. That evening, Willett dined with the family of Lieutenant Solomon Woodworth, possibly to discuss the formation of a ranging company.

Early on the morning of July 9, Docksteder's raiders left a guard at their camp and marched for Currytown, a previously untouched, predominantly rebel hamlet. According to William Sommer of New Dorlach, he and twenty-six other men from New Dorlach and Rynbeck, including 1TCM lieutenant Conradt Brown joined the party. These newcomers were painted and clothed like Indians to disguise themselves from their Currytown neighbours. Sommer later claimed that Joseph Brant and Bernard Frey had promised ten dollars for a scalp and fifty acres for every participant. Perhaps he lied, perhaps not, but we do know that neither Brant nor Frey were there. Along the trail, the party captured two scouts from McKeen's Company.

That afternoon, Willett sent Captain Gros and thirty-five Levies from Fort Plain to scout toward New Dorlach. Ironically, they had just returned from there after attempting to collect Tory beeves for the garrison. Smoke had been seen rising above Currytown and they were ordered to search over that way. At the Baxter settlement on the Currytown road, Gros was told that several hundred Indians had just passed through. He sent two men along their trail and went back to Bowman's Creek to await their report. One scout was the ex-Tryon ranger, William Nellis; the other, Jacob A. Young, a private from Dygert's 1TCM company. They followed along until they spotted packs lying about and Indians cooking, then reported to Gros who sent them on horseback to tell Willett.

The war party surrounded Currytown at approximately ten o'clock and caught many inhabitants at work in their fields. Jacob Dievendorf was tending a fallow field with two sons and a slave. The black man was seized and the sons ran, but were easily overtaken; one was tomahawked and scalped, the other made prisoner. The father ran in another direction, passed by the captive, Butterfield, and threw himself under a fallen tree. His pursuers ran up and demanded of

Benson J. Lossing, artist and engraver. (Benson J. Lossing. The Pictorial Field-Book of the Revolution, 2 vols. New York: Harper & Brothers, 1852.)

A scalping victim — Jacob Dievendorf of Currytown. The eleven-year-old who was felled by a tomahawk and scalped in the Indian camp at the swamp in New Dorlach. Lossing visited Jacob at Currytown seventy years later and made these sketches showing the scars, which had taken five years to heal.

Butterfield where he had gone. He coolly pointed in the opposite direction and saved Jacob from capture or death.

Jacob's wife fled their home with several girls and slaves. A large woman, she toppled a fence while climbing over. Undaunted, she pulled herself up and led her flock to the blockhouse. One of her brothers was plowing when the alarm sounded. After throwing off the horse's harness, he rode hard toward the Mohawk River (with several Indians in close pursuit) and evaded capture. Another brother was not so lucky; he escaped, but with a fatal wound.

A father and son were cutting timber in the woods and were killed and scalped, their bodies left at either end of a tree, just as they had fallen. Henry Lewis, two men, and woman were at Lewis's small, picketed blockhouse when the raiders burst into the settlement. Henry immediately fired three quick shots, the community's alarm signal. The eldest son of one of the men in the blockhouse was in a field when he heard the alarm. He ran home and hustled his family into the woods. Looking back, they saw Indians surrounding their house.

Jacob Tanner and family were nearly the last to reach sanctuary in the blockhouse. He carried a child in one hand and a firelock in the other. His wife followed with a babe in her arms and several clinging to her petticoats. When the Indians saw them escaping, a warrior threw up his rifle and fired. The ball passed over the head of the child in Jacob's grip and lodged in a picket near him. Brisk fire from the blockhouse prevented further pursuit. A scalped lad crawled to the blockhouse. Blood blurred his vision so he was unable to identify his uncle when he came out to save him and raised his hands, pleading not to be killed.

The raiders divided; some to plunder and burn, others to round up livestock. Several fortified houses had their doors forced and ten defenders were killed and one taken. Before long, twelve buildings were alight. A Tory's house was set afire, but a Native leader gave him permission to douse it once the raid passed. Whigs later thought the fire was a ruse to prevent their retaliation, but, whatever the case, the man could only save part of his building.

When the alarm sounded, a man went to recover a pair of horses hobbled nearby, but they had already been tied to a tree with a bark rope and the Indians were lying in wait. He was easily taken. The Indians carried away five men and an eleven-year-old girl. An old fellow was taken, but having been judged incapable of travel, was, as according to custom, killed, and scalped.

It was after four o'clock when the raiders disappeared. The settlement's cattle and horses had been either killed or driven away, except those turned loose in the woods by their owners. Docksteder reported burning a total of twenty houses, twenty barns, and four "iron shod wagons" and collecting sixty horses, fifty cattle, and thirty women and children. William Sommer, who had so many reasons to embellish his story, later said he had seen three children killed, one black and two white. If that were true, they would have been either too young or too upset to travel.

———————

As the smoke rising above Currytown had intensified, Willett sent Captain McKeen and a sixteen-man platoon to assist the settlement. He was to collect as many militiamen as possible on his march. When Gros's two messengers arrived at Fort Rensselaer, Willett was told that a war party of some "five or six hundred" was encamped near Dorlach. Undaunted, he ordered the Levies in the area to assemble at his HQ and sent out expresses to request assistance from local militia units.

On the march back to camp, the raiders were met at Flat Creek by several camp guards who, seeing smoke rising above Currytown, set off to join in the pillaging. After this reunion, the war party took a man from his house near the creek. When they drew near to camp, some of the New Dorlach and Rynbeck Tories split off to spend the night in their own beds.

McKeen's platoon arrived at Currytown after the enemy was gone and helped to extinguish some fires. Then they warily tracked the raiders as far as Flat Creek and halted to await support. By dusk, soldiers from three Levies' companies had assembled at Fort Rensselaer with volunteers from the 1TCM companies of Jost Dygert, Adam Lype, and Severinus Cook. As darkness fell, they set out with Nellis as their guide, travelling by way of Frey's Bush blockhouse, where they added a handful of militiamen. They continued to Bowman's Creek, met Gros's detachment and picked up McKeen's platoon at Flat Creek and a party of Schoharie militia. Willett now had 140 men, half Levies, half militia.

Nellis lost his way threading through the pitch-black woods and it was close to first light before they closed up to the raiders' camp in the cedar swamp. They had marched eighteen miles in stygian gloom from Fort Rensselaer.

The Tory renegade, William Sommer, recalled that the local men rejoined before dawn. His count of Docksteder's force was 100 Natives and some ninety-five whites, which presumably included the local Tories.

At first light, Willett divided his men into two elements, one under his own command and the other under Captain Robert McKeen, a Cherry

Valley native who had commanded companies in 1NY in 1778, in the levies in 1779, and 1780 as well as Tryon rangers and militia. Willett arranged his men in two parallel lines facing each other and they took cover behind trees, stumps, and brush. The lines were placed far enough apart to be reasonably safe from each other's covers. McKeen's men were held in reserve at the far end.

Then, the colonel employed a standard Native tactic and sent Lieutenant Jacob Sammons of Gros's with ten men to lure the enemy between his lines. They were told to get as close to the enemy camp as they dared, fire a volley and pull foot. Just as Sammons was leaving, a number of 1st Tryon men arrived and were absorbed into the ambush.

It was about six o'clock when the bait crested a rise and was spotted by an elderly Native woman who was out from the camp, perhaps to collect herbs. She raised a warning halloo, but the Levies had already seen the Indian pickets hiding behind tree boughs stuck in the ground and gave fire and withdrew. The pickets returned fire, whooped and broke cover in hot pursuit, followed by a horde of hallooing warriors. Sammons's men ran hard, but were so closely pursued by the fleet Indians that two men were overtaken and cut down. Although some of Willett's men left the ambush to assist, the trap was successful and a heavy fire greeted the warriors, which brought on a general action.

Near the beginning of the fight, Willett's QM serjeant, William Sole, was captured and bundled back to the camp by a pair of Indians, but he managed to escape before they could secure him.

At one point in the action, legend has it that Willett held his

Eames Collection. (Georg Friederici. "Scalping in America." Annual Report of the Smithsonian Institution, 1906.)

Prisoners' rope. Braided, natural vegetable fibre with metal cones and dyed moosehair in metal cones. As a primary objective of every war party was to take captives, certain men must have been designated to carry such a rope in a pouch.

hat aloft and shouted he would catch all the balls the enemy could send. Of course, if the firing was as brisk as claimed, the loudest yell would not have been heard for far, but such is the stirring stuff of which myths are born.

One militiaman saw that several shots had come from a big basswood stump. Resting his gun on a mate's shoulder, he fired dead centre into the stump and the firing stopped.

While Willett's men hotly engaged the Rangers in their front, the Natives sent a flank attack around their right to strike the rear. Another legend claimed that Willett then gave a second shout, "My men, stand your ground and I'll bring up the levies and we'll surround the damned rascals." Shout or no shout, McKeen recognized the threat and advanced his fifty men. Willett reported, McKeen "returned the attack with such spirit, that the enemy, dispersing in small parties, soon sought safety in flight," but not before the captain took two balls in the chest and his son, Lieutenant Samuel, a ball through his mouth. One fellow lost part of his ear and young McKeen bled profusely from perforated cheeks and lost teeth. The war party retired, abandoning most of their booty and stolen livestock.

With a retreat underway, the camp guards chose which captives to keep and which to kill. Eleven-year-old Jacob Dievendorf was untied from a tree and put astride a horse. When his guard looked away, Jacob leapt to the ground and ran, but his footfalls alerted the Indian who whirled and threw his tomahawk, knocking him down. He was scalped and left for dead. The girl and three men were struck down and scalped. Butterfield and three others were led off at a trot with ropes tied around their necks.

The Levies and militia collected their wounded. An inspection of the hollow stump revealed that two men had hidden inside and a trail of blood proved the militiaman's shot had hit home. Willett dryly commented that the fellow "will never get back to Canada." A corporal and three men built a litter to carry McKeen, while a serjeant assisted his wounded son. Others built litters and carried the wounded, then the exhausted troops set off.[10]

They were no sooner gone than another body of Tryon militia arrived and set about burying the dead. During their combing of the area for plunder, they discovered the murdered prisoners in the enemy's camp. Suddenly, young Jacob rose out of the bush, his face a mask of blood and leaves and a startled militiaman raised his musket, but another knocked it up and the shot went harmlessly overhead. Next, the blood-covered girl was found barely alive. Litters were made and the boy was carried to his father in Currytown where he joined a brother who had been scalped the day before. When the litter carrying the girl was just outside Fort Plain, she begged for water and, when given a cold draught, died instantly from shock.

Animals often made their way home when abandoned by raiders and this instance proved no exception when three horses came back to Currytown, as did several beeves.

———————

Although the war party had broken off and dispersed, their withdrawal could hardly be interpreted as a "compleat Victory." After reassembling at an agreed rendezvous, Docksteder sent a patrol to Fort Stanwix and then divided the balance into small parties to travel along New Dorlach's eastern boundary. One band came across Philip Hoffman and his wife in the act of hiding. Philip had been at Schoharie listening to Dominie Sommer (father of the Tory renegade William) preaching when news arrived about the firing of hundreds of small arms. The service instantly broke up and he rushed home to save his wife, as just the year before, they had narrowly escaped death, but their luck had run out and both were killed and scalped.

QM Serjeant Sole, who had earlier escaped the Indians' camp, arrived at a house in New Dorlach in the late afternoon where many people were gathered. When news came that a couple living nearby had been killed, he and two others went to investigate and found the Hoffmans.

Yet another killing occurred after the battle. In a vicious reprisal for a relative lost in the fighting, a luckless man was killed and his body mutilated — his nose, ears and an arm cut off. The raiders reassembled in a nearby valley and spent the night and next two days licking their wounds.

As this "swamp action" was immediately heralded as a major rebel victory, it deserves some analysis. Despite the duration and closeness of the fighting, Willett reported only five men killed and nine wounded and missing. Predictably, the enemy's loss was given as much higher at "not less than 40." When McKeen died at the fort, the colonel lamented him as "a brave, and very valuable officer"; his wounded son was noted as "a fine lad." Significantly, in short order, Willett had lost a second company commander in combat.

After a couple of days of reflection, the colonel sent a report to the governor that was so exuberant, it must have been penned for the newspapers: "We gained a compleat Victory over a party of 190 Indians under the command of the famous Joseph Brandt and near 100 Tories Commanded by one Barent Frey a Fugitive from this County … It was not in my power immediately to assertain the enemies loss which … appear[s] to be Between 80 and 90 Killed and Wounded. Near one half of which number are among the Slain. Our loss is Inconsiderable in number having had only 16 killed & wounded." This account sounded a note of victory very badly needed in Tryon. When William Sommer made his notorious confession a few days later, he claimed to have counted twenty-five dead, mostly Indians.

In contrast, Docksteder said, "he discovered at Durlach about 300 ambuscaded rebels under LCol Willett whom he immediately attacked, and after much firing killed twenty of them, but having only seventy in his party, he found it necessary to retire, they not pursuing him." He reported five Indians wounded, two dangerously, and the loss of most of the cattle. What a radically different account in virtually every detail of numbers! So, if Docksteder had not been thoroughly defeated, what had Willett really accomplished?

Most obvious was Willett's speed of reaction; every bit of intelligence was acted upon immediately. No dawdling or dithering, no delay to collect an overwhelming force. He risked trusting militia officers to respond and, in the interest of a rapid response, sent off scouts and small detachments, swiftly gathered his Levies and, when he was sure of the enemy's location, marched through the night to confront them with what he had at hand.

Bolstered by his forceful personality, all the troops, Levies and militia, officers and men, gave their very best. He employed sensible woods' tactics, even turned a Native tactic against them. He led from the front and was foremost in the combat and gave the Mohawk Valley folk heart, revitalizing their will to resist.

Although Henry Maracle was the only Butler's Ranger named, the number of white participants suggested a substantial presence, yet, oddly enough, no Butler's officer was named and Docksteder, who led the foray, was simply a 6NID lieutenant. No other Crown officer was recorded as participating and only one principal warrior was mentioned — Quahyocko, the least flamboyant of Sir William's mixed-blood sons. Docksteder extracted some useful information from his prisoners that confirmed intelligence already in Quebec, that is, Washington had ordered the Continentals from the north and sent 6,000 French from Rhode Island toward New York City.

Willett wrote to General James Clinton the day after the action. Because his regimental surgeon, Dr. Petrie, was at German Flatts attending many sick and wounded, it had been necessary to send some wounded Levies to the Schenectady hospital. He requested a surgeon from there be assigned to Fort Rensselaer and complained, "This place does not afford a gill of rum to bathe a single wound" and two barrels of the liquor that had been en route to him were "very irregularly" seized by the 2NY. To emphasize his need, he pointed out the severe duty and high fatigue endured by his men, which made rum "an article of importance."

While Docksteder and Willett clashed in the Mohawk, politics boiled in Vermont and northeastern New York. On July 8, Chittenden announced his intention to extend Vermont's western boundary to include the Kingsbury district on the upper reaches of the Hudson north of Fort Edward. As his rationale, he cited a massacre at Cambridge and "another Act of Flagrant hostility in Tomhannuck." In an appeal to the disaffected and dispirited, he claimed that the expansion would protect those "unfriendly to the American Revolution." Vermont's border would extend from the southeast corner of Queensbury to the southeast corner of the "provincial patent," then due north taking in Skeenesborough. As a blatant threat to New York, persons living in Kingsbury outside the new border, were told to move their effects "in to the Interior parts of this State; & all persons are hereby strictly forbid to Molest, Hinder, Hurt or plunder such persons while preparing to move."[11]

On July 6 at Quebec City HQ, the findings of a court martial of a number of deserters were promulgated. A man of the 8th and one of the 31st were awarded 1,000 lashes and another soldier of the 8th, "an object of mercy because of a disordered mind" was jailed. A man of the 33rd was acquitted and drafted into the 44th. Eight King's Rangers were judged "improper Subjects to serve His Majesty in this Country" and were to be shipped overseas. At least three, if not four, of the latter had been taken in arms at Forts Ann and George in the fall of 1780.

On July 9, Sir John provided Haldimand with his recommendations about the best route and method to waylay the Oneidas at Palmerstown, in the process, he revealed his extensive knowledge of wilderness raiding. He proposed the detachment take provisions for twenty days and travel from Crown Point to Schroon Lake and attack either Ballstown or Saratoga. Every day or two, they should make a depot of rations for their return march, lessening their load as they went. They should march slightly aside of the regular track. Two twenty-man scouts should be sent to the split in the path to cut off rebel parties and prevent discovery of the main force. Mathews wrote to Johnson the same day about Claus's report of the "strong resentment" of the Fort Hunters against the Oneidas "shutting up the communication" and, in particular, over the taking of the ranger, Randal Hewitt. They wanted immediate satisfaction and Haldimand was tempted to send them, but was waiting for Johnson's reply. Then, Mathews wrote Claus with Haldimand's approval of the project, "on the condition they show the rebel Oneidas no ill-placed tenderness, which they have long forfeited" — how well the governor understood Native customs.

On a pleasant note, Colonel Campbell reported that a party of St. Francis Abenakis returning from a scout had guided in two loyalists.

On July 9, Vermont's commissioner, Joseph Fay, arrived at Dutchman's Point to continue prisoner exchange talks and was greeted by Sherwood and Smyth. As well as being responsible for managing intelligence collection in New York State, the latter had been appointed to assist in the exchange discussions and the secret talks, which had now expanded to include the transfer of loyalist refugees who had sought sanctuary in Vermont. The impressive ninety-six-foot, twenty-six-gun *Royal George*, flagship of the Lake Champlain fleet, had been sent down from Fort St. John's to patrol offshore until Sherwood could complete his defences at the Point and the meetings were held aboard the vessel, which provided a most imposing venue. Sherwood was disturbed that Ira Allen had not come, as he considered Fay a lightweight. As if to prove the point, Fay confirmed he was only empowered to discuss prisoner exchanges. It transpired that Allen was in Philadelphia with the Congress to allay their suspicions (in theory), but the Quebec negotiators suspected he was angling for Vermont's acceptance as a state. An angry Sherwood said that Haldimand had suspended prisoner exchanges, but, Smyth, in a staged disagreement, contradicted and said that the governor was willing to have the talks proceed. By the time Fay left, he had promised that a list of British prisoners would be prepared. Sherwood forwarded a letter to Haldimand that Fay had brought from the Allens.

When the governor sent a copy to Sir Henry Clinton, he noted, "It is fraught with much insincerity or duplicity, the latter I fear is the real sense of it, which I am more inclined to this from his not coming with the flag." Although there was scant progress toward bringing Vermont into the British fold, the fact that hostilities were almost at a standstill was significant and, with Vermont disengaged from the fighting, she was free to distress her neighbouring states with political agitations and ambitions.

At Oswegatchie on July 10, Robertson reported that his scouts had brought in the restive ex-Continental, Jacob Klock Jr., and his Tory band. They had been found in great distress about two days' march north of the settlements. Robertson enclosed papers brought by Klock and news of a fort being built at German Flatts and of 1,000 boats under construction at Schenectady for an attack on New York or an expedition up the Mohawk against Canada. Robertson had sent a new scout "to that quarter" and was organizing another to go tomorrow. Loyalist converts were usually well met, if not fully trusted, and Klock was accepted at face value. He would soon try his hand at raiding.

After Captain Meyers's return from his major success at Ballstown, he was given the governor's consent for an independent company command separate from the King's Rangers, which must have been a blow to Rogers in his struggle to complete his battalion.

On July 12, Colonel Campbell, QID, reported that scouts from Kahnawake had intercepted rebel emissaries at Crown Point. Whether these infiltrators were fellow Kahnawakes or Stockbridges was unstated, but any contribution to Quebec's security by those wavering villagers was welcome.

Powell advised the governor of Butler's need for two staff officers. First, an adjutant, as the Rangers "are constantly sending out parties and are obliged to make out returns, exclusive of it being necessary to instruct their recruits in the use of arms." Second, "a Surgeon's Mate … as they frequently lose some of their men upon detachments for want of proper attendance [i.e. care]."[12]

Part of the 2NY left Albany on July 11. The regiment had been delayed near Schenectady waiting the completion of "34 Boats … to take our army from Elizabeth Town to Staten Island as soon as the French Fleet should appear off Sandy Hook in order to take New York." They marched to Albany on July 10 and encamped "on the Pattroons Flats." With great satisfaction, the colonel stated he had "the largest and most healthy Regiment in America not Excepting French, English or Germans and a fine Band of Musick." Healthier and happier no doubt for Willett's two barrels of rum.

Upriver at Fort Plain, Levies' Lieutenant Jacob Bockee wrote to his fellow subaltern, Pliny Moore, "I would Likewise inform You that Ever Since Coll Willett had that Skirmish at [Dorlach] we have Liv'd well Having No Less than Eight Cows to our mess and Beef & Mutton plenty and Sauce as much as we want[.] All we want is more Troops there being Ladies plenty[.]" How strange! If this livestock was recovered from the Currytown raid, was no effort was made to return the animals to their owners? As the garrison was always in need of provisions, fresh meat would have been greatly welcomed, but one would expect some restitution to have been made to the survivors, but perhaps there were none.

After finishing his reports to the Clintons, Willett travelled to Canajoharie on July 11 and stayed overnight. He was there next day when a nasty fire broke out, apparently from accidental or natural causes, as there was no mention of enemy action.

On July 12, Colonel Peter Vrooman reported great alarm in the Schoharie. After hearing of Willett's engagement at New Dorlach from his lieutenant at Cobleskill, enemy parties were seen in three locations close to the Middle Fort, "Crossing the roads that leads from this to Albany and Schenectady, one place two and another four, and at another six, perhaps gone to the Beaver Dam recruiting." The night before, QM serjeant William Sole arrived at the fort and told his tale of being captured early in the fight, his escape, the killing of the Hoffmans, and finding the tracks of 100–200 of the enemy. No one knew the outcome of Willett's action and, with the enemy being seen in the valley, anxiety was high. The colonel reminded Gansevoort that Schoharie was destitute of troops and pled for assistance at "all possible speed." Putman's company was sent from Fort Hunter, but how speedily is unknown.

On the day Vrooman wrote this plaintive letter, Gansevoort sent one of his own, exhorting Colonel Van Bergen at Coxsackie to raise his quota of every twentieth man from his regiment's classes for the second levy, especially as they were intended to defend his own frontier.

On July 13, Willett's chaplain, Reverend Daniel Gros, wrote to the governor about his four-week tour of the Mohawk:

> To my surprise I had almost forgot the repeated destructions this County has met with, if it had not been for the Ruins, indicating that the Inhabitants had had formerly the Comfort of Buildings.
>
> All along the River, and in the other settlements, the most remote ones excepted ... there is a prospect of as plentiful Crops, as has been in the Memory of Men, and every spot of ground flourishes with some kind of grain as much, if not more, as in time of the profoundest Peace.... The Hay harvest is at hand, and would have been almost finished now had it not been for the removal of the Troops, and the several incursions of the enemy since that time, which made it necessary to call every man under Arms for the comon Defence; and this has been done with the greatest alacrity imaginable. The Removal of the Troops, has not had that effect upon the Militia, which I feared it would have. Colonel Willet and I were enjoined by the General, to prepare them for that Catastrophe in time: and the hope that soon other troops will be sent, keeps up their spirits and rather animates them to the utmost exertions whereof we have several instances upon intelligence that the Enemy was discovered at Different places, which put it out of the power of Col. Willet, to send his men any where or to do anything else but to keep them in readiness, I wrote to two officers requesting them in the name of the Col. to assist at this critical juncture, when in one hour's time we had 76 effective men under march for such places, where it was thought they would be of service. And in the affair of Durlach, they gave full

proof of their determined zeal to Defend their Country. I make no doubt but the Militia, if well regulated with the assistance of some Troops, in my opinion 500, will be able to bid defiance to all the enemies that may be brought against them, and effectually protect themselves … I shall take the Liberty to point out such deficiencies, as have come under my knowledge, leaving the task of remedying them to your Excellency.

The qualifications of the officer commanding the Militia [Colonel Jacob Klock] are well known to you. I have only to add that he has of late become very unpopular[,] even suspected. The reason whereof I conceive to be that[,] besides his usual indolence and unconcernedness, his two sons, who have been suspected a good while ago and strenuously defended by him, actually went of[f] to the enemy and took along with them 11 or 12 others chiefly from the Col's Neighbourhood. There is a great cry that the Col. has lately sent his sons to Albany to bring up amunition, and when brought [it has] not yet [been] distributed, and People is left to guess wheter the Sons did tacke it to Canada in the whole or in part. This mackes the old gentleman so insignificant in the eyes of the whole County, that he is spoken of with contempt. He and the other field officers will in my opinion yield to be comanded[,] at least to have their men comanded[,] by an officer of Conduct and Ability. I have the particular pleasure to assure your Excellency, that Col. Willet is universally looked upon in this Light. I do not know what has been the reason, that I could not prevail with him to have a meeting of the field officers called and an opportunity given me to move this matter, which was almost the chief design of my going up with the Colonel; the reasons he alleged were, that he is waiting for instructions for that purpose from you. However, that may be, I could wish that the Militia would be in some manner coordinated with Col. Willet under proper restrictions to prevent jealousy or overbearance. Beg your Excellency will provide that Troops may be sent up... as soon as possible and a sufficiency of amunition dis-tributed among the Militia ...

P.S. General [Clinton] tells me that he is under some distant expectations of Troops from the Eastward ... Upon the examining into the amunition of those militia men who went with Col. Willet, none ... had more than 6 or 7 rounds, several none at all.

On July 14, Willett advised Brigadier-General Clinton that the small amount of ammunition at Fort Rensselaer had been badly depleted in the Dorlach swamp action and he had transferred 8,000 cartridges and 500 flints from Fort Herkimer, half of that post's supply. He decried the tiny amount and noted that more could not be made up for lack of paper and twine. He requested both and advised that the balls at Fort Herkimer were too large for most firelocks and requested a supply of smaller sizes.

He crowed in his brief account of the fight: "[T]he Enemy was not less than 200 strong in the late action Fourteen of their dead were found. Some undoubtedly were not found, so that we may reasonably suppose their loss in killed and wounded not to fall much short of Forty ... our strength was but one hundred and forty." He asked when more troops would be sent, what to expect in the way of provisions and rum, reemphasized his lack of flints and paper and amusingly chided that[,] without paper, "I shall be Forced to leave of[f] troubling you with any more letters."

The same day, he reported to the governor that William Sommer and another New Dorlach man had brought him a very strange letter signed by Lieutenant Conradt Brown that attempted to explain their settlement's lack of action at the time of Docksteder's raid. Perhaps the colonel's investigations had raised great fear in the settlement when it was realized he had discovered that the raiders had passed through Dorlach on the way to Currytown and no one had thought to warn him. Willett had heard the rumours of Dorlach's disaffection in earlier years, so the letter thoroughly aroused, rather than allayed, his suspicions. The two men were jailed and, within the next few days, a "horrid confession of villainy" had been wormed out of Sommer. Willett decided to break up the settlement and remove its livestock.

Willett's report became boldly outspoken, revealing his deep personal frustration. As Gros had mentioned in his letter, Willett had been keeping his own counsel, yearning for the resources he desperately needed to execute his commission. "I have already said much to your Excellency upon my own situation ... I have much more to say." He wrote of his upset on hearing from Major Throop that the three-year enlistment concept might collapse, as he had been relying upon it as a possible supply of stable manpower:

> When I reflect upon my present situation, And the situation I expect[ed] to have been in ... Two hundered and fifty levies with twenty artillery men Including Officers, Drums, Fifes and everything else, Except the Militia, is my whole force. And I have never been Instructed in the way by which I am to avail myself of the aid of the Militia — When any are wanting I can make requisitions, And so can any other man, And such as Chose may attend — Those that do not may let it along.
>
> I am exceedingly Dissaponted in this business. I did expect some Attention would have been paid to [the] plan I left with you. Or I certainly never would have risked my reputation and my everything upon so slender a Thread as it hangs at present — I wish earnestly to know if I have nothing to hope for from below. I do most humbly Intreat you to Inform me. Not one syllable have I had from you since I have [arrived] in this County. Nor had the least attention that I can learn been paid to our situation by the Ligeslature – It is true we have lately had some success over our enemies this way, But let it be remembered, that to [Heaven,] and not

to the aid we have received from below[,] are we wholly Indebted for this Advantage. Our late success has given excellent springs to the spirits of the people …

I protect the property of Tories, and others little better then Tories, bear all these burdens — Whilst such Miscreants remain at home in security and go wholly unpunished — This will not suit the feelings of such a Whig as I [know] myself to be — Any part of the World were this is to be the case cannot hold me.… [W]ould the Ligeslature afford me such reasonnable force as every Impartial Judge must acknowledge necessary — Formed and equipt in such a way as I could request And give me such power over the Militia as every good Whig in the Country would give their suffrage for?

Then he wrote to Major McKinstry at Saratoga:

[T]he savages have paid us a visit in this Quarter and done some damage. We have however had the satisfaction of retaliating upon them By giving of them a pretty sound drubbing. I should be glad to know … your situation at Saratoga — The Adjutant tells me he is not able to Comply with a regimental order of the 21st of May for want of the returns of Captains Gray & Dunhams Companies.… I must Insist upon such regimental Orders … being punctually Complyed with for the future — And youll please to order all the Companies under your Immediate direction to send at the beginning of every month a monthly return to the Adjutant as there is no other way for me to know that State of the regiment.

His busy day continued. He wrote to Villefranche at German Flatts, advising that he was sending twelve impressed cattle for the garrison's use and asked him to use fresh meat and preserve his salt rations for patrols and alarms. He was to send scouts to Oswego and, lacking hard cash, the colonel suggested they be paid in salt and a promise of rum when it arrived. They should be careful not to give false alarms or to wait too long in giving true ones. They should also look in at Stanwix and the fords "on the Oneida Lake." He wanted an estimate of the materials required for the construction and advice about the amounts of ordnance and QMG stores at the Flatts not needed by the local garrisons and how best to remove them.

The next day, he penned an angry letter to the governor about Sommer's confession. The renegade not only gave the names of local Tories at Currytown and the swamp fight, but also admitted to similar activities in 1777 and 1780. Outrageously, many of them had been "out" all three times. Willett sought permission to hang them and to have the power to remove all "Rascally disaffected Inhabitants" from the frontiers, as previous orders to militia commanders to do so had been ignored. He repeated his requests of the day before with less vehemence: "I wish to know what Force I may expect this way and I should be very glad of some directions from you, and be informed how to manage with so small assistance such complicated business as I am engaged in. [A]bove everything, I entreat you try to let us have men that we may beat the Enemy again, and again, should they (as no doubt they will) pay us any more visits ... for we are told of Troops being on this way from Bucks Island and from other parts of Canada."

Washington wrote to Brigadier-General Clinton on July 14 observing that the new fort at German Flatts was not likely to be completed "for Want of Workmen." As only a small force would be left in the neighbourhood, he had decided that the guns and stores would be insecure and must be taken to Albany, leaving only sufficient items for defence of the local posts. He had put the matter under Willett's direction.

His letter to Willett opened with favourable comments regarding his dispositions: "I have ever been of opinion that small stationary Garrisons were of no real utility. By having your parties constantly in motion and ready to unite upon occasion, the small parties of the Enemy will be checked and their Main Body may be suddenly attacked, if they commit themselves too far into the settlements." With these few words, the C-in-C had approved the essence of Willett's defensive strategy that was to prove so effective against the season's largest raid. He added, "A proportion of the Massachusetts Militia will be ordered to reinforce your command. Upon them and the Levies of New York you must place your dependance, for it will be impossible for me, while our present operations are in hand, to spare any of the Continental Troops."

In a short letter to Villefranche, Washington approved of what he had accomplished, saying, "it was certainly the wisest plan to repair the Old [works].… Strong Block Houses, and other fortified Houses, will be a great security against the incursions of small parties of the Enemy."[13]

Dr. George Smyth had listed fourteen of the most obnoxious rebels in the neighbourhood of Albany whose removal could have a devastating effect on rebel morale and would provide ideal exchange material for senior officers and important loyalists. Prominent were: General Philip Schuyler, Colonel Brinton Paine, Major Ezekiel Taylor and conspiracy commissioners, Samuel Stringer and John M. Beeckman. By mid-July, eight targets had been selected and Mathews had sent instructions to Sherwood about the composition of the parties. The governor insisted that two British Regulars be included, perhaps to provide discipline, and between four to six loyalists and, if necessary, Native guides. Sherwood and Smyth were to choose the loyalists and St. Leger, the Regulars. The parties would secretly assemble at Dutchman's Point. Three of the most successful Secret Service agents were chosen to lead parties: Bettys was to take Stringer at Ballstown; Meyers to take Schuyler at Albany and Howard, Bleecker at Hoosic. They were to be in position by July 31 and none were to strike earlier than that date so that no one group would set off a general alarm before the others could act.

On July 14, a supervising engineer with thirteen men of the 34th, a team of oxen and Volunteers Elijah Bothum and Thomas Sherwood, two serjeants, two corporals, and fifteen privates of Sherwood's Company left Fort St. John's to help build the blockhouse at Dutchman's Point.

That day, Ross reported David van der Heyden's success against Elsworth, enclosing papers found in the captain's pockets. The major then sent two strong, mixed parties to the Mohawk Valley, one led by Captain Crawford, another by Adjutant Humphrey Arden with orders to harass the inhabitants and drive their cattle to Fort Haldimand.

On July 16, Brigadier Maclean was sent the governor's orders: "[J]udging it expedient for the King's service, to occupy the island opposite Coteau-du-Lac, with buildings for the security and accommodation of Prisoners of War, I shall immediately send an officer from the engineer's department to superintend this service as well as some proposed improvements, in the navigation for the bateaux above The Cedars."

Haldimand wrote to Sir John about a difficult issue: "Several complaints having been made upon the subject of selling Negroes, brought into this Province by Scouting Parties, who alledge a Right to Freedome, and others belonging to Loyalists, who are obliged to relinquish their properties or reclaim them by paying the Money for which they were sold," he ordered him to make "the most minute Inquiry" and send Maclean a return of all blacks brought into the country, giving their names, identifying their former owners whether loyalists or rebels, by whom brought in, and to whom sold, for what price and where they are at present. Claus and Campbell were instructed to supply similar lists.

Sir John's list reported forty-one blacks, twelve of them female. Nineteen persons were from his own estate; fifteen others had been rebel-owned and at least a half dozen were serving in Herkimer's Bateaux company.

———————————————

———————————————

The continuing struggle to bring Willett's Levies to full strength led Governor Clinton to issue orders on July 17 to the captains and subalterns of the new men being raised and to the captains of the original companies that were still below full strength. Recruits were to have a good musket, a cartridge pouch or box that held seventeen rounds, a knapsack or haversack, and a good blanket. Oddly, neither bayonet nor hanger (short sword) was mentioned. Four newly appointed officers, Captains Abram

Livingston, Peter Van Rensselaer, Job Wright, and Lieutenant Joseph Van Ingen were sent to Schenectady to collect recruits from 2ACM. Instructions were given to Captain Thomas Skinner and Lieutenant Josiah Skinner, to receive recruits from Whiting's and Van Ness's. Captain Dunham was to send a subaltern to White Creek to receive Charlotte County's recruits from Paine's. Three original captains, Philip Conine, Benjamin Duboise, and Stephen White, were to receive recruits from Van Bergen's at Catskill. They were to accept "none but able bodied Men fit for active Duty" and take no deserters from the British service. Willett's Orderly Book contained a form letter patterned after Clinton's instructions, adding the need for a bayonet if possible. Recruits were to be taken "immediately into your charge" and trained for the service.

Willett wrote to Captain Marshall at Johnstown about the second levy. One man in every twenty was to be called out from the militia classes and there would be a considerable body of levies from Massachusetts. He optimistically theorized that, with these additions, the regiment had only a few more days of roughing it out. In a flurry of activity, he wrote to the various militia colonels to advise them of the names of officers he had assigned to receive their recruits: "I ... flatter myself that nothing in your power will be omitted in compleating and hastening on these troops. As every moment is a moment of importance and a delay of one day may be attended with very unhappy consequences." He further instructed his officers to keep a descriptive roll of the recruits and again emphasized the importance of a good gun, cartridge box or pouch and, if possible, a bayonet. After a very full day, he mounted his horse at 11:00 p.m. and rode out from Fort Rensselaer.

That day, Henry Glen, DQMG at Schenectady, sent a report to New York's QM about the boats being built in the town. His account was a painful litany of the agonies of the state's broken economy:

> I have used every exertion that lay in my power to prevail on the Proprietors of the Boards to let the Public have them. They say that it is impossible, unless they receive hard money for them, or we may as well cut their Wife's and Children's throats, for it is their only support

for the Necessarys of Life. As to sending soldiers or Persons to impress them, they seem to be determined not to suffer their Property to be taken from them any longer[,] at the risque of their Lives, as they have not been paid for their Boards etc. furnished the Public for these two years past, and no prospect of their being paid yet, this is their Language and what to do in the matter I do not know. I have this Spring when Congress and the Head of the Department's credit failed, pledged my own Credit to build sixteen new Boats for which I have made myself payable, and with the Expectation of receiving the Money in a few days, which I had the promise of and am daily ask'd for the Cash, and still no Money, all this I do not mind; no man longs more to make an end of the War than I do by carrying it on with Vigour, I am and always was willing to pledge my Life and little Property for the support of the War but am sorry to find the Virtue and exertions of the People are lost throughout the Whole Country.

On July 18, the governor sent Willett impress warrants giving him the power to "divest the disaffected of the Means of supplying the Enemy." Now, he had the means to obtain local subsistence for his troops. Clinton agreed that the Dorlach men were "undoubtedly guilty of high treason of the blackest hue" and merited severe punishment, but only the ordinary courts of justice could decide their fate, as they were not subject to martial law. They were to be "committed to close custody … until courts can be ordered for their trial." He thought it a pity they "had not fallen while in arms."

As recruiting the levies was not going well, he had approved extending the usual time allowed for recruiting.

Willett arrived at Albany on July 18 and spent eight days mustering recruits and organizing his command.

The governor wrote to Rev. Gros stating his pleasure that Tryon County "still afford[ed] such promising Prospects;" however, "[t]he

Legislature did not ... make any special Provision for the better Government of the Frontier Militia ... I have, therefore, issued an Order making them subject to the Call of Colo Willet on Cases of special Emergencies. This is all I could legally do and in this way the Evil you most dread will be least likely to take place." While not a perfect answer, this was a great improvement for Willett, who until now had counted upon voluntary cooperation. He hoped that when "the present Levies are brought into the Field ... & 600 Levies expected from Massachusetts arrive, that we shall be able to maintain a Force in Tryon County equal to what you conceive Competent for its defence."

This same day, Vermont's governor, Thomas Chittenden, prepared a bold proclamation that not only confirmed his republic's recent machinations, but must have set the teeth of every New York politician to grinding:

> Whereas the Legislature of this State at their Session in June last, for the Reasons hereafter exhibited, did extend their Claim of Jurisdiction from the North-West Corner of the Commonwealth of Massachusetts, Westerly in the same Direction with the North Line of Said Commonwealth, until It reaches the deepest Channel of Hudson's River; thence running Northerly in the deepest Channel of said River, to the Source thereof; and from thence a due North Direction to Latitude 45 deg North (or the southern Boundary of the Province of Quebec).
>
> AND Whereas, no Part of the Lands contained in said Claim, were ever included in any original Charter from the Crown of Great Britain to the Government of New York; Which Jurisdiction in its own Nature became null and void, in Consequence of the Declaration of Independence by the United States, and the Annihilation of kingly Power in America, And in consequence of a subsequent Commission from the same royal Authority to Governor Philip Skene, which vested him with the Powers

of Jurisdiction over the same Territory, and which on the Position of the Validity of royal Traditions and Boundaries, would fatally operate against the Claim of the state of New-York. And although there may have been what some People call a mutual Association and Connexion between the Inhabitants included in said claim and the State of New-York since the Declaration of Independence, yet the Nature of such Allegiance must be founded on a reciprocal Protection; for Government and Protection are by Nature so connected together, that the one cannot exist independent of the other; nor can any Allegiance be lawfully had or demanded by any Government, except at the same Time it affords the salutary Influences of Support or Protection to its Citizens.

AND whereas the Government of New-York, for a Number of Years, have been very deficient in succouring, defending or protecting the Citizens inhabiting the said claimed Territory, and of late have wholly abandoned them to the Ravages of the common Enemy; And whereas this State have been their main Support and Protection for several Years last past, and have lately entered into a governmental League and Combination with them, for the mutual happiness and Security of each other, under the same Constitution and Code of Laws; being urged thereto by the refusal of the Government of New-York to unite with this Government for their mutual Defence, and from the local Situation of both the Waters of Lake Champlain, and the British Government in Canada, from whence a powerful Force can suddenly invade this State including its last Western Union.

AND whereas Commissions both civil and military have been lately issued from the Supreme Authority of this State to Persons chosen, agreeable to the Laws and Customs thereof, in the several Districts and

Corporations within the Limits of the said western Claim of Jurisdiction.

I, have, therefore thought fit, by and with the Advice of my Council, to issue this Proclamation, and do hereby strictly require, charge and command all Persons of whatsoever Quality or Denomination residing within the said Western Claim of Jurisdiction, to take due Notice of the Laws and Orders of this State, and govern themselves accordingly on Pain of incurring the Penalties therein contained.

And I do hereby further strictly require and command all Magistrates, Justices of the Peace, Sheriffs, Constables, and all other civil, and all military Offices to be active and vigilant in executing the Laws aforesaid, without Partiality.

Given under my Hand, and the Seat of this State, at Arlington, this 18th day of July, A.D. 1781, and in the 5th year of the Independence of this State.

As if to emphasize the proclamation's consequences, Colonel Brinton Paine wrote to the governor from Saratoga: "I recd your Letter with the Enclosed Orders and shall Do all in my Power to put them in Execution, although I have but little hope to get the men as the inhabitants of Charlotte County have chosen their officers by order of Mr. Chittenden." A sloop had been discovered on Lake George and Paine expected "the Enemy Down soon." He hoped "you will grant us all releaf in your power; the Troops at this Garrison have been very short for Beef. I have purchased sum. Major McKinstry [seized] a Drove last night ... said to be purchased for the French army, which he will Give you an acompt."

On July 18, Enos Moore enlisted in Clark's company of Colonel Elisha Porter's regiment of MA Levies. Major Aaron Rowley led half of the regiment, including Clark's company, to the Mohawk Valley to serve in Willett's regiment, where Enos would have a few adventures.

John Woolaver, one of Willett's favourite couriers, was asked to obtain some "fat cattle" for the Fort Plain garrison. He was to either purchase them or arrange a trade for milk cows. He obtained several beeves at the Canajoharie Indian castle and he, his three brothers and brother-in-law, all 1TCM militiamen, drove them to the fort. After exchanging them for an equivalent number of milkers, they set out to drive them to the castle and, while crossing at a difficult ford, were ambushed by Indians. Woolaver's eldest brother and brother-in-law were killed; the other brother escaped with severe wounds to his thigh and shoulder and Woolaver was taken. A party of militia pursued unsuccessfully. The Indians kept Woolaver for twenty-two days before turning him over to the British at Niagara.[14]

The abduction parties set out from Fort St. John's on July 18. Contrary to Haldimand's instructions, they had fewer men than recommended. Each leader probably saw his needs in a different light. Although the number

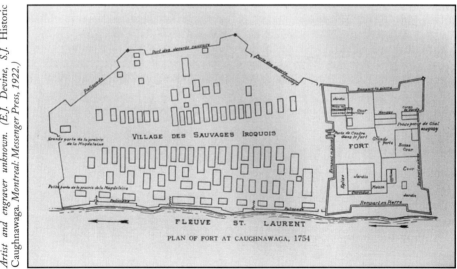

Artist and engraver unknown. (E.J. Devine, S.J. Historic Caughnawaga. Montreal: Messenger Press, 1922.)

Plan of the fort and settlement of Kahnawake (a.k.a. Caghnawaga or Sault St. Louis), 1754. The fort was surrounded by a loopholed, ten-foot-high stonewall. The palisade and fort probably deteriorated between the wars; however, the settlement remained a formidable place in 1781.

of Natives with each is unknown, in some cases, we know the number of whites. Bettys took four for the attempt on Stringer; Meyers, seven to lift Schuyler; Howard, five to abduct Bleecker, and a mystery man named Groves took three to take Colonel Paine.

Powell reported to Haldimand from Niagara that Colonels Johnson and Butler had persuaded him to send 100 Indians and fifty Rangers to "distress the rebels" at Curry's Bush, a decision that pointed to a possible disconnect in Indian Department strategy, as Docksteder had just destroyed the place. Captain Caldwell, BR, was chosen to lead the new foray.

Soon after emigrating from Ireland, William Caldwell had served as an officer under Virginia's Royal governor, Lord Dunmore. When the rebellion broke out, he left his Pennsylvania property and brought a party of recruits to Niagara. He was a 6NID Ranger during St. Leger's expedition in 1777 and, when Butler's Rangers was formed that fall, was given the second company. In 1778, he served at Wyoming, Minisink, and Cherry Valley and, in 1779, at Detroit and against the Sullivan Expedition. With Caldwell at the helm, this raid represented a major thrust from Niagara.

With all the rumours of Ethan Allen's activities, Powell thought it possible that Haldimand would send troops up Lake Champlain. He instructed Caldwell that, if he heard firm news that troops from Canada were at Fort Edward, he was to co-operate with the force commander. However well meaning, the incessant talk about Allen's secret activities must have upset the governor. In addition, Lieutenant John Hare, twenty-five Rangers and a party of Indians had gone out at the request of Captain Shenop, the Nanticoke, who had been so "very useful and active that it was impossible to refuse him." Powell found the Indians so anxious to sortie that it was difficult to restrain them, but reported he would not allow any more Rangers to go until he heard the governor's plans.

QID superintendent Colonel Campbell requested Haldimand's permission to pull down the houses of known rebel sympathizers at Kahnawake, who had perhaps been implicated by the rebel emissaries taken at Crown Point. The governor's patience had grown very thin and he approved this drastic punishment.

Mathews advised Brigadier Maclean that the rebel prisoner, Lieutenant-Colonel James Gordon, the 12ACM 2-I-C who had been taken at Ballstown by Munro in 1780, had abused his parole and sent intelligence to his wife. No proof could be brought without endangering the government's friends, so Gordon was to be arrested and sent to Quebec City.

At Oswegatchie, Robertson reported that Klock and his companions had told him that, if the tempo of raids continued as present, Schenectady would soon become the "Rebel Frontier." Certainly, Oswegatchie was doing its bit. Further, he advised, "Some of the Royalists that came from the Mohawk River asked leave to go on a Scout with some Indians and White Men with a view of getting off a number of their Friends as likewise some notorious Rebells." After Klock left, Robertson collected fourteen Indians and assigned a RHE serjeant and nine privates to join them. This party left on July 18. He anticipated the return of a small party that had been out nineteen days and also had two whites and five Indians scouting Fort Herkimer. Thus, as he sat writing, he had four scouting parties on the frontiers!

Vermont negotiator, Major Joseph Fay, wrote to Sherwood from Crown Point on July 18 to say that the schooner, *Carleton*, had picked him up near Ticonderoga. He would forward a list of thirty-six prisoners for exchange, including Major Zadock Wright, the QLR's 2-I-C who had been captured just after the Burgoyne campaign. At last, a glimmer of light in this snail-like process![15]

―――――――――――――――

―――――――――――――――

On July 19, in a Common Council meeting held at City Hall, Albany, Mayor Abraham Ten Broeck, the Aldermen, and common folk of the city resolved:

> That the Thanks of this Board be given to Colonel
> Marinus Willet, and the officers and troops under his
> command, for their bravery and military conduct in the

action of the 10th inst. Near Turlough, in Tryon County; who with an inferior force, defeated and put to flight the enemy under the command of Brandt and Frey;

That the Freedom of this city, be presented to Col Willet, in testimony of the high sense this Board entertains of his patriotism and distinquished merit.

Willett was present to receive this flattering address and responded with his "warmest acknowledgements." After a few pleasantries, he dramatically proclaimed, "I wish never to sheath my sword I have early drawn in defence of American liberty, as long as there is a soldier or a savage in the service of Britain, in any part of the States of America."

This same day, the Albany commission was hot on the trail of people who had supplied Meyers's serjeant, Joseph Smith. A woman was examined, but denied any knowledge of Smith's party. Then, five men and a wife were questioned and committed. Next day, two men were interrogated and, after their friend put up £100 bail for each, were released under a recognizance. With those two disposed of, the first of the New Dorlach transgressors was examined and jailed.

A small party of Indians raided a farm near Fort Paris in Stone Arabia, plundered and set the house afire and took away a girl and two boys, aged twelve and ten. When the girl was released, she hurried home to tell her father who had been asleep under an apple tree behind the house and had escaped the Indians' search. His youngest son was equally lucky, as he had been fishing nearby. The farmer snapped awake before his daughter found him and, thinking quickly, fetched milk from the cellar and doused the flames.

At Saratoga on July 21, McKinstry reported to Brigadier-General Clinton that scouts had found bark canoes in the Hudson River in Jessup's Patent, two of which had been pulled into a swamp only a short time before being discovered. On a different issue, Captain Silas Gray had led a party toward Crown Point to hunt for a prisoner, but a few miles short of his destination, he heard firing and turned back. Gray claimed he had found a 30-Ton barque and a forty-five-foot mast with a number of oars drifting along the shore of Lake George. McKinstry worried these signs foreshadowed an attack on his post and the adjacent settlements and asked for immediate help, as his few men were incapable of making "any Resistance worth naming." Having "primed the pump," he asked for salt provisions for his scouts and an armourer for the post, as a third of his men's firearms were unfit for service. Was it possible that the British had secretly transferred a 30-Ton vessel to Lake George? More likely, Gray had an overactive imagination or McKinstry was inventing evidence to magnify the plight of his post.

This same day, the Albany commission switched its attention away from Meyers and the New Dorlach Tories to interview a man suspected of helping Joseph Bettys.[16]

Loyalist Secret Service scout, Abraham Wing Jr., reported that he, Caleb Closson, and three other agents left Fort St. John's on July 17. Near Fort Edward, Wing sent his wife to Albany with a letter for Mrs. George Smyth and to ask where General Schuyler was at present. She returned with a mysterious Mr. St. John in tow and reported that Schuyler had come back from a visit to General Washington the day before she left Albany. Wing immediately set off for Quebec with his party and the courier, St. John. Did the two bark canoes belong to Wing's party? Was it any wonder there was so much concern about Tory wives?

On July 22, Haldimand wrote Powell that he was pleased to hear that the collection of intelligence would be practicable from Niagara and mentioned the Oneidas and whites who had closed down the previously free access enjoyed by his scouts and couriers. As to Ethan Allen, he cautioned, "There is no doubt a commotion in Vermont, in which Allen must have a principal share, but he has not gone the length reported ... nor is it known what his real intentions are." Blank commissions for the officers of the 9th and 10th companies were enclosed confirming Andrew Bradt as captain and Thomas Butler as first lieutenant. In a second dispatch, he mentioned the difficulty of assessing what the rebels intended by their withdrawal of the Continentals from the north and the chance that their concentration portended a design on Quebec. He also noted that he awaited the overseas' provisions' convoys with "utmost impatience."

Although Joseph Brant was serving at Detroit, he was not forgotten at headquarters. Haldimand wrote to Germain, indicating his appreciation for the Mohawk war captain: "[H]e has really great Merit and altho a bountiful acknowledgement of it May, in Some Measure; have Spoiled him, he Must be encouraged — were any thing to be done from Niagara, his Service Would be indispensably Necessary."

Sir Henry Clinton wrote to Haldimand on July 23 about the fragile communication system between their two headquarters. He had not received the letters that Haldimand mentioned sending in the hands of two ensigns, nor had he heard of them being intercepted. As to the Vermont talks, "If a Reunion of Vermont with the Mother Country can be effected it must be productive of happy consequences but I confess my suspicions of those People." Regarding Haldimand's request that he approach Benedict Arnold for information about rebel sympathizers in Quebec, he confirmed he would do so. Considering this had been first proposed last November, the matter was dragging on interminably. Of course, his original request may have been amongst the errant dispatches.

Captain Azariah Pritchard, KR, reported an adventure deep in rebel territory. Whether Sherwood, who was understandably sensitive about giving offence during his talks, knew of, or agreed to, the mission is unknown. Under St. Leger's orders, Pritchard had left Fort St. John's on June 22 with ten men and infiltrated through Vermont to the Connecticut River. From there, he sent a local man upriver for news. Mysteriously, four rebel deserters appeared at the fellow's place and warned that the man had been taken. When questioned, the local had confessed that Tories were at his house and offered to lead a party to take them. In the morning's dark hours, he gave the troops the slip and arrived home at 3:00 a.m. to warn Pritchard that forty-eight men were scant minutes behind. The captain decided his party was too big to hide in the woods and ordered six men to head for Canada as a diversion. With the other four, he crossed the river into New Hampshire and headed south. They soon came to their target, Whipple's farm, but found it guarded by twelve men. They lurked in the woods for three days, watching for an opportunity. In the dead of night, they crawled into position along a streambed that passed eighty-five yards from the house. They observed every motion until 4:00 p.m. the next afternoon and, when all but six guards were out of the house, assaulted. Although five shots were fired at them, the raiders were uninjured except for a slight wound to Corporal Barlow's hand; however, one guard was killed, another wounded, and four driven off. Pritchard dragged Whipple into the bush, but his feet and legs were horribly swollen with gout and, although utterly terrorized, he could not march and was coerced to sign a parole. Then, the party set off for Canada, evading all pursuit.

The captain explained in his report that he had not destroyed the farm as there were 5,000–6,000 bushels of wheat standing in the fields and 120 head of cattle grazing with 100 Continental beeves about to arrive for fatting and, by delaying a month, the maximum damage could be achieved; however, no record has been found of a follow-up raid.

In a crusty letter that presumed upon Robert Mathews's friendship, Walter Butler again wrote of his problems in raising money for a Regular captaincy; ventured into military politics; attempted to stop the passing of the Commissary General's receipts; questioned the expenses of the Ranger convalescents at Machiche and requested that his father be permitted to draw £5,000 from the Paymaster General for arms and clothing. On a more positive note, he wrote, "nothing would give him greater pleasure than … Service with the Rangers by way of Crown Point."[17]

On July 22, Major McKinstry advised Governor Clinton that he had seized ten cattle and thirty-four sheep that were being driven out of state and requested they be forfeited for the garrison's use. He thought the buyer was a flagrant violator of state law, as his purchases had driven up local prices and reduced the availability of provisions. The major must have been chagrined to be informed by the governor that there was no law preventing the shipment of livestock out of state and reminding him that impressments of stock procured for the French army and navy was forbidden. Here was a fine kettle of fish; the state was unable to supply McKinstry's men with their most basic needs, but the French were to be favoured. The major was rebuffed on a second note. He had asked that a small sum of money be paid to the three-years' men in lieu of some of the land bounty; however, Clinton advised that the legislature had risen without making further allowances for these men. In any event, the returns indicated that only seven men had been mustered for the three-years' service.

At Albany, Van Cortlandt had divided the "largest and most healthy Regiment in America" into two battalions, the second of which struck its tents and embarked in bateaux for West Point at 4:00 p.m. on July 23.

A 2TCM lieutenant had been killed the day before in the Tryon's Palatine District. No details have been found and his death survives as another random, violent act in the unremitting war of raids.

Four days after the officer's death, another attack occurred in the same district. Three brothers named Schuld, one a 2TCM serjeant, the others privates, were mowing hay two miles north of Stone Arabia with a youngster and a family slave. They had stacked their firelocks at the woods' edge and foolishly had gone to work without posting a guard. As the work took them nearer to the woods, the family dog growled, but they ignored the warning. Suddenly, a dozen Indians sprang from cover, gathered up the firearms, and dragged the men off; the only sign of their fate was their abandoned scythes. On their march, they were desperate for food and ate frog, rattlesnake, decaying horse, and, finally, the faithful dog. Soon after this incident, Willett wrote the governor a letter of deep despair apologizing for troubling him with "long details about such paltry affairs ... should I servive this campaign and preserve my reputation I shall count myself a Fortunate Man Indeed. I shall cease saying more upon this subject for the present. But I am truly sick of it."

One day while returning from hunting Indians, Willett stopped at George Herkimer's place. George's wife, Alyda, said he was out in the fields, but she would call him in and stepped up on a bench to blow a signal horn. Alarmed, Willett pulled her down. She was no sooner off her perch, than a rifle ball struck a nearby post. Willett hustled her into the house. Herkimer hurried in from the fields and joined in driving the sniper off.

The Herkimer Home. One of the most beautiful homes in the Mohawk Valley; its splendour reflected the prosperity of the Herkimer family who controlled the Little Falls carrying place.

Benson J. Lossing, artist and engraver. (Benson J. Lossing. The Pictorial Field-Book of the Revolution, 2 vols. New York: Harper & Brothers, 1852.)

On July 24, the Tory scoundrel William Sommer came before the Conspiracy Commission and was examined and recommitted. The next day, he and twenty-one men and a woman were arraigned. Ironically, the Tory, David Lewis of Currytown, was summoned to testify against them.[18]

By July 26, the abduction parties were well on their way when Sherwood was startled to discover that Dr. Smyth had given Pritchard permission to abduct General Jacob Bayley, the Cöos firebrand. The captain would stop at Dutchman's Point on his way out. As Joseph Fay was expected any day with his list of prisoners, Sherwood wanted nothing to mar this tiny bit of progress. While Bayley was against the Bennington mob, he lived in Vermont and that fact could tip the scale. He wrote to Smyth to halt Pritchard, but he was too late. When the captain appeared, Sherwood was prepared for a battle of wills, as he was handicapped by being unable to explain his reasons for wanting the attempt abandoned. Pritchard was not easily dissuaded. The two men held equal rank and the Ranger was eager to repeat his earlier success with Thomas Johnson, but Sherwood prevailed and a peeved Pritchard went on the comparatively mundane mission of collecting intelligence.

Sherwood's Loyal Blockhouse at Dutchman's Point was virtually complete. At ground level, there were the usual mess benches, bunk

Richard J Young, "Blockhouses in Canada, 1749–1841: A Comparative Report and Catalogue." Canadian Historic Sites: Occasional Papers in Archaeology and History (Ottawa: Parks Canada, 1980).

A Blockhouse. This extant eighteenth-century example built in 1750 at Windsor, Nova Scotia, has a twelve-foot-square footprint and rises twenty-six feet from the ground to the roof's peak. It was repaired during the Revolution and used to defend against rebel privateers.

beds, and cupboards. A ladder led to an overhanging, loop-holed second floor and a second ladder to a loft under the roof where Sherwood and Smyth shared privacy and quarters. When the building was finished, the Regulars returned to St. John's, leaving behind Lieutenant Dulmage, QLR, in command of a mixed thirty-man garrison of his men and King's Rangers. Sherwood thought that once the pickets were erected, fifty men with small arms could defend it against 300, although two or three swivels would be useful. "There is not so proper a place on the Frontiers as this for the residence and departure of secret scouts."

On July 26, Robertson reported several events. A party of twenty-five Indians ready "to go to War" had arrived at Oswegatchie on July 20 and he sent them off two evenings later with two Highlanders. That same day, a small party had returned with an Indian who had been shot in the leg and shoulder when he ran up to a rebel blockhouse to scalp a dead man and take another prisoner. Fifty Kanehsatake and Akwesasne warriors had arrived the day before, but a lack of rations prevented sending them out. Ross had asked for assistance to flesh out a formidable party at Fort Haldimand, so Robertson suggested they travel to the island, but they were reluctant to go without him being there to "speak to the Father." Was "the Father" Ross already seen as difficult? Before leaving for the island, he hoped to persuade another fifteen who had just arrived to accompany him. As Powell earlier noted, the Natives were eager for action.

Sir John reported the return of two parties from Tryon County with eight men, six of whom were to join the KRR. One party left Albany with news that all the enemy's Regulars at Saratoga and the Mohawk were to march south. He was distressed that Volunteer Spencer and others that he considered, "some of the best men I had," were prisoners and requested permission for his regiment to practice with powder and ball, as they had hitherto little opportunity.

About this time, Secret Service agent, Ensign Thomas Lovelace, was carrying letters to Colonel Cornelius Van Veghten, 13ACM, whose allegiance to the rebel cause was wavering. One chronicler labelled Lovelace as the worst sort of Tory: "brave, expert and cautious." After making the delivery, Lovelace and his two men sheltered in a swamp near Dovegat, five miles from Van Veghten's where two Tory families were already hiding. General Stark found out and sent Captain Holtam Dunham, WL, to take him. Dunham chose four men for the task — his lieutenant, his ensign, an orderly, and a private. In the dead of night, they entered the dense swamp and soon became separated, but Dunham continued on with two men. At dawn, the trio came to a bark hut and, finding Lovelace drawing on stockings, jumped out with levelled muskets. Dunham shouted they were surrounded and Lovelace and the four men quietly submitted. Papers secreted on the ensign indicated he had been sent to abduct an unnamed individual near Saratoga and it was thought that Van Veghten had been the target, which may have been a ruse to protect him as Smyth's new source.

Stark convened a court martial that sentenced Lovelace to death. He protested in vain, claiming status as a prisoner of war. Three days later, in what legend describes as "an awesome storm of rain, clashing thunder and vivid lightning," Lovelace was brought to a hill overlooking Schuyler's Fish Creek home and stood up in a cart in a hollow square of guards. A minister said a few prayers; a rope was placed around his neck, and the cart driven out from under him.

Lovelace left behind a widow and seven children. This was indeed a hard measure, and much later, a rebel general wrote that the tenor of the Tory's instructions and the fact that his party was armed "clearly barred the idea of his being considered as a spy"; however, the deed was done.

Willett wrote to Brigadier-General Clinton to warn him that the MA Levies were not being raised as had been hoped and, too agitated to wait for Clinton's action, he immediately wrote to Governor Hancock reminding him of Washington's expectations that 600 MA Levies would be raised for New York's defence and urging him to investigate.

On July 26, Lieutenant Adam Crysler, 6NID, with some twenty-five Schoharie Indians and Butler's Rangers, including his brother William and principal warrior Seth's Henry, infiltrated the Fox Kill valley, took two prisoners, and struck at Committee-man Jacob Zimmer's house, killing his son in front of his grand-mother and mother, Catharin, plundering

Unknown engraver. (Jeptha R. Simms. History of Schoharie County and Border Wars of New York …Albany: Munsell & Tanner, 1845.)

Becker's place under attack. This illustration shows the attempts to burn the gutters and roof and to set fire to the mill.

and firing the house, and killing a Hessian deserter from Burgoyne's army who had been working on the farm. After they left, the two women doused the house fire, but were unable to save the barn. On their march down the creek, the raiders took Zimmer's son Peter, who, on asking about his brother, was slyly told he was with the women.

The band killed two more victims on their way to Johannes Becker's, a former committee chairman and brother-in-law of Colonel Vrooman. No shots had been fired and the morning was particularly foggy, so the fires at Zimmer's were unobserved. Consequently, the party approached Becker's without discovery and killed his son John with an axe blow to the head. Two other sons, who were working in a cornfield, saw their approach and took flight and managed to successfully hide under the bank of the creek.

The party had still not fired their guns, as their main target was Becker, whose nine-year-old son Henry and Jacob Zimmer, a nephew of the murdered Jacob, were returning to the house with several other boys after driving hogs into a pasture. About eighty yards from the house, one boy exclaimed, "See the riflemen over there; they are painted like the Indians." Henry was wide awake and broke into a run, calling out "Indians! Indians!" but the raiders still held their fire and the boys made it into the house, tumbling into a cluster of younger children in the hallway.

Becker Sr. had been behind the house working when he heard Henry's shout. Running inside, he grabbed his firelock, rushed into a front room, thrust the barrel through a loophole and fired, breaking an Indian's arm.

An alert Mrs. Catherine Becker held open a heavy plank door to allow John Hutt, who had been out back making a whiffletree, to run inside. The furious barking of the Beckers' three large dogs had warned Hutt and, although he ran hard, a big Indian slipped past the animals and caught hold of him. When he raised the whiffletree to strike the warrior, he was released and he bounded into the house. The lady slammed the door and shot the bolt while the other warriors were killing the dogs.

The two-storied stone house was well suited for a stout defence and Becker, Hutt, and militiaman George Shell took posts at different windows while Catherine Becker and some women took the children upstairs. The raiders kept up a very brisk fire, sending twenty-eight balls through Hutt's window alone. Shell shot a raider who was hunkering along the creek bed carrying a firebrand with the obvious intent to set fire to the mill. Becker knocked the hat off another man who later proved to have been a Crysler.

The war party decided to burn out their prey and, under cover of "dead ground," piled combustibles in a wheelbarrow under a wooden downspout and lit it afire. Flames rapidly climbed the spout toward the gutters and shingles. Becker fortunately found a length of scantling in the room and worked to pry off the shingles. Catherine meanwhile descended to a cellar cistern and was shocked to discover an open door that the assailants could easily have entered. Pushing it shut, she slid home the bolts, then rushed upstairs with a pail of water. After a desperate struggle, Becker managed to dislodge the shingles and, as they fell to the ground, the Indians thanked him for the kindling. He poured the water through the hole and put out the burning spout. This stunt was performed over and over again, until the spout finally burnt off out of reach of new flames.

During the action, Becker's parents, who lived nearby, were seen fleeing toward the Lower Fort and were fired at by the war party; however, their concentration was on capturing Becker and the parents escaped.

The action had lasted too long and, in fear of retaliation, Crysler ordered a withdrawal. A party from the Middle Fort arrived just as the raiders left. By an odd atmospheric quirk, the firing had been heard there, but not at the Lower Fort, which was only half the distance away.

The man shot by Shell was alive and discovered to be a Scotsman named Erkert, who had been Becker's pre-war cooper. He soon expired and his scalp was lifted by a Schoharie Indian named Yan, who, ironically, was the son of David Ogeyonda, who had been crudely executed during the 1777 Tory uprising by Continental Dragoons after George Shell had botched an attempt at killing him.

After aborting the attack, the raiders headed toward Cobleskill, releasing captive Peter Mann near Schoharie town, perhaps because he was related to George Mann, a failed Tory leader of the same uprising. Cobleskill had been warned to be ready for Crysler and the people were herded into Fort Duboise and the militia turned out; however, the war party evaded interception, burned several properties and captured George Warner Jr., who had foolishly left the fort to take care of his father's place.

———————

That afternoon, a second war party led by Fort Hunter War Captain David Hill Karonghyhontye, and the Schoharie warrior, Seth's Joseph, and seven others captured a pair of fathers, their two sons, one eighteen, the other ten, and five girls harvesting wheat. Two other lads escaped to give the alarm. The party moved up the Schoharie Kill and, after a mile, stripped the girls naked and released them, perhaps relying on embarrassment to delay discovery. As soon as the boys gave the alarm, Colonel Vrooman sent Captain Gray and a detail of Levies in pursuit, but he gave up that evening without seeing anything of the party and without finding the girls. That night, the war party camped thirteen miles from the wheat field. A porcupine was killed, had its quills singed off and was roasted and divided by tomahawk. The captives refused to eat. At night, they were partially stripped and tightly bound. When a storm came up, they all took shelter under the canopy of a large tree, their bodies intertwined to prevent escape. When the eighteen-year-old pled with Hill to loosen his bonds, he complied and, in the dead of night, the lad wormed his way out of the ropes, removed an Indian's head from his stomach, and carefully unwound a tumpline from around his neck. Jumping to his feet, he crashed into the brush. The Indians sprang awake and unsuccessfully gave chase. Next morning, two captives who were suspected of assisting with the escape were prepared for ritual death, but the lad's father gave an explanation for his son's escape that saved them. On the twenty-day trip to Niagara, the war party was desperate for food. They ate unripe apples, corn, and pumpkins, a colt abandoned by Docksteder's men, and, for four days, had nothing to eat.

———————

That evening at Albany, Willett heard of the eruptions at Schoharie and immediately wrote Colonels Wemple, Clyde, Visscher, and Klock, advising that he would leave the city with a detachment of the 2NY in wagons and on horseback to pursue the raiders and urged all of them to turn out troops to do the same. Wemple was to march directly to Schoharie while the Tryon troops were to meet him near New Dorlach. The senior officer at Fort Rensselaer was instructed to march all the Levies he had, leaving only a small guard to guard the stores and cattle. The men were to take five days' bread and not lose a moment. The 2NY troops arrived in Schoharie on July 28, found the war parties gone, turned about, and were back in Albany at nine o'clock that night.

———————————————
———————————————

In a most surprising event, Captain Holtham Dunham and Lieutenant Benoni Grant were arrested on July 27 by Major McKinstry on charges of "unofficer and ungentleman Like Behavour," to wit, encouraging their men to desert and speaking with contempt of a court martial at which Dunham was sitting. Both were confined to quarters. Considering the captain's exemplary performance in the taking of Lovelace, there was clearly more to this story.

On July 28, Governor Clinton sent Washington disturbing news about the eagerly awaited MA Levies. A Berkshire County brigadier had told Willett that very few men had been raised and, in any event, his county was only expected to contribute 193 men and he had no orders to march them to Albany. Clinton worried that the enemy would be greatly encouraged to make incursions in the harvest season and urged the C-in-C to investigate this issue and expedite the march of the "Eastern Levies."

On July 28, Bettys's and Meyers's abduction parties separated near Ballstown. With Meyers gone, Bettys made an incredibly irrational decision and, lusting after a girl, abandoned his mission. Ever the rake, Bettys had Jellis Legrange's daughter in his sights. In total disregard for his responsibilities, let alone the security of the other parties, he told his men they would have to snatch Stringer themselves, as he had other business. Bettys went south to Legrange's at Normanskill and spirited the girl away. His men panicked and headed back to Canada.

Legrange was already under suspicion, so he had no qualms about improving his lot by reporting Bettys. As the commissioners were perfectly familiar with Tories offering half-truths to disguise their personal involvement, troops were sent to the Legrange home to make a thorough search. Even the girl's brother joined the hunt for his sister and her notorious lover. Parties ranged high and low over the very area where Meyers and his men were hiding before making their attempt on Schuyler.

Meyers had his first word of Betty's indiscretion from Mrs. Smyth when he boldly visited her in Albany. She was expecting a dispatch for Haldimand, which she promised to send to Meyers when the "ferment in the Country ceases." On July 31, Legrange visited the commission to report that Meyers was in the area with several men and had been in Albany the day before. Another man said that his wife had seen Bettys that very day and was told where the Tory would hide that night. Yet another 2NY detachment was sent to investigate. Meanwhile, Meyers lay low near the river below Albany waiting for the hubbub to die down.

On July 30, Lieutenant James Parrot's abduction party was twenty-five miles from New City when they were discovered and forced to abandon their original plan to take an individual from near that town. Parrot decided it would be just as useful to abduct Second Major John Younglove, 16ACM, who had been an arch foe of the Tories from the outset of the rebellion and had served on the Committee of Sequestration for Albany County's northern district. The previous October, Younglove had been involved in moving loyalists from their properties to the interior regions of the state. He was an ideal target indeed.

Parrot scouted Younglove's house and found it guarded by four men with another five living in a hay barrack beside it. Slipping by the barrack, his party surrounded the house. Parrot shouted a demand to surrender or he would fire on the house and was answered by, "fire and Be Damb'd I can fire as fast as you." When Parrot's men saw a gun being levelled, they fired. Still Younglove refused to surrender, so Parrot ordered the family to get away from the entryway, as he was about to force his way inside. He shot through the door and Mrs. Younglove jerked it open to reveal a mortally wounded man lying on the floor. Parrot gathered up the rebel guards and set off for Canada. En route, he somehow heard that his victim had expired and, confidently reported Younglove dead, but he was mistaken, as the fellow lived on for many years.[19]

On Sunday morning, July 29, people from around Stone Arabia were gathered together for religious services when an express arrived with news that Jacob Klock Jr. had come down from Canada and was hiding in the woods about six miles away with his Tories and Indians. As was customary, the men had come to the services with their arms and accoutrements and Oriskany veteran, Captain Henry Miller, a lieutenant and a serjeant quickly assembled their 2TCM militiamen. A runner was sent to Fort Paris to get help and twenty-five Willett's Levies under Lieutenant Jacob Sammons of Gros's company joined.

Klock's party included six men who had gone north with him four weeks before, nine other whites and fourteen Natives. According to one of the region's earliest historians, the band left Oswegatchie without firm plans and along the way decided to strike a blow in the area of Fort Hess and, in particular, to attack the Bellinger family where they expected to find plenty of booty and six girls, aged fifteen to twenty-five. This chronicler claimed that an incentive for Tories to conduct these raids was to "pamper the[ir] hellish lust" for violating captive females. True or not, such a stimulus would likely have only applied to the whites in the party, as rape was not the Native way. Philip Helmer, one of Klock's confederates, had been left out of this odious plan and was shocked to hear of it, as he loved one of the Bellinger girls. Repelled by his associates, he watched for a chance to warn the intended victims.

Eleven days out, the band arrived in the Palatine District and hid in a field. That night, a Tory and an Indian went to a supporter's house and wakened the family. They were received "with great joy and [given] as much bread, smoked meat, butter and cheese as they could carry away." The friend promised to tell some local Tories that the party had arrived and where they were hidden. This interaction pointed to a considerable degree of disaffection in the area. The two men returned to the party at dawn. At about ten o'clock, two locals arrived and, after some discussion, the band moved to another location and the newcomers left to collect additional volunteers. Helmer was sent with an Indian to search out some vulnerable targets. Near Fort Hess, he persuaded the native to climb a tree overlooking the countryside while he circuited the nearby farms. From high atop the tree, the Indian saw Helmer heading toward a cluster of buildings and, suspicions aroused, climbed down and ran after him. Catching up, the Native, with lowering, black looks, remonstrated with him, but Helmer innocently protested he had not realized his danger and the pair continued their scout. On their way back, the Native's suspicions had subsided and Helmer said he would collect a local farmer's black slave as a recruit. The Indian continued on to the band's hideout, while Helmer removed the paint from his face and went directly to Fort Hess to alert the neighbourhood.

Captain Miller had collected a force of about forty men. He chose seven local men as trackers and followed closely behind them with the main body. Klock's party had moved again, this time to a heavily wooded ridge near Mother's Creek on Lampman's farm. The new site provided excellent observation of the back trail, but when Miller's scouts were seen at about 2:00 p.m., the Tories thought they were reinforcements brought along by their morning visitors and hailed and waved them in. This allowed the rebels to get in amongst the trees and catch the raiders lounging on the ground. Militiaman Andrew Gray killed the Indians' war captain and two other Natives were wounded. Scrambling to their feet, the raiders fired a few shots, hitting one Levy in the breast. When the rebels charged, the raiders bolted, jumping down a steep bank into thick brush, leaving behind their packs, blankets, hats, and a couple of guns. Someone scalped the dead Native and the trophy was carried back to Fort Paris.

Klock's chastised party reassembled at Canada Creek and set off for Oswegatchie. This decisive repulse of a foray that could have had such a tragically different outcome, confirmed the revived spirit of resistance that had been stimulated by Willett and Gros. The skirmish was to live on in Tryon's collective memory under names such as the battle of Lampman's (or Landman's) Farm, or Mother's (or Mudder's) Creek.

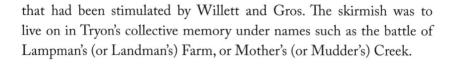

On July 30, Washington wrote to Governor Clinton from his HQ at Dobbs Ferry to confirm that, as soon as he had decided to withdraw the Continentals, he had asked Governor Hancock of Massachusetts to raise 600 Levies from his western counties to assist in defending New York's frontier. Until he received Clinton's letter to the contrary, he had thought this request had been complied with. He again urged Hancock's speedy compliance.

At a depot deep in the Mohawk region, Captain Caldwell by chance met up with Lieutenant Hare's party and the pair decided to combine efforts. The raiders now totalled eighty-seven Rangers and 250 Senecas and Delawares. The war captains had noted a severe lack of provisions and unilaterally decided to attack Monbackers, a flourishing settlement in Ulster County's Rochester region west of Poughkeepsie. Although very much against his orders, Caldwell had little choice but to agree.

At Albany on 6:00 a.m. on July 31, the 2NY Light Company struck tents and embarked in bateaux for West Point.

It would be weeks before Haldimand received a July 31 letter from Germain's Under Secretary that advised of "[the] most certain & precise Intelligence ... of the Plans and Intentions of the Enemy." He wrote:

> The French Court have absolutely refused to send any more Troops to the Continent, they have put Mr Rochambeau under Washington's orders but with the exception of not making Detachments from his Army....

It was Washington's request that the whole of the French Troops should have gone by Sea to Virginia but the French Admiral would not venture to convoy them & that project was therefore laid aside. No attempt is to be made upon New York [City] after the French Troops join Washington until de Grasse arrives from the West Indies with his Fleet and long before that can happen, Sir Henry Clinton will have received his Reinforcement of near 6,000 Europeans. This Intelligence, which may be entirely relied on, will fully prove to you that no attempt will be made by France or the Rebels on the side of Canada and leaves you entirely Master of your own operations & to carry on what Enterprises you may judge proper to undertake on the Frontiers of the Revolted Provinces in Co-operation with and support of the Southern Army.[20]

CONSTANTLY INFESTED WITH PARTIES OF THE ENEM

I Shou'd Hope to Give Good Account of Him

*I*nside Vermont, talk of treason had become rampant, which led one Assembly member to demand that Chittenden's official papers be laid before the members. After heated debate, his resolution was approved and the governor produced several letters that referred solely to prisoner exchanges. This was such a credible reason for negotiations that both rabid Whigs and the spies from other states were satisfied.

On July 30, Mathews advised Maclean that the son of James Gordon, the Ballstown colonel, was also implicated in spying and was to be left at Montreal where he and "his most intimate associates" could be observed. Meanwhile, Thomas Johnson was busily making observations at Fort St. John's:

> Everything was then pursued to carry on two expeditions, one against Schenectady and the other against Albany, hand barrows, wheel barrows, a new construction of Bateau very light and portable, artillery carriages, and light Trucks [carriages] or hand wagons, fashioned so that six men would sit on a bateau large enough to carry 15 men and baggage and run with it

three or four miles in an hour, and every other thing
necessary to force a rapid march or retreat with the
greatest expedition. Nothing prevented their intended
expedition but the want of provisions. But before that
arrived[,] information came that General Starke with a
body of troops was marching toward Saratoga; this put
them into great consternation.

While the Mohawk Valley basked in the outcome of the
Lampman's Farm affair, Joseph Bettys's men arrived at St. John's and
confessed the failure of their mission, adding considerably to Smyth's
and Sherwood's anxiety.

At Niagara, Walter Butler again indulged his anger in a letter of
August 2 in which he took offense at Mathew's description of Butler's
Rangers as "a Corps of Loyalists." Presumably, this was seen as a slur,
as it lumped the Rangers with the struggling smaller corps in lower
Quebec. Then, he lashed out at Guy Johnson over some slight cast upon
his father, making an idle threat in the process. Mathews's head must
have been spinning over all this crankiness.

Haldimand replied to Powell concerning the Rangers's requirement
for an adjutant and promising that a suitable candidate would be found
amongst the Regular regiments in lower Quebec. As for a surgeon's
mate, the general hospital was short of staff, but many young men were
expected with the fleet and one would be sought from amongst them.

The governor then wrote a top secret dispatch to Sir Henry Clinton,
advising that a full account of the Vermont talks could not be sent, as his
dispatch vessel was unable to sail. In the interim, he offered an opinion:

> [I]t appears to me infinitely more Dangerous to yield to
> the delays urged by that People than to bring them to
> a declaration[,] since from the best Information these
> Delays are only to gain time to strengthen themselves to
> Act no doubt in cooperation with Congress — They are
> busily forming Magazines, have raised a considerable
> number of men, and in a few months will be an

important Ally or a formidable Enemy to either side, from the whole Tenor of their Conduct I cannot think they will adopt ours.

To carry on the Deception[,] Ethan has quitted the Service but Ira goes Commissioner to Congress instead of coming here with the Flag — This is to avoid the Test of a Discovery, I think it cannot fail to produce. An intercepted Letter dated Albany, the 15th July from Schuyler to Washington is just sent in ... It congratulates him upon the confirmation that a Detachment of Count de Gras's Fleet will join that of Mons. De Touche, for the Attack of Quebec and agreeing with him that every Demonstration for an attack upon New York should be given, That De Rochambeau should not march with the Troops until the Fleet leaves Boston, he is to penetrate by Coos.

This letter appears to have been conveyed to me by design to prevent a Diversion in your favor, where I conceive the Blow is Levelled. — I wait in the utmost anxiety to hear from you & in the most painful suspense for Provisions, without which my Efforts must be very ineffectual.

In a second letter to Sir Henry, Haldimand expanded on his problems. Quebec had subsisted for the past fortnight on the fortuitous, but temporary relief of a merchant's cargo that had arrived from Cork. Now, the season for westerly winds had set in and there had been no word of the expected fleet. Five or six rebel Privateers were cruising the Gulf of St. Lawrence, giving him great anxiety for the safety of the victuallers, which were unlikely to escape their vigilance. What little of last year's grain remained was selling at inflated prices and worms had greatly damaged the current crop. The hay was so badly affected that the *habitants* were slaughtering their cattle while they remained fat. Obviously, Thomas Johnson's observations were accurate; however, later that day, events took a turn for the better when some ships of the Trade Fleet and three captured rebel Privateers arrived in Quebec's basin escorted by two RN frigates. The seamen advised that several merchantmen had been taken in the Gulf and others at sea by a French or Spanish Ship of the Line. Their charges safe, the frigates turned about and headed for the Gulf to protect the rest of the fleet.

———————————————

———————————————

On August 1, Captain Aaron Hale's newly formed company of Willett's marched to the Schoharie to take up garrison duty. At Albany, a lieutenant recommended to the governor by Brigadier Van Rensselaer and Colonel Whiting brought in 17ACM's recruits, then, for no apparent reason, deserted. Upriver in Canajoharie District, Nicholas House, 1TCM, was taken by a war party.

Willett was still in Albany when he sent orders to his new major, Josiah Throop, instructing him to march all the new Levies in the city to Fort Rensselaer without loss of time, taking all the bateaux from Schenectady that he could man, loaded with flour and any other stores. He was to forward the flour on to Fort Herkimer in wagons, with a dozen of the best, fat cattle from Fort Rensselaer and a strong party of guards and drovers. Guards were to be supplied for the inhabitants harvesting their crops and preference given to the more distant farms. They were to take up a concealed position from where they could see the fields and the harvesters, who should also post sentinels while they worked. The major was to have his men cut hay for public use from abandoned farms and any fields where the whole crop could not be taken off by the owners. Captain House at Fort House would advise him about what grass near the river should be cut. Throop was to keep out scouts to prevent the posts and guards from being surprised and he was to conform in detail to the orders given to the officer commanding at Rensselaer.

While Willett was writing to Throop, 2NY troops marched from Albany to Saratoga to hunt an enemy party that had taken four Kingsbury men and alarmed the district.

In response to Washington's inquiry, the governor of Massachusetts, John Hancock, expressed surprise that his levies, which were being

THE OLD SCHUYLER MANSION, ALBANY, N. Y.

left: Major-General Philip Schuyler (1733–1804). One of the more significant rebel New Yorkers of the Revolution.

right: Schuyler Mansion, Albany. The house raided by Captain Meyers in his attempt to abduct Major-General Schuyler.

raised for service in New York, were tardy and gave assurances that he would hasten them on.

On August 2, the Albany conspiracy commission released a New Dorlach Tory on a recognizance for good behaviour and £100 bail. Considering the nature of his crimes, his release suggests that the jails were still overflowing.

The same day, the captain of Schenectady's militia artillery company marched his men to Fort Plain, presumably to receive training from Moodie's Regulars.

On a sad note, Ann Ramsey, the wife of David, who had been taken by Meyers at Ballstown a few months earlier, appealed to the governor to exchange her husband, as her large family was on the edge of penury. It was months before he offered the news that the Commissary of Prisoners had been told to spare no pains to effect Ramsay's exchange.

Of far greater moment, New York's congressional delegates submitted a memorial from the state legislature about Vermont. In 1779, Congress had resolved that New York, New Hampshire, and Massachusetts should allow it to settle all issues of jurisdiction between them and the people of the Grants, in order to avoid internal dissention and maintain domestic peace and good order. The three states were to cease enforcing their laws over the Grants and Congress would view any violence committed against the "Tenor, true intent & meaning" of the resolution as a breach of the peace of the union. In keeping with this resolution, New York passed a law authorizing Congress "to hear and determine all differences & disputes relative to jurisdiction;" however, the state contended that the intent of these resolutions had been repeatedly flouted by "the pretended State of Vermont," as it had made new encroachments far beyond the original limits of the Grants. It was clear that, in the midst of fighting a protracted war for independence, no progress had been made to resolve this highly contentious internal issue, which Haldimand continued to aggravate.

Willett advised Villefranche that Throop had marched with part of Skinner's new Levies' company and would bring flour and a dozen cattle to Fort Herkimer. Volunteer Randolph Wilson, who was at Herkimer, was appointed lieutenant in Skinner's company. Villefranche was to send men from his garrison to guard the harvesters at German Flatts, even if this meant a temporary halt to construction. When the colonel was through at Albany, he would come to Fort Herkimer and replace the present levies with new, and add as many more as needed. If Captain Marshall could be spared, he was given permission to go to Albany on personal business; if not, he was to stay until the harvest was complete. Artillery captain Moodie had the right to enlist men from the Levies, but his recruits must first complete their term of service before transferring.[1]

On August 4, Governor Clinton wrote to Frederick Weissenfels, former 2NY lieutenant-colonel and colonel of Levies, who had expressed concern over the "neglect of his previous services" and had requested a command in the new Levies. Frustrated, Clinton gently chided that he had "expected an earlier Intimation" of his intentions. Nevertheless, he gave command of a second regiment of Levies for the frontiers to the veteran and instructed him to call without delay to receive his orders.

A six-man patrol from House's 2TCM company was ambushed on its way to hunt Indians at Fort Walradt. Lieutenant John Zimmerman and his cousin, Serjeant Jacob Zimmerman, were killed outright. Two other Zimmermans escaped and Peter Hellegas and a second Jacob

Zimmerman were taken. After scalping the dead men, the Indians led the captives into the woods. They had gone a short distance when Jacob's clothes were seen to be covered in blood from a throat wound. He was told to spit. As the discharge was clear, he was saved and the party set off at a hard trot. Men from 2TCM pursued, but failed to overtake.

On August 5, Washington wrote to Governor Clinton deploring the inability of the states to fill their Continental battalions and their expectation that what few troops he had would be assigned to state defence. "Instead of offensive Measures[,] a defensive Plan must be adopted — instead of an active & decisive Campaign ... we must end our operations in Languor & Disgrace — & perhaps protract the War, to the Hazzard of our final Ruin." With that off his chest, he advised the actions he had taken to forward the MA Levies.

In keeping with these concerns, the governor sent Major Elias Benschoten, a 1780 Levies' veteran, to visit the colonels of the Dutchess County regiments who had not furnished their full quota of Levies. He was to demand that they supply men from their delinquent classes and to warn that those who did not comply would be fined according to law.

As the terms of so many of Willett's first wave of Levies were falling due, he was very concerned about the slow arrival of the replacement wave. He advised the governor that the Albany County regiments of Whiting, Van Ness, Van Alstine, and Henry Rensselaer had sent most of their quota, but none had been received from the other twelve, even though he had urged compliance. He planned to make another tour of the posts and distribute the extra ordnance stored at Fort Herkimer.

August 6 marked the failure of another abduction. Lieutenant Mathew Howard, KLA, had added thirteen men to his party of four loyalists and two Regulars, many of them escapees from the Convention Army. They easily carried off John Bleecker, but when he failed to appear for supper, his wife alerted the neighbourhood. Word reached Bennington that Tories were afoot and a party was quickly raised. When Howard discovered he was hotly pursued, he released the captive and, soon after, his party was overtaken and quietly submitted. The pursuers had missed Bleecker and thought the Tories were just another group running off to Canada; however, the jig was up when secret orders were found on Howard's person. In addition to Howard, the pursuit had made quite a haul: Volunteers Daniel Carr, KLA, and Hazelton Spencer, KRR; a corporal and private of the 34th; a King's Ranger and escaped prisoners of the 9th, 47th, and 53rd regiments who had been lurking about. A court sentenced Howard to death and, when Stark visited Bennington, he and his friend, Vermont colonel, Samuel Herrick, yanked the Tory from the guardhouse, fixed a rope around his neck, uttered dire threats, then threw him back in the cell. Ensign Roger Stevens, KR, who had been taken earlier while on some other mission, saw Howard tearfully wringing his hands and told him they only meant to scare him, yet the ordeal was thrice repeated. The final time, he was jerked aloft. He lived to escape later with the help of local sympathizers.[2]

Captain Meyers's attempt on Schuyler presented a radically different story. Of note, Schuyler had been forewarned that an attempt might be made and wrote:

> [T]he British in Canada are not ashamed … to steal away individuals … and even … offer rewards for some particular persons. On the 29th ult. I was informed … that parties were lurking about the place to carry me off, and in the course of the last week this intelligence was confirmed by the Commission for detect'g conspiracies, by information given to General Clinton by a person escaped from Canada, by Colo McKinstry from Saratoga, by others whose names it would be dangerous to them to name should this letter miscarry, some of which assured me that two hundred guinas had been

promised for delivering me to Canada. This repeated information induced me to take measures to prevent a surprise … My Gates and outward doors in the rear of my house were closed and secured at sunset.

Meyers assaulted Schuyler's mansion between seven and nine o'clock on August 7. A newspaper account said the raiders boldly walked up and made a call. "[R]efused admittance at the back gate, they forced it, entered the kitchen, and had proceeded to the back hall, before they were met by four white men and two blacks, who on discovering them [went] for their arms." Meyers had to knock down two doors before gaining access to the hallway, which gave Schuyler and his family time to gain the upper floor. The general noted that "Captain Myer … at the head of 18 or 20 men" broke in before his guards could fetch their muskets. They "entered the kitchen and had proceeded into the back hall" where they "were met by the men who had gone for the arms." The guards and black servants defended gallantly, giving Schuyler "time to get out of my front Hall and to gain my bed room where my arms were deposited." Schuyler wrote to Henry Glen, "[B]y firing I alarmed the town [which] turn[ed] out with alacrity and expedition, the villains carried off one of my men, wounded another, and took some of my plate. I have to Intreat you to request the Onieda, Tuscaroras and Cajhuawagas to turn out … divide into parties … [and] take up every suspected person."

Meyers recalled the event slightly differently:

After I entered the house I met with an opposition of seven men with which a carnage insued which lasted near a quarter of an hour, in which I and my party killed one and wounded two, and took two prisoners and the other two made their escape … not having sufficient men to surround the house [Schuyler] made his escape out of a window, the centry I had planted at the door said he heard two pistols fired after he made his escape towards the town which I supposed to be to alarm the town.

Schuyler reported, "Some of the party then attempted to surround the house, whilst others entered it. Those in the quarter exposed to my fire, retired on the first discharge, altho I repeated my fire frequently to alarm the town. In the meantime Myers with some of the party had got upstairs into the saloon leading to the bedroom, but retired with precipitation on hearing me call to the citizens to hasten up and surround the house ... tho the citizens made all possible dispatch to come to my relief ... they came too late."

Meyers's captives were John Cockley, 1NY, and John Tubbs, an army courier assigned to the general. John Ward, 1NY, was wounded, but not severely. Typically, the names of the faithful blacks were not recorded. Unlike Howard, the wily Meyers beat a rapid retreat and, dividing his party into small teams, eluded all pursuit. Once burned, twice shy — Washington instructed General Clinton to quickly reinforce the general's personal guard to twelve men.

When the Albany Conspiracy Commission met the next day, they ordered troops to block Meyers's likely escape routes. A company was ordered to the Niskayuna road and to remain there until the next day while other detachments scoured the area. Colonel Beeckman was to order out part of his regiment to guard the Hudson shore at the Kinderhook Dock to prevent a crossing. All was in vain.[3]

The abduction attempt, led by Lieutenant David Jones, KLA, a notable veteran of the 1777 campaign, also went amiss. St. Leger opined that the failure was due to Jones's lacklustre performance, and Jones asked Mathews to assure the governor that the country had been so utterly alarmed by the actions of the other parties that, he was prevented from executing his mission. Similarly, Groves, William Ferguson, and Serjeant Peter Taylor, KR, all failed.

While outrage over the abduction attempts was sweeping the upper Hudson, Willett focused on his officer corps. He had retained some first wave captains: Conine at Catskill, Duboise at Schoharie, White at Ballstown, Putman at Fort Hunter, and Gros at Rensselaer. By August 7, his new captains, Abram Livingston, Peter Van Rensselaer, John Harrison, and Thomas Skinner had joined Major Throop at Fort Rensselaer. Aaron Hale went to reinforce Duboise at Schoharie and Job Wright to Saratoga. They were "to take rank agreeable to their former commissions." Lieutenant Jacob Winne replaced John Fonda as quartermaster and a talented, flexible young officer, Joseph Van Ingen, was appointed Hale's first lieutenant. During Joseph's service, he would act as a surgeon at the Schenectady hospital and a conductor of ordnance at the Continental armourers' shop.

On August 7, two New York congressmen wrote to the governor from Philadelphia enclosing a copy of Lord George Germain's letter to Sir Henry Clinton about the attempts of some leading Vermonters to form a coalition with Britain. They pointed to the danger of Vermont extending its claims and "spreading Disaffection to our Cause" and assured him that "Everything in our Power shall be exerted to obtain Security for our State beyond the Limits originally set up for the Grants, and preserve some Dignity in the cession on the part of the United States."

The governor wrote his brother James telling him about Germain's intercepted letter, which confirmed the rumours that Vermont's leaders "had formed a criminal connection with Great Britain." He hoped that the bulk of the Grants people would repudiate it. But, adding fuel to the fire, he received a letter from the president of congress, enclosing a copy of the proposed legislation concerning Vermont. New York and New Hampshire were to surrender their claims to the lands west of Connecticut River and pave the way for the republic to enter the union. His blood pressure must have jumped a notch.

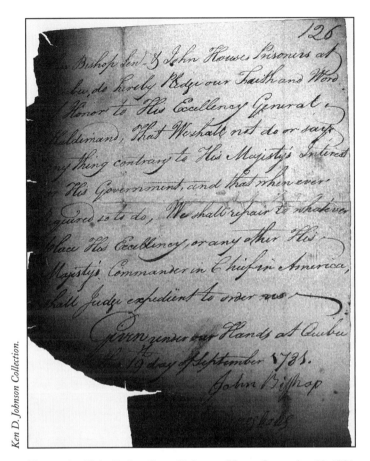

Ken D. Johnson Collection.

The parole of John Bishop Sr. and Johannes House, September 19, 1781. Canadian records indicate that Bishop was taken from Otter Creek in 1778 and House from Tryon County in 1779. They pledged to "not do or say anything contrary to His Majesty's Interest or His Government."

Then, to scrape at his sensitivities, Colonel Paine and two other Charlotte County luminaries requested an immediate supply of ammunition for their militia because they had found it necessary during a recent alarm to apply to Chittenden for a supply and had promised him repayment. They stressed the obvious importance of keeping the militia in their exposed part of the state amply supplied so that patrols could be kept out to determine enemy intentions and added the news that "the Treacherous" Dunham had escaped confinement and was at large.

The long-awaited prisoner exchange with Vermont got underway on August 7 when Major Jonas Fay met Sherwood and Smyth on board the *Royal George* offshore the Loyal Blockhouse. Fay had thirty-four British prisoners cached on the east side of the lake. He was quick to complain about the condition of the rebel prisoners. Sherwood was equally quick to retort, as he was no fool and had made a careful search of the rebels to be exchanged and found letters sewn into coat linings exposing loyalists in Albany and Schenectady, despite a solemn oath taken by each man that he would "neither say or Do anything prejudicial to His Majesty's Government." He reported to Mathews the next day that, when Major Zadock Wright of Peters's Corps was released, he displayed the "incipid enthusiasm of a Shuffling Quaker" and refused the exchange. Fay had brought no news about the reunion with Britain and Sherwood wrote that Vermonters wanted "Two strings to their bow."

Five days into their march, Captain Caldwell's force was closing on Monbackers. On August 8, Lieutenant Robert Nelles, 6NID, was reconnoitering when he fell in with a rebel patrol and took two prisoners who claimed that an attack was anticipated. The raiders were now forty miles from a small post called Lackawaxen, at the junction of the river of that name with the Delaware on the border of Ulster County and Pennsylvania. The fort was located in a cut worn through the mountains by the river and anyone passing was only ninety yards from the pickets. Caldwell thought there was a good chance to surprise the garrison and proposed an attack, but the Indians were unwilling to risk alarming the country.

The remarkable Mohawk region drama enacted by John Service of the Royal Yorkers' 2nd Battalion came to an end. It will be recalled that Major Ross had sent John on a dangerous mission in May. He had been a rebel captured in arms during Sir John's October 1780 raid, which, considering the nature of the mission, explains his selection. His instructions were to return south, surrender as a deserter, gain the authorities' confidence, collect specific intelligence and return to Carleton Island. Accordingly, he surrendered and, when examined by Governor Clinton and "a committee of the executive council," provided a bogus account of Carleton Island's defences and was fully accepted. He re-entered the valley, perhaps as a new Levy, and, over two months, visited every fort (except one), noting details of their strength. As a final ruse, he was furloughed to New Jersey and then came back to the island with six young recruits and word that the inhabitants were secreting provisions in expectation of a visit by Sir John. Service was sent to lower Quebec for a further debriefing with a strong recommendation for a reward and was given a twenty-dollar gratuity by the governor.[4]

On August 6, a Quebec City court martial tried two men of the 84th. A rebel prisoner had given them a route map to New England and papers to be delivered to the authorities there. One man was freed for lack of evidence; the second was judged guilty and sentenced to be "hung by the neck 'till he is dead, and hung in Chains, to deter others." There was no forgiveness for desertion to the enemy.

Major Edward Jessup warned the governor about "Mr. Allen and the Green Mountain boys." They were "acting a Double part to Amuse government and Secure themselves in Peacable possession of their Country." There was nothing new about this contribution; however, Jessup further offered that, if the governor wanted Ethan Allen brought to Canada with his papers, he would go with a small party who knew the country and bring him in. He apologized for interfering, but knew Allen and his followers and could not help but

Watercolour by Henry Rudyerd, 1788. (Library and Archives Canada, CO40330.)

Oswegatchie, the nearest of the Upper Posts. A staging area for the movement of supplies up the St. Lawrence and a post from where a great many scouts and raids were organized.

share his thoughts. Jessup's thoughtful and useful services were earning him the governor's warm regard.

The war party that had taken Jacob Zimmerman arrived at Oswegatchie about August 12. The trip had been harrowing, as blood oozed constantly from his throat wound and he often felt faint and ready to drop. Every time his captors saw fresh blood on his clothes, they halted and made him spit. Each time, he passed their crude test and the march resumed. Unable to swallow solid food, the Indians fed him roasted cornmeal gruel and plastered his wound with medicinal plants to prevent infection. He was unable to raise his arm because of his swollen neck and had to be carried across many streams. The Indians were fully aware that his value increased as they drew nearer to home base, as the reward for a captive was greater than a scalp. Everyone was relieved when the post came in sight. Men came out to greet the party and Zimmerman recognized Tories from the Valley. They asked him what was left to eat in the Mohawk and he told them truthfully that much of the grain was destroyed, but those with extra shared with those in need. He praised Willett as an active and good officer, then asked to have the ball removed from his neck. Apologetically, they told him that nothing could be done without the Indians' permission, but fortunately, they did consent and he was taken to the post surgeon. When the man cut out the ball, he stated that Jacob had been very close to dying.

On August 9, General John Stark arrived at Albany to take command of the Northern Department. In a report to Washington, he advised that during a visit with Chittenden, he had been promised assistance to repel the common foe. He believed the offer genuine, as before he arrived at Bennington, McKinstry had warned the Vermonters of a British incursion and, in only a few hours, 150 men rode to his assistance. Of his terrorizing of Howard, nothing was said.

When Stark arrived at Saratoga, he found there were no MA Levies and only ninety men in the garrison, so he returned to Albany to collect the second-wave Levies. He wrote to complain of the great difficulty in finding an express and asked for a permanent arrangement to be made. And, there was not a single drop of rum in the department and he noted, the men out scouting the woods "deserved a little grog." In a second letter, he mentioned the jailing for debt of a Massachusetts soldier who was on special duty at the Continental armoury. He blustered that the arrest was an attempt to prove the superior force of civil government over the military and that the city was full of the disaffected. The jailing was a Tory plot to cripple the army in the face of its pressing

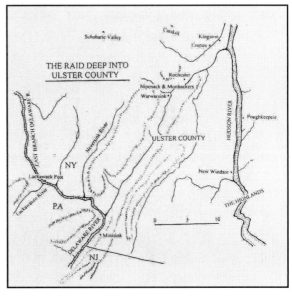

Gavin K. Watt, 2008.

The Raid Deep into Ulster County.

needs for men and the enormous public expense to raise them. The letter was a jumble of angst and distrust that seemed to say more about Stark's state of mind than any inherent threat in the incident.

That day, Governor Clinton warned Albany County's two brigadiers: "the present critical situation of the Northern & Western Frontiers renders it necessary that the militia … be held in the most perfect Readiness." Their regimental commanders were to update their classes and form them according to law, so, if only a part of the militia was wanted, they could "be drawn out with Care & Expedition."

He wrote to Willett advising that he had told Washington in the strongest terms of the dangers to the frontiers once the Continentals were removed and, in consequence, the retention of the 2NY at Albany had been approved until the MA Levies arrived. He requested a report on the number of new Levies and what Willett's expectations were for additional men. He also wanted an accounting of the "old" Levies, listing desertions; deficiencies in numbers supplied by each militia regiment and a return of the three-years' men.

In reaction to the assault on Schuyler, the Albany commission brought in Dr. Smyth's bailsman on suspicion of corresponding with Canada and being privy to the attack. His house was searched, as was the home of a woman said to have housed Meyers. Two men from the Nistageune Road who were suspected of assisting Meyers were examined. The escaped traitor, Holtham Dunham, had been run to earth and taken back to Saratoga and put in close confinement.[5]

On August 9, Haldimand advised Sir John that another prisoner exchange would shortly take place. Brigadier-General Maclean had been directed to have the rebel women and children being held in and about Montreal ready to depart in a minute's warning. Johnson was to provide a list of the old and infirm men who wished to return home. They would be required to formally attest to never "in any Respect … oppose the King & His Government." Anyone whose residence was far from Lake Champlain was to be held back.

Walter Butler wrote to Mathews about the Rangers' new 10th company and made some telling comments concerning Benjamin Pawling, the corps' senior subaltern. Although a good man, he did not think him proper to command a company. "He at all times does his duty with cheerfulness … but there is a certain something in many men that they can't in a length of time acquire what others will obtain in a few months … I could wish we had a few more Officers who were acquainted with the Service. They would be of use in a young Corps. Those are my private sentiments, and I can declare no motive, but the good of the Service induces me to mention them."

Aboard the *Royal George* off Dutchman's Point, Master and Commander William Chambers, the commodore on the lake, concluded an extremely important accord with Major Jonas Fay. Hostilities were to cease forthwith and Vermont would not remove any abandoned guns from Ticonderoga. The republic was out of the war and the first real step to return it to the British fold had been achieved.

Haldimand had earlier advised London of his concerns that his highest-ranking officer was the colonel of the Anhalt Zerbst regiment. As he had so little confidence in his German troops, he requested a British officer of senior rank to take command in Canada and, on August 11, Germain sent word that Major-General Alured Clarke, the proprietary colonel of the 31st Regiment, would sail for Canada.

Caldwell's raiders "ghosted" past Lackawaxen fort at ten o'clock on the night of August 11 and were at Warwarsink early next morning. As the region was in traditional Delaware territory, Caldwell expected their war captains to guide the raid, but as soon as the force entered the settlement, they faded away, which might have proven disastrous if the Rangers and Senecas had not been self-reliant. Warwarsink had six strong forts and several fortified stone houses. The Senecas recklessly attacked the first fort and had three men killed and two wounded, so Caldwell urged them to concentrate on houses, mills, and barns where plunder would be found. Two mills and thirty large storehouses were destroyed and, when defenders in one storehouse refused to surrender, they were burned alive. Ironically, when Caldwell wanted to move on, the Senecas balked, as they were glutted with booty. Robert Lottridge, 6NID's Lower Senecas captain, persuaded a number to join the Rangers and the party marched to Nipenack, burned two mills, many houses, and much grain, then continued on to Monbackers.

By happenstance, Colonel John Cantine of Ulster's 3rd Regiment was at Monbackers that morning. The day before, townfolk had heard firing and seen smoke from several fires rising above Warwarsink, so Cantine sent a warning to Albert Pawling, colonel of the local Levies. He in turn sent orders to his juniors to turn out and prepared himself for the field. Pawling's brother Levi asked for help from a nearby 1UCM major who put together some men and set off for Monbackers.

Caldwell's men overran the settlement, destroyed houses and storehouses and killed an Ulster militiaman. An Oneida serving with the Senecas was mortally wounded, but there were no injuries to the Rangers. As Esopus was just twenty-five miles away, Caldwell had hoped for some useful intelligence, but he only found a couple of newspapers.

About 4:00 p.m., Levi Pawling received an express from Albert advising that the enemy was retreating. Cantine was in pursuit, but had insufficient men to attack. Levi was asked to appeal to Colonel Snyder to send more men from 1UCM. About 8:00 p.m., Levi received a second note from Albert saying he expected the enemy to retreat via Lackawaxen, but his and Cantine's forces were too small to interfere. Albert's request for help to Colonel Elvingdorph, 4UCM, mentioned that an enemy deserter said there were nearly four hundred raiders, two had been killed and five wounded, one mortally. Elvingdorph had difficulty collecting men and was only able to join Albert as the moon began to rise. The night was dark and rainy and the men were reluctant to go on. Snyder was even tardier and came with only ten men who were equally timorous. Levi reported, "Such deadness of military spirit I never saw before."

On a more positive note, Clinton later wrote that the Levies at Monbackers had taken "to the houses and defended them with Spirit and … saved the greater part of the Settlement," which may very well have been true.

Working with Natives was often difficult. They had their own agenda and rarely shared it with their European allies. A large number of horses and cattle had been taken, but, for some reason, the Senecas killed the beeves and left the Rangers with only a handful of horses to subsist on. When the Delawares rejoined, they claimed to be closely followed, so Caldwell sent Hare on ahead and hung back to observe, but no pursuit appeared. Catching up with Hare, he heard that a serjeant and eleven men had unwittingly followed some Indians who had decided to disperse. Separation was a common hazard of wilderness warfare and Caldwell could only hope his men would find their way.

When news of Warwarsink reached Schoharie, the ever-nervous Vrooman fretted that the enemy would come northwards and attack his district. He appealed to his brigadier who sent men from 2ACM and 4ACM and some Oneidas.[6]

There was more trouble in Ulster County. Lieutenant-Colonel Jansen, 4UCM, wrote of his problems in recruiting new Levies. He was ordered to raise thirty men from the regiment's seven companies, but four were exempt, having earlier provided twenty men, and the other three could not be expected to raise that many. As Willett indicated, other regiments faced similar difficulties.

On August 11, a 5ACM lieutenant reported to the commission that while he was away from home the night before, armed men came to abduct him and greatly abused his wife. He was permitted to lead a search and next day brought in a fellow whom he said had assisted Bettys. The man was committed and disappeared from the records.

On August 13, the commission read a note from McKinstry about Moses Harris Jr., whom he had sent down from Saratoga under guard on suspicion of buying provisions to supply parties from Canada. That Harris was so soon released raises the question of whether this was a charade to hide his role as a double agent. The commission next probed an odd event. An Indian woman living in the city with a Tory soldier's wife reported finding a murdered man in the woods. Mayor Ten Broeck investigated, but no corpse was found and an abduction plot was suspected. Under examination, she confessed that a party of men told her to go to the mayor with the story. The Tory's wife and another woman were questioned, but denied knowledge of the affair.

When Clinton congratulated Schuyler on his escape, the governor advised that a third attempt to seize his person was at present organizing in New York City. His informant named the culprits, all of whom were well known to him. In answer to Schuyler's appeals, he had sent forty beeves to help feed the Levies and urged the state agent "to pay particular attention to the Troops on the Frontiers."

Clinton then wrote to Brinton Paine advising that he had directed Gansevoort to deliver a suitable proportion of the powder that had been held in Albany for militia use since last spring. Paine must have wondered why his appeals had not been answered earlier. The commissary of military stores had been ordered to immediately forward a quantity of lead to Albany and the brigadier would send a supply to Paine when it arrived. In a third letter, he informed his brother James that he had word that the Berkshire and Hampshire Counties men were "embodied & ready to move … they may be early expected in Albany."

On August 14, a 150-man force from Carleton Island, which included several Mohawks, struck Fort Timmerman in the Palatine District. The post was the fortified home of Serjeant Conrad Timmerman and was placed to guard the mills on Timmerman Creek with a garrison of Levies and Oneidas. The men were away at Fort Nellis and Colonel Peter Bellinger's mother and several Oneida women vigorously fired through the loopholes, including Senagena, wife of Honyere Doxtator, the famous Oriska war captain who had plundered Molly Brant's home in 1777. As Senagena had openly strutted about in Molly's finery, her death or capture would have been sweet revenge for the Mohawks; however, the women's defence was stout and the raiders turned away. After burning some houses, barns, and wheat stacks, the raiders were driven off by Willett at the head of a body of Levies and 2TCM militia. The Indians killed their looted livestock and easily outdistanced the pursuit. A local man suggested a detour to gain the enemy's front, but the attempt failed. Two nights and three days later, the tired, hungry rebels turned back.

Also on August 14, the commission jailed Bettys's brother-in-law in Albany. He was considered "notoriously disaffected to the American Cause" and to have known that Bettys was in the country without giving proper warning.

The commission examined the alleged traitors Dunham and Grant on August 16. They were charged with holding a secret meeting in the woods with the Tory David Jones and some others from Canada and attempting to desert when discovered. Their depositions were sent to the governor and they were recommitted for later examination.[7]

An illness had spread to both sides of the Niagara River. Powell reported the 8th had forty sick with only its Light Company fit for active service. He commented that the regiment had been so long at this frontier posting, "that they are really worn out with the unremitting fatigue." The Rangers were worse off with sixty ill. To this grim news, he added another complaint about Major Rogers. Captain Peter Hare's nephew had been in lower Quebec on his way to join his uncle as a Volunteer, but was detained by Rogers. Butler hoped the governor would order the lad's release. In a second letter, the brigadier sent Butler's recommendations for the 10th company's officers and Benjamin Pawling was suggested as captain, the very man whom Walter had declared unfit scant days before. If Pawling were promoted, there would be four first lieutenant vacancies in the corps, an untenable situation, as that rank often commanded the company in the absence of the captain. Joseph Ferris was senior second lieutenant, but, because of his recent arrest, Butler was unsure of his suitability. If all vacancies were settled within the corps, there would be six second lieutenant vacancies, but only three suitable Volunteers with sufficient service. John Hare, the subject of the recruiting wrangle with Rogers, was a fourth, but too young to be a viable contender.

―――――――――――――

―――――――――――――

Stark wrote to Washington from Albany on August 15 to complain about the removal of his paymaster, his general lack of staff officers, and his personal low level of pay. In a crossover letter of the same day, Washington instructed Stark to consider Howard's Tories as prisoners of war and to have them closely confined to prevent escape. This likely disappointed the vindictive New Hampshireman; however, the C-in-C had been more sympathetic about two other issues. Orders had been issued to pay for express couriers and to forward a supply of rum.

In a strange overlap of authority, Stark instructed Willett's captain, Abraham Livingston, who had been deranged from his brother James's 1st Canadian Regiment, to march his company of new Levies from Albany to Schoharie and take post on the most convenient and advantageous piece of ground. He was to keep scouts out to prevent surprise and, if militia joined him, he was to give them the same provisions as his own men. His troops must not commit "wanton mischief ... upon the persons or property of the inhabitants."

Brigadier-General James Clinton sent the very welcome and long-awaited news to his brother that one hundred Massachusetts troops had arrived in Albany that morning. They were immediately assigned to Schoharie and would march with Livingston and some local militia. John Stark had formally replaced James as department commander. James would soon leave Albany with the few remaining Continentals.

Stark wrote Governor Clinton about a request made by several reputable New York gentlemen for permission to send a prisoner exchange flag to Canada. In a second letter, he waxed poetic about the idea of exchanging George Smyth's son Terrence for a long-serving captain of Warner's regiment, who was a proven soldier firmly attached to the cause, contrasting him to Smyth, who was simply a youth with no power to do any essential service to the King. A few days later, Clinton agreed to the proposal, providing the captain was a citizen of the state.

At Fort Herkimer, harsh military justice was meted out when two deserters from Willett's were taken there for execution. The men were sat upon their coffins and a serjeant and six privates fired at one and a corporal and six at the other. After the parties fired, two musketmen advanced and delivered a *coup de grace*, firing balls into their heads.

The last of the 2NY left Albany by bateaux on August 20, the same day that Willett sent Captain Elihu Marshall to that city to forward all new Levies as fast as they arrived.

A New York Congressman advised Governor Clinton that everything was in place to establish Vermont as a state in the union within the limits of its first claim, but the politics had become too entwined with people on New Hampshire's side of the Connecticut River to proceed.

Colonel Weissenfels's report to the governor on August 21 about his success in raising his regiment in mid-state was at such odds with Willett's experiences that one must conclude men were avoiding service on the northern frontiers. Although he began recruiting after Willett, his men were the best "with respect to the Exterior appearance ... that have been raised in this State," and their arms were "in good order and all Bayonetted." What a strange contrast!

During re-examination, Willett's traitorous officers, Dunham and Grant, betrayed a man who had fed David Jones's party while it was hiding in the woods waiting to abduct Major McKinstry. Then, the commission examined a lieutenant about a young fellow who feared being jailed after returning from running away with Bettys. The lad was forgiven on condition that he told everything he knew.[8]

On August 17, a very irate Meyers arrived at Fort St. John's. While outraged by Bettys's thoughtless actions, he had been embarrassed to learn that pieces of Schuyler's silver plate had been looted during the attack and dutifully reported the theft to St. Leger, who for the moment ignored the issue, as the failures were occupying his mind. Later attempts to recover the items were fruitless and there seems to be no record of the culprits being punished.

Captain Sherwood sent Corporal David Crowfoot, QLR, to Arlington to question a loyalist sympathizer about the attitudes of everyday Vermonters toward a possible reunion. Before Crowfoot's return, Sherwood discovered that his arch-rebel uncle, Seth Sherwood, who had been captured the year before, had been allowed the freedom of Montreal by Sir John and was being recommended for exchange. This was a keen embarrassment, for as Smyth said later, "The Indulgence given Prisoners to return home on Parole ha[s] been detrimental to our Friends" and Seth had "not a little Contributed to the afflictions of many worthy inhabitants." While this prickly issue was hanging over him, Captain Pritchard returned with four prisoners from a patrol of the Connecticut Valley and reported that Jacob Bayley was taking an interest in an arrangement with Britain. Perhaps Crowfoot had also returned, as Sherwood reported that one-fifth of Vermonters favoured reunion in order to gain trade access to Canada, another fifth were true loyalists and the rest rabid rebels. While these odds were quite unfavourable, he urged a continuation of the talks for their short-term benefits.

Canada's chronic shortage of trained artillerists had led Haldimand to form a composite company of Hanau Artillery in 1780, using Burgoyne's remnants and some Hanau infantrymen who had been left behind with Carleton as sick, but the problem persisted and gave rise to further expedients. On August 20, Ross reported he had begun teaching his soldiers at Fort Haldimand "the exercise of the great guns."

The grueling work on Fort Haldimand's ditch and bomb-proofs was complete. "Half a Portfire was used every day … for blowing the Ditch [and] holes for the charges were drilled by hand at a rate of about twelve inches per hour."

In a letter to Mathews, Meyers revealed his anger over the treatment of his serjeant,

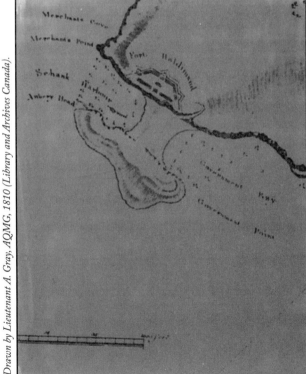

Drawn by Lieutenant A. Gray, AQMG, 1810 (Library and Archives Canada).

Fort Haldimand, Carleton Island. Situated on a high cliff on the southwest corner of the island, the fort commanded the oddly shaped peninsula below where the storehouses and naval works were located, as well as the two small, but reasonably sheltered harbours.

Joseph Smith. Butler's lieutenant, Andrew Bradt, had met Smith and his recruits on the frontier and seized the men. When Smith objected, Bradt put him under arrest, which raised an unholy kerfuffle that lasted for weeks. Bradt wrote an arrogant explanation to HQ; he knew of no Captain Meyers and, in any event, what right did he have to recruit in Butler's Rangers's territory? As Meyers had great influence at HQ, Smith was released.

A major prisoner exchange occurred on August 22. Vermont's prisoners were sent to Pointe au Fer and Sherwood took his to Skenesborough, where he heard that Howard's abduction party had been exchanged, but without Howard and the two Regulars. There was a joyful reunion between Smyth, his wife and son Thomas; then Joseph Fay and Ira Allen arrived and wanted to take Sherwood and Smyth to Pawlet for a conference, but the doctor had just taken a tumble getting out of a bateau, so the meeting was instead held at Skenesborough. The loyalists were told that an election had confirmed Chittenden's leadership and the republic had extended its western boundary to the Hudson River, supposedly to the inhabitants' satisfaction, which put Skenesborough in safe territory for the exchanges. Most important, to expedite reunion, Ira proposed that Haldimand send a proclamation outlining the terms offered.

When back in Canada, the colourful Dr. Smyth reacted to the failed abduction attempts by criticizing his agents, writing that three of them haunted him "like Hamlet's Ghost; the first is a simpleton, the second … a knave, & the last … unfit for anything Except weaving Lindsey Woolsey." On a different topic, he condemned the many layabouts at Fort St John's: "There is a Number of Active & Able Body'd Beef devourers here, eating up the King's Royal Bounty … I wish his Excellency would permit anyone he pleased to adopt such bodily Exercise for those Gulp and Swallow Gentry as may keep them from Scorbutic and Indolent habits." Smyth and others were scandalized by Bettys, as the scoundrel's wife Abigail and their children were still at Ballstown and Joseph was refusing to give up "his Desdemona" even when confined to barracks by St. Leger. He was unable to utter a single syllable of intelligence and "Hums & Ha's as his own Vindication." When his girl was finally found, Smyth thought it pointless to send her home, as Bettys would take off after her and, in the process, "ruin many of His Majesty's loyal subjects."

On August 23, Ross reported the return of Crawford and Arden. They had destroyed one of the Valley's few remaining mills and several houses fifteen miles below Herkimer. Although the militia outnumbered their troops and Indians three to one, they claimed to have driven them into their forts. Although his Mississaugas had done well, Crawford reported that the Akwesasnes and other Canada Indians had not, but gave no explanation. It is likely that this was the raid that skirmished with the Oneida women and was so vigorously pursued by Willett.

Stark wrote to Governor Clinton on August 22 about a large quantity of grain in the Schoharie Valley that the owners were willing to sell on favourable terms. As crop destruction was an enemy strategy, he wanted to remove it to Schenectady. This would require a large number of teams and wagons and he requested a press warrant. So, less than a year after Sir John's huge raid had ravaged the Valley, and despite raiding throughout the crop cycle, the farmers had managed to raise grain well beyond their needs. As Stark said, this fertile valley was indeed a primary target. A few days later, the governor acknowledged the grain's value and vulnerability; but, as it belonged to individuals, he could not grant impress warrants. If it was purchased for the Army, he could grant a warrant for as many teams as necessary. If the owners refused to sell, he hoped Stark would persuade them to have the grain sent to the state's interior so as not to tempt the enemy.

Stark requested Washington's approval to retain three Continental armourers; two for Willett and one for Saratoga, noting, "when a gun is out of repair (though perhaps a trifle would put it in order), a soldier is rendered unfit for duty; and it is very improbable that any man can be found with the militia capable of performing that service." He closed by advising that two hundred MA Levies had arrived and seventy more were expected tomorrow.

_____

_____

On August 24, Major-General William Heath advised Stark that Washington had assigned him to command all troops and posts north of Peekskill. He asked that all reports and troop returns be sent to him as well as "the earliest and best intelligence of any motions or designs of the enemy." News was to be sent immediately as well as periodic advice about supplies. Rum was being sent to Claverack, one-tenth of which was intended for Stark's northern department, the balance for West Point, even though his eighteen Regular regiments below were without "a single drop."

Heath was born in 1737 at Roxbury, Massachussetts. He was active in the militia prior to the Revolution and the colonel of Boston's artillery in 1770. An accomplished writer, he published essays on military discipline and skill at arms and was also a politician in the provincial general assembly and a committeeman and congressman in 1774 and 1775. His Revolutionary War military experience began as a brigadier at Concord. He organized and trained troops at Cambridge and, in June 1775, was appointed a Continental major-general. Dedicated and talented, Heath was an ideal replacement for Washington at this critical juncture.

Stark wrote to a long-time friend reporting that his new department was the most disagreeable he had ever served in; there was no forage, no horses to transport provisions and no camp kettles. If these problems were not remedied, he predicted the troops would go home.

Major General William Heath (1737–1814). Heath replaced Washington in command of the north when the latter moved against Cornwallis in Virginia.

In another shocking comparison to Willett's and Stark's troubles, Weissenfels commented in a weekly return: "I have drawn ammunition, Flints, Canteens, Camp Kettels, axes, for the men, and spontoons for the officers, and are so far, in perfect readiness to march."[9]

By August 25, only part of the rum had arrived at Fort Rensselaer; however, as the tardy arrival of the new Levies was of far greater concern, Willett philosophized, "half a loaf is better than no bread" and added, "[T]his is the most convenient frontier ... for the enemy to approach, either from Niagara, Buck's [Carleton] island, or Oswegotchie (from all which places we have been visited this campaign); nor would it be a new thing for the enemy to move this way through Lake Champlain." He continued:

> [T]he immediately painful part of my business here, is the daily applications that are made to me by numbers of suffering inhabitants ([who are] among the best of whigs, being always ready to turn out in case of alarm), for guards to enable them to save their grain, a considerable quantity of which is still in their fields, in great danger of being spoiled — and it is not in my power to help them. Very considerable quantities of grain may be had in these parts for public use ... But, in order to procure grain for the public use, the quarter master should furnish us with bags; indeed, this appears to me to be an object of such importance that it ought to spur the quarter master to make large exertions ... At present I have a large guard at Turlock [New Dorlach,] with a number of hands at work endeavouring to secure as much of the harvest of that place as possible. This makes my force, which was otherwise very scant, bare indeed.
>
> The whole force now at this place, including ten who are sick, is 51; and most of the posts above and below are entirely destitute. I am not a little desirous of removing a part of the stores from Fort Herkimer, agreeably to an order I received some time ago from ... General Washington, which the want of strength has hitherto prevented.

I can not therefore help thinking it strange that 100 men, beside the two companies stationed at Schoharie, and which is the full proportion for that place, should be sent for and detained there, while this more exposed and extensive country remains so exceedingly bare. Of this I imagined Governor Clinton was well apprised. By his letter to me of the 13th inst., immediately after the disaster at [Warwarsink,] in which, after continuing to guard against a possible appearance of that party of the enemy in this quarter, he lets me know that he had ordered reinforcement for Schoharie from General Ganesvoort's brigade of militia, until the entire departure of the enemy should be ascertained. Yet after this, his reinforcing that place with part of the quota of troops intended for this river, which is more exposed than that place, is what I could not have expected ... I shall be much obliged to you to mention the difficulties I labor under to him ... that I may likewise write upon this business as soon as possible, as much may depend upon it. I am in danger of having a famine of paper. I shall therefore be much obliged to you, sir, to order some this way.

Willett was far too agitated to wait for Stark to react and wrote to the governor on August 25, stating his opinion that Schoharie was well off for troops compared to the Mohawk, which was "constantly infested with parties of the enemy, more I am well assured than any other frontier we have." He pled with Clinton not to alter the troop placements that had been so carefully developed with Brigadier-General Clinton: "[T]his mode of deranging our dispositions put me not a little out of my guesses." Clinton replied a few days later, assuring Willett that he would continue to be solely responsible for the arrangement of the troops in the Mohawk and Schoharie.

On Sunday, August 26, raiders captured two 2TCM men named Pickard at Bowman's Creek and a party of Mohawks attacked Cobleskill, allegedly assisted by local Tories from New Rynbeck. Although many people were at church in Schoharie, others sheltered in Fort Duboise and a few men were at their homes enjoying a quiet Sabbath. Two brothers were visiting a friend's rebuilt house when the raiders struck, killing one man, taking two prisoners, and setting the buildings afire. In the afternoon, the war party moved toward the fort, burning a farm, and capturing five men. Most warriors gave the fort a wide berth by hugging the riverbank out of musket range, but an eager pair ran to set fire to two barns near the pickets and were driven off. The raiders spent the night at a farm and burned it next morning. Retracing their steps, they discovered the twelve-man garrison had razed the fort overnight. When Willett reported this event a few days later, he complained that no request had come to him for aid, although he had men close by in New Dorlach. The loss of the fort and houses forced the abandonment of Cobleskill and the inhabitants took shelter in Schoharie's Lower Fort until the war's end.

On August 27, Stark wrote that a spy who had been aboard the enemy's shipping at Crown Point said the British intended to "make a push upon this place, to alarm the New-Hampshire Grants by way of Castleton, and gather all the tories in this quarter, who are to be met by Gen Howe's army near this place." All of this was patent nonsense, but it served its purpose of keeping Stark in a froth. He acted on another piece of misinformation that day when he congratulated Governor Chittenden in such freely offered sentiments that his personal opinions on the Grants' issue became crystal clear: "[N]o intervening circumstance on the grand political system of America, since the war began, has given me more real pleasure than to hear of your acceptance into the Union — a measure that I ... always did think, was highly compatible with the real interest of the country." He claimed that the citizenry of Albany were "fully convinced that to be separate will be more for the interest of both States than to be united ... nothing can wound a generous mind more than the mortifying thought of making a large country miserable; and the people of your State, by their utter detestation of the management of New-York, must have been wretched under their government."

Commissioner Dr. Samuel Stringer, the object of Bettys's aborted abduction, sent the governor information that a large packet of dispatches from Canada had been brought into Albany on August 26 and, if Clinton knew the route used by the enemy's expresses, the packet might be seized.

Vermont became belligerent with New York's officials in the recently annexed regions. Chittenden chastised Colonel Yates of the Hoosic and Schaghticooke District for "exercising the authority of New York within the western Claims of this State by draughting and forcibly compelling sundry Inhabitants on the East side of the Hudson" into the service of New York. People in the Western Union needed "no authority but what is derived from this State." Yates was to "desist exercising your power over any of those People [or], Sir, the Consequences will be inconvenient." He replied: "You are wrong in supposing that I act as Colonel in despite [of] and to create disregard to the Jurisdiction claimed by Vermont. As a Colonel of Militia in the State of New York, you can be no Stranger that I have taken an Oath of Office, for the faithful discharge of that Trust … long before the time it was even in contemplation that Vermont would assume a Jurisdictional Claim westward from the Grants to Hudsons River. Do you conceive Sir I can dispense with this oath because a few

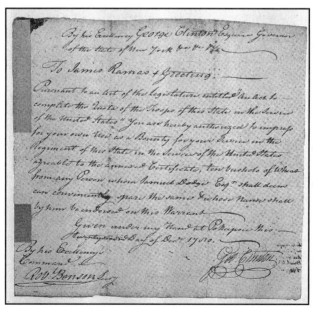

A plate from James A. Roberts, comptroller. (New York in the Revolution as Colony and State 2 vols. Albany: State of New York, 1904.)

Press Warrant. This 1780 example of Governor Clinton's warrant for pressing wheat is an example of the official format employed.

discontented Whigs (supported by the Tories of our District) have joined in Union with you[?]" As if in answer to this letter, the following was posted: "Vermont State Elections: Notice is hereby given to the Inhabitants of the Town of [Schaghticooke] to meet … in Tomhanock on tuesday the fourth day of September next at 9 o'clock … in order to elect a Governor, Lieutenant governor and twelve counsellors and two representatives for the year ensuing, also a State treasurer by order of the Selectmen." The challenges to New York's authority could not have been clearer; all were grist to Haldimand's mill.

On August 28, Willett told Stark that a supply of beef was coming at last. In his typically supportive way, he wrote of Tryon's militia: "No people can be more alert and ready to turn out on news of the approach of an enemy than the militia of this quarter … none deserve more attention."

The governor wrote Stark on August 28 to approve sending a Flag to Canada to arrange an exchange of New York citizens and enclosed a list of Tories to be offered. Those who were citizens of New York were to make written application to him before they would be released. In justice, prisoners held the longest should be selected first. As to collecting grain, he sent an impress warrant for forty wagons for ten days. The disaffected were to be "the objects of the impress, which I am sure will not be disagreeable to you."

On August 29, Stark advised Heath that he was unable to make regular departmental returns for lack of paper: "I desired Colonel Willet to send me a return twenty days ago, but it has not come yet [as] He has nothing to make it on." Stark promised to send all the intelligence that came his way and began with the disagreeable news of the Cobleskill raid: "[T]hey bent their course towards Cherry Valley, where it is very probable we shall hear of some other instances of their unparalleled clemency." There were some prisoners of war in his area, "very improper persons to be at large," some under bond to appear on certain days, others moving freely about. He had ordered them seized and wanted to trade them for some Massachusetts and Warner's men who had been taken while on frontier service.

That day, a past member of the state Legislature wrote to Governor Clinton that the New City was convulsed over Vermont's claim to control the region. The "usurper's civil and military officers" had been sworn in and were men "of little or no property," often supported by Tories. They had coerced people into compliance and several affrays had resulted, which without his interference would have had fatal results. Similar to Yates, Lieutenant-Colonel Henry Van Rensselaer, 6ACM, had received a letter forbidding him to exercise his commission over the people in the Western Union. Neutrality had been urged on both sides until Congress made its decision, but this would scarcely have impressed Clinton who needed all Yorkers to firmly support the state.

The U.S. Hospital Department noted its inability to comply with Willett's request for an additional physician and surgeon. The Albany commission released a few more of the less offensive Dorlach Tories on £100 bail each. The next day, the commission advised the governor that several Tory women, who were "the cause of infinite Mischief," had asked to join their husbands in Canada, which he approved some days later. Reverend Stuart had requested to be exchanged for Colonel Gordon, 12ACM, and to go to Skenesborough where the British vessels were to lie till September 20.

At month's end, Stark again wrote to Governor Clinton about the intolerable state of affairs in his department. He had no forage and the QM could do nothing. He could not conduct business without a forage depot, or at very least, an immediate supply. Over the past month, only swamp hay had been delivered and none of that for the last ten days. As to the almost daily requests he received for provisions, he could send none, as the QM had no money to hire teams and no authority to press them.

On August 31, Willett seized goods from Tryon's disaffected: 27 cattle on the hoof; 460 pounds of dressed mutton; 926 pounds of beef; 23 barrels of flour, and 43 pounds of rough tallow. He also sent five bateaux upriver to Fort Herkimer to bring down stores and a marching detachment to deliver ten prime beeves. The bateauxmen were told to bring back only two barrels of powder, as "our conveniency" was not as good as Herkimer's. Major Villefranche was ordered to send down Moodie with a 6-pdr and apparatus and as much shot, musket ball, and QMG stores as the boats could carry, leaving enough to complete the works and equip the garrison. If the work at Herkimer could be left to a competent officer, the major was to come down to oversee the construction of a blockhouse at Fort Plain, bringing with him all the artificers not needed above.

Willett had taken twelve men each from Whelp's, Skinner's, and Van Rensselaer's to create a ranging company and put them under Lieutenant Randolph Wilson, the former British Regular. They, and half of Harrison's were to be gun escort and the other half augmented the boat guard.

Accordingly, Villefranche passed command of Fort Herkimer to Peter Van Rensselaer, a former 1CDN captain who posted his guards as follows: at Fort Dayton, a subaltern, serjeant, two corporals, and twelve privates; at Herkimer, a subaltern, two serjeants, two corporals, and eighteen men; at the Little Falls' mills, a serjeant, corporal, and six men and a corporal and three privates each at two houses and a storehouse.

Five White Creek men wrote to Governor Clinton about Vermont's "Unjust Claim" advising that only a few of the 150 freeholders had been told about a public meeting held by Vermont's supporters, which resulted in representatives being elected by a mere eight men. At a second meeting, there was a general turnout and the vote was 2:1 in favour of New York, but the pro-Vermont representatives went ahead and chose civil and military officers and declared their intention to levy taxes and raise men. A great many outraged citizens had "Entered into a Combination both in this District and Black Creek to oppose it with their Lives & fortunes." They feared the British might come and they had no ammunition, nor were there "field officers worth Notice in the County, nor Guards, excepting a few from Vermont." Although there were 200 troops at Saratoga, the enemy could easily penetrate between Skenesborough and Fort Edward and scouts were needed in that quarter as there were at least ten enemy scouting parties lurking about. Raising men for New York would be difficult, as the classes were intermixed with Vermonters and the republic was raising men for its own service. Clinton was in a vice; he was waging a war against the British in north, south and west while his erstwhile co-revolutionists tore at his guts.[10]

On September 2, Haldimand received news that must have given him much satisfaction; Vermont had extended its western boundaries into parts of New York not previously in contention. The republic's Assembly was to meet on October 1 and he advised Sir Henry Clinton that he would influence their thinking by sending a large force to take post at Crown Point for the season. He would also send strong parties to strike in the Mohawk and on the Pennsylvania frontier, which he hoped would be of assistance.

Haldimand wrote Sir John to inquire if changes were required to the list of officers the baronet had recommended for appointment in 2KRR, as he planned to issue commissions forthwith. Perhaps adjustments were requested, as over two months passed before "forthwith" took place, weeks after Ross and his officers returned from a most stresssful adventure on the Mohawk.

Haldimand wrote Powell regarding Meyers's complaint about Bradt's seizing of his recruits. He made it clear where his sympathies lay, describing Meyers as "a most active and zealous partisan" and hinted that the hotheaded Bradt should have known better, pointing out that he had just recently been promoted to a company. Powell was to prevent anything of the kind happening in the future and tell Butler to advise Bradt of "the impropriety of his conduct." Clearly, it was unwise to upset the governor's favourites.

On September 1, one of the most brutal, malicious raids of the season struck the home of Captain William Dietz, a 3ACM company commander. His farm was in the Switzkill Valley at the south end of Beaver Dam close to the Hellebergh, two settlements notorious as nests of Tories. The Dietz and Weidman families were the only Whigs in Beaver Dam, but whether Dietz was an overzealous rebel is unknown. Yet, his capture was clearly not a random act. A mixed war party threaded its way through the Schoharie settlements and, just before nightfall, fell on the Dietz place and slaughtered William's wife Maria; their four children; William's father, old

Johannes; his mother Maria; and a Scots servant girl in an orgy of blood. Only the captain and a young hired hand, John Brice, were spared. Cruelly, both were tied to a tree to watch the murders. Brice's unsuspecting brother, Robert, returned from Weidman's gristmill while the atrocity was underway and blundered into a sentinel. When taken to the scene, he found Brice and the captain surrounded by mangled corpses. After setting the farm afire and tying the booty to the family's horses, the war party set off.

Private George Borthwick was stationed at Weidman's stockade near Beaver Dam and gave the alarm when he saw smoke rising, then went with a party that discovered the massacre. A second detachment set out on pursuit that night, but soon gave up, fearing the enemy was 300 strong. When word arrived at Schoharie, Vrooman sent a body of troops that included some locals who accurately predicted the enemy's route. Two days later, they overtook the war party and opened fire, hitting a raider and recovering the horses and plunder, but not the captives.

Lieutenant John Jost Dietz, a family relative, led a burial party from the Lower Fort. Hogs had gorged on the bodies, making the scene of slaughter much worse than these war-hardened men had grown to expect. The corpses were borne to the Dutch Reform Church and interred in a common grave. William Dietz suffered an agonizing march to Niagara with the horror of the murders flashing behind his eyes. Soon after arriving at the fort, he fell into deep depression and died, although the Brice youngsters survived the war and came home. The vicious nature of the Dietz massacre was a feature in the *Pennsylvania Gazette*:

> On Saturday last, a party of his *Most Sacred Majesty's* savage subjects, went to the house of one … Fietz, at Beaverdam … where they performed a most extraordinary piece of bravery, that should be told to the world: They murdered the old man and his wife, both of them at least 70 years of age; his son's wife and five children … his son, being a captain of militia, was kept alive to be an eye and ear witness to the horrid cruelties perpetrated on his dear relatives … The conduct [of] this affair, confirms an account I have heard [from] released

captives brought from Montreal, that Colonel Clause should damn his copper-coloured brethren, and say, he wished they would kill old men, women and children, and not trouble him with them.

On September 1 Willett's strength return listed sixteen captains and two of which had no company assignments. Seven companies had over fifty rank and file; five over thirty. Duboise's company, which drew primarily from the Tory informer, Van Veghten's regiment, had only twenty-one. All told, the Levies had enrolled 749 rank and file, but on the day of the return only 503 were fit for duty. Fifty-three were deserters, a truly upsetting number considering the regiment had existed for just three and a half months, but it was not noted whether these deserters included men who were selected by their class and failed to report, or whether they had reported for duty, then run off. Of the 749 men, 434 (58 percent), had enlisted for the nine-months' service, and 315 (42 percent) for four months. Seventy-three nine-months' men were from Tryon and seventy-five from Charlotte and Dutchess. Of the four-months' men, thirty-eight were from Tryon and thirty-two from Rensselaerwyck.

Willett wrote that "green" officers posed a problem in the preparation of returns, which seems very odd, as the majority had seen extensive service. In the hopes that an officer of reputation and experience would produce regularity, he had appointed Andrew Finck as brigade major. His recruiters had enlisted forty-seven three-years' men; twenty-two had been mustered, five were on furlough, and only nineteen had actually joined, a tiny gain scarcely worth noting. Since then, some had enlisted out of the Levies, perhaps for artillery or Continental service. Half were with Wright at Saratoga and the others scattered from Schoharie to Fort Herkimer. He recommended they be concentrated into a single company at one location and then pointed out that McKinstry had 500–600 NY and MA Levies at Saratoga and all of New England at hand in time of need, so the three-years' men should be clothed and sent to Tryon. He recommended holding supplies of uniforms to encourage new recruits to enlist from the short-term Levies. This would be a great incentive with the approach of cold weather, as most were poorly clothed.[11]

On the first of September, General Stark complained to the president of Congress that it was three years since he had received cash from the public as pay, except $2000 he had in 1779 at Rhode Island. He had been advanced some paper currency, the remainder of which the hardened patriot chose not "to convert to hard cash on principle." That same day, Clinton wrote to Stark about an exchange of women and children and forwarded his letter to Haldimand to be sent by a Flag for this purpose. Reverend Stuart and his "Negro man" were to be exchanged and, in their place, two captains received from Canada.

On September 3, Hugh Mitchell, a Schenectady luminary who had formerly been on the town's committee of safety and conspiracy commission, wrote Clinton about the Tory families seeking exchange. He saw no harm in releasing women without families, but mothers with sons near military age would pose a risk, as they would soon join their fathers and add to Canada's military strength. He proposed a *quid pro quo* scheme — mothers and sons to be exchanged for like family members held prisoner in Canada. As an aside, he opined that local Tories were to blame for the Dietz murders and recommended razing Beaver Dam. Clinton replied two days later, accepting Mitchell's ideas for the exchange of Tory women and their teenaged sons. He expressed grief over the Dietz tragedy and registered surprise that the disaffected had not been removed from the frontiers as had been ordered in the spring.

General Heath had not received Stark's earlier report about conditions in the Northern Department when he complained about the continued lack of reports. He also sent the welcome news that Henry Laurens, the ambassador to the French, had returned home with "a large sum of specie, and a quantity of clothing of all sorts." Ironically, the United States was once again sustained by the French monarchy, while fighting to throw off the British version.

At Saratoga, McKinstry wrote to recommend Lieutenant Abraham Fonda to command the company of three-years' men originally intended for the disgraced Holtam Dunham. Like Willett, he believed clothing would improve the chances of attracting more recruits and might even induce a number of MA Levies to enlist.

On September 4, the governor was advised by the corporation and militia field officers of Albany that they had obtained positive information that a force from Canada was coming to burn and loot the city. It was critical that troops be stationed to protect public buildings, stores, and magazines, as the city's guards and night watches were insufficient and the militia ill-disciplined and inadequate. Stark had been approached to transfer a company from Saratoga, but said this required an order from Heath, so Clinton was asked to obtain the C-in-C's approval for one or two companies of sixty men each.

In the meantime, Stark took action and appointed Captain Elihu Marshall, WL, to be responsible for city security. Marshall had a great deal of experience as a brigade major in 1778 and 1779 and as commander of the Main Guard at Morristown in 1780 and later that year as inspector of brigade. He was to continue to execute his responsibilities to victual and forward new Levies to the regiment and would, until further orders, keep back twenty Levies in the city as a constant guard. During his "leisure time," he was to inspect public works, as Stark believed there was "every reason to think that the most flagrant abuses are committed, and the most wanton dissipation of public property." He was authorized to impress teams and Stark noted that the wagons of doubtful characters were ideal for public purposes. Any MA Levies who arrived without arms were to be supplied and Marshall was to obtain receipts from their officers, making them accountable to the commissary of military stores.

Willett's morale received a major boost in the first days of September when Major Aaron Rowley of Colonel Elisha Porter's Massachusetts's regiment arrived at Fort Rensselaer with four companies of three-months' Levies under Captains Clark, Heacock, and two others. The balance of Porter's was led to Stillwater by Major Barnabus Sears and added significantly to Stark's troops in the Saratoga region.

By September 5, word of the Dietz atrocity was across the Northern Department. Willett wrote to Captain Aaron Hale at Schoharie that, although he was pleased that the raiders had been forced to yield their plunder, "to omit pursuing them when an opportunity offers and ... to be so cautious as not to attack them, is omitting to do all in our power to chastise a set of wretches." His letter clarified a rather surprising, little-known rule of frontier service: "The plundering that the party has retaken is their lawfull prise[;] they have a right to sell it and divide the proceeds among them. Or should plunder have been taken from distressed Whigs they have an opportunity of evidencing their sympathy by restoring it to its former owner if they cho[o]se."

That day at Fort Rensselaer, Captains Abraham Livingston and Anthony Whelp and two lieutenants, one of the Artillery, the other of Willett's, were arrested for their "ungentlemen and unofficer like manner" and "disturbing the Garrison at an unseasonable time of night[,] insulting the Commandant and refusing to obey his orders." They were confined to quarters within the pickets of the fort. All the men giving evidence against these Yorkers were MA Levies, Lieutenant Holdridge of Clarke's Company and a corporal and two privates of Marsh's. While this had partisan overtones, Willett was far more concerned about discipline and the lack of respect shown to his person was intolerable. A few days later, the offenders further disgraced themselves by breaking arrest and leaving confinement. Having already lost three captains, two to combat, and a fourth to treason, a less confident commander may have experienced a twinge of self-doubt.

The Schenectady artillery detachment training and doing duty at Fort Plain buried victims of yet another raid and chased the Tory, Barney Kane, a Canajoharie district blacksmith who evaded them and joined 2KRR on August 25.

———————————————

On September 5, Haldimand wrote to Powell about a proposal Guy Johnson had privately made to the home government to roll his tiny unit of Foresters into a 10th company of Butler's Rangers. Perhaps Johnson saw himself sliding over top of Butler as the corps' commandant, which would raise his profile, and perhaps his pay. Haldimand was again affronted to be bypassed and dryly noted that, if the Foresters' function in 6NID was valid, they should remain a separate corps. He instructed Powell to describe the roles they played in the field and in quarters, so that he might better judge the case. As it was, he could not see the least justification to expand their numbers and in future their activities were to be reported in 6NID returns. Further, he trusted the Foresters provided their own clothing similar to the Rangers who had the same pay. Johnson had opened himself to yet more scrutiny and, in the process, added to his burden of paperwork.

Haldimand mentioned a rebel newspaper report about Willett's victory over Brant and conjectured that Caldwell was meant; however, the reference was to Docksteder and the victory was more in the writing than in reality. In a separate letter, he wrote of Butler's wish to have Benjamin Pawling command the 10th Company:

> I imagine the Colonel's recommendation in this and some former occasions have been in compliance with the request of the Corps and to testify his inclination to oblige them. Otherwise, I am persuaded he would rather seek to introduce a few officers of longer standing and more experience to a rank on which the discipline and conduct of a young Corps so immediately depend. Nothing but my wishes to gratify Colonel Butler, who was so sanguine for the preferment of his nephew, could have induced me to promote Mr Bradt so early in the rank of Captain independent to the prejudice it must be to the Corps in particular to advance so rapidly young officers who have neither time nor opportunities to acquire a sufficient knowledge of their profession. I consider it to be a great injustice to the Army, and may be productive of bad consequences in cases where important commands may devolve to the eldest officer.

He approved filling up the Rangers' first lieutenantcies by seniority, "as they may have time in that rank to learn their profession," and, supported advancing Ferris, "as … it would be unjust to stop it merely because he had been in arrest when the 9th Coy was mustered." Serjeant William Smyth, 47th, had been appointed the Rangers' adjutant and would join the corps in its clothing. "He is the son of an Officer who bears a very respectable character and is himself a decent, modest man. He has served in this country the last and present war, some part of the time in the light infantry."

Mathews advised Butler about items sent for the farmers settled across the river. The governor, whose strong interest in agriculture has been noted, approved supplying them with a blacksmith paid at the King's rate and charged to the engineers. Western Quebec's first loyalist settlement was progressing.

Sir John wrote to Haldimand about replacing Humphrey Arden, who had resigned as 2KRR's adjutant and returned to the 34th. Isaac Mann, the Loyal Volunteers' former adjutant, had in some manner "blotted his copybook" and Johnson and Leake had withdrawn their recommendations, so Ross suggested Serjeant William Fraser of the 34th.

Although the advice from Britain that there would be no attack on Canada had still not arrived, as has been noted, the lateness of the season persuaded Haldimand to "let loose the hounds." He informed Ross he would renew the previous years' strategy of raiding the frontiers and destroying supplies. Expeditions would go to Crown Point, Pennsylvania, and the Mohawk. Detachments from Carleton Island were to join in the latter effort and Robertson would visit Ross to consult about employing troops from Oswegatchie. The three movements were to take place about October 1, "in order to make the consternation general and divide the force of the enemy." As Sir John's movement had been exposed the year before, Ross was to keep the plans profoundly secret. He was to send one or two vessels to Niagara to transport troops and set up a provisions' depot at Oswego guarded by a Carleton Island detachment. It was left to him to decide about commanding the Mohawk expedition, as the governor thought the venture "too inconsiderable" and needed no further proof of his zeal and activity.[12]

September 6 proved another fateful day in the Mohawk Valley when the newly raised company of Rangers left Fort Plain to march to Fort Dayton under the command of acting Captain Solomon Woodworth, who hailed from Mayfield north of Johnstown. He had distinguished himself for great daring and persistence in the spring of 1780 by fending off an attack on the Sacandaga blockhouse and then tracking and killing the raiders. Later that year, he served as a lieutenant in Harper's Levies and the following March in 3TCM.

Woodworth had drawn men from Gros's, Putman's, and Heacock's companies at Fort Plain, while Lieutenant Randolph Wilson had his platoon at Fort Herkimer. Orderly Serjeant John Dunham was also from Mayfield and had lost members of his family in a raid. For its first operation, the forty-nine-man company united at Fort Plain. They were to march over the Adirondacks to the St. Lawrence and take prisoners from one of the British posts.

The rangers arrived at Fort Dayton just before evening and, before sun-up of September 7, they set out with six Oneida scouts in support. A witness recalled they made a fine appearance and were in great spirits, yet the company lacked its full complement of officers and Wilson was relatively unproven on the frontier. As the men had been drawn from six companies, many were strangers to one another. Presumably, the long trek north would serve as a "shake-out."

The rangers were unaware that a seventy-four-man war party of Cayugas and Onondagas was camped nearby, having arrived in the area just the day before. In command was the Onondaga sachem, Tiahogwando, assisted by Lieutenant Joseph Clement, 6NID. When the war party heard three cannon discharges at daybreak, a young warrior was sent to reconnoitre.

The rangers were marching up West Canada Creek when at mid-morning they came across freshly made tracks in the damp grass. The Oneidas asserted these were made by a much larger party and, to prove it, had Woodworth march the company alongside them for some time. As the new tracks were only half as big, the Oneidas recommended going back for more men, but Woodworth declined. Jacob Shew, Woodworth's close friend from Mayfield, suggested sending a runner to bring on

Putman's Company from Dayton, but Solomon would brook no delay and delivered a taunting lecture, giving the men a chance to turn back if they were afraid. No one rose to the bait. As he was so eager to get on, he refused to halt for breakfast, but did promise to proceed with caution. Dividing the company into three columns, Woodworth led the centre with Wilson abreast on the left and Dunham on the right. A van was sent on ahead and the Oneidas formed a rearguard.

Meanwhile, the young Indian scout spied the rangers following yesterday's tracks and ran to tell the war party of their strength and composition. Taking up their arms and packs, the warriors hid a short distance from the camp to await developments.

After a march of about three miles, the company came to the abandoned campfires. The hidden Natives heard some rangers exclaim, "Damn them, they are gone off." The Indians knew the rangers would soon follow their new tracks and, with their customary stealth and discipline, moved along the trail to find favourable ground. Coming across a number of fallen trees, they set up a semi-circular ambush and dispatched a body of warriors to get in behind the rangers and cut off their retreat.

The company came along the trail in tactical columns. When the van was as close as a pistol shot, a signal triggered the ambush. More than half the rangers were cut down at the first fire and the survivors went to tree. Woodworth and his friend Shew hid behind a large sugar maple, but Shew felt strangely vulnerable sharing the same shelter, so, after reloading, he sprinted to another maple about six yards off. Three balls struck him as he ran — one through his clothes, another through his queue, and a third grazed his ankle. No sooner was he behind the second tree than Woodworth arrived and abruptly took a ball in the chest. Dropping his rifle, he slumped forward gasping, "O Lord! I'm a dead man." Blood pumped from the wound, slathering over Shew, and he died without another word.

In the rearguard, Oneida Moses Yokum was severely wounded in the hip and his "brothers" rushed him away. Their worst fears had come to pass and they had no desire to fall into the hands of their vengeful brothers.

When the ambushers broke cover to take prisoners, David Putman joined Shew at the tree just as he sprang up and tore off down the back trail. After a distance, Shew tripped over a root, fell flat on his face, and his knapsack stuffed with food and a prized brass camp kettle flew away. Scrambling to his feet, he heard a whoop from down the back trail, which, from an earlier captivity, he knew signalled that a prisoner was close at hand. Spotting a fallen tree tangled in some bushes, he crawled under and was just out of sight when Putman come crashing down the trail. He whispered to him, but was not heard. Putman was no sooner gone than three Indians pounded along in pursuit, running so close that Shew could have tripped them with his gun barrel. A second group followed, again just missing treading on him. Soon after, he heard an exultant yell. He learned later that Putman and another men had been taken, and that Wilson and several others that preceded him had been captured, although the lieutenant was not amongst the men taken to Canada. Perhaps he was recognized and disposed of as a deserter. Two men, one of whom had had his firelock shot out of his hands in the opening fire, escaped the Native cordon and made it back to Fort Dayton and reported that Shew was dead, as both had seen his blood-soaked body fall. Shew lay hidden for several hours listening to the elated Natives scalping and gathering up a rich haul of booty. When he was sure they were gone, he emerged from his hide and took an indirect route back to Dayton where he was greeted as a dead man risen.

Lieutenant Clement interrogated the captured rangers and discovered their mission had been to take prisoners at Carleton Island or Oswegatchie and immediately sent a runner to warn Ross and Onasadego, an Onondaga chief, to warn Colonel Johnson at Niagara and deliver news of the party's success. His tally of enemy losses was three officers (probably including Dunham) and nineteen privates killed and eight privates taken, which is oddly at variance with rebel records. Two Onondagas had been severely wounded.

Henry Glen's report to Governor Clinton said the rangers had been forty strong and that two officers and twenty-six privates were killed and only twelve escaped. Marshall wrote to Stark saying that, of two officers and thirty-nine men, only fifteen escaped, eleven were killed, and the balance taken. For sheer fantasy, nothing matched John Schermerhorn's account. He said the rangers were furiously attacked by about 400 Indians who killed the whole company except him and six others who were captured and the Indians said they had about 100 warriors killed. Whatever the exact numbers, for Willett and Tryon County, the ambush was a disaster. The colonel had now lost his fourth company commander in a single campaign. Of course, it was a signal victory for the Six Nations and the department, the kind that would live in tales around their campfires for decades.

Word of the disaster reached Willett at Fort Rensselaer on September 8 and he immediately rode to Dayton. Next day, two survivors and five Oneidas led Putman's and Severinus Klock's company, 4TCM, to scour the ambush site for victims. They found twenty-five mutilated and dismembered corpses, which to Europeans was an ugly and unsettling feature of Native warfare. Of necessity, the bodies were tumbled into a large pit. When Willett returned to Fort Rensselaer, he sent a message to Marshall in Albany saying the enemy was in strength at the Flatts and he was to immediately march all the new Levies on hand with as many rations as possible.[13]

John Taylor, a zealous Albany Whig, wrote to Clinton about the enemy's plan to burn the city. Citizens were preparing to carry off their valuables and the city militia had been under arms for three nights without food or rest. Bettys and Meyers were lurking in the vicinity, yet the officers refused to remove the disaffected. He added that Stark had taken Dunham and Grant to trial in Saratoga.

There was a prisoner exchange at Skenesborough on September 7 with William Marsh acting as Crown commissioner. Moses Harris Sr. had come from Canada and, when examined by the Albany commissioners, he eagerly babbled away. His rambling story — a tale with overtones of double espionage — was sent to the governor. "[O]ld Capt. Harris" had been taken by Carleton in 1780. While in Quebec, he met Hugh Mosier from Hicks Hollow in Dutchess County, who had met up with a Butler's Rangers' lieutenant in Coxsackie last spring. Mosier and ten others went with the Ranger to Fort Niagara, but he argued with the officer and was sent to Montreal, ending up in the same house as Harris and told him that Meyers had enlisted most of the Hicks Hollow men. Harris spent a night at Fort St. John's with a former Kingsbury man named Bremon whose Tory soldier son visited with twelve Indians and spoke of plans to attack Castleton, Albany, and Schenectady. During the voyage to Skenesborough, a sailor said there "would be an expedition on foot very quick." To make this tale more credible, Harris's operator had allowed him to "leak" Quebec's garrison strengths and tell of the severe crop damages and the high cost of food.

When Major-General Heath heard the news of Albany's immediate peril, he recognized that Stark had insufficient troops to respond and ordered Major Samuel Logan to march two companies of Weissenfels's Levies to the city. They were to be under Stark's orders while in the northern district, but not to be removed from Albany, unless some extreme event should warrant it. Nor was Stark to move any troops from Saratoga to cover the city.

That same day, the governor wrote to Mayor Ten Broeck and Brigadier-General Ganesvoort, enclosing Heath's letter to Stark for forwarding. The letter was most reassuring, as it told Stark to ask for more assistance if Logan's two companies proved inadequate. The mayor and brigadier were counselled to include attributions for all their intelligence, so that he could assess its credibility and he closed with the exciting advice that the British army in Virginia had been completely blocked up by the French fleet.

On September 7, Powell reported the news that a raid had killed a man and burned twenty houses at Canajoharie. Another had killed a man near Fort Pitt, but rebel vigilance had prevented the taking of a prisoner. He thought other parties in that quarter might have more success. Spies had been found in the Natives' new villages near Niagara, raising great fears for the safety of the corn crops.

Mathews advised John Butler that Walter had been denied permission to travel to lower Canada to settle the regiment's accounts. William Smyth, the Rangers' new adjutant, would be allowed subsistence on the regiment's rolls from August 18 and his commission would bear that date so that he could be fitted out and prevented from commencing his new role in difficulty. Mathews hoped Smyth would be found useful and deserving, as he had "an excellent character and deports himself with modesty and propriety." Such repeated songs of praise might have worried a less trusting man. Crossing in the mail was Powell's report that the Rangers' 10th company was complete, mustered, and "a good one." Captain Caldwell's missing men had been heard from and were expected to rejoin soon.

On September 10, troops of the Hanau Jäger Corps boarded twenty-four bateaux at Sillery near Quebec City to travel to Sorel to await further orders. The concentration for the Lake Champlain venture was underway.[14]

On August 9, Marshall advised Stark that he had held back the only available express horse in case intelligence came from the west. Aware of the general's disdain for Albanians, he found fertile ground when he wrote, "The same slothfulness, too prevalent here, has prevented me from sending the rum and other stores this day." Only two hogsheads had arrived, hardly enough for the whole district! Stark wrote Heath to request ammunition, as his department did not have enough to fight even a single action.

That day, the governor sent an explanation to General Heath about the troop dispositions in northern New York. He noted the recent augmentation to Willett's by new Levies from Albany and Tryon, but was unaware of the regiment's current strength or how many MA Levies had arrived. The frontiers of Albany and Tryon Counties were closer to the enemy's posts and more exposed than Ulster's or Orange's and reinforcements were difficult to collect in emergencies, so, if additional forces could be spared, they would be of real service. Although Stark had general command in the north, Clinton had great confidence in Willett and asked Heath to continue him in command and allow him to organize his troops as he saw fit. There was no more news about Ten Broeck's concerns for Albany's safety and he suspected there was more sense in guarding the city's approaches than in keeping a large internal guard, as a small detachment and the city militia should intimidate arsonists.

Stark opened a correspondence with Haldimand about prisoner exchanges, noting that his British prisoners were as eager to be released as the Americans held in Quebec. He recommended the terms decided upon by Washington and Sir Henry Clinton and requested the numbers and ranks of men held in Canada and a suggestion for an exchange site.

Schenectady commissioner Hugh Mitchell wrote Stark about the Tory wives who wanted to join their husbands in Canada, noting Clinton's approval in principle. Shifting to military matters, he explained that before Stark arrived to take the northern command, he had asked Willett to leave a twelve-to-fifteen-man detachment in town to assist the commissary department and apprehend Tories. Willett had promised to comply, but had probably been unable because of pressing business and lack of men. He renewed the request, stating that the town's militia would not answer the purpose.

The governor advised McKinstry that clothing could not be given to the three-years' men before they were mustered, particularly when those already in service could hardly be supplied. In any event, the time for raising three-years' regiments had expired and he could not extend it. Those recruited would be mustered and officers appointed to their command. When the legislature sat on October 1, he would ask for approval to protect the three-years' service and extend the time for completion. He also approved Lieutenant Abraham A. Fonda to replace Captain Dunham.

On September 10, Captain Marshall reported to Stark that he had just returned from up the Mohawk where he found 9,000 cartridges in inventory and the artillerymen making even more from some three tons of loose powder. In view of Stark's anguished appeal for ammunition for Saratoga, the general must have been astounded by this news.

Due to the chronic scarcity of writing paper, Schuyler wrote Heath under a flying seal, passing the letter through the governor. He had heard rumours that the British were offended at being duped by the Vermonters and intended to attack them, but he was unpersuaded. There was intelligence that a brigade of troops was assembling at Fort St. John's and naval preparations were being made there and he thought their real goal was to come down the lakes to either the Mohawk or Hudson. Alarmingly, he advised that two couriers from Canada had passed through Albany, and although discovered, had managed to escape.[15]

On September 10, word was afoot in Poughkeepsie that 120 men, women, and children taken on the frontiers of New York had arrived for exchange. That same day, Mitchell sent the governor his suggested list of Tory women and children.

Next day, Stark acknowledged Heath's dispatches of September 3 and 7, commenting that the C-in-C's former letters must have been lost. He again explained the reasons for not making returns and reported the strength of the Saratoga garrison: 2 majors, 7 captains, 11 lieutenants, 27 serjeants, and 360 rank and file, but there were only ten cartridges per man and none in stores. (Had Marshall's advice about Willett's surfeit gone astray?) He complained about the lack of a deputy adjutant general. His disdain for Albanians was palpable:

> Albany is a very dangerous place to put men into; for, were I to send a company there, I should expect they would have one half of them in jail, and the other half to keep them there … Albany is able to turn out 500 men for its own defence; and a larger body than fifty can not well come against them; and, if ten virtuous citizens are not able to defend themselves against the assaults of one sculking rascal of a tory or an Indian, it is very remarkable, as they have got forts and walls to cover them, almost beyond the power of human force to shake. But, my dear sir, if you have men to spare from

the army, I expect they will be soon wanted at this place, as I have this day almost certain intelligence of there being a large detachment of the enemy at St. Johns, destined for this quarter.

He apologized for his inability to send an express, as his only resort was a trusty foot soldier with his provisions on his back. If the enemy approached, he would need to send expresses to Hampshire and Berkshire Counties, Albany, and the Grants, but he had no horses or riders. Nor was there money to pay expenses, nor forage.

Governor Clinton advised Willett that he had appointed Captain Job Wright to take charge of the three-years' recruits at Saratoga. Wright had advised the recruits would be of little value, as they were mostly unarmed and, as there was nothing to give them, he thought it would accomplish little to send them to the Mohawk. Clinton agreed that a great many more might accept the three-year term if he could clothe those already enlisted, but that was beyond his power.

At the encouragement of General Schuyler, a party of forty-four Oneidas, Tuscaroras, and Kahnawakes had gone to Philadelphia to appeal to Congress for clothing and provisions for the coming winter. The Indians received official apologies for the previous sparse support of their physical needs and, on September 11, they were heartened to hear that the union, in recognition of their allegiance to the cause and loss of their communities, would soon avenge their injuries. "The faithfull Oneidas, Tuscaroras and Cachnawagas will then experience the good consequences of their Attachment to us and yourselves and your Children, when they share in the blessings of our prosperity."

DQMG Henry Glen wrote from Schenectady to advise the governor that:

> [A]ll the force they can Spare in Canada was on the 25th ulto. at St. Johns in order to Come across Lake Champlain & its said they mean the Vermounters & that Sir John is in the Expedition & to have a Sepreate Command. I am a little of opinion Sir John will Come

something near this Quarter. As there is a possibility of Albany or this Town being their object, both valuable, & an Eye sore to them. I could wish we had some more Assistance; if Sir John should come as low down as in this Neighberhood.... [I]f my friend Colo. Willett was to move his force as Low as Johnstown & [Caughnawaga] might be of Service to this place & Gen Starck cutt of[f] his communication to send a Sufficient force Across from Saratoga.... Our town [is] at last Clossd. [picketed] & in pretty Good condition[,] could I But Convert some of the Inhabitants[.] I should be happy to learn wether we cant without delay have some assistance from the Easthren Brethren or from General Heath?

Although the British had agreed to cease hostilities with Vermont during the talks, the Canada Indians had their own agenda. A

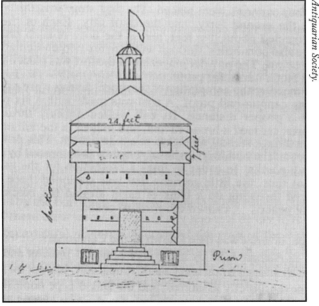

Robert B. Roberts, New York's Forts in the Revolution. *Cranbury, NJ: Associated University Presses, 1980, ex U.S. Revolution Papers, American Antiquarian Society.*

Fort Plain Blockhouse. Built of logs about two feet in diameter, covering a large redoubt. Note the prison that was primarily used to control the disaffected.

detachment of Vermont troops posted at Peacham sent four men to guard the Caspian Lake blockhouse on the Hazen Road. The men were enjoying a careless moment when two were struck dead and the other two carried off to Canada. The results of this eruption on the progress of the negotiations are unknown.

A war party attacked the Chyle settlement in the German Flatts district. Captain Henry Eckler and his eldest son were harvesting when they saw smoke pouring out of their buildings. After telling his son to hide in the woods, Eckler ran into the house and was confronted by Quahyocko Brant Johnson's shout, "Captain Eckler, do you surrender?" He bellowed, "No, I do not!" and bolted out the back door for the woods. Just as the Indians opened fire, his foot caught and he took a tumble. The Natives whooped in triumph, but he quickly regained his feet, vaulted a high brush fence at the edge of the field, and hid under a fallen elm. The raiders searched the top and hollow of the tree, but could not find him. Allegedly Quahyocko said, "The long-legged Dutchman is too many for us; he used to get away from me but now he has got way from both of us." An older daughter stooking wheat had been scalped and Eckler's wife, Christiana, and the younger children were taken. She was warned that the party would be moving rapidly and the youngsters must keep tight together and, on no account, cry; however, at a halt to drink from a stream, a four-year-old began weeping that she wanted to go home. Before her mother could react, a warrior grabbed the child's hair, scalped her and threw her lifeless body into a tree. Christiana now had her second warning. They arrived at Niagara after a long, rugged trek, but were held for a few more days before being given to the garrison, cold and hungry, but otherwise whole.

While Quahyocko's party attacked the Ecklers, a band of Mississaugas captured two men at the ruins of Stanwix and ran them off to Canada.[16]

On September 15, Heath thanked Governor Clinton for his detailed explanation of frontier dispositions and assured him that Willett, "of whom I have the highest opinion," would not be interfered with. Although he had sent two of Weissenfels's companies to Albany, he had heard since that Ballstown was a more likely approach route for an attempt on the city and thought it may be wise to send one there. Clinton was given the option of where to locate the balance of Weissenfels', except for a company already committed to Orange County. If he thought the northern frontier was inadequately covered and Weissenfels' would be more serviceable there, the regiment would be sent north. If he thought two companies were sufficient, but that it would be better to station one at Ballstown, he should do so. "I request your opinion freely in these matters ... My wish is to afford the frontiers the best protection in my power, compatible with ... the effectual security of the ... Highlands."

Major Logan of Weissenfels' wrote Stark from Albany to report that when he marched a company of his detachment out of the city in response to the general's instructions there was such an uproar that he had to call a halt. The city's officers reminded him that his orders were not to leave unless in an emergency and gave him a copy of the mayor's letter emphasizing this, which Logan forwarded to Stark.

A letter from Schuyler repeated Heath's orders and enclosed an appeal from the mayor and councilmen. Although Stark must have resented this interference, he was very circumspect in his reply, noting that he had only ordered half of Logan's detachment to Saratoga and "[t]he remainder, with the united efforts and spirited exertions of the citizens of Albany, must ... be competent to its defence ... You must be sensible, sir, that no party of more than fifty or sixty could get there undiscovered ... On the other hand, Albany may for a few days turn out 150 men for guards, every night [which] with the regular guards of troops which will be left, will be an infallible bar against any descent upon the city." Bitterly, he again displayed his disdain for Albanians saying that he had no hopes of their help and citing their fumbling response when the city's militia was called upon to aid Schoharie.

Several Tories, who had been permitted to live amongst the general populace, had been proven complicit in recent treasonous plots and Albany County's administration was finally moved to take action. Colonel Phillip P. Schuyler, 3ACM, rounded up 70–100 families of "the most notoriously disaffected" at Beaver Dams and adjacent hamlets and brought them to Albany for dispersal.

While at Stanwix in 1777, Willett had earned a reputation for disliking Frenchmen when he had Captain La Marquisie dismissed for incompetence, but there was no hint of any such prejudice in his letter of commendation for the émigré engineer who had been assigned to German Flatts. "Major Lewis Villefranche has had the direction of several works on these frontiers. In the execution of which he has paid the greatest attention, and that beside his having the ordering and directing of the fortifications at the German Flats he had the command of that important post for two months during which time he has conducted himself with propriety that merits my approbation." On September 17, Willett again set off to tour his command, riding to Fort Hunter, where he remained for the next day. Meanwhile, Dunham and Grant's trial began at Saratoga with MA Lieutenant-Colonel Barnabus Sears as president.

Also that day, Heath wrote Stark about repeated reports of the enemy making canoes and small bateaux at Fort St. John's and the arrival there of hardtack baked at Montreal. The large number of small craft raised speculation about British plans; perhaps they would attack the Connecticut River towns rather than Saratoga. Stark was to keep a sharp lookout and be ready to react. Heath had sent the balance of Weissenfels' to Albany to join Logan, which put 350 new troops in the district. "They are an exceedingly fine corps, and generally officered with old continental officers." Stark was to leave a company at Albany and post the rest as he saw fit. (It seemed he had prevailed over the whinging Albanians!) Several of Hazen's Canadiens had deserted when the regiment moved south and Stark was to send any that were caught to HQ.

On September 19, the Albany commissioners reported their examination of five exchanged prisoners, which confirmed information gleaned from other sources, that is, some 300 of Sir John's men had been seen crossing the St. Lawrence on their way to Fort St. John's, where they would be joined by whites and Natives from as far away as Niagara to attack either the Mohawk or Hudson River. Albany was an oft-mentioned target and the large quantity of hard tack baked at Montreal was confirmed. On this same day, Reverend James Stuart, parole in hand, with his wife and three young children left Schenectady for Skenesborough.

While Willett rode to Caughnawaga on his tour, Stark wrote to Heath in some alarm. He had received no replies to his several reports about the lack of resources — no musket ammunition, no horses, forage, or paper. Venting again, he disparagingly described the fears of "sacred" Albany.

In a second letter, he reported to Washington that some Tories and seven of Hazen's deserters had been seized and would be sent below. He was unimpressed that forty-seven enemy Indians were said to be coming to Saratoga to make a treaty "while their young men are cutting our throats." The officer carrying his dispatch had found fifty-five shells, twelve boxes of musket balls, a vise, and a pair of hand screws that the British had jettisoned in the river near Saratoga in 1777. There were rumours that some guns had also been sunk, but he had too few men to make a search.[17]

———————————

———————————

On September 13, Sir John sent the discharges of seven KRR privates convicted of mutiny in the Coteau-du-Lac affair to HQ. As their punishment was complete, they were being sent aboard the King's ships of war "to serve abroad at his pleasure." Considering the severity of their floggings, could they possibly have been of any value as ratings?

On September 14, Secret Service operative William Marsh reported that he, an officer, and sixteen soldiers had taken 177 men, women, and children to Skenesborough and had waited two days before exchanging twenty-three loyalist families who had been escorted by fifteen Vermont troops.

St. Leger wrote to Mathews stating his disgust with the endless bickering between Jessup and Rogers over recruits, suggesting that an "appeal to cold iron [shackles?] might make the provincial officers better bred to each other."

The Hanau Jägers arrived at Sorel and found new orders to proceed to Chambly. On departure, they left their invalids and baggage in the care of their sick QM captain.

On September 17, Sir John reported that two of Leake's men, who had been captured near the Hudson River, betrayed three Royal Yorkers he had sent to Johnstown and who had been fortunate in managing to escape. Haldimand observed, "As it is probable they have been intimidated by the Threats of the Rebels[.] You would do well to represent in the Strongest Terms to all Scouts the Dangerous

Consequences of Yielding to those Inquisitions, and how unnecessary it is to their Personal Safety, for whatever the Enemy may threaten, they will not venture to take their Lives, unless Dispatches are found upon them, which is always to be avoided."

Haldimand's instructions for the mounting of three major expeditions had been sent express up the St. Lawrence on September 7, but, because of contrary winds, did not reach Ross until September 20. Recognizing the urgency, he immediately forwarded them to Powell.

In the fawning phraseology of the time, the major's reply to the governor made it very clear he was eager for employment: "I am much honoured by Your Excellency wishing to give me a greater command. Thinking that my presence here will not be absolutely necessary for a time, I have, by Your Excellency's permission, taken the resolve of commanding this party, nor do I think any party too inconsiderable could I at any time execute Your Excellency's intentions, or be of any Service in commanding it."

Considering that Ross's battalion was quite young, his keenness to take the field invites some analysis, although he would, of course, also command veteran Regulars and Provincials and not simply rely upon his own men. 2KRR had the following troops at Fort Haldimand: 3 captains, 7 lieutenants, 3 ensigns, an adjutant and surgeon, 15 serjeants, 15 corporals, 18 drummers, and 169 privates. An additional 76 privates were unavailable, as they were serving as artificers in the fort, warehouses, and shipping yard. Of those who could be employed, several factors had contributed to their discipline and skill at arms: the professionalism of the adjutants seconded from the 34th; the experience of the thirty-plus men who had transferred from 1KRR; the presence in the garrison of two veteran companies (one of the 34th and Leake's) and, lastly, the battalion's frequent mounting of dangerous, long-range parties to the frontiers.

Ross advised that Lieutenant Anthony Wingrove, 34th, had returned from Niagara to report that the garrison was sickly and that Powell would be unable to put more than 150 men into the field. Consequently, he planned to take more men from Carleton Island. "[I]f the Mohawk River is in the same state that it was in a short time ago, the intended party may do as they please until a force is collected from about Albany to oppose

The schooners *Maria* and *Carleton* in action, 1776.

Detail from unattributed engraving. (Digitales Archiv Marburg document 29.)

them, but I am sorry to inform Your Excellency that this scout has [been] talked of in Canada, as I received accounts of it the same day [your] orders arrived here." In view of Sir John's experiences the year before, this was disquieting news, but Ross was unfazed and expected to be at the rendezvous on October 1 and to write again from there.

On September 22, John Butler sent a dispatch to HQ with several enclosures: first, a muster roll of his 10th company and the suggestion it should be known as the lieutenant-colonel's under the command of a captain-lieutenant; second, a request for a certificate confirming he had raised ten companies, which entitled his officers to half-pay; third, with amazingly little additional comment, Walter's request for a majority; fourth, a list of the farmers' needs on the Canadian side and his proposal that it would be better if responsibility for their settlement were given to Powell; and, fifth, a report from Detroit that Brant's advance party had defeated elements of George Rogers Clark's army, killing thirty-seven and taking sixty-four.

The Lake Champlain expedition continued to develop in lower Quebec. On September 22, the Jägers were at Fort St. John's, whence they were instructed to stage forward to Pointe au Fer. They were to take four weeks' provisions and be prepared to camp in the woods.

The next day, Pritchard was sent with a KR party to destroy the grain and forage of Vermont's most inveterate rebels. This deliberate default of the truce would demonstrate the far reach of the Crown. Commodore Chambers reported that the gunboats and tenders were ready and that he would station the schooner *Maria* and galley *Trumbull* half way between Isle aux Noix and Pointe au Fer. Days later, he reported sending the victuallers to join the other vessels at Pointe au Fer with provisions for 2,000 men for thirty days. The sloop *Lee*, which had been taken from the rebels in 1776 with the *Trumbull*, and the other vessels could handle 500 men with ease and the *Maria* and *Trumbull* could take 500 more. He suggested the stores would be handier to the troops if they were "depoted" at Crown Point rather than aboard the *Royal George*.

Unknown to the rebels, their expectation of Sir John's imminent descent on the frontier was put to rest when he was given permission to visit England where he hoped to resolve several issues, in particular to obtain an establishment for the KRR NY similar to that enjoyed by the RHE.

At Pointe au Fer, Lieutenant-Colonel von Kreutzbourg observed a rebel colonel sail past on his way to be exchanged for Dr. Smyth and reflected in his journal that, if the expedition was not already known, that fellow would soon break the news.

The governor sent Powell some alarming news. An audit had found severe irregularities in the accounts of Forsyth and Taylor, Niagara's Indian trade merchants, and Guy Johnson's presence was required in Montreal. Butler was to take command of 6NID in his absence. Guy's oft-cavalier management of expenses was coming home to roost, but weeks were to pass before this instruction arrived.

Captain Robertson reported on September 27 that he had sent an officer, two serjeants, two corporals, and twenty-six of his "most active" men to join Ross at Carleton Island. The next day, he sent off a third corporal with twenty-two Indians, probably local Oswegatchies and Akwesasnes.[18]

The governor's dispatches forwarded by Ross on September 20 did not arrive at Niagara till September 28. Powell was instructed to consult with Johnson and Butler about routes and numbers of troops. He was to equip and dispatch as many Rangers and Indians as possible to the Mohawk and Pennsylvania frontiers. The raids' strategic goals were to destroy grain and forage, cattle and mills, but to avoid killing women or children or any form of cruelty. And, there was one other critical objective — extirpate the rebel Oneidas! As these orders had taken three weeks to arrive, there was no time to waste and Powell promptly met with Johnson and Butler. On September 29, he wrote, "The Mohawk River has been so long the theatre of action for troops and Indians from this post and Carleton Island, very little field remains for further operations in that quarter, for the people have been so much accustomed to those incursions that they now secure what grain they raise in fortified houses where it would be imprudent to attack them." The two Provincials recommended assembling at Oswego and advancing to Onondaga Falls, or an island on the south side of Lake Oneida, where the boats could be left under guard. A party might be sent to destroy the mills at Canajoharie and rejoin the main body at Cobleskill, then proceed against Duanesborough, "a settlement which has not yet been molested." Any attempt to combine with the Crown Point force would be risky, but if it was necessary, the Sacandaga River route through Jessup's Patent should be used. Niagara's troops and Indians would embark on October 5 and possibly arrive at Oswego on October 8. All being well, the raid would be at Duanesborough by October 22. Powell had heard from Ross that he would command and, with the late season, it was left to him to make any alterations. Willett was expected to send out a party from German Flatts, so the force had been enlarged. Niagara would send: Lieutenant Thomas Coote and the surgeon, 2 serjeants and 33 privates of the 8th; Captain Walter Butler and 150 Rangers with 8 officers and 9 serjeants; and, Captain Gilbert Tice and 3 6NID subalterns to manage 200 warriors. Ross was expected to take 150 rank and file with officers and 50 Indians. Niagara would send a second party of Indians to Shamokin at the junction of the Susquehanna River's two branches.

On September 29, Ross reported the return of two trusty men he had sent to the Mohawk in early August. They had heard no intimation in the Valley that an attack would come from the west. The rebels had slightly increased their strength and Willett had 300 men at Fort Plain and about 400, including militia, at Stone Arabia and its environs. Ross commented, "Could I draw him out with his garrison, I shoud hope to give a good account of him. It will probably be no difficult matter to accomplish it as he turns out on all occasions." He said there were reports in Albany that 5,000 troops were about to descend from Canada and that no preparations were being made to oppose them. Perhaps his two "trusty" men had left before the MA Levies reinforced Stark or Logan's two companies arrived at Albany. Ross's report seemed to reek of over-confidence.

To encourage the Six Nations to support these new ventures, Guy Johnson gave presents to three significant men. A "Rich Brocade Waistcoat" to Sayenqueraghta, the Confederacy's principle War Captain; a "Scarlet Coat & Waist-coat" to an unnamed Cayuga chief and a "Ruffled Shirt & Feathers" to Christian, a loyal Oneida. Independent of the preparations for Ross's excursion, the colonel ordered Lieutenant Adam Crysler to proceed with a twenty-eight-man party of Oquagas to raid the Schoharie Valley.

On September's last day, Powell reported that Corporal Jacob Buskirk and Private Mathew Van Dyke of Butler's, and Grenadier John Dingwall, 1KRR, had arrived the night before with ten recruits. Dingwall had fallen behind during the Schoharie raid the previous fall and worked his way to Lunenburg where he met up with a BR's recruiting party. They gathered recruits until September 4, then left for Niagara bringing news of some actions around New York City that hinted of a distinct lack of coordination between the rebels and their French ally.

A BR's return listed 9 captains; 9 first and second lieutenants, 28 serjeants; 19 drummers, and 438 rank and file at Niagara, and 46 at Detroit. Twenty-three were prisoners of the rebels. The total of all ranks enlisted was 599.

On September 29, Haldimand wrote to Sir Henry Clinton on a broad matter of strategy. He had heard thoroughly alarming news of the C-in-C's concept for an operation that would involve the main army advancing from New York City to strike north up the Potomac and Susquehanna Rivers. A force of 2,000 troops sent south from Canada would join in the area of Fort Pitt. The naivete of the proposal was distressing and frustrating, as it so clearly illustrated Clinton's total lack of appreciation for the conditions of Haldimand's command. "The proposed diversion taking Place in the Winter is inadmissible as it never can be done except by water and the Lakes and Rivers from Montreal upwards cease to be navigable in the month of November." A force of 2,000 men would be the whole of his active British troops and it was

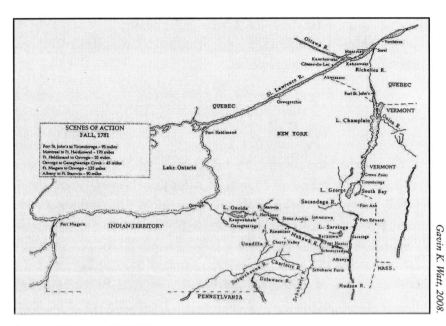

Scenes of Action — Fall 1781.

Gavin K. Watt, 2008.

not worth the risk to detach that many men on the supposition that the French had laid aside their designs on Canada. Besides, it was impossible to support so large a force at such a distance from their base and he gave numerous examples of the difficulty of keeping the upper posts supplied while relying on overseas convoys.

Of course the Vermont negotiations dragged on in the midst of preparing for the expeditions and Haldimand's efforts to fend off Sir Henry's wild scheme. On September 30, Sherwood and Smyth reported they were "of the opinion that Messrs Chittenden, Allen and Fay with a number of the leading men in Vermont are making every exertion in their power ... to bring about a reunion with government." In alarm, Congress was employing several agents in Vermont to counteract the scheme, one of whom was General Bayley, whom Pritchard just scant days before had said was leaning towards the reunion. As Bayley was a chief obstacle to the talks, Sherwood suggested he be gotten out of the way.[19]

Earlier in the year, a sawmill had been built on the Lacolle River about a mile from the Richelieu to provide planks and boards for the improvements being made at Fort St. John's, Chambly, and Ile aux

Noix. A blockhouse and barracks were under construction to defend the sawmill as was a lighthouse on a height of land between Ile aux Noix and Pointe au Fer for relaying messages.

Willett advised the governor that there were more than sufficient arms to equip the three-years' recruits at Albany, so General Stark should have no difficulty. He again offered the opinion that clothing was the most likely method of getting new recruits. Best of all would be to couple a financial bounty with a good suit of clothes as soon as the recruit entered the service. Along that same theme, his Levies were in desperate need of clothes and, very soon, would be fit for little more than garrison duty and many not for that. He then revealed his deep-seated frustrations that surely gave the hard-pressed governor some angst: "And should men for permanent service be rais'd for the defence of our frontiers and a plan adopted for their Defence that looks to me as if it would answer the Expectation of the publick[,] no man living would be readier to Exert himself ... But to serve another Campaign with the embarrassments that has hitherto[,] and is like to Continue[,] to attend this — I hope will never fall to my lott again." He apologized for being such a trial, but his situation demanded it, as there had been so many unexpected obstacles in his path.

On September 23, orders were issued at Fort Rensselaer for the lieutenant of Livingston's company to take the men not employed by the QM to Fort Herkimer to relieve Skinner's. He was to use six empty bateaux and an artillery detachment to recover some ordnance. Captain Harrison at Fort Walradt would supply a thirty-man boat guard as far as the Little Falls landing. Regimental orders instructed company commanders that next month's returns were to record physical descriptions of deserters and recruits and the militia regiment they came from. A court martial was set to try the officers charged with inappropriate conduct.

Stark wrote to Heath on September 24 acknowledging receipt of his five letters and registering incredulity that his own letters had been mislaid. He fully agreed about the likelihood of an imminent attack, as the British had repaired 80–100 bateaux, which he saw as a threat to Saratoga or the Mohawk, but not, as some were saying, the Connecticut River. He stressed his post's lack of ammunition, horses, forage, cash, and paper — items critical for the conduct of public business. Some thirty enemy agents were lurking in his area and he had sent out parties "to trepan them," but feared his poor messaging system would prevent success.

Heath wrote to advise Stark that his letters of the September 9 and 11 had at last arrived. He had only received one other, which he had sent on to Congress so the members would be apprised of conditions in the north. Cartridge paper, thread, 30,000 musket cartridges, and 1,500 flints had been sent north from West Point and should already be on the water. As writing paper had gone to Albany some time ago, he wished to have a district return made October 1. With so much lost mail, he repeated the dispositions mentioned earlier. He was embarrassed about the lack of cash and express horses and riders and assured Stark he had made representations on his behalf.

On September 26, a letter sent to Coxsackie reported that the French had defeated the Royal Navy, which had limped back into New York City with a few shattered ships. The writer elatedly claimed that Cornwallis had been taken, which was just a trifle premature.

As the prisoner exchanges were ongoing, Stark ordered Captain Heacock of Porter's Levies to take a Flag of Truce from Skenesborough to the British shipping on Lake Champlain. He was to search out a certain captain and see if he had the authority to conduct business. If so, Heacock should spend a few days in talks, but if the fellow had to seek permission in Canada, he was to return and make a report. During his travels, he was to fly his Flag and have his drums frequently beat a parlay, especially if a boat or party was encountered. It went unstated that these perambulations would yield useful intelligence.

Raiding was continuing apace in the Mohawk during the preparations for Ross's expedition. A seven-man war party took Conrad Ittig near Fort Plain and, at nightfall, halted at a deserted log building. The Natives made a fire and, while preparing a meal, discussed the poor results of their foray without realizing Ittig understood their dialect.

They grumbled about their single prisoner and having taken no scalps or booty. Ittig understood that they had decided to kill him in the morning and go farther afield. In preparation for sleep, he was secured with cords laid across his chest and thighs and knotted to the warriors, which was certainly an odd precaution if they planned to dispose of him. (And, why wait till day; why not that night?) When the Indians were asleep, he felt around and found a piece of broken window glass. After slowly sawing through his bonds, he sat up, slipped from under the rope over his legs and coolly examined his captors in the pale moonlight slanting through the window. Moving ever so quietly, he raked up the coals and again scrutinized the Indians; all were sound asleep. Creeping to the door, he pushed it open ever so carefully, then burst out at a full run, heading for the moonlit woods. He knew his captors' watchdog would give alarm, so was unsurprised when the animal barked and chased him. Glancing back, he saw them rush from the building, rifles in hand. He was almost at the trees when he tripped and the balls passed harmlessly overhead. Scrambling up, he burst into the trees, running to a giant hollow basswood log he had seen the day before. He was no sooner hidden than the dog ran past in full throat, followed closely by the thudding footfalls of the warriors. After a few tense minutes, the animal came padding back, obviously having lost the scent. Then, the Natives returned and sat on the log to discuss how he could have disappeared — perhaps he climbed a tree, or, ever superstitious, had been helped by the devil.

When morning approached, an Indian went to a nearby field, shot a sheep and brought it back to roast against the hollow log where the others had built a fire. Heat built up quickly and steam and smoke entered through every wormhole. While stifling a coughing fit, he tried to block them with leaves and was at the point of surrendering when the mutton was ready. The Natives began to eat and the fire was allowed to die down. When finished, a warrior was left behind to watch for him and the rest of the party set off for the settlements. The guard sat on the log for some time, then got up and stood nearby, but Ittig was very, very patient and, when all human sounds had faded, he slowly came out of hiding and carefully looked about. No one was in sight and he set out at a trot for Fort Plain.

A seven-man scout of Willett's Levies from Fort Herkimer had an encounter with another war party. After patrolling for seven miles, they stopped to rest in an apple orchard at a deserted farm at Fall Hill. They had just begun to eat some fruit when they heard a shrill whoop. Springing up, they saw a huge party of Natives enter the orchard. Choosing instant flight, they leaped over a fence into the road and ran for their lives. A volley missed them all, but the Indians were in hot pursuit. After some distance, a young fellow began to lag and two men hung back to help. To lighten their load, they cast away their guns and, running an hour-long race, drew near to Fort Herkimer. The single remaining warrior was so determined, he failed to see his danger and, when the three men reached the pickets, rifles barked, and the he fell dead in his tracks.

Another raid plundered and destroyed a Palatine District farm. William Feeter joined with his fellow Stone Arabia militiamen to pursue, but they gave up after a day or two of futile chase. He recalled that small parties of two or three Indians frequently caused alarms till late in the fall.

On September 27, Captain Marshall forwarded a partial return of Willett's Levies and Robert Van Rensselaer's militia brigade to the governor. Although Willett had asked repeatedly, Major McKinstry failed to send a return for the three Saratoga companies and, for some reason, Gansevoort did not send a 1st brigade's return, although he was in the same city as Marshall. The captain requested that Clinton clarify a technicality about the new Levies, as he was involved in a controversy with Lieutenant-Colonel Henry K. Van Rensselaer, who was twelve men short of his quota. The colonel claimed it was Marshall's duty to collect the recruits. Although Marshall thought otherwise, he would comply; however, he had been sending men to Willett as fast as they came and, if collection was also his duty, he would have to keep back a party for the purpose. He would await the governor's advice.

The return showed Willett's Levies with 638 rank and file, 542 as fit for duty, 34 sick, 36 on command, 20 on extra service, and 6 on furlough. At Schoharie, Catskill, Ballstown, and Saratoga were 201, leaving him with 437 in Tryon, to which were added 160 MA Levies for a total of 597, which were distributed as follows: 120 between Forts House, Walradt,

Timmerman, and Stone Arabia; 60 at Forts Clyde, Plain, Windecker, and Willett; 85 at Forts Hunter and Johnstown; and 332 in and around Fort Rensselaer.

Willett had heard that the local Tories were eagerly anticipating another punitive expedition from Canada that would set the Valley back on its haunches and he happily taught a few of them a lesson. Over seven days, he collected 5 head of cattle; 165 pounds of mutton; 1,861 pounds of beef; 23 barrels (147 pounds) of flour; 106 pounds of rough tallow, and 339 pounds of hides.[20]

7

THE HAMMERS FALL

They Broke and Fled with Precipitation

**Comparative Chronology of
the Ross and St. Leger Expeditions, Fall 1781**

Date	Rebel Command	Ross Expedition	Leger Expedition
Sept.			
20		Ross receives Halidmand's orders.	
27		84th detachment goes to Oswego.	
28		Orders arrive at Niagara.	
Oct.			
01			29th, 31st, and 44th regiments alerted.
03	Stark reports enemy at Lake George.	Ross at Oswego. His scouts take prisoners in Mohawk Valley.	
05		Troops and Natives sail from Niagara.	

Date	Rebel Command	Ross Expedition	Leger Expedition
06	Willett requests Logan's companies.		
08	Stark reports enemy concentrating at Pointe au Fer.		
09	1st Albany Brigade called out. 2nd Brigade warned for service.		British Lights and Jägers at Pointe au Fer. Haldimand's proclamation arrives at Fort St. John.
11	200 New Hampshire Militia called out. Stark again reports enemy at Lake George.	Force departs Oswego.	Sherwood and Smyth leave Ile au Noix.
12		At Onondaga Falls. Several Mohawks desert.	Sherwood and Smyth at Crown Point.
13	Vermonters agitate in Hoosic. New Hampshire Continentals Brigade sent north.	At Three Rivers. Onondagas bring prisoners.	
14	Wemple requests troops for Schnectady. Willett raises alarm. 2nd New Hampshire arrives at Albany.	Scouts take prisoners at Fort Herkimer.	Haldimand issues orders to St. Leger.
15	Willet cancels his alarm. 200 Massachusetts Militia arrive at Albany. Stark admits his false alarm. Western Union in turmoil.		Haldimand at Fort St. John's. 29th Lights and Provincials at Pointe au Fer.

Date	Rebel Command	Ross Expedition	Leger Expedition
17	Albany hears of Yorktown siege.	At Ganaghsaraga Creek.	St. Leger sails from Pointe au Fer.
18		East of Old Oneida.	Jägers and Provincials set sail.
19			At Crown Point.
20	Stark to stand down New York Militia. Lord Stirling sent north.	At Unadilla River.	At Ticonderoga.
21	Heath advises he may use southern New York militia against Sir Henry Clinton.		Sends patrol to meet Ross. Provincials move boats to Lake George.
22		At ruins of New Town Martin.	British kill Vermont serjeant.
23	Enemy at Crown Point. Albany County brigades alerted.	At Young's Lake.	
24	Enemy at Ticonderoga. Willett discovers Ross.	Burns Currytown and Noses. March all night to Warrensborough.	Jessup launches onto Lake George. St. Leger apologizes to Vermont.
25	Hall Battle. Stark hears of Yorktown surrender.	Destroys Warrensborough. Fights Hall Battle.	
26	Willett waits at Stone Arabia.		Jessup sends out three parties.
27	Willett goes to Fort Herkimer.	Hill sent to burn boats.	Attack on Sugar Loaf outpost.
28	Willett leads 400 troops and 60 Natives to catch Ross.		Sherwood and Smyth at Castleton. Talks suspended.

Date	Rebel Command	Ross Expedition	Leger Expedition
29	March to the Hurricanes.	Finds Carleton Island track.	
30	Butler killed at Canada Creek.	Rearguard overtaken at Ford.	

Nov.

Date	Rebel Command	Ross Expedition	Leger Expedition
01	Vermont troops at Fort Ann.		Jessup returns to Ticonderoga.
04			St. Leger moves to Chimney Point.
07		Ross at Carleton Island.	
10	Stark reports enemy gone to Canada.		St. Leger leaves Chimney Point.
16			Chambers docks at Fort St. John's.

*A*s the month turned, the persistent rumours of Albany and Schenectady's imminent destruction held the rebels' focus, to the point where they almost ignored the more vulnerable western frontiers. Yet, from Fort Niagara alone, seventy-five war parties had sortied out in the first ten months of the year. Some of the Native leaders who were ill were encouraged in these efforts by Guy Johnson's luxurious gifts of "tea, brown sugar, eight barrels of port wine, four of Madeira [and] 100 pounds of chocolates."

On October 1, Haldimand reported to Sir Henry Clinton about the return of his agents from a meeting with Ira Allen and Joseph Fay. Although he was concerned that the majority of Vermonters were anti-reunion, Allen and Fay reasoned they would accept terms if a proclamation were issued that recognized the Eastern and Western Unions and was simultaneously supported by a force on the lakes. While Haldimand properly sought his superior's instructions, he recognized how slow and unsure communications could be and had already taken action: "I shall Issue the Proclamation, worded with as much Caution as Consistent with my Hopes of its Success." No offensive measures were to be taken against Vermont: "on the contrary every appearance of Hostility will be carefully avoided." As the other frontiers would be "distressed," he hoped to convince Vermonters that the British intended to protect them, but if the worst came to the worst, the proclamation could allow Ira Allen to claim the British, not he, had taken the initiative.

The 29th regiment's Grenadier and Light companies had surrendered with Burgoyne in 1777 and when word of their exchange and drafting at New York City came in September, Haldimand ordered the regiment to reconstitute them from its own resources. On October 1, the new flank and several line companies were warned for the Champlain expedition, as were the Lights of the 31st and 44th.

———————————————
———————————————

With obvious satisfaction, Willett advised Governor Clinton on October 2 that there had been no desertions in the past six weeks since he had executed two culprits and transferred a third to the Continentals. In view of such productive results, he sought advice about apprehending and punishing time-expired deserters. His peace of mind was disrupted the next day when he noted in his orderly book that three of his delinquent officers had again broken arrest during his absence from Rensselaer.

Raiding along the Mohawk continued — a man was taken at Stanwix's ruins and another skirmish occurred near Fort Timmerman. In a third incident, fifty discharged NY levies set off for home from Fort Plain, but had gone only a mile when Indians attacked. They fired a ragged volley, but there seemed to be hundreds of warriors and they hotfooted back. A party of Levies turned out to pursue, but gave up about seven miles from Lake Oneida.

Heath advised Stark that Villefranche had reported that the Northern Department had no shortage of ammunition; indeed, the quantity was much too large, considering the vulnerability of its storage. "There were not less than twenty odd casks of powder, each containing 200 pounds, beside a large quantity of fixed ammunition on the Mohawk River." A majority was at Fort Herkimer, which Heath viewed as "one of the most advanced posts," with a number of spare guns. The powder was to be reorganized in the different forts and a reserve held in the rear, from where the advanced posts could draw supplies. The extra guns were to be dealt with similarly and Stark was to immediately order Willett to take action. Stark must have felt chastised like an errant subaltern and have fumed that such critical information arrived on his doorstep from his superior. Here he had been complaining of a lack of ammunition when an excess was stored in his own department. Obviously, he had not received Marshall's report. As a further poke to his sensitivities, Heath again noted that a supply of paper had been sent to Albany in September and pointedly renewed his request for a speedy departmental return.

Colonel Weissenfels reported to Governor Clinton from Saratoga about his experiences in Vermont's Western Union during his march north from Albany. A Mr. Fairbank, whom Chittenden had commissioned lieutenant-colonel, had collected men at New City to choose a captain and lieutenant for the local company to replace New York's appointees. Weissenfels saw this as a public insult to the governor's authority and attempted to dissuade him, but he persisted. Suspicious that Fairbank and his confederates were seeking an armed confrontation, he had chosen to leave.

On October 3, Stark wrote to Gansevoort in alarm about "the advance of the enemy to this side of Lake George," but failed to explain in what numbers. This news triggered an avalanche of activity.

On the Mohawk River, Captain Jacob Small, 4TCM, and a soldier were collecting a winter supply of apples near a small, empty blockhouse located between Herkimer and Little Falls. Small was aloft picking when an Indian shot him dead, lifted his scalp and rushed the accompanying soldier into the woods. On October 4, a father was killed and his son taken at their uninhabited home at Fall Hill. Willett wrote that three or four "unknown rascals" committed this deed, which suggested Tory perpetrators rather than Native, but the proximity to Small's killing implies otherwise.[1]

———————————————
———————————————

On October 2, Lieutenant-Colonel Butler received a defiant letter from his captains, John McDonell, Barent Frey, and Peter Hare, in which the phrase "in order to prevent any ill consequences" was prominent. The Rangers were unaccustomed to having officers thrust on them from outside and the three officers were outraged that Captain John McKinnon, who had a patronage appointment from HQ, claimed seniority back to his 1778 commission from Sir Henry Clinton. They suspected there had been some particular reason for his reduction in the Southern Army and argued he had no right to more consideration than a half-pay lieutenant. Butler was asked to lay the case before Powell for resolution.

Two significant incidents occurred before Haldimand's expeditions were to dominate the scene. On the October 5, Lieutenant-Colonel Thomas Johnson was paroled at St. John's. Sherwood had informed him of the Vermont negotiations and was in high hopes he would use his substantial influence to win over the communities east of the Green Mountains.

Unattributed artist. (Library and Archives Canada, C-011057.)

above: Unattributed artist. (Library and Archives Canada, C-011058.)

left: Reverend John Stuart (1740–1811). Rector of Queen Anne Parsonage at Fort Hunter and loyalist spy. Stuart fled to Canada and became the chaplain of the 2nd Battalion, King's Royal Yorkers.

right: Typical of so many minister's wives, Jane Stuart not only had her husband and three boys to worry about, but also a large number of hangers-on who attached themselves to their party.

On the day of Johnson's parole, Reverend John Stuart wrote to Dr. Smyth from Brown's Point, where he had arrived with fifty people, including his wife, three small sons, and slaves. He had been forced to post a £400 bond and wait for the exchange of a rebel colonel, but when the fellow failed to appear, the commission relented and gave him leave. Now, his party was stranded until boats came from Canada and he feared plundering by Vermonters, as there was no Flag for protection. By October 6, Stuart and party were at Crown Point where Commodore Chambers reported they had so much baggage that the *Carleton* could not accommodate it. In any event, the vessel had a Flag of Truce aboard and taking on refugees was out of the question, so he offloaded provisions and sent them to Windmill Point for pick up by the *Trumbull*. Stuart's party was at Fort St. John's by October 9.[2]

A MOST DARING AND DESPERATE VENTURE

By October 3, Ross was at Oswego with his most important assistant, Captain William Ancrum, who commanded the 34th's Light Company and a party of seventy-five line troops. Ancrum had a great deal of North American experience, including serving as St. Leger's adjutant general in

1777. He was unpopular for his violent temper, but, in strange contrast, was known for great generosity. Although it is unrecorded, he likely served as Ross's second-in-command.

As to other Regular infantry, Ross had an RHE subaltern, two serjeants twenty-nine rank and file, and a section of eleven Hanau Jägers under a corporal. His Provincials included Leake's veteran Independent Company with First Lieutenant William McKay, Second Lieutenant Henry Young, 3 serjeants, 2 drummers, and 42 and file, and 150 Rankers of 2KRR with Adjutant Fraser, Surgeon Kerr, and all the combatant officers from the island.

Despite several requests, there is no evidence that Land Pattern arms had been issued to 2KRR. A month later, the QMG's return for Quebec City alone listed 4,300 English Pattern arms with bayonets and scabbards and 1,000 Carbines. It seems incredible that 250 stand of military arms with bayonets could not be found for troops sent on a dangerous mission deep into enemy territory, yet this was more typical of Haldimand's administration than not. The grip of his strict frugality is often palpable in these details.[3]

At noon on October 5, Captain Gilbert Tice, a very experienced, senior 6NID officer, and 109 Indians embarked on the *Caldwell*. Another 100 were expected to join at Oswego from the Genesee. Also boarding was Lieutenant Thomas Coote with two serjeants and twenty-eight men of the 8th (King's), Captain Walter Butler, two captains, four subalterns, seven serjeants, two drummers, and 150 Rangers. By two o'clock, they were under sail for Oswego. The next day, they were in sight of Great Asodus when a hard gale drove them across the lake to Toronto. Such delays were most unwelcome, as the season was rapidly closing.

On October 6, Willett asked Stark for permission to divert Logan's two companies from Ballstown to Johnstown, where they would provide additional protection for Stone Arabia. His request was denied, which was later to lead to recriminations. The colonel also asked about the expiration

Detail from a sketch attributed to Lieutenant John André, 1775. (William L. Clements Library.)

above: Detail from a sketch by Edward Hicks, Halifax 1781.

left: Three Light Bobs at a frolic with some Canadiens and Natives. Their cap trimmings are believed unique to each regiment. They wear jackets, breeches, and what appear to be moccasins.

right: A sentry in a jacket, cap-hat with a single, feathered cock, and overalls being spoken to by a casual non-commissioned officer while an apparently inebriated Light Bob in plumed cap, jacket, breeches, and spatterdashes lolls nearby.

date for the services of the MA Levies and mentioned his dire need for surgeons. The regiment's doctor was at German Flatts and unable to visit other posts and his mate was at Saratoga. A mate from the General Hospital was at Fort Rensselaer, but he could only attend to needs in that immediate area. That day, raiders captured a 2TCM lieutenant.

While Ross anxiously awaited Niagara's contingent at Oswego, a twelve-man detachment of 1KRR Light Bobs, including John Cough Jr., his stepbrother Jacob Ross, the Parker brothers, William and John, and Nicholas Schafer from Johnson's Bush, was holed up at Cough's father's place in Philadelphia Bush. Young Cough was a bold fellow, so it was likely his idea that the lads indulge in a silly exploit on the night of October 7 and endangered their mission of collecting intelligence and recruits. Being young, and probably "in liquor," they set off under cover of night, infiltrated through Johnstown to the fort and took potshots at the duty sentry. Although Light Infanteers were chosen for their marksmanship, these fellows may have been too drunk and their fusillade missed, but the sentry coolly returned fire and shattered Cough's knee. When the duty drummer beat the alarm, the Light Bobs panicked and lugged their groaning comrade the six miles back to his father's place. A local doctor refused to attend, dreading the consequences of helping a Tory soldier. Local women visited over the next three days, but it was finally decided that Cough needed medical assistance. After some more stalling, John Sr. finally sent a younger son to the father-in-law of Captain John Littel, the fort's commandant. The lad told the whole sad tale and, the next day, a Royal Yorker sentinel saw a militia party coming and he, John Sr., and most of the Tories took off for the woods. Littel and his four men took young Cough and a few dispirited Tories prisoner and hung a bed between two horses as a crude litter. Militia private, Stephen Shew, harboured a keen resentment of Tories, as he had been taken in 1778 and badly used by his Native and white captors. As the group marched along, Shew frequently startled one of the horses, which jolted the litter and caused John to moan and thrash about in pain. Near the fort, the wife of a Continental spotted Cough and exclaimed, "There comes that d_____ tory who was going to kill us the other night." Cough's brilliant idea had certainly paid him more than he bargained for.

On October 7, Captain François Dambourgès, RHE, who was in command at Carleton Island in Ross's absence, reported that another eight Natives had gone to join Ross the day before. The Niagara contingent's vessel was becalmed on October 7, but the next day had fair winds and, at ten o'clock the following morning, joined a most impatient Ross.

Powell reported from Niagara that Serjeant John Rowe and six Rangers had arrived from the Hellebergh. They brought news that Schuyler had been told by a Quebec informer that Sir John was to attack Albany and people from as far away as Schoharie were bringing cattle and grain to the city. Ranger scout Private Abraham Scott had heard that New England troops were moving north to Lake Champlain to confront 3,000 British troops coming down from Canada.

Johnstown Court House. Detail from a nineteenth-century sketch.

Orders were posted at Fort Rensselaer on October 9 to stop the selling of liquor after tattoo beating or on Sundays. The same day, Tryon County's Court of General Sessions of the Peace sat in the Johnstown Courthouse. The members could scarce have imagined that they and their predecessors would be engaged in mortal combat later in the month less than a mile from where they sat. Willett's brigade major, Andrew Finck, was foreman of the grand jury that indicted sixteen former residents as enemy adherents, adding to the ninety-four others charged in the June session. Walter Butler, the young lawyer who had appeared in the courthouse on many occasions and whose father John had sat as a justice of this very court, would be leading the enemy's Rangers. Overseeing the loyal Indians would be Gilbert Tice, the owner of the tavern where the members often retired for refreshment after a day of legal affairs. Such interweaving of former friends and acquaintances was typical of this bitter civil war.

Gansevoort wrote to the governor from Albany enclosing a letter from Stark about the enemy force expected on Lake Champlain. He thought Sir John would attack farther westward, especially as he had heard that a thirty-man enemy party had been seen in the vicinity of Ballstown.[4]

In an October 10 report, Ross made two curious observations, prompting questions as to the rationale for why his expedition was proceeding. First, he wrote, "Should I be so fortunate as to get into the Country unexpected, what little remains may be destroyed, but by last accounts the Corn is all threshed off and in their Stockaded Forts," that is, the grain was out of reach. Second, "Duanesboro, the place particularized by Brigadier Powell, is but a small settlement within eight miles of Schenectady." That is, it was insignificant!

Nonetheless, Tice and the Indians moved off the next day at one o'clock with the Rangers following immediately behind and marched to Half Way Creek on the Oswego River. Later that day, Lieutenant John Ryckman, 6NID, came from the Genesee villages with the disturbing news of his failure to recruit any warriors. They had claimed a lack of moccasins, which was seen as a very weak excuse; however, early next day, ten Niagara Mohawks used the same excuse when they defected and set off to "accomplish something" before returning to Niagara. By custom and training, Natives were thoroughly independent men and often left expeditions on their own accord, but for this to occur so early in the proceedings seems an ill omen. The concern that they may carelessly betray the expedition must have lain heavily on Ross's mind. He later claimed that many Niagara officers said that Guy Johnson could have sent useful chiefs and warriors, rather than those whom Ross viewed as "nothing more than the refuse of the different Tribes without a leading man amongst them." This dismisssive comment ignored the presence of David Hill Karaghgunty, a Fort Hunter war captain of substantial reputation. Yet, in fairness to the major, the better-known leaders such as Old Smoke, Cornplanter, Brant, and Deserontyon were not with him. The first two were raiding Pennsylvania and Brant was at Detroit. As to Deserontyon, despite Fort Hunter's great disappointment, Haldimand would not permit them to participate in concern they would confide in the Kahnawakes, who might leak details to the rebels. Captain David escaped this ban by being at Niagara all summer. Ross was frustrated by the Natives' attitude, reporting later that, from the outset, "they began not only to make difficulties of everything but to counteract and procrastinate whatever I proposed to them." A bitterness settled on him, as he was fully aware of the importance of willing Native support.

On October 11, Willett wrote to Stark, informing him that spies in Montreal said 800 men had gone up the St. Lawrence in early September to relieve the upper posts. He asked if troops could be drawn from

Stark's area, noting that his own district was so remote from the thickly populated parts of the state that rapid support could not be expected in an emergency, but vowed that if the British came, he would do "everything in his power … to cause them to regret their enterprise."

The next day, Lieutenant Bockee at Fort Plain wrote to his friend Lieutenant Moore at Ballstown, "the Enemy have made themselves Scarce[.] I Expect they'l pay you a Visit."

———————————

On October 12, Ross's expedition was camped at the big falls on the Oswego River. The next day, the force negotiated three small rapids and camped at Three Rivers. A party of nine Onondagas appeared and presented Tice with a scalp and a prisoner for him to interrogate. Perhaps this was Captain Small's scalp lock and the prisoner was the militiaman taken apple-picking near Fall Hill. About this time, the ten Mohawks who had abandoned Ross took two prisoners. For some inexplicable reason, they told the captives what they knew of the major's plans. Having now "accomplished something," they headed for Niagara, but a day later, released a captive who had fallen lame, instead of following custom and killing him. Their decision smacked of a deliberate attempt to sabotage the expedition, suggesting that Ross had insulted them when they chose to leave. Later, the major posited that their betrayal explained the rebels' vigilance. The expedition's boats set off from Three Rivers on October 14 with the Indians and Rangers marching overland. That evening, everyone camped at the ruins of Fort Brewerton at the far west end of Lake Oneida.[5]

———————————

On October 14, Colonel Wemple, 2ACM, wrote Gansevoort from Schenectady to request reinforcements from the militia brigade, which he knew had been called out to meet Stark's alarm. Unaware that Ross was targeting a settlement only eight miles west of town, he saw the threat emanating from the north, not the west. Yet, the very next day, Willett expressed word to Marshall in Albany that alarm guns had fired at Fort Herkimer. The captain was to march upriver with all the levies under his command without loss of time. Willett noted that Stark could easily handle any threat from the north, so Marshall was not to leave any men behind, other than oldsters and invalids in the little forts. This message arrived at Albany on October 16 and Marshall immediately wrote to advise the governor, then hurried on the men, but for some reason, chose not to march himself.

Even in the midst of the Fort Herkimer alarm, the dreary business of purging Tryon of the disaffected continued. Major Finck, who also served as a county commissioner of conspiracies, provided the governor with a list of twenty-three men, fifteen wives, young women above the age of fourteen, and forty-seven children — a total of ninety-nine persons suitable to send north. In a second enclosure, he listed Tryon folk who had been taken prisoner since early spring and could be exchanged for these Tories.[6]

On October 17, Ross sailed from Fort Brewerton's ruins to Ganaghsaraga Creek. That such an obvious, open route was safe spoke volumes about the successful purging of the rebel Indians. Prior to the war, the Tuscaroras' main village of Ganaghsaraga had been a short distance up this creek, but now, an enemy force of 600 men was able to land there with little fear of detection. After caching a supply of provisions, he detailed twenty sick and lame men to guard the food and boats. David Hill reported that the Six Nations' warriors joined the expedition here. Perhaps these were the men who chose to serve under his personal leadership. If not, who were the Indians on the *Caldwell*, or the Onondagas at Three Rivers, or the Mohawks who abandoned the force, if not Iroquois? Whatever was meant, Ross needed a prisoner from German Flatts and Hill sent eight men to take one.

———————————————————
———————————————————

In a bizarre twist, Willett's second dispatch to Marshall cancelled the alarm. Fort Herkimer's guns had only been fired to warn of the killing of two people and capturing of a third by a small party that disappeared. Perhaps this was the 4TCM private who was wounded and captured while collecting firewood. Evidently, the lame man released by the Mohawks had not yet arrived home to warn of the very real threat looming just inside Indian Territory.

———————————————————
———————————————————

The expedition camped two miles beyond Old Oneida on October 18. That night, Second Lieutenant Frederick Docksteder, BR, an accomplished officer and brother of John, was suddenly "attacked by a Violent Disorder." He died next morning and, after his burial, the force moved off, heading for Herkimer's Lake. That evening, the camp was at a small creek flowing south from the lake where five Onondaga scouts brought Tice a prisoner from Little Falls who said that Sir John was at Crown Point with a large army.[7]

On October 20, the camp was on a branch of the Unadilla River when Captain David delivered a prisoner from Fall Hill, who provided the same information. Two days later, the force marched past Croghan's Lake and camped at the abandoned hamlet of New Town Martin. Next day, they passed the upper end of the burned shell of Cherry Valley, then marched past Tunnicliff's and, that evening, camped beside a creek running out of Young's Lake.

———————————————————

Unaware of Ross's proximity, Willett sent out Gros's and Putnam's companies towards Schoharie on October 22 to collect Tory cattle. Serjeant Jacob Tanner of Putnam's recalled marching "through the Wilderness fifteen miles to Hamis Mills where they remained over night." Having found no beeves, the Levies turned about next morning. Tanner and Frederick Ulman got permission to visit their families at nearby Currytown and set off toward home. At night, they slept in a cedar swamp near New Dorlach and were up at dawn. They had gone less than 200 yards when they came across Lieutenant John Hare's ten-man Indian scout, which had slept in the same swamp. The two Levies ran down Flat Creek's bed, flinging aside their packs and guns to hasten their retreat. After three miles, they were far enough ahead to climb a hill, throw themselves on the ground, and watch their pursuers pass by below. Judging it safe, they took a different direction and came across a funeral of a fellow who had been killed while hunting. When told of the Indians, the ceremony broke up and everyone headed home, but Rudolf Keller, his wife, and three men were quickly captured. After a plea by her nephew, Royal Yorker Henry Keller, Mrs. Keller was released with six other females. Another mourner was near home when a giant Indian seized his bridle and several others jerked him out of the saddle. Hare's party now had six prisoners and his warriors reckoned they were too far behind the main column, so were content to turn back for the boats. As to Tanner and Ulman, on their way to Currytown, they fell into an ambush set by Henry Brant, Joseph's cousin, who had already taken Ulman's parents.

In the afternoon of October 24, the raid marched past the deserted hamlet of Argusville and came to the outskirts of Currytown, which Docksteder's raid had so effectively destroyed in July. Natives slipped into the hamlet, avoided Lewis's blockhouse, and plundered the rebuilt buildings. No fires were set in case smoke would signal their presence. As word of the raid spread, people took shelter in the woods. One family was found and taken, but a son escaped and ran to report to Willett. Four miles from the fort, he was lamed after stumbling over a fence and had to find other men to carry his message. The raid surged forward and captured a serjeant and private of Yates's 3TCM company, then went north toward the river on a road over Stone Ridge where they took another prisoner.

As twilight fell, a Native party came up to Lieutenant Joseph Printup's place. He was at home with his brother-in-law Jacob Frank, John Loucks, and John Van Alstyne, all militiamen in Yates's Company. Printup had just cleaned his firelock and was returning the rammer when he said, "Now I am ready for the Indians." Moments later, Natives loomed out of the dusk. Frank and Loucks ran out of the house and up a hill; Frank was shot down and scalped, but Loucks escaped. In the meantime, Printup had loaded and fired at the Indians as they rushed the house. A warrior closed with him and thrust his muzzle into the lieutenant's chest. Printup just had time to push the barrel down when the trigger was pulled and the ball caught him square in the meat of his thigh. Frustrated, the Indian was about to finish him when a Tory acquaintance in the party stepped in and saved him. A short distance down the road, his captors halted to kill him, but again the Tory interposed. Printup leaned on Van Alstyne who had also been taken in the fracas, and hobbled along. As darkness fell, the column moved on.

Most of the Van Epps family escaped ahead of the raid, but a curious young Evert set out in the dark to see for himself. He had crossed a bridge and was opening a small swing gate when he heard the cocking of firelocks. A voice thundered, "Who's there?" Unable to see anything, he was tempted to turn and run, but something told him to freeze. In a wink, he was surrounded and taken.

When the column arrived at a brook in a small ravine, Van Alstyne whispered to Printup that, if not for him, he could escape. The officer told him to go ahead and Printup broke away and ran up the ravine to safety. The Indians chose not to fire and alarm the locals. Once again, Printup's life was threatened, and again, the Tory intervened.

It is quite remarkable that Ross's column could "ghost" through Willett's district from its far western margin to close to its eastern edge without raising a major alarm. While this feat revealed the weaknesses of Willett's intelligence system and was a tribute to the skills of the raiders, it was also a measure of the desolation of the settlements south of the river and the paucity of Willett's manpower. And of note, so inured were the inhabitants and Levies to constant attack, even the killings and captures by the clouds of Indian scouts that scoured ahead of the column had not raised undue anxiety.

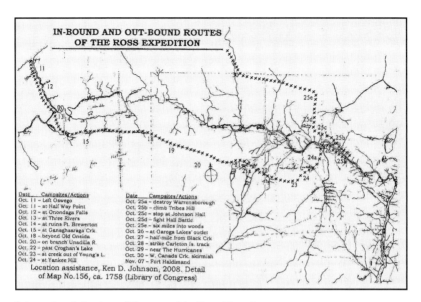

Inbound and Outbound Routes of the Ross Expedition.

Tice reported taking several prisoners as his Indians marched up the road to the river. The captives claimed that 600 militiamen were at Schenectady, 400 were with Willett at Canajoharie, and 500 were at Schoharie. These grossly inflated numbers suggest that someone had at last coached people how to respond to interrogation. Scouts brought in two more prisoners, likely Tanner and Ulman. They warned Ross that his expedition was known and the militia was waiting for his approach. Yet the major was an easy march from his intended target and it was unlikely he would be blocked from his purpose; however, withdrawal could be an entirely different matter. As noted, Ross had concluded that Duanesborough was "a trifling place" and that "the only Settlement of any Consequence now on the River was Warrensborough." The rebels were said to think the place totally secure, as it was located centrally between Fort Hunter, Schoharie, and Schenectady. Someone said it was a nest of rebels from the very beginning; however, many of the farmers were loyalists, which later was to give Willett reason to exult over the ruin of their properties. Pragmatically, ownership mattered little, as every source fed the rebels.

War Captain David Hill recalled closing up to the river at Anthony's Nose, where his men began to destroy farms that had been overlooked the previous fall by Johnson. Hill reported that rebels attacked his party on three occasions and almost killed "young David," likely his son or a near relative. Soon after, Ross ordered the expedition to cease burning and to head for Schoharie Creek. The men marched through the night to arrive on target before morning. "[T]he weather was most unfortunate, heavy Rains and the worst of Roads for fourteen Miles, the Troops labored hard to keep together, and notwithstanding every exertion several were … left behind on the March."[8]

Henry Lewis of Currytown reported to Willett at eight o'clock that evening that a large raid was at hand. Now, Willett's genius for inspiring and organizing came alive. "[E]very means was instantly taken to Collect the forces of the County in order to oppose them without loss of time." Supplies were assembled and the men's haversacks filled. Levies from local posts and nearby militia companies were called in. Expresses were sent to Forts Clyde and Plain to order Levies and militia to march without delay. At nine o'clock, he wrote to Major Rowley at Stone Arabia to advise that the enemy had passed through the lower part of Currytown in considerable force about sunset and were marching toward the river. "I am collecting all the forces in this quarter, and shall advance toward them as quickly as possible. As they are in your quarter, I have no doubt of your exertions in collecting as many of the men of your regiment as possible … without loss of time. And as it is likely you may be somewhat acquainted with the particular route of the enemy, sooner than I shall, I wish you to take such a position as you may think best, and make me acquainted with it, together with the whole of your situation, and every information." Rowley was to forward Willett's letter to Schenectady by express so that appropriate action could be taken there.[9]

At 3:00 a.m., the expedition forded the Schoharie Kill south of the post and settlement of Fort Hunter. There were two versions of what happened next. Hill reported that six soldiers deserted into the fort and warned the garrison, which caused an alarm gun to be fired and, when the inhabitants streamed into the fort, his warriors burned their properties. Ross reported that thirteen soldiers were lost during the forced march to Warrensborough, one 8th, seven 34th, two 84th, two 2KRR, and one Leake's. Doubtless, the raiders were fatigued and downhearted by the awful weather and endless marching, but to the extent of deserting seems questionnable. A rebel account claimed that a sortie took twelve stragglers and Peter J. Quackenboss, who was stationed there, said he personally captured five.

The raiders marched to within a mile of Warrensborough and climbed into the woods atop Yankee Hill, where Ross had the exhausted troops lie on their arms until daylight. When dawn broke on October 25, Tice was ordered to detach himself with his officers, Indians, and some Rangers to destroy the settlement while the troops blocked the roads to fend off any attacks.

The hamlet of Warrensborough, or Warrensbush, was on South Chuctanunda Creek about two miles from the Mohawk. It was central to the Patent and clustered around a road junction — one road came south over the hills from Fort Johnson, a second came east through the creek valley and a third from Fort Hunter to the west. Six houses, a tannery, a potash works, a trading post, and a mill formed the village. The farms of the seven-mile-long Patent were located in the creek's valley, along tributaries and on either side of the three roadways. Ross reported, "I made the necessary arrangement to destroy the Settlement as expeditiously as possible, appointing a Rendezvous for the whole. [I]n this particular only did the Indians become useful[;] they mixt with part of the Rangers[,] Effected everything that could be required, before 12 O'clock the whole Settlement for seven miles was in flames, near 100 farms, three Mills and a large Granary for Public Service were reduced to Ashes, the Cattle and Stock of all kinds were likewise destroyed. The Inhabitants fled precipitately in the Night."

As usual, Ross's grudging praise of his Indians ignored their essential services as scouts and flank guards.

The widow of Captain Samuel Pettingell, 3TCM, who had been killed at Oriskany in 1777, was living in the southwest corner of the village. She and her thirteen children had struggled to lay up sufficient cattle feed and personal supplies for the coming winter. Early that fateful morning, they spotted a party of Tice's Indians and ran to the woods, taking refuge under an overhanging bank in "a cove-like recess in the creek's gorge." The fugitives held their breath when they heard furtive steps crossing over a nearby slate rock. One of the girls began to sob and her mother smothered her mouth with an apron. When uncovered, the girl had to be shaken vigorously to revive her. That night, the family stole back home and found their property looted and burned, except for a single stack of wheat.

Captain William Snook, Pettingell's successor, heard of Ross's arrival and sent his subaltern to warn the neighbours. Meanwhile, a well-known Mohawk, known as One-Armed Peter because of his disability, captured two sisters and a girl. When one woman stumbled and fell, Peter insisted on taking the child she had been carrying. Such kindness was so incongruous in the face of the killing, burning, and looting, that it was later thought, perhaps uncharitably, that he had used the child as a shield. When they arrived at a crossroad, he returned the infant and asked the women if they had any money. One of them untied her pocket and gave it to him; he extracted two coins and returned it. Suddenly, he gave a stentorian yell, which was immediately answered by others and the girl fainted dead away. Once his friends arrived, Peter freed the captives.

When the Rowland family escaped, they carried their most important possessions to a pole platform built well above ground in a dense thicket of tall hemlocks. For hours, they silently watched the smoke from their home and their neighbours' rolling over the treetops. They were terrorized when several Indians passed through the woods, particularly when one abruptly stopped under their platform, but he simply adjusted his pack, then hurried off to catch up with his fellows.

The Guile family farm was on the bank of the Mohawk and one of the last in the Patent to be destroyed. Their buildings, 260 bushels of grain, and two tons of hay were torched. Nineteen-year-old Ray Guile, who had just signed up for the Levies, lurked about the farm, itching for revenge. With his musket charged with two balls, he crept up to 200 feet from a soldier who had hung back, shot him, then stripped off his hat and long sword. Just as he tumbled the body into the river, Captain David McMaster, 3TCM, whose beat was in the area, arrived with some men and ordered Guile to join in following the enemy.

One of the patent's loyalists who lost property was Alex Campbell who, in a petition to the British government, claimed £117.12 for the loss of his potash works and utensils.

When the raiders were done, they had killed two inhabitants, destroyed 22 houses, 18 barns, the commercial enterprises, over 7,000 bushels of grain, 109 tons of hay, and killed or removed 250 livestock. Although this represented only a fraction of what had been destroyed in the 1780 raid, it was a tragedy for the owners. Lieutenant Alex McDonell of Butler's recognized the enormity of the deed by characterizing Warrensborough as "one of the first settlements on the Mohawk River," which, in both senses of "first," was indeed an historic fact.[10]

Ross had planned the best route of withdrawal. As an initial step, he instructed Captain Hill to secure the ford over the Mohawk near Fort Johnson. Tice recalled, "We finished about 10 o'clock in the morning and joined Major Ross within 12 miles of Schenectady. Then wheeled about, marched up the Mohawk River [and] crossed at Fort Johnson." Although Ross had been given orders to cooperate if possible with the Lake Champlain expedition, he dismissed the idea, later reporting that he had heard nothing of its progress. As to his withdrawal, he wrote, "I always ... designed retreating to Carleton Island, but imparted it to none so that the Prisoners who fell into the Enemy's hands the night before, could make no discoverys. [T]o Retreat as I came must give the Enemy every advantage, they having the Command of the River could get in my front at pleasure. There was also an other Circumstance which equally determined me, it was not impossible that the Boats and Provisions left at Canasarago might fall into their hands, which they could not fail to have information of, in that case a march from thence to Niagara or Carleton Island without provisions and almost barefooted at this Season of the Year, presented a disagreeable Prospect.

Time, distance, Security … in short everything argued for the Retreat to this Island."

The Mohawk was swollen by heavy rains and the troops had difficulty fording. Ross noted, "some Militia began to shew themselves on the Banks." Once over, the expedition marched to Fort Johnson and began to climb the road just to the east that led over Tribes Hill and on to Johnstown.

———————

Rebel troops had been assembling at Fort Rensselaer during the night and early morning. Putman's company came from Fort Plain to join Gros's, Elsworth's, and Whelp's. Militiamen from Jacob Diefendorf's, Rynier Van Evera's, and Adam Lype's 1TCM companies arrived from Fort Plain and Canjoharie. Major Abraham Copeman, 1TCM, and his captain, Jost Dygert, brought seventy-five and others came from Fort Clyde. As speed of reaction was critical, Willett left early next morning with a small train of wagons and Moodie's 3-pdr brass gun. As they marched along the south shore, William Feeter of Klock's company joined with two other men from Stone Arabia. When an express from downriver said that Ross had crossed to the north shore at Fort Johnson and was on his way to Johnstown, Willett sent his men across the Caughnawaga ford, losing four ammunition boxes in the process. More 2TCM men joined on the north shore and William Wallace arrived. A commissioned veteran of the Continentals and Levies, Wallace was currently a serjeant in Fonda's 3TCM Exempts. As a Johnstown man, he knew the area intimately and Willett chose him and Feeter to scout ahead and report the enemy's situation.[11]

———————
———————

Of course, the progress of the Lake Champlain expedition was simultaneously affecting rebel actions. It is important to digress for a moment to understand the responses in the lower Mohawk Valley. Even before the news of Ross's appearance broke, Gansevoort had sent instructions to his brigade's colonels: "General Stark at Saratoga … informs me that the enemy are advancing in force [on Lake George] and [he] expect[s] to be attacked within three days — you will … without delay give orders for your regiment to collect as soon as possible at the Half moon with three days provisions, where you will receive farther orders — and send from thence wagons to this place for such necessaries as you may stand in need of with proper returns for the same." All companies of Exempts were to receive the same orders.

The express carrying this order must have crossed along the road with one from Schenectady's Colonel Wemple, who was reporting Major Rowley's warning about Ross. Gansevoort received Wemple's dispatch at one o'clock. It read, "just now an other Express is Arrived who brings the Disagreeable news that the enemy are in great force and were this afternoon at 3 o'clock engaged at fort Hunter. A body of 350 Red Coats have been seen marching along the Road about 14 miles above this place …We have reasons to believe that the enemy are strong. We Expect to be attacked this night. If possible send us some reinforcement soon." He added a postscript, "For god sake send some ammunition."

While these messages crisscrossed, Wemple ordered Schenectady's improved defences to be manned. When Gansevoort received Wemple's report, he advised Major-General Lord Stirling (who had just arrived to take overall command in the north) that his brigade's regiments from east of the Hudson had still not arrived at Albany. In consequence, Stirling ordered the New Hampshire brigade, which had just arrived from the south, to halt its march to Saratoga and head west for Schenectady. Then, Stirling had Gansevoort collect fifty of the city's mounted militia and send them off. Next, he sent instructions to Brigadier-General Van Rensselaer to rush on troops from his brigade to counter Ross's threat.

When Wemple received Willett's express with the report that Ross had crossed the Mohawk and was marching to Johnstown, he sent it to Albany, adding, "For god sake let us have some men to go and join that brave officer and endeavour to relieve him. The more so as he has no provisions in the fort not sufficient to support his men above one day … I mean to send up as many men as I can spare from those few I have here, hardly sufficient if the whole was to stay to defend this place as there appears a great Manovre of the Enemy. I am not clear that it is safe for me to leave this place … naked of men." The colonel organized volunteers from 2ACM's five companies and sent them upriver. When Van Rensselaer's Claverack men arrived after a long, forced march, he pushed them forward. Yet, for all the excitement caused by Ross, the Lake Champlain threat was very real and, as soon as Stirling received news that Ross had gone northwards, he had the NH brigade reverse about and head to Saratoga. One can hear the men groan![12]

Captain John Littel, 3TCM, commanded a small garrison in Fort Johnstown drawn from his own company and the Exempts. When he heard that the enemy was coming up Tribes Hill road, he chose eleven men to guard the fort, including three of Sir John's former tenants, and then formed a scout composed of Exempts' Lieutenant Zeph Batcheller with Serjeants John Eikler and Henry Shew; Corporal Jacob Shew and nine privates. The scout set off down the road accompanied by Lieutenant Isaac Saulkill of Whelp's, who was riding express to Schenectady. About noon, they bumped into Ross's van five miles east of Johnstown. The Indians opened fire, dropping Saulkill dead in the road. Littel gave orders

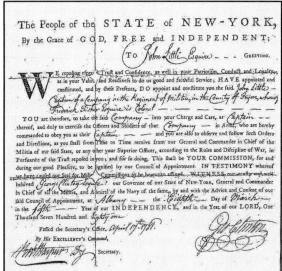

Detail of a reproduction of the original in J.F. Morrison's collection.

Governor Clinton's commission to Captain John Littel, dated April 17, 1781. This document appoints Littel as captain of a company in Fisher's (Visscher's) 3rd Tryon County Militia battalion.

to return fire, but Jacob Shew shouted disagreement. Some men dove into the woods on the left, others on the right.

After stopping for a short rest after climbing Tribes Hill, Ross's force set off again with Hill's warriors in the van. The Indians moved forward with their customary skilled blend of caution and speed and managed to surprise Littel's scouts and kill Saulkill, quickly securing his mount and sending his dispatches down the column to Ross. Resuming the march, they set fire to buildings on both sides of the road and collected more horses and livestock. And, to judge from Ray Guile's report, McMaster's men crossed the Mohawk, trailed the raiders uphill, and sniped at the rear guard.

Ross's column burst into Johnstown and was in midtown before any alarm was given. Perhaps the Town Constable and a friend did something brave or were simply in the wrong place; both were killed. Although the main body bypassed the fort, some flankers provoked sentry Stephen Shew, who gave fire. The tiny garrison turned out, but after a few exchanges of musketry and some shot from the fort's small guns, the enemy moved off. As so much of Johnstown belonged to Sir John's family and friends, the raiders burned very little and moved through town to the grounds of Johnson Hall and halted.

Scottish-born widow Rebecca Van Sickler visited Ross's troops, perhaps to search for an old-country relative or, as likely, for her two sons who were in the Levies, as one had narrowly escaped death earlier as a Woodworth's ranger. Passing by the rebel prisoners, she saw Printup's mangled thigh and persuaded Ross's officers to allow him to stay at her home, which may well have saved his life.

Once the raiders were gone from the fort, several men sortied out to give chase and met up with Captain Littel, who had made his way back into town. He ordered them to return to the garrison and then set off to pursue the enemy. Littel came across John McMartin and ordered

334 | A dirty, trifling, piece of business

him to turn out and, when John arrived at the fort with musket in hand, he found "the utmost confusion & disuray prevailing Every where." Meanwhile, Littel snuck up to the Hall fields and saw the raiders butchering and roasting livestock.[13]

William Wallace rejoined Willett two miles from Johnstown about three o'clock, and reported exactly what Littel was observing; the enemy was preparing food at the Hall.

Major Rowley had originally moved his MA Levies and 2TCM militia to block Ross's line of retreat along the river's north bank, but when he heard that Ross had gone north, he joined Willett southwest of Johnstown.

The colonel now took a significant tactical gamble and divided his force. Rowley was sent with Clark's and Heacock's companies and a body of men from 1 and 2TCM on a wide left hook through woods and around a swamp to cut Ross off. As soon as Rowley was on his way, Willett marched the NY Levies and some militia into Johnstown.

Frederick Ulman was able to observe the colonel's progress from the cover of some woods where his Native captors were holding the prisoners taken the day before. Once in town, Willett picked up some stragglers and drew out the fort's garrison, leaving only a few old men as guards. He had Levies from six companies and a smattering of militia and began organizing for an attack. Sources say there were no more than 412 men — 228 with Willett and 184 with Rowley. Willett must have realized he was substantially outnumbered, but he did not hesitate.[14]

While Ross waited for the troops to eat a quick meal and prepare supplies for the retreat, he grew very uneasy about the lack of specific information about the enemy. From his examination of prisoners and captured dispatches, he had expected a strong reaction, but where was it? So far, rebel opposition was weak and fragmented, not at all in keeping with predictions, so he decided to send out several scouting parties. Identifying who was assigned has proven difficult. Later, Ross reported that only one subaltern, five serjeants, and forty-one rankers of 2KRR were in the battle, which would mean that two subalterns, three serjeants, and fifty-two rankers were on some other duty. It makes sense that Ross would select Tryon County men for scouting and he partially confirmed this theory when he reported on November 16 that two 2nd Battalion soldiers "sent out as Spies just before the action at Johnstown have returned to this place a few days ago." Probably, the scouts were divided into small packets and sent in different directions. Whatever the case, as so few Royal Yorkers were missing at the end of the expedition, these fifty-seven men, whatever their duty, must have rejoined the column after the action.

During the halt, provisions and goods were impressed from Janet Grant, Angus McNaughton, and John McDonell, all loyal local Scotsmen: seven sheep; one and a half barrels of salt beef; thirty skipples (see page 454 for definition of skipple) potatoes; twelve skipples Indian corn; ten skipples flour; two firkins butter (one firkin equals roughly 40.9 kilograms); one piece Linen; one ell plaid (one ell equals roughly the distance from the elbow to the wrist); thirteen shirts; one greatcoat; fourteen small cloaks; twelve blankets; six silk handkerchiefs; six hand towels; two tanned hides; a fuzee (fusil) and dirk and, enigmatically, a Bible and psalm book. This haul was valued at £35 17S and Ross paid £3 10S on the spot.

When the major asked David Hill to recommend a good route of retreat, he offered little help, saying, "we wou'd go in the Woods where it was fit for Indians to fight." Hill thought Ross "well satisfied" with this insight. Fortunately, the major had other local experts to consult. Tice recalled being ordered at about three o'clock to march with the Indians by "the nearest and best way to Carleton Island." This was about the time that Rowley left Willett to go on his flanking movement. Lieutenant McDonell noted a later start time, "In the evening, we drew off from that once hospitable gate [Johnson Hall]," but this seems too late.[15]

Littel watched Willett enter town, then took his scouts to "where the enemy had built their fires and saw them retreating into the woods about half a mile north of Kingsborough." His scouts "pursued as fast as they could run and came up close to the woods" and, from the cover of trees, opened fire on Ross's rearguard.

Alex McDonell recalled the expedition's rear was scarcely moving when the enemy made its appearance. As the expedition's front had already entered the woods, he reckoned that its strength was obscured, which tempted the rebels to pursue "their imaginary prey with amazing celerity." He continued, "We marched about half a mile into the woods, and the Rangers being ordered to form and cover the retreat, were disposed in excellent order by Captain Butler; we were placed in ambuscade, each being concealed behind a tree and lying flat on the ground. The last man of our Rear had scarce passed us when the pursuers came within shot. They were suffered to approach very near before they had any intimation of the ambush. The signal, however, being made they were soon convinced of their mistake by a general and very effective discharge."

Littel's serjeant, John Eikler, ducked when he was showered with bark from a bullet strike causing the captain to caustically remark, "why do you dodge when you see the bark fly[,] you are in no danger." However, a second ball hit Eikler in the chest, and then another grazed Littel's leg. The pressure was too much and the scouts retreated, abandoning their fallen serjeant. One fellow assisted his limping captain. In McDonell's words, the Rangers sprung up and "reversed the chase with the greatest alacrity."

Back in town, Willett had dispatched Major Finck and fifty men to reinforce Littel and buy more time to organize his attack. Finck's men advanced across the Hall fields and were met by Littel's scouts hotfooting from the woods. After the captain's leg was bandaged, Finck led the combined detachment back in and they had advanced only a short distance when they were met by fire. Finck's men drove the Rangers back, hotly pursuing them a half a mile only to brought up short by Ross's main body arrayed along a ridge. Finck and Feeter were the first to catch attention, but the balls struck trees ten to fifteen feet above their heads, as the British had failed to adjust for downhill firing. Right after this volley, Feeter saw an Indian hiding nearby and dropped him, but Finck ordered a retreat when he spotted Rangers manoeuvring to get in behind.

At about four o'clock, Ross's column was a quarter mile into the woods when he was told that the rebels were "just in our Rear." Judging that fatigue would prevent his troops from outpacing the pursuit without losing a great many men from his rear units, he formed for action.

As noted earlier, Ross had been eager to command an expedition into the Mohawk and his ambition could scarcely have been satisfied with burning some farms and taking a few prisoners. Over the past months, rebel prisoners had sung the praises of Willett, and Ross saw him as a worthy opponent whom he yearned to fight. He had written, "Could I draw him out with his garrison, I shoud hope to give a good account of him." There would be little martial glory in returning to Canada after accomplishing so little, so Ross showed little reluctance to confront his pursuers.

He found a height of land and formed his companies along the ridge. Firing was heard from the back trail, followed by a short delay, and then a brisk resumption. Scattered musketry continued until Finck's men came through the trees. Butler's Rangers melted to the flanks and uncovered Ross's main body positioned along the crest. The companies volleyed and the rebels pulled foot when the Rangers moved to get in their rear. Ross ordered his line troops to doff knapsacks and then put his little army in motion, a tactic that followed the standard British doctrine of instantly capitalizing on an enemy's retreat.

Willett's NY Levies and militia arrived at the Hall fields and advanced over ground littered with dismembered animals and smouldering cooking fires where they were joined by Finck's men as they retreated from the woods. Willett sent Finck and his men to the right flank to guard Moodie's 3-pdr and continued forward. He was repeating methods that had worked so well for him in earlier engagements — rapid pursuit to grip the enemy, then close up and launch a sharp attack. As the infantry advanced, Moodie dragged his gun to a rise from where he could enfilade the British if they emerged from the woods. Willett shifted his infantry into an adjoining field that was used by the British earlier and marched in two parallel columns. His right column exchanged fire with Ross's skirmishers, forcing them to retire precipitously into an adjacent wood. Willett recalled, "In this pleasing situation, without any apparent cause, the whole of the wing turned about and fled ~~in the most shame~~." Others recalled Ross's skirmishers exiting the wood line and being pushed back by a charge. Isaac Mason of Putman's said that the line closed to within eight rods of the British front, gave fire, charged and broke their line. Presumably, he referred to Ross's skirmishers, who retreated, reformed with the line troops, advanced and broke Willett's men. Another man said that Ross's Regulars advanced aggressively, "the very countenance of which made the Rebels give way," and give way they did, in full flight. McDonell of Butler's wrote, "When we got into the clear fields, and they had perceived our small numbers, they attempted to form, but were too closely followed to effect a long stand, particularly when they perceived the rest of the party advancing, which joined us on hearing our fire." His recollection suggests that Willett's troops were caught in the midst of forming line from column when they broke.

Tice and his Indians had been a mile into the forest when they got Ross's order to join Butler's Rangers. They came on at speed, spurred by the sound of firing. When Ross's lead infantry emerged into the open fields and began to form front, Moodie's gun galled them with a brisk fire, at which point Butler's Rangers changed front and volleyed. Just then, the Indians arrived and immediately added to the fire. Then, "with their usual yells," both Indians and Rangers assaulted. In Ross's laconic words, the Rangers fired a few "platoons," and charged. After a brief show of resistance, the gun crew and guards fled with a precipitation equal to the others and the Rangers secured the piece, taking seven men prisoner. McDonell wrote, "We took a field piece and a baggage waggon with a large quantity of ammunition." Other Rangers and Natives ran after the fleeing rebels.

It may have been during this short, sharp action that Major Finck gave vent to his legendary temper and struck a shirker to the ground. No matter, no officer was able to rally the men and they ran through the fields toward the security of the town. Captain Littel was again wounded in the brief fight by a tomahawk blow to the shoulder. He managed to get away with Henry Shew leading him by the hand. With a game leg and throbbing shoulder, he could only hobble along. He urged Shew to leave him to his fate, as Fort Johnstown was a mile and a half off, but Shew bravely persisted and, miraculously, they arrived safely in town.

Willett stood in the field exhorting his panicked men to reform, but they ignored him and streamed by. A Massachusetts veteran thought that Willett's troops were young and untried, but this is an odd explanation, as most Levies had seen years of service. Ross reported, "They broke and fled with precipitation in full view for more than a Mile." He complained of a lack of "a good Body of Indians (few of those present venturing to engage)," absurdly musing that their failure spoiled his chance to "crush the spirit of rebellion on the Mohawk River."

Was this rout simply due to the sudden appearance of disciplined redcoats, the flash of their bayonets, and spirited, disciplined advance? Perhaps. Certainly, the Levies were no more fatigued than Ross's men, in fact less so, for they had marched far less. And, they were no wetter, as both sides had tramped through the rain and forded the river. Ross's sudden, cheap victory was inexplicable and fed a dangerous sense of contempt and superiority in him and his men. The raiders dropped their guard, lost cohesion, and fragmented into small groups, some pursing the Levies, others scattering to search for booty before the Indians beat them to it. Ross thought that many rebels owed their lives to some men stopping to kill the wounded.[16]

Of course, some rebels turned to give fight, taking up positions at defensible points. A few halted at a hedge running eastward from Johnson Hall, but after a few rounds, ran off. Last to leave was militiaman Joseph Wagner. Just before he set off, he shot at a "genteelly clad," long-haired officer who had sprung through an opening in the hedge. The man fell and Wagner swore a hundred muskets fired at him in retaliation as he scampered to safety.

James Crosset and William Scarborough had arrived late and ran to join the troops. When they came to the Hall fields, they found their fellows in full flight with the British in close pursuit. James shot at one or two, then took a bullet through his hand and wrapped it in a hanky before returning fire from behind a hemlock stump, but he was soon killed and Scarborough was captured by a party of Scotch troops. A Captain McDonald recognized William as the fellow who had bested him in a politically motivated brawl before the war. Enraged by the memory of his humiliation, he ordered the prisoner shot. Three Highlanders obeyed, but bungled the job. McDonald drew his sword and swung it at Scarborough, who caught the blade in its descent. The captain wrenched it free, almost cutting through William's hand and then killed him with a second blow.

Ross's men chased the flying rebels through the fields, past dying cooking fires and littered carcasses, down the road and across the bridge over Canada Creek, almost to the doors of St. John's Anglican Church, where the fugitives had broken in a window to gain refuge. During the chase, Captain Stephen White of Willett's was overrun and captured. At times, the pursuers' firing had been so intense that Scarborough's mother's home near the Hall farm had thirteen bullet holes in its siding. When Finck joined Willett at the church, he was ordered to get a few volunteers and retake the gun. The major co-opted his three brothers and George Stansell. They crept out of town, through some woods and were hunkered behind a fallen tree when Stansell was shot through the lungs. Hoisting him up, the Fincks beat a hasty retreat. Back in town, the major organized a second try, but again had no success and returned with nothing more than a cocked hat and a bottle of brandy. Willett was equally unsuccessful in inspiring his troops to make a second effort.[17]

Ross recalled thinking the fighting was over, when Rowley's left hook suddenly appeared in his rear.

When the flanking force separated from Willett at about three o'clock, William Wallace was in the lead with his vanguard of Tryon militiamen, many less than sixteen years old. He went along the river road south of Johnstown, across the creek near a mill until they were quite a distance north of the Hall, then downward to the east along the north side of the Hall Creek and through the woods to the edge of the open fields. The militia took up positions along the edge of the woods and opened a desultory fire on those British that were within view. Rowley joined Wallace; neither had any notion of Willett's debacle and fully expected to coordinate their efforts with his, so they were confused when the 3-pdr fired at any militiaman who showed himself. Rowley told Captain Clark to send a man to the gun crew and tell them they were in danger of hitting friends. Private Enos Moore was sent and, as he drew near the gun, he shouted to an officer, whom he thought was Continental artillery captain Andrew Moodie. The officer shouted back that Moodie was not there; these men were Butler's Rangers and, to Moore's shock, the Rangers opened left and right and the gun fired. He scampered back to the woods. This was Rowley's first intimation that something was terribly amiss and, from the enemy's possession of the fieldpiece, he concluded that Willett had attacked and been repulsed. Wallace recalled "the enemy in different places on the Hall farm," a wide dispersion that could have provided an excellent opportunity, but Ross's officers near the woods were quick off the mark and sent troops to outflank the militia. Rowley advanced his Levies and had them in position before this attack went in. Now, the tables were turned and, along the wood line, the rebels outnumbered the British. Wallace recalled Rowley's men advancing and firing on the enemy, who immediately diverted men to their right along Hall Creek. Rowley ordered Wallace to challenge these fellows and, taking some volunteers, he ran to meet them. He told his men not to fire until ordered, but one man fired, and killed the British commander, or so Wallace thought. When Wallace gave fire from the front and Rowley from the flank, the British quickly withdrew.

In the fields, Ross's troops were reassembling in files and sections while brisk musketry continued near the woods. Major Rowley was struck by a ball in the ankle and was taken to the rear. Other officers such as Clark, Heacock, and Wallace forced some British to shelter behind a fence, where they made a firm stand. Other rebels retook the fieldpiece, but not before the Rangers spiked the touch-hole, stripped the cart of musket ammunition, and blew up the gun charges. Low-intensity fighting surged to and fro for almost an hour, during which time the Stone Arabia militia led by Captain John Breadbake and Lieutenant John Zeilie arrived.

Somehow, they had combined with McMaster and his Warrensborough men, who also joined the fray. Independent rebel skirmishers roamed the fields and kept the British from mounting a decisive response. Rebel accounts have left the impression that this random fighting was entirely in their favour, yet at some point, Lieutenant Jacob Myers, 2TCM, was killed; Captain Samuel Clark and his lieutenant, Dudley Holdridge, were severely wounded and Lieutenant John Zeilie was taken prisoner, while, despite rebel claims to the contrary, Ross had no commissioned casualties throughout the battle.

At long last, Willett returned to the fray with Tryon and Albany Militia reinforcements and some Levies. Enos Moore derisively said that Willett brought no more than twenty men, but other sources say he arrived with 100. Romantically, John Duesler of Putman's deposed that Willett came up to the recaptured gun, laid his hand on the barrel and shouted, "hurra for Lady Washington." Another veteran recalled Willett as the first man to lay his hand on the gun, as if the retaking of the piece had been sharply contested and a matter of great moment. Perhaps it was, as another witness said there had been a fight over the gun, "with the loss of several lives by the enemy around about the field piece," as well as some Whigs. Perhaps Ross was expected to pack the gun through the wilderness; a thought which may not have been pure fantasy, as he later apologized to Haldimand: "I am sorry it was impracticable to bring off the field piece, there was no possibility of taking it farther than the Edge of the Wood." Yet, if there were a fight to recover the gun, no one would know it from Ross's dry account.

William Wallace's report closed ecstatically: "Thus, for a second time, the militia of Tryon County defeated the enemy with a very inferior number." He continued, "At Oriskany, the enemy were two to one in a battle of about five hours and were completely drove back [and] left Herkimer unmolested to make beirs and carry their wounded off." On the contrary, the odds at Oriskany had been quite even, and, if the mortally wounded Herkimer had been "unmolested," the gruesome toll of dead and wounded of his shattered brigade was quite the opposite. Wallace expanded lyrically, "Then 250 drove Ross from the field with seven or 800 men — like bulldogs, hold fast or die with the holt."

Butler's lieutenant, Alex McDonell, saw it this way: "The evening was now so far advanced that we could hardly distinguish our own men from the enemy." Like all British accounts, his estimate of the opposition was fanciful: "They had just been joined by a fresh body of 600 men, exclusive of small platoons of thirty or forty which continually flowed into them, so that their numbers amounted to 1400 and upwards when night parted us."

Of course, Ross shone a favourable light on the final stages of the fighting, reporting that Rowley's detachment "suffered much and nothing but night coming on prevented their Total destruction, the darkness favored their escape."

Ross's men gathered at their knapsack depot. Thirty-two were missing, some had deserted, some were wounded, some lost. Among the deserters was Nicholas Herkimer, a Niagara volunteer, who was later to give Major Finck details of Jacob Klock's abortive July raid. Simon Moss, a former Harper's Levy, switched allegiances again and stole away from the Royal Yorkers. A Highland Emigrant deserted, some said in disgust over Scarborough's murder.

———

At eight o'clock that evening, Jacob Winne, Willett's QM, wrote to Henry Glen from Veeder's Mills in Caughnawaga. He said the enemy was in Johnstown and Willett had been defeated, losing his fieldpiece and retreating to the fort in the town. Winne had been on the way to join him when he got the news and returned to the mills. He planned to march to Johnstown that night with some Tryon militia.

———

Tice reported that three Indians were killed and four wounded in the fighting. One of the dead was a brother of the noted Tuscorara sachem, Saqueresa. Two Onondagas and Christian the Oneida were wounded. Turning to fight had cost Ross in terms of dead: eight soldiers and three Indians and in wounded: ten soldiers and four Indians for a total of twenty-five — just over 4 percent of his original strength of 583 — a greater loss than Johnson's of the year before, but not crippling. Compared to "Woodworth's disaster" of the previous month, Ross's loss in dead and wounded was moderate for a much more extensive action. Some rebels reported Ross's "missing" as high as fifty men, including Indians, whom he failed to record. Yet, the meticulous Major Finck recalled only thirty-seven to thirty-nine prisoners. Incredibly, Van Slyck's 2ACM company claimed to have captured twenty-seven. A handful of Ross's casualties may have been local loyalists, such as Frederick Bell, whose brother Thomas had joined 2KRR the month before, and who was killed in the action. Perhaps he had planned to "come off" with the troops, but such men would not have been in Ross's computation. Ensign Sutherland heard later from local informants that five Royal Yorkers, three Jägers, and eight Regulars gave up, "quite dispirited, through fatigue, having thrown away their arms," which varies little from Ross's accounting.

For whatever reasons, Ross exaggerated the size of his opposition:

> The Action, considering circumstances, ended most fortunately. By the Prisoners we found that the number of the Enemy in every attack far exceeded our numbers, besides many other disadvantages, without Cannon and much fatigued, several officers taken assert that more than twelve hundred men were in pursuit of us (amongst whom were four hundred Continentals from Schenectady) and that the greatest part, if not the whole, were engaged, so that the smallest Computation there could not be less than a thousand men, which was nearly three times our numbers. It is impossible to ascertain the loss of the enemy, but it must have far exceeded the King's troops, which in Killed and wounded is but trifling. The Enemy lost many Officers, and in one Spot Twenty men lay dead in the field. Night and the darkness of the woods prevented knowing our own Loss, and in consequence of both, together with the Effects of extreme fatigue a considerable number is missing.

How misleading! Ross was confronted in the Hall Battle by fewer troops than he had at his own disposal. Yes, there were likely 1,200

Levies and militia or more in pursuit, but accounts show them to have been spread far and wide.[18]

Rebel casualties were similar to Ross's, although British accounts consistently exaggerated. Tice said the rebels had about seventy killed in the Hall Battle, "among whom was Captains Garrason[?] & Selley with two Lieutenants which I saw & knew. Sutherland reported, "one Captain of Militia[?] and 1 Lieutenant of nine months men, Kill'd with about 50 Private[s], and several taken Prisoners." Tice brought sixteen prisoners to Niagara and claimed to have had double that number, but said the main guard allowed many to escape. Of course, his numbers included those taken prior to the Hall Battle. In February 1782, a British intelligence report gave rebel casualties as fifty killed or wounded exclusive of prisoners taken. Surely, Willett's official return to the governor was the most reliable: "York Levies killed, one Lieutenant, Six Rank and File; Wounded, four; Missing, One Captain, three Rank and File; Massachusits Levies, wounded One Major, One Captain, One Lieutenant, Five Rank and file; Militia killed, five rank and File; Wounded one Lieutenant[,] Eleven R. & file; Missing One Lieutenant" — forty-one total casuals.

This little confrontation at Johnstown can scarcely be considered a battle in the classic sense; it was nothing more than an extended skirmish, yet, as the largest armed conflict in the north in 1781, it earns a place in history on that score alone. To review — Ross had been in the process of withdrawing when the rebels closed with his rear. As the better of two choices, he chose to turn and fight, just as Sir John had the year before at Klock's Field. It was not Ross's intention to hold a piece of ground, but to bloody Willett's nose and sufficiently punish his pursuers while gaining time and space so he could continue his retreat. His initial attack did just that, forcing Willett's men to break and run. Ross had not anticipated Rowley's flank attack, which garnered some success, but neither forced his surrender, nor prevented his withdrawal. Clearly, Willett suffered a severe reverse at the outset and only Rowley's arrival put a better face on affairs. Ross's casualties were not major, nor were Willett's. Nonetheless, judging from the pace of Ross's retreat over the following days, his desire to avoid further punishment was a strong motivator. To sum up, Ross had won the first round; he had destroyed much of his target, done some collateral damage, and beaten off a pursuit.

———————————

The evening of the battle, a war party arrived at Duncan McGregor's home several miles north of Johnstown. Armed with his sword and musket, McGregor hid at the back of the house, vowing to himself to kill anyone who abused his wife and then take flight to the woods — a desperate plan with little chance of success. He watched a Tory ask for Johnny-cake, which his wife provided with some milk. He saw another ask about a painted chest. His wife said it belonged to a relative in Albany and the man replied, "He belongs to the rebel army I suppose." The chest was split open and books and clothes tossed onto the floor. The raiders took the clothing, but mindful of the lady's hospitality, left without burning the house, fortunately for McGregor.

The main column marched six more miles before halting for the night. The Indians still held Tanner, Ulman, and fourteen others prisoner, but, as already noted, the main guard had many others, of whom several were allowed to escape for reasons that will become apparent.

———————————

Torches were used to search the Hall fields and the bodies of Crosset and Scarborough were found and drawn by sled to Fort Johnstown. A chunk of meat was discovered in the mouth of another corpse, which was thought to be a sign of Native derision. Joseph Wagner and friends looked for the man he had shot in the hedge gap. When he was found lying nearby, Wagner admitted to shooting him and offered to take him to the fort for medical care. The man exclaimed, "I would rather die on the spot than leave it with a d_____ rebel," so he was left to his fate. Several lost, dispirited enemy soldiers were found wandering about and were held overnight in the fort while many of Willett's men slept at the Hall. Their colonel's work was hardly done; he sent William Feeter home to Stone Arabia to ask families and friends of wounded men to come and care for them. Feeter, who had not eaten since early morning, travelled twelve miles on this mission of mercy. Presumably, other men were sent on the same errand to other local settlements. Fresh troops arrived throughout the night including some of dead captain Elsworth's company between 2:00–3:00 a.m. The prisoners who had "escaped" from Ross's main guard arrived before daylight with news that the British would march to Stone Arabia for provisions, so Willett set out for there at daybreak with a force about equal in size to Ross's.[19]

Troops left behind to search for more bodies found three friendly and seven enemy. Sir John's ex-tenants, who had been ordered into Fort Johnstown prior to the action, assisted 3rd Tryon's men to dig a mass grave for a common burial. They recalled interring thirty-eight rebels killed in the open fields and around the bridge over Canada Creek and thought more lay in the woods. The corpse of a large Indian was covered over by a pile of rocks; perhaps it was thought improper to bury a savage with the whites, whether Christian or not. Sergeant John Eikler of Littel's, one of the first struck down, was found alive in the undergrowth. He was taken to his home in town and soon expired.

Most of Elsworth's men had remained in Johnstown and were joined by part of White's company, which, in response to rumours, had completed an incredibly circuitous march from Ballstown, to Fort Rensselaer, to Herkimer, back to Rensselaer, and then to Johnstown. Some other Levies joined the two part companies and they set off at ten o'clock with orders to cut off Ross's retreat and destroy his boats at Lake Oneida.

At the same time, a group of MA Levies and 2nd Albany militia escorted the British prisoners to Fort Hunter and took the wounded to the Albany General Hospital.

In keeping with the system of rapid deployments to counter threats, Colonel Wemple, 2ACM had the greatest part of his regiment, some Albany city militia and about thirty Oneida warriors on their way upriver before 6:00 a.m. As they passed Fort Hunter, Oothout's 2ACM company joined from the garrison. In the afternoon, Colonel Schuyler's 3rd Albany marched through Schenectady on its way west. The pursuit of Ross was gaining momentum.[20]

On October 26, Ross asked Tice and Hill to secure the boats at Lake Oneida. Hill's men thought the mission too risky, but Tice changed their minds that evening in the camp a half-mile beyond the Garoga Lakes' outlet. Next morning, the war captain set out with four warriors.

Willett waited at Stone Arabia all of October 26 and the following night before concluding that Ross would not appear. It seems the wily Scot had allowed prisoners to escape with false intelligence as a ruse to buy time for his escape. As the British had not turned south, Willett was convinced there was no danger of a "sudden stroke below the Little Falls." On the morning of October 27, he marched for German Flatts to put himself between Ross and his boats, which was just as well, for when he arrived there, he found that the Levies he had sent to destroy the boats had "returned without doing their duty." A soldier of Livingston's company recalled, "a party of men & friendly Indians were ordered to go to Fish Creek above Fort Stanwix to destroy the boats & property of the enemy, [but] we met with hostile Indians & were driven back." It is unclear whether these Indians from the expedition or an entirely independent war party.

Having been duped once, Willett needed positive information about Ross's route and expressed orders to Littel to immediately send out scouts to track the expedition. Littel already had a small party out and, early on October 26, they captured two soldiers who had fallen behind and found the knapsacks of those who had surrendered earlier. They came back with their captives and booty, but with no firm idea of the enemy's route.

The resilient Littel had sufficiently recovered from his two wounds to lead a new effort and, with Jacob Shew and the reformed Tory recruiter, William Laird, set off on October 27. They made good time, as there was little chance of stumbling into the enemy. The weather was bitter and, when they came to Ross's campfires on October 26, they raked up the coals to warm themselves. Pushing on, they tracked the column a little farther. Then, satisfied that the route headed north, they backtracked and camped at the old fires.

———————

There were a few roads through the Mayfield and Jerseyfield patents and Ross took the most easterly one, following it for several miles until stopping on a ridge a half-mile from Black Creek to camp the night of October 27. A drove of cattle had been slaughtered along the march, but this had been quickly consumed and, from that point on, the expedition chiefly depended on horseflesh. When they set out the next day, Tice made bold to note that they had been undisturbed by the enemy in front or rear.

———————

Littel and his scouts had tracked Ross for about twenty-eight miles and were back at Fort Johnstown on the morning of October 28. A horse stood fed, watered, and saddled, and Littel chose Peter Yost to make the forty-mile ride. Meantime, Willett had been joined at Fort Herkimer by the companies of 1 and 2ACM and their Oneida companions. On their way upriver, these men had seen how easy it was to sort out Tories' farms from Whigs', as the latter were intact and the former were plundered and burned. These scenes hardened their resolve. When express rider Yost arrived with word of Ross's northern route, Willett concluded "that the enemy having given up the hope of arriving at their Boats were directing their march to Buck Is, or Oswaugashee." Again, his terrific energy and genius for improvisation came to the fore. He spent the day "furnishing the Choicest of the troops & Sixty Oneida Indians" with four-and-a-half-days' provisions. By early evening, 400 men had been ammunitioned and provisioned and, to "stimulate" the Oneidas, he promised each a blanket. Exactly how the "Choicest" men were selected is unknown, but for sure, the colonel did not pass through the throng and choose his favourites. Likely, the NCOs were instructed to select the fittest, most rested, and most keen and they did their job. An examination of seventy of the 400 chosen reveals that a few of Moodie's artillerists volunteered as infantry and that nine Levies' companies were represented. Of the militia, five were from 2ACM, one 3ACM, one 14ACM, three 1TCM, one 2TCM, two 3TCM, and one 4TCM — a diverse group indeed. For senior officers, Willett had Brigade Major Finck, Colonel Peter Bellinger, 4TCM; Lieutenant-Colonel Volkert Veeder, 3TCM; and Major Abraham Copeman, 1TCM. How such a disparate group melded into an operational tactical unit is a mystery.

That evening, Willett's force marched out of Fort Herkimer and crossed the Fort Plain ferry to the river's north shore. The troops paralleled West Canada Creek, forded it a mile north of Fort Dayton, then continued to a brook, which they traced up the Jerseyfield road, then went north until stopping for the night in a thick wood in the Royal Grant. As snow had fallen and it was bitterly cold, the troops were permitted fires. Supposedly, Willett offered a reward to any volunteer who would climb a tall tree and look about for the enemy. One fellow came forward, threw off his coat, and shinnied up the trunk. He shouted down that he could see a light a short distance off to the northeast. After consulting his compass, the colonel decided where Ross was encamped and ordered the intrepid Lieutenant Jacob Sammons of Gros's to take two men and scout it out. Sammons knew the area well and was able to find Ross's camp without disturbing his guards. Leaving one man huddled in the cold woods to watch the enemy, he returned with the other. Supposedly, he reported the enemy was well armed with bayonets, which surely was no surprise, as the use of cold steel was a known specialty of the British infantry.[21]

Willett's men were on the move early, but not soon enough to catch Ross's column. They marched all of October 29, slogging another twenty miles through a snowstorm before Willett called a halt at a well-known landmark called The Hurricanes and sent out an Oneida scout to confirm Ross's location, which presumably was accomplished.

Ross reported that, due to bad weather, the expedition did not strike the Carleton Island track until October 29. That evening, the Six Nations' warriors told him they would leave the column the next day and "march home through their own country." Presumably, the Canada and Mississauga Indians were to remain with the column. Following tradition, Ross went to Tice's fireplace to shake hands with the League Iroquois and thank them for their good behaviour. Later, he vented a firestorm of complaints over his virtual abandonment: "the natives had left him without any regard to the column's safety … they fled to a man at the smallest alarum … they had never been of much service and now they were none … the expedition was still only a day's march above German Flats and the day was late, the troops fatigued, snow had fallen and the Indians failed to scout the area."

Conditions were terrible. Corporal Andrew Embury of Leake's recalled marching for "a no. of days through the Snow; and ha[d] to lay down on it at night in the open wilderness when the weather was very Severe."

Ross's two servants hung back to dry clothes at the fire with Tice's man when the troops marched off next morning. Although the British Indians may not have feared pursuit, the 6NID officers were more cautious and Ryckman went on patrol with two Brant's Volunteers.

At first light, Willett sent Lieutenant John Thornton of White's to locate the enemy's trail. Thornton divided his squad into files and partnered himself with an artillerist. They had gone quite a distance without finding any sign, then, just as they mounted a ridge, they came across traces of Ross's camp almost hidden by fresh snow. Thornton sent word back to Willett and moved on with his partner. He had not expected to find the enemy near at hand, so was surprised to hear voices slightly in his rear. Glancing back, he saw Ryckman and his men, and realized he had inserted himself between them and Ross's main body. The pair hid in the underbrush and watched the patrol pass. After a time, they cautiously followed the fresh tracks, at any moment hoping their own advance party would catch up. Dawn was breaking when they entered a little beech plain on The Hurricanes at about eight o'clock. A sudden shot crashed out from a treetop ahead and the artilleryman sprang two feet into the air from the ball's impact. As Thornton knelt beside his dead companion, he saw the ambusher run off. He waited until the vanguard came up and joined them to continue the chase. At Black Creek, they came across about forty men, some organizing provisions, others drying clothing. A sharp firefight ensued. Ryckman and the three officers' servants were taken with their mounts; several were killed. Those who fled abandoned packs, food, and blankets. Quickly reorganizing, the vanguard continued pursuit.[22]

The rattle of small arms fire failed to carry to Ross's column in the snow-deadened woods and the troops marched on unconcerned; however, an ominous sound did roll over the hills from the southeast in the form of the progressive cannon discharges of a *feu de joie*. Ross mused about what prompted this celebration and only later realized it marked Cornwallis's defeat in Virginia. Then came a shock: "soon afterwards one of [the rebels'] advanced Partys fired at an Indian in our Rear, which was the first intimation I had of the Enemys approach." Now, the pursuit became a footrace, the raiders setting out at a trot in Indian file, hotly pursued by Willett's vanguard. The weather was damp and bitter cold, creeks were swollen and many deep; fast flows had to be crossed. At the widest, deepest fords, Ross's men kept their feet by walking four abreast carrying poles. A pursuing militiaman recalled that some creeks had frozen over and his mates, who took off their trousers to keep them dry, worried that ice would cut their legs. Willett was amazed by his opponents' endurance, "Not withstanding the Enemy had been 4 days in the Wilderness with only half pound of horse flesh for each man per day[,] In this famished Situation Major Ross with such of his men as could keep way with them trot[t]ed more then thirty miles before he Stoped." At a particularly nasty ford across West Canada Creek, the raiders drove hard and got across about 2:00 p.m. It was here that Ross posted Captain Butler with a body of Rangers as a delaying tactic.

About the time that Ross's column were fording West Canada Creek, four Oswegatchies and a Delaware caught up to Tice with news that a large party of rebels was pursuing Ross. Tice's people kept very still, but could hear no firing. Puzzled over what to make of the news, they marched on. Somewhere along the route, the Indians killed and scalped the prisoner, Jacob Myers, who had been taken near Currytown, as he was simply too old to keep up.[23]

Willett's Indians were in the vanguard well ahead of the main body with some Levies and a fit body of 2ACM militia led by Lieutenant Teunis Swart of Van Patten's Company. The colonel reported, "Our Indians were very usefull[;] they pursued them with their Common alertness upon such occations ... they are the best Cavalry for service in the Wilderness." Such a contrast to Ross's attitude!

What happened next is the subject of a great many tales told by men who witnessed the event or came upon its aftermath. Some claim that Walter Butler rode his horse across the ford and dismounted just as the first men of the vanguard closed up. Many reports leave the impression that the skirmishing that followed was short and sharp and that Butler was killed almost immediately. Lieutenant Alex McDonell wrote that the rearguard "had scarce crossed when the rebels appeared on the opposite side. They expected to overtake us before we could ford the creek, which is very deep and rapid. As soon as they perceived us, they gave a general discharge. We returned the compliment and kept up a pretty brisk exchange of such favours for near ten minutes, when the gallant Captain Butler was unfortunately shot through the head by a rifle ball." Levy Philip Graff recalled, "coming down a hill to the creek we rec'd a very strong fire from the enemy who had crossed the West Canada Creek, which was returned from Willett's men with spirit." Another said the southern bank was covered by huge hemlocks and thick undergrowth. Heavy, dense fog hung over the creek as the vanguard came up, which suddenly lifted and the British delivered a warm fire, causing the soldiers to draw back apiece. A few witnesses recalled a verbal exchange between Butler and the vanguard. One remembered Butler taunting, "Shoot and be damned," and another, "kiss [my] posterior." All could be true, as Butler was known to speak his mind. If McDonell and Graff are to be believed, the claims that Butler was at the stream's edge taking a drink from a tin cup are unlikely; however, that he may have been shot while directing the defence from behind a tree is credible. Graff recalled the Tory captain peering around a tree and being shot through his hat and upper head. He then staggered and fell and the Native marksman ran through the other warriors, forded the creek, and found his victim tottering up and down in great agony. Butler stared his assailant in the face as the Indian shot him through the eye and coolly stripped off his scalp. If so, Butler would have been amongst the last of the Rangers to withdraw, as, according to this version, the Indian was totally unopposed. But note, if this tale were true, Butler would have had two head wounds, yet most accounts say only one.

The identity of the Native marksman is another matter of debate. Most accounts name Colonel Louis, the Kahnawake leader of the rebel Oneidas and Tuscaroras on so many of their forays. One Levy gave the name as "Lewey;" another as "Louis Nic," both variants of Colonel Louis, although "Black Louis" was his most common nickname. Other witnesses named entirely different Natives, such as Harmanus, a Schoharie, or Anthony, either a Mohawk or Oneida Sachem. One veteran said the Native stripped off Butler's regimental, donned it, and boastfully strutted about the shore, an act of bravado entirely in keeping with the warrior code.

In contrast, Lieutenant Thornton said he was one of the first men across the creek. He found Butler lying dead near a tree and, pulling the captain's gold-laced hat from his head, saw the bullet hole. As Thornton was wearing lightweight linen pants, he stripped the corpse of its warmer woollen pair. If he is to be credited, then all those who recalled the Indian crossing the creek and immediately scalping Butler had to be wrong, as he would hardly have replaced the hat after the scalping, nor was it likely the warrior could have pulled off the jacket without dislodging the hat.

Levy John Duesler recalled coming to the edge of the far shore and seeing a man waving a paper and shouting it was Butler's commission. As most rebel reports gave Butler's rank as major, this document became a subject of their derision, as it was only his 1776 ensign's commission from the 8th Foot and made it appear that he had puffed himself up. Henry House saw Butler's "dead body lay on the ground with his Scalp taken off and was nakit." Richard Casler remembered an Indian with Butler's scalp and coat and seeing a dead serjeant of Rangers. Philip Graff said he saw three dead Rangers, two of them serjeants and a private shot through the body. These accounts reflect Ross's return of BR casualties, a dead and wounded serjeant and three dead and one wounded privates.

In the melee, an 84th private was wounded and a 34th private went missing with three 2KRR privates. This mix of units was further proof that the column's stragglers had no sooner crossed the creek than the vanguard was upon it. Despite the loss of his corps' senior captain, Lieutenant McDonell's newspaper article prosaically commented, "The skirmish being ended, we continued our march for Carleton Island." Willett was far more dramatic in describing the British withdrawal and Butler's death: "[O]ne man's being Knocked in the head or falling off into the woods never stoped the Progress of his Neighbour, not even the fall of their favourite Butler, could attract their attention so much as to Induce them to take even the Money or anything Else out of his Pocket, altho he was not Dead when found by one of our Indians, who finished his business for him and got a Considerable Booty." Most rebel accounts, including Willett's, state that the vanguard took no casualties in this affray, which could indicate, as McDonell said, that they came upon the Ranger rearguard before it had time to take up defensive positions or that the large hemlocks on the south shore sheltered them from fire. On the other hand, Finck's recollection was that the action was by no means bloodless for the rebels. He reported that ten to fifteen men were killed during the pursuit, which would have included the morning's casualties as well as those suffered at the ford.[24]

Ross offered this explanation for pushing on beyond the crossing: "The Enemy had greatly the advantage of Ground & their favorite object of firing at a distance, wherefore I ordered the Troops to move forward in order to take possession of the first favorable Spot that offered." He sent his sick and wounded farther along and waited in position for nearly an hour before concluding that Willett did not intend further pursuit and then resumed the march. In contrast, Willett reported to Lord Stirling, "we pursued them as Closely and warmly as possible untill quite Night," which was hardly corroborated by Ross's recollection of getting across the creek at two o'clock in the afternoon, unless his "first favorable [defensive] Spot" was several miles beyond the ford. Willett said that, if he had followed the enemy for a day or two longer, his troops would have been in scarcely better condition than the enemy, as his Indians and many men had cast aside their blankets and provisions to "pursue them with greater vim," and these were twenty miles to the rear. He made no mention of fearing an ambush, which certainly must have been a great inducement to turn back.

He reported: "The woods were strewed with the packs of the Enemy; Provision they had none. A few horses they had amongst them when first we fell in with them, they were obliged to leave; except five, which were sent a Considerable way in front, with some of their Wounded and a few Prisoners." This was an observation that had to be made by a deserter or straggler who fell into his hands after the pursuit was abandoned. He waxed poetic to the governor over the likely fate of the enemy. "[T]o the Compassion of a starving Wilderness, we left them in a fair way of Receiving a Punishment better suited to their Merit than a musquet ball, a Tomahawk or Captivity." To Stirling: "I shall not attempt to give your lordship an account of the enemies loss through the whole of this affair — But shall leave it to the fields of Johns town[,] The Hills[,] the Mountains[,] the Deep and Gloomy Marshes[,] the Rivers and the Brooks in the Desolate region for more than twenty miles in length[,] thirty miles in width of North of Fort Schuyler thro which they have & thro which they are to pass the rest through snow." These images circulated among the rebel high command as if actual fact. How chagrined they all would have been to know that Ross marched his men without further loss for seven days in atrocious weather, even to the extent of crossing rivers on rafts. Perhaps, he had thought ahead and strategically located provisions' depots along the pathways south of the Island. If not, his men would have been close to starvation. A particular observation of Willett's deserves repetition: "The man who sent such a fine Detachment of Troops upon such a Paltry Business … will be best able to say how great their loss has been and to him I leave it." Certainly, the strategic damage done was minimal compared to the 1780 expeditions and scarcely warranted the lost manpower exacted from Haldimand's meager resources.

Predictions by Niagara's officers that targets were now so deep inside enemy territory, and so inconsequential as to be too risky to undertake, had been fully proven. Adding to the hazards of deep penetration was

Willett's energetic and persistent reaction, which meant that the days of quick, cheap in-and-out thrusts were gone.

Willett crowed to the governor, "[T]he affair might have turned out better, yet it is a most Capital stroke in favour of the County of Tryon." While this has the appearance of exaggeration, the colonel had expected Ross to raid farther up the valley on his return march to his boats, although the major at no time showed any inclination to do so. With this possibility in mind, Willett understandably believed he had prevented far greater destruction and, from the shelter of his success, he risked being critical of his immediate superior: "Was I disposed to find fault I think I have cause to do it the calling away Major Logan with those two Companies … from Johnstown by General Stark, has undoubtedly been an Essential Injury to us; such an Addition to our strength at Johnstown must have assured us a most Compleat victory … and the Calling of those Troops from this Quarter to a part where they have the whole Eastern world at hand to Reinforce them, appeared to me as unaccountable at that time as it has Proved Injurious since." Willett's remarks were as fatuous as Ross's claim that the Indians had spoiled his opportunity to "crush the spirit of rebellion in the Valley." There was no reason to think two more companies would have led to Ross's defeat at Johnstown.

Of course, all this analysis came days later. For now, Willett's men were far from home and the expedition's dregs had yet to settle. It was dubiously claimed that, when the vanguard crossed West Canada Creek, a five-year-old white girl was found crying piteously under a fallen tree where an Indian had abandoned her to better make his retreat. It was also recalled that a mortally wounded Tory was sent back down the track on horseback under guard, but soon died and was buried. Another account claimed that, once Butler's killer recrossed the creek, he strode up to the British prisoners with his victim's scalp in hand and struck it against a tree, shouting, "Take the blood." Turning to Ryckman, he shoved the hair in his face and the lieutenant snapped his head back to avoid the repugnant stroke.

358 | *A dirty, trifling, piece of business*

When the artillerist's body was prepared for burial, it was found that his coat, which he had tucked up under his belt, had been perforated five times by a single bullet. The soldiers buried him in the cavity of a toppled tree by cutting through the trunk and righting the roots. While other dead were being buried at Jerseyfield, Willett gave a Tory prisoner to the Oneidas to avenge the stabbing death of one of their men. The man had been found with a bloody knife in his hand and was presumed guilty. Anticipating his fate, he asked the Whig officers if they were going to allow his murder and, in answer, they silently stood by and watched him being tomahawked. During the return march, the Oneidas carried their enemy scalps on a trophy pole as they marched through the woods and settlements. The sanguinary trappings of frontier warfare were by no means only found amongst the Crown's forces.

News of Butler's death and Cornwallis's surrender was celebrated in Johnstown with a prolonged peeling of the Court House bell and a huge bonfire in a nearby street. In Schenectady, Whig homes were illuminated and Tories who showed reluctance to follow suit were threatened with mob action. Not long after, Butler's jacket and officer's insignia were sold in the town and his scalp was traded at Albany.

When the Warrensborough lad, Ray Guile, came home, a small ball was removed from just under the skin below his knee. After being hit in the Hall Battle, he had carried this missile all through the arduous Canada Creek pursuit. Within days, he was well enough to enter the Levies, but, after his adventurous experiences, was assigned the dull task of building a blockhouse in his home settlement.

Immediately after the Hall Battle the rebels ordered the removal from Johnstown and vicinity every inhabitant in the least suspected of being disaffected. After so many attempts at this, it is a wonder that any were left.

That most militant Christian, Reverend Daniel Gros, wrote of his joy over Willett's several victories and the death of "bloody Butler," lamenting that illness during the past two months had prevented him from sharing in the honour.[25]

It will be recalled that Captain David Hill had been sent to prevent the boats cached at Lake Oneida from falling into enemy hands. When he arrived on October 31, he found the craft untouched and destroyed them, then left for Niagara. Hill made no mention of the twenty sick and lame men left behind as a guard, so presumably, they had returned to Oswego after waiting for a set number of days. When Tice arrived on November 3, he found the cache of supplies gone and six bateaux cut to pieces and sunk in the lake. At midnight, six Butler's Rangers arrived with news of how the rebels had overtaken the main column, pursued it to "Large Canada Creek" and killed Captain Butler. Next morning, the men hauled a boat ashore and, using pieces of board, repaired five large holes and set off for Oswego.

In the style that so endeared him to his subordinates and won their respect and loyalty, Willett fulsomely praised those who had a hand in punishing the invaders. He addressed the Massachusetts Levies in General Orders: "his thanks to Major Rowley and the Officers and Soldiers under his command for their Services since they have been upon this frontier, and Especially to those few troops of this Corps who were with Major Rowley in the Action of the 25th Ultimo at Johnstown, whose Bravery Demands Particular Acknowledgments."

Of the Tryon and Schenectady men he wrote:

> Colonel Willett presents his Particular thanks to the Militia of this County for their alertness in turning out to oppose the enemy in their late Incurtion … he finds himself Compeled In the Strongest terms to Testify his approbation of the behaveayer of those few brave men amongst them whish Composed a part of the left wing that so Nobly fought and repulsed the enemy in the Action of the 25 Ultima at Johnstown.
>
> It gives him particular pleasure to acknowledge to those few Choise Souls who went out with him into the Wilderness in pursuit of the enemy. To the men of Colonel Bellinger's regt Commanded by the Colonel himself. To the men of Colonel Clydes regt Commanded by Major Coopman. To the men of Colonel Clocks regt Commanded by Captn Backbread

To the men of Colonel Vishers regt Commanded by Lt Colo Veder And to those few Militia from Schnectidie Commanded by Captain Jellis J Fonda.

The Spirit that has been exhibited — upon this occasion must Convince the enemy That These are a people not to be trifled with. And will undoubtedly Damp that Dirty Spirit of Enterprise that can have nothing but the Destruction of Individuals for its object …The Particular attention[,] great Diligence and manly Deportment of Andrew Finck, Esquire through the whole of this Affair … merits everything that can be said in his praise. He is Requested to Accept…Sincere Acknowledgement of his Services.

To his Levies and Continentals: "The Patience and Fortitude that has Discovered itself in the officers and Soldiers of the Levies throughout the whole of this fatigue does them great Honor. And the few Artillery men, under the Command of Capt. Moody with the Rest of his Officers, who Voluntarily became Musqueteers that they might participate in these Toils, merits Particular Applause."

————————

Ross, who had received as much, or perhaps even more, resilient and dedicated service from his men had only this to say in his report to Haldimand: "The Troops have suffered much in their Limbs by the wetness of the weather and likewise by hunger, all which they have endured with that fortitude which becomes soldiers." He expressed sincere regrets over the death of Walter Butler, "whose loss to the Service in General and to the Corps in particular is much to be lamented."

At month's end, a domestic matter arose that may have somehow meshed with Ross's expedition. Two friends, Peter Bellinger and Nicholas Bell, planned a trip to near Little Falls to pay a debt. Bell's wife chided Peter to take care of her husband. In equally good humour, Bellinger promised he would take care of her if he failed to bring back her husband. It was all in jest, but the event proved anything but comical, as a couple of miles above the Falls, Bell was killed in an ambush. Bellinger shot an assailant and ran for his life and, after some distance, shook off pursuit. True to his word, he later married the widow. Were these the Indians that had stopped Willett's troops from destroying Ross's boats or were they just another one of the flood of random war parties that terrorized the region?[26]

THEY CANNOT HAVE THE LEAST HOPE OF SUCCESS

Now let us step back in time and place and follow the affairs of the Lake Champlain expedition. Although raiding in the Champlain, upper Hudson and lower Mohawk valleys lacked the intensity of the upper Mohawk, it was of constant concern for the inhabitants and garrisons. In October, one of Porter's MA Levies was taken near the ruins of Fort George and, in the midst of "neutral" Vermont, three men were lifted, probably by Canada Indians. As Schenectady was specifically threatened, the city's regiment was on rotation guarding its various small posts. With no great fondness, a militiaman recalled a three-week stint at Teunis Swart's fort, a palisaded brick home armed with a small field piece near the Mohawk's fourth flat.

When Major Logan came to Albany with Weissenfels's two companies, he took local command and informed Captain Marshall that his appointment had been at the city's particular request. Fully expecting Logan would remain for some time, Marshall sent most of the Levies he had kept back for guard and administrative duties upriver to the regiment. To his surprise, Logan and his companies were sent to Ballstown and he had difficulty scheduling reliefs for his puny six-man city guard or supplying escorts for convoys.

On October 8, Stark reported to Heath that the supply of ammunition had at last arrived, but noted that the twenty-four sheets of paper sent to serve both the garrison and his headquarters would only last a few days. Willett would send the excess ammunition reported by Villefranche to Schenectady for safekeeping. Small enemy parties were everywhere. Two enemy soldiers had been captured the night before and confessed to being part of a five-man party that had split up just a few miles above Saratoga.

Thomas Lovelace, the commander of the Tory party whose instructions had been forwarded to Heath, had been hanged in compliance with his court martial. His four men were sentenced to imprisonment for the duration and sent to Albany. Stark enclosed a strength return and urged the C-in-C to send reinforcements if he judged it sensible, reasoning that the season was so far advanced, there would be no time to react if the enemy appeared. He had promises of support from Vermont, but was quite skeptical and was disappointed that he had not received official news about the French fleet or the southern army.

The governor wrote Stark in response to his complaint about the jailing of soldiers for tavern debts. He was "fully impressed with its destructive consequences" and promised to ask the Legislature to prevent future abuses.

Stark used up one of his few pieces of paper to advise Gansevoort that two British regiments, one of Jägers and "all their Tories" had concentrated at Pointe au Fer with marching orders for Saratoga. He asked for 200–250 militia with six days' rations to be sent as soon as possible to help him retard the enemy's advance until a sufficient force could be organized to give battle. Gansevoort received this letter the next day and immediately wrote to fellow brigadier, Robert Van Rensselaer, advising that he had called out his regiments from the districts most directly threatened, although he was unsure of what response he would get from Hoosic and Schaghticoke district, as it lay within Vermont's new claim. He believed a general turnout of the county's militia might convince the enemy to cancel his plans, which, with the lateness of the season, would shut down his efforts for 1781, and perhaps for the rest of the war. Gansevoort then sent Stark a list of the regiments he had called out: Yates's and Van Veghten's were ordered to Saratoga and Wemple's and Van Bergen's were to assemble and be ready to march. The rest of the brigade would march to Albany from where he would lead it to Half Moon to await Stark's orders.

On November 10, Heath ordered NH militia Colonel Reynolds at Fort No. 4 to detach his major and 200 men to join Stark. This left Reynolds with another 200 that could move to aid Stark, or to the Connecticut River settlements, should the enemy strike there. Due to the large number of troops concentrating at Saratoga, the lack of flour was a concern. Marshall discovered that Albany citizens who were willing to help had none to spare, so he sent a Commissary of Issues to procure supplies, by force if necessary (in particular from Tories around Saratoga, Half Moon and Schoharie). Schuyler offered Stark "whatever beef he ha[d] fit for the knife" and all the wheat at his Saratoga property. To keep everyone on edge, one of Weissenfels's men was taken at the ruins of Fort Ann, but whether while patrolling or hunting is unknown.[27]

On October 9, the Light Companies of the 31st and 44th Regiments moved into camp at Pointe au Fer and two more Jäger companies joined von Kreutzbourg. He recorded that his three Jäger companies had 121 combatants, a number mysteriously below their nominal strength of 100 each.

Haldimand's very carefully crafted proclamation for Vermont arrived at Fort St. John's. Everything was coming together for St. Leger's movement up the lake.

On October 11, Captain Sherwood and Dr. Smyth left Isle aux Noix aboard the eight-gun row galley *Trumbull*. After a stop at the Loyal Blockhouse, they sailed for Crown Point to find out if their scouts had been in contact with Ira Allen or Joseph Fay. En route, Serjeant Andrew Rikely, KR, came aboard with the alarming news that the keeper of one of the Service's safe houses had betrayed his party. Fortunately, Caleb Clossen had managed to escape with Sherwood's dispatch for Sir Henry Clinton, but Rikely and Serjeant Lemuel Caswell, QLR, were taken in irons to Saratoga where they witnessed Thomas Lovelace being hanged at Stark's door. Under pressure, Rikely agreed to show the rebels where the agents had hidden their boat and was sent with an eighteen-man party. At an opportune moment, he struck down two, disarmed another, and escaped.

Sherwood was outraged over Lovelace's execution. "This barbarous Murder of my worthy friend … stings me to the heart! I hope in God His Excellency will permit us to retaliate either by hanging up some of the rascals we have prisoners … or by taking and hanging on their own ground some of those inhuman butchers." Predictably, however, Haldimand refused to condone such a contravention of the rules of war.

On October 11, Stark wrote his friend and fellow Bennington veteran, Vermont general, Samuel Safford, about British activity and requested help. Later that day, he sent Gansevoort the startling news that the enemy was "on this side of Lake George," urging, "For God's sake hurry on with all the Force you can collect as perhaps this may be the Last Information I can Give you until they are in reality here. I can Give no information of their Force but we must be prepared for the Worst."

In a letter to Governor Clinton, Heath expressed distress over Stark's execution of Lovelace. He noted that the man had been carrying written instructions to seize a prisoner and was leading an armed party and, as such, could hardly be considered a spy. He could not grasp "upon what principle he was executed" and was concerned the incident would bring considerable difficulties and suggested it would be best to keep mum about the affair.

The flurry of dispatches continued. An aide of Governor Clinton's wrote to Robert Van Rensselaer giving approval for a full assembly of the county's militia. He was to hold his brigade in readiness to support Stark or reinforce Willett.

At 8:00 a.m. on October 12, Schuyler sent an express to the governor about Stark's report that the enemy had landed at Lake George, recommending that Clinton "hasten up" to Albany, "or much evil may arise."

Max Rosenthal, engraver, 1885, after an earlier print. (New York Public Library Digital Gallery, image 417882.)

Yet, for all the excitement, the warning was false, as St. Leger was still at Fort St. John's. Stark's inadequate intelligence system must have confused intensive patrolling with an invasion, thus raising an acute level of anxiety in the rebel command.

Lieutenant-Colonel Barry St. Leger, 34th Regiment (1733–1789). This rather unpredictable, touchy, yet proficient officer led a confusing, almost farcical expedition on Lake Champlain in the fall of 1781.

That same day, Colonel Wemple, 2ACM, wrote to Gansevoort from Schenectady with his own report that the enemy was on Lake Champlain. He was still concerned about a thrust from a second direction and reminded the brigadier that the town was vulnerable from both north and west. He had scouting parties out to Schoharie, to Jessup's Patent and to the Salt Springs. He reported the arrival of two fieldpieces from Albany the evening before without ammunition and asked for a supply of powder and ball for 6-pdrs. As the town's security was of great concern, he urged speed.

Schuyler re-entered the scene, advising Stark that, due to the enemy's arrival, he had sent two expresses to Gansevoort urging him to hasten on the militia and had written to MA General Rossiter for reinforcements. A letter bound for Canada had been intercepted which said a team of arsonists would soon come to burn Albany, so he had ordered Indian scouts to assist the militia in intercepting these incendiaries and instructed all other Natives to join Stark.

Heath wrote Stark on October 12 that he had set up a chain of expresses between his HQ and Saratoga. He required reports of the size and structure of the enemy's force, who was in command and details of their movements. He cautioned that it would take about thirty hours for word to reach him. Heath was still unaware of Stark's bogus news of a landing at Lake George and warned that, from the size of the bateaux the enemy had built, the intention may be to move up the lateral rivers to the head of the Connecticut. He reasoned that, as long as the British remained at Pointe au Fer, there would remain doubt as to their intentions and he anticipated much deception on their part.

Heath informed Governor Clinton of Schuyler's news that the enemy had completed seventy new bateaux at St. John's and that carpenters were repairing others. Further, all the troops at Montreal, except city guards, had been sent to Fort St. John's, where 1,000 Regulars and Irregulars and seventy Indians had accumulated. Another 800 were said to have gone up the St. Lawrence to relieve the western posts and, to judge by their baggage and stores, this appeared to be their destination (perhaps this was 1KRR performing the duty of supplying the upper posts). He had warned the eastern states of a possible thrust to the Connecticut

River and confessed, "I am very apprehensive [that] if the enemy make a serious move at the northward, Sir Harry [Henry Clinton] will make one on this side."[28]

Adding to the alarm over an invasion, the discord between New York and Vermont heated up. On October 13, Lieutenant-Colonel John Van Rensselaer reported that, since last May, Vermont had employed every artifice to exercise authority in Hoosic District. When the head of one of his classes refused to provide a nine-months' man, he ordered him detained, but pro-Vermonters rescued the fellow and said they would pull down the colonel's house if he attempted to exercise the state's authority. Since then, Vermont had seized and sold at public *vendue* the effects of many friends of New York. On September 13, he had received a threatening letter from Chittenden, which said in part: "If you persist in your opposition you may depend on it you will be taken care of … on the next account I have of your continuing your notorious, insulting and obsene conduct." Such were relations between two states supposedly fighting a common enemy.

In a letter to Gansevoort written at eight o'clock the morning of October 13, Governor Clinton advised, "The enemy's force is so formidable at New York & in such perfect readiness for some capital movement as to justify an apprehension of an attempt agt the posts in the southern parts of the state and to make it necessary to be prepared agt it." Such unrest and anxiety up and down the state was precisely what Haldimand hoped to create.

When Stark's dire news of a landing at Lake George reached Heath, he was totally persuaded of its veracity and ordered Massachusetts colonel, Benjamin Tupper, the NH brigade's senior officer, to select his best-clothed men and a detachment and fieldpiece from the 3rd Continental Artillery and immediately march for Albany. If winds were favourable at Fishkill, he could embark on vessels, if not, he must march on with all expedition. When he arrived at Albany, Tupper would express a report to Stark and continue to Saratoga, or to wherever he was ordered to march. If he got certain news that the enemy had retired, he was to return to the Highlands Department, leaving behind the 2NH. He was to draw three days' provisions, fill the men's cartridge pouches and transport 15,000 spare musket cartridges. The C-in-C then wrote Stark advising of this new disposition and instructing him to return these troops the moment they were judged unneeded. He explained that, although 2NH was low in numbers, it had excellent troops and more field officers than 1NH; therefore some companies of Levies might be incorporated. He sent Governor Clinton the same news and asked that the state quartermaster procure forage and wagons for the troops and the state agent provide flour, not only for the troops in the north, but for the Highlands, which were also in great need.

On October 14, Gansevoort informed Stark that the 2NH, a gun, and crew had arrived and that his own brigade was speedily assembling. He added an extremely prescient comment: "It appears very probable to me that the enemy are not serious in making an excursion from the northward, as they cannot have had the least hope of success." He thought the enemy only intended to distract in the north and their blow would fall to the west. He asked permission for his militia to leave Half Moon and march to Schenectady and he sought approval that the 6ACM, which presumably was already at Saratoga, be sent to Half Moon. To seal the issue, he had already ordered Brigadier Van Rensselaer's brigade to Schenectady. One has to wonder how the hypersensitive Stark enjoyed being second-guessed by an Albanian militia officer, a breed he had so little use for. It would matter little that Gansevoort had been a Continental officer with a reputation for skillful leadership earned in the defence of Stanwix in 1777 — after all, he was a New Yorker. In another unilateral decision, Gansevoort had told Colonel Van Bergen, 11ACM, that, as troops were pouring in from every quarter, his regiment's services could be dispensed with. He was to return to his district of Coxsackie/ Groote Imbocht and arrange his men for maximum security, keeping out a sufficient number of good scouts.[29]

On October 12, Sherwood and Smyth arrived at Crown Point and were disconcerted to find that no one was there to receive Haldimand's proclamation. This same day, Thomas Johnson arrived home at Newbury in Coös. He had finally been persuaded to promote a reconciliation with Britain and decided to allay his fears of committing treason by taking on the role of double agent. He planned to correspond with Haldimand to discover his plans and pass them on to the rebels, a tense double game that was almost to be his undoing.

Although Stark's alarm had triggered a great deal of activity and anxiety, Haldimand's orders for St. Leger were not even prepared until October 14. He was instructed to proceed to the upper end of Lake Champlain and take post at Crown Point. He would not engage in hostilities unless attacked, but would carefully observe Vermont, "not trusting too far their friendly disposition." He would send a detachment up Lake George "to cause such terror and dismay on the west as they possibly can." To accomplish this task, he would take trucks from Fort St. John's to convey bateaux overland from Champlain. He would leave St. John's as soon as the 29th's Lights and line troops arrived, taking the troops that could be spared from the St. John's and Isle aux Noix garrisons. At Pointe au Fer, he would put under orders two British Light

Detail of a watercolour after von Germann's 1776 original. ("The Von Germann Watercolours of the American Revolution 1776-1783." Gansevoort, NY: Corner House Historical Publications.)

Companies and the Jägers and would stay on the lake as long as the season admitted, or "unless any event should happen to make it necessary for you to return sooner." Haldimand arrived at St. John's on October 15 to answer any questions St. Leger might have and see the expedition off. That same day, the 29th Lights entered the Pointe au Fer camp under the

A Hesse Hanau Jäger. This image portrays a Jäger in his dress uniform. By 1781, it is likely that the coat and cocked hat had been laid aside as impractical for campaigning.

command of Lieutenant William Farquhar, an experienced officer who had raided up the lake on at least two previous occasions.

Von Kreutzbourg noted that Major Jessup arrived the next day with "150 Loyalists and Rangers," an amazing number, as according to Haldimand, the KLA was no larger than 127 effectives and, like all loyalist corps, many men were with the Engineers, Secret Service, and on other duties. No matter how important this expedition, Jessup could not have freed up all of them, indicating that Major Nairne had likely sent men from McAlpin's, which had returned 116 in May.

Haldimand's adjutant, Captain Brehm, arrived with Jessup and gave von Kreutzbourg his first intimation that St. Leger would lead the expedition. The two colonels had endured a hostile relationship in 1777, to the extent that von Kreutzbourg labelled St. Leger unfit for command and lacking in initiative, but there was no hint in the German's journal that he continued to hold such opinions. Foolishly, Brehm recommended that winter clothing be obtained for the Jägers, but nothing could be done, as their baggage was at Chambly. That evening, Major William Monsell arrived with 100 line infantry of the 29th and Major Alex Dundas with 100 of the 34th. Possibly because St. Leger was colonel of the 34th, his second major, Robert Hoyes, was given command of the Light companies of the 29th, 31st, and 44th.

Von Kreutzbourg also noted the arrival of "Major Rogers with 150 Rangers, and Colonel Peters, with as many Loyalists." Rogers mustered 182 in April and may have brought 150 King's Rangers, but Peters could never have raised 150, as the QLR had no more than eighty-two in April and, if McAlpin's reinforced Jessup, there were no units left to shore up Peters. Perhaps, von Kreutzbourg heard that Rogers and Peters had 150 men and assumed each brought that many. The colonel estimated St. Leger's little army at about 900 men, but it was more likely no larger than 750.

With marked foreshadowing, Haldimand gave Jessup senior command of the loyalists, which assuredly galled Peters and certainly upset Rogers, as both were senior in the Provincial line. As to Natives, the governor wrote, "I have not Sent a Single Indian across Lake Champlain, knowing the Impossibility of Restraining them to Discrimination, chusing rather to riske the Loss of their Services Should Vermont

Courtesy Parks Canada.

Captain Jessup's belly box and belt. Another very rare artifact of a Provincial soldier. As the inner flap is inscribed with only rank and surname, the owner is somewhat in doubt; however, it was only Joseph Jessup who held the rank of captain during the Revolution.

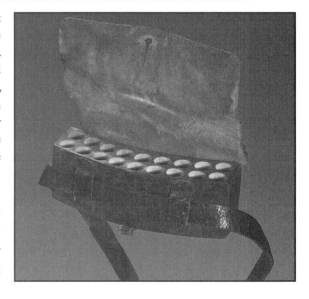

Attack, than the Danger of exasperating that People by trusting the Indians amongst them."[30]

On October 15, Captain Marshall wrote a sarcastic letter to Major Caleb Stark, who was serving as his father's aide at Saratoga: "I suppose you are under no great apprehensions while the Albanians and the contiguous militia are at your backs. Their patriotic spirit never shone more brilliantly than at this juncture. And their resolution and firmness, I am sure you cannot doubt; for larger numbers of them have been severely handled heretofore by the Governor, for their [inactivity] on similar occasions … Great spirit and determination is evinced by their officers — swearing death and vengeance against the delinquents. Of some [regiments], two companys, and of some three have already marched. I hear a certain general swear, 'God d___m him, if he did not make them smart.' So the next account, after the alarm subsides, will be bloodshed and slaughter among our friends in this quarter; shrieks, cries, and deadly agonizing groans already vibrate on the drums of my ears." As side issues, Marshall advised that the treasonous Dunham had escaped before his court martial could be held and confirmed that the 2NH and the 6-pdr would move north as soon as wagons were obtained.

Schuyler advised Stark that Rossiter of Massachusetts had arrived in Albany and 800–900 of his militiamen were expected that evening. As Reid's 2NH was already in town, he suggested to Rossiter that he wait for further news about the need for his men and asked Stark to send advice as soon as possible in order to save the public the expense of provisions. He added that all was quiet in Willett's district.

Everyone was now doubting the alarm and Stark settled the issue by writing to advise Heath that it had been premature. The expenditure of so much good will, energy, and resources must have been troubling. Yet, that very same day, Schuyler reported to Governor Clinton that the enemy was between Crown Point and the ruins of Gilliland's Mills. Again, this was incorrect, as St. Leger's main force was forty miles north of Gilliland's. Perhaps, a scout had seen Sherwood or noted some naval activity. With great pleasure, Schuyler described the spirited militia assembling from all quarters and enthused that Reid's 2NH gave them so much confidence that they looked forward to meeting the enemy.

His observation about the militia's high spirits ignored the ugly upheaval between New York and Vermont, which had been agitated by Stark's request for aid from both jurisdictions. Gansevoort's concern about his regiments in the Western Union proved fully justified. In 4ACM's district, a gang of malcontents had even plotted to capture him. Colonel

Henry Van Rensselaer sent his major and 100 men to apprehend them and, in the ensuing fracas, two men were wounded, one mortally. All of the villains escaped except a fellow named Fairbank from New City, a former 4ACM private whom Chittenden had commissioned a colonel. Even he soon escaped, which suggested skullduggery. Of course, Vermonters saw the event in a different light. General Safford told Stark that he had sent orders "to the militia, now considered in this State [i.e., Vermont], in the neighbourhood of New City" to assemble in support of Saratoga. Lieutenant-Colonel Fairbanks reported that he had gathered a number of men and that NY's Colonel Van Rensselaer came with a party of militia, took them prisoner, broke open their houses, and distressed their families. Safford mused, "Such conduct appears very extraordinary at this time, when every man ought to be rather employed in the defence of his country, than in destroying his neighbours' property. What Colonel Van Rensselaer designs, is best known to himself; but it has the appearance of preventing men going to defend the frontier ... The inhabitants of this western territory are willing to do their duty under Vermont, but are prevented by York. And now, sir, if you judge it lies within your province to quiet those disorders, I must entreat you to do it. That we may be united is my sincere desire. The dispute of jurisdiction must be settled between the States; but if such conduct is persisted in before, I must repel force by force."

Spinning this further, Vermont colonel Eben Walbridge, of Mapleton, sent Colonel Henry Van Rensselaer a list of demands. He warmed to the topic by saying his only motivation was to settle the dispute honourably and peacefully. He chastised him for taking prisoners and threatened that they must be released and all damages made good and, in future, the people would be left unmolested until Congress settled the issue, or Van Rensselaer would answer for it.

A citizen in nearby Schaghticoke district wrote to Governor Clinton about a meeting held by several friends of New York at which they found a handbill posted by two, "so-called" Justices of the Peace appointed by "the free-men of Vermont." It said the pro-Yorkers were to cease "advising the people ... trying to disaffect them ... spreading evil reports and raising sedition." Then, one of the justices arrived with armed men and ordered them to disperse, but they paid no regard and finished their business.

Stark was thrust into the middle of this turmoil by a letter from Colonel Samuel Robinson of Bennington, which flippantly ignored all of New York's prior jurisdictional rights in the Western Union. "I am surprised to learn that the militia of Albany county have no other business upon their hands, at this time of general alarm and danger, than to distress the inhabitants of Vermont, as if they considered the British from Canada not sufficient for our destruction, at a time when all our militia are under marching orders, and most of them have already marched. This they think a proper time to manifest their spite and malice ... Part of my regiment has marched to Castleton. I shall this morning follow with the remainder. If your honor can not find the militia of Albany some other employment, I shall march my regiment to that quarter, and try powder and ball with them ... I pray your honor to check them if possible." Obviously, Stark was expected to order New York's militia out of the Western Union, but that was quite beyond his authority.

Gansevoort advised the governor that, because of Schoharie's vulnerability, he had not called out Vrooman's 15ACM and would send 300 Claverack men of 8ACM there as soon as they arrived. As Stark had taken Logan's two companies of Weissenfels' from Tryon County, he would send Van Rensselaer's brigade to Schenectady and would go there the next day to be in a better position to march when the enemy's movements were known. He emphasized his brigade's severe shortage of ammunition and provisions.

John Taylor of Albany wrote to the governor about John Cough Sr. of Tryon's Philadelphia Bush, who had been near Hoosic when he approached the home of one Woodworth to beg food and shelter. By sheer coincidence, Woodworth was the brother of Solomon, the ranger captain killed in the Indian ambush in September. Cough was not long in the house before rashly criticizing New York in favour of Vermont. Next, he revealed himself a Tory and, when Woodworth played along, he told the story of his son John being wounded at Fort Johnstown. The gossipy Cough said that the eleven soldiers who had come with John were unable to leave Tryon, as Oneidas had destroyed their canoes and the woods were full of rebel scouts. So, he decided to flee to Vermont to escape the consequences of these lads being found in his care. Woodworth offered to assist them to get away and Cough told him where they were hiding. Woodworth informed the conspiracy commissioners and they ordered him to lead a party to capture the Tories with Major Finck's assistance. Only two were taken, as nine had left for Canada two days before. With the bit in his teeth, Woodworth approached Stark for some men to pursue them, as he knew their intended route. Whether this was allowed is unknown. Taylor's letter provided other valuable news — a packet of dispatches was abroad in Tryon County destined for Canada, which he thought could be seized. As the enemy had taken one of Stark's scouting parties, he sent 250 men to the Scotch Patent to drive off cattle to keep them out of enemy hands. Lastly, Colonel Willett had reported the firing of guns the previous day at German Flatts, which, as noted in the tale of Ross's raid, had proved to be a false alarm.

———————

On October 17, General Heath sent a cryptic letter to Governor Clinton about the Central Department. Due to recent intelligence, he had ordered 1,500 NY militia to be held in readiness with five to six days' provisions. To allay suspicion, this would be done under the pretense of supporting the northern frontier, although there was another purpose that he dare not commit to paper. If the militia was already under orders to turn out, properly equipped, and provided for on the shortest notice, he thought it would be unnecessary to issue further orders. Clinton was to decide.

———————

The same day, Marshall advised the governor about the German Flatts alarm and the receipt of Willett's second express saying it had blown over. He feared "the whole alarm [across the north] will prove abortive, for now we are so well prepared I could almost wish them to come." Next day, Schuyler wrote Stark that a large body of militia had crossed the ferry near his house and added the exciting news that the British were besieged at Yorktown in Virginia.

Governor Clinton wrote Gansevoort to explain that the legislature had not found the time to discuss Vermont's expansion beyond their former claim. To avoid any altercation that might encourage the enemy, he had "submitted to insults which otherwise would not have been borne" and he would continue to do so, although he still worried that Vermont militia would assist the enemy. The brigadier should exercise his authority in all districts of his brigade and enforce the state's laws against those who disobeyed his lawful orders. Clinton cautioned that his opinions were based on Henry Van Rensselaer's accounts and, if these were exaggerated, it was his earnest desire not to bring affairs to extremities, at least before the end of the campaign. He closed with the alarming advice that he was unable to supply any ammunition, as Washington had sent the state's total share to Albany last spring. Only 500 pounds had come since and it was reserved for "the other exposed parts of the State." Nor could he supply provisions.

Imagine Gansevoort's predicament — his brigade was to defend against an enemy thrust on Lake Champlain; he dare not ignore another strike that was expected out of the west; elements of his brigade were in revolt, which he was expected to quell and Albany, the county's largest city and his family home, was threatened by arson.[31]

On October 17, St. Leger arrived at Pointe au Fer aboard the schooner *Maria* and, shortly after, sailed with the line companies for Ile la Motte, leaving behind the three Light companies, Jägers, and Jessup's. When von Kreutzbourg went to sail the next day, he found the Lights had taken his boats. Fortunately, Jessup's was able to cram between twenty and thirty into each craft, and they sailed at five o'clock in the morning, moved through heavy fog and arrived at Ile la Motte at eight o'clock. Shortly after their arrival, St. Leger set sail for Valcour Island with the first division. Four hours later, the Jägers sailed with the 29th and 31st Lights, but in confusion, von Kreutzbourg sailed past Valcour. When St. Leger saw them pass, he decided to continue to Crown Point and, in so doing, bypassed von Kreutzbourg, who had put in at Schuyler's Bay. Von Kreutzbourg spent the night at the bay and joined St. Leger at Bullwaga Bay at 3:00 p.m. on October 19. In spite of this farce, no harm was done.

Commodore Chambers recalled St. Leger's anger when he found that Ensign Roger Stevens, who had been sent with a Flag and dispatches for Sir Henry Clinton several days before the expedition sailed, had been so idle in executing his duty as to arrive at Crown Point a day after the colonel. He grumbled that the ensign had not gone as far in five days as the expedition had in eighteen hours. Stevens and the Flag were detained aboard a vessel.

At daybreak of October 20, St. Leger left for Ticonderoga with the gunboats. The order of sailing was sixteen men to a gunboat, each armed with a single cannon, leading eighteen bateaux containing the 31st. These were followed by Rogers's and Jessup's in thirty boats escorted by another five gunboats manned by the 29th and 31st. The Jägers brought up the rear. Clearly, Chambers's report was incomplete, as he made no mention of the 34th, 44th, or Peters. The heavily burdened *Lee* was to follow with the provisions; however, winds were contrary and, although the gunboats carried sixteen oars each, they could make no headway. An order was given for them to anchor and the rearguard passed through. At five o'clock, the unarmed boats arrived at Ticonderoga and, at a signal, 100 Lights disembarked and formed the left wing, and 100 Jägers formed the right. Other Jägers led by Lieutenants von Stosch and von Horn, occupied the old French lines, while the rest of the Lights took post along the waterfront across from Mount Independence and Sugar Loaf Hill. With these positions secured, the other troops landed and formed around the ruins of the fort. That evening, the Rangers and loyalists marched to the Lake George Landing. An officer, two NCOs and twenty-five Jägers took post behind the Landing on Mount Hope, which blocked the trail coming north from Fort George. Another officer, three NCOs, and thirty Jägers were posted on Sugar Loaf, which commanded both Ticonderoga and Independence.

General Heath wrote to Stark on October 20 with instructions to release the NY militia if there was any doubt about the enemy's advance,

Major-General Lord Stirling, William Alexander (1726–1783). Sent north to stiffen the resolve of the officers and troops of the Northern Department.

Benson J. Lossing, artist and engraver. (Benson J. Lossing, The Pictorial Field-Book of the Revolution, 2 vols. New York: Harper & Brothers, 1852.)

as they were needed at home for the harvest and there were insufficient provisions to keep them unnecessarily. To bolster Stark's resolve, Heath listed the substantial force that had been assembled to assist him, in the process painting an excellent picture of the U.S. Army's organizational efficiency in the face of chronic shortages. In addition to Albany County's militia, there was the NH Continental brigade, elements of Porter's, Willett's, and Weissenfels's Levies and a detachment of Reynolds's NH Militia. Further, he had sent Major-General William Alexander (Lord Stirling) to Albany to assess the situation, a decision that betrayed a tacit lack of confidence in Stark, Schuyler, and Gansevoort, the three senior officers who were on the scene and somewhat at odds over Vermont.

Stirling was a Scottish immigrant who had owned a substantial ironworks in New Jersey before the rebellion. He rose rapidly in the Continental Army and became one of Washington's most trusted officers. He had been a delegate to the Continental Congress and, as a Jerseyman, could be relied upon to appear neutral in the Grants dispute.

In an October 21 private letter to the governor, Heath confided his plan to hold the southern NY militia in readiness to react against a British attempt to reinforce Cornwallis in Virginia and, because of the danger of a leak, he ordered they were not to be told the reason for their assembly. The Highlands army had received only part of its bread allowance over the last four to five days and, if any movement was to made, at least that many days' supply must be on hand and 400–500 barrels of flour must be sent immediately.

Stark had confided his concerns to Schuyler that Lord Stirling was coming north to relieve him, receiving the reply that there was little fear of that happening, as his lordship was only on a short-term assignment. At the same time, he strongly praised the Massachusetts Levies, who had so rapidly responded to the alarm. "The conduct of the Berkshire militia is one of those events which place human nature in an amiable and dignified light. How ridiculous is the idea of conquering a country whose inhabitants, with so much alacrity, abandon the sweets of domestic ease and private concerns, when put in competition with their country. This is the true spirit of patriotism, which I earnestly hope will pervade every quarter of the United States. My thanks are small matters, but as they are gratefully bestowed, they acquire some value." This generous sentiment was notable, as Schuyler was entirely aware that his relief from the Northern Department's command in 1777 had been due to the machinations of a New England cabal.

Just when the rebel command had more or less relaxed, Colonel Tupper sent word on October 23 that a large body of the enemy had landed at Crown Point the Friday before. When Lord Stirling was informed of this new development, he ordered Brigadiers Van Rensselaer and Gansevoort to get their men ready to move. On October 24, Stirling wrote to the governor from Albany to report intelligence from Bennington that the enemy was now at Ticonderoga. He thought the details were too vague to warrant calling out the New York militia again, but Tupper had marched his NH brigade that morning to Saratoga. Of course, to everyone's alarm, this very day Ross's raiders broke from cover in the Mohawk Valley, which caused a flurry of expresses to be sent around the country and led to major changes in troop dispositions.

At Ticonderoga on October 21, St. Leger's Provincials used the truck carriages to move boats overland from Lake Champlain to the Lake George landing. Thirty-six men were in front of a truck, twenty-four on each side, and a party in the rear to manhandle each boat an exhausting two-and-a-half miles.

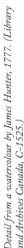

Detail from a watercolour by James Hunter, 1777. (Library and Archives Canada, C-1525.)

Gunboat and small craft. A typical British gunboat accompanying a bateau and ships' boats on Lake Champlain. Some of the outworks of Ticonderoga are in the background.

Meanwhile, two gunboats were stationed on South Bay off Mount Independence to cover that approach. One boat chased a pair of canoeists up the bay until the alarm gun was heard at Skenesborough. While cruising on Champlain, Chambers picked up some men from the west shore who had come from Johnstown as part of John Cough Jr.'s party and sent them to St. Leger for debriefing.

After swearing Von Kreutzbourg to secrecy on October 22, St. Leger apprized him of the Vermont negotiations. Either he misheard St. Leger, or he was grossly ignorant of the area's geography, or, just as likely, was told a pack of half-truths. What he recorded in his journal was a weird jumble of oddities. To wit, the expedition would be based at Ticonderoga and co-operate with Major Ross, who had, not long before, set out from Oswego with 300 Regulars and 400 Natives. Ross would join St. Leger "at Oneida Lake along the Mohawk River near Saratoga." The famous Ethan Allen and his Green Mountain Boys would join them and, with this additional strength, Albany County's sympathizers would be won over and assist the expedition to winter in the country. Early next year, they would mount an expedition against Boston, "aided by a strong detachment of Clinton's army." Was St. Leger toying with the German? His journal continued: "If something unforeseen should happen to hinder any part of this plan, a strong scouting party was to be sent out over Lake George. It was to collect sympathizers, burn rebels' homes, and after a 12 to 14 day absence, return to us. If Major Ross has the same order, Ethan Allen should be apprized of it, so he could act accordingly." Probably as a ruse to explain their inactivity, von Kreutzbourg was left with the impression that Vermont's troops would co-operate with the expedition and was told that St. Leger had already sent an officer and five Rangers through the woods to Ross, who was in the vicinity of Fort Stanwix, to tell him of their location. Another party would get intelligence near Albany and a third would go to Vermont to take some soldiers prisoner, whom St. Leger planned to set free with communications for Ethan Allan. Von Kreutzbourg wrote that St. Leger sent an incredible 350 troops "across the lake to escort sympathizers to Canada," but because of adverse intelligence, they returned. From other information, it is possible that Colonel Peters accompanied this detachment.

St. Leger wrote to Captain Mathews to report the arrival of Caleb Clossen, "who stands high in the estimation of his officers for Zeal and Veracity" and who was returning from delivering the governor's dispatches. He advised, "The whole country is in warm alarm, at the approach of the *formidable Armament* they expect." Stark had ordered the militia from all directions to Saratoga and confiscated the cattle of the disaffected and secured that of the Whigs. While many militia regiments quickly responded, others were reluctant. He had spoken to two confidential persons, well known to Smyth and Sherwood, who said that 2,000–3,000 men could be raised with ease to oppose St. Leger's advance. Caleb had been safe-housed with a Colonel Smith, a previous transmitter of Haldimand's dispatches, and while there, his host received a threatening order from Chittenden not to raise a single man for New York.

St. Leger reasoned, "This intelligence must necessarily change the offensive mode of operations" in order to favour Ross's advance by the Mohawk, or facilitate his return. As to his own operations, in prudence, he would, "make every appearance of doing, what I could have wished to do, in reality, by giving them every jealousy in my power, of their own safety, keeping them in suspense as long as possible, and thereby to prevent their sending any Detachment to the Westward: For this purpose, I shall enter Lake George, with the Loyalists, part of de Creuzbourg's Corps, some light Infantry and a party from the 29th and 34th making every show of the advance of great numbers by extensive fires and slow movements — and, thus, spin out the time, till I conceive the blow on the Mohock may be struck, and the Season reminds us of the propriety of a return to Canada."

That same day, St. Leger sent Ensign Walter Sutherland, 1KRR, and five men to the Mohawk to meet Ross. The ensign was to tell the major that St. Leger would hold his troops ready to assist. The three men of John Cough's 1KRR party told similar stories to Clawson's, reporting that 117 troops (Logan's two companies) had been pulled from Johnstown to reinforce Saratoga, as there was no word of an attack from the west. Of course, Ross was deep in rebel territory west of Cherry Valley when these men made their report.

The next day, 205 Provincials, sixty British Lights and forty Jägers formed up at the Landing under Jessup's command with fourteen days' rations and fifty rounds each. Von Kreutzbourg noted that Jessup and his officers and men had been born in this country and were thoroughly familiar with the topography and trails.

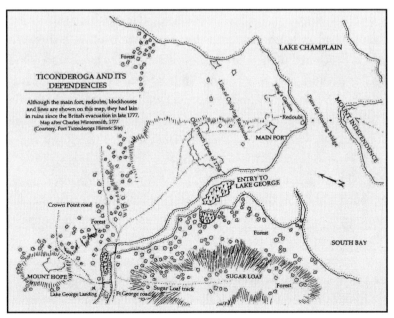

Ticonderoga and Environs.

Then, there was the bizarre tale of the party sent into Vermont. It all began when Captain Sherwood grew impatient waiting for Ira Allen and suggested to St. Leger to send a detachment across the lake to capture a Vermont patrol. The prisoners were to be brought to Ticonderoga, given Haldimand's proclamation, and released to go home. Accordingly, a British officer and twelve men were sent across to Mount Independence and ambushed a serjeant and five men on the Hubbardton road. When ordered to lay down their arms, the Vermont serjeant levelled and a British soldier killed him. The patrol returned on October 22 with the corpse and the prisoners and St. Leger now faced a diplomatic fiasco.[32]

Word had still not reached Heath about another sighting of the enemy on Lake Champlain when he wrote Stark on the October 25. He again suggested it was doubtful the British would come south on the lake and cautioned him about calling out the NY militia prematurely. In pointed emphasis, he once more reminded him of the strength of his force of Regulars, Levies, and militia. Clearly, his faith in Stark's judgment had suffered over the false alarm! He explained that Major-General Lord Stirling had been sent northward, "[w]hen matters looked very threatening" and, if necessary, he would take command during the emergency. Stark would "find great relief and support from his lordship, should the enemy advance in force. If they should not come in force, he will not interrupt ... your command." This essential "fluff" was followed by specific orders about troop dispositions. The 10MA, which was part of the NH brigade, and the artillery detachment with its 6-pdr, was to be sent south as soon as they could be safely spared, that is, after Stark was "pretty certain" that the enemy was not in considerable force, or would not advance, or had turned back.

Heath realized that troops were necessary to garrison Saratoga district over the winter and, as Weissenfels's men were only engaged until the beginning of December and Willett's till the beginning of January, the two NH regiments would be assigned and their absent detachments sent north when the Highlands army went into winter quarters. Stark was to consult with Stirling and Schuyler about where to post these troops and in what numbers. He was to consider the Mohawk River's needs and other parts of the frontiers and take the best measures in his power for provisions, fuel, and forage. After a bit more handholding, Heath wisely told him to assure the NH Continentals that "they may depend on equal justice being done them in the distribution of clothing, or any public stores." The C-in-C was well aware that far too many Regulars had missed critical issues in the past when squirreled away in backwater postings. The historic news of Cornwallis's surrender on October 17 was oddly tucked away in a postscript. Perhaps the significance of Britain's loss of a second major army was not yet apparent.

Although Lord Stirling chose not to call out Albany County's militia, Gansevoort took matters into his own hands and ordered Taylor and Yates to once again assemble the whole of their regiments without delay, including their Exempts. They were to be provided with two days' provisions and to march to Saratoga. As to Vermont's threats, the brigadier countered with one of his own, declaring that courts martial would be called after the stand-down.

Faced with a valid alarm, Stark proved he had a head on his shoulders and calmly wrote to Governor Clinton on October 26 about the future of the northern frontier. To ensure the district's safety, he thought it absolutely necessary to build a proper post near Saratoga where there were already barracks and other advantages that made it the best location. Someone with power must be accountable to procure supplies, or advance funds to procure them. His patience was exhausted in making fruitless applications to Congress's officers. He had no other recourse than to apply to Clinton, as he was "more interested in the protection of this frontier than any other man — being the father and guardian of the people." Should speedy measures not be taken, he thought that "the northern and western frontiers must be evacuated as far as Albany; and, indeed, Albany itself."

Brigadier-General Roger Enos of Vermont advised Stark that one of his captains had returned from Mount Independence where he had spied on the British for most of a day. They were repairing Ticonderoga's fortifications and nearly 200 oxen were dragging cannon and stores from their boats. What a strange observation! Where could the British have found that many draft animals? The captain reported seeing smoke from many fires rising behind the old French lines where he supposed most of their army was camped. Later, Colonel Walbridge reported no sign of enemy activity on Lake George, but promised to advise of any changes.

At nine on the evening of October 24, Jessup's Provincials launched onto Lake George, covered from the landing by the 31st's Lights and Jägers on the flanks at Mounts Hope and Sugarloaf. Jessup's men "sailed most peaceably three miles, landed on a small island, built many fires, and without taking the least precaution against surprise, slept undisturbed and passed the night thus."

Von Kreutzbourg wrote an interesting account of St. Leger's surprising skill at managing his foreign troops, a talent he had distinctly

Unattributed painting, Friederich von Riedesel Papers. (Niedersaechsisches Staatsarchiv Wolfenbuettel, Acta 237, N/89.)

German Jägers. Although this image is of Brunswick Jägers of von Barner's Light Infantry Battalion, the uniforms and arms are very similar to that employed by the Hesse Hanau Jäger regiment in garrison.

lacked four years before. The Irishman made several small concessions that appealed strongly to the Germans. Although the boats had been withdrawn from the British, the Jägers were allowed to keep theirs. The British were only given a day's supply of rum, but the Jägers were allowed whatever quantity their colonel wished. Watches were relieved at ten o'clock, but the Jägers could choose their own times. No soldiers were allowed to leave camp to hunt, except Jägers. Such favours created happy relations and St. Leger's mess benefited.

With Sherwood's and Smyth's agreement, St. Leger overplayed his hand and released the patrol's survivors with a bundle of the dead serjeant's clothing and an open letter of apology to Chittenden, phrased "in as unallusive terms as I could to any ... Negociation between the Kings Government and Vermont." The letter was quickly in General Enos's hands, who, as an confidant to the Allens, understood the text's allusions. He sent the letter to Castleton with a few of his own dispatches, but failed to reseal it and the curious courier shared its strange contents with folks along the way. By the time it was delivered to the Assembly, many people were agitated to understand its meaning, amongst them a virulently pro-Whig army officer who confronted Ira Allen for an answer. Under pressure, Ira fumbled an explanation and then retired with the Board of War, all of whom were aware of the negotiations. They furiously altered Enos's dispatches to produce a set of bogus letters to share with the public and calm their anxieties. These were read in the legislature, but all else was ignored once news of the British surrender at Yorktown broke upon the town.

While this uproar was simmering in Vermont, Chambers was cruising Lake Champlain. On October 22 and 23, the *Royal George* rode in middling breezes while the sailors were "working up Junk," probably plucking oakum from old cable. On October 24 at 1:00 p.m. in "Light Airs and Rain," the *George*'s cutter returned from Ticonderoga and an hour later took off six Connecticut men from the Vermont shore. The next day, in moderate northerly winds, she loosed her sails to dry and sent a tender to St. John's on routine business. On Friday, October 26, Chambers tumbled the six Connecticut men into a bateau and sent them to St. John's in southerly fresh breezes and rain. Next day was fair with fresh breezes, when a boat came alongside with a sutler who had a permit to proceed to the expedition and was allowed to pass.

After two nights on the island in Lake George, Jessup's detachment set sail the evening of October 26. When a fire was seen in the woods on the east shore, a captain and twelve men were sent to investigate. They returned four hours later without finding the fire's exact location, but reported hailing and, hearing no answer, concluded the firelighters were friendly. Jessup was satisfied with this strange tale and sailed on, stopping at three or four islands to set several large fires. A second patrol of the same size was sent to the east shore to work inland and secure prisoners and came across a rebel hunting party. When ordered to surrender, one fellow threatened to shoot the patrol's corporal and the eight loyalists fired, killing two and wounding a third, who escaped. A fourth man said that no one between Saratoga and Stillwater was aware that troops were on Lake George (the loyalists must have wondered about the value of setting all those fires). He said his superiors knew of the expedition's strength and General Stark had ordered all locals capable of service into his camp. Some had come, most had not and those who did found no clothing or provisions and went home. Incredibly, Jessup sent an unarmed group to visit their wives and children south of the Mohawk — surely a risky venture considering the region's turmoil and the distances to be travelled.[33]

On October 26, Major-General Heath wrote to Governor Clinton in frustration: "It is really surprising that accounts from the northward are so vague and uncertain. At one time, the enemy are beyond the lakes, at another this side of the lakes, at another, between them — and sometimes it is not known where they are." Shifting topic, he again advised the desperate need for flour in the Highlands Department. The troops had gone five to six days virtually without bread and there was a great deal of muttering. That morning the artificers had refused to work. He again pled with Clinton for immediate assistance, as the army depended upon New York for flour and New England for meat — an interesting revelation for anyone doubting the efficacy of the British strategy of destroying crops, stock, farms, and farmers.

The next day, Lord Stirling sent a lengthy report to Clinton about the measures taken to reinforce Willett in response to Ross's emergence near Schenectady on October 25. He mentioned diverting Tupper's NH brigade to the west and then, in reaction to General Enos's advice that the enemy were on Lake George, countermanding his orders and sending the brigade north to Saratoga.

On the morning of October 26, Gansevoort received a report about the alarming first phase of the Johnstown battle. When Stirling was advised, his lordship saw that the Albany County militia might not arrive in time and suggested to Stark that he send reinforcements, but his mind was set at ease in mid-afternoon when two dispatches arrived. First was Willett's report of the evening of October 25, asking Marshall for ammunition, which, from its tone, allayed fears that his back was to the wall. The second was from Willett's surgeon saying that Ross had retired into the woods.

Major Myndert Wemple confirmed to Gansevoort his receipt of orders to send all troops belonging to the brigade to Saratoga, except 2ACM, which had left town the morning before, but he noted this would leave the town with only eighty young and old townsmen and forty of 4ACM. He begged leave to detain the latter, as the enemy could thrust at Schenectady from the bottom of Lake George. While Wemple worried about Schenectady's security, the 8ACM (1st Claverack), which had just come back from its deployment to Caughnawaga on the Mohawk, was sent to Stillwater with 7ACM (Kinderhook). Half of 8ACM remained at Stillwater under its first major while the balance went to Saratoga with Brigadier-General Van Rensselaer.

On October 27, Clinton wrote a wildly optimistic letter to an unknown recipient, "If proper measures are taken at Saraghtoga it will be almost impossible for the enemy to return to Crown Point." What gave birth to this flight of fantasy? Certainly none of the actions taken up to that day, and, in case the governor thought his troubles were on the wane, a letter was on its way advising that Vermont had appointed commissioners with full powers to treat with New Hampshire and New

York to achieve statehood. Clinton also wrote to Heath, agreeing that the uncertainty of northern intelligence was most perplexing. From the Bennington report about the enemy landing in strength at Ticonderoga, he thought the British had two forces on Champlain and that the one at Crown Point would attack Tryon County via Schroon Lake. Poor Clinton was on an emotional seesaw. First, he fantasized that the British were going to be cut off from returning to Crown Point and, two days later, he feared they would mount a second strike through the Adirondacks.

At two o'clock on the afternoon of October 29, Colonel Peter Yates wrote to Major Wemple at Schenectady from Saratoga, where he had taken 14ACM (Hoosic and Schaghticoke). He made several useful observations. He thought the enemy was advancing very slowly on Lake George and, like the governor, speculated they had a second party out to the westward attempting to join up with Ross. Yates urged Wemple to keep a sharp lookout, as this second party could very well strike at Schenectady while keeping Saratoga off guard by threatening along Lake George. When Colonel Abraham Wemple returned to Schenectady from upriver next day and read Yates's letter, he wrote to Gansevoort, reporting the prisoners taken from Ross had said that a strong party from the north was to join them. This, coupled with Yates's conjectures, gave him concern that Schenectady was still a primary target. He had detained some county militia and recommended posting a regiment downriver at Niskayuna and the rest in the town.

On October 31, Stirling advised Gansevoort that there was now no doubt that the enemy was in force on Lake George and moving south. He ordered all elements of his brigade, not already in motion, to be immediately marched to Saratoga with five to six days' provisions. He then sent the governor the same information and reported that both Albany County brigades were marching to Saratoga.[34]

On October 27, a forty-man party, somehow identified as "Green Mountain Boys," attempted to surprise the Sugar Loaf post, but the Jägers were alert and fought them off. Von Kreutzbourg adjusted his dispositions, reducing the Sugar Loaf outpost to one corporal and six Jägers; adding twenty-five men to the Mount Hope detachment and posting a picket of one NCO and fifteen men on the Crown Point road. The 31st Lights were marched over the creek to the Jägers' camp, leaving a corporal and three Lights to outpost the far side of the bridge. The 31st was to build a redoubt on a nearby height to defend the road. A "latrine rumour" said that Stark's army had grown to 9,000 and included fifty Oneidas. What a tribute to the Natives' value; at only half of 1 percent of the alleged army, they received specific notice!

Von Kreutzbourg noted the arrival of boatloads of refugees from around Albany and the Green Mountains seeking refuge. The German proved to be a naturalist, writing in his journal that New York's weather was different than Quebec's with days as warm as summer, clear and calm with little rain; only nights were cold. Red deer and wildfowl were plentiful. Red cedar was prolific, which did not grow at all in Canada, nor did many of the bushes and plants.

While the "games" were playing out on Lake George and around Ticonderoga, Ira Allen and Jonas Fay wrote Sherwood to urge a delay in the broadcasting of Haldimand's proclamation, as the timing was inappropriate due to suspicions raised by St. Leger's letter and the news from Virginia. Upon receiving this letter, Sherwood and Smyth decided to take a Flag to Castleton and attempt to reopen the negotiations. Along the road, they were often met with open hostility and arrived on October 28 in the midst of a hornets' nest stirred up by the virulent, influential Whig colonels, the two Samuels, Herrick and Safford, who became even more aroused when they saw the Flag. In a secret meeting, the council proved willing to strictly maintain the truce, but would not support further talks. Sherwood in turn pledged that no hostilities would be committed east of the Hudson. The council pointed out that, if Cornwallis had actually surrendered, the United States would have troops free to move against Vermont, and Canada for that matter.

On October 27, St. Leger reported the return of Secret Service agent, Ensign Thomas Sherwood, QLR, the captain's cousin. He said the alarm had spread and Schenectady was demanding the return of those forces that had been drawn to Saratoga and as many more as Stark could spare. When he delivered his dispatches to Albany, he was told the militia had assembled at Saratoga on October 16, only to be discharged on October 19. St. Leger must have been pleased, as his efforts were intended to create just such confusion.

In fair weather at 6:00 a.m. of October 28, another sutler came alongside the *Royal George*. He also had correct papers and was sent on to the army. Early that afternoon, a bateau full of families from St. Leger appeared and Chambers supplied provisions before they sailed north. The tars worked up junk in the rain on October 29 and, the next day, *Carleton's* tender arrived from St. John's and reported losing its commander overboard in a squall. At half past three, musket fire was heard at Crown Point. A boat was manned and armed and sent to investigate and Captain Sherwood and eight others were taken off. He had left St. Leger and was heading for St. John's to file reports. Chambers immediately sent him on his way. The next day, musket fire was again heard from Crown Point and a boat was manned and armed and picked up three sutler's men who had walked north from Ticonderoga. At 10:00 a.m., yet another sutler appeared, had his papers examined and was permitted to go forward.

Roger Stevens, who had earlier been confined for dilatory conduct, redeemed himself when he came back from Shaftsbury with a fulsome, although not entirely palatable, report:

> [T]he People's Report …That there was 2,000 British Troops left at Tyconderoga & 400 advanced towards Saratoga …. the Encampment … was 6,000 troops and that they were fortifying Tyconderoga and Mount twist[?] & generally said that if every soul in the States was Soldiers they would not be able to drive them from Mount twist & Tyconderoga this winter. The common People seem'd very spirited against the British Troops … I was inform'd by a Loyal Gentleman that General Starks sent a letter to

the State of Vermont that there was a large body of People within five miles of [Schenectady] burning all before them & desired the Governor [Chittenden] to endeavour to cut off the Retreat of the British Troops into Canada. The Report was that the British Troops was too numerous for Vermont to attempt a thing of the kind … Two Rebel Gentlemen from Hartford Reported that there was twenty five tun of gold and silver Rec'd from France, one tun of which was intire gold, they said they saw it deposited in Carriages & sent to pay General Washington's army and that Ld Cornwallis was surrounded & that they expected to have him very soon in their Custody.

Due to the reports of unrest in Vermont, St. Leger decided to move to Chimney Point as soon as Jessup returned. Expecting the rebels to be in hot pursuit, he had Major Rogers take post with twenty-three

Montage by Christopher Armstrong, 2008 of two watercolours by Charles Randle, 1776. (Library and Archives Canada, 1996-82-1&2.) Details of rigging, structure, and armament. (Robert Malcomson. Warships of the Great Lakes 1754-1834. Annapolis, MD: Naval Institute Press, 2001.)

Some vessels of Commodore Chambers' Lake Champlain fleet of 1781. (left to right) The fifty-nine-foot schooner *Carleton* carried twelve 6-pdrs and six swivels. The seventy-four-foot galley *Trumbull* carried two 18-pdrs in the bow; four 4-pdrs in the stern; two 6-pdrs abeam, and 18 swivels. The forty-three-foot sloop *Lee* carried eight 6-pdrs and four swivels. The sixty-six-foot schooner *Maria* carried fourteen 6-pdrs and six swivels. A longboat is in the foreground. The *Trumbull* and *Lee* had been captured from the rebels in 1776.

Rangers at the Lake George Narrows supported by the 31st Lights 300 paces behind and Major von Franken with two companies of Jägers 200 paces behind them. Von Kreutzbourg and three companies were 200 paces in their rear and the 44th Lights formed the rearguard. The rebels were in for a shock if they tried to fulfill Governor Clinton's fantasy. The troops stayed in the woods with pickets stationed and patrols on the adjacent hills for the entire day, but were undisturbed.

At 3:00 a.m. on a squally 1st of November, the sloop *Lee* arrived from Ticonderoga alongside the *Royal George*. Early in the evening, the *Carleton* came down from Mill Bay where Chambers had stationed her because the rebel Flag that was aboard could not be permitted to observe St. Leger's army.

At Lake George, Lieutenant von Horn's early morning scout of Jägers and King's Rangers returned at six o'clock having killed two and taken several prisoners in a sharp action. Two hours later, Jessup appeared. St. Leger later reported that the major had conducted himself "with great address" and was particularly pleased with the information brought from the Scots Patent and New City. Stark was "bound fast at Saratoga" and "absolutely refused the request of the People of the Mohawk either to march in person to their assistance, or send a Detachment (saying) he should have enough to do, to stop the progress of an Enemy in great force marching towards him." Presumably, it was Jessup's unarmed party that had gone south of the Mohawk that brought back news that Ross's men were "destroying many things, burning everything and escaping, that they [had] behaved as trusty King's henchmen." Wounded rebel officers at Albany "could scarcely lament enough the number of their men killed and deserting."

With Jessup back, the expedition sprang into action, loading the major's boats onto the trucks and hauling them to Lake Champlain. By 4:00 p.m., all was complete. At 8:00 a.m. on November 2, von Kreutzbourg was ordered to withdraw and the companies that had been placed to cover Jessup's arrival were pulled out in the reverse order of their posting. At 5:00 p.m., the detachments on Mount Hope and Sugar Loaf vacated after lighting several fires as a ruse. A boat had been spotted on Champlain's shore below Sugar Loaf to pick up its small garrison. All the newly built bridges were taken up and embarkation was set for six the next morning; however, strong gales and rainsqualls delayed departure.

At 11:00 a.m. on November 3, Lieutenant Crofts, 34th, passed the *Royal George* en route to Quebec with St. Leger's dispatches. The rain let up at Ticonderoga towards 11:00 p.m. and von Kreutzbourg thought the weather was breaking. St. Leger ordered him to sail for Chimney Point the next morning and, at 6:00 a.m. his division set off, but there was some confusion, as St. Leger, who had been distressed by the abnormally heavy rainfall, stayed behind. His failure to inform his 2-I-C reeked of his past behaviour. When his absence was noticed, von Kreutzbourg returned to Ticonderoga. His troops stayed on the shore in an unceasing rain all that day and the next night. Yet, the quartermasters of the expedition must have sailed, as Chambers saw troops setting up camp at Chimney Point and ordered the *Lee* to deliver them provisions.

On November 2, Stark had advice from General Enos that he had arrived at Fort Ann the previous evening with a body of troops. As Fort Ann was located in the Western Union, the deployment was an interesting compromise. It was very doubtful that St. Leger would risk offending Vermont by sending troops any distance down South Bay, especially after Sherwood had pledged no hostilities east of the Hudson. So, by placing troops to block that route, Vermont supported Stark at virtually no risk. Prior to marching, Enos had secured five days of beef, but had no bread. He complained about the volume of cartridges Stark supplied and observed that the New Hampshire regiments were similarly destitute. He said he would go no further unless there was some "absolute occasion." Even as he wrote, guns and small arms were heard near Fort Edward. He would send scouts to investigate; however, if the enemy was not found, he would march his troops home.

On the November 3, Stirling wrote to the governor from Saratoga, where he had moved his HQ to take command of the Northern Department. He reported the garrison had saluted the Yorktown victory with fourteen guns, the last to compliment "our friends in Vermont, who have with great alertness joined us to repel the attempts of our common enemy." Did Clinton's teeth grit? Patrols had come in two days before to report there was no sign of the enemy beyond the narrows of

Lake George and only a few at Ticonderoga. With the advanced season's heavy rains, swollen rivers, impassable fords, and lakes soon choked by ice, he thought there was no need to keep the militia in the field any longer. After consulting Stark and the other senior officers, they had been released that morning with a commendation:

> Major General Lord Stirling … takes the earliest opportunity to relieve the Malitia from the severe service they have necessarily been engaged in; he requests them to accept his warmest thanks for the readiness and spirit which Brigadier General Starks assures him they have repeatedly shewin in leaving their peaceful homes to partake in the hardships & dangers of War, in repelling the attempts of an invading Enemy, a behaviour which will ever prove the highest security to their Liberty & property. He desires the Commanding Officers of Regiments may march them into their respective districts & dismiss them with the fullest approbation of their Conduct. The General with great satisfaction takes this opportunity to thank General Stark for his attention to the motions of the Enemy, and the prudent and spirited measures he has taken to render their designs abortive, he also with pleasure returns his thanks to all the Officers and Soldiers of the Army for their Steady and proper behaviour on this occasion.

Stirling ordered the construction of two closed redoubts on the high ground above the barracks to prevent surprise, which fit well with Stark's earlier recommendations to the governor. His lordship believed it prudent to keep the two NH regiments at Saratoga and the 10MA at Albany, indicating he was unaware of Heath's earlier orders to have the latter return to the Highlands as soon as the alarm was over. He noted the need to put troops on the Mohawk River before Willett's enlistments expired.

On November 4, Leonard Gansevoort Jr. wrote a friend about the gun salutes, bell ringing, drinking, and feasting in Albany that had marked

Cornwallis's surrender, adding sentiments that boded ill for the disaffected: "I hope your good Whigs at Cooksackie will also celebrate the Day[;] Nothing will excuse you for not doing it[.] Let every Heart be glad[,] Let every Friend to his Country rejoice and let those dastardly Villians the Torys with dejected Spirit and drooping in Silence and Sorrow curse the Day that they became Enemies to their Country ... It gives me Pleasure to see the Mortification of those Miscreants whose Souls are as Black as Hell and whose Minds are as dark as the Midnight Shades." There was more news. The day before, Willett's report had arrived at Albany advising his success in catching Ross at West Canada Creek and killing Butler. From Leonard's letter, it was clear that Walter's death was not the signal event in Albany that it had been in the Mohawk Valley, but he did say, "I think the Expedition has been a pretty dear One to the Enemy" and added, "Lord Stirling writes that the Enemy are not advancing further than Ticonderoga so that we need fear nothing from there." Of course, this was of far more moment to the city than Walter's demise.

The next day, Stark informed Chittenden that he had resumed command of the Northern Department and, if necessary, had orders to call out the New York and Vermont militia to protect the frontiers of both states. He observed, "with great satisfaction, the alacrity with which both have taken the field on every requisition; but, accountable as I am to superiors, and inexcusable as I should be if I neglected to advise them of any circumstances which carry the aspect of iniquity, I wish to receive the most authentic information respecting the sergeant of the Vermont militia who was slain." The diplomatic gaffe had come to the fore.

> I expect your excellency will enable me to furnish a minute detail of it to Congress, by affording me a perusal of the original letter, which the British commanding officer is said to have written to you upon the occasion. This will be returned you by a safe hand, and a copy transmitted to Congress ... The report, as brought to me, is that, upon the party's arrival at Ticonderoga, the British officer expressed great displeasure that the citizens of Vermont had been disturbed; that he sent for the corpse

of the deceased sergeant, caused it to be interred with military honors, and then dismissed the captured party with what liquor and provisions they chose to carry away, and delivered them a letter of apology to your excellency. If this be true, it indicates a deep stroke of policy on the part of the enemy, to raise a suspicion in the minds of all Americans that the Vermonters are friendly to them or that they have really some encouragement from some people in Vermont ... That the principal portion of the people of Vermont are zealously attached to the American cause, no honest man can doubt; but, that like every other State, it contains its proportion of lurking traitors, is a reasonable supposition; and if these, by their machinations, have brought upon the people injurious suspicions, there is no doubt but the latter will severely punish the miscreants as soon as their misdeeds are fully developed.... Your compliance with my request will probably afford me one of the means; and I pray most earnestly your acquiescence, that I may detail the whole business in its true light.

On November 6, Congressman Livingston, the newly appointed U.S. secretary for foreign affairs, sent Willett's recent report to Governor Clinton, which read, in part:

The Enemys Attempts to the Northward have not, contrary to my Expectations, ended in a mere Matter of Amusements. I do not believe that there have been more than 400 of them if any, at Ticonderoga, and no design of fortifying them there, tho repeated Accounts to that Purpose from the Grants. On the Western Frontier, a Major Ross with upwards of 600 of the Enemy made his first appearance at Warrens Bush where he destroyed 20 or 25 Houses. On his Return he was attacked at Johnstown, by Colo. Willett with an inferior Force who remained in Possession of the Field with 40 Prisoners, chiefly British. Major Ross then retreated with Rapidity but was overtaken at Canada Creek by Colo. Willett, who cut off a Part of his Rear, among whom Major Walter Butler fell a sacrifice to the Oneidas. There is the highest Probability that the Remainder of the Party, extremely fatigued and almost destitute of Provision and having before them a great extent of Wilderness will never be able to reach their Boats.

It appears that Willett deliberately attempted to undermine the man who had denied him assistance by giving a very low estimate of St. Leger's strength without having any real knowledge of the facts. He also appears to have perpetuated the rumour about Butler's rank, perhaps to enhance the significance of his death. And, to excuse his decision not to pursue Ross farther, even after running him to ground, he fantasized that the wilderness would consume the raiders. This report hinted at a nasty, petty side of Willett's highly ambitious character. Yet, when Stirling wrote to Clinton this same day, he very deservedly praised Willett's many virtues: "[He] seems to have acted ... a Vigilant, prudent, experience'd Officer, & altho the Enemy finally evaded his pursuit, his Conduct was such as must reflect the highest honor upon his Military Character."[35]

A signal was fired at "half past two AM" on November 4 and the balance of St. Leger's force set sail from Ticonderoga and arrived at Chimney Point at nine o'clock. The Jägers found their tents were too torn up to be pitched and von Kreutzbourg recommended that everyone move into the woods, to which St. Leger gave his characteristic, "It is very well." Great care was taken to make the camp secure, although the gunboats still lay at Ticonderoga due to winds of almost storm level intensity. Next morning at 9:00 a.m., smoke was observed above the west shore and Chambers sent armed boats to investigate. They returned with eleven Royal Yorkers led by Ensign Sutherland. He was sent to St. Leger. On November 6, the colonel wrote to HQ with a report of the ensign's patrol. During his travels, people had told him that St. Leger had come with 8,000 troops, almost ten times more than reality.

The exchange Flag had been transferred to the *Lee* and St. Leger sent Captain Sherwood, who had come back up the lake, to converse with "his friends" in Vermont and accompany a rebel captain to Skenesborough. Although the colonel would wait for his return, he thought the governor would not wish to expose the troops to inclement weather now that the expedition's military object was complete. That same morning, Chambers sailed in a very light wind and at 9:00 a.m. he sent the eleven Royal Yorkers over to the *Trumbull*. After retrieving his boats, he got under way and worked down the lake on a routine patrol. At half past one, the wind fell and he anchored south of Mill Bay, but at nine o'clock in the evening, he sailed again, working down the lake to anchor at Button Mould Bay at midnight. The next morning, he got under way at 8:00 a.m., worked down to the Narrows and at 5:00 p.m. passed Split Rock. The weather calmed and the ship was rowed to anchor in Blood's Bay. On November 8, there were strong gales and squalls, and at 6:00 a.m., the *Carleton*, *Trumbull*, and two victualling ships came down the lake from Crown Point. Chambers ordered the two warships to accompany their charges as far as Cumberland Head, and then make their best way for St. John's. At 1:00 p.m., there was a very hard squall and snowstorm and the ship struck a rock as it was being put about; however, with the great swell, the crew got her off with no harm done. By four o'clock, she was anchored in heavy snow off Valcour Island.

Von Kreutzbourg received orders to leave Chimney Point the next morning. The order of embarkation would be the Jägers, Jessup's, Rogers', the gunboats (one supposes with the Line infantry), and the three Light Companies in the rear. On the evening of November 8, the gunboats got a head start with the intention of waiting on the further side of the Point, but, with fair weather, they continued north. Despite strong contrary winds, the signal was given at 8:00 a.m. for the rest of the boats to depart. The men pulled on the oars with all their might, but in three quarters of an hour, had only gone 200 yards. Waves pounded the boats tossing them dangerously together, so the colonel signalled a return. In only five minutes, the exhausted Jägers were back ashore to find the other boats lying calmly at anchor. St. Leger had seen the difficulties and cancelled the order, which no doubt made the German feel like a fool. On November 10, the wind fell and everyone set off. St. Leger's expedition was at an end.

Sherwood reported to the governor that he had met for a few hours with Colonel Eben Walbridge, Vermont's senior officer at Skenesborough. Walbridge approved of the proclamation's details, but lamented the impossibility of their approval in the present situation. The "Ruling Men in Vermont were at present mostly friends to a reunion … and that the Idea had become familiar to Many of the Populace … everything was going on Well till the News of the bad Success of Great Britain by Sea and Land had Circulated through the State. This had in a great Measure Overturned all that had been done, and (if affairs did not take a Sudden turn) he fear'd would finally prevent a Reunion… there was Still a very Considerable number that dreaded the Arbitrary Measures which they had reason to Expect from Congress, who had lately threatened to divide Vermont among the Three Claiming States, except she immediately Comply'd with the Terms offered last Spring. — He did not yet know what effect these threats would have, but should any thing interesting occure he would Communicate it to me." Walbridge and several of his subordinates told Sherwood that, after Yorktown, the French admiral had sent eleven ships of the line and a body of troops to the West Indies and had retained twenty-four ships of the line against the British twenty-two. Before winter set in, his fleet would support an attack on New York City and, if New York fell, Charlestown would be next, then Canada next spring.

While St. Leger sailed to Canada, the legacy of his expedition lived on. Chittenden deftly dodged the bullet of Stark's probing letter by sending the account of the slain serjeant to Washington with other matters relating "to the welfare of the independent states of America." He noted that, although Vermonters favoured independence, Congress refused to recognize their state and, faced with the constant threat from Canada, some careful "management" had been necessary. This disingenuously explained away the talks and St. Leger's faux pas and may have satisfied General Washington, but certainly not New York State.

Stirling returned to Albany and replied to Stark's report on November 10 that he believed the enemy had returned to Canada. He hoped to hear soon about a prisoner exchange, as he had fifty prisoners to send downriver before winter if his offer was not accepted. He promised Stark some small personal items and two of the best iron cannon he could find. He would communicate Stark's plan for employing Reynolds's NH militiamen to HQ and ask that the NH Continental carpenters be sent to Saratoga. In closing, he shared details of Willett's latest encounter with Ross and, like so many rebel officers, indulged himself with images of the Scotsman's force perishing in the wilderness.

Haldimand had received no official confirmation of Cornwallis's fate and he betrayed much concern in his dispatch to Sir Henry Clinton of November 14: "Anxiety for the Fate of affairs in the Chesapeake obliges me to dispatch a Runner to you. On that Event the Conduct of Vermont will turn, if unfortunate, she will be our most dangerous Enemy, otherwise Affairs are in a good train — The Detachment under Colonel St Leger has had every effect I could expect. The Vermonters appear conciliated and a large Body of the Enemy are drawn from all Quarters to Albany — But these Efforts will prove feeble unattended to the Southward." St. Leger's activities, which had so mystified the enemy, were to Haldimand's satisfaction and, judging from his letters to Ross, his actions were equally approved of. Yet, both had accomplished so very little. The next day, Benjamin Davis, QLR, set off to deliver the dispatch to New York City.

The exertions of St. Leger's expedition were far from over. On November 13, between the hours of 7:00 and 11:00 a.m., in light winds and fair weather, a parade of bateaux loaded with troops passed the *George* going down the lake. By 5:00 p.m., the wind had fallen off and the ship had to be rowed and towed to anchorage. At daylight, the anchor was hoved in and the ship was rowed and towed for Ile aux Noix, but just below Hospital Island, she ran firmly aground. Chambers fired four guns to signal for help and, at half past 2:00 a.m., three bateaux came alongside manned by 44th soldiers. All the guns and a part of the ballast were swung over into the boats and, at 5:30 a.m., the ship floated free and was rowed and towed to anchor off the island. The next day, the wind continued, light and frosty. Soundings of the island's shoals revealed less than five feet of water and, even in the deepest channel, bottom was frequently touched. Chambers thought the water was abnormally low due to hard winds that had blown from the north for so many days and decided to offload everything before taking the ship further.

At Ile aux Noix, Roger Stevens wrote in his journal that St. Leger returned to Canada after hearing of Cornwallis's surrender, which was misleading, as that news was a side issue. There was no choice; he had to get off the lake before navigation closed. Lieutenant Enys, 29th, recalled that word of Yorktown reached St. Leger through a Flag of Truce from Stirling. The Flag's officer gossiped that he would have come three days earlier except his lordship was so drunk over the news, he was unable to do his duty.

At daylight on November 16, the *George* got under way in light winds and by 11:00 a.m. was anchored off Fort St. John's in a grand display of sails, rigging, yards, and spars. The next day, the river froze over at 5:00 a.m. in severe frosty weather. The gunboats arrived with news that the *Trumbull* was nearby and the *Carleton* at Isle aux Noix. All the chickens were coming home to roost. At six o'clock, all the ships' and gunboats' powder was sent ashore while the rest of the crews returned the unused stores and took in the guns.

Von Kreutzbourg glumly wrote about the "futile" expedition. "Its only accomplishment was the interrupting of the rebel General Sterling, who was to follow Major Ross as he was leaving Carleton Island. Nothing more significant happened before its conclusion. 1,500 men were sent out, several houses and barns were burned, and 84 of the men lost." His grasp of geography was no better at the close than at the outset, nor was his appreciation of the mission's purpose. Who was at fault here – St. Leger or the man himself? Surely his total of 1,500 troops referred to both expeditions. If eighty-four men were really missing that would mean St. Leger somehow lost thirty-five men to Ross's forty-nine! These questions remain unanswered.[36]

Von Kreutzbourg's disgruntled assessment ignored the fact that the rebels at no time mounted offensive operations to disrupt St. Leger at Ticonderoga or against Jessup when he was hanging out on a limb on Lake George. As Colonel Louis and his most active warriors had been in the Mohawk Valley chasing Ross, even rebel patrolling had been timid at best and the only active strike on St. Leger's outposts was attributed to the "Green Mountain Boys."

Although Haldimand's two major expeditions had achieved their military goals and greatly agitated the rebel high command, they had little strategic value, as Sir Henry Clinton's attention was focused on Cornwallis's plight at Yorktown and he chose not to capitalize on the northern distractions to attack the enemy's lines around New York City.

The political goal of delivering Haldimand's proclamation to Vermont, which was intended to persuade that republic to declare for Britain, had failed for the nonce, but efforts would continue in the following years.

THE END

Mutiny at Coteau-du-Lac, June 25, 1781

Mutineers	Penalty Assessed	Background	Date of Capture
John Carter/ Garter	1,000 lashes/ deportation	2TCM	April 3, 1780
William Edwards	1,000 lashes/ deportation	Harper's Levies	October 23, 1780
Peter House/ Howse	acquitted	Harper's Levies	October 23, 1780
Seth Jacquay	1,000 lashes/ deportation	MA Levy	October 19, 1780
Nathaniel Miller	500 lashes/ deportation	unknown	
Peter Sharp	1,000 lashes/ deportation	Harper's Levies	October 23, 1780
Nicholas Smith	500 lashes/ forgiven	Harper's Levies	October 23, 1780
Seffrinus Tygert	1,000 lashes/ deportation	Harper's Levies	October 23, 1780

Andrew Van Waggoner	1,000 lashes/ deportation	Deserter*	unknown
Jacob Piper	1,000 lashes	4TCM	unknown

The Court
President: Major John Adolphus Harris, 1/84RHE.
Members: Major James Gray, 1KRR; Captains William Monsell, 29th; George Lawes, 1/84; Alexander Fraser, 34th and QID; and Thomas Scott, 53rd.

Sources
GO, Carleton and Haldimand, 1776–83, LAC, HP, AddMss21743. Cruikshank and Watt, *KRRNY* and Watt, *Burning*, 234–36, 346; **One Forgiven**: Fraser, *Skulking*, 60 ex New York Genealogical and Biographical Society, Asa Fitch Papers, No.244 James Rogers; **Von Waggoner**: von Papet, *Canada During the American Revolution*, Burgoyne, ed., 185. LAC, HP, AddMss21789, 214. Reuter, *Brunswick Troops*. Lists Johann Steckhane, Private Musketeer Regiment "Specht," released in Canada, July 23, 1783.

JACOB KLOCK'S TORIES, JULY 1, 1781

On April 24, 1780, Jacob J. Klock resigned his commission as a 1NY ensign, due to family upheaval. He deserted to the enemy on July 1, 1781, after being denied a company of new levies. The following is a list of men who deserted with Klock. Those who came back on the raid of July 29 are marked with an asterisk.

---

* Van Waggoner was discovered to be Johan Steckhane, a deserter from the Brunswick Regiment von Specht at Ticonderoga in 1777. He was returned to the German troops and was released in Canada on July 23, 1783.

Name	Later Service	Settlement in Canada
John Anguish*	Frey's Coy, BR	Drew rations at Fort Erie until 1786
John Bangle	no record	
"Old" Adam Bangle	Alex McDonell's Coy, 1KRR	At Royal Township No.1, 1784
Henry Heiney/ Haynor		Haynor, in Canada at Niagara, 1786
Philip Helmer*	Returned to the rebels.	
Nicholas Herkimer*	BR, to Oct. 26, 1781	At Cataraqui Township No.1, 1785
Adam Klock	Crawford's Coy, 2KRR	At Cataraqui Township No.3, 1784
Jacob I. Klock*	no record	
Jacob J. Klock	Volunteer, 2KRR	Deserted in 1782
Nicholas Rosencrantz*	Second lieutenant, Genevay's Coy, BR	Nassau District, Canada 1792
Matt's Wormwood*	Genevay's Coy, BR	Near Fort Erie, 1785

Sources
Resignation: *PPGC, VI*, 790. Egly, *Van Schaick*, 79; **Who Deserted and Who Raided:** Simms, *FNY, II*, 517–18.

NEW DORLACH AND RYNBECK INHABITANTS
Who Assisted Docksteder at Currytown, July 9, 1781

Godleap Bowman
Martis Bowman
Conradt Brown
John Coenradt/Conradt
David Coughman

Jacob Coughman
George Cross
Michael Fichter
Andres Ficther
Jacob Fraunce

Henry Frandts/Frauts

Michael Fredericks

Ann Frets

Earnest Frets

Henry Haines/Hanes

Henry Haines/Hanes Jr.

Jacob Haines

Jacob Hanes Jr.

Christian Hanover

Chas Hearwager

Coenradt Hopper

Jacobus Hopper

Henry Loucks

Christian Merkle

Frederick Merkle/Mirch

Matthias Merkle/Mirch

Michael Merkle/Mirch

Christian Minor

Christian Olman/Ottman

Christopher Redick

John Summer

William Summer

George Walker

Sources

"Affidavit of Wm Sommer," PPGC, VII, 80–81.

WILLETT'S LOST SENIOR OFFICERS OF THE 1781 CAMPAIGN

Name	Fate	Date
Samuel Clark	Severely wounded	October 25
Holtham Dunham	Traitor/deserter	July 27
Peter Elsworth	Killed in action	July 6
Abraham Livingston	Under arrest	September 5
Robert McKean	-do-	July 10
Aaron Rowley	Severely wounded	October 25
Anthony Whelp	Under arrest	September 5
Stephen White	Captured	October 25
Solomon Woodworth	Killed in action	September 7

The "Captain McDonald" Mystery

Identifying the Captain McDonald of Scotch troops who murdered William Scarborough in Johnstown during the Hall Battle is a challenge. The first thing to recognize is that "McDonald" could very well be "McDonell," as those surnames were often used interchangeably and pronounced as "McDonal" and "McDonel" respectively. The only detachment of Scottish troops with Ross was from the Royal Highland Emigrants (84/RHE) and those men likely wore some items of distinctive Highland clothing such as Scots Bonnets.[1]

The men were drawn from Captain Daniel Robertson's Company at Oswegatchie, although the captain did not personally join the expedition. A year later, regimental returns showed two subalterns in Robertson's: Lieutenants Lauchlan Maclean and Archibald Grant.[2] One of these two may have led the detachment to the Mohawk the year before. Maclean had been recruited in the Carolinas and captured at Moore's Bridge in 1776. He subsequently escaped and made his way to Canada. So, he was hardly the man who had a pre-war altercation with Scarborough in Johnstown. Details of Grant's background are unknown; however, his surname is a long step from McDonald. Although Maclean and Grant were in Robertson's in 1782, it may have been that one of the McDonell officers in 1RHE had performed duty with Robertson in 1781. Two prime choices would be Lieutenants Ranald and Ensign Archibald McDonell, who, as will be discussed below, beat their cousin to within an inch of his life in a drunken fracas on Carleton Island.

———————

It is possible that Scarborough's captors spoke with a distinctive Scottish brogue, but this would have been as true of many Royal Yorkers as of the Highland Emigrants and accent alone seems unlikely to have elicited the description, "Scotch troops."

———————

Another possibility is that Captain McDonald was an officer from one of the other detachments on the expedition and, when he came across Scarborough, he ordered the Scotch troops to kill him. For instance, if McDonald was a Royal Yorker, his red jacket would have been faced blue with gold buttons, which at a glance, would appear exactly the same as those of the Emigrants, and the observer may have concluded that he was their officer. Following this train of thought — although McDonald was identified as a captain, in this time period, there was no difference in the uniforms worn by captains and subalterns. So, perhaps the Royal Yorker's ensign, Ranald McDonell (Leek), of Johnstown was the culprit. He had taken up arms in 1775 under Sir John and was one of six Scottish hostages taken by Schuyler when Johnson, his friends, and tenants were disarmed in the winter of 1776. Perhaps Scarborough, who was recognized by his peers as high handed in the cause of "liberty," gave one of the McDonells a drubbing at that time. Ranald spent three years incarcerated in Reading, Pennsylvania, before he escaped and joined the British Army in Philadelphia. From there he went to New York City and on to Canada where he joined the Royal Yorkers. Although the Leek branch of the McDonells was not known for bad tempers, given Ranald's experiences, it would not be difficult to imagine him losing his head and killing Scarborough out of hand.

———————

A far more likely perpetrator was Captain James McDonell (Scotus) as his family was known to have fierce tempers. As noted above, while James was in garrison at Fort Haldimand, he became embroiled in "a nasty disagreeable Drunken Squabble" with two of his cousins and [was] severely beaten.[3] After the war, James was so intemperate in his speech toward Major Holland, the chief surveyor of the new townships, that all of his privileges were withdrawn by Haldimand and only restored after he offered abject apologies.[4]

Then, looking back at the RHE again, if one of those McDonells was with Ross, he must be a suspect, as anyone, drunk or not, who can beat someone almost senseless shows an abnormal propensity for violence.

———————

Another possibility exists; perhaps McDonald was an officer of one of the other participating corps. As there were none of that name in Leake's Independent Company, that formation can be ruled out, as can the 8th, 34th, Hanau Jägers, and Indian Department for the same reason. That leaves Butler's Rangers; however, that regiment's jackets were green and it is difficult to imagine any observer thinking a Ranger officer was in command of the Highland Emigrants. Nonetheless, to spin this thread to its end, the information as to which of Butler's officers attended the expedition is sparse. We know that Captain Walter Butler commanded the Rangers and that there was at least one other captain present. Only one captain named McDonell served in the Rangers and he was John (Aberchalder); however, from what is known of his background and character, the commission of such a crime seems very unlikely.

There is no doubt that Lieutenant Alexander McDonell (Collachie) participated, as he wrote the report printed in the Quebec *Gazette* in November. Could he have been the man? One would expect that his article would have mentioned the incident, but, of course, not in the same light as the observer recalled, but nothing was said. There was one other lieutenant named McDonell in Butler's with the given name Chichester. He was the brother of Captain John (Aberchalder); however, the same comment applies to him as to his brother; he is an unlikely candidate for murder.

———————

Of course, the other possibility is that the story was untrue; McDonald did not exist and Scarborough was not murdered. He simply fell in action and the manner of his death was invented.

NOTES

CHAPTER I: THE GOVERNOR OF A STRATEGIC BACKWATER

1. **Haldimand**: "Captain-general and Governor in Chief of his Majesty's Province of QUEBEC, and the territories depending thereon in AMERICA; Vice-admiral of same. General and Commander in Chief of His Majesty's Forces in the said Province and the Frontiers thereof" was the title employed by Haldimand at the head of a proclamation of January 18, 1781. See, General staff (Historical section), ed., "The War of the American Revolution, The Province of Quebec under the Administration of Governor Frederic Haldimand, 1778–1784," in *A History of the Organization, Development and Services of the Military and Naval Forces of Canada From the Peace of Paris in 1763 to the Present Time With Illustrative Documents*, Vol. 3 [hereafter, *HSGS*] (Ottawa: King's Printer, n.d.), 193, ex *The Quebec Gazette*; **British strategy**: Piers Mackesy, "Could the British Have Won the War of Independence?" Bland-Lee Lecture, Clark University, 1975; **The War's Extent**: Piers Mackesy, *The War for America 1775–1783* (Lincoln and London: University of Nebraska Press, 1992); **West Indies**: *Ibid.*, 184–88. "For England, the islands held the lure of compensation for her losses in America, finance to pay for the war, a favourable balance of trade, an economic lever to coerce America. For the chance of conquering the French West Indies and 'avenging the faithless and insolent conduct of France,' the King had said he was willing even to come to terms with America. As early as the end of January, he had been contemplating a complete withdrawal from the rebel colonies, retaining only Canada, Nova Scotia and Florida. This ultimately led to a redistribution of troops for an offensive against the French West Indies and the abandonment of Philadelphia. These orders reduced the forces in America to the defence of Britain's undisputed possession of the flanks of the rebellion, with only two posts in the rebel colonies themselves, New York City and Rhode Island. Canada and Newfoundland would be reinforced from home; but for Nova Scotia

and the Floridas, which lay within Clinton's command, he would have to provide part of the reinforcements from his own depleted force. And no replacements would be sent: no new regiments except the three already promised for Nova Scotia; and no recruits, for they were needed to fill the battalions at home. Clinton was forced to draft his weakest regiments, return the Marine battalions home and one of his cavalry regiments, which was thought not to be required for the anticipated defensive war, was dismounted and also sent home."

2. **Christened**: François-Louis-Frédéric, "Frederick Haldimand," in *Dictionary of Canadian Biography* [hereafter *DCB*], *Vol. V (1801–1820)*; Jean N. McIlwraith, "Sir Frederick Haldimand," in *The Makers of Canada*, Vol. 3 (Toronto: Morang & Co., Ltd., 1911), 2–5, 15; Lord Loudoun, C-in-C America in 1757, wrote of Haldimand and his friend Henri Bouquet, "These two Lieut Colonels will do extremely well, and are very good officers"; **Portrait**: Gives little indication of his capability for endurance, persistence, and great determination. A much later portrait shows him in a pensive, almost timid, frame of mind. None of his driving energy or humour is evident. He looks worn down by the heavy load of his responsibilities; **Women/ Gifts**: McIlwraith, 76, 77.

3. **Military Career**: *DCB, Vol. V, s.v.* "Haldimand;" McIlwraith, 21, 26; William Eyre to Robert Napier, L. George, July 10, 1758, in *Military Affairs in North America 1748–1765*, Stanley Pargellis, ed. (1936; reprint Hamden, CT: Archon Books, 1969), 420; Francis Parkman, *Montcalm and Wolfe* Vol. 2 (2 vols.) (Boston: Little, Brown, and Co., 1884), 242–43; A second instance of Haldimand being given command of elite troops, a clear mark of the confidence placed in his Prussian and Swiss Guards' experience; *DCB, IV, (1771–1800) s.v.* "Thomas Gage." Despite Gage's impressive innovations in the development of light infantry, he had a reputation as a timid, lethargic military leader, although he was seen as a very solid civil administrator; **Quebec Troubles**: *Ibid.*, Gage had experienced similar difficulties in Montreal district and wrote that, "the sooner these Croix de St. Louis, with the rest of the idle Noblesse, leave the Country, the better it will be for it."

4. **Gardens**: Haldimand's interest in all forms of gardening: floral, herbal, and vegetable, gave him a lasting reputation as one of America's first experimental gardeners. McIlwraith, 33, 57, 71. **Vermont**: Haldimand to Tryon, September 1, 1773, McIlwraith, 89, 90, 105–107, 113, 118; Gage to Haldimand, July 3, 1774, *ibid.*, 97; *DCB s.v.* "Haldimand"; Haldimand to Samuel Holland disclaiming responsibility for Concord, *ibid.*, 102–103; Macksey, 40. King George approached Catherine the Great of Russia for troops, but she declined; *DCB, IV (1771–1800) s.v.* "Hector Cramahé." Cramahé entered the army in 1740. By 1758, he was

captain of the 15th Regiment at the sieges of Louisbourg and Quebec. He entered diplomatic service as secretary to Quebec's first British governor. He was appointed lieutenant-governor in 1771 and continued in the province for twenty-two years. Cramahé was very active in promoting the Quebec Act and in the defence against the 1775 American invasion. He was well regarded by Carleton, but did not enjoy a warm relationship with Haldimand. The traders in Albany, New York, were far more threatened by Quebec's boundary restoration than those in New England, but all negative impacts were grist for the mill of agitation; **Praying Indians**: The term was applied to the Roman Catholic Christian Indians whom the French had encouraged to set up satellite communities around their towns as a protective screen. These Indians became zealous partisans of the French cause and were greatly feared by the British-Americans. The term differentiated them from "savage" Indians, although by the time of the revolution, several other nations were also predominantly Christian, albeit Anglican or Protestant.

5. Gustave Lanctot, *Canada & the American Revolution, 1774–1783*, trans. Margaret M. Cameron (London, Toronto, Wellington, Sydney: George G. Harrap & Co. Ltd., 1967), 23. ex *Journal of the Continental Congress, 1784–1789,* Vol. I, 31–40, and *ibid.*, 24, 31–40 ex *Journal of Continental Congress*, Vol. I, 72; **Propaganda**: Lanctot, 27–29; **Populations**: James A. Henretta, "American Revolution," in Microsoft® Encarta® Online Encyclopedia 2005. http://encarta.msn.com. In 1770, the Thirteen Colonies had a total population of 2,500,000 people, 567,000 of which were black. The American colonies grew so explosively that the population rose to one-third of that of the British Isles. Robert Famighetti, "Estimated Population of American Colonies, 1630–1780" in *1998 World Almanac and Book of Facts* (New York: World Almanac, 1998), 378. ex Bureau of the Census, U.S. Department of Commerce. In 1780, Virginia had the largest population at 538,000. Massachusetts at 317,700, and New York at 210,500 (exclusive of 47,600 in the contested region of Vermont); Ernest J. Lajeunesse, *The Windsor Border Region — Canada's Southernmost Frontier* (Toronto: The Champlain Society, 1960), lii–lxxiv.

6. **Habitant**: Lanctot, 4. In France, the rural people were known as peasants, a pejorative term suggesting a dull intellect and subservient nature. Lanctot quotes the French officer Bougainville describing the differences between the Canadien officers and their French counterparts. "We seem to belong to another, almost an enemy, nation." Lanctot notes that "the same rivalry existed between Canadian priests and French members of the higher clergy, and the subservience of the French vassal to his lord was unknown in Canada, where the tenant farmer seized every opportunity to display 'a sort of independence.' Accustomed to 'liberty,' and 'naturally indocile,' Canadians were inclined to recognize 'neither rule nor regulation'"; **Fur Trade**:

Donald Creighton, *The Empire of the St. Lawrence* (Toronto: Macmillan, 1956), 1–21; **Corvée**: a Canadien term describing obligatory labour by the habitants on public duties such as military transportation, road-building, and clearing. This very useful form of public service was a unique feature of Quebec life and was retained by the British Administration.

7. **French Intentions**: Mackesy wrote concerning 1779 and 1780: "We know now that the French did not intend to conquer Canada for the Americans; but the rebels' hopes and dispositions, the promises held out to the Canadians, the reports of the French troops' equipment and commanders, all suggested that Quebec, Newfoundland or Halifax might be their objective. And Quebec and Halifax were very weak. It had been impossible to spare reinforcements from England for Canada; and Clinton, having failed to get troops through to the St. Lawrence in the autumn, had switched everything he could spare into his southern offensive at Charleston." Mackesy, 326. See also Lanctot for a very thorough examination of the invasion threats and Canadien reaction; **Vessels on Lakes**: Report, January 1785, *HSGS, III*, 251 ex HP, B145, 120; **Artillery**: Christian Rioux, "The Royal Regiment of Artillery in Quebec City," in *History and Archaeology* 57 (National Historic Parks and Sites Branch). Ottawa: Environment Canada, 1982), 29. Burg took the most experienced men, leaving two NCOs and twenty-four men at Quebec City. In total, he took three companies (coys) and left Carleton one to defend Canada. By September 1777, the company in Quebec City had grown to approximately forty all ranks; LAC, HP, WO42/37, 268. General return of the Army in Canada, St. John's October 1, 1777; *ibid.*, 269–276. A state of ordnance at Quebec City — October 1, 1777; *ibid.*, 278–282. Similar return for Montreal, Chambly, and St. John's — October 27, 1777.

8. **Quebec Militia**: *HSGS, II,* 43. British militia, Quebec City — 8 coys consisting of 29 officers, 819 other ranks. Canadien militia, Quebec City — 8 coys of 41 officers, 819 other ranks. District of Quebec — 54 coys of 113 officers, 6,945 other ranks. Montreal City — 9 coys of 31 officers, 528 other ranks. District of Montreal — 87 coys of 258 officers, 6,483 other ranks. District of Three Rivers — 23 coys of 61 officers, 1,924 other ranks. Detroit settlements — 6 coys of 28 officers, 484 other ranks; **Detroit Militia**: In contrast, in the later war years, Detroit Militia companies, mixed Anglo and French, went on active campaign and performed sterling service, perhaps as they were a long way from French and rebel influence. *HSGS, III,* 9; **Riedesel Comment**: Jean-Pierre Wilhelmy, *German Mercenaries in Canada* (Beloeil, QC: Maison des Mots, 1985), 166fn.

CHAPTER 2: THE BACKGROUND TO THE 1781 CAMPAIGN

1. Vermont declared independence on July 8, 1777, not only from Britain, but also from New York. The text of the declaration may be found on Yale University's website: http://www.yale.edu/lawweb/avalon/states/vt01.htm; B. Robinson to E. Allen, March 30, 1780 quoted in its entirety in Hazel C. Mathews, *Frontier Spies* [Hereafter, *Spies*] (Fort Myers, FL: author, 1971), 121, 122. Robinson was the lieutenant-colonel of the Loyal American Regiment, part of the NYC garrison; As early as March 3, 1779, Germain requested that Sir Henry Clinton encourage Vermont to return to allegiance. Mentioned in Germain to Haldimand, April 16, 1779, CO42/39, 19, No. 23; Germain to Haldimand, March 17, 1780, CO42/40; Haldimand to Germain, September 13, 1779, CO42/39, 261; The men in on the secret were Thomas Chittenden, Moses Robinson, Samuel Safford, Ethan Allen, Ira Allen, Timothy Brownson, John Fassett, and Joseph Fay. Frederic P. Wells, *History of Newbury, Vermont, From the Discovery of the Coös Country to Present Time* (St. Johnsbury, VT: The Caledonian Company, 1902), 92, 93; Henry W. De Puy, *Ethan Allen and the Green-Mountain Heroes of '76* (Buffalo: Phinney & Co., 1853), 129. Ethan had five brothers: Heman, Heber, Levi, Zimri, and Ira, who, in his quiet, energetic way, became as influential as Ethan. The two sisters were Lydia and Lucy; **Ticonderoga**: Chilton Williamson, *Vermont in Quandary 1763–1825* (Montpelier: Vermont Historical Society, 1949), 51, 52 ex *Correspondence of Thomas Gage, II,* 199; **Crown Point**: Ethan Allen to Albany Committee of Safety, Ticonderoga, May 12, 1775. Mathews, *Spies,* 119–20; **Declaration**: For complete wording, see De Puy, 380–81; **Chittenden**: *Ibid.,* 385–86; **Impropriety**: Williamson, 69–70, 79.

2. **Brattleborough**: Report of Samuel Minott. Mathews, *Spies,* 119, ex Public Papers of George Clinton [hereafter PPGC] Document 2315; **Bayley**: NY Brigadier-General Jacob Bayley commanded the militia of Cumberland and Gloucester Counties in 1776 (Michael Barbieri research). In September 1777, he was commissary general of the U.S. Northern Department (Neil Goodwin research). Bayley was a notorious rebel and a member of the Commission (?) of Safety and Court of Confiscations. He was particularly unpopular with loyalists; **Bayley/Allen**: Williamson, 79; **Eastern Union**: *Ibid.,* 82–84; **Germain**: *Ibid.,* 91 ex *Sir Henry Clinton Papers, Box for July 1–28, 1778*; Ida H. and Paul A. Washington, *Carleton's Raid* (Canaan, NH: Phoenix Publishing, 1977), 33–61. A 354-man expedition was led by Major Christopher Carleton, 29th Regiment; **Otter Creek**: Haldimand to Germain, November 21, 1778. Williamson, 88–89 ex HP, B54, 61–72; Germain to Clinton, March 3, 1779, *ibid.,* 91–92 ex HP, B63, 135; **Haldimand's Attitude**: Mathews, *Spies,* 122; **Sherwood**: Hadden, 113fn. As Burgoyne was not free with praise for his loyalists, the compliment is particularly noteworthy.

3. **May 1780 Raid**: Ernest Cruikshank and Gavin K. Watt, *The History and Master Roll of The King's Royal Regiment of New York*, revised ed. (Campbellville, ON: Global Heritage Press, 2006). *KRR NY*, 41–43; **Levies**: Law for Raising Troops for the Defence of the Frontiers. PPGC, V, 600–601; **Militia Leadership**: William Harper to Governor Clinton, February 16, 1779, Kenneth D. Johnson, *The Bloodied Mohawk: The American Revolution in the Words of Fort Plank's Defenders and Other Mohawk Valley Partisans* [hearafter *Bloodied Mohawk*] (Rockport, MA: Picton Press, 2000), 134–36. Harper was utterly vitriolic, in particular regarding Colonel Jacob Klock and, to a lesser extent, Colonel Frederick Visscher. Harper had not experienced the Oriskany bloodbath, so his judgments must be viewed in that light, but the evidence he provided, assuming accurate, must have been highly distressing. One fact was obvious, the Tryon County Militia had not recovered from the 1777 campaign; **George Clinton**: Brief biography found in: www.robinsonlibrary.com/america/unitedstates/1783/biography/clinton-g.

4. **Incapable German Troops**: Hanau Jägers were the only German regiment to see service on the frontiers during Haldimand's regime. Colonel von Kreutzbourg's diary noted, "When requesting the General for the relief of my commando at Carleton Island by other troops of Jägers, even he confessed that he could not rely upon any Braunschweig or Zerbst Jäger to the same high degree as he could my Jägers," John C. Zuleger, trans. "Narration of Hesse Hanau Jäger Corps in America," in Hessian Papers, Morristown NHP, NJ., 130; Haldimand was scathing in his appraisal of his other Germans, Haldimand to Germain, September 13, 1779, CO42/39, 65. He wrote, "I cannot help here observing to your Lordship, the very little use these Troops are, in general, in this Province — They are lazy and inactive unwilling to Work, which here constitutes the greatest part of a Soldier's Duty and cavel at every little extraordinary, or what appears to them extraordinary duty, and so prone are they to desertion, that I dare not trust them at any of the Frontier Posts"; **Peters**: "The Evening before the Convention of Saratoga was Signed Your Memorialist went off by Permission of General Burgoyne, with Colonel Peters & others to Canada," Captain Simeon Covell, QLR, AO13/54s, 169–70; **Peters's Escape**: Mary B. Fryer, *King's Men, the Soldier Founders of Ontario* (Toronto: Dundurn Press, 1980), 223; **Jessup**: *Ibid.*, 195; **Mackay**: "Narrative of Captain Samuel Mackay," McCord Museum, McGill University; **Adams's Rangers**: Adams to Sir John Johnson (SJJ), Montreal, August 11, 1780, MG13, WO28/5,64, and Muster Roll dated Boucherville, January 23, 1778, LAC, HP, AddMss21827, 136–67; **Guarding Chest**: *Ibid.*, 134 endnote F ex HP, AddMss 21827, f.25; **Convention relaxed**: Earle Thomas, *Sir John Johnson, Loyalist Baronet* (Toronto: Dundurn Press, 1986), 78.

5. **Plan for 2KRR**: Daniel McAlpin to be Major, seven coys with designated captains, two coys without. There were 20 officers selected, an adjutant, 30 serjeants, 30

corporals, 10 drummers, and 269 rank and file, Sorel, October 15, 1778, LAC, WO28/10, Part 1, 142–56; **Plan Collapses**: Haldimand to SJJ, Sorel, October 19, 1778 and SJJ to Haldimand, Montreal, October 29, 1778, Cruikshank and Watt, *KRR NY*, 23; **McAlpin**: Houlding, *King's Service*. Daniel McAlpin was adjutant 42nd Regiment, March 25, 1749, lieutenant 2/60 when raised on February 10, 1756, captain of same August 7, 1771, retired March 28, 1779, 2/60 at Plains of Abraham where he did signal service. J. Fraser, *Skulking for the King: A Loyalist Plot* (Erin, ON: Boston Mills Press, 1985), 31; Transcript of roll of McAlpin's 2/60 Coy, New York, October 24, 1772, *ibid.*, 174 ex Public Record Office (PRO), WO12/6935 and Haldimand to SJJ, May 17, 1779, *ibid.*; **Leake's Coy**: Haldimand to SJJ, May 1779. Leake married SJJ's sister-in-law, Margaret Watts, in NYC in 1783; **Arms indent**: Haldimand to Germain, November 1, 1779, CO42/40.

6.   **2KRR Beating Order**: Cruikshank and Watt, *KRR NY*, 43–44; **Forming 2KRR**: SJJ to Haldimand, Montreal, July 20, 1780, LAC, WO28/5, 33; **Ross as Major**: Haldimand, Quebec, July 1, 1780, LAC, HP, AddMss 21745/1, f.31; **Gumersall**: Memorial of Thomas Gummersall to SJJ, Oswego, September 8, 1783, LAC, HP, AddMss28173, 176–78; **Ross's Map**: "Course of the River Mississipi … Taken on an Expedition to the Illinois … 1765. By Lieut Ross of the 34th Regt." (London: Robert Saver, 1775). The map illustrates Britain's Seven Years' War gains and establishes the future western boundary of the new United States. British and Americans used the map during the American Revolution as the most authoritative map of the Mississippi Valley. Thomas Jefferys, *The American Atlas: or A Geographical Description of the Whole Continent of America …* (1776; reprint Amsterdam: Theatrum Orbis Terrarum, 1974); **Ross's Career**: Twenty-seven years in 34th and four in 2KRR; breveted major in 34th, June 12, 1782; major, May 20, 1785; retired February 17, 1789, Houlding, *King's Service*; **Ross's Wounding**: "List of Officers Killed, and Wounded of Br Genl. Fraser's Advance Corps at Huberton July 7th 1777," Claus Papers, Vol.1, 240; **1778 Raid**: Jeptha R. Simms, *Frontiersman of New York Showing Customs of the Indians, Vicissitudes of the Pioneer White Settlers and Border Strife in Two Wars with a Great Variety of Romantic and Thrilling Stories Never Before Published* [hereafter, *FNY*], Vol. 2 (2 vols., Albany: Geo. C. Riggs, 1883), 217–23. Simms gave Ross's rank incorrectly as lieutenant; **Mohawks Retrieved**: Gavin K. Watt, *Rebellion in the Mohawk Valley: The St. Leger Expedition of 1777* [hereafter, *Rebellion*] (Toronto: Dundurn, 2002), 302–03, 406fn885.

7.   **King's Favour**: General Orders (GO) signed Francis LeMaistre, Deputy Adjutant General, HQ, Quebec, September 4, 1780, Archives of Ontario, Ms521(1), Edward Jessup Papers; "The Orderly Book of the King's Loyal Americans and the Loyal Rangers," dated from September 4, 1780 to October 23, 1783, [hereafter Jessup OB]; **Axe vs. Firelock**: Haldimand to Sir Henry Clinton (SHC), May 26, 1789, Cruikshank

and Watt, *KRR NY*, 28; **Best, Most Active**: Haldimand to Germain, September 13, 1779, *ibid.*, 32; **Indian Fusils**: Cruikshank and Watt, *ibid.*, 63 and Regimental Orders (RO),October 14–15, 1780, noted in Gumersall to SJJ, Oswego, September 8, 1783, LAC, HP, AddMss21873, 176–78; **Recruiting Allowed**: Haldimand to Peters, Quebec, September 6, 1780, Jessup OB; **Nairne**: Stanley, *Canada Invaded*, 101–02; **Sherwood**: Mathews, *Spies*, 125; Mary B. Fryer, *Buckskin Pimpernel, the Exploits of Justus Sherwood Loyalist Spy* [hereafter, *Pimpernel*] (Toronto: Dundurn Press, 1981), 111–23; **Carleton's Raid**: Watt, *Burning*, 91–119, 348–51, 353–55; **Ballstown**: *Ibid.*, 119–36, 355–56, 347–48; **SJJ Raid**: *Ibid.*, 157–250, 357–59, 345–47; **VT Raid**: *Ibid.*, 137–49, 356–57; **Expenditures**: Isabel Thompson Kelsay, *Joseph Brant 1743–1807: Man of Two Worlds* (Syracuse: Syracuse University Press, 1984), 299–300; **Requisition**: Kelsay, 299; **Colonel G. Johnson**: Haldimand to Germain, Quebec, January 26, 1780, Lieutenant-Colonel William A. Smy, trans. and ed., "The Butler Papers: Documents and Papers Relating to Colonel John Butler and His Corps of Rangers 1711–1977," (u.p., circa 1994) [hereafter Smy Transcripts] ex LAC, CO, Q17 /1 & CO42/40, 63–64.

8. **Plan of Attack**: Letter of instruction prepared by Order of Congress to Benjamin Franklin, *HSGS, III*, 182–84; **Oquaga**: The letter showed "Oncaquaga." Oquaga was in Indian Territory and served as headquarters for Brant in 1776 and later for mixed parties of BV, BR, and loyalist recruits; **Cataraqui**: "Cadaroque" in Congress's letter. This is a decent harbour on Lake Ontario's north shore, which was the site of Fort Frontenac, razed by Bradstreet in 1758; **Chasseurs**: This French term likely indicates riflemen; **Second Handbill**: Lanctot, 194 ex LAC, HP, Quebec Series, 181–82; Haldimand to SHC, Quebec, October 26, 1780, *HSGS, III*, 186 ex LAC, HP, B147, 268; Haldimand to Germain, Quebec, October 26, 1780. *ibid.*, 180–82 ex Series Q17/1, 152; **Oneidas Move to Niagara**: Joseph T. Glatthaar and James Kirby Martin, *Forgotten Allies – The Oneida Indians and the American Revolution* (New York: Hill & Wang, 2006), 271–72, and Haldimand to Bolton, Quebec, September 1, 1780, Smy Transcripts, ex HP, AddMss21756: "The treacherous conduct of the Oneida Indians, and the impossibility of effecting anything against the enemy in that quarter while they remain in the rebel interest, has brought me to a resolution to force them to obedience, or to cut them off … For [that] purpose, I shall send a strong detachment into that Country under the command of Sir John Johnson." Obviously, the loyal Indians got wind of Haldimand's resolve and took action to persuade the Oneidas to come to Niagara before Johnson mounted his raid; Watt, *Burning*, 80–81; **Oneidas Leave/Harvest**: *HSGS, III*, 187 ex LAC, HP, B147, 283–85. Although unstated, these harvests were likely at the Mohawk settlement of Canajoharie, which had been bypassed by SJJ's raid that October. Honyery Tewahangaraghkan (Doxator) and many other Oriska inhabitants had occupied abandoned Mohawk homes at Canajoharie after the failed siege of Stanwix. Watt, *Rebellion*, 270–71; **Carleton**

Island: Cruikshank and Watt, *KRR NY*, 61–63; Ross to Mathews, Coteau-du-Lac, October 17, 1780, LAC, HP, AddMss21818, 201. Ross complained of "a great many Old and Infirm men sent me from the 1st Battalion whose Services cannot be in the least depended on and destitute of everything"; **Rebels as Recruits**: Haldimand to SJJ, November 6, 1780, Cruikshank and Watt, *KRR NY*, 62.

9.   **Smoked Meats**: Jeptha R. Simms, *History of Schoharie County, and Border Wars of New York; Containing also a Sketch of the Causes Which Led to the American Revolution; etc.…* (Albany: Munsell & Tanner, 1845), 453–54; Simms has the event occurring in 1781, but the following source indicates the fall of 1780: Samuel Tallmadge, *Orderly Books of The Fourth New York Regiment, 1778—1780: The Second New York Regiment, 1780–1783 with Diaries of John Barr, 1779–1782*, Almon W. Lauber, ed. and trans. (Albany: University State of New York, 1932); Talmadge, 532–35. [Hereafter *4&2NY OB*]; **Smyth Letter**: *Minutes of the Commissioners for Detecting and Defeating Conspiracies in the State of New York, Albany County Sessions, 1778–1781*, Vol. 2, Victor Hugo Paltsits, ed. [hereafter *Conspiracies*] (Albany: New York State, 1909), 561; **Walden Meyers**: *Ibid.*, II, 565–66. There were many variations of this name, for example, Johan/Hans/John Walden Meyers/Waltermyer. See, Mary B. Fryer, *Loyalist Spy, The Experiences of John Walden Meyers during the American Revolution* (Brockville, ON: Besancourt Publishers, 1974), 1–5; **Garret**: *Conspiracies*, II, 579; **Patrick Smyth**: *Ibid.*, 579–80. Brother of Dr. George Smyth. Mathews, *Spies*, 9–10, 54, 198, see index. Patrick was at Sorel in 1785. Crowder, 95; **George Smyth**: Mathews, *Spies*, 50–54; Officers of 3NY to Van Cortlandt, November 11, 1780. Jacob Judd, ed., *The Revolutionary War Memoir and Selected Correspondence of Philip Van Cortlandt*, [Hereafter, *Cortlandt Memoir*] (Tarrytown, NY: Sleepy Hollow Restorations, 1976), 389–90; T.W. Egly, Jr., *History of the First New York Regiment* [hereafter, *1NY*] (Hampton, NH: Peter E. Randall, 1981), 177. Discipline in 1NY was generally more rigid than in 3NY.

10. Haldimand to SHC, Quebec, November 16, 1780, *HSGS, III*, 189 ex LAC, HP, B147, 278–80; **Carbines**: LAC, HP, MG21, B158, 221; **Capture Canada**: Lanctot, 193. Confirming Haldimand's theory, some rebel leaders considered the capture of Canada as a bargaining chip to regain any state occupied by the British at the close of the war; **Indians**: Most concerning were the Lakes' and Ohio Nations, which had demonstrated their attachment to France during the Pontiac Uprising of 1763. Less so, but still a worry were the Seven Nations of Canada, the Mississaugas. and the League Seneca; **Hazen's Road**: Mathews, *Spies*, 72–73. The Bayley-Hazen Road, built 1778–79 by 110 men through Jacob Bayley's leadership. Co-named after Hazen. The fifty-mile road led from Coös in the Connecticut River Valley over the hills to a feature in the Green Mountains known as Hazen's Notch; Haldimand to

Germain, Sorel, October 15, 1778, LAC, CO42/37, 198. Mentions the building of the road and that Hazen had visited the St. Francis Indians and predicted an invasion of Canada. See, Frederick W. Baldwin, "The Hazen Military Road," www. rootsweb.com/~vermont/HistoryHazenMilitaryRoad.html (accessed March 2005); **Hazen**: In the expedition against Crown Point in 1756 and Louisbourg in 1758. With Wolfe in 1759. Distinguished himself at Sillery, April 28, 1760. Lieutenant in 44th, February 1761. Residing at St. John's when war broke out. Furnished supplies and other aid to Montgomery's army. Raised a small regiment in 1776, later known as the 2Cdn. His Quebec property destroyed by the British. His brother John resided in Newbury, VT, *ibid.*, 4-8; Haldimand to Germain, Quebec, November 28, 1780, *HSGS, III*, 190 ex LAC, HP, B57-2, 309–14.

11. **Strength, Small Corps**: These corps were in a constant state of flux. The totals of Officers and ORs are found in LAC, HP, AddMss21827, part II, May 1, 1781. At peak strength in 17777, the KLA, QLR, and LV were each close to meeting the establishment figure. The QLR and LV were hammered at Bennington, August 16, 1777. During the campaign, both AR and AV were both at two-coy strength, each having a coy serving on bateaux, as was a coy of the KLA; **Nairne Organizes**: December 9, 1780, Jessup OB; **Independent Coys**: Entry for December 5, 1780, *Ibid.*; **Officers 2KRR**: Haldimand to SJJ, December 11, 1780, LAC, HP, MG21, B159, 131–32; H.M. Jackson, *Rogers' Rangers, A History* (Toronto: self-published, 1953), 181–85 ex LAC, HP, B160 AddMss21820; **Patrol**: Entries, December 9–10, 1780, *4&2NY OB*, 844; **Tryon Survey**: Kelsay, 301; SHC to Haldimand, NYC, November 8, 1780, *HSGS, III*, 191 ex *HP, Q18*, 130; **Sherwood's New Responsibility**: Fryer, *Pimpernel*, 126–27; **Carleton Island**: Bond, 12; **Molly Brant**: Lois M. Huey and Bonnie Pulis, *Molly Brant, A Legacy of Her Own* (Youngstown, NY: Old Fort Niagara Association, 1997), 9, 13, 37; **Protecting Harvest**: *HSGS, II*, 187 ex HP, B147, 283–85; **Desertonyon**: Claus to Mathews, Ernest A. Cruikshank, "The Coming of the Loyalist Mohawks to the Bay of Quinte," *OHSPR* 26 (1930): 394 ex HP, B114, 160–61.

CHAPTER 3: WINTER TURMOIL ON THE WESTERN FRONTIER
1. **Reform Continental Line**: Robert K. Wright Jr., *The Continental Army* (Washington: Army Lineage Series, Center of Military History, U.S. Army, 1989) 153–63; Huntington to Governor Clinton, Phil, October 6, 1780. T.W. Egly Jr., *History of the First New York Regiment* [hereafter, *1NY*] (Hampton, NH: Peter E. Randall, 1981), 175; **Amendments**: Washington to Governor Clinton, November 6, 1780, *ibid.*, 176; **Reorganization/Rearrangement**: Wright, 158–60. Excellent detail of reorganized infantry and artillery regiments; **5NY**: (New York) Pension Application [hereafter, (NY) PA], W1525, widow of Marinus Willett; **NY Line**: *4&2NY OB*, 8–9, Wright, 157, and Egly, *1NY*, 176–81; **Derange**: Contemporary term meaning to throw into

confusion or to disturb the normal state, working or function. A deranged officer was one who was not part of the current arrangement of a regiment, that is, he had been knocked out of the new arrangement and was without assignment; Governor Clinton to Robert Van Rensselaer, June 29, 1780. Johnson, *Bloodied Mohawk*, 143 ex PPGC, V, 894; Van Rensselaer to Governor Clinton, Fort Paris, July 5, 1780, *ibid.*, 144 ex PPGC, V, 919; **At Stanwix**: *4&2NY OB*, 554–55, 741; **Mutiny**: Carl Van Doren, *Mutiny in January, The Story of a Crisis in the Continental Army...* (New York: Viking Press, 1943), and Wright, 163. A "precipitating factor" that led to the crisis in the PA Line was the army's reorganization; **VT prisoners**: McHenry; Clyde to Governor Clinton, January 6, 1781. PPGC, VI, 551–53; Return dated December 2, 1780. James F. Morrison, *Col Jacob Klock's Regt, Tryon County Militia* [hereafter, *Klock's Regt*] (self-published, 1992), inside back cover; **Richter's Coy**: (NY) PA W16396 widow of Johann Jost Scholl. Johnson, *Bloodied Mohawk*, 546; **4TCM Return**: J.F. Morrison research. Herkimer Family Papers, SC11965, No.13, NYSL.

2. **Convoy**: *Correspondence of the Van Cortlandt Family of Cortlandt Manor 1748–1800*, Jacob Judd, tr. and ed. (Tarrytown: Sleep Hollow Restorations, 1977) [Hereafter, *Van Cortlandt Correspondence*] 394–96; **Tories Examined**: *Conspiracies, II*, 618, 22–24; **East Union**: Williamson, 100–01; **1NY**: Egly, *1NY*, 183; **Rebel Indians**: Barbara Graymont, *The Iroquois in the American Revolution* (Syracuse: Syracuse University Press, 1972), 242. People of all three nations occupied these deplorable huts, although Schuyler referred only to Oneidas. Schuyler to Huntington, Albany, January 18, 1781. Maryly B. Penrose, ed., *Indian Affairs Papers, American Revolution* (Franklin Park, NJ: Liberty Bell Associates, 1981), 269. Schuyler had written in a similar vein on December 2, 1780, *ibid.*, 265–66, and Graymont, 243. Schuyler wrote a third letter on December 26, 1780; Glatthaar and Martin, 380fns28, 30. Provides a careful analysis of the number of rebel Indians at Schenectady; **Abraham Wemple**: The Oneidas later recalled his kindnesses. He "turned out an Ox for us and gave Us Bread when We were hungry, Drink when We were dry, and his House was our own." Alan Taylor, *The Divided Ground: Indians, Settlers, and the Northern Borderland of the American Revolution* (New York: Vintage Books, 2007), 147.

3. **Karaghgunty**: Captain David Hill Karonghyontye, likely; **Nanticokes**: Penrose, *Indian Affairs Papers*, 187; Haldimand to SHC, January 3, 1781, HSGS, III, 192 ex *HP, B147*, 287–88; **Wheat/Unrest**: *Ibid.*; Cramahé to Haldimand, January 5, 1781. *Ibid.*, 192–93 ex *HP, B95*, 94–99; Haldimand to Cramahé, n.d. and unsigned, *Ibid.*, 193 ex *HP, B95*, 100–01; **Fraser's Coy**: William Fraser to Haldimand, Isle aux Noix, August 26, 1778. He had chosen "four Serjeants and fifty Rank and file … all very fit for the duty of Rangers" from "the different corps of Royalists (Sir John Johnsons excepted)." He requested clothing and light arms. LAC, HP, AddMss21874, 52, and a Roll of

William Fraser's Coy, Verchère, December 1, 1780, prepared after returning from the Ballstown expedition of October, listed 1 captain, 2 lieutenants, 3 serjeants, 3 Corporals, and 52 rank and file, WO28/10, Part 2, f.254; **Clothing & Orders**: RO, Verchère, January 4 and 20, 1781, Jessup OB; Cruikshank and Watt, *KRR NY*, 65–66; **Mathews**: Ensign, 8th, February 28, 1761. Served under the Duke of Brunswick. In 1768, he was stationed with the 8th, in Quebec. Made lieutenant in 1770. Appointed adjutant on April 10, 1775. Stationed at Fort Niagara for the early years of the war. Made captain on July 5, 1777. A study examining the health of the Upper Posts, written by Mathews and his fellow officer, the DAG, Francis Le Maistre, caught the eye of Haldimand and led to him being brought to HQ as the governor's military secretary, a role in which he excelled for several years. During that time, he formed a personal friendship with his superior. Made major in 53rd, January 1785. He was most significant in the settlement of the loyalists in upper Quebec. Postwar, he served at Detroit with the 53rd and Carleton recognized his talents and dedication, but he returned home and commanded the 53rd in October 1793 in the defence of Nieuwpoort, Belgium. Major of the Chelsea Hospital, October 6, 1801. Mathews married Mary Simpson, a noted Quebec beauty who had been Horatio Nelson's first love. *DCB, Vol. V* (1801–1820); **Scouts**: SJJ to Mathews, January 15, 1781, LAC, HP, MG21, B158, 231; Robertson to Brehm, January 15, 1781. LAC, HP, AddMss21780, 116–17.

4.   **Sherwood/St. Leger**: Fryer, *Pimpernel*, 127; **Haldimand's Proclamation**: HSGS, III, 194; **Townfolk**: Haldimand to Germain, *ibid.*, 203; Mathews to SJJ, January 18, 1781 LAC, HP, B159, *138*; St. Laurent to HQ, January 24, 1781, LAC, HP, AddMss21794, 9; **G Johnson's Foresters**: Haldimand to Germain, LAC, HP, AddMss21717, Part 2; **Stanwix Raid**: Kelsay, 306; **Bradt**: Cruikshank, *Butler's Rangers*, 91. Cruikshank identifies Bradt as John, not his older brother Andrew. John's commission as second lieutenant was allowed to date February 20, 1781, but he was a Volunteer at the time of this raid; "Return of Indian War Parties of Colonel Guy Johnson's Department now on Service," April 21, 1781, Graymont, 245 ex HP, B109, 146; Robinson to Ethan Allen, NYC, February 2, 1781. Mathews, *Spies*, 127–28 ex Nye, VT State Papers, V.VI (1941), 38.

5.   Pierre Van Cortlandt to NY Congressional delegates, November 29, 1781, *Van Cortlandt Correspondence*, 400; Governor Clinton to Congress, February 5, 1781, Graymont, 240; Klock and Deygart to Governor Clinton, February 6, 1781, PPGC, VI, 635; **Van Cortlandt/Stanwix**: *Cortlandt Memoir*, 58, and Van Cortlandt to Henry Glen, Fort Schuyler, February 6, 1781, *Van Cortlandt Correspondence*, 407; **Davis Attack**: Simms, *FNY, II*, 283; **Mohawk Valley Forts**: Morrison research. An undated list of forty-seven forts and fortified homes that existed during the war. Several of these have the same name, although located in distinctly different places;

Sleigh: General Clinton to Governor Clinton, January 17, 1781, PPGC, VI, 585; **Discipline**: *4&2NY OB*, 563–64; **Ansley**: Simms, *FNY, II*, 506–07; Amos, his wife and three children settled at Cataraqui Township No.1 (CT1), 1784, Crowder, 61; **Confiscation**: PPGC, VI, 642–44; **Malcontents**: *Ibid.*, 607–13.

6. **Board of Officers**: GO, HQ Quebec, January 29, 1781, Jessup OB; Campbell to Mathews, Montreal, February 8, 1781, LAC, HP, AddMss21771, 8; **Mutiny**: Dundas to Mathews, Isle aux Noix, February 11, 1781, LAC, HP, AddMss21792, 71; Mathews to Jessup, February 15, 1781, LAC, AddMss 21823, 83–84; **Herkimer**: Johan Jost was the elder brother of Nicholas, the TCM brigadier-general mortally wounded at Oriskany. At this time, Jost was in the 6NID as an overseer of Bateaux. He received St. Leger's praise for his work in clearing Wood Creek and forwarding supplies. Later served as the dept's commissary; **Bateaux Coy**: between 5–10 black men were soldiers in this company, many of whom had been slaves before the war. Incredibly, even after loyal service, in 1783 they were ordered returned to their owners, if proper proof was provided. Mathews to SJJ, October 6, 1783, LAC, HP, B159, 203; **Indian Arms**: Mathews to Maclean, February 19, 1781, LAC, HP, AddMss21791&21773, 177; **Powell**: Signed his correspondence as Watson Powell. For the sake of brevity, I have used Powell only, but Watson Powell would be more correct. Lieutenant in 46th, 1753. Captain in 64th, 1756. Served in French West Indies, 1759. With 64th in America, 1768. Major in 38th, 1770. Lieutenant-Colonel in 5rd, 1771, at Minorca. Arrived in Canada ith 53rd, Spring 1776. Appointed brigadier in Carleton's Second Brigade (20th, 34th, 53rd, 62nd) on June 10, 1776. Transferred to First Brigade (9th, 31st, 47th, 53rd) in November 1776. Commanded Second Brigade (20th, 21st, 62nd) under Burgoyne. Sent to command Ticonderoga with 53rd and Prinz Friedrich's Regiment as garrison. Powell "suffered the disgrace of a surprise," on September 27, 1777. Evacuated/destroyed Ticonderoga on November 8, 1777. Commanded Montreal District, 1777–78. Commanded St. John's District, 1779–80. Commanded Niagara and far Upper Posts, 1780–82. Made colonel in the army on February 19, 1779. Made General on November 20, 1782. Made colonel of 69th on April 16, 1792. Made colonel of 15th on June 20, 1794. Made lieutenant-general, May 3, 1796. General, January 1, 1801. Died, July 14, 1814, Hadden's OB, 464–67; Mathews to John Butler, Quebec, July 13, 1780, Smy Transcripts ex HP, AddMss21765; **Thomas Butler**: His father was persistent in recommending him for a coy. In the absence of a captain, First Lieutenant Butler commanded the 10th Coy, but never received a captaincy; **10th Coy**: Mathews to Powell, Quebec, January 8, 1781, Smy Transcripts, LAC, HP, AddMss21764; John Butler to Mathews, Niagara, December 4, 1780, *ibid.*, LAC, HP, AddMss21765. Butler advised HQ that he had appointed Barent Frey to command the 7th Coy and Andrew Bradt the 8th. Frey's appointment "stuck" and Bradt's did not; Powell to Hald, February 19, 1781; *Ibid.*, HP, AddMss21761;

Lieutenant-Colonel William A. Smy, *An Annotated Nominal Roll of Butler's Rangers 1777-1784 with Documentary Sources* [hereafter, *Annotated Roll*] (St. Catharines: Friends of the Loyalist Collection at Brock University, 2004), 6–10. Lewis Genevay, one of Haldimand's secretaries, later received command of the 10th Coy; A 1784 roll of officers listed the captains by seniority. Three captains had died on service, Charles Smith and Walter Butler were killed in combat and Andrew Thompson drowned. They had been regimental appointments, as were the following survivors: 1st senior., William Caldwell. 3rd, Peter Ten Broeck. 4th, Peter Hare. 6th, Bernard Frey. 9th, Andrew Bradt. The following captains came from outside the regiment: 2nd senior, John McDonell Aberchalder. 5th, George Dame. 7th, John McKinnon. 8th, Lewis Genevay. LAC, HP, AddMss21827, 348; **Indians' Needs**: Kelsay, 299.

7.   Egly, *1NY*, 184; Governor Clinton to Washington, Albany, February 20, 1781, PPGC, VI, 651; Washington to General Clinton, New Windsor, February 16, 1781. George Washington, *The Writings of George Washington from the Original Manuscript Sources, 1745–1799* [Hereafter, *Washington Writings*] XXXIX Vols., John C. Fizpatrick, ed. (Washington: U.S. Government Printing Office, 1937), V.21, 234; Washington to General Clinton, New Windsor, February 20, 1781. 200 barrels of salt provisions were being sent to Clinton at Albany and he was to "throw a supply of three Months' into Ft Schuyler, before the Roads are broken up." *Ibid.*, 258. Washington to Blaine, HQ, February 20, 1781. "On the 6th instant there were only fourteen days Beef at Ft Schuyler; that the Troops at Albany and Schenectady were obliged to be billeted upon the Inhabitants for want of Meat, that part of the Country was so intirely exhausted of Meat, that it could not be purchased," *ibid.*, 259; **State Assembly**: Penrose, *Indian Affairs*, 270; **Blankets**: Graymont, 243; **Punishments**: *4&2NY OB*, 566; **Provisions**: *Ibid.*, 562, 566–67; Field Officers, 2ACM to Governor Clinton, February 27, 1781. Willis T. Hanson, *A History of Schenectady During the Revolution* (Author, 1916), 114–15; **Blockhouse Locations**: *Ibid.*, 115fn; **H.K. Van Rensselaer**: *Conspiracies, II*, 636.

8.   **Crawford's Scout**: LAC, HP, AddMss21787 and Mathews to Campbell, March 12, 1781 for a discussion of Crawford's report, LAC, HP, AddMss21773, 182; Campbell to Mathews, Montreal, February 8, 1781, LAC, HP, AddMss21771, 8; **Crofts**: Willes/Wills. Born in Ireland, 1750. Ensign and quartermaster for the 34th, 1770–78. Lieutenant in 1772. Retired in 1786. Houlding, *King's Service*; **Killing**: Campbell to Mathews, Montreal, February 22, 1781, LAC, HP, AddMss21771, 12, and Colin G. Calloway, *The American Revolution in Indian Country: Crisis and Diversity in Native American Communities* (Cambridge: Cambridge University Press, 1995), 73, 77–78; **Abenaki Rangers**: Bayley to Washington, Newbury, September 16, 1782. Wells, 400 and roll of Captain John Vincent's Ranging Coy in the U.S. service

from St. Francis, May 1, 1780. Listed one Captain, one ensign, two serjeants, and thirteen rangers, *ibid.*, 409. For details on the Abenaki communities, see Calloway, 65–84 and *Collections of New York Historical Society*, 12 [1879]: 189; **Palmerstown**: Campbell to Mathews, February 26, 1781, LAC, HP, AddMss 21771, 14.

9. Haldimand to Smyth, February 28, 1781. Mathews, *Spies*, 56 ex HP, B182, 314–17; Haldimand to SHC, February 28, 1781, *HSGS, III*, 200 ex HP, B147, 292; **Brant's Strike**: *4&2NY OB*, 744–45 and Simms, *Schoharie*, 454–55, 55fn. For a slightly different account, see Simms, *FNY, II*, 488–89; **2NY Routine**: *4&2NY OB*, 567–68; **Fish's Detachment**: William W. Campbell, Jr., *Annals of Tryon County; or the Border Warfare of New York* (Cherry Valley, NY: The Cherry Valley Gazette Print, 1880), 178–80; **Drill Incident**: Simms, *Schoharie*, 454–55, 55fn, and *FNY, II*, 488–89; **Niagara**: Kelsay, 306; **Ferris**: G. Johnson report, LAC, HP, AddMss21770; **Vermont**: Fryer, *Pimpernel*, 130–31; **Jessup**: LAC, HP, AddMss21774, 163; **Robertson**: HP, AddMss 21780, 118, **Ross**: HP, AddMss21784, 65; **Rogers's Recruiting**: LAC, HP, AddMss 21874, 184–86; Rogers to Mathews, January 5, 1781, Fryer, *King's Men*, 249 ex LAC, HP, AddMss21820, 106–107; Robertson to Haldimand, Oswgtch, March 7, 1781, LAC, HP, AddMss 21780, 119.

10. **Hoosic Road**: *Conspiracies, II*, 646, 651, 654, 657; **Johnson/Trail**: NH State Papers, V.XVII, V.4, 210 and Mathews, *Spies*, 106–107; **Pritchard**: Claim of Azariah Pritchard, Montreal, October 29, 1787, Alexander Fraser, ed., *Second Report of the Bureau of Archives for the Province of Ontario*, 2 vols. [hereafter, Fraser] (1904; reprint, Baltimore: Genealogical Publishing Co., Inc., 1994), i, 349; **As Captain**: Fryer, *King's Men*, 251, roll of KR, September 8, 1780, ex LAC, HP, AddMss21810, 83 and Wells, 93. Claims Pritchard used Johnson's kidnapping as a lever to earn his captaincy, but the roll of September 8, 1780 refutes this; **Kidnapping**: Mathews, *Spies*, 107–10 and Sherwood to Mathews, March 10, 1781, Fryer, *Pimpernel*, 129; **3TCM adjustments**: *Fernow, Vol. XV, State Archives Vol.1*, [hereafter *V.XV, SA1*] 296; **Andrew Wemple**: Smy, *Annotated Roll*, 195; **Lord/Lard/Laird**: Watt, *Burning*, 117–18, 134; Stefan Bielinski, "Abraham Ten Broeck," www.nysm.nysed.gov/albany/bios/t/abtbroeck6.html (accessed January 1, 2005); **Ball**: Smy, *Annotated Roll*, 41. Commissioned first lieutenant on August 15, 1780, arriving that day at Niagara with forty recruits. An accomplished recruiter!; **Smyth/Women**: *Conspiracies, II*, 611–13, 620. Women's names: Elsie Elizabeth Finkle, Margaret Finkle, Margaret Seman, Catharine Seman, Maria Stever, Eva Houser, and Christian Benneyway.

11. **2KRR Indian Arms**: LAC, HP, AddMss21788, 88; **QM stores**: Return, October 1, 1780, LAC, HP, AddMss21849, ff.95–100; Ethan Allen to Huntington, Marcy 9, 1781, *ibid.*, 129; Snyder to Governor Clinton, March 9, 1781 and Governor Clinton

to Snyder, March 20, 1781, PPGC, VI, 673–76; **Van Rensselaer Inquiry**: Albany, March 12, 1781, *ibid.*, 692–703; **Bettys/Beaver Dam**: *Conspiracies, II*, 653–55; **Hewson/Smyth**: Hewson was discharged on March 24 after giving £100 bail, *ibid.*, 661,667–68 and Bond of George and Patrick Smyth and William Shepherd, March 19, 1781, PPGC, VI, 708; **Sherwood/Johnson**: Mathews, *Spies*, 110 ex Johnson's Journal found in Reverand Grant Powers, *Historical Sketches of the Discovery, Settlement and Progress of Events in the Coos Country* (Haverhill, NH: 1841); SJJ to Haldimand, March 15, 1781, LAC, HP, B158, 203; **Deserontyon**: Ernest A. Cruikshank, "The Coming of the Loyalist Mohawks to the Bay of Quinte," OHSPR, 26 (1930) ex HP, B114, 170; Haldimand to SJJ, Quebec, March 19, 1781, LAC, HP, B159, 140; **NYS Act**: Pliny Moore, "The Year 1781 at Saratoga — Col. Marinus Willett's Regiment of Levies from the Pliny Moore Papers" [hereafter, Pliny Moore Papers] *Mooresfield Antiquarian*, II (1938), 61. These "unappropriated" lands were primarily in Indian Territory and excluded those formerly held by the Oneidas and Tuscaroras.

CHAPTER 4: SPRING: THE CALAMITIES OF THE COUNTRY

1. Entry for March 22, 1781, *4&2NY OB*, 570–71. The abuse was undoubtedly verbal, or the penalty would have been far more severe; **Maximum Penalty**: For a superb six-part study of punishment, see John K. Robertson, "'39 lashes on his naked back …': Military Justice in the Revolutionary War Armies," *The Brigade Dispatch, Vols. XXXIII and XXXIV*; **Schenectady Defence**: Hanson, 115,115fn, 16; Clinton to Schenectady Magistrates and Field Officers, Albany, March 24, 1781, PPGC, VI, 715–16; Governor Clinton to Haldimand, Albany March 27, 1781, *ibid.*, 723–27. A list of 159 persons accepted by Lieutenant Allan McDonell at Crown Point in 1780 was originally attached to this letter, but not transcribed; General Clinton to Governor Clinton, Albany, March 29, 1781, *ibid.*, 728; NY Legislature to Washington, March 30, 1781, *ibid.*, 729; "Letters of the Rev. John Stuart.," James J. Talman, ed., *Loyalist Narratives From Upper Canada* (Toronto: The Champlain Society, 1946), 338.

2. **Confiscations**: *Conspiracies, II*, 672–73; **Militia Ineffectiveness**: Washington to Congress, September 15, 1780, R.K. Wright, 156; **Enlistments**: Washington to Governor Clinton, New Windsor, December 15, 1780, PPGC, VI, 509; **Levies**: Henry Livingston to Governor Clinton, Philadelphia, April 16, 1781, *ibid.*, 785, and R.K. Wright, 162; **Willett**: William M. Willett, *A Narrative of the Military Actions of Colonel Marinus Willett, Taken Chiefly From His Own Manuscript* (New York: G&C&H Carvill, 1831), 2,11, 28–32, and Howard Thomas, *Marinus Willett, Soldier-Patriot 1740–1830* (Prospect, NY: Prospect Books, 1954), 5, 19–20, and Larry Lowenthal, *Marinus Willett, Defender of the Northern Frontier* (Fleischmanns, NY: Purple Mountain Press, 2000), 9–18; **St. John's**: Egly, *1NY*, 20.

3. **Threats & Punishments**: *4&2NY OB*, 572–74; **Matross**: Gunner's apprentice, assists in loading, firing, and sponging guns. They carry firelocks as guards for the guns. Smith, *Dictionary*, 161; Congressional minutes, April 2, 1781, PPGC, VI, 734; **Smyth**: *Conspiracies, II*, 675; **Stuart**: His bond, April 4, 1781, PPGC, VI, 736 and *Conspiracies, II*, 683; The individuals considered suitable for Smyth's exchange were: Colonel James Gordon, taken by Captain John Munro's raid, October 17, 1780; Captain Jeremiah Snyder of Esopus County taken May 6, 1780; Captain Alex Harper taken by Brant, April 9, 1780; Tryon committeeman Adam Fonda taken by SJJ, May 22, 1780, McHenry, 14, 20, 24, 28, 34; Stuart to White, Schenectady, April 17, 1781, "Letters of Rev John Stuart," Talman, 338–39; **Stirling**: Alex McDougall affected the title "Lord Stirling" by which he was commonly known. Washington to Stirling, Poughkeepsie, April 6, 1781, PPGC, VI, 741–45; Governor Clinton to John Jay, Poughkeepsie, April 6, 1781, *ibid.*, 746; Governor Clinton to Duane, Poughkeepsie, April 6, 1781, *ibid.*, 749–50; **Shinop Withdraws**: Smy Transcripts, HP, AddMss21767, 211; **Taken on Delaware**: Jasper Edwards, McHenry, 29, 64; (NY) PA S9277 of Christian Bellinger. Johnson, *Bloodied Mohawk*, 306; **2NY's Lights**: J.F. Morrison research, return dated July 1, 1781, Revolutionary War Rolls 1775–83, Series M-246, Roll 67, Folder 25, NA, Washington.

4. **Sickness/Niagara**: Wilbur H. Siebert, *The Loyalists and Six Nation Indians in the Niagara Peninsula* (Ottawa: The Royal Society of Canada, 1935), 89, and Calloway, 139–40; **Indian Stores**: Butler to Haldimand, Calloway, 144 ex HP, AddMss21765, 213; **Upper Posts Provisions**: April 2, 1781, Cruikshank and Watt, *KRR NY*, 75; Rogers's Memorial, April 3, 1781, LAC, HP, AddMss21874, 205; Rogers and Peters to Haldimand, LAC, HP, AddMss21875, 212; **Provincial Squabbles**: LAC, HP, AddMss21743; **BRs/Provisions**: Powell to Haldimand, April 7, 1781, Smy Transcripts and Haldimand to Powell, April 22, 1781, *ibid.*, HP, AddMss21764. The governor replied that, unlike the rest of the army, the corps had never paid for provisions while in garrison and was expected to provide its own provisions in the field.

5. Robertson to Haldimand, Oswegatchie, April 9, 1781, LAC, HP, AddMss21780, 121; Haldimand to Robertson, April 11, 1781, *ibid.*, 122–24; **Deserontyon's Party**: Deserontyon to Claus, Carleton Island, April 12, 1781, LAC, HP, AddMss21774, 170, and "Return of Indian War Parties of Col Guy Johnson's Dept now on Service," April 21, 1781, Graymont, 245 ex LAC, HP, B109, 146. Deserontyon had 44 men, mostly Tuscaroras. They set off toward Canajoharie; **Brawl**: Penrose, Indian Affairs, 270–72, includes Mary Brant's letter ex LAC, HP, B114, 180–81; **Brant/Detroit**: Lieutenant Daniel Servos to Claus, April 12, 1781, *ibid.*, 272, and Kelsay, 309. Kelsay mentions Brant to Claus, Fort Erie, April 11, 1781; **Ross**: Ross to Haldimand, Carleton Island, April 17, 1781, Cruikshank, "Loyalist Mohawks," 396 ex LAC, HP,

B127, 227; Mathews to Butler, Quebec, April 12, 1781, Smy Transcripts, HP, AddMss 21741; **Second Blockhouse**: entry of April 12, 1781, Jessup OB; Haldimand to SJJ, April 12, 1781, LAC, HP, B159, 141–42; **2NY Men**: J.F. Morrison research. Fernow noted Samuel Mitchell, George Reed, and Jonathon Benjamin killed, James Ivory wounded, Corporal Jonathon Albright and David Lambert taken; **Walradt**: often spelled Walrath. (NY) PA S11684 of Peter Walradt. Johnson, *Bloodied Mohawk*, 628; **Abeel**: Affidavit, December 20, 1781, PPGC, VII, 606–607, and Stone, *Brant*, *II*, 172, and Butler to Mathews, Niagara, May 20, 1781, Smy Transcripts, HP, AddMss21765; Governor Clinton to General Clinton, April 6, 1781, *Conspiracies, II*, 676; Duboise to Governor Clinton, Cats Kill, April 27, 1781, PPGC, VI, 800–802; **Lansingh**: *Conspiracies, II*, 678; Entry for April 11, 1781, *4&2NY OB*, 575.

6. **Court-martial**: Haldimand to Powell, April 11, 1781, Smy Transcripts, HP, AddMss21764; **Appointments**: Haldimand to Powell, April 11, 1781, *ibid*, HP, AddMss21756; Washington to General Clinton, April 12, 1781, *Washington Writings, Vol. 21*, 452; Entry of April 13, 1781, *4&2NY OB*, 575–76. It is unclear when Colonel Van Cortlandt left Stanwix and Lieutenant-Colonel Cochran resumed command, although March 26 seems likely; Gansevoort to Governor Clinton, Albany, April 14, 1781 and Clinton to Gansevoort, April 19, 1781, PPGC, VI, 765–67; Benson to Willett and Weissenfels, April 15, 1781, PPGC, VI, 773–74; *Conspiracies, II*, 681–82; **Clossen**: Captured by rebels, 1777 while spying. Escaped, rejoined army. After Burg's defeat, went to Canada. Joined Major Jessup, but not found on KLA rolls. Thereafter in Secret Service. Sergeant, LRs, 1783, www.collectionscanada.ca/education and LAC, WO 28/10, Part 4, 457–73; **Rikely/ Reakley**: Serjeant, KR. Fryer and Smy, Provincial Rolls, 82, 98. Clossen and Rikely were frequent Secret Service operatives. Mathews, *Spies*, index, 126; Washington to Clinton, New Windsor, April 15, 1781 and anonymous report. PPGC, VI, 770–73.

7. Paine to Governor Clinton, Stillwater, April 16, 1781, *ibid.*, 775–77; Governor Clinton to Paine, April 27, 1781, *ibid.*, 777–78; SJJ to Haldimand, April 16, 1781, LAC, HP, B158, 205–206; Haldimand to SJJ, April 15, 1781, and end of April. Cruikshank and Watt, *KRR NY*, 67–69; Peters to Sherwood. Fryer, *Pimpernel*, 129 ex HP, B180, 7; **Jacob James Klock**: Second Lieutenant, August 26, 1775 2TCM. Second Major Tryon City County Battalion of Minute Men, Late 1775 to early 1776. Ensign, Finck's Coy, 1NY, November 21, 1776. Resigned 1NY, May 16, 1780. Egly, *1NY*, 151–52; Klock to Governor Clinton, April 18, 1781, *ibid.*, 789–90; M. Visscher to Governor Clinton, Albany, and Younglove to Yates, Cambridge, both April 18, 1781, PPGC, VI, 787–89; *Conspiracies, II*, 686; **Ruiter**: 1777 LV listed Lieutenant John Ruiter starting service on August 1, 1777, LAC, HP, MG21, B167a, Part 1, 109. Ruiter, first lieutenant, Meyer's Coy, LR, May 30, 1782.

8.   Mathews to Powell, April 20, 1781, Smy Transcripts, HP, AddMss21764; Marsh to Haldimand, Isle aux Noix, April 21, 1781, Jennifer S.H. Brown and Wilson, *Colonel William Marsh, Loyalist and Vermont Patriot* (n.p. [work in progress], 2007), ex HP, AddMss21821, ff.236–37; Return of Indian War Parties of Colonel Guy Johnson's Dept now on Service, April 21, 1781, Graymont, 245, ex LAC, HP, B109, 146; G. Johnson to Haldimand, April 23, 1781, LAC, HP, AddMss21767, 219; **The Raid**: Chris P. Yates to Glen Throop Wider, ed., "The Glen Letters — That We May Remember," *New York History, Vol. XXVI, No.3 (July 1945)*; **Bowen**: Watt & Morrison, *British Campaign*, 77. Watt, *Rebellion*, 224, 238, 264. William R. Bowen, a Tribes Hill native, had been captured with William No, Walter Butler in August 1777 and jailed until 1780, when he either escaped or was exchanged; **Burial Party**: (NY) PA S23221 of Robert Flint Johnson, *Bloodied Mohawk*, 401; Deserontyon's report. LAC, HP, HP, AddMss21761, 65; **Aaron Hill**: Hill to Claus, LAC, HP, AddMss21774, 180.

9.   *4&2NY OB*, 577–79; Smyth to Haldimand, April 26, 1781. Mathews, *Spies*, 57; **Schoharie Defences**: Simms, *Schoharie*, 450–51, and pension application of Barend Stubrach. Jeff O'Connor research; Governor Clinton to Charlotte County magistrates, April 27, 1781, PPGC, VI, 799–800; Governor Clinton to Willett, Poughkeepsie, April 28, 1781, *ibid.*, 807–809; **War Party**: A fourteen-man Delaware war party from Fort Niagara led by John Chughnut. As Chuknut was the Delaware name for Newtown, perhaps he was John of Chuknut. No mention of BRs or 6NID officers attending. G. Johnson report May 19, 1781, LAC, HP, AddMss21770; **Minisink 1779**: Vernon Leslie, *The Battle of Minisink, A Revolutionary War Engagement in the Upper Delaware Valley* (Middletown, NY: T. Emmett Henderson, 1976); **Minisink 1781**: Governor Clinton to Pawling, April 28, 1781, PPGC, VI, 810–11; General Clinton to Governor Clinton, Albany, April 29, 1781, *Doc No.158. Historical Magazine* ex History Society of PA, Gratz Collection, Case 4, Box 18, Folio A.D.S. Item X00530; Entry, April 30, 1781, *Conspiracies, II*, 696.

10. **Servos**: Cruikshank and Watt, *KRR NY*, 76; **Ditch**: Bond, 12–13; **Portfire**: A rolled paper case that contains an explosive composition and is used for firing charges; **Five Scouts**: SJJ to Haldimand, May 3, 1781, LAC, HP, B158, 207; **Corn Crops**: Calloway, 145; **Carleton Island**: Cruikshank and Watt, *KRR NY*, 75; **Schuyler Attempt**: SJJ to Haldimand, May 3, 1781, LAC, HP, B158, 207; Robertson to Haldimand, Oswegatchie, May 10, 1781. The prisoners were John Brant and John Minks. Both men enlisted in 2KRR. LAC, HP, AddMss21780, 129; St. Leger to Haldimand, St. John's, May 1781, LAC, HP, AddMss21794, 40; **Pointe au Fer**: In the winter of 1781, Ensign Roger Stevens, KR, maintained an outpost here with about twenty men. The site was garrisoned throughout the war and relinquished in 1796. Mathews, *Spies*, 95, and Russell P. Bellico, *Sails and Steam in the Mountains, A*

Maritime and Military History of Lake George and Lake Champlain (Fleischmanns, NY: Purple Mountain Press, 1992), 149.

11. **German Prisoners**: *Conspiracies, II*, 697–98; **West Point**: Egly, *1NY*, 186; *4&2NY OB*, 749; **Rebel Prisoners**: McHenry and Fernow, *V.XV, SA1*, 545; **Discipline**: *4&2NY OB*, 579–80; *Conspiracies, II*, 699–704; Schuyler to Governor Clinton, Saratoga, May 4, 1781, PPGC, VI, 840–43; **Cochran's Proposal**: Robert B. Roberts, *New York's Forts in the Revolution* [hereafter Roberts, *NY Forts*] (London and Toronto: Associated University Presses, 1980), 213–14; Washington to General Clinton, New Windsor, May 4–5, 1781, *Washington Writings, Vol. 22*, 29. The shad were packed using three pecks of salt to a 220-pound barrel of cleaned fish; General Clinton to Van Cortlandt, May 6, 1781, *Van Cortlandt Correspondence*, 415–16; Washington to Reed, New Windsor May 5–7, 1781, *Washington Writings, Vol. 22*, 45–50; Washington to General Clinton, May 7, 1781, *ibid.*, 51–52.

12. Germain to Haldimand, May 4, 1781, HSGS, III, 201–202 ex LAC, HP, Q18, 49–50; William Butler to Lernoult, May 6, 1781, Smy Transcripts. *WO28/4*; **Vermont Flag**: Dundas to Mathews, Isle aux Noix, May 7, 1781, LAC, HP, AddMss21792, 79, and Fryer, *Pimpernel*, 132; Smyth to Haldimand, May 8, 1781, Mathews, *Spies*, 57 ex LAC, HP, B180, 348; **Ira's Comments**: Williamson, 102–103; Dundas to Mathews, Isle aux Noix, May 9, 1781, LAC, HP, Add Mss21791, 80; Sherwood to Mathews, *Spies*, 127, and Fryer, *Pimpernel*, 131–33; Treaty Terms, May 9, 1781, LAC, HP, AddMss21774; Alun Hughes, "John Butler and Early Settlement on the West Bank of the Niagara River," *The Butler Bicentenary – Commemorating the 200th Anniversary of the Death of Colonel John Butler* (Colonel John Butler Branch, United Empire Loyalists Association of Canada, 1997.)

13. Fernow, V.XV, SA1, 545–46; James F. Morrison, *The Mohawk Valley in 1781, a Brief History of the Battles, Skirmishes and Raids* [hereafter *1781*] (Gloversville, NY: Author, 1991), 1; NYSL, Special Collections and Mss, Audited Accounts, Vol. C, 229. **Captured**: Privates John J. Failing, 2TCM, and Thomas and John Shoemaker, 4TCM; (NY) PA S22985 of Jacob Shew. He recalled this event taking place in the summer, yet Stanwix was evacuated on June 2, 1781. James F. Morrison, *A History of Fulton County in the Revolution* [hereafter *Fulton*] (Gloversville, NY: Author, 1977), 41; Schuyler to Governor Clinton, Saratoga, May 10, 1781, Mathews, *Spies*, 132–33; Cochran's report, May 11, 1781, *Van Cortlandt Correspondence*, 417–18; LAC, HP, AddMss21842, 339, and G. Johnson to Haldimand, May 19, 1781. LAC, HP, AddMss21767, 228; **Allen**: 6NID rolls rarely listed Volumes. On a roll signed by SJJ as Superintendent General Inspector General of Indian Affairs, December 1783, Allen was described as "unworthy from late bad conduct." He did not settle in

Canada prior to 1789; Cruikshank, "Loyalist Mohawks," 396 ex HP, B127, 230, and *B114*, 101; Ross to Haldimand, May 12, 1781, LAC, HP, AddMss21787, 281, and Add Mss21774, 181; Powell to Haldimand, Niagara, 13May81, Smy Transcripts, LAC, HP, Add Mss21761.

14. Governor Clinton to Schuyler, May 13, 1781, PPGC, VI, 859–60; Schuyler to General Clinton, Saratoga, May 13, 1781. Stone, *Brant, II*, 147–48; Cochran to Van Corlandt, Stanwix May 13, 1781, *Van Cortlandt Correspondence*, 419; Washington to General Clinton, May 14, 1781, *Washington Writings, Vol. 22*, 83–84; **Stanwix Fire**: *4&2NY OB*, 581, 750, and Cochran to General Clinton, Stanwix, May 14, 1781, PPGC, VI, 877; **Petit**: Simms, *FNY, II*, 491, and LAC, HP, AddMss21842 and Willett Thomas, 113; **Laboratory**: Place where quick-matches, fuses, caseshot, hand grenades, etc. are prepared.

15. Schuyler to General Clinton, Saratoga, May 15, 1781, PPGC, VI, 880–81; **Atayataghronghta**: a.k.a. Lewie/Lewis/Louis Cook or Black Louis. The only Native lieutenant-colonel in the rebel service. Born of black and Indian parents in 1740 on the Schuyler family's Saratoga plantation. Captured as a youth by a Kahnawake war party and adopted. Louis was one of the most respected and feared enemies of the loyal Indians and their allies. Theodore C. Corbett, *A Clash of Cultures on the Warpath of the Nations: The Colonial Wars in the Hudson-Champlain Valley* (Fleischmanns, NY: Purple Mountain Press, Ltd., 2002), 117, 135, and "The Life of Colonel Louis Cook," Rev. Eleazer Williams (unpublished., circa 1851, transcribed by Darren Bonaparte, 2001). Williams says that Louis was promoted by Congress to lieutenant-colonel of Cavalry in 1780; **Rodgers et al**: Williamson, 101–102; **Theft**: *4&2NY OB*, 581; General Clinton to Governor Clinton, Albany, May 16, 1781, PPGC, VI, 876; General Clinton to Cochran, Albany, May 16, 1781, *ibid.*, 878–79; *4&2NY OB*, 582; General Clinton to Van Cortlandt, Albany, May 16, 1781. PPGC, VI, 880; Washington to General Clinton, N Windsor, May 18, 1781. *Washington Writings, Vol. 22*, 99; **New Law**: Benson to Gansevoort, May 15, 1781. Gansevoort Papers, No.18-130; General Clinton to Governor Clinton, Albany, May 17, 1781, PPGC, VI, 881–82; General Clinton to Governor Clinton, n.d., *Van Cortlandt Correspondence*, 430; Elsworth to Governor Clinton, May 17, 1781, PPGC, VI, 883–84.

16. Kelsay, 307 ex LAC, HP, AddMss21761, *P t2*, 72; **Brant's Captaincy**: "Return of Six Nations' Department," May 16, 1781, listed six captains and their responsibilities. A seventh was listed as a rebel prisoner. Brant was responsible for the Mohawks and Oneidas, a group of 877 souls, the second largest of the six theoretical coys. LAC, HP, AddMss21770; **Ball**: There were two lieutenants named Ball: First Lieutenant Jacob Ball, commissioned August 4, 1779, and his son, First Lieutenant Peter Mann

Ball, commissioned August 15, 1779. Smy, *Annotated Roll*, 40–41; **War Parties**: G. Johnson's report, May 17, 1781, LAC, HP, AddMss21770; St. Leger to Haldimand, Fort St. John's, May 17, 1781, LAC, HP, AddMss21794, 45; **St. Leger's Temper**: Some who suffered St. Leger's wrath: Colonel von Kreutzbourg, Captain Hertel de Rouville, Reverend Scott, Captain John Munro; **Rumours**: Hanson, 116 ex *Washington Papers, Library of Congress*; **Cambridge articles**: M. Visscher to Governor Clinton, May 19, 1781, PPGC, VI, 884–85; McClung to Governor Clinton, May 19, 1781, *ibid.*, 885; Governor Clinton to Robert Van Rensselaer, Poughkeepsie, May 19, 1781, *ibid*, 892–93; **Willett's Levies**: Willett's report, Albany, May 19, 1781, *ibid.*, 895–97. Some liberties have been taken with names and abbreviations. The latter section of the report has been broken into paragraphs for greater clarity; **Gross's**: Biographies of Johann Daniel and Lawrence Gros, see Johnson, *Bloodied Mohawk*, 423–24; **Spy**: (NY) PA W5825, widow of William Nellis; **Bayley**: Calloway, 79.

17. Sherwood report, June 5, 1781. William Marsh Brown, ex LAC, HP, B176, 128–29; **British Proposal**: Wells, 399; **Carscallen/Bothum**: Eula C. Lapp, *To Their Heirs Forever* (Belleville, ON: Mika Publishing Co., 1977), 233–34, ex HP, B178/I; Butler to Mathews, May 20, 1781, Smy Transcripts, HP, AddMss21765; **Balsly**: Morrison, *1781*, 1; (NY) PA R7581 of George H. Nellis. Johnson, *Bloodied Mohawk*, 500; **Stanwix**: *4& 2NY OB*, 582, 751; **Return 1**: Misc. Mss: Willett, Marinus. NYHS; **Return 2**: "A Return of a Regiment of Levies raised for the immediate Defence of the Frontiers of this State Commanded by Marinus Willett, dated Albany 21May81." PPGC, VI, 900–901; General Clinton to Van Cortlandt, Albany, May 22, 1781, *Van Cortlandt Correspondence*, 423; *4&2NY OB*, 583, 751; **Spears**: Perhaps spontoons (a type of spear), as carried by officers, or more likely, a cruder form of iron-tipped pole arm as used to repel boarders on ships, an ideal close-quarters weapon to defend fort entryways; **Paper**: With the massive volume of correspondence and reporting that took place, be assured that Haldimand's Canadian Department appears to have never lacked paper; Conine to Bronck, May 22, 1781, *Bronck Family Papers*, 34–35.

18. Haldimand to Sherwood, May 21, 1781, Fryer, *Pimpernel*, 133 ex LAC, HP, B179-1, 40; Claus to Mathews, May 21, 1781, LAC, HP, AddMss21774, 182; **Handbill**: PPGC, VII, 27; G. Johnson report, LAC, HP, AddMss21770; **Hoff/Huff**: Both men were on a "List of Capt Brants' Volunteers," September 4, 1782, LAC, HP, AddMss21771, 104. Captain Hill's Report, May 4, 1781, Penrose, *Indian Affairs*, 274; **Ferry**: The serjeant was named Walrath, as were two privates. The other two were named Cargar. Morrison, *Klock's Regt*, 6, 14, 16. Morrison, *1781*, 2. Fernow, V.XV, SA1, 546. McHenry; **Leaked Dispatch**: Hansen, 117; Washington to Congress, May 27, 1781, *FNY, II*, 490; **Scalped Children**: (NY) PA W19231, widow of John Etting. Johnson, *Bloodied Mohawk*, 389–90; *Conspiracies, II*, 720–21; Egly, *1NY*, 189; **Engineer**:

Washington to du Portail, May 28, 1781, *Washington Writings, Vol.22*, 127. Three days later, the C-in-C ordered Major Villefranche to Albany to report to Brigadier-General Clinton, *ibid*, 142; Washington to General Clinton, HQ New Windsor, May 28, 1781 in Egly, *1NY*, 188; **Fort Herkimer Attack**: Simms, *FNY, II*, 283; Morrison, *1781*, 1. The wounded men were Abram Wholeber, scalped twice, and Nathan Shoemaker; **Wholeber**: spelled various as Wholeben, Woleber, Wolever, and Wolleber. Abram was a 4TCM Oriskany veteran; **Quakers/Disaffected /Smyth**: Entry from May 30, 1781, *Conspiracies, II*, 723–24, 726; **Smyth/Howard**: Mathews, *Spies*, 58–59. The author cites Howard's memorial in Cruikshank (68–69), "Some Loyalists from NY ..."; **Finck**: Egly, *1NY*, 51, 81, 151, 177–78. John B. Koettertiz, "Andrew Finck, Major in the Revolutionary Wars." Address to Herkimer County Historical Society, 1897.

19. Robertson to Brehm, Oswegatchie, May 27, 1781, LAC, HP, AddMss21780, 131; **T. Sherwood**: Mathews, *Spies*, 55, 104 ex LAC, HP, B176, 123; William Butler to Mathews, May 30, 1781, Smy Transcripts, HP, AddMss21765; G. Johnson's report, *ibid*, HP, Add Mss21770; **John Johnston**: Indian Department captain, 1764. Recommissioned in 1775. Prisoner of enemy, September 2, 1782, AddMss21770. His stepbrother William ranked as captain, June 1783. See, "Return of Officers of the Indian Department Recommended for Half Pay," circa 1784, LAC, HP, AddMss21827, f.353. Officers at Niagara, December 4, 1783, showed John Johnston as an extra captain, perhaps another man had been promoted while Johnston was a prisoner. Johnston died in 1785. His wife was 64 in 1783, so, assuming John was near her age, he was in his sixties during this raid; Maclean to Munro, Montreal, May 31, 1781, LAC, HP, B158, 216. Cruikshank and Watt, *KRR NY*, 48–49; **Dunbar's Order**: LAC, HP, B158, 222–23.

20. **John Walden Meyers**: Fryer, *Loyalist Spy*, 103–108; **De Spitzer**: Hanson, 158; **Banker's**: (NY) PA R10927 of John B. Veeder. Johnson, *Bloodied Mohawk*, 619; **Reddick**: Confession of William Sommer, PPGC VII, 79–81. John Reddick, Grenadier, 1KRR, enlisted on August 15, 1777. George Reddick, Duncan's Coy, 1KRR, enlisted on November 17, 1780. Cruikshank and Watt, *KRR NY*, 293; **Harris**: Moses was a true double agent. He was jailed at Albany as a ruse and allowed to escape to Canada to pass false intelligence to Dr. Smyth. On another occasion he was trapped by Joseph Bettys, fled for his life, and found refuge with a friend of Schuyler. He was suspected by Secret Service agents Clossen and Rikely, his former neighbours. He retired after being wounded fleeing rebel scouts and was liberally rewarded by Schuyler. Mathews, *Spies*, 104–105; **Stanwix**: *4&2NY OB*, 751–52. (NY) PA W6370, widow of Simon J. Vrooman; (NY) PA S11513 of Jacob Tanner; **Veeder's Mill**: Caleb Stark, trans. and ed., *Memoir and Official Correspondence of Gen. John Stark, with Notices of Several Other Officers of the Revolution* (Concord, MA: G. Parker Lyon, 1860), 263–

64; Egly, *1NY*, 188; **Hazen's**: Wright, 59, 157, 317–18; **DeWitt**: *Conspiracies, II*, 729–30; **Schoharie attitudes**: Gavin K. Watt, *The Flockey 13 August 1777* (King City, ON: author, 2002). Jeff O'Connor, *Thunder in the Valley* (Schoharie: The Schoharie County Historical Society, 2002); Vrooman to Gansevoort, June 2, 1781, Gansevoort Papers, 18, 130; **Meyers**: Fryer, *Loyalist Spy*, 103–108; **Oneidas**: *Van Cortlandt Correspondence*, 424–27; **Back Nations**: Perhaps Mississaugas who spoke an Algonkian dialect.

21. Robertson to HQ, June 1, 1781, LAC, HP, AddMss21780, 133–35; G. Johnson's "General State of the Corps of Indians and Department of Indian Affairs … Niagara," June 1, 1781, LAC, HP, AddMss21769, *122*; Sherwood to Haldimand, June 2, 1781, Fryer, *Pimpernel*, 133; **Gill/Whitcomb**: LAC, HP, AddMss21777, 282–86; SJJ to Haldimand, June 4, 1781, LAC, HP, B158, 224; Mathews to Sherwood, June 5, 1781, Fryer, *Pimpernel*, 134 ex LAC, HP, B179-1, 72. Long Isle is presently known as North Hero Island; **Garett**: *Conspiracies, II*, 730–31; Washington to General Clinton, June 5, 1781, Egly, *1NY*, 189; *4&2NY OB*, 752; **Johnstown**: Morrison, *Klock's Regt*; **Dygert**: Variously Deygart, Dychard, Tygert; Williams to Governor Clinton, White Creek, June 5, 1781, PPGC, VII, 11–13; Van Cortlandt to General Clinton, Fort Herkimer, June 5, 1781, *Van Cortlandt Memoir*, 157–58; **Fort Haldimand**: Cruikshank and Watt, *KRR NY*, 75; McKinnon to Haldimand, Quebec, June 6, 1781, Smy Transcripts, HP, AddMss21734; Haldimand to SJJ, June 7, 1781, LAC, HP, B159, 147; **Rebuke**: Cruikshank and Watt, *KRR NY*, 70; Butler to Powell, and Powell to Haldimand, June 7, 1781, Smy Transcripts, HP, AddMss21761; **Dame/Turney**: Powell to Haldimand, June 7, 1781, *ibid.*; James J. Talman, ed., "The Journal of Adam Crysler." *Loyalist Narratives From Upper Canada* (Toronto: Champlain Society, 1946), 59; **Duboise's Soldier**: (NY) PA W25200, widow of Jerone Barhydt and Hanson, 131.

22. **Gros's Coy**: George House and David Schuyler. Fernow, V.XV, SA1, 545; Morrison, *1781*, 2; *Conspiracies, II*, 733; **Parkers**: Difficult to establish relationship between the various Parkers; **Waits**: Private George and Corporal Joseph Wait were in 1KRR, but how they relate to John and Jane is unknown. Cruikshank and Watt, *KRR NY*, 329; Paine to Governor Clinton, Saratoga, June 9, 1781, and Chittenden to Paine, Arlington, June 9, 1781, PPGC, VII, 19–20; **End of Stanwix**: *4&2NY OB*, 752; **Meyers/Ballstown**: Fryer, *Loyalist Spy*, 110–12; Captured were First Lieutenant Epenetus White, Second Lieutenant Henry Banta and his brother, Ensign Christian. (NY) PA W24704, widow of Hendrick Banta. Johnson, *Bloodied Mohawk*, 299. Date of this attack is in debate. Banta's widow gave it as June 11. A. Rumsey to Governor Clinton, Ballstown, PPGC, VII, 157. Fernow, V.XV, SA1, 271, 545. Stone, *Brant, II*, 212fn; Prisoner list taken June 13, 1781 from Ballstown, LAC, HP, AddMss 21821. It is understandable that the Regular was returned to British service, but hard to comprehend why the Frenchmen were not allowed to stay with Meyers after they

had proven themselves so useful. Perhaps Haldimand was concerned about what they might tell the Canadiens they met while in service. Probably they were sent to Britain; **Munro's Raid**: Watt, *Burning*, 121–30, 357–58; *Conspiracies, II*, 734; Hansen, 190–94; Lieutenant Benjamin Mooers, "Orderly Book of the 2nd Canadian Regiment," [hereafter Cdn Regt OB] NYSL, Special Collections and Mss, No. 8175; **Two Serjeants**: Butler to Powell, June 12, 1781, Smy Transcripts, HP, AddMss21761; SJJ to Haldimand, June 14, 1781, LAC, HP, B158, 225; Smyth to Haldimand, Fort St. John's (FSJ), June 14, 1781, Mathews, *Spies*, 59 ex LAC, HP, B176, 131.

23. **Deserters**: *4&2NY OB*, 587; *Conspiracies, II*, 735; *Canadian Regiment OB*, Mooers Ms; General Clinton to Governor Clinton, June 16, 1781, and Cannon to General Clinton, circa June 15, 1781, PPGC, VII, 25–27; **Awl**: Possibly Johannes/John Ault of Johnstown, although his petition to the government suggests he enlisted 1KRR in 1780. Michael Ault enlisted in 1KRR on May 6, 1777, and Nicholas on May 22, 1780. Relationship of these three not proven. Cruikshank and Watt, *KRR NY*, 170; **Parker**: The Parkers had already been taken to Albany when this was written. Perhaps Cannon referred to James, who had been allowed to return to Johnstown; **Commissary**: Hughes to Governor Clinton, Albany, June 16, 1781, PPGC, VII, 27–28. Roberts, *II*, 79; *Conspiracies, II*, 736–36; G. Johnson Report, LAC, HP, AddMss21770; **Docksteder**: As John Docksteder would very soon figure prominently in the Mohawk Valley, I concluded this officer must be his brother Frederick; Powell to Haldimand, Niagara, June 16, 1781, Smy Transcripts, HP, AddMss21761; E. Rae Stuart, "Jessup's Rangers as a Factor in Loyalist Settlement," *Three History Theses* (Toronto: Ontario Department of Public Records and Archives, 1961), 43; Nelles to G. Johnson, Niagara, June 19, 1781, LAC, HP, AddMss21767, 197–98; **Sherwood's Post**: Mathews, *Spies*, 47–48.

24. General Clinton to Van Cortlandt, June 18, 1781, *Van Cortlandt Correspondence*, 431–32; **Villefranche**: Jean Louis Ambroise de Genton, Chevalier de Villefranche, major of Continental Engineers, *Washington Writings, Vol. 24*, 42fn; **Ballstown Scout**: (NY) PA S11665 of John Wasson. Johnson, *Bloodied Mohawk*, 633; **Hewit/ Empey**: Variously, Randal/Randell, *Conspiracies, II*, 737–39, 741, 744; William Empey returned to duty in 1KRR, September 1783. The given name of the lad Stevens is unknown. In December 1783, Aaron (21) and John (19) Stevens were serving in the 6NID at Niagara with their father Nicholas; **Tripp**: Fled to Canada and joined Meyer's Coy. Fryer and Smy, Provincial Rolls, 94; Younglove to Governor Clinton, Cambridge, June 20, 1781, PPGC, VII, 34–35; Marinus Willett, "Col Marinus Willett's Letter and Orderly Book, Fort Rensselaer 1781." (Hereafter, *Willett OB*) Charles Gehring, trans. Typescript, James F. Morrison, Doc. No.15705, NYSL, Albany, Arch & Mss, 2–3. I have introduced paragraphing to improve

clarity; "Letterbook of LCol Carl von Kreutzbourg, 31Mar 77 to 31Oct83," John C. Zuleger, trans., Hessian Papers, Morristown National Historic Park, NJ, 108; **Crawford**: LAC, HP, AddMss21787, 239.

CHAPTER 5: THE BLOODY EARLY SUMMER ON THE FRONTIERS

1. **"These troops"**: It is unclear what troops are referred to, but most likely Hazen's Canadian Regiment. General Clinton to Governor Clinton, Albany, June 21, 1781. Includes several quotations from Washington's orders to James Clinton, PPGC, VII, 37–38; *Van Cortlandt Correspondence*, 58; Regimental Order (RO) June 21, 1781, *Willett OB*, 27; "Willett's itinerary, June 8–November 8 1781," Johnson, *Bloodied Mohawk*, 276; Washington to Board of War, N Windsor, June 21, 1781, *Washington Writings, Vol. 22*, 244–45; *Canadian Regiment OB*; **Schell Raid**: Lyman Draper Mss, F10, 127–30. Wisconsin Historical Society and Simms, *FNY, II*, 283. Morrison, *1781*, 2; Elizabeth, Christian's widow, applied for his back pay as a private, 4TCM, from July 8, 1781, until the time of his death. NYSL, Special Collections and Mss, Audited Accounts, Vol.A, 157; Canadian Regiment OB.

2. **Bunker Hill**: Richard M. Ketchum, *Decisive Day, The Battle for Bunker Hill* (Doubleday & Company, Inc., 1962), 146–49; Washington to Stark, New Windsor, June 25, 1781, *Washington Writings, Vol. 22*, 263–64. Caleb Stark, trans. and ed., *Memoir and Official Correspondence of Gen. John Stark, with Notices of Several Other Officers of the Revolution … *Stark, 211–12. Editor Caleb Stark wrote: "The expedition against Cornwallis was now in secret contemplation. The movement was only known to Congress, Washington, Robert Morris, Rochembeau, the French agent Chevalier de La Lucerne, and Lafayette. Previous reports had been circulated, that on the arrival of the French army, an attempt would be made on New-York"; **Prisoners**: Privates Henry Deck, George House, and David Schuyler were taken. (NY) PA S14423 of David A. Schuyler. Johnson, *Bloodied Mohawk*, 549; NYSL, Special Collections and Mss, Audited Accounts, Volume C, 227–28. An account of May 21, 1783, claimed David Schuyler Jr., a private in Captain Tiger's Coy, Clyde's 1TCM, was taken July 8, 1781. Similarly, an account of May 3, 1785, indicated Private George House, Clyde's 1TCM, was taken on July 9, 1781. Of interest, both men claimed militia pay for their time in captivity; Fernow, V.XV, SA1, 545; (NY) PA S19340 of George House; Willett's letter of June 28, 1781, noted that two Levies serving at Fort Windecker had not been seen for two days. Morrison concludes they were taken June 26, 1781.

3. SJJ to Haldimand, June 21, 1781, LAC, HP, B158, 226; Haldimand to Powell, June 24, 1781, two letters. Smy Transcripts, HP, AddMss21764; G. Johnson to Haldimand, Niagara, June 24, 1781, LAC, HP, AddMss21767, 197; **KRR Return**: LAC, HP, AddMss21751, 27; GO, Carleton and Haldimand, 1776–83. LAC,

HP, AddMss21743 and Cruikshank and Watt, *KRR NY*, Master Roll and Watt, *Burning*, 234–36, 346; **Commanding Officer, Coteau**: I cannot determine who this was, but Thomas Gumersall is likely; **One Forgiven**: Fraser, *Skulking*, 60 ex NY Genealogical and Biographical Society Asa Fitch Papers, No.244 James Rogers; **Levy**: The author recognizes that this word used as a noun is collective, but to differentiate between militiamen who had joined the Levies versus those who had not, the word is used frequently in this book in the singular, eg. "a MA Levy"; **Von Speth**: Claimed a soldier named Wagner or Von Waggoner. Von Papet, Lieutenant Friedrich Julius, *Canada During the American Revolutionary War: Lieutenant Friedrich Julius von Papet's Journal of the Sea Voyage to North America and the Campaign*, Bruce E. Burgoyne, ed. (Westminster, MD: Heritage Books, Inc., 1998), 185. LAC, HP, AddMss21789, 214. Reuter, *Brunswick Troops*. Lists Johann Steckhane, Private Musketeer Regiment "Specht," released in Canada, July 23, 1783; **Son of Victim**: *(NY) PA R1750* of John Carter.

4. **Abenakis**: LAC, HP, AddMss21777, 290; Return 2Regiment Artillery, June 27, 1781, PPGC, VII, 69; General Clinton to Glen, Van Cortlandt Correspondence, 433; Canadian Regiment OB; Washington to Stark, Stark, 213; Willett to General Clinton, Fort Rensselaer, June 28, 1781, Willett OB, 3; Meeting of June 28, 1781, *Conspiracies, II*, 740–41.

5. G. Johnson report, June 28, 1781, LAC, HP, AddMss21766, 53 and AddMss21770; **Nelles**: Lieutenant, 6NID, 1757–60. Captain, 1779. Return of Officers 6NID, circa 1784, LAC, HP, AddMss21827, f.353; A young Mississauga chief was treated for a dangerous wound in his back between July 3–11 by Surgeon Kerr at Carleton Island, perhaps received on this raid. LAC, HP, AddMss21772, 112; **Jacob J. Klock**: Johnson, Bloodied Mohawk, 462; (NY) PA S13013 of William Feeter; *Canadian Regiment OB*; **2ACM**: Hanson, 187, 248; **Viele's**: Johnson, *Bloodied Mohawk*, 290; **Expropriation**: Roberts, *II*, 230; **Smyth**: Mathews, *Spies*, 61; Mathews to Sherwood, Quebec, July 4, 1781, *ibid.*, 63 ex LAC, HP, B179, 57, and B176, 189–91; Haldimand to SHC, n.d., HSGS, III, 207 ex LAC, HP, B147, 400–401; **Caterpillars**: i.e. Armyworms. "Common east of the Rocky Mountains ... travelling in dense armies, devouring all crops along the line of march. This native pest has been serious on cereal and forage crops since early Colonial times. It fluctuates in importance, reaching epidemic numbers at varying intervals ... usually worse after a cold spring ....There may be 2 or 3 generations in a year with the first most injurious. Wheat, corn, oats, and rye are favorite food plants and may be devoured down to the ground." Cynthia Westcott, *The Gardener's Bug Book* (Garden City, NY: American Garden Guild and Doubleday and Company, Inc., 1956), 84–85; T. Johnson to Washington, 1782. Wells, 398–99.

6. **Katzeburgh**: (NY) PA S14371 of John Roof and (NY) PA S28608 of Jacob Snell. Johnson, *Bloodied Mohawk*, 537and 570 respectively; Willett to General Clinton, n.d., Willett's OB, 3–4; Willett to Wemple and Beeckman, n.d., *ibid.*, 4; **Timber**: Fryer, *Pimpernel*, 138 ex LAC, HP, B176, 142; **Haldimand's Order**: Jessup OB; Butler to Lernoult, July 1, 1781, Smy Transcripts. HP, AddMss21765; SJJ to Haldimand, July 1, 1781, LAC, HP, B158, 227; **Fort Herkimer**: Watt, *Burning*, 229–30; Powell to Haldimand, July 2, 1781, Smy Transcripts. HP, AddMss21761; **Ball**: First Lieutenant Peter Mann Ball returned to duty and served without further incident. He commanded McKinnon's Coy in 1783. Smy, *Annotated Roll*, 41; Petition of E. Phillips and D. Windecker to Haldimand, July 2, 1781, Smy Transcripts. HP, AddMss21874; Elizabeth was the wife of Nicholas Sr. Dorothy was the wife of Hendrick. Smy, *Annotated Roll*; Haldimand to SJJ, July 5, 1781. LAC, HP, B159, 150; Claus to Haldimand, July 5, 1781, LAC, HP, AddMss21774, 200–201; **Hewitt**: *Conspiracies, II*, 744; Haldimand to St. Laurent, July 5, 1781, Mathews, *Spies*, 67 ex LAC, HP, B135, 234. St. Laurent to Sherwood, n.d., *ibid.*, 67.

7. Egly, *1NY*, 191–92 ex General Clinton to Governor Clinton, July 11, 1718. A detachment was sent to bring in those who ran to the Grants and one was recovered. He was sent to West Point where a court martial sentenced him to death, which was approved by Washington and performed on August 25, 1781; **Smith**: LAC, HP, AddMss21842 and *4&2NY OB*, 754; Benson to Gansevoort, July 6, 1781. Gansevoort Papers, 18–131; Willett to Washington, Fort Herkimer, July 5, 1781, Johnson, *Bloodied Mohawk*, 177–80; **Fortification**: In a likely apocryphal story, it was said that Willett and Villefranche doubted the utility and strength of a top-heavy blockhouse that stood outside the stockade of Fort Plain. As a test, they had a six-pounder ball fired at the building, which penetrated both walls and struck the earth beyond. This was greeted by much hilarity by the observers until it was realized they had been relying on the blockhouse for their security. Thomas, 133.

8. **2NY**: *Van Cortlandt Memoir*, 58; Willett to Governor Clinton, German Flatts, July 6, 1781. William Willett, 79–80; Governor Clinton to Paine, Poughkeepsie, July 6, 1781. PPGC, VII, 62–63; "Return of New Levies Commanded by Colonel Pawling," Naponagh, July 6, 1781, *ibid.*, 65; **Commissary**: Lansing to McKinstry, Albany, July 6, 1781. Pliny Moore Papers, 61–62; **Fishing**: Van Cortlandt Memoir, 58. (NY) PA W16905, widow of Garret Clute. Johnson, *Bloodied Mohawk*, 338; **Scouting**: (NY) PA S23244 of Henry Grem/Grim. TCMN, V.XIX, No.6 and Johnson, *Bloodied Mohawk*, 421; (NY) PA S2311 of Giles Hickcox, *ibid.*; (NY) PA W26899, widow of Gottlieb Pitcher, *ibid.*; **Volunteers**: Fernow, V.XV, SA1, 296; **Steele's Creek**: (NY) PA R9525 of Thomas T. Schoemaker cites this as Shult's Creek; **Van der Heyden**: Ross to Haldimand, July 14, 1781. LAC, HP, AddMss 21787, 231. Ross

to Haldimand, August 5, 1781, *ibid.*, 237. Perhaps David contracted a fever on this raid, as he was bled at Carleton Island on August 26. LAC, HP, AddMss21772, 112; **Maracle**: His arrival at Dorlach, see "Affidavit of William Sommer," PPGC, VII, 80–81; It may be that Maracle took Brant Johnson for Joseph Brant, or simply reported that Brant was coming, and started the misreport of the former's participation. *Ibid.*, 79–81; LAC, HP, AddMss21842, 374; Second journal of Thomas Johnson, Trois Rivières, July 7, 1781. Wells, 389.

9. *Conspiracies, II*, 742; **Smith**: Was recruiting for Meyers at the time of this robbery. Serjeant in Meyers's Independent Coy. Fryer, *Loyalist Spy*, 215; **Wheat Harvest**: (NY) PA S234 of George Anthony; **Docksteder**: Spelling variations — Dachsteder, Dochsteder. John and his brother Frederick were Mohawk Valley farmers recruited in 1775 by Henry Hare. Before the war, John had been a lieutenant in Guy Johnson's Tryon Militia regiment and had spent seven months in a rebel jail. He spoke several Iroquoian dialects. Paul L. Stevens, "His Majesty's 'Savage' Allies: British Policy and the Northern Indians During the Revolutionary War — The Carleton Years, 1774–1778," doctoral dissertation for the Department of History, SUNY at Buffalo, 933; **Quahyocko**: Francis Whiting Halsey, *The Old New York Frontier, Its Wars with Indians and Tories, Its Missionary Schools, Pioneers and Land Titles* (New York: Charles Scribner's Sons, 1917), 304. Gives the name as Quackyack. He was known by three names: Quahyocko Brant Johnson, William Brant Johnson, and Brant Kaghneghtago; John Docksteder to G. Johnson, July 31, 1781, LAC, HP, AddMss21767; **Size of Raid**: Although Docksteder reported his strength at seventy, Daniel Claus reported from Montreal on July 26, 1781, that "Doghstoder's and Brant Johnson's" numbers as about 150 whites and Indians from Niagara. As Claus and Brant Johnson were close friends, I have accepted that number over Docksteder's; **Butterfield**: (NY) PA S44351 of James Butterfield. Claimed he had been a MA captain in Alden's regiment at Cherry Valley in 1779 and the next year as a lieutenant in Dubois's NY Levies. No record has been found to support his claim to have been a three-years' captain; secretary of the Commonwealth, *Massachusetts Soldiers and Sailors in the War of the Revolution* (Boston: Wright and Potter Printing Co., 1896), 262. Lists James Butterfield of Acton, MA, with service f/1776-80 as a fifer, light infantryman, and as a corporal in Alden's 6MA at Fort Herkimer in 1779. Can this be the same man?; **Provisions**: Sommer Affidavit, PPGC, VII, 79–81.

10. **Gros**: Willett's OB indicates that men were sent out on July 8 on these errands, had no success and returned to Fort Plank/Plain next day, only to be sent out again. See Johnson, *Bloodied Mohawk*, 180; **New Dorlach**: James F. Morrison, *The Battle of New Dorlach, Tryon County July 10, 1781* (Gloversville, NY: Author, 1991); Campbell, *Annals*, 181–83. Simms, *FNY, II*, 494–97, 501. Willett to Clinton, William Willett,

80–82. **Schoharie men**: (NY) PA W16971, Catherine, widow of Major Cornelius Eckerson, 15ACM; and (NY) PA S5825 of William Nellis; (NY) PA W16244, widow of John Duesler; (NY) PA R11960 of Jacob A. Young; (NY) PAs S28806/ 127161 of Samuel McKeen; S23379 of David Quackenboss; S11684 of Peter Wallradt. Johnson, *Bloodied Mohawk*, 486, 527, 628, respectively; (NY) PA S9277 of Christian Bellinger; Benson J. Lossing, *The Pictorial Field-Book of the Revolution or, Illustrations, by Pen and Pencil, of the History, Biography, Scenery, Relics, and Traditions of the War for Independence* (2 vols., New York: Harper & Brothers, 1851), I, 293–94; Sommer Affidavit, PPGC, VII, 79–81; (NY) PA W19237, widow of Philip Failing. Failing recalled the division of Willett's force into two elements and the setting up of parallel lines; **McKeen**: Fernow, V.XV, SA1. Egly, 1NY, 82. His widow Janet applied for seven years' half pay from 1782–88. New York State Library (NYSL), Special Collections and Manuscripts, Audited Accounts, Vol. A, 116; Transcript *PA Gazette*, 8 August 1781 and study by Harry E. Mitchell dated November 3, 1914 in my possession; (NY) PA W2461, widow of William Van Slyke; Willett's OB, 9; (NY) PA S5825 of William Nellis. He deposed that Willett's men opposed 300 of "Sir John Johnston's green coats," one presumes taking BR for KRR, yet the KRR was in redcoats by this time and were not on the raid. Nellis also claimed that all but two of McKeen's men were killed, as were 30–40 principally British. He also claimed that Willett lost about 100 men; **Tryon Reinforcement**: (NY) PA S23036 of Martin A. Van Alstine; **Willett's Shouts**: Thomas, 127; **William Sole**: Vrooman to Gansevoort, Gansevoort Papers, 18–131; **Other Details**: Halsey, *Old New York Frontier*, 304; (NY) PA S23224 of William Forgason; (NY) PA, W6370, widow of Simon J. Vrooman; (NY) PA S14453 of Henry Shults; (NY) PA R8538 of Peter J. Quackenboss; W16688, widow of Abraham D. Quackenboss; R8537 of Abraham J. Quackenboss; (NY) PAs W12099, widow of Peter Flagg; W1662, widow of Budd Stuart; S10016 of George Van Slyke. Johnson, *Bloodied Mohawk*, 397, 583, respectively; **Stump**: Simms, *Schoharie*, 461–62 and *FNY, II*, 501.

11.   (NY) PA S23179 of Henry Croutz. Johnson, *Bloodied Mohawk*, 354; **Death of Young Girl**: *Lossing, I*, 294–95; Willett to Governor Clinton, transcribed as July 1, 1781, but obviously written on July 11, 1781. William Willett, 81–82; Docksteder to G. Johnson, July 13, 1781, LAC, HP, AddMss21767; Daniel Claus, Montreal, July 25, 1781. Claus reported rebel casualties as Captain McKeen, mortally wounded and his son and nine privates, wounded. Johnson, *Bloodied Mohawk*, 83–84; **Maracle**: Smy, *Annotated Roll*, 122; Willett to Governor Clinton, July 13, 1781, Willett's OB, 9; Docksteder report; **Hoffmans**: Mitchell account and *Sommer Affidavit* and Watt, *Burning*, 322, 24. Simms, *Schoharie*, 455–62. *FNY, II*, 501; **Mutilation**: (NY) PAs S21258 of Daniel Hadcock. Johnson, *Bloodied Mohawk*, 425; Roberts, *NY in the Rev*, 172, 175; Willett to General Clinton, July 11, 1781, Stone, *Brant, II*, 160; Five wounded were in Albany

hospital in August and may have been from the Dorlach action. Dr. John Cochran, *Surgeon to Washington, Dr. John Cochran 1730–1807*, translated transcribed by Morris H. Saffron. (New York: Columbia University Press, 1977), 185; Intelligence provided to Haldimand, September 2, 1781, Mathews, *Spies*, 129.

12. Quebec OB, BL, AddMss21743, f.81. Website, The Loyalist Institute, http://www. royalprovincial.com/military/orderly/orderly.htm KRs sentenced to deportation were: Serjeant Benjamin Bennet (possibly Serjeant Joseph Bennett, taken at Fort George), Gideon Fanner, Cahin Flinds (possibly Calvin Hinds taken at Fort George), Samuel Hindman, Emanuel Humphries (possibly Emry Umphrey taken at Fort Ann), Isaac Pownell, Ephraim Thomas, and Esara Wood (possibly Iser'l Wood taken at Fort George); SJJ to Haldimand, July 9, 1781, LAC, HP, B158, 229; Mathews to SJJ, July 9, 1781, LAC, HP, B159, 151; Mathews to Claus, July 9, 1781, LAC, HP, AddMss21774, 188; Campbell to HQ, July 9, 1781, LAC, HP, AddMss21772; **Dutchman's Point**: Fryer, *Pimpernel*, 139; Haldimand to SHC. Mathews, *Spies*, 131; **Royal George**: Bellico, 165. HSGS, III, 251 ex LAC, HP, B145, 120; Robertson to Brehm, Oswegatchie, July 10, 1781, LAC, HP, 21780, 140; **Klock**: Simms, *FNY, II*, 517–18; **Meyers's Indian Coy**: Meyers to Mathews, St. Johns, July 8, 1781, LAC, HP, AddMss21821; **Campbell**: LAC, HP, AddMss21772; Powell to Haldimand, Niagara, July 12, 1781, Smy Transcripts. HP, AddMss 21761.

13. **2NY**: *Van Cortlandt Memoir*, 58–59; Bockee to Moore, July 11, 1781. Pliny Moore Papers, 66–67; Willett's itinerary, Johnson, *Bloodied Mohawk*, 277; Vrooman to Gansevoort and Gansevoort to Van Bergen, July 12, 1781, *NYPL, Gansevoort Papers*, 18–131; (NY) PA R8538 of Peter J. Quackenbush; Reverend Gross to Governor Clinton, Albany, July 13, 1781, PPGC, VII, 74–76; **Ball Sizes**: Possibly some soldiers were armed with .75 calibre, British-pattern muskets and others with .69 calibre French; Willett to General Clinton, Fort Rensselaer, July 14, 1781, Willett's OB, 4–5; Willett to Governor Clinton, Fort Rensselaer, July 14, 1781, *ibid.*, 5–6; Willett to McKinstry and Willett to Villefranche, July 14, 1781, *ibid.*, 7; Willett to Governor Clinton, Fort Rensselaer, July 15, 1781, PPGC, VII, 78–80; Washington to General Clinton, Dobbs Ferry, July 14, 1781, Washington Writings, Vol .22, 375; Washington to Willett, July 14, 1781, *ibid.*, 378; Washington to Villefranche, July 14, 1781, *ibid.*, 379.

14. **Smyth's List**: Fryer, *King's Men*, 284 ex LAC, HP, B179-2, 57 and Fryer, *Pimpernel*, 139–41. Mathews, *Spies*, 63–64; Ross to Haldimand, Carleton Island, July 14, 1781. LAC, HP, AddMss21787, 231. Cruikshank and Watt, *KRR NY*, 76; **Prison Island**: Mathews to Maclean, July 15, 1781, Neil Goodwin research, LAC, HP, AddMss21791, 164; **Survey of Blacks**: Haldimand to SJJ, July 16, 1781, LAC, HP,

B159, 152. John Ruch, "Blacks Among the Loyalists," in *The Loyalists of Quebec, 1774–1825, A Forgotten History* (Montreal: Heritage Branch, UEL Association of Canada, 1989). Ruch's article and transcript of SJJ's list are confusing as the dates seem incorrect. Despite their service in the boats, their former owners demanded their restoration in 1783. Haldimand ordered this be done if sufficient proof of ownership was provided; J.F. Morrison contends that, in this context, a firelock referred to long arms unable to mount a bayonet, eg. rifle, trade musket, fowler; Governor Clinton on recruiting, July 17, 1781, PPGC, VII, 86–89; Willett's OB, 9–11; Glen to Hughes, July 17, 1781, Hanson, 117, 18fn ex Letter Books of Colonel Hugh Hughes, NYHS; Governor Clinton to Willett and to Reverend Gross and to Lush, July 18, 1781 and Chittenden's Proclamation, July 18, 1781, PPGC, VII, 90–96, 100; (MA) PA W2264, widow of Enos Moore; **MA Levies in Willett's Regiment**: That the MA companies became an integral element of WL is indicated in (MA) PA S30954 of Henry Covell, which stated he "went as one of the Classitees from Hancock Berkshire County in the State of MA to fill up Colonel Marinus Willetts Regiment." He joined WL at Fort Plain and was transferred to Woodworth's Ranging Coy. **Woolaver**: variously spelled, Wholeben, Wolleber, Woolerod, Woolever, Woolver, and "Pension Application of John Woolaver." *Stone Arabia Battle SAR Chapter Newsletter*, September 1998. (NY) PA W19659, widow of Peter Woolever, and (NY) PA W16244, widow of John Duesler; **Militia Pursuit**: Details of Private Henry Murphy, TCMN, Vol. I, No.10.

15. **Abduction Parties**: Mathews, *Spies*, 68fn–69fn ex LAC, HP, B176, 22; **Groves**: Likely John Greaves, a loyalist courier; **Caldwell**: Smy, *Annotated Roll*, 61. Caldwell's career continued apace in 1782. Operating out of Detroit, he was engaged at Sandusky (Ohio) in June 1782 where his coy and the attached Indians achieved a major victory. Later that year, he orchestrated a second major victory at Blue Licks, Kentucky. He was a star performer in the Northern Department. Postwar, he served as deputy superintendent of Indian Affairs in the Western District of Upper Canada. During the War of 1812, he led an effective force of rangers operating with the Natives; Powell to Haldimand, July 19, 1781, Smy Transcripts, HP, AddMss21761; **Hare**: Watt and Morrison, *Campaign of 1777*, 77, 82. John Hare Jr. served in the ID rangers through the St. Lawrence Expedition. Smy, *Annotated Roll*, 99. John Hare, First Lieutenant, December 25, 1779. In June 1781, there was only one Hare in the rank of lieutenant at this time. Served in Dame's Coy, 1783; Campbell to Haldimand, July 19, 1781, LAC, HP, AddMss21772; Mathews to Maclean, July 19, 1781, LAC, HP, AddMss21791, 118; **Gordon's 1780 Capture**: Watt, *Burning*, 124–30; Robertson to Brehm, Oswegatchie, July 19, 1781, LAC, HP, AddMss21780, 142; Sherwood to Mathews, July 27, 1781, Fryer, *Pimpernel*, 140 ex LAC, HP, B176, 183.

16. **Willett Honoured**: "Warfare in the Mohawk Valley — Transcriptions from the *Pennsylvania Gazette*, 1780–783," a personal handout by William B. Efner, city historian, transcriber (Schenectady: 1948). William Willett, 138–39; *Conspiracies, II*, 747–50. **Two Boys**: Circumstantially, the captors were Canada and/or Mississauga Indians. The timing of this small raid is known only as mid-summer. The boys were ultimately restored to their family. Simms, *FNY, II*, 522–23; On July 22, "George the Mississauga" was treated for a shoulder wound at Carleton Island, LAC, HP, AddMss21772, 112; McKinstry to General Clinton, July 21, 1781. NYSL, Doc.No.4470.

17. Wing report, July 21, 1781. Mathews, *Spies*, 68 ex LAC, HP, B176-1, 167; Haldimand to Powell, July 22, 1781, Smy Transcripts. HP, AddMss21764; Haldimand to Powell, July 23, 1781, Cruikshank and Watt, *KRR NY*, 73; Haldimand to Germain, July 23, 1781, Kelsay, 316 ex HP, AddMss21764, 216; Henry Clinton to Haldimand, NYC, July 23, 1781, HSGS, III, 205 ex HP, B147, 321–3; **Ensigns**: Ensign Walter Prentice, 1/84RHEn was given a duplicate set of dispatches, but was shipwrecked en route. G.G. Campbell, ed., *Ensign Prenties's Narrative — A Castaway on Cape Breton* (Toronto: Ryerson Press, 1968). The fate of the second ensign has not been determined; Pritchard's report July 23, 1781, LAC, HP, AddMss21794, 90; **Whipple**: A very common, prominent name in New England. Two men of this surname signed the Declaration of Independence. A Whipple from Portsmouth, NH, marched a large militia reinforcement to Saratoga in 1777. Pritchard did not supply a given name; General Order, Quebec, July 23, 1781, Smy Transcripts. HP, Add Mss21743; **Balls**: Smy, *Annotated Roll*, 40–41, **Freylick**: *Ibid.*, 91; W. Butler to Mathews, July 23, 1781, Smy Transcripts. HP, AddMss 21765.

18. McKinstry to Clinton, July 22, 1781, and Clinton's reply, July 23, 1781, PPGC, VII, 102–104; Lieutenant's death, July 22, 1781, Fernow, V.XV, SA1, 550; *4&2NY OB*, 755; **Schulds**: Also spelled Schultz, Shultes, Shults, Shultz, Shutts, Sultes; Simms, *FNY, II*, 514–15 and McHenry, 46, 60. Gives date of capture as July 26, 1781. NYSL, Special Collections and Manuscripts, Audited Accounts, Vol. A, 295–96. Gives the capture as July 26, 1781; **Despair**: Willett to Governor Clinton, n.d. Thomas, 130; **George Herkimer**: As George had been taken at Steele's Creek on July 6, it is not known how he managed to be back home during this event; **Herkimer Home**: *Ibid*, 131; **Alyda**: Penrose, *Mohawk Valley*, 260. Alyda Schuyler married George Herkimer in 1767 and (NY) PA W19659 widow of Peter Woolever. He was in this action; *Conspiracies, II*, 751–52.

19. **Pritchard/Bayley**: Fryer, *Pimpernel*, 141; **Loyal Blockhouse**: Stuart, Jessup's OB, 44 ex HP, B176, 184; Robertson to Brehm, Oswegatchie, July 26, 1781, LAC, HP, AddMss 21780, 146; SJJ to Haldimand, July 25, 1781, LAC, HP, B158, 230;

Lovelace: Heath to Governor Clinton, Continental Village, October 11, 1781, PPGC, VII, 391–93 and Mathews, *Spies*, 115–16, 198. Lists Lovelace as a QLR lieutenant, yet a detailed search of that regiment's rolls does not list him in any rank. Similarly, Fryer, *King's Men*, 296, lists him as a KLA ensign, yet that regiment's rolls do not show his name and *Lossing, I*, 92–93 and Fryer, *Pimpernel*, 153; **MA Levies**: Willett's OB, 11–12; **Tenor of Orders**: Heath to Governor Clinton, Continental Village, October 11, 1781, PPGC, VII, 391–93; **Schoharie Raids**: Jeff O'Connor, "The Story of Fort DuBoise 1779–1781," *Schoharie County Historical Review* (Spring 1999), Simms, *FNY, II*, 503–12. Efner, "PA Gazette, 08&29Aug," 6, 7. *4&2NY OB*, 756; **Catharin Zimmer**: Née Bater. Born in Germany. Married Jacob March 22, 1746 at the Dutch Reformed Church of Schoharie ex Jeff O'Connor; **Johannes Becker**: Several accounts give him the rank of major, perhaps confusing him with his son Jost, who was second major, 15ACM. Of course, Johannes may have held the rank before or after the war; **Catherine Becker**: Born in 1745, Catherine Kniskern, daughter of Henry, married circa 1762–1769; **Erkert**: as this fellow was a Scotsman, the spelling was most likely Urquhart. No one of this surname served in BR. A William Urquhart of Tryon County served in 1KRR; **Ogeyonda**: Watt, *Flockey*, 80; **Naked**: Folk were often said to be "naked" when they were only in shirts or shifts, so one cannot tell whether the girls were totally exposed in this instance. *4&2NY OB*, 756; Pliny Moore Papers, 65 and (NY) PA S11226 of John Pettit. Johnson, *Bloodied Mohawk*, 517; Governor Clinton to Washington, Poughkeepsie, July 28, 1781, PPGC, VII, 143–44; **Willett's Reaction**: Willett's OB, 12–13; **Bettys/Meyers**: Mathews, *Spies*, 67–70 & Fryer, *Pimpernel*, 143; Fryer, *Loyalist Spy*, 128–29 and *Conspiracies, II*, 755–56; **Legrange Daughter**: No source reveals the age of this lady; **Younglove**: *Ibid.*, 540 and Roberts, *NY in the Revolutionary War, II*, 243. In State Assembly, July 11–25, 1782 and June 23–March 23, 1783, *ibid.*, 158; PDF of Parrot report, www.collectionscanada.ca/education.

20. **Religious Services**: Both Stone Arabia churches had been destroyed in October 1780. Morrison believes it unlikely that new facilities had been built by this time. Services were likely held in the open or at a local barn; **Klock's raid**: (NY) PA S10690 of Willam W. Fox and (NY) PA W13941 of Elisabeth, widow of Peter Suts. Morrison, *1781*, 17 and examination of Nicholas Herkimer, November 3, 1781. Simms, *FNY, II*, 517–21 and (NY) PA S13013 of William Feeter and Bockee to Pliny Moore, Fort Plain, July 29, 1781, Pliny Moore Papers, 66–67. Bockee stated that 25 Levies participated and gave much credit to Lieutenant Sammons, his fellow Levies officer; **Rape**: Recognizing that references to sexual violence were infrequently reported, I have found only one incidence of Native involvement in forty years of research. On June 2, 1780, Captain Alex Fraser reported from Carleton Island that the Mississaugas refused to surrender their captives and

"publickly ravished the women yesterday in their Camp, a circumstance that can hardly be called aggravated by their being children to Loyalists." C.C.J. Bond, "The British Base at Carleton Island," *OHPSR*, Vol. LII (1960); **War Captain**: (NY) PA W21221, widow of Andrew Gray. Peter Sits/Suts gave evidence that Gray had killed a Sachem of Indians and, in his own application noted above, identified the Indian as "their chief warrior." Henry Gramps/Kremps/Krembs, another participant, noted that the "chief of the Indians" was killed. (NY) PA W16273, widow of Henry Gramps; Washington to Governor Clinton, Dobbs Ferry July 30, 1781. PPGC, VII, 147–48; **Caldwell /Hare**: Caldwell to Powell, Oquago, August 19, 1781. Smy Transcripts, HP, Add Mss21761; **2NY Light Coy**: *4&2NY OB*, 756; Knox to Haldimand, London, July 31, 1781, *HSGS, III*, 206–207 ex Q18, 99–101.

CHAPTER 6: CONSTANTLY INFESTED WITH PARTIES OF THE ENEMY

1. **Chittenden's Papers**: Williamson, 104; Mathews to Maclean, July 30, 1781, LAC, HP, Add Mss21791, 122; T. Johnson to Washington, April 30, 1782, Wells, 393, 398–99; **Truck Carriage**: The truck was a wheel made of one piece of wood. The carriage was on four trucks of twenty-four inches diameter, had two flat side-pieces, ten inches broad, and served to carry guns, ammunition boxes, or any other weights. Smith, *Dictionary*, 247; W. Butler to Mathews, Niagara, August 2, 1781, Smy Transcripts, HP, AddMss21765; Haldimand to Powell, Quebec, August 2, 1781, ibid, HP, AddMss21764; Haldimand to SHC, Quebec, August 2, 1781, HSGS, III, 207–208 ex LAC, HP, B147, 338–40; Haldimand to SHC, Quebec, August 2, 1781, *ibid.* ex LAC, HP, B147, 383–88; Haldimand to Nova Scotia Lieutenant-Governor and Rear Admiral Sir Richard Hughes, Quebec, August 2, 1781, *ibid.*, 209 ex B150, 97–98; Governor Clinton to Lush, Poughkeepsie, July 18, 1781, PPGC, VII, 96; **House**: (NY) PA W18046, widow of Nicholas House. Johnson, *Bloodied Mohawk*, 442. Fernow V.XV, SA1, 545; Willett OB, 13; **Kingsbury**: *4&2NY OB*, 756 and McHenry. Luther Cady, Abraham Foster, Silas McWithy, and Rutalf Caller captured Kingsburgh, August 2, 1781 and Roberts, *NY in the Rev*, 123. First three men had been in the Charlotte City militia; Hancock to Willett, Boston August 2, 1781. PPGC, VII, 171–72; *Conspiracies, II*, 756; (NY) PA W9210, widow of Henry H. Peck, Crousehorn's Artillery Coy. Johnson, *Bloodied Mohawk*, 513; A. Ramsey to Governor Clinton, Ballstown, August 23, 1781 and Clinton to A. Ramsey, October 14, 1781, PPGC, VII, 157–58; NYS memorial re: VT, August 3, 1781, *ibid.*, 164–66; Willett to Villefranche, Albany, *Willett OB*, 14.

2. Governor Clinton to Weissenfels, Poughkeepsie, August 4, 1781, PPGC, VII, 149; Bockee to Moore, Fort Rensselaer, August 4, 1781, Pliny Moore Papers, 66; **Zimmermans**: Zimmerman and Timmerman seem to be alternate spellings for this surname. Fernow, V.XV, SA1, 546, 550 and (NY) PA W20002, widow of

Jacob Zimmerman and W16489, widow of Lieutenant John Zimmerman. Johnson, *Bloodied Mohawk*, 429. Date of this raid is in debate. One application gives August 1, 1781, the two Zimmermans gave August 10. K.D. Johnson states the Haldimand Papers give August 7, 1781 ex AddMss21843, 278 and "The Indian Frontier," in *Revolution Remembered*, 285–87, gives August 9; **Pursuit**: (NY) PA S21258 of Daniel Hadcock. Johnson, *Bloodied Mohawk*, 425; Washington to Governor Clinton, Dobbs Ferry, August 5, 1781, PPGC, VII, 166–67 and Washington's instructions to Lincoln. *Washington Writings*, V.22, 470–71; Governor Clinton to Benschoten, August 6, 1781, PPGC, VII, 169–70; *Willett OB*, 15; Willett to Governor Clinton, Albany, August 6, 1781, PPGC, VII, 170–71; **Howard**: Fryer, *Loyalist Spy*, 130–31. Schuyler to Governor Clinton, Albany, August 9, 1781, PPGC, VII, 186. Mathews, *Spies*, 71–72. *Pennsylvania Gazette*, August 29, 1781. Efner, 7; **Stevens**: Ernest A. Cruikshank, "The Adventures of Roger Stevens, A Forgotten Loyalist Pioneer in Upper Canada," *OHSPR*, 33 (1939), 11; **Herrick**: Geo H. Hepson, *Herrick's Rangers* (Bennington, NY: Bennington Museum Series #1, n.d.).

3. **Schuyler Attempt**: Schuyler to H. Glen, Albany, August 7, 1781, Kevin Richard-Morrow, "The Attempt to Abduct General Phillip Schuyler and the Great Kidnap Plot of 1781," in *The Burning Issues*, Vol.14, No.1 (March 2006). Mathews, *Spies*, 69–70. Simms, *FNY, II*, 516. Schuyler to Governor Clinton, Albany, August 9, 1781. Egly, Ted W. Jr., *General Schuyler's Guard* (Author, 1986), 6–8 ex PPGC, VII, 184–86. *Ibid.* Some sources contend that Schuyler was without a formal guard until after this incident, but Egly proves otherwise, and *Pennsylvania Gazette*, August 29, 1781. Efner, 7–8 and Bayard Tuckerman, *Life of General Philip Schuyler 1733–1804* (New York: Dodd, Mead and Co, 1903), 246. Tuckerman contends that Indians were with Meyers and that one threw his tomahawk at Margaret Schuyler, who was running through the hall with her younger sister in her arms. He says the axe missed Margaret and struck the banister, leaving a mark that was visible at his time of writing. Schuyler's account to Governor Clinton made no mention of Indians or that any of his children had been in imminent peril. Nor does Egly, who only mentions Schuyler's family obliquely. Presumably, Egly researched this incident thoroughly; **Meyers's Casualties**: Fryer, *Loyalist Spy*, 133–36. Indicates that several local men had joined the party, one of whom was killed during the attempt. Says Meyers attempted to get them to come off to Canada without success. Also notes that two 34th Regulars were wounded; Washington to Schuyler, and Washington to General Clinton, Dobbs Ferry, August 15, 1781. The C-in-C directed Clinton to leave a small 2NY guard of an NCO and his weakest men. *Washington Writings*, V.23, 2–4 and *Conspiracies, II*, 758–59.

4. **Jones**: D. Jones to Mathews, Verchère, August 19, 1781, LAC, HP, AddMss21821, 282; David was the fiancée of Jane McCrae, who was killed by Crown Indians

in July 1777 when they were bringing her to Burgoyne's camp for her marriage ceremony; **Ferguson and Tyler/Taylor**: LAC, HP, AddMss21842, 417, 421. Neither leader had been identified and I have made educated guesses; **WL Officers**: Willett OB, 27; **Van Ingen**: Hanson, 240; **Congressmen**: Duane and l'Hommendieu to Governor Clinton, Philadelphia, August 7, 1781, PPGC, VII, 175–76; Governor Clinton to General Clinton, August 7, 1781, *ibid.*, 173–74; President McKean to Governor Clinton, Philadelphia, August 8, 1781, *ibid.*, 177–78; Paine et al to Governor Clinton, August 8, 1781, *ibid.*, 178; **Prisoner Exchange**: Fryer, *Pimpernel*, 143. Fryer, *King's Men*, 295–96. Mathews, *Spies*, 80; **Nelles**: Caldwell's report provided only his rank and surname. As Hendrick Nelles was a Captain at this time, his son Robert is likely the individual referred to; Cruikshank, *Butler's Rangers*, 93–94; Caldwell to Powell, August 19, 1781. Smy Transcripts. HP, AddMss 21761. Powell to Haldimand, September 7, 1781. *ibid*; **Prisoners**: Silas Bowker, Pawling's Levies, taken on the Delaware. McHenry, *Rebel Prisoners at Quebec*. A. Hines mentioned in Pawling's report, April 13, 1781, PPGC, VII, 190–192. James Hines served in Pawling's. Roberts, *NY in Rev*, 84; **Service**: Cruikshank and Watt, *KRR NY*, 76.

5.   Quebec OB, BL, AddMss21743, ff.83, 86. The Loyalist Institute (http://www. royalprovincial.com); Ed Jessup to Haldimand, Verchère August 8, 1781, LAC, HP, AddMss21821; **Zimmerman**: (NY) PA W20002, widow of Jacob Zimmerman. Johnson, *Bloodied Mohawk*, 661. "The Indian Frontier," in *Revolution Remembered*, 285–87. Stone, *Brant, II*, 215. Stone named Oswego as the British post and McHenry lists Jacob Tumberman/Timberman taken on July 1 or 7, 1781; Stark to Washington, Albany, August 9, 1781 and Stark to Governor Clinton, n.d., Stark, 213–16; Governor Clinton to R. Van Rensselaer and to Gansevoort, Poughkeepsie, August 9, 1781, PPGC, VII, 183; Governor Clinton to Willett, August 9, 1781, *ibid.*, 187–88; *Conspiracies, II*, 759–60. Pliny Moore Papers, 65.

6.   Haldimand to SJJ, August 9, 1781, LAC, HP, B159, 155; W. Butler to Mathews, Niagara, August 10, 1781, Smy Transcripts, HP, AddMss21765; **Chambers/Fay**: LAC, HP, AddMss 21792, 131–34; **Clark**: Germain to Haldimand, Whitehall, August 11, 1781, LAC, CO42/40, 73; **Caldwell Raid**: Cruikshank, *Butler's Rangers*, 93–94. Caldwell to Powell, August 19, 1781, Smy Transcripts, HP, AddMss21761. Powell to Haldimand, September 7, 1781. *Ibid.* and General State of the Corps of Indians and Department of Indian Affairs, Niagara, September 2, 1782. LAC, HP, AddMss21770 and Levi Pawling to Governor Clinton, April 13, 1781, PPGC, VII, 190–92; **Place Names**: Pawling's report spelled Monbackers as Mumbakers, Lackawaxen as Leghweek; **Loyalist Deserter**: this fellow was said to be named Vrooman. Smy, *Annotated Roll*, lists four of that name, all of whom settled in

Canada. Of course, the fellow could have been an irregular volunteer. Governor Clinton to Schuyler, August 14, 1781, PPGC, VII, 195; Simms, *Schoharie*, 466.

7. Jansen to Godwin, Shawangunk August 11, 1781, PPGC, VII, 193; *Conspiracies, II*, 761–63; Governor Clinton to Schuyler, August 14, 1781. PPGC, VII, 193–95; Governor Clinton to Paine, August 14, 1781, *ibid.*, 179–80; Governor Clinton to General Clinton, August 14, 1781, *ibid.*, 197; Willett's report, Fort Rensselaer August 19, 1781. Johnson, *Bloodied Mohawk*, 85–86; **Fortt Timmerman**: (NY) PA S23019 of Honyere Doxtator. *Morrison's Pensions*. For the fort's location and ownership of the core building, see J.F. Morrison, "Mohawk Valley Forts" and Johnson, *Bloodied Mohawk*, 284 and (NY) PA S13013 of William Feeter, which said the blockhouse was occupied by Jacob Timmerman's family; **Bradbig's**: (NY) PA R3182 of Johannes Ecker. Johnson, *Bloodied Mohawk*, 380; **Prisoner**: Fernow, V.XV, SA1, 545 and Morrison, *Klock's Regt*, 15; **Dunham/Grant**: *Conspiracies, II*, 765–66. One has to wonder, did Thomas Lovelace first influence Dunham?

8. Powell to Haldimand, Niagara, August 16, 1781, two letters. Smy Transcripts, HP, AddMss21761; **Stark on Militia**: Stark, 217 and Gansevoort to Bronck, August 15, 1781. Bronck, 35–36; Washington to Stark, Dobbs Ferry, August 16, 1781. Stark to Livingston, August 16, 1781, Stark, 218–19; General Clinton to Governor Clinton, Albany, August 18, 1781, PPGC, VII, 209–10; Stark to Governor Clinton, August 18, 1781, Stark, 219; Stark to Governor Clinton, Albany, August 18, 1781, PPGC, VII, 228–29; Governor Clinton to Stark, August 23, 1781, *ibid.*, 229–30; **Executions**: (NY) PA R571 of Job Barstow and (NY) PA S6001 of John Riker. Johnson, *Bloodied Mohawk*, 301, 535 and Simms, *Schoharie*, 469; *4&2NY OB*, 757; Willett OB, 31; **Vermont**: Duane to Governor Clinton, Philadelphia, August 20, 1781, PPGC, VII, 232; Weissenfels to Governor Clinton, Fishkill, August 20, 1781, *ibid.*, 240; *Conspiracies, II*, 766–67.

9. **Silver plate**: Fryer, *Loyalist Spy*, 136; **Seth Sherwood/Vermonters**: Sherwood to Mathews, August 19, 1781, Fryer, *Pimpernel*, 145, 467. Watt, *Burning*, 101, 253; **Hanau Artillery**: *HSGS, III*, 69–70 ex HP, B54, 25–30; Ross to Haldimand, Carleton Island, August 20, 1781, LAC, HP, AddMss21787, 253; **Ditch/Bombproofs**: Bond, 13; **Meyers re: Bradt and Smith**: LAC, HP, AddMss21821, 320, 323, 33; **Smith**: Did not appear on later muster rolls. A Joseph Smith, who was Meyers's servant before the war, was a witness to Meyers's claim in 1787. Perhaps, he was Meyers's batman for the duration; Bradt to HQ, August 29, 1781, LAC, HP, AddMss21821. Various letters of Smyth to Mathews. Fryer, *Pimpernel*, 147–49 ex LAC, HP, B176, 289–93. Fryer, *King's Men*, 285. Mathews, *Spies*, 70 ex HP, B176, 247; Ross to Haldimand, Carleton Island, August 23, 1781, LAC, HP, AddMss21787, 250; **Grain**: Stark to Governor Clinton,

Albany, August 22, 1781, and 810825; Clinton to Stark, Poughkeepsie, August 25, 1781, Stark, 222; **Armourers/MA Levies**: Stark to Washington, Albany, August 23, 1781, Stark, 220–22; Heath to Stark, August 23, 1781, Stark, 221; Washington to Heath, Dobbs Ferry, August 19, 1781, *Washington Writings*, V.23, 21; **Heath**: William Heath, *Memoirs of Major-General William Heath, Containing Anecdotes, Details of Skirmishes, Battles, etc., during the American War* (Boston, 1798); James Grant Wilson, John Fiske, and Stanley L. Klos, eds. *Appleton's Cyclopedia of American Biography*, (6 vols., New York: D. Appleton and Company, 1887–1889, and 1999); **Disagreeable**: Stark to Pickering, Albany, August 25, 1781. Stark, 225; Weissenfels to Governor Clinton, Fishkill, August 25, 1781, PPGC, VII, 254.

10. Willett to Stark, Fort Rensselaer, August 25, 1781, Stark, 223–24; Willett to Governor Clinton, Fort Rensselaer, August 25, 1781, and Clinton to Willett, Poughkeepsie, August 29, 1781, PPGC, VII, 252–54; **Bowman's Creek**: Johnson, *Bloodied Mohawk*, 278; **Pickard/Pickerd**: Fernow, V.XV, SA1, 546 and Morrison, *1781*, 3; **Warner**: *ibid.*; Jeff O'Connor, "The Story of Fort DuBoise 1779–1781," in *Schoharie County Historical Review* (Spring 1999); **Faulty Intelligence**: Stark to Laurens, Albany, August 27, 1781. Stark, 225; Stark to Chittenden, August 27, 1781, Stark, 226; Stringer to Governor Clinton, Albany, August 27, 1781, PPGC, VII, 261; Chittenden to Yates, August 24, 1781 and Yates to Chittenden, Schaghticooke, August 27, 1781, *ibid.*, 266–68; **Election Notice**: *Ibid.*, 302; Willett to Stark, Fort Rensselaer, August 28, 1781, Stark, 227–28; Governor Clinton to Stark, August 28, 1781; Stark to Heath, August 29, 1781, *ibid.*, 228–30; **New City**: Bancker to Governor Clinton, New City, August 29, 1781. PPGC, VII, 300–301; **Hospital**: Dr. John Cochran, *Surgeon to Washington, Dr. John Cochran 1730–1807*, Morris H. Saffron, trans. (New York: Columbia University Press, 1977), 140–41; *Conspiracies, II*, 773; Albany Commission to Governor Clinton, August 29, 1781, PPGC, VII, 271–72; Stuart to Governor Clinton, August 29, 1781, *ibid.*, 274; Stark to Governor Clinton, Albany, August 31, 1781, Stark, 231; NYSL, Special Collections and Manuscripts, Audited Accounts, Vol. A, 168; Willett OB, 18; **White Creek**: Williams, McCraken, McCallister, Rusel, and Armstrong to Governor Clinton, White Creek, August 31, 1781, PPGC, VII, 276–77.

11. Mathews, *Spies*, 129; Haldimand to Sir Henry Clinton (SHC), Quebec, September 3, 1781, HSGS, III, 209 ex HP, B147, 341; **Moratorium**: Jessup OB; **Forthwith**: Haldimand to SJJ, September 3, 1781, LAC, HP, B159, 156; Haldimand to Powell, Quebec, September 4, 1781, Smy Transcripts, HP, AddMss21764; **Dietz**: No Crown records of this raid have been discovered. Judging by the brutality, it seems the Natives were Schoharies, as these Mohawk affiliates were known as inveterate partisans with a deep grudge against the area's whites. However, Schoharies rarely targeted women

and children, so one must suspect the whites in the party. The raid may have been led by Adam Crysler, as he appears to have participated in a great many of the raids in the Schoharie vicinity. In fact, the frequency of raids into the Schoharie indicates that Crysler and the Schoharies laid up in some out-station in Indian Territory such as Oquaga or the abandoned southern reaches of Tryon rather than travelling back and forth from Niagara. Simms, *Schoharie*, 499–501. He placed this event in 1782; McHenry, *Rebel Prisoners at Quebec*. This source confirms that John Brice, Robert Brice (Bruce), and William Dietz (Tids) were captured in 1781. James R. Brice, *History of the Revolutionary War… Brief Account of the Captivity and Cruel Sufferings of Captain Deitz, and John and Robert Brice …* (Albany: author, 1851), 3–6. Mark Sullivan, "Obituaries of Schoharie County Veterans," *Schoharie County Historical Review* (Fall-Winter 1997). Mitchell to Governor Clinton, Schenectady, September 5, 1781, PPGC, VII, 295–96. (NY) PA S12192 of Francis Becraft. Harold H. Miller, "The Dietz Massacre" (n.p., March 2004) and *Pennsylvania Gazette*, September 19, 1781. Efner, 8; "Return of the Regiment of N.Y. Levies Commanded by Marinus Willett … from the formation of the Regiment to ye 1st Sept 1781," PPGC, VII, 285; **Dunham/3-Years' Men**: McKinstry to Governor Clinton, Saratoga, September 3, 1781, *ibid.*, 297; **Finck**: Served as brigade major, September 5, 1781. Koettirez commented that Finck was comfortably located, well-connected and had a good income. He educated his family and entertained in good style. Over the years, he grew less popular at home, as he had an aggressive temper and was outspoken. He had a superior education to his neighbours and let it be known. Koetteritz, 11, 14 and *NYSL, Special Collections and Manuscripts, Audited Accounts, Vol. A* and Willett to Governor Clinton, September 2, 1781, PP-GC, VII, 289–91.

12. Stark to Congress and Governor Clinton to Stark. Stark, 232–34; Mitchell to Governor Clinton, September 5, 1781, PPGC, VII, 295–96. Hanson, 190; Heath to Stark, Peekskill, September 5, 1781, Stark, 234–35; McKinstry to Governor Clinton, Saratoga, September 3, 1781, PPGC, VII, 297; Albany City to Governor Clinton, September 4, 1781. Stark, 235–36; **Marshall**: *4&2NY OB*; Stark to Marshall, September 4, 1781. Stark, 237–38; Willett to Hale, September 5, 1781. Willett OB, 2021; **MA Levies**: J.F. Morrison research and (MA) PA W20264, widow of Enos Morse; **Arrests**: Willett OB, 31–32; How this dereliction of duty was resolved has not been found. A number of researchers have commented that the senior militia officers were reluctant, seemingly to the point of being afraid, to remove dangerous Tories from their farms. We can only speculate on their reasoning; Governor Clinton to Mitchell, Poughkeepsie, September 5, 1781, PPGC, VII, 296–97; (NY) PA W9210, widow of Henry H. Peck of Crousehorn's Artillery Coy. Johnson, *Bloodied Mohawk*, 513; Haldimand to Powell, September 5, 1781, two letters, Smy Transcripts, HP, AddMss21764; Mathews to J. Butler, September 6, 1781, *ibid.*, HP, AddMss21765;

Adjutant Smyth/Smith: Smy, *Annotated Roll*, 173; SJJ to Haldimand, Montreal, September 6, 1781, LAC, HP, B158, 232–33; Haldimand to Ross, September 6, 1781, Cruikshank and Watt, *KRR NY*, 76–77 and Smy Transcripts, HP, AddMss21784.

13. **Woodworth's Past Service**: Nathaniel S. Benton, *History of Herkimer County* (Albany: J. Munsell, 1856), chapter V. J.F. Morrison believes that Woodworth was not promoted to captain to command this company and retained the rank of lieutenant. I have accepted the many accounts that give his rank as captain. Whatever the case, Solomon commanded the company during this event; **Tiahogwando**: Variously, Teaqwanda, Daiquanda; **Ambush**: Simms, *FNY, II*, 508–12. J.F. Morrison., "The Ambush of Lieutenant Solomon Woodworth and his Party of Scouts," (Author, n.p., n.d.). Morrison, *Fulton County*, 20, 53; Johnson, *Bloodied Mohawk*, 375; (NY) PA S22985 of Jacob Shew and Colonel Guy Johnson, "Account of an Action between a party of seventy four Onondagas & Cayugas under Daiquanda & Lieut Jno [Jos] Clement of Colo Johnson's Dept & a party of the Rebels near the German Flats." Note spelling of Tiahogwando. LAC, HP, AddMss21767 & (NY) PA W6370, widow of Lieutenant Simon J. Vrooman of Gros's Coy. Stated that Woodworth and Wilson went out with forty-two men who were all killed except four Indians who escaped, Simms, *Schoharie*, 469. Marshall to Stark, Albany, September 12, 1781, Johnson, *Bloodied Mohawk*, 87. (NY) PA W17785, widow of John L. Schermerhorn, *ibid.*, 545. Daniel Frederick Bakeman/Beekman claimed to be a survivor of this ambush. When he died in 1869 at 109, he was the "last surviving soldier of the Revolution." Roberts, *NY Forts*, 435en81. Taylor to Governor Clinton, September ?, 1781, PPGC, VII, 304; **Joseph Clement**: Fraser, *II*, 965–66, 977. Stevens, *Savage Allies, XXI*, 1385; **Prisoners**: Fernow, V.XV, SA1, 544. Lists Corporal David Putnam, Privates Joel Savage, John L. Schermerhorn, and Stephen Valentine, taken September 7, 1781. McHenry lists David Potman/Putman, Joel Savage, Stephen Valentine, and Ebenezer Pease German Flatts, September 7, 1781; **Burial**: Morrison, *Klock's Regt*.

14. Taylor to Governor Clinton, September ?, 1781, PPGC, VII, 304; Statement of Captain Moses Davis [Harris,] Albany, September 11, 1781, *ibid.*, 320–21. To add to the likelihood that Harris's tale was an espionage ploy, the name Bremon, or variant thereof, cannot be found amongst the loyalist troops in Canada. A Moses Harris was listed with Carleton's prisoners taken near Fort Ann as a private of Webster's Regiment, Charlotte City militia. Watt, *Burning*, 354; Heath to Stark, September 8, 1781. Stark, 243; Heath to Ten Broeck and Gansevoort, September 8, 1781, *ibid.*, 244; Powell to Haldimand, September 7, 1781, Smy Transcripts, HP, AddMss21761; Mathews to J. Butler, September 7, 1781, *ibid.*, HP, AddMss21765; Powell to Haldimand, September 7, 1781, *ibid.*, HP, AddMss21761; entry for September 9, 1781, "Letterbook of Lieutenant-Colonel Carl von Kreutzbourg, March 31, 1781 to October 31, 1781."

Letter Q. [Hereafter Von Kreutzbourg letterbook] John C. Zuleger, trans. (Lidgerwood Collection. Hessian Papers. Morristown National Historic Park, NJ).

15. Marshall to Stark, Albany, September 15, 1781, Stark, 245; **Hogshead**: 52 Imperial gallons; Stark to Heath, Saratoga, September 9, 1781, *ibid.*, 246; Governor Clinton to Heath, September 9, 1781, PPGC, VII, 315–16; Stark to Haldimand, Saratoga, n.d. Stark, 236–37; Miller [Mitchell] to Stark, September 9, 1781, Stark, 246–47. Although transcribed as "Miller," this fellow was most likely Hugh Mitchell, a prominent Schenectady politician. See also, Hanson, 19, 43, 190 and Roberts, *NY in Rev, II*, 195, 229; **Schenectady Militia/2ACM**: The Schenectady militia had always shown great zeal in their duty and would do so again. Perhaps the persecution of former friends had lost its appeal; Governor Clinton to McKinstry, September 9, 1781, PPGC, VII, 298; Marshall to Stark, September 10, 1781, Stark, 247; Schuyler to Heath through Governor Clinton, September 10, 1781, PPGC, VII, 318; *Pennsylvania Gazette*, September 17, 1781. Letter dated Fishkill, October 4, stated that a KRR detachment (about 250) arrived at St John's at the end of August. This was likely the arrival of Jessup's KLA. Efner, 9.

16. *Pennsylvania Gazette*, September 26, 1781, *ibid.*, Efner, 9; Mitchell to Governor Clinton, September 10, 1781, PPGC, VII, 319; Stark to Heath, September 11, 1781, Stark, 247–49; Governor Clinton to Willett, September 11, 1781, PPGC, VII, 292; **Rebel Indians**: A superb study of the treatment of the Oneidas and Tuscaroras after the war is found in Glatthaar and Martin, *Forgotten Allies*. For the visit to Congress, see 279–80; Glen to Governor Clinton, Schenectady, September 12, 1781, PPGC, VII, 324–25; **Caspian Lake**: Wells, 96–97. Baldwin, *Hazen's Road*; **Raid Story**: Simms recorded that when Eckler was walking near Fort Herkimer in the summer of 1781, he was accosted by Joseph Brant and escaped capture by hiding under the roots of a tree. *Schoharie*, 487. *FNY, II*, 535. Yet, Joseph Brant was in Detroit all summer, so the Indian leader must have been Quahyocko Brant Johnson; **Eckler**: He was unemployed in the militia after his coy disintegrated. Morrison believes there was either a captain in the beat where he resettled, or insufficient men to make a new company; "Captain Henry Eckler of Herkimer County" adapted by Mrs. Eunice Cooper in 1972 from an essay written by Bonnie Eckler in May 1968 for the annual Yorker Club convention, Jr. branch, NYSH Association (http://www.rootsweb.com/%7Enyherkim/eckler.html); **Mississaugas**: The captives were Jacob Dennis and Abraham Halley. McHenry *Rebel Prisoners at Quebec*.

17. Heath to Governor Clinton, Continental Village, September 15, 1781, PPGC, VII, 332; **Continental Village**: Hans DePold, Bolton Town Historian, http://revroad@ctssar.org. In October 1776, the main U.S. HQ was at Continental Village, north of

Peekskill. In 1781, Wash headquartered in the Appleby house about three quarters of a mile west of the Odell house where Rochambeau stayed. Heath must have followed Washington's lead; Logan to Stark, Ten Broeck to Logan, and Schuyler to Stark, September 15, 1781. Stark, 251–53; Stark to Schuyler, September 16, 1781, *ibid.*, 253–54; Colonel Schuyler to Gansevoort, September 16, 1781, Stone, *Brant, II*, 178; Commendation of Villefranche, September 16, 1781, Willett OB, 33; **La Marquise**: Watt, *Rebellion*, 62, 92, 126–27; **Villefranche**: On March 4, 1782, the major was thanked by Congress for his many good works on the Mohawk River. His correspondent said, "I am very sensible of the Zeal, professional knowledge and Activity you have shewn during your Services in the Country and shuld be happy in contributing to your advancement; but it is a matter in which I have not in the least interfered those Gentlemen of your Corps who have obtained promotion owe it intirely to their good fortune in having assisted at a successful Operation and to the representations which were made in Congress by General Du Portial in consequence thereof." Like Willett, Villefranche had served in a backwater and could expect no promotion. *Washington Writings*, Vol. 24, 42–43; Willett's Itinerary, Johnson, *Bloodied Mohawk*, 278; **Court Martial**: Pliny Moore Papers, 65; (NY) PA S11226 of John Pettit. He recalled that Dunham and Grant were found guilty of corresponding with the enemy and they were sent off to West Point in irons; Heath to Stark, Continental Village, September 17, 1781, Stark, 254–55; Heath to Governor Clinton, Continental Village, September 17, 1781, PPGC, VII, 335–36; Albany Commission to Governor Clinton, September 19, 1781, *ibid.*, 339–40; Marshall to Stark, September 19, 1781, Stark, 255–56; Stuart Letters, 342; Stark to Heath, September 20, 1781, and n.d. Stark, 256–57; **Enemy Indians**: these may have been Kahnawakes or St. Francis Abenakis. Other nations seem most unlikely; **Hand Screw**: a large, ratcheted hand tool for raising heavy weights.

18. SJJ to Le Maistre, September 13, 1781, LAC, MG13, No. 24, 76; Marsh to Haldimand, Fort St. John's, September 14, 1781, Brown, Marsh, St. Leger to Mathews, September 15, 1781, LAC, HP, AddMss21794, 139; Lieutenant-Colonel Carl von Kreutzbourg, "Relation of the Secret Expedition under the Command of Colonel St. Leger on September ninth, 1781" [hereafter, Von Kreutzbourg Relation] found in the "Narration of Hesse Hanau Jäger Corps in America." Letter O. John C. Zuleger, trans., Hessian Papers. Morristown National Historic Park, NJ, 32; SJJ to Haldimand, September 17, 1781, LAC, HP, B158, 234; Haldimand to SJJ, September 20, 1781, LAC, HP, B159, 159; Using a 2KRR return of officers and the State of the Garrison of Carleton Island on December 11, 1781, it can be deduced which officers were likely available for the expedition. **2Bn Return**: Cruikshank and Watt, *KRR NY*, 130–31. **State**: LAC, WO 17/1574&75, 229. Available captains were Thomas Gumersall, James McDonell and, William Redford Crawford. Lieutenants were

John Howard, Philip Lansingh, Hazelton Spencer, Oliver Church, and adjutant, William Fraser. Ensigns were Alex McKenzie, Ranald McDonell, and John Hay. Unfortunately, I have not been able to determine which of these men participated; Ross to Haldimand, Fort Haldimand, September 20, 1781, LAC, HP, AddMss21787, 256; **Wingrove**: Born, England, 1752. Served only in the 34th. Ranked ensign, December 12, 1781. Ranked lieutenant, August 1, 1777 and, although a lieutenant infantry officer, went with St. Leger to Stanwix while his coy went with Burgoyne. Ranked, captain-lieutenant, May 14, 1788 and as adjutant, August 1, 1788, to beyond 1792. Houlding, *King's Service*. Watt and Morrison, *British Campaign of 1777*, 28; Butler to Mathews, September 22, 1781, Smy Transcripts, HP, AddMss21765; Von Kreutzbourg Relation, 32; **Pritchard**: LAC, HP, AddMss21821, 332; Chambers to Haldimand, September 23, 1781. LAC, HP, AddMss21802, 112–13; General Return of Vessels on Lake Champlain, January 1, 1779. *HSGS, III*, 85 ex LAC, HP, B144, 140–49; Haldimand to SJJ, circa September 27, 1781, Cruikshank and Watt, *KRR NY*, 74; Von Kreutzbourg Relation, 34; Haldimand to Powell, Quebec, September 27, 1781, Smy Transcripts, HP, AddMss21764; Robertson to Haldimand, Oswegatchie, September 27, 1781, LAC, HP, AddMss21780, 153.

19. Haldimand to Powell, September 7, 1781 — received September 20. Smy Transcripts, HP, AddMss21764; Cruikshank and Watt, *KRR NY*, 78; Powell to Haldimand, Niagara, September 29, 1781, Smy Transcripts, HP, AddMss21761. An appended list showed an unnamed 8th captain as a participant, but his role was unstated; **Coote**: Born in Ireland. Lieutenant in the newly raised 91st Foot, January 18, 1760. 1762 — served in Portugal. On supplementary list on disbandment. When 8th was augmented in Ireland, Coote joined as lieutenant, August 15, 1775. Captain-Lieutenant, 34th, November 1, 1780, which date clashes with his command of the 8th's detachment in October 1781. Captain, June 28, 1786. Retired, February 20, 1788. Houlding, *King's Service*; Ross to Haldimand, Fort Haldimand, September 29, 1781, Smy Transcripts, HP, AddMss21787; **Gifts**: Calloway, 146; **Christian**: Most likely, Christian the Oneida (Kristianko Thonigwenghsoharie, Washer Away of Blood). Christian was one of eleven Oneidas given officer's rank by Congress in June 1779. He and ten other warriors were coerced to leave Old Oneida in June 1780. Glatthaar and Martin, 236, 272; **Crysler**: Order issued, September 28, 1781. *Crysler Journal*, 59. Crysler's constant employment against the Schoharie certainly earned him the lasting enmity of his old neighbours; **Oquagas**: This mixed-nations community may also have included the handful of Schoharies who had been driven from their villages; Powell to Haldimand, Niagara, September 30, 1781, Smy Transcripts, HP, AddMss21767; **BR Return**: WO28/4; Haldimand to H. Clinton, Quebec, September 29, 1781, *HSGS, III*, 210–12 ex LAC, HP, B147, 381–87. This lengthy letter offered a superb account of the difficulties of waging war from Canada; **Bayley**: Wells, 97–98.

20. Young, Richard J., "Blockhouses in Canada, 1749–1841: A Comparative Report and Catalogue," [hereafter, "Blockhouses"] in *Canadian Historic Sites: Occasional Papers in Archaeology and History* (Ottawa: Parks Canada, 1980), 31–32 ex Twiss to Haldimand, January 12, 1782, LAC, HP, MG21, G1, B154, 371; Willett to Governor Clinton, September 22, 1781, *ibid.*, 351–52; Willett OB, 33–34; Stark to Heath, Saratoga, and Heath to Stark, Continental Village, September 24, 1781, Stark 260–61; **Cornwallis**: Bronck, 37; Stark to Heacock, Saratoga, September 26, 1781, Stark, 262; **Ittig**: Simms, *FNY, II*, 537–38. *Schoharie*, 488–90. Simms say he was captured by 7 Mohawks; **Dogs**: For another account of the Natives' use of dogs for guarding and tracking, see Freemoyer, *Revolution Remembered*, 294–95; **Orchard**: (NY) PA S12116 of Zenas Barker and Simms, *FNY, II*, 532–33; **Family farm**: (NY) PA S13013 of William Feeter; Marshall to Governor Clinton, Albany, September 27, 1781, PPGC, VII, 363–64; **McKinstry**: Previous major, 8ACM. Morrison comments, "John McKinstry proved to be one of the less successful appointments to Willett's Levies. From the outset, the relationship seems strained. Perhaps there was jealousy between the two. Despite Willett's many request for returns from McKinstry, none were made." Of course, we know from Stark's correspondence, there was no writing paper at Saratoga. Morrison continues, "Eventually McKinstry was promoted to LCol by Gen Stark, but on what authority is unknown, and for some reason, Maj Throop seems to have joined McKinstry in Stillwater"; **Willett's Return**: Johnson, *Bloodied Mohawk*, 181 ex Willett's Letter Book, MSS SC16670; **Confiscations**: NYSL, Special Collection and Manuscripts, Audited Accounts, Vol. A, 163, 221; **Skipple**: Schepel, a traditional unit of dry volume. The Dutch schepel is usually translated as "bushel" in English. The schepel was roughly 0.75 bushel or about 26 litres. It weighed approximately thirty pounds of wheat. Of course, the bushel has a different weight for each commodity, making conversion difficult. From September 21 to November 30, Willett impressed 185 skipples of wheat from Tryon citizens to feed his hungry levies. Twice in November and once in December, he signed for cattle, beef, mutton, flour, tallow, and hides taken from the disaffected. Reimbursement appears to have been made in 1785, but it is unclear what, if anything, was paid to the disaffected.

CHAPTER 7: THE HAMMERS FALL

1. Preface, PPGC, VII, xii–xiii; **War Parties**: Calloway, 144 ex HP, AddMss21769, 122, 124, 146, 165; Haldimand to SHC, Quebec, October 1, 1781, *HSGS, III*, 212 ex LAC, HP, B147, 374–47; Haldimand to St. Leger, Quebec, October 1, 1781, LAC, HP, AddMss21795, 280; Williamson, 106; Enys, 53; Willett to Governor Clinton, Fort Rensselaer, October 2, 1781, PPGC, VII, 370; **Small Raids**: (NY) PA R6461 of Dietrick Loucks; **Discharged Men**: (NY) PA S14669 of Abraham J. Terwilliger. His account raises the question of discharged Levies carrying off public

firelocks, but, of course, they may have been personally owned. Johnson, *Bloodied Mohawk*, 88–89, 477; Heath to Stark, Continental Village, October 1, 1781, Stark, 262–63; Weissenfels to Governor Clinton, Saratoga, October 3, 1781, PPGC, VII, 371; Willett OB, 32; Stark to Gansevoort, Saratoga, October 3, 1781. Stark, 273; **Small**: Simms, *FNY, II*, 534–35. *Schoharie*, 469; J.F. Morrison places this incident at about October 4; **Private**: McHenry shows the name as Caster, aged forty-one, taken October 15, 1781 at German Flatts; **Father and Son**: Willett to Stark, October 6, 1781, Stark, 263–64.

2. **McKinnon**: John McDonell, B. Frey, P. Hare to Butler, Niagara, October 2, 1781, Smy Transcripts. WO28/4 and McKinnon to Lieutenant-Colonel Butler, Niagara, October 9, 1781, *ibid*. WO 28/4. McKinnon wrote:

> I find that some of the Capts of this regt is much dissatisfied and has wrote against me for holding a former Commission in the Provincial Army as a Capt, as they apprehend, from the date of that Commission I shall claim rank in the Provincial Line. I humbly appeal to BGen Powell of the validity of the same, or to be determined in any other manner, by Gen Powell, as he shall think fit. The C-in-C knows that I raised and commanded a coy under the command of LGen Howe in the Regt of Roman Catholics. My Commission is dated Feb 25th 1778. That regt was drafted into [an]other Corps. I was put with the rest of the Officers upon half pay till we was provided for. Thinking myself ill used, I went to England and was sent out to Canada by Lord Geo Germain, recommended to the C-in-C. His Lordship's letter testifies the same.

Butler's captains had no way of knowing how accurate their concerns were, as McKinnon had been discharged from the service in disgrace after a 1778 court martial at Long Island, NY. How much more vociferous would they have been if this information had been available. Todd Braisted research. PRO, WO71/87, 173–76; **T. Johnson**: Wells, 94–97; **Stuart**: Fryer, *Pimpernel*, 151–52 ex LAC, HP, B177-1, 25–2.8 Talman, Stuart Letters, 340–41; Chambers to Haldimand, October 6, 1781, LAC, HP, AddMss21802, 123.

3. **Ancrum**: Watt & Morrison, *Brit Campaign of 1777*, 28; Although W. Butler listed the 34th with 100 all ranks, Ross's and McDonell's reports listed seventy-five; A study of the 34th Regiment by Don Hagist indicates that Second Lieutenant Anthony Wingrove, another veteran of the St. Leger campaign, was likely the subaltern with Ancrum in 1781; Ancrum was Light Company CO in an October

1782 return. See, WO12/4866, Part 2; Lieutenant Alex McDonell's article, *Quebec Gazette*, 22 November 1781 [hereafter McDonell Article], Smy Transcripts; **Hanau Jägers**: Listed in Ross's November 6 return. Justin Boggess's research indicates this was likely corporal August Einfeld, Major's Coy. He and Corporal George Wille and eighteen Jägers had been at Carleton Island for two years, seven months, under the command of Lieutenant van den Velden until November 1781, when the lieutenant was recalled to lower Quebec and Einfeld took command. Einfeld was the Capitaine d'Armes in Major Franken's (Hildebrand's Coy) in 1777, but was not with the St. Leger Expedition; **2KRR**: From a December return, the captains available to attend were: Thomas Gumersall, James McDonell and W.R. Crawford. The possible first lieutenants in order of seniority were: John Howard, Phillip Lansingh, Hazelton Spencer, and Oliver Church. No second lieutenants were available. By seniority, the possible ensigns were: Alex McKenzie, Ranald McDonell, and John Hay. "State of the Garrison of Carleton Island 14 December 81," WO17/1574, 229; **Small Arms**: The following is Captain John Munro's July 30 1781 explanation of the difficulties faced by Sir John and himself to ready their detachments in the fall of 1780:

> When Sir John Johnson went off with his detachment the Men and Arms were picked from the whole Regiment — when I rec'd my Orders, I had no Arms fit for Service, many of the Men which went with me were Recruits [who] did not receive their Cloathing and the party in General in want of every thing fit for the Service they were [enter]ing upon, which obliged me Imediately to employ all the Gunsmiths, Taylors, Shoemakers &c in the Regiment and Montreal in order to get ready. I made application to the Kings Stores For Arms and Other Articles, and all I received was 12 pair of Shoes and Six Blankets for which I gave my obligation to return the Same in Quantity and Quality, I supplied every Man with 2pr of Shoes, Trousers, Knapsacks, &c &c *for which they have pay'd* — I found myself under the necessity of purchasing all those necessary to Complete the Men for the duty which they had to perform. The Articles which I have charged in said Acct. were of the cheapest sort that could be found, and for the other Articles it was Impossible to avoid them unless I would suffer the Men to die in the woods. The Men also observing all the Loyalists Completely Cloathed at St John's, who had only to go by water with Major Carleton to Crown Point, and remarking that their Brother Soldiers which went with Sir John Receiv'd all Necessarys for a Campaign. (LAC, HP, AddMss21821, 268–69.)

4. Captain Gilbert Tice, "Journal of the Proceedings with the Indians on the late Expedition in October 1781," [hereafter, Tice Journal], LAC, HP, B107, 301; Powell to Haldimand, Niagara, October 10, 1781, HP, AddMss21765; McDonell Article; **Great Asodus**: Modern Sodus Point, NY; Willett to Stark, October 6, 1781. Stark, 263–64; **2TCM Lieutenant**: George Loucks. Fernow, V.XV, SA1, 546; **Cough**: Morrison, *Fulton*, 51–52. Simms, *FNY, II*, 579–81. Simms stated John Jr. was exchanged in 1782 and rejoined his regiment, although military records do not confirm this; **Local Women**: Likely Elizabeth Frey, née Herkimer, daughter of loyalist Han Jost. Penrose, *Mohawk Valley in Revolution*, 253; Dambourgès to Mathews, Carleton Island, October 7, 1781, Smy Transcripts, HP, AddMss21787; Tice Journal; Powell to Haldimand, Niagara, October 9, 1781, Smy Transcripts, HP, AddMss21761; **Liquor**: Willett OB, 34; **Court Session**: Colonel Charles Briggs, curator of Johnson Hall, "Chronology," Tryon County Court Records, Montgomery City Department of History and Architecture, Old Court House, Fonda. I am beholden to Briggs for the artifice of personality juxtapositioning; Gansevoort to Governor Clinton, Albany, October 9, 1781. Gansevoort Papers, 18–137.

5. Ross to Haldimand, Oswego, October 10, 1781. Ross spelled Duanesborough as Dunsboro. Smy Transcripts, HP, AddMss21784; Tice Journal; **Lachine Mohawks**: Graymont wrote, "They were very much hurt that they had not been sent to help Ross and continually importuned Claus to send them out on service. Claus tried to humour them by telling them that the Canada Indians were never teasing him so much to be sent out and they replied that the Canada Indians had not had their homes destroyed." She noted that, although a peace between the U.S. and Britain might be drawing near, the Mohawks had no desire for peace. She also noted that the Mohawks were not entirely occupied with war. Having been "particularly accustomed to the comforts of civilization, desired that … they should not lapse into barbarism." Brant requested that Guy Johnson supply his people with a schoolmaster at Niagara. Lack of schooling was also a concern at Lachine and a Native schoolmaster, Paulus Sahanwad, and a clerk, were supplied — both men were Fort Hunters. About this time, Claus completed an Anglican primer in Mohawk, which was printed in England and copies sent to Niagara. Graymont, 251–52 ex Claus to Haldimand, HP, B114, 204; Ross to Haldimand, Oswego, November 7, 1781 [hereafter, Ross Report], Cruikshank and Watt, *KRR NY*, 80, and information provided to Ross by Brant. Ross to Haldimand, June 26, 1782 [hereafter, Brant Information], Smy Transcripts, HP, AddMss 21784; Willett to Stark, Fort October 10, 1781, October 11, 1781, Stark, 273; Bockee to Moore, Fort Plain, October 12, 1781, Pliny Moore Papers, 73; **Onondagas**: Tice Journal. Morrison thinks the scalp may have been Small's and the prisoner Jacob Casler, yet McHenry dates Casler's capture as October 15; **Released Prisoner**: Brant Information; Tice Journal.

6. Wemple to Gansevoort, Schenectady, October 14, 1781, Gansevoort Papers, 18; Willett to Marshall, Fort Rensselaer, October 15, 1781. Johnson, *Bloodied Mohawk*, 89. Johnson did not indicate the letter's recipient, but Marshall's later letter to Clinton clarifies the issue; **Militia**: As all Levies were drawn from the militia, the term "militia" was often used in contemporary correspondence when "Levies" was meant. A document's context must be examined to determine when Levies was meant to be understood. In this specific case, Marshall was stationed in Albany to collect the new Levies as they arrived and forward them to the regiment. Marshall had no militia under his direct command other than those joining Willett's; Marshall to Governor Clinton, October 17, 1781, PPGC, VII, 413. Here's another instance of "militia" being used to indicate Levies. There is an outside chance that Marshall, as Albany's commandant, would have had the authority to order out Gansevoort's militia coys to assist Willett, but I have concluded this was very slim. With Stark already clamouring for assistance at Saratoga, it would seem most unlikely that men of 1ACM would have been sent westward. Perhaps, Marshall sent his small twenty-man guard. It is unknown why he himself did not march. Stark may have ordered him to stay in Albany as post commandant; Finck to Governor Clinton, October 16, 1781, *ibid.*, 407–08. The governor agreed to the exchange of these persons in a letter of October 28.

7. **Ganaghsaraga**: Also spelled Kanaghsoraga; Ross Report and Tice Journal; "David the Mohawk Chief to Coll. Johnston," Niagara, November 11, 1781 [hereafter, Hill Report], LAC, HP, MG21, B10, 309–11; **4TCM Private**: (NY) PA R17772 of Abraham Wolleber; Marshall to Governor Clinton, October 17, 1781, PPGC, VII, 413–14; **Docksteder**: Butler to Mathews, Niagara, December 7, 1781, enclosed a memorial by Frederick's brother, Lieutenant John, which read:

> That the brother of your memorialist, from his attachment to Government and zeal for His Majesty's Service left his family and friends on the Mohawk River, where he lived in easy circumstances, and came to this post in the year 1776, where he served in the Ind Dept and afterwards as Sjt in LCol Butler's Corps of Rangers, in which station he behaved so as to procure a recommendation from the Commanding Officer in consequence of which Your Excellency was pleased to appoint him a Lieutcy in the said Corps. He was called out in the detachment of that Corps on the late expedition to the frontiers under Maj Ross, and on the march against the rebels was attacked by a violent disorder which deprived him of life, and has left his widow and a young child in distressed circumstances and without any means of present subsistence or support but from

Your Excellency's well known bounty and benevolence which your memorialist hopes will be incited to afford her some relief. (Smy Transcripts, HP, AddMss21765 and LAC, HP, B105, 304.)

8. (NY) PA S9277 of Christian Bellinger, Morrison's Pensions; **John Lewis**: Audited Account, Vol. A, 135. **Philip Bellinger**: *Ibid.*, 278; **Bowman**: Fernow, V.XV, SA1, 550; **Ross Report**: Ross recalled that rebel alarm guns had already been fired when the Indians chose not to burn Currytown. If this was the case, their gunfire failed to warn Willett, as he did not receive news of the expedition until 8 p.m. and that from a refugee, not gunfire; **Hare's Party**: Tice Journal; (NY) PA W4104, widow of John Wood. Johnson, *Bloodied Mohawk*, 646; **Raid Details/Printup**: Simms, *Schoharie*, 470–77. *FNY, II*, 539; **Tanner/Ulman**: (NY) PA S11513 of Jacob Tanner. Johnson, *Bloodied Mohawk*, 89–90, 587. Fernow, Vol. XV, SA1, 296. (NY) PA W6730, widow of Simon J. Vrooman; (NY) PA S14743 of Frederick Ulman; **Keller**: Henry Keller was 18 in 1781. He had joined the KRR on May 3, 1780. He did not settle in Canada after the war. Perhaps because of this kind act, he was accepted back into Mohawk Valley society, as a man of this name wrote a will at German Flatts in 1812; **Evert Van Epps**: McHenry, *Rebel Prisoners at Quebec*; **Ross Report**: Ross recalled marching for eight days from Ganaghsaraga, but that would make the date October 25, which could not be correct; **Burned Farms**: Willett's Letter Book, 1781, 29. Willett listed thirty-one persons who lost farms and crops at Warrensborough. Many of their surnames appear on the rolls of the KRR and BR; **Anthony's Nose**: Hill Report and Glen to Stirling, Schenectady, October 26, 1781, PPGC, VII, 443–44 and Ross Report.

9. Willett to Stirling, November 2, 1781. Johnson, *Bloodied Mohawk*, 90; "Memoir of Marinus Willet," Stark, 340; **Expresses**: (NY) PA W16688, widow of Abraham Quackenboss of Gardenier's Company, 3TCM. Abram was sent to warn some troops at Flat Creek, southeast of Canajoharie. Johnson, *Bloodied Mohawk*, 526–27; (NY) PA W6126, widow of Henry Smith. Smith, Gros's Coy, WL was chosen as the express to Fort Paris in Stone Arabia as he had earlier served in Miller's Coy, 2TCM, which frequently did duty there.

10. **Deserters**: Hill Report; **Garrison Sally**: St. Leger to Mathews from intelligence gathered by Ensign Walter Sutherland, 2KRR, Chimney Point, November 6, 1781 [hereafter, Sutherland Report], LAC, HP, MG21, B134, 175. Sutherland was at Johnstown on a Secret Service scout four days after the battle and received many insights for local loyalists. He reported that the twelve men taken at Fort Hunter were stragglers cut off by a sally from the fort. Claus to Mathews, Montreal, November 29, 1781, Claus Papers, 175. Claus also comments on Sutherland's

findings; **Garrison Member**: (NY) PA R8538 of Peter J. Quackenboss. In 1780, he was in Gardinier's Coy, 3TCM and, circumstantially, in Putman's Coy, WL, in 1781; Ross Journal; McDonell Article; **Warrensborough**: Built on land owned by Sir Peter Warren, an uncle of Sir William Johnson (SWJ). The latter came from Ireland to manage his uncle's Mohawk Valley properties and from there built his empire. **Tales of Warrensborough**: "Some History, Traditions, Folklore of the Town of Florida," address by Robert M. Hartley, Mohawk Valley Historical Associaton 1936 Yearbook. The Pettingells later thatched over the floor joists and barely survived the winter on the remaining stack; (NY) PA R4017 of Ray Guile. Guile believed the man he killed was an officer. His uniform and "uncommonly long sword" suggests Guile was correct. However, the only commissioned officer lost by Ross was Walter Butler, and his death occurred much later. For some reason, Willett's enumeration of property losses at Warrensborough did not mention the Guiles' buildings which Ray's brother Stephen reported destroyed; **Alex Campbell**: Fraser, II, 360–61. Campbell said that SJJ had been instrumental in the destruction of the works. Oddly enough, Johnson did not refute this fact when he witnessed Campbell's claim. Also, Campbell reported his works as being in Schenectady, but, as that place was not under direct attack, I concluded this was a loose reference and Warrensborough was the true location; **Inhabitants' Deaths**: Willett to Stirling, October 26, 1781, PPGC, VII, 443.

11. **Putman's Coy**: (NY) PA S13497 of Samuel Hubbs. Johnson, *Bloodied Mohawk*, 444–45; (NY) PA S13013 of William Fetter; (NY) PA S22985 of Jacob Shew; **Diefendorf's Coy**: (NY) PA W22528, widow of Jacob Waggoner of Diefendorf's. Johnson, *Bloodied Mohawk*, 625–26; **Jost House's Coy**: (NY) PA W16920, widow of Conrad Countryman, *ibid.*, 348; **Lype's Coy**: (NY) PA W18543, widow of Henry Murphy of Lype's. Wounded in right arm and later pensioned. *Ibid.*, 495–96; **Van Evera's Coy**: (NY) PA S22662 of Orderly Serjeant (O/Sjt) Adam Brown, Van Evera's, *ibid.*, 323; **Ammunition Boxes**: Stirling to Clinton, Albany, October 27, 1781, PPGC, VII, 449–50; **Wallace**: A Johnstown native. Enlisted in 1776, private in John Visscher's Coy, 3TCM. January 1777, entered Hanson's Coy, 1CDN, first lieutenant on May 6, 1777. Served Saratoga campaign. Resigned August 1779 due to father's health. Family home burned in SJJ's May 1780 raid. Enlisted as lieutenant, Demuth's Coy, Dubois's NY Levies. Fought at Klock's Field in October 1780. Enlisted in Fonda's 3TCM Exempts in 1781 and served as serjeant. J.F. Morrison profile. TCMN, Vol. XXI, No. 5.

12. Wemple to Ganse, Schenectady, October 24, 1781. Gansevoort Papers, 18-8240; **Guarding Schenectady**: (NY) PA R10978 of Ensign Lawrence Vrooman, Jellis J. Fonda's Coy; **Volunteers**: A conclusion drawn from a page by page review of Hanson; **Schenectady's Five Coys**: Commanded by Jellis J. Fonda, John Mynderse,

John Van Patten, Thomas Banker, and Jesse Van Slyck. Fernow, Vol. XV, SA1, 263; **Claverack Men**: (NY) PA S14258 of Second Lieutenant Jonathon Reynolds, Barret's Coy, 2Claverack. Claimed he was at the Johnstown battle, although (NY) PA W18546, widow of Nicholas Myers, Philips's Coy, 1Claverack stated that the Claverack men marched to Caughnawaga, then heard that Ross's force had been repulsed and turned about for home. Johnson, *Bloodied Mohawk*, 533, 498; Stirling to Governor Clinton, Albany, October 27, 1781, PPGC, VII, 447–48.

13. **Littel's Scout**: (NY) PA, S22985 of Jacob Shew; **Tenants**: Claus to Mathews, Montreal, November 29, 1781, Claus Papers, 175. Sutherland spoke to three "friends to government" who told him that they had been ordered to duty in the fort and "were spectators of the action"; Simms, *FNY, II*, 543–44; *Hill Report*; **Sniping at Column**: (NY) PA R4017 of Ray Guile; (NY) PA W1090, widow of Stephen Shew; **Bypassed Fort**: Sutherland Report. He reported that [Ross] "pass'd thro Johnstown, the 24th without regarding the Fort." Certainly a deliberate assault on Fort Johnstown would have been noted by either Ross, Tice, Hill, or McDonell. Not a word was written; **Noon**: McDonell Article; **Simon Veeder**: Hanson, 259; (NY) PA W18479, widow of Isaac Mason; **Van Sickler**: Simms, *Schoharie*, 470–77. Printup's thigh healed and he was able to return home. Jim Morrison provided the lady's given name and identified her son; (NY) PA S13013 of William Feeter; (NY) PA S28807 of John McMartin. Johnson, *Bloodied Mohawk*, 487.

14. **Rowley**: (MA)PA W20264, widow of Enos Moore; Willett's Letter Book, NYSL, Mss SC-6670. See also, Johnson, *Bloodied Mohawk*, 90; (NY) PA S14743 of Frederick Ulman; **Willett's Force**: (NY) PA W18479, widow of Isaac Mason. Stated that Willett had about 400 men "of all descriptions," but does not define whether that was the number before Rowley was split off; J.F. Morrison, *Hall Battle*. Jim states that Willett deployed 400 men. Again, it is not clear if that included Rowley's flank attack or not and (NY) PA W6370, widow of Lieutenant Simon J. Vrooman, Gros's Coy. "We overtook the enemy at Johnstown and had an action with them. We had 228 men under Col Willet." Now, if Vrooman's memory was sound, Willett's force was split with approx 180 of 412 going with Rowley and approx 230 with Willett and (MA) PA, W20264, widow of Enos Moore stated the "Attack commenced by a division of 200 under Col Willett."

15. Ross Report; **Impressed Provisions**: Walter Sutherland Papers, HP, LAC, B158, 296–97, 301. When Sutherland arrived four days after the battle, he paid a further £4 "hallifax Currency" to these people. As of April 29, 1783, Sutherland had not received payment from the government for his generosity. On May 14, 1783, Ross acknowledged Sutherland's payment to the Johnstown folk and asked him to pay off

the balance of the debt, as he had no opportunity to do so from Oswego. B158, 302 and on June 6, 1783, Sutherland arranged to send the balance with "a Trusty man of Sir John's Regiment going to Johnstown as soon as leave will be granted (B158, 284) however, by June 30, no funds had reached him to give to the trusty man, but, if they were sent immediately, he could give them to Ensign Jacob Glen, 1KRR, of Schenectady, who was at Dutchman's Point and apparently about to venture to Johnstown. Nor had any funds been given Sutherland for his time and expenses incurred by his repeated jaunts over the past three years into enemy territory, except for one scout for which Colonel Claus had paid. He was owed for 188 days of scouting, under extremely hazardous conditions. In contrast, Sherwood and Smyth paid their men 2S 6P/day. (B158, 306); Hill Report; Tice Journal; McDonell Article.

16. Simms, *FNY, II*, 543–44; **Knapsacks**: *TCMN*, V.5, No. 6; (NY) PA S13013 of William Feeter; McDonell Article; Ross Report; (NY) PA W18479, widow of Isaac Mason; **Finck Striking Man**: (NY) PA W22687, widow of Job Wood. Wood witnessed Finck's action. Johnson, *Bloodied Mohawk*, 647–48; **Young Troops**: (MA) PA W20264, widow of Enos Moore; Willett to Stirling, November 2, 1781, Willett's letter book, NYSL Mss SC16670. Johnson, *Bloodied Mohawk*, 91. The struck-out words were in his original book and reflect his thinking about the event; **Littel**: Deposition, RG233 and evidence of Henry Shew. Littel's shoulder wound later prevented him from earning a livelihood. A doctor deposed that Littel was in great pain and unable to use his right arm and that he was in low circumstances with a wife and large family and his only income was as county sheriff. By 1798, Littel was no longer sheriff and was without income. He deposed that a tomahawk had caused the wound. John Mason and William Lord stated they had seen the wound the evening of October 25 and it was a contusion made by the head of a tomahawk or some other blunt instrument; **White Captured**: (NY) PA W6370, widow of Simon J. Vrooman.

17. **Wagner**: Simms, *FNY, II*, 547–48. His recollection posses a mystery similar to Guile's earlier story, i.e., who was the officer shot by Wagner? During the whole raid, Ross lost only one commissioned officer, Walter Butler. Perhaps Wagner's victim was a Gentleman Volunteer, who, as a man of means, was wearing a better class of clothing; **Scarborough and Crosset**: Simms maintained that both these men were in Littel's Coy, 3TCM. J.F. Morrison reckons that Crosset may have been John Crossard of Putman's Coy. Scarborough (né Crowley, son of Jeremiah) was also listed in Putman's in Fernow. In any event, both men could have been selected from Littel's to serve in WL and, therefore, were in both organizations; **McDonald**: Simms, *Trappers*, 95–97. See appendix for discussion of this officer's identity; *Sutherland Report*.

18. **Winne/Winney**: Gansevoort Papers, 18. Roberts, *NY in Revolutionary War*, 128; Wallace account. Morrison, *Battle of Johnstown*; **Killed Officer**: Once again, we have a report of the death of a British officer, in this instance by Wallace's volunteers, but Ross had no officers killed in the Hall Battle. Perhaps, this was the 34th Sjt reported killed in Ross's return; (NY) PA W18479, widow of Isaac Mason; **Spiked Gun**: W12099, widow of Peter Flagg. TCMN V.XIX, No. 10; Ross Report; (MA) PA W20264, widow of Enos Moore. Moore reported Rowley was wounded in "the second fire," presumably a second volley-like exchange; **Stone Arabia Reinforcement**: (NY) PA S28690 of Hugh Connelly, Snook's Coy, 3TCM; **Myers's Death**: Fernow, V.XV, SA1, 550; **Deserters**: Herkimer, see Simms, *FNY, II*, 519. Moss, see LAC, HP, AddMss 21794, 176; **Lady Washington**: (NY) PA W16244, widow of John Duesler; **First Hand on Gun**: (NY) PA W2084, widow of Conrad Edick, Elsworth's Coy, WL. Morrison Pensions; **Fight for 3-pdr**: (NY) PA W16273, widow of Henry Gramps/ Krembs; Tice Journal. Who Tice meant by Captain Garrason is a mystery. Seely was obviously Zeilie, who was captured, not killed; **Saqueresa**: Penrose, *Indian Affairs*, 1–3; **Small Arms' Cartridges**: Glen to Stirling, October 26, 1781, PPGC, VII, 443–44; **Ross's estimate**: LAC, HP, AddMss21787; Sutherland Report; **Van Slyck**: Hanson, 247–48; (NY) PA S43563 of Andrew Finck. Johnson, *Bloodied Mohawk*, 395; **The Bells**: Cruikshank and Watt, *KRR NY*, 175. Simms, *FNY, II*, 545, 547fn.

19. (NY) PA S11513 of Jacob Tanner; (NY) PA R11782 of David Wood; Willett to Clinton, Fort Rensselaer, November 4, 1781, PPGC, VII, 481–82; **Classic Battles**: See Brant Nosworthy, *Anatomy of Victory & Battle Tactics 1689–1763*; McGregors: Simms, *FNY, II*, 547fn; This may have been an independent war party; Torches: William Willett, 84; **Wagner**: Simms, *FNY, II*, 548. Wagner later that morning saw several Oneidas. One carried a long-haired scalp that resembled his victim's; **Sled/ Meat**: Simms, *Trappers*, 97, 97fn; Glen to Stirling, October 26, 1781, PPGC, VII, 443–44; (NY) PA S13013 of William Feeter; **Elsworth's**: recollection of Henry Grim. TCMN V.XIX, No. 6; British Intelligence Report, received February 28, 1782. Archivbezeichnung — 237 N 96, #16. Nieders, Staatsarchiv, Wolfenbuettel, Braunschweig, Germany.

20. (NY) PA S5504 of Daniel Herrick, White's Coy, WL; (NY) PA W1090, widow of Stephen Shew; Claus to Mathews. Sutherland's report. Smy Transcripts, HP, AddMss 21774; (NY) PA S28690 of Hugh Connelly; (NY) PA S15059 of Martin Crannell, Elsworth's Coy. Crannell went on the march to Stone Arabia, which suggests that troops from all coys were selected for duties depending on their physical condition; **Eikler/Indian**: Simms, *FNY, II*, 544–45; **Burial**: (NY) PA R6996 of Jeremiah Mason; (NY) PA R8537 of Abraham J. Quackenboss, Gardinier's Coy, 3TCM; (NY) PA W19604, widow of Myndert B. Wemple, J. Wemple's Coy, 3TCM; **Guards**: Nicholas

G. Veeder guarded the Tories. He became famous as Schenectady's last surviving Revolutionary War soldier. Hanson, 257–58. Frederick Weller, see 268–69 and (MA) PA W20264, widow of Enos Moore of Clark's Coy. Enos was also a guard; Glen to Stirling, Schenectady, October 26, 1781, PPGC, VII, 443; **Oneidas**: The initial thirty had swollen to sixty by the time they joined Willett. Glatthaar and Martin, 281. The authors point out that two weeks earlier, the Oneida sachems had declined Schuyler's request to assist, claiming too many of their men were scouting and hunting; **Oothout**: Hanson, 195; a British intelligence report of February 28, 1782 advised that thirty-seven prisoners taken from Ross were sent to Stony Point, NY, from where most escaped and made their way to New York City. Archivbezeichnung – 237 N 96, #16.

21. **Reason for Failure**: (NY) PA S22868 of Peter Lambert, Livingston's Coy, WL; Hill Report; Tice Journal; Simms, *FNY, II*, 545–46; **Laird/Lord**: Watt, *Burning*, 117–18, 134; **Horseflesh/Bad Weather**: Ross Report; Willett's Letter Book; **Choicest**: So described in Willett to Stirling, November 2, 1781. Johnson, *Bloodied Mohawk*, 91. PPGC, VII, 472; **Blankets**: Certificate of Marinus Willett, January 29, 1792, Smy Transcripts. Daniel Ehle Collection, Johnstown Museum. Eleven years after the event, Willett's promise to the Oneidas had still not been kept by the U.S. Government; **Ferry**: (NY) PA R11498 of Conrad Widrig, Staring's Coy, 4TCM. Conrad was a ferry guard when the force crossed the river; **Route**: Simms, *FNY, II*, 546; **Camp in Woods**: (NY) PA W16244 of John Duesler. In contrast, Simon Vrooman recollected sleeping in an open field. Of course, with 400 men, some might have slept in woods and others in fields. (NY) PA W6370, widow of Simon J. Vrooman; **Royal Grant**: A group of settlements including Shells Bush, Remensnyders Bush, Klocks Bush, Snells Bush on west side of East Canada Creek and Youkers Bush and Krings Bush on the east side of East Canada Creek and Yankee's Bush about seven miles north of Little Falls. Johnson, *Bloodied Mohawk*, 288–89; **Fires & Snow**: Recollections of Philip Graff. *TCMN* V.VI, No. 7; **Climb Tree**: Thomas, 139; **Bayonets**: Lossing, I, 291.

22. Willett's Letter Book; (NY) PA W6370, widow of Simon J. Vrooman; Ross Report; Tice Journal; **Oneidas track**: Johnson, *Bloodied Mohawk*, 93; **Embury**: Andrew's land petition included an account of his extensive services. AO, UCLP, E Bundle, 18, #35; **Brant's Volunteers**: Tice Journal. This was the only source I found to mention BV as part of the Ross expedition; **Thornton**: Simms, *FNY, II*, 546–47. Benton, Chapter.V; (NY) PA W16244 of John Duesler; Stirling to Stark, HQ Albany, November 6, 1781, Stark, 288; (NY) PA R7533 of Serjeant Frederick Meyer, Harrison's Coy, WL.

23. **Feu de Joie**: Ross Report and St. Leger to Mathews ex Sutherland: "That, Early, in the Morning of the 30th Octr when he/Mr Sutherland,/ was preparing to return,

he heard a heavy firing of Cannon and Musquetry at Fort Arabic [Fort Paris, Stone Arabia]; from which, he concluded, that Major Ross was return'd; he, therefore waited, to gain farther Intelligence." LAC, MG21, B134, 177. Claus to Mathews ex Sutherland. "At, 12 o'Clock, he counted 13 discharges of Cannon, at Johnstown Fort; he, being about two Miles from the last, and seven, from the first mention'd place — That, a Man, he sent to Johnstown, reported to him, that the firing was occasion'd by the Enemy's rejoicing at the news of the Capture of Lord Cornwallis and his Army: which, an intelligent person, whom he sent to Fort Arabic, confirm'd; Adding, that an Express with the Account, had arriv'd there, the night before, and that the Officers and Soldiers had been drunk, firing, and rejoicing all night." *Ibid.*, 177–78; Ross Report; **Trot**: Willett to Stirling, Fort Rensselaer, November 2, 1781, Johnson, *Bloodied Mohawk*, 91; **Poles**: Simms, *FNY, II*, 547; **Ice**: Recollection of Lodowick Moyer. *Ibid.*, 550; Tice Journal; **Myers**: Simms, *FNY, II*, 539.

24. Willett to Stirling, November 2, 1781, Johnson, *Bloodied Mohawk*, 91–92; **Swart**: Hanson, 221–22; **Horse**: Account by soldier in the vanguard, Johnson, *Bloodied Mohawk*, 93; McDonell Article; **Fog**: Benton, Chapter V; Account of Philip Graff, Van Rensselaer's Coy, WL, Smy Transcripts. *The Mohawk Democrat* (Fonda, NY) 27 February 1913; (NY) PA R4017 of Ray Guile; **Louis Nic**: (NY) PA S16252 of Nicholas Smith; **Lewey**: (NY) PA S19478 of John Stalker and (NY) PA R21851 of Tall William. He deposed that Laucy Nic shot Butler and took his clothing. He later calls him Lewey Nic. He said that an Oneida named John Canada took some coin and Black William hung Walter's shoe buckles around his neck; **Harmanus**: (NY) PA S13445 of Fifer Rozel Holmes, Van Rensselaer's Coy, WL; **Anthony**: Testimony of Daniel Ohlendorf, Simms, *FNY, II*, 549–50. Glatthaar and Martin, 382fn59. The authors suggest this may have been Anthony Shonoghleoh, a rebel Oneida who became a principal warrior after the Revolutionary War; (NY) PA S10540 of George Danbar/Dunbar says Captain John, an Oneida Indian; (NY) PA W21383 of Henry House; (NY) PA W16244 of John Duesler; (NY) PA W6637 of Richard Casler; (NY) PA S43563 of Andrew Finck. Johnson, *Bloodied Mohawk*, 395.

25. Ross Report; Willett to Governor Clinton, Fort Rensselaer, November 2, 1781, PPGC, VII, 472–75; Willett's Letter Book, draft Willett to Stirling, November 2, 1781. Johnson, *Bloodied Mohawk*, 90–93; **Child**: Simms, *FNY, II*, 547; **Wounded Tory**: *Ibid.*, 551; **Sacrificed Tory**: Benton, Chapter V. (NY) PA S10697 of Thomas Folger and Hanson 165; **Scalp Brandishing**: Memories of Philip Graff. *The Mohawk Democrat* (Fonda, NY) 27 February 1913; **Bury Artilleryman**: Simms, *FNY, II*, 546–47; **Scalp Pole**: (NY) PA S28690 of Hugh Connelly; **Illumination**: Hanson, 120fn and Smy Transcripts. Evan, Elizabeth, *Weathering the Storm: Women of the American Revolution* (New York: 1975), 281; **Bell and Bonfire**: Lew Decker, Fulton County Court House,

http://www.carogatimes.com; Reverend Gros to Clinton, November 4, 1781, PPGC, VII, 484; **Jacket, Insignia & Scalp**: M. Paul Keesler, *Kuyahoora, Discovering West Canada Valley* (Newport, NY: Mid-York Sportsman, Inc., 1999), 35. Bronck Family Papers, 38–39. The insignia may have included his gorget, sash, and epaulettes; Claus to Mathews, November 29, 1781, Smy Transcripts, HP, AddMss21774.

26. Hill Report; Tice Journal; **Prisoners**: Simms, *FNY, II*, 550; GO, Fort Rensselaer, November 2, 1781, PPGC, VII, 483–84. Willett Mss. #SC-15705, Johnson, *Bloodied Mohawk*, 147–48; Hanson, 167; Ross Report; **Bell**: Simms, *FNY, II*, 533, 554 and (NY) PA W11434, widow of Thomas T. Shoemaker, 4TCM. A 4TCM party immediately pursued the Indians.

27. Joshua Spencer at Buffteville, John Serjeant on the Onion River and Thomas Wooster Jr. at Upper Cohös. McHenry; **Stint**: Nicholas Lighthall, Van Patten's Coy. Hanson, 180, 221; Marshall to Stark, Albany, October 7, 1781, Stark, 264–65; Stark to Heath, Saratoga, October 8, 1781, *ibid*, 265–66; Governor Clinton to Stark, Poughkeepsie, October 8, 1781, PPGC, VII, 386; Stark to Gansevoort, Gansevoort Papers, 18–137; Gansevoort to Van Rensselaer, Albany, October 9, 1781, *ibid.*; Gansevoort to Stark, Albany, October 9, 1781, *ibid.*; Heath to Stark, Continental Village, October 10, 1781, Stark, 267–68; Marshall to Stark, Albany, October 10, 1781, *ibid.*, 268–69.

28. Sherwood to Mathews. *King's Men*, 296 ex LAC, HP, B176, 314–15. Lovelace's widow Lois petitioned for a continuation of her pension on January 25, 1783. LAC, HP, Add Mss21875/2; Von Kreutzbourg Relation, 34; **Proclamation**: *King's Men*, 287; **Rikely et al**: Fryer, *Pimpernel*, 152–53; Stark to Safford, Saratoga, October 11, 1781. Stark, 277; Stark to Gansevoort, Saratoga, October 11, 1781, PPGC, VII, 391; **Safford**: Born in NH. Major, Green Mountain Boys, July 27 to December 1975. Lieutenant-Colonel of Warner's Continental Regiment, July 5, 1776. Deranged, January 1, 1781. Appointed Brigadier-General of VT Militia, 1781–82 after these events; Heath to Clinton, Continental Village, *ibid.*, 391–93; **Aide**: Benson to Robert Van Rensselaer, Poughkeepsie, October 11, 1781, *ibid.*, 393–94; Schuyler to Governor Clinton, Albany, October 12, 1781, *ibid.*, 395–96; Wemple to Gansevoort, circa October 12, 1781, Gansevoort Papers, 18–140; Schuyler to Stark, Albany, October 12, 1781, Stark, 271; Heath to Stark, Continental Village, October 12, 1781, *ibid.*, 271–72; Heath to Governor Clinton, October 12, 1781, PPGC, VII, 394–95.

29. Affidavit of Lieutenant-Colonel Van Rensselaer, October 13, 1781, *ibid.*, 389–90; Clinton to Gansevoort, October 13, 1781, *ibid.*, 398; Heath to Tupper and Heath to Stark, Continental Village, October 14, 1781, Stark, 273–74; 10MA had been

removed from 1MA Brigade on June 18, 1781 and assigned to the NH Brigade of the Highlands Department. On October 14, 1781, the NH Brigade was relieved from the Highlands Department and assigned to Stark's Northern Department. On November 12, 1781, the 10MA was relieved from the NH Brigade and assigned back to the Highlands Department. Wright, *The Continental Army*, 211; Heath to Governor Clinton, October 14, 1781, PPGC, VII, 399–400; Gansevoort to Stark and Gansevoort to Van Bergen, October 14, 1781, Gansevoort Papers, 18–140.

30. Haldimand to St. Leger, October 14, 1781, LAC, HP, AddMss21794, 153. *HSGS, III*, 212–13 ex LAC, HP, B134, 153–54; Von Kreutzbourg Relation, 34; **Loyalist Corps' Strength**: GO, circa October 1781 for Haldimand regarding the various loyalist corps. LAC, HP, MG13, W028/5, 171–72; "Effective Roll of the Corps of Loyalists Commanded by the late Major Daniel McAlpin," i.e. American Volunteers, May 1, 1781, LAC, HP, MG21, B167b, (AddMss21827, Pt.2) ff.276–277; **Farquar**: 1778 raid, see I.H. and P.A. Washington, 47–50. 1780 raid, see Enys, 28, 32, 42, 44, **St. Leger and Von Kreutzbourg, 1777**: Watt, *Rebellion*, 267–68; "Subce Wanted for a Detachment of the Kings Rangers," October 25, 1781–April 24, 1781, LAC, HP, AddMss21751, 43; Rogers to Mathews, FSJ, December 3, 1781. "Maj Jessup was as much surprised as he, that he was to take command on the late expedition, as he [Rogers] takes rank before Jessup." LAC, HP, AddMss21820, 97. I believe that Haldimand had no intention of slighting Rogers. His decision would have been based on Jessup's seniority in the Canadian Department and, his desire to observe Edward's performance in a key role as part of his decision-making about the future of the many small corps; Haldimand to Germain (most private), Quebec, October 23, 1781, LAC, HP, AddMss21715, 36–40; **Two Majors**: Both Dundas and Hoyes were 34th majors at this time, although, when Dundas took command of the 8th after the St. Leger 1781 expedition, his commission as lieutenant-colonel was backdated to January 11, 1781. Houlding, *King's Service*.

31. Marshall to C. Stark, Albany, October 15, 1781. Stark, 269–70; Schuyler to Stark, Albany, October 15, 1781, *ibid.*, 283; Stark to Heath, Saratoga, October 15, 1781, *ibid.*, 278; Schuyler to Governor Clinton, Albany, October 15, 1781, PPGC, VII, 404; **Fairbanks Fiasco**: Gansevoort to Governor Clinton, Albany, October 15, 1781, *ibid.*, 402–403. Taylor to Governor Clinton, Albany, October 17, 1781, *ibid.*, 405–407. Safford to Stark, Bennington, October 17, 1781, Stark, 277. Walbridge to H. Van Rensselaer, Mapleton, October 17, 1781, PPGC, VII, 592; **Meeting**: Rowland to Governor Clinton, circa October 15, 1781, *ibid.*, 591; Samuel Robinson Jr. commanded a coy in the battle of Bennington and rose to the rank of colonel. In 1779–1780 he represented the town in the assembly and was for three years a member of the board of war. He was the first justice of the peace appointed in town under the authority of VT in 1778, and during the same year one of the judges of a special court.

The website makes this interesting judgment: "Colonel Robinson was one of the few persons who managed a correspondence with the British general Haldimand during the Revolutionary war, securing VT from invasion." http://www.famousamericans. net/samuelrobinson; Robinson to Stark, Bennington, October 16, 1781, Stark, 275–76; **Cough**: Taylor spelled this name "Cook," a common variation; Heath to Governor Clinton, October 17, 1781, PPGC, VII, 410–11; Marshall to Governor Clinton, October 17, 1781, *ibid.*, 413–14; Schuyler to Stark, Albany, October 18, 1781, Stark, 272; Governor Clinton to Gansevoort, October 18, 1781, PPGC, VII, 415–16.

32. Von Kreutzbourg Relation; Chambers Journal. LAC, HP, AddMss21802; **Ticonderoga**: It has not been found how or when St. Leger altered his orders to take post at Crown Point and went to Ticonderoga instead. However, he could not put boats into Lake George from Crown Point and Sherwood expected VT's representatives to come to Ticonderoga to receive Haldimand's proclamation, so the decision made perfect sense; Heath to Stark, Continental Village, October 7, 1781. Stark, 278; Heath to Governor Clinton, Continental Village, October 21, 1781, PPGC, VII, 431–32; Schuyler to Stark, Albany, October 22, 1781. Stark, 281–82; Lieutenant-Colonel Fletcher to Tupper, Fort Warner and Stark to Tupper, Saratoga, and Stirling to Clinton, Albany, October 23, 1781, PPGC, VII, 437–38; Heath to Stark, Stark, 280–81; Stirling to Governor Clinton, Albany, October 24, 1781, PPGC, VII, 438–39; Von Kreutzbourg Relation; Chambers to Mathews, Crown Point, October 20, 1781, LAC, HP, AddMss21802, 126; **Peters**: Fryer, *King's Men*, 228; **VT Scout**: Fryer, *ibid.*, 287–88. *Pimpernel*, 154; St. Leger to Chittenden, Ticonderoga, October 23, 1781, LAC, HP, AddMss21794, 161; St. Leger to Mathews, October 22–23, 1781, *ibid.*

33. Heath to Stark, October 25, 1781, Stark, 280–81; Gansevoort to Taylor and Yates, Albany, October 25, 1781, Gansevoort Papers, 18; Stark to Governor Clinton, October 26, 1781, Stark, 279; Enos to Stark, Castleton, October 26, 1781, *ibid.*, 282; **Enos**: A CT-born, Seven Years' War veteran. Commanded a regiment in Arnold's 1775 Quebec expedition, but when faced with starvation, he turned back. A court martial was required to recover his reputation. Twice a CT regimental commander, before moving to VT, where he was commissioned brigadier-general. A daughter married Ira Allen, which placed Enos in the Allens' camp; Von Kreutzbourg Relation, 37–39; **Enos's Express**: This was Simon Hathaway, see Bellico, 189; Stone, *Brant, II*, 200–03 and Fryer, *King's Men*, 287–88; **Yorktown**: Fryer, *Pimpernel*, 154–55; **Jessup's Activities**: see Von Kreutzbourg Relation.

34. Heath to Clinton, Continental Village, October 26, 1781, PPGC, VII, 441–42; Stirling to Clinton, Albany, October 27, 1781, *ibid.*, 449–50; Stirling to Gansevoort, Saratoga, October 31, 1781, *ibid.*, 461–62; Major Wemple to Gansevoort, Schenectady, October

27, 1781, Gansevoort Papers, 18–8240; **7&8ACM Turnout**: (NY) PA W18546, widow of Nicholas Myers, 8ACM; **Clinton's Optimistic Thought**: Clinton to unknown, Poughkeepsie, October 27, 1781, PPGC, VII, 450–51; **VT Commissioners**: Elisha Payne to Clinton, Charlestown, October 27, 1781, *ibid.*, 444–47; Clinton to Heath, Poughkeepsie, October 28, 1781, *ibid.*, 451–52; Colonel Yates to Major Wemple, Saratoga, October 29, 1781, Gansevoort Papers, 18–8240; Colonel Wemple to Gansevoort, *ibid*; Stirling to Clinton, Saratoga, October 31, 1781, *ibid.*

35. Von Kreutzbourg Relation; **Castleton**: Lieutenant-Colonel H.M. Jackson, *Justus Sherwood: Soldier, Loyalist and Negotiator* (Toronto: author, 1958), 35; **Herrick**: At capture of Ticonderoga by Allen and Arnold, 1775. Lieutenant-Colonel, regiment of Green Mountain Rangers, 1777. Fought under Stark at Bennington. Prominent role in attack on Ticonderoga, September 1777; St. Leger to Mathews, Ticonderoga, October 27 and 29, 1781, LAC, HP, AddMss21794, 165, 67; St. Leger to Mathews, Ticonderoga, November 10, 1781, *ibid.*, 179; Chambers Journal, LAC, HP, AddMss21802, 130; Von Kreutzbourg Relation; Cruikshank, *Roger Stevens*. Had Mount Independence at some time been renamed Mount Twist[s], after the chief egineer, Captain William Twiss(?); Enos to Stark, Fort Ann, November 2, 1781. Stark, 284; Stirling to Governor Clinton, November 3, 1781, PPGC, VII, 478–80; Gansevoort to Bronk, November 3, 1781. Bronck Family Papers, 38–39; Stark to Chittenden, Saratoga, November 4, 1781, Stark, 285–86; Livingston to Clinton, November 6, 1781, *ibid.*, 487; Stirling to Clinton, Albany, November 6, 1781, PPGC, VII, 479–80.

36. Chambers Journal. LAC, HP, AddMss21802, 131; Von Kreutzbourg Relation; St. Leger to Mathews, Chimney Point, November 6, 1781, LAC, MG21, B134, AddMss21794, 17778; Sherwood to Haldimand, November 17, 1781. Justus added a postscript: "I very much fear that any further negotiation with Vermont will be but time and Labor lost Except Affairs take a more favorable turn to the Southward — I am almost persuaded that our adverse fortune in that part is the only obstacle now in the Way"; Chittenden to Stark, Arlington, November 10, 1781, Stark, 286–87; Many Vermont apologists developed rather twisted explanations for the negotiations. For example: "Our truce with Canada was rather a help than a hindrance to the last great struggle of the war — the operations against Cornwallis. It was either unknown to Washington, or understood by him to be a political manoeuvre … By this policy of Governor Chittenden, an army, equal in force to that of Burgoyne, was kept inactive in Canada — amused by the finesse of the governor, and his able coadjutors, till the war was virtually ended by the surrender at Yorktown"; Stirling to Stark, Albany, November 10, 1781. Stark, 291; Haldimand to Henry Clinton, Quebec, November 14, 1781, HSGS, III, 214–15, ex LAC, HP, B174, 387; **Davis**: Mathews, *Spies*, 74fn; Cruikshank, *Roger Stevens*; Enys, 53; Von Kreutzbourg Relation, 42–43.

APPENDICES

1. Kim Stacey, *No One Harms Me with Impunity — The History, Organization, and Biographies of the 84th Regiment of Foot (Royal Highland Emigrants) and Young Royal Highlanders, During the Revolutionary War 1775–1784*, (manuscript in progress, 1994). Of Stacey's description of the Emigrants' late war uniform, the only truly distinctive item would be a blue Kilmarnock bonnet mounting a unique, brass badge, with a blue tourie and bearskin flash. This bonnet would have been markedly different than the cap-hats or round hats worn by the other troops. The Emigrants may also have worn a black leather baldric carrying a belt axe and bayonet, but more likely they employed a simple waistbelt mounting a sliding frog and bayonet to the left of the belly box and the dirk to the right. Other than the dirk, these accoutrements would have been similar to most redcoats.

2. No return has been found for 1781; *Ibid.*, Lauchlan Maclean ranked as ensign on June 14, 1775. He was appointed QM and served in that capacity in 1778. He was a lieutenant, October 20, 1781 and captain, October 17, 1781. Archibald Grant had entered the regiment at the outset and was ranked as ensign on June 14, 1775, and a lieutenant on June 21, 1777.

3. Fryer, *Allan Maclean*, 167. In February 1780, James McDonell of the KRR was in a drunken brawl with his cousins, Lieutenants Archibald and Ranald McDonell, and QM Duncan Murray, all of 1/84RHE.

4. Haldimand to Ross, Quebec, August 23, 1784. Cruikshank, *The Settlement of the United Empire Loyalists on the Upper St. Lawrence*, 155, ex LAC, B64, 181–82.

BIBLIOGRAPHY

PRIMARY SOURCES
Archival

Archives of Ontario
AO13/54.
Ms521(1), Edward Jessup Papers.
The Orderly Book of the King's Loyal Americans and the Loyal Rangers, dated from September 4, 1780 to October 23, 1780.
Ms622, (a miscellaneous selection of Haldimand Papers).
Upper Canada Land Petitions, E Bundle, 18, #35.

British Library
Haldimand Papers.
AddMss21717, Vol. 1, Part 2, Letters to the Ministry, 1780–84.
AddMss21734, Vol. 3, Letters from various persons to General Haldimand, 1781–82.
AddMss21741, Register of Letters from the Adjutant-General's Office at Quebec, 1780–83.
AddMss21743, General Orders issued by Carleton and Haldimand, 1776–83.
AddMss21745, Vol.1, Register of Military Commissions.
AddMss21751, Vol. 3, as above, 1781–82.
AddMss21756, Correspondence with Officers Commanding at Mackinac and Niagara, 1777–82.
AddMss21761, Letters from Officers Commanding at Niagara, 1781.
AddMss21764, Letters to Officers Commanding at Niagara, 1779–83.
AddMss21765, Correspondence with Officers at Niagara,1777–84.
AddMss21766, Correspondence of Haldimand with Colonel Guy Johnson, 1779–83.

AddMss21767, Part 1, Correspondence with Colonel Guy Johnson, 1778–81.

AddMss21767, Part 2, Correspondence with Colonel Guy Johnson, 1782–83.

AddMss21769, Vol.1, Letters and Papers relating to Indian Affairs, 1777–81.

AddMss21770, Vol.2, Letters and Papers relating to Indian Affairs., n.d. and 1782–87.

AddMss21771, Vol.1, Letters from Lieutenant-Colonel J. Campbell and others, 1778–81.

AddMss21772, Vol. 2, Letters from Lieutenant-Colonel J. Campbell and others, n.d., 1782–87.

AddMss21773, Letters to Lieutenant-Colonel J. Campbell and others, 1779–82.

AddMss21774, Correspondence with Lieutenant-Colonel Daniel Claus, n.d. and 1777–84.

AddMss21777, Correspondence with Various Indian Residents, etc., n.d. and 1777–84.

AddMss21780, Correspondence with Officers Commanding at Oswegatchie, 1778–84.

AddMss21784, Register of Correspondence with Officers Commanding at Carleton Island, Oswego, Cataraqui, 1781–83.

AddMss21787, Letters from Officers Commanding at Carleton Island, 1778–84.

AddMss21788, Letters to Officers Commanding at Carleton Island, 1779–83.

AddMss21789, Vol.1, Letters from Officers Commanding at Montreal, 1778–81.

AddMss21791, Letters to Officers Commanding at Montreal, 1778–84.

AddMss21792, Correspondence with Officers Commanding at Isle aux Noix, n.d., 1778–83.

AddMss21794, Vol. 2, Letters from Officers Commanding at Fort St. John's, 1781–84.

AddMss21795, Copies of Letters to Officers Commanding at Fort St. John's, 1778–84.

AddMss21802, Vol. 2, Letters from officer of the Provincial Navy, n.d., 1776–84.

AddMss21818, Letters from Officers of the KRR NY with Returns etc., n.d., 1776–83.

AddMss21819, Letters to Officers of the KRR NY, 1779–83.

AddMss21820, Correspondence with Lieutenant-Colonel Rogers and Major Rogers commanding the Royal Rangers, n.d., 1779–84.

AddMss21821, Vol. 1, Letters from Officers of the Loyalists, 1777–82.

AddMss21823, Letters to Officers of the Loyalists, 1779-83.

AddMss21827, Part 1, Muster Rolls, Accounts etc., Corps of Loyal Americans, 1776–83.

AddMss21827, Part 2, Muster Rolls, Accounts etc., Corps of Loyal Americans, 1776–83.

AddMss21842, Papers of Secret Intelligence, n.d.

AddNss21843, Papers and Correspondence relating to Rebel Prisoners, n.d., 1778–83.

AddMss21873, Memorials from Officers and Soldiers of the Army, n.d., 1778-84.

AddMss21874, V.1, Memorials from Prov Corps and Loyalists n.d. and 1777-82.

AddMss21875, V.2, as above, n.d., 1783-84.

Johnstown Museum, Johnstown, NY
Daniel Ehle Collection.

Library and Archives Canada
Claus Papers, Vol. 1, Correspondence, 1760–77.

Haldimand Papers
MG13 (WO28/5)
    No.23, Royal Regiment New York. Field Officers' Letters from 1781–82.
    No.24, Royal Regiment New York. Field Officers' Letters — from 1778–88. Provincial.
    No.31, Royal Regiment New York. Field Officers' Letters for 1783, Provincial.
    No.53, Papers concerning the 2nd Brigade. Royal Regiment New York. 1780. MG21.
    B10, Correspondence with Sir William Johnson and papers on Indian Affairs, 1759–74.
    B105, Correspondence with Officers at Niagara and Papers, n.d., 1777–84.
    B107, Vol. I of Correspondence with Colonel Guy Johnson, 1778–81.
    B112, Vol. II of Letters from Lieutenant-Colonel J. Campbell and others, 1780–83
    B114, Correspondence with Lieutenant-Colonel D. Claus, 1777–84.
    B134, Vol. 2, Letters from Officers Commanding at Fort St. John's.
    B158, Letters from officers of the Royal Regiment of New York with returns, etc. 1776–84. (AddMss21818)
    B159, Copies of Letters to officers of the Royal Regiment of New York, 1779–83. (AddMss21819)
    B167a, Muster Rolls, Accounts, etc. … relating to the Corps of Loyal Americans, n.d., 1776–85.
    B167b, as above.
    B177, Letters from Captain Sherwood and Dr. Smyth, n.d., 1782.

Colonial Office Records
CO42 (Canada, Original Correspondence).
42/39 (Q16), 1779 — Returns of regiments.
42/40, British North America, Original correspondence, 1779–80.

War Office Records
17/1574, British Provincial and German Troops serving in Canada, 1780.
17/1575, as above, 1781.
28/4, Headquarters Records and Returns, America, 1775–95.
28/5, as above.
28/6, Headquarters Records and Returns, Upper Posts, 1782–83.
28/10, as above.
42/37, Ordnance Records, 1777.
71/87, Judge Advocate General's Office, Courts Martial

Library of Congress
Papers of George Washington. Series 4, General Correspondence.

McCord Museum, McGill University, Montreal, Quebec
"Narrative of Captain Samuel Mackay."

New York Historical Society (collections of)
Willett, Marinus, Papers of: Miscellaneous Manuscripts.

New York State Library
Special Collections and Manuscripts, Audited Accounts, Vols. A and C.

Nieders, Staatsarchiv, Wolfenbuettel, Braunschweig, Germany
Archivbezeichnung — 237 N 96.

Public Record Office
War Office Records
12/4866, Part 2, 34th Regiment of Foot, Pay Lists, 1760–87.
28/2, 34th Regiment of Foot, Field officers' Letters, 1777–89.
28/10, Part 4, 457–73, Muster Roll of the Loyal Rangers dated Rivière du Chêne, January 1, 1783.

State Library of Virginia, Richmond
The Lidgerwood Collection
HZ-1 (2). General Riedesel Correspondence. Lewis Biegigheiser, translator.

U.S. National Archives and Records Center
Revolutionary War Rolls 1775–1783. Microfilm Reel 78, Series M246.

Pension Applications (Photocopies, Transcripts, and Excerpts)
Key: S = survivor   W = widow of   R = rejected

Massachusetts Pension Applications,
Covell, Henry, S30954.

New York Pension Applications,
Anthony, George, S234.
Banta, Hendrick, W24704.
Barhydt, Jerone, W25200.
Barker, Zenas, S12116.

Barstow, Job, R571.

Becraft/Benaft, Francis, S12192.

Bellinger, Christian, S9277.

Brown, Adam, S22662.

Butterfield, James, S44351.

Carter/Garter, John, R1750.

Casler, Richard, W6637.

Clute, Garret, W16905.

Connelly, Hugh, S28690.

Countryman, Conrad, W16920.

Crannell, Martin, S15059.

Croutz, Henry, S23179.

Danbar/Dunbar, George, S10540.

Deusler/Duesler, John, (widow Catharine), W16244.

Doxtator, Hon Yere, S23019.

Ecker, Johannes, R3182.

Eckerson, Cornelius, (widow Catherine), W16971.

Edick, Conrad, W2084.

Etting, John, W19231.

Failing, Philip, W19237.

Feeter/Vetter, William, S13013.

Finck, Andrew, S43563.

Flagg, Peter, W12099.

Flint, Robert, S23221.

Folger, Thomas, S10697.

Forgason, William, S23224.

Fox, William W., S10690.

Gramps/Krembs, Henry, W16273.

Grem/Grim, Henry, S23244.

Guile, Ray, R4017.

Hadcock, Daniel, S21258.

Herrick, Daniel, S5504.

Hickcox, Giles, S2311.

Holmes, Rozel, S13445.

House, Henry, (widow Nancy), W21383.

House, Nicholas, W18046.

Hubbs, Samuel, S13497.

Krembs, *see* Gramps.

Lambert, Peter, S22868.

Little, John, RG233, File No.HR9A — F1.1.

Loucks, Dietrick/Richard, R6461.

Mason, Jeremiah, R6996.

McKeen, Samuel, S28806&127161.

McMartin, John, S28807.

Meyer/Myer, Frederick, R7533.

Moore/Morse, Enos, W20264.

Murphy, Henry, W18543.

Myers, Nicholas, (widow Cornelia), W18546.

Nellis, George H., R7581.

Nellis, William, S5825.

Nellis, William, W5825.

Peck, Henry H., W9210.

Pettit, John, S11226.

Pitcher, Gottlieb, W26899.

Printup, Joseph, S14225.

Quackenboss, Abraham D., W16688.

Quackenboss, Abraham J., R8537.

Quackenboss/bush, Peter J., R8538.

Quackenbush, David, S23379.

Reynolds, Jonathon, S14258.

Riker, John, S6001.

Roof, John, S14371.

Schermerhorn, John L., W17785.

Schoemaker, Thomas T., R9525 and widow, W11434.

Scholl, Johann Jost, W16396.

Schuyler, David A., S14423.

Shew, Stephen, W1090.

Shew, Jacob, S22985.

Shoemaker, *see also* Schoemaker.

Shults, Henry, S14453.

Smith, Henry, W6126.

Smith, Nicholas, S16252.

Snell, Jacob, S28608.

Stalker, John, S19478.

Stuart, Budd, W1662.

Suits/Suts, Peter, widow Elizabeth, W13941.

Tall, William, R21851.

Tanner, Jacob, S11513.

Terwilliger, Abraham J., S14669.

Thornton, John, W20085.

Timmerman, *see* Zimmerman.
Ulman/Olman, Frederick, S14743.
Van Alstine/Alystyne, Martin A., S23036.
Van Alstine, Peter, S14762.
Van Slyke, George, S10016.
Van Slyke, William, W2461.
Veeder, John B., R10927.
Vrooman, Lawrence, R10978.
Vrooman, Simon J., W6370.
Waggoner, Jacob, W22528.
Wallradt, Peter, S11684.
Wasson, John, S11665.
Wemple, Myndert B., W19604.
Widrig, Conrad, R11498.
Willett, Marinus, (widow Margaret), W1525.
Wolleber, Abraham, R17772.
Wood, David, R11782.
Wood, Job, W22687.
Wood, John, W4104.
Woolever, Peter, W19659.
Young, Jacob A., R11960.
Zimmerman, Jacob, W20002.
Zimmerman, John, W16489.

Pennsylvania Pension Applications
Mason, Isaac, W18479.

Wisconsin, State Historical Society
Lyman C. Draper Manuscripts
Joseph Brant Papers, Series F, Vol.10.
Captain John Deserontyon's Services, 14F49.

PRIMARY SOURCES — PUBLISHED
Newspapers and Periodicals

The Mohawk Valley Democrat (Fonda), July 10, 1913.
The Quebec Gazette, November 22, 1781.

Documents, Maps, and Contemporary Works

Barr, John (1779–1782) and Samuel Tallmadge (1780–1782), et al., Diaries thereof. *Orderly Books of The Fourth New York Regiment, 1778–80 — The Second New York Regiment, 1780–83 with Diaries.* Edited and transcribed by Almon W. Lauber. Albany: University of the State of New York, 1932.

Clinton, George. *Public Papers of George Clinton, First Governor of New York, 1777–95, 1801–04.* 6 Vols. New York and Albany: State of New York, 1902.

Cochran, Dr. John. *Surgeon to Washington: Dr. John Cochran 1730–1807.* Transcribed by Morris H. Saffron. New York: Columbia University Press, 1977.

Crowder, Norman K. *Early Ontario Settlers: A Source Book.* Baltimore: Genealogical Publishing Co., Inc., 1993.

Dann, John C. *The Revolution Remembered: Eyewitness Accounts of the War for Independence.* Chicago: University of Chicago Press, 1980.

Fernow, Berthold, ed. *Documents relating to the Colonial History of the State of New York XV, State Archives, Vol.1.* Albany: Weed, Parsons and Company, Printers, 1887.

Fraser, Alexander, ed. *Second Report of the Bureau of Archives for the Province of Ontario.* 2 vols. 1904. Reprint, Baltimore: Genealogical Publishing Co., Inc., 1994.

Fryer, Mary B. and Lieutenant-Colonel William A. Smy. *Rolls of the Provincial (Loyalist) Corps, Canadian Command American Revolutionary War Period.* Toronto: Dundurn Press, 1981.

General Staff, Historical Section of, ed., III, "The War of the American Revolution, The Province of Quebec under the Administration of Governor Frederic Haldimand, 1778–1784," in *A History of the Organization, Development and Services of the Military and Naval Forces of Canada From the Peace of Paris in 1763 to the Present Time With Illustrative Documents [HSGS].* 2 vols., Canada, King's Printer, n.d.

Hadden, Lieutenant James M. *A Journal Kept in Canada and Upon Burgoyne's Campaign in 1776 and 1777.* Edited by Horatio Rogers. Albany: Joel Munsell's Sons, 1884.

Lajeunesse, Ernest, ed. and trans. *The Windsor Border Region: Canada's Southernmost Frontier, A Collection of Documents.* Toronto: Champlain Society, 1960.

McHenry, Chris, compiler. *Rebel Prisoners at Quebec 1778–1783*. Author, 1981.

Paltsits, Victor Hugo, ed. Minutes of the Commissioners for Detecting and Defeating Conspiracies in the State of New York, Albany County Sessions, 1778–1781. 2 Vols. Albany: State of New York, 1909.

Penrose, Maryly B., ed. *Indian Affairs Papers, American Revolution*. Franklin Park, NJ: Liberty Bell Associates, 1981.

———. *Mohawk Valley in the Revolution, Committee of Safety Papers and Genealogical Compendium*. Franklin Park, NJ: Liberty Bell Associates, 1978.

Roberts, James A., comptroller. *New York in the Revolution as Colony and State*. Albany: New York, 1897 — reprinted in 2 vols., 1904.

Secretary of the Commonwealth. *Massachusetts Soldiers and Sailors in the War of the Revolution*. 17 vols. Boston: Wright and Potter Printing Co., 1896.

Smith, Captain George. *An Universal Military Dictionary, A Copious Explanation of the Technical Terms &c. — Used in the Equipment, Machinery, Movements, and Military Operations of an Army*. 1779. Reprint, Ottawa: Museum Restoration Service, 1969.

Stark, Caleb, transcriber and ed. *Memoir and Official Correspondence of Gen. John Stark, with Notices of Several Other Officers of the Revolution. Also, a Biography of Capt. Phinehas Stevens, and of Col. Robert Rogers*. Concord, MA: G. Parker Lyon, 1860.

Washington, George. *The Writings of George Washington from the Original Manuscript Sources, 1745–1799*. Edited by John C. Fitzpatrick. 39 vols. Washington: U.S. Government Printing Office, 1937.

UNPUBLISHED TRANSCRIPTS, LETTERS, DOCUMENTS, AND JOURNALS

Covell, Captain Simeon. *The Memorial of Simeon Covell, Captain in the Queens Loyal Rangers*. PRO, AO13/54, f.169–70.

Dusten, Captain Moses. *Orderly Book of Capt. Moses Dusten 2nd New Hampshire Regiment — December 15, 1781–July 24, 1783*. Albany: New York State Library (NYSL), Department of History and Archives, NY. Mss.11391, Vol. 2.

Gansevoort, General Peter. *Military Papers of General Peter Gansevoort.* Transcribed by the State Historian. Submitted 1906, NY State Archives.

Mackay, Captain Samuel. "The Narrative of Captain Samuel Mackay." Montreal: McCord Museum, McGill University.

McMillan, Hugh (collection of). Letters from and related to Lieutenant Walter Sutherland, 2KRR NY. Researched and transcribed by Heather Devine and Barbara Rogers from the Haldimand Papers.

Mooers, Lieutenant Benjamin. *Orderly Book of the 2nd Canadian Regiment.* Albany: NYSL, Special Collections and Manuscripts, No.8175.

Morrison, James F., unpublished study of the NYSL, Mss and Special Collections, Audited Accounts, Vol. A.

Rimaldy, Virginia, transcriber. Orders of the Field Jaeger Corps from May 7, 1777 to April 30, 1783.

Smy, Lieutenant-Colonel William A., transcriber and ed. "The Butler Papers: Documents and Papers Relating to Colonel John Butler and his Corps of Rangers 1711–1977." [Smy Transcripts] u.p., 1994.

Willett, Marinus. Col Marinus Willett's Letter and Orderly Book, Fort Rensselaer 1781. Transcribed by Charles Gehring. Typescript, James F. Morrison. Document No.15705, NYSL, Albany, Archives and Manuscripts.

Published Memoirs, Depositions, Diaries, Journals, Poems, and Correspondence — American
(See also State pension depositions noted previously)

Beecher, Raymond, ed. *Letters from a Revolution 1775–1783: A Selection From the Bronck Family Papers.* Albany: The Greene County Historical Society and the NYS American Revolution Bicentennial Commission, 1973.

Glen family. Throop Wilder. "The Glen Letters — That We May Remember." *New York History*, Vol. XXVI, No.3 (July 1945).

Heath, Major-General William. *Memoirs of Major-General William Heath by himself.* Edited by William Abbatt. New York: editor, 1901.

Lesser, Charles H., ed. *The Sinews of Independence — Monthly Strength Report of the Continental Army.* Chicago: The University of Chicago Press, 1976.

Moore, Pliny. "The Year 1781 at Saratoga — Colonel Marinus Willett's Regiment of Levies from the Pliny Moore Papers." *Mooresfield Antiquarian* II (1938): 59–76.

Prenties, Ensign Walter. *Ensign Prenties's Narrative — A Castaway on Cape Breton.* Edited by G.G. Campbell. Toronto: Ryerson Press, 1968.

Van Cortlandt family. *Correspondence of the Van Cortlandt Family of Cortlandt Manor 1748–1800.* Edited and transcribed by Jacob Judd. Tarrytown, NY: Sleepy Hollow Restorations, 1977.

Van Cortlandt, Philip. *The Revolutionary War Memoir and Selected Correspondence of Philip Van Cortlandt.* Edited and transcribed by Jacob Judd. Tarrytown, NY: Sleepy Hollow Restorations, 1976.

Von Papet, Lieutenant Friedrich Julius. *Canada During the American Revolutionary War: Lieutenant Friedrich Julius von Papet's Journal of the Sea Voyage to North America and the Campaign …* Edited by Bruce E. Burgoyne. Westminster, MD: Heritage Books, Inc., 1998.

Washington, George. Papers of George Washington. Library of Congress. http://memory.loc.gov/ammem/gwhtml/gwhome.html

———. *The Writings of George Washington from the Original Manuscript Sources, 1745–1799.* Edited by John C. Fizpatrick. 20 vols. Washington: U.S. Government Printing Office, 1937.

BRITISH, GERMAN, AND CANADIAN

Crysler, Adam. "The Journal of Adam Crysler." In *Loyalist Narratives From Upper Canada.* Edited by James J. Talman. Toronto: Champlain Society, 1946.

Enys, John. *The American Journals of Lt John Enys.* Edited by Elizabeth Cometti. Syracuse: Adirondack Museum and Syracuse University Press, 1976.

Gumersall, Captain Thomas. "Memorial of Thomas Gummersall to Sir John Johnson, Oswego, September 8, 1783." LAC, HP, AddMss28173, 176–78.

Hill, David Haronghyoutye, Fort Hunter War Captain. "A letter from David the Mohawk Chief to Coll. Johnston dated Niagara, November 11th 1781." LAC, HP, MG21, B10, 309–11.

Jefferys, Thomas. *The American Atlas.* 1776. Reprint, Amsterdam: Theatrum Orbis Terrarum, 1974.

Johnson, Colonel Guy. "Account of an Action between a party of seventy four Onondagas & Cayugas under Daiquanda & Lieut Jno [Jos] Clement of Colo Johnson's Department & a party of the Rebels near the German Flats." LAC, HP, AddMss21767.

McDonell, Lieutenant Alexander. Report of Ross Raid. *The Quebec Gazette,* 22 November 1781.

"Narration of Hesse Hanau Jäger Corps in America." Translated by John C. Zuleger. Hessian Papers. Morristown National Historic Park, NJ.

Pargellis, Stanley, ed. *Military Affairs in North America 1748-1765.* Reprint, North Haven, CT: Archon Books, 1969.

Sommer, William, *Affidavit of.* PPGC, VII, 80–81.

Stuart, John. "Letters of the Rev. John Stuart." In *Loyalist Narratives From Upper Canada.* Edited by James J. Talman. Toronto: Champlain Society, 1946.

Sutherland, Lieutenant Walter. "Letters From and Related to Lieutenant Walter Sutherland, 2KRR NY." Researched and transcribed by Heather Devine and Barbara Rogers from the Haldimand Papers. Hugh McMillan Collection.

Tice, Captain Gilbert (Six Nations' Indian Department). *Journal of the Proceedings with the Indians on the late Expedition in October 1781.* LAC, HP, B107, 301.

———. letter to Guy Johnson, dated Niagara, November 15, 1781. LAC, HP, B107, 312.

Von Kreutzbourg, Lieutenant-Colonel Carl. "Relation of the secret expedition under the command of Colonel St. Leger on September ninth, 1781." In the "Narration of Hesse Hanau Jäger Corps in America." Letter O. Translated by John C. Zuleger. Hessian Papers. Morristown National Historic Park, NJ.

————. "Letterbook of LCol Carl von Kreutzbourg, 31Mar77 to 31Oct83." Letter Q. Translated by John C. Zuleger. Lidgerwood Collection. Hessian Papers. Morristown National Historic Park, NJ.

SECONDARY SOURCES — BOOKS

Bellico, Russell P. *Sails and Steam in the Mountains, A Maritime and Military History of Lake George and Lake Champlain.* Fleischmanns, NY: Purple Mountain Press, 1992.

Benton, Nathaniel S. *A History of Herkimer County, Including the Upper Mohawk Valley, from the Earliest period to the Present Time.* Albany: J. Munsell, 1856.

Brice, James R. *History of the Revolutionary War … Brief Account of the Captivity and Cruel Sufferings of Captain Deitz, and John and Robert Brice …* Albany: author, 1851.

Brown, Jennifer S.H. and Wilson. *Colonel William Marsh, Loyalist and Vermont Patriot.* Work in progress, 2007.

Calloway, Colin G. *The American Revolution in Indian Country, Crisis and Diversity in Native American Communities.* Cambridge: Cambridge University Press, 1995.

Campbell Jr., William W. *Annals of Tryon County; or the Border Warfare of New York.* Cherry Valley, NY: The Cherry Valley Gazette Print, 1880.

Corbett, Theodore C. *A Clash of Cultures on the Warpath of the Nations, The Colonial Wars in the Hudson-Champlain Valley.* Fleischmanns, NY: Purple Mountain Press, Ltd., 2002.

Creighton, Donald. *The Empire of the St. Lawrence.* Toronto: Macmillan Company of Canada Limited, 1956.

Cruikshank, Ernest A. and Gavin K. Watt, *The History and Master Roll of The King's Royal Regiment of New York.* Revised edition. Campbellville, ON: Global Heritage Press, 2006. Previous edition, *King's Royal Regiment of New York with the Additions of an Index, Appendices and a Master Muster Roll.* Toronto: Gavin K. Watt, 1984. Regimental history originally published, *OHSPR*, 27 (1931).

————. *Butler's Rangers: The Revolutionary Period.* 1893. Reprint, Niagara Falls, ON: Lundy's Lane Historical Society, 1975.

De Puy, Henry. *Ethan Allen and the Green-Mountain Heroes of '76.* Buffalo: Phinney & Co., 1853.

Devine, E.J. (S.J.) *Historic Caughnawaga.* Montreal: Messenger Press, 1922.

Dictionary of Canadian Biography. http://www.biographi.ca/index-e.html.

Egly Jr., T.W. *History of the First New York Regiment.* Hampton, NH: Peter E. Randall, 1981.

———. *General Schuyler's Guard.* Author, 1986.

Everest, Allan S. *North Country Pioneer: Pliny Moore of Champlain, New York.* Plattsburgh: Clinton County Historical Association, 1990.

Famighetti, Robert. "Estimated Population of American Colonies, 1630–1780." In *1998 Word Almanac and Book of Facts.* New York: World Almanac, 1998.

Fraser, J. *Skulking for the King, A Loyalist Plot.* Erin, ON: Boston Mills Press, 1985.

Frazier, Patrick. *The Mohicans of Stockbridge.* Lincoln, NE and London: University of Nebraska Press, 1992.

Fryer, Mary Beacock. *Loyalist Spy: The Experiences of Captain John Walden Meyers During the American Revolution.* Brockville, ON: Besancourt Publishers, 1974.

———. *Buckskin Pimpernel: The Exploits of Justus Sherwood Loyalist Spy.* Toronto: Dundurn Press, 1981.

———. *Allan Maclean, Jacobite General, The Life of an Eighteenth Century Career Soldier.* Toronto: Dundurn Press, 1987.

———. *King's Men: The Soldier Founders of Ontario.* Toronto: Dundurn Press Limited, 1980.

Glatthaar, Joseph T. and James Kirby Martin. *Forgotten Allies: The Oneida Indians and the American Revolution.* New York: Hill and Wang, 2006.

Graymont, Barbara. *The Iroquois in the American Revolution.* Syracuse: Syracuse University Press, 1972.

Halsey, Francis Whiting. *The Old New York Frontier: Its Wars with Indians and Tories, Its Missionary Schools, Pioneers and Land Titles.* New York: Charles Scribner's Sons, 1917.

Hanson, Willis T. *A History of Schenectady During the Revolution to which is appended a Contribution to the Individual Records of the Inhabitants of the Schenectady District During that Period.* Author, 1916.

Hepson, George H. *Herrick's Rangers.* Bennington: Bennington Museum Series #1, n.d.

Houlding, J.A. "The King's Service: The Officers of the British Army, 1735–1792." n.p., n.d.

Huey, Lois M. and Bonnie Pulis. *Molly Brant, A Legacy of Her Own.* Youngstown, NY: Old Fort Niagara Association, 1997.

Jackson, H.M. *Rogers' Rangers, A History.* Toronto: author, 1953.

———. *Justus Sherwood: Soldier, Loyalist and Negotiator.* Toronto: author, 1958.

Johnson, Ken D. *The Bloodied Mohawk: The American Revolution in the Words of Fort Plank's Defenders and Other Mohawk Valley Partisans.* Rockport, MA: Picton Press, 2000.

Keesler, M. Paul. *Kuyahoora, Discovering West Canada Valley.* Newport, NY: Mid-York Sportsman, Inc., 1999.

Kelsay, Isabel Thompson. *Joseph Brant 1743–1807 Man of Two Worlds.* Syracuse: Syracuse University Press, 1984.

Ketchum, Richard M. *Decisive Day, The Battle for Bunker Hill.* Doubleday & Company, Inc., 1962.

Kidder, Frederic. *History of the First New Hampshire Regiment in the War of the Revolution.* 1868. Reprint, Hampton, NH: Peter E. Randall, 1973.

Lanctot, Gustave. *Canada & the American Revolution, 1774–1783.* Translated by Margaret M. Cameron. London: George G. Harrap & Co. Ltd, 1967.

Leslie, Vernon. *The Battle of Minisink: A Revolutionary War Engagement in the Upper Delaware Valley.* Middletown, NY: T. Emmett Henderson, 1976.

Lossing, Benson J. *The Pictorial Field-Book of the Revolution or, Illustrations, by Pen and Pencil, of the History, Biography, Scenery, Relics, and Traditions of the War for Independence*. 2 vols. New York: Harper and Brothers, 1851.

Lowenthal, Larry. *Marinus Willett, Defender of the Northern Frontier. New Yorkers and the Revolution*. Fleischmanns, NY: Purple Mountain Press, 2000.

Luzader, John F. "Construction and Military History." In *Fort Stanwix: History, Historic Furnishing, and Historic Structure Reports*. Washington: Office of Park Historic Preservation, National Park Service, U.S. Department of the Interior, 1976.

Mackesy, Piers. *The War for America 1775–1783*. Lincoln, NE and London: University of Nebraska Press, 1992.

Malcomson, Robert. *Warships of the Great Lakes 1754–1834*. London: Chatham Publishing, 2001.

Mathews, Hazel C. *Frontier Spies*. Fort Myers: Hazel C. Mathews, 1971.

McIlwraith, Jean N. "Sir Frederick Haldimand." In *The Makers of Canada, Vol. 3*. 11 vols. Toronto: Morang & Co., Limited, 1911.

Morrison, James F. *A History of Fulton County in the Revolution*. Gloversville, NY: Author, 1977.

———. *The Mohawk Valley in 1781, a Brief History of the Battles, Skirmishes and Raids*. Author, 1991

———. *Colonel Jacob Klock's Regiment, Tryon County Militia*. Author, 1992.

———. *The Battle of New Dorlach, Tryon County July 10, 1781 — Now Known as Sharon Springs, Schoharie County*. Gloversville, NY: Author, 1991.

Nosworthy, Brent. *Anatomy of Victory & Battle Tactics 1689–1763*. New York: Hippocrene Books, 1990.

O'Connor, Jeff. *Thunder in the Valley*. Schoharie, NY: The Schoharie County Historical Society, 2002.

Parkman, Francis. *Montcalm and Wolfe*. 2 vols. Boston: Little, Brown, 1884.

Reuter, Claus. *Brunswick Troops in North America, 1776–1783 — Index of all Soldiers Who remained in North America.* Toronto: German-Canadian Museum of Applied History, n.d.

Roberts, Robert B. *New York's Forts in the Revolution.* London and Toronto: Associated University Presses, 1980.

Senior, Hereward and John Ruch, eds. *The Loyalists of Quebec 1774–1825: A Forgotten History.* Montreal: Heritage Branch, UEL Association of Canada, 1989.

Siebert, Wilbur H. *The Loyalists and Six Nation Indians in the Niagara Peninsula.* Ottawa: The Royal Society of Canada, 1935.

Simms, Jeptha R. *Frontiersman of New York Showing Customs of the Indians, Vicissitudes of the Pioneer White Settlers and Border Strife in Two Wars with a Great Variety of Romantic and Thrilling Stories Never Before Published.* 2 vols. Albany: George C. Riggs, 1883.

———. *History of Schoharie County, and Border Wars of New York; Containing also a Sketch of the Causes Which Led to the American Revolution; etc...* Albany: Munsell & Tanner, 1845.

———. *Trappers of New York: or, A Biography of Nicholas Stoner and Nathaniel Foster; Together with Anecdotes of Other Celebrated Hunters and Some Account of Sir William Johnson and His Style of Living.* Albany: J. Munsell, 1871.

Smy, Lieutenant Colonel William A. *An Annotated Nominal Roll of Butler's Rangers 1777–1784 with Docu-mentary Sources.* St. Catharines: Friends of the Loyalist Collection at Brock University, 2004.

Stanley, George F.G. *Canada Invaded 1775–1776.* Toronto and Sarasota: Samuel Stevens Hakkert and Company, 1977.

Stevens, Paul L. *A King's Colonel at Niagara 1774–1776.* Youngstown: Old Fort Niagara Association, 1987.

Stone, William L. *Life of Joseph Brant — Thayendanegea — Including the Indian Wars of the American Revolution.* 2 vols. New York: Alexander V. Blake, 1838.

Taylor, Alan. *The Divided Ground: Indians, Settlers, and the Northern Borderland of the American Revolution.* New York: Vintage Books, 2007.

Thomas, Earle. *Sir John Johnson, Loyalist Baronet.* Toronto: Dundurn Press, 1986.

Thomas, Howard. *Marinus Willett, Soldier-Patriot 1740–1830.* Prospect, NY: Prospect Books, 1954.

Tuckerman, Bayard. *Life of General Philip Schuyler, 1733–1804.* New York: Dodd, Mead and Company, 1903.

Van Doren, Carl. *Mutiny in January: The Story of a Crisis in the Continental Army.* New York: Viking Press, 1943.

Washington, Ida H. and Paul A. *Carleton's Raid.* Canaan, NH: Phoenix Publishing, 1977.

Watt, Gavin K. and James F. Morrison. *The British Campaign of 1777 – Volume 1, The St. Leger Expedition. The Forces of the Crown and Congress.* Second ed. Campbellville, ON: Global Heritage Press, 2003.

Watt, Gavin K. with research assistance by James F. Morrison. *The Burning of the Valleys, Daring Raids from Canada Against the New York Frontier in the Fall of 1780.* Toronto: Dundurn Press, 1997.

———. *Rebellion in the Mohawk Valley, the St. Leger Expedition of 1777.* Toronto: Dundurn Press, 2002.

———. *The Flockey 13 August 1777 — The Defeat of the Tory Uprising in the Schoharie Valley.* King City, ON: author, 2002.

Wells, Frederic P. *History of Newbury, Vermont, From the Discovery of the Coös Country to Present Time.* St. Johnsbury, VT: The Caledonian Company, 1902.

Westcott, Cynthia. *The Gardener's Bug Book.* Garden City, NY: American Garden Guild and Doubleday and Company, 1956.

Wilhelmy, Jean-Pierre. *German Mercenaries in Canada.* Beloeil, QC: Maison des Mots, 1985.

Willett, William M. *A Narrative of the Military Actions of Colonel Marinus Willett, Taken Chiefly from His Own Manuscript.* New York: G.&C.&H. Carvill, 1831.

Williamson, Chilton. *Vermont in Quandary, 1763–1825*. Montpelier, VT: Vermont Historical Society, 1949.

Wright, Robert K. Jr. *The Continental Army*. Washington: Army Lineage Series, Centre of Military History, United States Army, 1989.

Young, Richard J. "Blockhouses in Canada, 1749–1841: A Comparative Report and Catalogue." In *Canadian Historic Sites: Occasional Papers in Archaeology and History*. Ottawa: Parks Canada, 1980.

SECONDARY SOURCES
Articles, Monographs, Booklets, Newsletters, Catalogues, and Theses

Bond, C.C.J. "The British Base at Carleton Island." *OHSPR* 52 (1960.)

Briggs, Charles Burton. "A Chronology of the Fulton County Court House and the Fulton County Jail." Fulton County Bar Association, Feb. 16, 1972.

Burleigh, H.C. *Deforests of Avesnes and Kast, McGinness*. Author, n.d.

Christman, Richard. "225 Years Ago: Torch, Tomahawk Ravage Cobleskill." *Schoharie County Historical Review* (Spring 2003).

Cruikshank, Ernest A. "The Coming of the Loyalist Mohawks to the Bay of Quinte." *OHSPR* 26 (1930).

———. "The Adventures of Roger Stevens, A Forgotten Loyalist Pioneer in Upper Canada." *OHSPR* 33 (1939).

Efner, William B., "Warfare in the Mohawk Valley Transcriptions from the Pennsylvania Gazette, 1780–1783." Personal handout. Schenectady, 1948.

Green, Ernest. "Gilbert Tice, U.E." *OHSPR* 21 (1924).

Hartley, Robert M. "Some History, Traditions, Folklore of the Town of Florida." Mohawk Valley Historical Association 1936 Yearbook.

Hughes, Alun. "John Butler and Early Settlement on the West Bank of the Niagara River." *The Butler Bicentenary, Commemorating the 200th Anniversary of the Death of Colonel John Butler.* Colonel John Butler Branch, United Empire Loyalists' Association of Canada, 1997.

Koettertiz, John B. "Andrew Finck, Major in the Revolutionary Wars." Address delivered to The Herkimer County Historical Society, 1897.

Mackesy, Piers. "Could the British Have Won the War of Independence?" Bland-Lee Lecture, Clark University, 1975.

Miller, Harold H. "The Dietz Massacre." N.p., March 2004.

Mitchell, Harry E. "Battle of New Dorlach." N.p., November 3, 1914.

Morrison, James F., ed. "Captain Christian House's Company (Seventh Company) Colonel Jacob Klock's Regiment of Tryon County Militia (Second Regiment)." Author, July 1976.

———. "The Ambush of Lieutenant Solomon Woodworth and his Party of Scouts." Author, n.p., n.d.

———. *Colonel James Livingston, The Forgotten Livingston Patriot of the War of Independence.* Johnstown: Colonel James Livingston Historic Research Committee, 1988.

———. "Men from the Third Battalion [TCM] Who Served in the Levies." *TCMN*, Vol. XIII, No.4 (1993).

———. *The Battle of Johnstown, October 25th, 1781.* Gloversville, NY: Third Battalion of Tryon County Militia, 1991.

———. *Colonel Jacob Klock's Regiment, Tryon County Militia.* Gloversville, NY: author, 1992.

O'Connor, Jeff. "The Story of Fort DuBoise, 1779–1781." *Schoharie County Historical Review* (Spring 1999).

"Pension Application of John Woolaver." Stone Arabia Battle Chapter (Sons of the American Revolution) Newsletter (September 1998.)

Richard-Morrow, Kevin. "The Attempt to Abduct General Philip Schuyler and the Great Kidnap Plot of 1781." *The Burning Issues,* Vol. 14, No.1 (March 2006).

Robertson, John K. "39 lashes on his naked back ... Military Justice in the Revolutionary War Armies." *The Brigade Dispatch*, vols. XXXIII and XXXIV. Milford, CT: Brigade of the American Revolution, 2003/2004.

Rioux, Christian. "The Royal Regiment of Artillery in Quebec City." *History and Archaeology* 57. National Historic Parks and Sites Branch. Environment Canada. Ottawa, 1982.

Ruch, John. "Blacks Among the Loyalists." In *The Loyalists of Quebec, 1774–1825, A Forgotten History*. Montreal: Heritage Branch, United Empire Loyalists' Association of Canada, 1989.

Stacey, Kim. "No One Harms Me with Impunity — The History, Organization, and Biographies of the 84th Regiment of Foot (Royal Highland Emigrants) and Young Royal Highlanders, During the Revolutionary War 1775–1784." Manuscript in progress, 1994.

Stevens, Paul L., "His Majesty's 'Savage' Allies: British Policy and the Northern Indians During the Revolutionary War — The Carleton Years, 1774–1778." Doctoral diss., State University of New York at Buffalo.

Stuart, E. Rae. "Jessup's Rangers as a Factor in Loyalist Settlement." *Three History Theses.* Toronto: Ontario Deptartment of Public Records and Archives, 1961.

Sullivan, Mark. "Obituaries of Schoharie County Veterans." *Schoharie County Historical Review* (Fall-Winter 1997).

Tryon County Militia Newsletter. Vol. I, No.1 (1983); Vol. I, No.2 (1983); Vol. I, No.10 (1983); Vol. II, No.8 (1984); Vol. II, No.9 (1984); Vol. II, No.10 (1984); Vol. V, No.4 (1986); Vol. V, No.6 (1986); Vol. VI, No.7 (1987); Vol. VII, No.3 (1988); Vol. XIII, No.10 (1993); Vol. XV, No.8 (1995); Vol. XIX, No.5 (1999); Vol. XIX, No.6 (1999); Vol. XIX, No.10 (1999); Vol. XXI, No.5 (2000).

Williams, Rev. Eleazer. "The Life of Colonel Louis Cook." u.p., circa 1851. Transcribed by Darren Bonaparte, 2001.

Websites

Baldwin, Frederick W. "The Hazen Military Road." http://rootsweb.ancestry.com/~vermont/HistoryHazenMilitaryRoad.

Biography of George Clinton. http://Robinsonlibrary.com/america/unitedstates/1783C ontinentalVillage.

DePold, Hans, Bolton Town Historian. htttp://www.connecticutsar.org.

Decker, Lew. "Fulton County Court House." http://carogatimes.com.

Dictionary of Units of Measure. http://www.unc.edu/~rowlett/units/.

Eckler, Captain Henry of Herkimer County. Eckler, Bonnie, 1968. Adapted by Cooper, Eunice, 1972. Yorker Club Convention, NYHS Convention. http://Rootsweb. com/%7Enyherkim/eckler.

Famous Americans. http://famousamericans.net/samuelrobinson.

Fort Klock Historic Restoration. http://threerivershms.com. (Acessed January 2005.)

Fulton County, New York, military page: http://rootsweb.com/~nyfulton/Military. (Accessed December 2004.)

Henretta, James A. "American Revolution." Microsoft® Encarta® Online Encyclopedia 2005. http://encarta.msn.com © 1997–2005 Microsoft Corporation.

Johnson, Ken D. "In Defense of the Facts." http://geocities.com/fortplankhistorian. (Accessed January 2005.)

Loyalist Institute, The. http://royalprovincial.com.

Morrison, James F. and Berry Enterprises. Morrison's Pensions. http://morrisonspensions. org.

Parrott report. http://collectionscanada.ca/education.

Stark, John, biographical information.
http://seacoastnh.com/Famous_People/Framers_of_Freedom/John_Stark.
http://virtualvermont.com/history/jstark.html

Ten Broeck, Abraham. Biographical notes. Stefan Bielinski. http://www.nysm.nysed. gov/albany/bios/t/abtbroeck6.html. (Accessed January 1, 2005.)

Town of Caroga, NY. http://www.carogatimes.com/Johnstown. (Accessed November 2004.)

Tryon County Militia. http://www.geocities.com/tryoncountymilitia/history. (Accessed December 2004.)

Tryon County New York General website. http://www.rootsweb.com/~nytryon/l1782. html. (Accessed December 2004.)

Yale University website. http://yale.edu/lawweb/avalon/states/vt01.

INDEX

1. All page entries in bold indicate that the subject is in an image or on a map.
2. A Native's affiliation is designated by a two- or three-letter abbreviation after his/her name, e.g. Abenaki (Ab); Delaware (De); Kahnawake (Kah); Tuscarora (Tu).

Abductions, 18, 19, 88, 117, 174, 210, 217, 225, 232, 242, 245–48

Abeel, Anthony, 105, 137

Abeel, David, 105, 137

Albany, NY, Attitudes Regarding, 113, 287, 289, 293, 294, 370–71

Allen, Ebenezer, 2, 50, 51, 125

Allen, Ethan, 17, 38, 39, **40**–43, 49, 50, 77, 88, 91, 108, 110, 111, 119, 121, 131, 137, 144, 176, 179, 218, 221, 240, 251, 301, 379, 380

Allen, Ira, 17, 39, **40**, 41, 50, 75, 100, 110, 111, 122, 123, 136, 201, 240, 264, 311, 363, 382, 385, 389

Ancrum, William, 315, 316

Anderson, Joseph, 16, 145, 146

Anguish, John, 405

Ansley, Amos, 79

Anthony's Nose, NY, **172**, 325

Antill, Edward, 166, 170, 173

Argusville, NY, **172**, 323

Arlington, VT, **79**, 137, 156, 216, 262

Army
British, 23, 25, 39, 45, 51, 55, 84
Artillery/Artillerists, 24, 34, 56–58, 80, 263
Engineers, 46, 56, 75, 116, 369

8th (King's) Regt, 16, 33, 73, 102, 124, 168, 169, 200, 259, 299, 315, 327, 354, 409
Light Coy, 259

29th Regt, 33, 51, 73, 376, 401, 404
Light Coy, 311, 368, 369, 375, 380, 398

31st Regt, 33, 200, 255
Light Coy, 311, 363, 369, 375, 376, 380, 384, 389, 392, 393

34th Regt, 16, 47, 33, 66, 80, 83, 102, 245, 281, 296, 327, 355, 364, 369, 376, 381, 393, 404, 409

44th Regt, 35, 200, 400
Light Coy, 311, 363, 369, 375, 376, 392, 398

47th, 33, 102, 245, 280

53rd Regt, 33, 80, 245, 404

60th (Royal Americans) Regt (RA), 4, 15, 22, 26, 46

84th (RHE), 14, 34, 45, 48, **49**, 64, 75, 80, 102, 103, 117, **151**, 200, 219, 226, 251, 298, 315, 317, 327, 340, 343, 355, 404, 407, 408

French, 24, 33, 54, 55, 63, 69, 73, 174, 189, 199, 216, 224, 237
Canadien Militia, 24, 25, 54, 55

German, 229
Anhalt-Zerbst, 35, 255
Brunswick Regt, 33, 35, 404
Von Barner's Jägers, **384**
Hesse Cassel Regts, 35
Hesse Hanau
Artillery, 34, 263
Jäger Regt, 16, 34, 35, 164, 287, 295, 297, 315, 345, 362, 363, **368**, 369, 375, 376, 380, 381, **384**, 385, 388, 389, 392, 397, 398, 409

Provincial, 23, 45, 51, 64
Adams's Rangers (AR), 14, 46, 64
American Volunteers (AV) (McAlpin's), 14, 46, 64, 369
Butler's Rangers (BR), 14, 16, 34, 45, 48, 76, 81, 86, 102–06, 111, 121, 124, 125, 131, 137, 154, 155, 157, 160, 168, 179, 189, 196, 199, 202, 218, 221, 223, 228, 236, 239, 255–57, 260, 264, 279, 280, 286, 287, 297–300, 313, 317, 318, 327, 329, 336, 337, 341, 343, 353, 369, 405
McDonell's Coy, 145

9th Coy, 160, 179, 221, 280
10th Coy, 179, 221, 255, 260, 279, 280, 287, 297
Drummond's Independent Coy, 64
Fraser's Independent Coy, 51, 64, 65, 73
Herkimer's Bateaux Coy, 80, 81, 145, 211
King's Loyal Americans (KLA), 14, 16, 45, 48, 51, 83, 87, 244, 245, 247, 369, **370**, 375, 376, 381, 384, 386, 398
King's Rangers (1st Bn), 65
King's Rangers (2nd Bn) (2KR), 14, 16, 35, 51, 74, 87–89, 117, 200, 202, 226, 245, 248, 297, 363, 369, 376, 392, 398
King's Royal Regt of New York (1st Bn) (1KRR), 14, 16, 34, 44–48, 59, 73, 80, 83, 92, 96, 108, 117, 145, 146, 155, 161, 169, 296, 298, 300, 316, 365, 381, 397, 398, 405
King's Royal Regt of New York (2nd Bn) (2KRR), 14, 16, 34, 46, 47, 59, 73, 83, 109, 116, 154, 169, 178, 251, 279, 295, 296, 298, 314–315, 323, 327, 334, 335, 343, 345, 355, 403–05, 407
   Arming of, 48, 62, 315
   Officers for, 64, 65, 274
Leake's Independent Coy (LIC), 15, 46, 59, 110, 295, 296, 315, 327, 351
Loyal Volunteers (LV), 15, 45, 280
Quebec Militia, 33, 35, 63, 83
Queen's Loyal Rangers (QLR), 15, 16, 45, 48, 64, 65, 102, 109, 137, 143, 151, 160, 219, 226, 250, 262, 363, 369, 390, 400
Royal Highland Emigrants, *see* 84th Regt
United States
   Continental, 33, 53, 54, 68, 73, 80, 96, 99, 221, 254
   Artillery, 81

Lamb's 2nd Regt, 18
Moodie's Coy, 66, 99, 127, 139, 170, 187, 207, 242, 272, 279, 330, 337, 338, 349, 351, 358, 359
Third Regt, 366, 382
Engineers, 142, 154
Massachusetts, 69, 271, 382, 394
New Hampshire Brigade, 15, 69, 331, 332, 366, 367, 371, 377, 378, 382, 383, 387, 393, 394
New York, 17, 61, 70, 90, 244,
   1st Regt (1NY), 15, 17, 68, 71, 78, 81, 82, 98, 99, 110, 118, 126, 130, 142–44, 148, 152, 165, 181, 182, 195, 247
   2nd Regt (2NY), 17, 61, 68, 70, 81, 85, 86, 99, 101, 105, 106, 113, 115, 117, 118, 126, 129, 130, 158, 161, 165, 202, 231–33, 236, 241, 242, 254, 261
   3rd Regt (3NY), 61, 98
   4th Regt, 59, 66, 68
   5th Regt, 68, 97
   Hazen's Canadian Regt, 14, 148, 157, 158, 165, 166, 170, 173, 294, 295
Levies, 99, 101
   Massachusetts, 51, 167, 169, 212, 214, 227, 232, 237, 241, 244, 253, 254, 258, 261, 266, 276, 277, 287, 300, 305, 316, 346, 359, 378, 403
      Clark's Coy, 216, 279, 334
      Heacock's Coy, 278, 282, 334
   New York, 51, 90, 97, 99, 107–10, 114, 125, 167, 210, 276
      Pawling's, 115, 188
      Weissenfels', 17, 242, 261, 286, 292, 293, 300, 315, 360, 363, 377, 382

Willett's (WL), 15, 17, 129, 130, 132–34, 141, 154, 170, 191–98, 207, 211, 214, 254, 276, 279, 305, 377, 382
   Conine's Coy, 133, 138, 139, 165, 248
   Duboise's Coy, 133, 134, 138, 155, 165, 276
   Dunham's Coy, 132, 133, 138, 187, 208
   Elsworth's Coy, 133, 138, 151, 165, 188, 189, 330, 347
   Gray's, Coy, 138, 187, 208
   Gros's Coy, 17, 134, 135, 138, 148, 155, 168, 191, 195, 234, 248, 282, 322, 330, 350
   Hale's Coy, 241, 248
   Harrison's Coy, 248, 273
   Livingston's Coy, 248, 302, 348
   Marshall's Coy, 133, 159
   McKean's Coy, 133, 191, 193
   Putman's Coy, 133, 148, 203, 248, 282, 283, 322, 330, 337
   Skinner's Coy, 242, 248, 273, 302
   Van Rensselaer's Coy, 248, 273
   Whelp's Coy, 132, 134, 138, 165, 187, 273, 330, 332
   White's Coy, 133, 161, 187, 248, 346, 351
   Woodworth's Coy, 17, 190, 281, 333
   Wright's Coy, 248, 276
Militia, 96, 100, 377
   Massachusetts, 28, 53, 55, 210, 365, 377
   New Hampshire, 55, 167, 377, 400
   New York, 44, 53, 77, 107, 114, 167, 377
      Albany County, 14, 51, 383,
      1st Brigade, 17, 90, 388

2nd Brigade, 17, 44, 305, 331, 332, 367, 373, 388

1st Regt (1ACM), 88, 285, 347, 349

2nd Regt (2ACM), 14, 82, 134, 147, 173, 178, 212, 257, 320, 332, 347, 349, 353, 359, 362, 365, 387

3rd Regt (3ACM), 133, 274, 293, 347, 349

4th Regt (4ACM), 134, 178, 257, 371, 372, 387

6th Regt (6ACM), 88, 134, 272

7th Regt (7ACM), 134, 387

8th Regt (8ACM), 134, 373, 387

9th Regt (9ACM), 133, 134

11th Regt (11ACM), 60, 105, 133, 137, 362

12th Regt (12ACM), 133, 157, 160, 219

13th Regt (13ACM), 108, 133, 227, 363

14th Regt (14ACM), 133, 349, 388

15th Regt (15ACM), 17, 134, 148, 149, 194, 373

16th Regt (16ACM), 17, 110, 132, 133, 161, 233

17th Regt (17ACM), 133, 142, 241

Schenectady Artillery Coy, 94, 242, 279

Van Slyck's Coy, 147, 345

Tryon County Brigade, 15, 17, 44, 51, 89, 98, 124, 135, 182–86, 195, 205, 232, 271, 359

1st Regt (1TCM), 70, 112, 135, 153, 191, 194, 241, 303, 330, 349, 350, 359

2nd Regt (2TCM), 15, 17, 70, 109, 140, 153, 224, 234, 259, 268, 316, 334, 342, 350, 359, 403

3rd Regt (3TCM), 15, 90, 135, 282, 323, 324, 328, 329, 350, 359

Littel's Coy, 332, 346

Fonda's Exempts, 330, 331

4th Regt (4TCM), 70, 242, 243, 285, 313, 330, 350, 359

Ulster County, 15, 91, 115, 256, 257

Vermont, 167, 295, 382, 395

Green Mountain Boys, 17, 39, 40, 42, 43, 111, 168, 251, 379, 388, 402

Abenaki Rangers, 83, 135

Warner's Continental Regt, 40, 51, 261, 271

Arden, Humphrey, 47, 82, 211, 265, 281

Arnold, Benedict, 50, 62, 222

Awl, Johannes, 159

Ball, Jacob, 179

Ball, Peter, 90, 179

Ballstown, NY, 51, **79**, 123, 132, 133, 138, 142, 157, 160, 179, 187, 200, 202, 219, 238, 242, 248, 264, 292, 293, **301**, 305, 315, 318, 320, 346, 360

Bangle, Adam, 405

Bangle, John, 405

Barlow, Abner, 89, 223

Batcheller, Zeph, 332

Battles/Skirmishes
Bennington 1777, 41, 44, 65, 167, 364

Cowpens 1781, 82

Hall Battle 1781, 334–46, 358, 387, 407–09

Klock's Field 1780, 51, 345

Lampman's Farm 1781, 234–39, 343

Monbackers 1781, 250, **253**, 255–57

New Dorlach 1781, 190–97

Oriskany 1777, 67, 98, 135, 234, 328, 342

Ticonderoga 1758, 23, 97, **381**

Woodworth Ambush 1781, 281–85

Yorktown 1781, *see* Cornwallis

Bayley, Jacob, 17, 42, 83, 88, 109, 135, 136, 225, 262, 301

Beaver Dam, NY, **79**, 90, 92, 118, **148**, 149, 203, 274–77, 293

Becker, Catharine, 229, 230

Becker, Henry, 229

Becker, Johannes, **228**–30

Becker, John, 229

Beeckman, John, 178, 210

Beeckman, John H., 247

Bell, Frederick, 345

Bell, Mrs., 359, 360

Bell, Nicholas, 359, 360

Bell, Thomas, 345

Bellinger family, 234

Bellinger, (Colonel) Peter, 70, 133, 350

Bellinger, Peter, 359, 360

Bennington, VT, **79**, 142, 143, 225, 244, 245, 253, 373

Bettys, Abigail, 264

Bettys, Joseph, 16, 91, 118, 157, 160, 171, 210, 218, 221, 232, 233, 239, 258, 259, 262, 264, 269, 285

Bishop, John Sr., 249

Black Recruits, 99, 118, 179, 211

Blair, John, 110, 132, 162

Bleecker, John, 210, 218, 244, 245

Blockhouses, **63**, **141**, **226**, **291**

Bockee, Jacob, 203, 320,

Borthwick, John, 275

Bothum, Elijah, 137, 151, 210

Bowman, Godleap, 405

Bowman, Martis, 405

Bradt, Andrew, 81, 106, 179, 221, 264, 274, 280

Bradt, John, 76

Brant, Henry, 323

Brant, Joseph Thayendanegea (Mo), 16, 53, 67, 76, 81, **84**, 85, 87, 92, 93, 103, 104, 115, 130, 131, 139, 147,

148, 189, 191, 198, 222,
280, 297, 319
Brant, Mary/Molly Wary
Gonwatsijayenni (Mo), 67,
104, 178, 259
Brattleborough, VT, 42, **79**
Breadbake, John, 341, 359
Brice, John and Robert, 275
Brown, Conradt, 191, 206, 405
Bucks Island, *see* Carleton Island
Burgoyne, John, 28, 33, 40, 45, 47,
48, 81, 111, 147, 229, 263
Capitulation, 34, 46, 311
Buskirk, Jacob, 300
Butler, Catherine, 89
Butler, John, 16, 34, 36, 46, 53,
81, 102–104, 106, 121, 137,
145, 179, 202, 218, 239,
260, 274, 279–81, 287,
297–99, 313, 318
Butler, Thomas, 81, 104, 106,
179, 221
Butler, Walter, 16, 113, 121, 144,
145, 179, 223, 239, 255,
260, 287, 297, 299, 318,
336, 352, 395, 396, 409
Death of, 353, 354, 357–59
Butterfield, James, 190–92

Caldwell (sloop), 315, 317, 321
Caldwell, William, 16, 218, 236,
250, 255–57, 280
Campbell, Alexander, 329
Campbell, John, 16, 36, 48, 80, 81,
83, 93, 201, 202, 211, 218
Canadians (Anglophones), 30,
31, 35, 63
Canadiens (Francophones), 24, 25,
30–33, 35, 37, 55, 61, 63,
72, 73, 87, 158, 165, **189**,
190, 294, 295
Canajoharie, NY, 86, 133, 138,
166, **172**, 177, 184, 185,
203, 286, 299, 325
Cansopi (De?), 131
Cantine, John, 256, 257
Carleton (schooner), 219, **297**, 314,
390, **391**, 392, 398, 401
Carleton, Christopher, 51, 58, 95,
Carleton, Sir Guy, 16, 29, 30,
33–35, 45, 60, 81, 263
Carleton Island, 56, 59, 62, 67, 76,
83, 92, 93, 103, 119, 120,
125, 138, 140, 146, 209, 251,
259, **263**, 267, 281, 283, 296,
298, 299, 317, 329, 335, 349,
350, 355, 401, 407
Carr, Daniel, 245

Carscallen, Edward, 137
Carter/Garter, John, 403
Casler, Richard, 354
Castle Town/Castleton (VT), **41**,
176, 269, 286, 373, 385
Catskill, NY, **79**, 132, 133, 138,
139, **148**, 165, 187, 212,
248, **253**, 305
Caswell, Lemuel, 363
Caughnawaga, NY, **79**, 148, 166,
170, **172**, 173, 291, 294,
330, 343
Causland, James, 102
Chambers, William, 16, 255, 297,
314, 376, 379, 385, 386,
390, 392, 396, 398, 400, 401
Cherry Valley, NY, 66, 112, **172**,
190, 194, 195, 218, 271,
301, 322
Chimney Point, NY, **41**, 391, 393,
397, 398
Chittenden, Thomas, 17, 39, 41,
111, 136, 156, 188, 199,
214–16, 238, 249, 253, 264,
269, 270, 301, 312, 365,
372, 385, 391, 395, 399
Church, Oliver, 157, 168
Clark, George Rogers, 104, 160, 297
Clark, Samuel, 341, 342, 406
Claus, Daniel, 16, 36, 75, 92, 103,
109, 139, 181, 200, 201,
211, 276
Claverack, NY, **79**, 133, 134, 266,
332, 373, 387
Clement, Joseph, 282, 283
Clinton, George, 17, **44**, 60, 61,
70, 77, 81, 82, 91, 94, 97–99,
101, 107–108, 113, 115,
118, 125, 128, 130–131,
143, 153, 156, 158, 160,
162, 165, 183, 184, 186–88,
203, 211–13, 216, 224, 232,
236, 242, 244, 248, 251,
258, 261, 265, 268, 270–73,
277, 278, 285, 288, 290,
292, 301, 311–312, **332**,
362, 364–67, 371, 372, 374,
383, 386–88, 392–95
Clinton, Sir Henry, 16, 28, 43, **44**,
62, 65, 66, 82, 84, 91, 121,
131, 158, 174, 201, 222,
237, 239, 240, 248, 274,
288, 300, 301, 311, 313,
363, 366, 379, 400, 402
Clinton, James, 17, 70, 81, 86, 95,
99, 100, 106–107, 115, 120,
126, 128, 130–131, 139,
142, 147, 152, 154, 158,

161, 165–166, 170–171,
177, 181–182, 199, 203,
206, 209, 220, 228, 245,
247, 259, 261, 268
Clossen, Caleb, 16, 108, 221,
363, 380
Clyde, Samuel, 70, 134, 230
Cobleskill, NY, **148**, 203, 230, 268,
271, 299
Cochran, Robert, 17, 69, 105, 106,
113, 117, 119, 124–29, 139
Cockley, John, 247
Coenradt/Conradt, John, 405
Cohoes, *see* Cöos
Colonel Louis Atayataghronghta
(Kah), 17, **127**, 128, 139,
161, 253, **354**, 401
Conine, Philip, 133, 212, 248
Conspiracy Commissions
Albany County, 59–61, 71,
78, 82, 90, 92, 99, 105, 118,
131, 141, 142, 147, 155–57,
161, 171, 190, 210, 220,
221, 225, 233, 242, 247,
250, 254, 272, 285, 294, 374
Schenectady, 157, 160, 277,
288, 331
Tryon County, 17, 143, 321
Continental Congress, 30, 39, 40,
42, 43, 45, 53, 54, 71, 72, 77,
85, 91, 99–101, 110, 120,
123, 141, 162, 166, 167, 178,
188, 201, 239, 240, 242, 272,
301, 303, 372, 377, 395, 399
Conyne, Peter, 90
Cooeyman's, NY, 60, **79**, 107,
146, 147
Coon, John, 157
Cook, Severinus, 194
Cöos Region (VT), 18, **41**, 62, 83,
88, 109, 136, 175, 190, 225,
240, 368
Coote, Thomas, 299, 315
Copeman, Abraham, 330, 350, 359,
Cornwallis, Earl Charles, 266, 352,
377, 383, 385, 389, 391, 393,
395, 399–402
Cough, John Sr., 316, 317, 373, 374
Cough, John Jr., 316, 317, 379, 381
Coughman, David, 405
Coughman, Jacob, 405
Counties, New York
Albany, 91, 114, 132, **172**, 287,
293, 379
Cambridge, 78, 110, 128,
131, 133, 153, 199
Duanesborough, 134, **148**,
299, 318, 325

Hoosic and Schaghticoke, 270, 362, 372
Jessup's Patent, **79**, 116, 142, 220, 299, 365
Kingsbury, 51, **79**, 107, 199, 286
Livingston Manor, 71, 78, **79**, 130, 133, 134
Queensbury, 51, **79**, 200
Rensselaerwyck (Manor), 60, **79**, 82, 91, 133, 134, 276
Schoharie, 92, 100, 105, 132, 138, **148**, 230, 248, 267, 269, 293, 300, 305, 317, 325, 363, 365, 373
White Creek, 110, 153, 212, 273
Charlotte, **41**, 110, 113, 114, 132, 133, 153, 216, 249, 276
Argyle/Scots, 78, **79**, 84, 374, 392
Cumberland, **41**, 111
Dutchess, 114, 132, 134, 165, 187, 276, 286
Gloucester, **41**, 111
Orange, 115, 188, 287, 293
Tryon, 51, 66, 72, 82, 100, 105, 114–115, 129, 132, 163, 174, 182, 203, 213–214, 220, 227, 272, 276, 285, 287, 305, 321, 357, 373–374, 388
Canajoharie District, 112, 134, 155, 171, **172**, 241, 279
Chyle Settlement, 292
Jerseyfield Patent, 349, 358
Johnson's Bush, 316
Kingsborough, **79**, 335
Mayfield Patent, **79**, 282, 349
Mohawk District, 133, **172**
Palatine District, 134, 143, **172**, 224, 234, 259
Philadelphia Bush, 316, 373
Royal Grant, 350
Ulster, 44, 115, 188, 250, **253**, 287
Rochester, 236, **253**
Coxsackie, NY, 60, **79**, 105, 118, 133, 140, 203, 286, 303, 395
Cramahé, Hector, 30, 73
Crawford, William Redford, 16, 83, 154, 164, 211, 265
Crofts, Wills, 83, 393
Cross, George, 405
Crosset, James, 339, 340, 346
Crowfoot, David, 262
Crown Point, *see* Forts

Crysler, Adam, 16, 155, 228, 230, 300
Crysler, William, 228
Currytown, NY, **172**, 189–94, 198, 203, 206, 209, 218, 225, 323, 326, 352, 405
Cuyler, Abraham, 88

Dambourgès, François, 317
Dame, George, 155, 168
Davis, Benjamin, 400
Davis, John, 59
Davis, Peter, 78
De Grasse, Admiral, 237, 240
Derangement, Continental Line, 68, 69, 90, 143, 260
Deserontyon, John (Mo), 16, 67, 76, 92, 93, 103, 104, 125, 319
Deserters, British, 78, 85, 92, 114, 116, 295, 327
Rebel, 115, 117, 158, 261, 276, 311, 312
De Spitzer, Gerrit, 147
Deygart, Peter S., 78, 153
Diefendorf, Jacob, 303
Dievendorf, Jacob, 191, **192**
Dievendorf, Jacob Jr., 196, 197
Dievendorf, Mrs., 192
Dietz, Johannes, 149, 275
Dietz, John Jost, 275
Dietz, Maria, 274
Dietz, Maria (2), 275
Dietz, William, 274, 275
Dingwall, John, 300
Docksteder, Frederick, 160, 322
Docksteder, George Adam, 59
Docksteder, John, 16, 190–96, 199, 218, 230, 280, 322, 405
Doxtator, Honyere (One), 259
Drummond, Peter, 64
Duboise, Benjamin, 133, 134, 212, 248
Duesler, John, 342, 354
Dulmage, John, 104, 226
Dundas, Alexander, 66, 122, 369
Dunham, Holtham, 17, 108, 132, 133, 156, 212, 227, 232, 249, 254, 259, 262, 277, 285, 288, 294, 371, 406
Dunham, John, 282–84
Dutchman's Point, 160, 178, 201, 210, 225, 255
Dygert, Jost, 194, 330

Eastern Union, **41**, 42, 71, 75, 128, 311
Eckler, Christiana, 292
Eckler, Henry, 292

Edwards, William, 403
Eikler, John, 332, 336, 346
Elkins, Jon Jr., 89, 109
Elkins, Jon Sr., 89
Ellice's Mills, 75, 161
Elsworth, Peter, 130, 133, 186, 188, 190, 211, 406
Elvingdorph, Jonathon, 257
Embury, Andrew, 351
Empey, William, 161, 179
Empire, British, 21, 32, 122
English, 22, 32
Enos, Roger, 383, 385, 387, 393
Enys, John, 401
Erkert, ?, 229
Esopus, NY, **79**, **253**, 256
Expeditions
Burgoyne's 1777, 33, 45, 219,
Carleton's 1780, 51, 65, 137, 175, 200, 286,
Lake Champlain 1758, 23, 24, 88, 117, 156, 201,
Munro's 1780, 51, 157, 219,
Ross, 1781, 178, 307-361
St. Leger's 1777, 36, 218,
St. Leger's 1781, 307–10, 361–404
SJJ May 1780, 44, 70,
SJJ October 1780, 51, 91, 99, 141, 146, 149, 251, 265, 326
Sullivan/Clinton 1779, 36, 55, 135, 218

Fairbank, 312, 313, 372
Fall Hill, 305, 313, 320, 322
Farquhar, William, 369
Fay, Jonas, 250, 255, 389
Fay, Joseph, 17, 50, 75, 101, 104, 142, 201, 219, 225, 264, 301, 311, 363
Feeter, William, 330, 336, 346
Ferguson, William, 248
Ferris, Joseph, 179, 260
Fichter, Michael, 405
Ficther, Andres, 405
Finck, Andrew/Andreas, 17, 143, 276, 318, 321, 336, 337, 340, 343, 345, 350, 355, 374
Firelocks, 48, 86, 171, 193, 206, 224, 229, 284, 324
Carbines, 62, 315
Fusils, Indian, frontispiece, 48, 62, 315
Muskets, 46, 48, 55, 78, 86, 171, 211, 212, 223, 315, 328
Musketry, 24, 336, 337, 353
Fish, Nicholas, 86, 94, 117
Fishkill, NY, 114, 144

Flags of Truce, 50, 96, 100, 122, 137, 153, 201, 240, 271, 277, 303, 314, 376, 389, 392, 398, 401

Flogging, British Army, 169, 403 U.S. Army, 79, 82, 94, 99, 128, 138

Fonda, Abraham, 277, 288

Fonda, Jellis J., 359

Fonda, John, 248

Florida, 26–28

Forsyth and Taylor Merchants, 298

Fort Edward, NY, 23, 61, 71, 78, **79**, 80, 96, 109, 148, 153, 156, 199, 221, 273, **301**, 393

Fort Hunter, NY, 133, 314, 325, 326

Forts (Blockhouses)
Ann, **41**, 43, 51, 55, 58, **79**, 100, 175, 200, **301**, 363, 393
Brewerton, 320, 321
Caspian Lake, 292
Caughnawaga, QC, **217**
Chambly, **63**, 295, 369
Clyde, **172**, 306, 326, 330
Coteau-du-Lac, **47**, 48, 58, **63**, 81, **145**, 169, 211, 295, **301**, 403
Crown Point, 40, **41**, 95, 161, 202, 218–20, 223, 269, 281, 298, 299, **301**, 314, 363, 367, 371, 378, **381**, 387–90
Davis, 19, 78
Dayton, 70, 71, 85, 87, 103, 166, **172**, 273, 281–85, 350
Detroit, 36, 37, 53, 56, 62, 104, 110, 116, 130, 131, 148, 160, 168, 218, 222, 297, 300, 319
Duboise, **148**, **172**, 269
Frey's Bush Blockhouse, 194
George, 43, 51, 55, 58, **79**, 80, 164, 175, 200, 360, 376, **381**
Haldimand, 56, 67, 116, 154, 164, 178, 211, 227, **263**, 296, **301**, 408
Herkimer, 59, 71, 78, 103, 117, 129, 130, 139, 142, 143, 148, 152, 154, 156–58, **172**, 179, 182, 188, 190, 206, 219, 241, 242, 261, 267, 272, 273, 276, 282, **301**, 302, 305, 312, 321, 322, 346, 349, 350
Hess, 234, 235
House, 19, 150, **172**, 241, 305
Hunter, **79**, 138, **148**, **172**, 173, 203, 248, **301**, 306, 327, 347
Johnson, **79**, **172**, 327, 329, 330

Johnstown, **79**, **172**, 179, 306, 316, 332–34, 338, 346, 349, 373

Isle aux Noix, **63**, 80, 92, 117, 122, 152, 153, 298, 301, 363, 368, 400, 401

Lackawaxen, 250, **253**, 255, 256

Lewis, **172**, 192, 193, 323

Lower Fort, **79**, **148**, 149, 229, 269, 275

Loyal Blockhouse, **63**, 179, 225, 226, 250, 363

Middle Fort, **148**, 149, 155, 203, 229

Midway Fort, **148**, 149

Mount Hope, 376, **381**, 389, 392

Mount Independence, 376, 379, **381**, 383

Niagara, 23, 24, 26, 36, 37, 51, 53, 56, 62, 81, 86, **102**, 105, 110, 124, 125, 137, 138, 154, 155, 157, 160, 179, 217, 218, 259, 267, 284, 286, 298, 300, **301**, 311, 356, 359

No.4 Charleston, **41**, **79**, 362

Ontario/Oswego, 23, 24, 26

Oswegatchie, **63**, 75, 87, 103, 138, 150, 181, 202, 219, 226, 234, 235, **252**, 267, 281, 283, **301**, 349, 407

Paris, **172**, 220

Pitt, 53, 125, 160, 287, 300

Plain, 101, 118, 127, 140, 141, 171, **172**, 173, 198, 203, 216, 242, 273, 279, 281, **291**, 299, 303, 304, 306, 312, 320, 326, 330

Plank, *see also* Plain, 95, 147, 171

Pointe au Fer, **63**, 89, 117, 131, 152, 264, 297, 298, 302, 362, 363, 365, 368, 375

Rensselaer, 162, 171, **172**, 185, 193, 194, 199, 206, 212, 232, 241, 248, 267, 285, **301**, 302, 316, 330, 346

St. John's, 50, 54, **63**, **74**, 76, 87, 88, 98, 108, 109, 117, 122, 136, 139, 152, 157, 174, 175, 179, 201, 210, 217, 221, 222, 238, 239, 262, 286, 289, 290, 294, 297, **301**, 313, 314, 363–65, 368, 386, 390, 398, 401

Schuyler, *see* Stanwix

Sorel, **63**, 287, 295, **301**

Stanwix, 34, 53, 58, 59, 61, 66, 68, 69, 71, 76–79, 82, 85, 86,

94, 97–99, 101–06, **112**–18, 120, 124–30, 138–41, 143, 148–52, 154, 156–58, 164, 181, 197, 209, 292, 293, **301**, 312, 348, 380

Sugar Loaf Hill, 376, **381**, 388–92

Ticonderoga, 23, 33, 34, 39, 40, **41**, 43, 60, 70, 97, 137, 164, 169, 219, 255, **301**, 376, 379, **381**–84, 390–97, 401

Timmerman, 168, **172**, 259, 306, 312

Upper Fort, **148**, 149, 155

Walradt/Walrath, 19, 110, **172**, 243, 302, 305

Weidman, 149, 275

West Point, 81, 118, 142, 148, 173, 182, 224, 236, 266, 303

Willett, 171, 306

Windecker, 171, **172**

Yamaska Blockhouses, **63**, 73, 76, 104

Frandts/Frauts, Henry, 406

Frank, Jacob, 321

Fraunce, Jacob, 405

Fraser, Alexander, 80, 404

Fraser, William, 64, 315

Fraser, William (2), 281

France, Court, 53, 121, 236
Language, 22, 25, 28, 31

Fredericks, Michael, 406

Frets, Ann, 406

Frets, Earnest, 406

Frey, Barent/Bernard, 191, 198, 313

Freylick, Benjamin, 179

Fur Trade, 25, 30, 32, 150

Gage, General Thomas, 23, 26, 28

Gansevoort, Leonard, 394, 395

Gansevoort, Peter, 18, 61, 89, 95, 105, 106, 129, 147, 203, 254, 257, 258, 268, 286, 313, 318, 330, 331, 362, 364, 365, 367, 371, 373–78, 383, 387, 388

Garret, Simeon, 60, 146, 147

German Language, 22

German Flatts, NY, 70, 78, 87, 128, 130, 132, 133, 141, 142, 161, 165, 166, 170, 171, 178, 182, 202, 208, 209, 292, 294, 299, 316, 321, 348, 351, 374

Germain, Lord George, 29, 38, 39, 43, 52, 56, 62, 76, 121, 155, 174, 222, 236, 248

Gibson, John, 89

Gill, Joseph Louis (Ab), 152

Gilliland's, **41**, 109, 371

Glen, Henry, 170, 212, 246, 285, 290, 343
Gordon, James, 218, 238, 272
Graff, Philip, 354
Grain, *see also* Seeds, 26, 32, 51, 55, 56, 66, 73, 75, 85, 175, 265, **270**, 297, 329
Grant, Archibald, 407
Grant, Benoni, 232, 259, 262, 285, 294
Grant, Janet, 335
Granville, NY, **79**, 110, 119, 128
Gray, Andrew, 235
Gray, James, 16, 59, 146, 404
Gray, Silas, 132, 133, 220, 221, 230
Gros, Johann Daniel, 18, 135, 161, 204, 207, 213, 236, 258
Gros, Lawrence, 18, 133–35, 193, 194, 248
Groves (Greaves, John?), 218, 248
Guile, Ray, 328, 333, 358
Gumersall, Thomas, 47, 59, 145

Haines/Hanes, Henry, 406
Haines/Hanes, Henry Jr., 406
Haldimand, Frederick, 16, **22**, 23–37, 39, 43, 45–59, 61–66, 72–76, 80, 81, 84, 87, 88, 92, 94, 95, 100, 103–06, 109, 111, 113, 121–23, 131, 136, 139, 144–46, 154–57, 160, 168, 174, 179, 181, 200, 201, 218, 221, 222, 236, 239, 240, 242, 247, 251, 254, 264, 271, 274, 277, 279–81, 288, 295–97, 300, 311, 313, 315, 319, 342, 356, 359, 364, 366–68, 382, 400, 402
    Foreign Birth, 21, 22, 24, 26, 28, 29
Hale, Aaron, 241, 278
Half Moon, NY, **79**, 133, 362, 363, 367
Halifax, NS, 28, 33, 54, 55, 168
Hancock, John, 228, 237, 241
Hanover, Christian, 406
Hare, John, 218, 236, 257, 323
Hare, John (2), 260
Hare, Peter, 260, 313
Harper, John, 135
Harris, John Adolphus, 80, 404
Harris, Moses Jr., 107, 119, 144, 148, 258
Harris, Moses, Sr., 285, 286
Harrison, Joseph, 302
Haynor/Heiney, Henry, 405
Hazen, Moses, 148
Hazen Road, **41**, 80, 88, 89, 292

Heacock, Samuel, 303, 341
Hearwager, Chas, 406
Heath, William, 18, **266**, 271, 277, 278, 286–94, 302, 303, 312, 360, 365–67, 374–77, 382, 383, 386, 388, 394,
Hellebergh, NY, **79**, 105, 118, 123, 137, **148**, 157, 274, 317
Hellegas, Peter, 243
Helmer, Nicholas, 405
Helmer, Philip, 234, 235, 405
Herkimer, Alyda, 224
Herkimer, George, 166, 188, 224
Herkimer, Johan/Han Jost, 81
Herkimer, NY, 118, 265, 313
Herkimer, Nicholas, 343
Herkimer Home, **172, 225**
Herrick, Samuel, 245, 389
Hewitt, Randall, 161, 179, 181, 200
Hewson, Daniel, 85, 92, 104, 158, 160
Hill, David Karaghgunty (Mo), 16, 72, 230, 319, 321, 322, 325, 326, 329, 333, 335, 348, 358, 359,
Hoffman, Philip and Mrs., 197
Holdridge, Dudley, 279, 342
Hoosic, NY, **79**, 88, 110, 133, 142, 143, 210, 365
Hopper, Coenradt, 406
Hopper, Jacobus, 406
Hough, Philip (Mah), 72
House, Christian, 243
House, Henry, 354
House, Johannes, 249
House, Johannes Jost, 241
House/Howse, Peter, 403
Howard, Mathew, 109, 143, 210, 218, 244, 245, 247, 253, 260
Howe, General Sir William, 28
Howse, Nicholas, 241
Hoyes, Robert, 80, 369
"Hudibras" *see* George Smyth
Hudson Highlands, NY, 148, 293, 366, 367, 377, 383, 386, 393
Huff, Hendrick, 140
Huff, John, 140
Hurricanes, The, 350
Hutt, John, 229, 230
Hutton, Timothy, 134

Indian Castles and Towns
    Akwesasne (Mo), **63**, 92, 226, **301**
    Bécancour (Ab), 24, 37, **63**
    Canajoharie (Mo), 67, **172**, 190, 217
    Fort Hunter (Mo), 16, 36, 48,

51, 230, 314, 319
    Ganaghsaraga (Canasaraga) (Tu), **301**, 321, 329
    Indian Castle, *see* Canajoharie
    Kahnawake (Mo), 17, **63**, 109, 150, 202, **217**, 218
    Kanawolohale (One), 66, 85, **301**, 322
    Kanehsatake (Mo), **63**, 226, **301**
    Old Onedia, *see* Kanawolohale
    Oswegatchie (Ono), 37, **301**
    St. Francis (Ab), 25, 37, **63**, 83, 152, 169, 201
    Stockbridge (Mah), **79**
Indian Department
    Six Nations (6NID), 14, 16, 35–37, 48, 52, 53, 84, **102**–04, 111, 116, 125, 130, 151, 160, 172, 178, 190, 218, 250, 256, 282, 285, 298, 299, 315, 319, 323, 351, 409
    Brant's Volunteers (BV), 14, 16, 92, 140, 351
    Claus's Rangers, 51, 161
    Foresters, 76, 279, 280
    Quebec (QID), 15, 16, 35, 48, 51, 80, 81, 145, 404
Indian Nations
    Six Nations Confederacy, 36, 53, 56, 67, 160, 172, 181, 285, 300, 321, 350, 351
    Cayugas, 282–84, 300
    Mohawks, 16, 48, 58, 67, 75, 92, 109, 117, 130, 139, 149, 150, 179, 181, 200, 268, 319, 320, 321, 328
    Oneidas, 58, 67, 71, 77, 83, 87, 103, 117, 128, 129, 139, 149–51, 178, 179, 200, 201, 221, 246, 256, 257, 259, 265, 282, 283, 290, 298, 343, 347, 349, 350, 354, 358, 373, 389, 396
    Onondagas, 67, 93, 282–84, 320, 321, 343
    Oquagas, 155, 190, 300
    Senecas, 53, 116, 124, 131, 160, 236, 256, 257
    Tuscaroras, 67, 71, 125, 178, 246, 290, 321, 354
    Affiliates of Six Nations
    Mahican/Mohicans, 72
    Nanticokes, 72, 101
    Schoharies, 228
    Allies of Six Nations
    Canada Indians (Seven Nations of Canada),

frontispiece, 24, 30, 36, 37, 51, **136**, 181, 265, 291, 350, 360
  Abenakis, 24, 25, 37, 83, 152, 169, 201
  Akwesasnes, 37, 75, 265, 298
  Kahnawakes, 17, 37, 71, 127, 181, 246, 290, 354
  Kanehsatakes, 37
  Oswegatchies, 37, 75, 117, 149, 298, 352
  Delawares, 72, 131, 236, 255–57, 352
  Lakes Nations, 36, 104
  Chippewas, 123, 124
  Mississaugas, 80, 123, 124, 172, 188, 265, 292, 350
  Stockbridges, 112, 151, 202
Indian Territory, 53, 55, 149, 160, **301**
Ittig, Conrad, 303, 304

Jacquay, Seth, 403
Jansen, Johannes, 257
Jessup, Ebenezer, 45, 46, 48
Jessup, Edward, 16, 45, 80, 251, 252, 295, 369, 381, 386, 391, 392, 401
Jessup, Joseph, 46, **370**
Johnson, Brant Quahyocko (Mo), 190, 199, 292
Johnson, Elizabeth Brant, 178
Johnson, Guy, 16, 36, **52**, 53, 76, 81, 111, 116, 123, 124, 151, 155, 169, 172, 218, 239, 279, 280, 284, 298, 299, 311
Johnson, Sir John, 16, 34, 44, 46, 58–62, 65, 66, 70, **73**, 75, 76, 79, 84, 87, 92, 104, 109, 116, 118, 139, 146, 149, 152–57, 168, 179, 200, 211, 227, 254, 262, 274, 281, 290, 291, 294–98, 317, 318, 322, 326, 332, 345, 347, 408
Johnson, Thomas, 18, 88, 89, 92, 109, 135, 175, 189, 190, 225, 238, 240, 313, 368
Johnson, Sir William, 24, 36, 67, 190
Johnson Hall, **172**, 333–40
Johnston, John, 125, 145
Johnstown Court House, **318**, 358
Johnstown, NY, 44, 86, 89, 116, 125, 138, 147, 152, 153, 159, 166, **172**, 179, 212, 282, 291, 315, 330–35, 340, 343, 346, 356, 357, 381, 395, 407–09

Jones, David, 247, 259, 262

Kane, Barney, 279
Keller, Henry, 323
Keller, Mrs., 323
Keller, Rudolph, 323
Kerr, Dr. Robert, **178**, 315
Kinderhook, NY, 60, **79**, 134, 146, 147, 247, 387
King George III, 26–29, 38, 39, 48, 71, 75, 77, 124, 157, 176, 214, 254, 261, 264
Klock, Adam, 405
Klock, Jacob, 18, 78, 99, 110, 134, 143, 153, 205, 230
Klock Jacob I., 405
Klock, Jacob J., 18, 78, 110, 143, 172, 202, 205, 219, 234, 235, 343, 404, 405
Klock, Severinus, 285, 330

Lachine, QC, 36, 47, **63**, 92, 139, 181
La Fayette, Marquis de, 55
Laird/Lord, William, 89, 348
Lansingh, Philip, 105, 109
Laurens, Henry, 53, 56, 110, 277
Leake, Robert, 46, 281
Lee (sloop), 298, 376, **391**–93, 398
Legrange, Jellis, 171, 232, 233
Legrange, Miss, 232, 233, 264, 265
Lernoult, Richard, 121, 122, 135, 179
Lewis, David, 225
Lewis, Henry, 192, 326
Littel, John, 89, 317, **332**, 333, 335–37, 348
Little Falls, NY, 75, 82, 128, 143, 161, **172**, 225, 273, 302, 313, 322, 348, 359, 360
Livingston, Abraham, 211, 212, 260, 261, 279, 406
Livingston, Henry, 134
Livingston, James, 148
Locks, Navigation, **47**, 48, 58
Logan, Samuel, 286, 293, 294, 300, 315, 360, 373, 381
Lottridge, Robert, 256
Loucks, Henry, 406
Loucks, John, 324
Lovelace, Thomas, 227, 228, 232, 362, 363
Lype, Adam, 194, 330

McAlpin, Daniel, 46, 49
McAlpin, James, 64
MacBean, Forbes, 80,
McDonald, Captain, 340, 407–409

McDonell, Alexander (Collachie), 329, 335–37, 343, 353, 355, 409
McDonell, Archibald, 407
McDonell, James (Scotus), 408
McDonell, John (Aberchalder), 145, 179, 313, 409
McDonell, John (2), 335
McDonell, Ranald, 407
McDonell, Ranald (Leek), 408
McGregor, Duncan, 345
MacKay, Samuel, 45
McKay, William, 315
McKean/McKeen, Robert, 133, 191, 193–98, 406
McKean, Samuel, 196, 198
McKinnon, John, 81, 106, 154, 155, 313
McKinstry, John, 115, 132, 133, 138, 188, 208, 216, 220, 221, 224, 232, 245, 253, 258, 262, 276, 277, 288, 305
McMartin, John, 333, 334
McMaster, David, 329, 333
Maclean, Allan, 17, 46, 87, 109, 145, 146, 152, 155, 169, 211, 219, 238, 254
Maclean, Lauchlan, 407
McNaughton, Angus, 335
Machiche, QC, **63**, 179, 223
Mann, Isaac, 281
Mann, Peter, 230
Maracle, Henry, 189, 190, 199
Maria (schooner), **297**, 298, 375, **391**
Marsh, William, 111, 136, 285, 295
Marshall, Elihu, 133, 212, 242, 261, 278, 285, 287–89, 305, 312, 321, 322, 360, 363, 370, 374, 387
Mason, Isaac, 337
Mathews, Robert, 17, 73, 76, 80, 104, 110, 139, 144, 174, 200, 201, 210, 223, 238, 239, 247, 250, 255, 263, 295, 380
Merkle, Christian, 406
Merkle/Mirch, Frederick, 406
Merkle/Mirch, Matthias, 406
Merkle/Mirch, Michael, 406
Meyers, John/Johan Walden, 17, 60, 71, 146, 156–61, 190, 202, 210, 218, 220, 221, 232, 233, 242, 245–47, 254, 262, 263, 274, 285
Miller, Henry, 234, 235
Miller, Nathaniel, 403
Minisink, NY, 115, 218, **253**
Minor, Christian, 406

Missisquoi Bay, 62, **63**, 76
Mitchell, Hugh, 157, 277, 288, 289
Monbackers, NY, 16, 236, 250,
   253, 256, 257
Monsell, William, 369, 404
Moodie, Andrew, 18, 66, 94, 118,
   158, 186, 242, 272, 330, 337,
   338, 341, 359
Moore, Enos, 216, 341, 342
Moore, Pliny, 188, 203, 320,
Mosier, Hugh, 286
Moss, Simon, 343
Munro, John, 17, 51, 145
Murchison, Duncan, 83
Mutiny, British, 145, 169, 403
   Rebel, 69, 80, 85, 182
Myers, Jacob, 352

Nairne, John, **49**, 64, 369
Navy, French, 33, 54, 55, 202, 241,
   286, 303, 362, 399
   Royal/Prov'l, 16, 25, 31, 33, 35,
   54, 56, **74**, 117, 241, **297**,
   303, **379**, 385, 386, **391**,
   392, 400, 401
   U.S., 33, 53–55, 240
Nelles, Hendrick, 172
Nelles, Robert, 160, 250
Nellis, William, 135, 191, 194
Nelson, Moses, 112, 113
New City, NY, **79**, 100, 233, 271,
   312, 372, 392
New Dorlach, NY, 147, **148**, **172**,
   189–94, 198, 203–206, 213,
   220, 221, 232, 242, 267,
   269, 272, 323, 405
New Fane, VT, **79**, 157
New Hampshire Grants, NY
   (*see also* Vermont), 27,
   39–**41**, 80, 100, 101, 108,
   118, 119, 131, 137, 153,
   157, 175, 242, 248, 269,
   290, 395
New Rynbeck, NY, **148**, **172**, 191,
   194, 269, 405
New York City, 21, 22, 26–29, 38,
   43, 57, 60, 88, 97, 98, 105,
   113, 125, 144, 146, 174, 189,
   199, 203, 258, 300, 303, 311,
   366, 399, 400, 402, 408
New York State
   Finances, 96, 101, 212
   Legislature, 45, 82, 107, 207,
   208, 214, 215, 242, 271,
   362, 374
Newbury, VT, **41**, 88, 89, 368
Newfoundland, 54, 55
Niagara, IT, (*see also* Forts), 58, 67,

72, 85, 86, 103, 104, 110,
116, 123, 140, 221, 222, 275,
286, 296, 298, 319, 320, 329
Nipenack, NY, **253**, 256
Niskayuna, NY, **79**, 123, 247, 388
Noses, The, 59, **172**
Nova Scotia, 54, 65, 226

Old Smoke Sayengaraghta (Se),
   160, 300, 319
Olman/Ottman, Christian, 406
Onasadego (Ono), 284
One-Armed Peter (Moh), 328
Oswego, IT (NY), 23, 24, 51, 53,
   110, 111, 209, 281, 299, 314,
   315, 359, 379
Oswegatchie, *see* Forts

Paine, Brinton, 18, 108, 156, 187,
   188, 210, 212, 216, 218, 258
Palmerston, NY, 83, 87, 103,
   128, 200
Parker, Isabel, 155, 156
Parker, James, 155, 156
Parker, John, 92, 155, 316
Parker, William, 155, 156, 179
Parker, William (2), 316
Parole/Pass, 61, 96, **249**
Parrot, James, 160, 233
Pawling, Albert, 115, 188, 256, 257
Pawling, Benjamin, 255, 260, 280
Pawling, Levi, 256, 257
Peacham, VT, **41**, 292
Peekskill, NY, 118, 174, 189, 266
Peters, John, 17, 45, 46, 48, 64, 87,
   103, 109, 369, 376, 380
Petrie, Dr. William, 161, 199
Pettingell, Mrs., 328
Pettingell, Samuel, 328
Pettit, Samuel, 126, 127
Philadelphia, PA, 22, 30, 85, 160,
   201, 218, 248, 290, 408
Phillips, Elizabeth, 179
Pickard, ?, 268
Piper, Jacob, 404
Porter, Elisha, 216, 377
Poughkeepsie, NY, 236, **253**, 298
Powell, Henry Watson, 17, 81,
   103, 106, 110, 111, 130,
   155, 168, 179, 202, 218,
   221, 239, 259, 274, 279,
   286, 287, 296–98, 300, 318,
Printup, Joseph, 324
Prison Island, 145, 169, 211
Prisoners' Exchange, 43, 49, 95,
   101, 122, 139, 219, 250,
   261, 264, 271, 277, 288,
   294, 303, 314

Pritchard, Azariah, 17, 88, 92, 109,
   136, 222, 225, 262, 297, 301
Putman, David, 284
Putman, Garrett, 133, 135

Quackenboss, Myndert W., 90
Quackenboss, Peter J., 327
Quebec Act, 28–32,

Ramsey, Ann, 242
Ramsey, David, 157, 242,
Redick/Reddick, Christopher, 147,
   148, 406
Reynolds, Colonel, 362, 377, 400
Richter, Nicholas, 70
Riedesel, Baron Frederick, 37
Rikely, Andrew, 108, 363
Robertson, Daniel, 17, 75, 87, 103,
   117, 143, 150, 202, 219, 226,
   227, 281, 298, 407
Robertson, Neal, 64
Robinson, Beverly, 38, 43, 77, 91
Robinson, Samuel, 373
Rochambeau, le Comte de, 55, 66,
   165, 236, 240
Rodgers, John, 128
Rogers, James, 17, 35, 65, 87, 102,
   111, 202, 260, 295, 369, 391
Rogers, Robert, 65, 102
Rosencrantz, Nicholas, 405
Ross, Jacob, 316
Ross, John, 17, 47, 59, 67, 83, 87,
   102, 104, 116, 154, 189,
   211, 227, 251, 274, 281,
   296–300, 314–61, 379, 380,
   387, 392, 395, 396, 400, 401
Rossiter, General, 365, 371
Rowe, John, 317
Rowland family, 328
Rowley, Aaron, 216, 278, 326, 331,
   334, 340–45, 359, 406
Royal George (ship), 201, 250, 255,
   298, 385, 390, 392, 393,
   400, 401
Ruiter, Henry, 117, 131
Ruiter, John, 110
Ryckman, John, 319, 351, 352, 357

Safford, Samuel, 364, 372, 389
St. John's Anglican Church, 340
St. John's, QC, *see* Fort St. John's
St. Leger, Barry, 17, 34, 75, 76,
   80, 109, 117, 131, 160, 181,
   210, 222, 262, 264, 295, 314,
   363, **364**, 368, 369, 371, 375,
   376, 379, 380, 382, 384, 385,
   389–93, 397–402
Salt Springs, NY, **49**, 365

Sammons, Jacob, 18, 195, 234, 235, 350

Saratoga, NY, 23, 43, 51, **79**, 83, 87, 116, 117, 124, 126, 128, 132, 133, 138, 143, 156, 166, 167, 179, 184, 187, 200, 216, 220, 227, 228, 239, 241, 245, 248, 253, 254, 258, 265, 273, 285, 276–78, 289, 293–95, **301**, 303, 305, 312, 316, 331, 332, 360–67, 380–83, 387, 388, 390–93, 400

Saulkill, Isaac, 332, 333

Scarborough, William, 339, 340, 343, 346, 407–09

Schafer, Nicholas, 316

Schaghticoke, NY, **79**, 124, 133, 271,

Schell, Demas, 166,

Schell, Frederick, 166,

Schell, John Christian, 166

Schell, Marks, 166

Schermerhorn, John, 285

Schmid, Luc, 83

Schuld Brothers, 224

Schuyler, Philip, 18, 71, 82, 108, 117, 118, 124–28, 142, 151, 156, 171, 174, 189, 210, 218, 228, 233, 240, **242**, 245–47, 254, 258, 262, 289, 290, 293, 317, 363, 365, 371, 377, 378, 383, 408

Schuyler, Philip P., 133, 293, 346

Scott, Abraham, 317

Scott, Thomas, 80, 404

Sears, Barnabus, 278, 294

Secret Service, British, 16, 17, 38, 43, 46, 65, 77, 79, 91, 100, 107, 108, 111, 131, 137, 141, 143, 144, 146, 155, 157, 165, 168, 189, 221, 227, 295, 314, 369, 390

Senagena (One), 259

Service, John, 116, 251

Seth's Henry (Sch), 228

Seth's Joseph (Sch), 230

Shaftsbury, VT, **49**, 390

Sharp, Peter, 403

Shell, George, 229, 230

Shenop, Captain (Nan), 72, 101

Sherwood, Justus, 17, 43, 44, 49–51, 66, 75, 92, 109, 122, 123, 136, 139, 151, 160, 174, 178, 181, 201, 210, 219, 225, 239, 250, 262, 264, 301, 313, 363, 367, 371, 380, 382, 385, 389, 390, 398, 399

Sherwood, Seth, 262

Sherwood, Thomas, 143, 151, 210, 390

Shew, Henry, 332, 339

Shew, Jacob, 124, 282, 283

Shew, Jacob (2), 332, 348

Shew, Stephen, 317, 333

Simons, Titus, 64

Skenesborough, NY, **41**

Skinner, Josiah, 212, 242

Skinner, Thomas, 212

Skirmishes, *see* Battles

Small, Jacob, 313, 320

Smith, Joseph, 190, 220, 264

Smith, Nicholas, 403

Smyth, Dr. George, 17, 59–61, 84, 90, 92, 99, 100, 104, 111, 113, 123, 139, 142, 157, 158, 160, 174, 181, 201, 210, 225, 239, 254, 261, 262, 264, 298, 301, 363, 367, 380, 385, 389

Smyth, Mrs., 221, 233, 264

Smyth, Patrick, 60, 174

Smyth, Terrence, 60, 61, 142, 261

Smyth, Thomas, 60, 108, 264

Smyth, William, 280, 281, 287

Snook, William, 328

Snyder, Jacob, 92

Snyder, Johannes, 91, 256, 257

Sole, William, 195, 197

Sommer/Summer, William, 17, 190–94, 197, 198, 206, 207, 225, 406

Sorel, QC, **63**, 73, **301**,

Spencer, Hazelton, 118, 227, 245,

Split Rock, **41**, 181, 398

Stansell, George, 340

Stark, Caleb, 370

Stark, John, 18, 166, **167**, 171, 227, 228, 239, 245, 253, 254, 260, 261, 265–72, 277, 285, 287–89, 291, 293, 294, 300–03, 313, 315, 318–20, 331, 357, 361–63, 366, 367, 371–78, 380–83, 386, 389–95, 399, 400

Steele's Creek, NY, 188, 190

Steuben, Frederick, 86

Stevens, Roger, 245, 376, 390, 401

Stillwater, NY, **79**, 126, 387

Stirling, Lord, 18, 100, 331, 332, 355, **377**, 378, 382, 383, 387, 388, 393, 394, 397, 401

Stone Arabia, NY, 51, 116, 125, 143, 147, 149, 153, 159, 161, **172**, 220, 224, 234, 299, **301**, 306, 315, 326, 330, 341, 347, 348

Stringer, Samuel, 210, 218, 269

Stuart, Jane Okill, 294, **314**

Stuart, Reverend John, 17, 92, 96, 100, 104, 272, 277, 294, **314**

Summer, William, 406

Sutherland, Walter, 345, 381, 397

Swart, Teunis, 352

Switzerland/Swiss, 21, 26, 29

Sylvester, Levi, 88,

Tanner, Jacob, 148, 192, 193, 322, 323, 325, 345

Taylor, Ezekiel, 133, 158, 160, 161, 210, 383

Taylor, John, 285, 373

Taylor, Peter, 248

Ten Broeck, Abraham, 90, 219, 258, 286, 288

Thonigwenghsoharie, Christian Kristianko (One), 300, 343

Thornton, John, 351, 354

Three Rivers, QC, 24, 25, **63**, 190

Throop, Josiah, 163, 207, 241, 242

Tiahogwando (Ono), 282

Tice, Gilbert, 299, 315, 318, 320, 322, 325, 327, 329, 335, 338, 345, 348–52, 359

Timmerman, Conrad, 259

Tomhannock, NY, **79**, 200, 271

Tribes Hill, NY, 59, **79**, **172**, 330, 332, 333

Tripp, Robert, 161

Trumbull (galley), 297, 298, 314, 363, **391**, 398, 401

Tryon, Governor William, 27, 39

Tubbs, John, 247

Tupper, Benjamin, 366, 378, 387

Turney, John, 103, 155, 168

Tygert, Seffrinus, 403

Ulman, Frederick, 322, 325, 334, 345

United States, Finances, 69, 101, 106,

Valcour Island, **41**, 375, 398

Van Alstine, Abraham, 134, 244,

Van Alstyne, John, 324

Van Bergen, Anthony, 60, 133, 203, 212, 367

Van Cortlandt, Philip, 18, 61, 68, **69**, 70, 79, 82, 120, 126–29, 138, 139, 143, 154, 161, 165, 170, 186, 224

Van der Heyden, David (Mis), 188, 189, 211

Van Dyck, Cornelius, 71, 128, 142

Van Dyke, Mathew, 300

Van Eps, Evert Jr., 324
Van Evera, Rynier, 330
Van Ingen, Joseph, 212, 248
Van Ness, Peter, 134, 212, 244
Van Rensselaer, John, 366
Van Rensselaer, Henry K., 82, 88,
    134, 244, 272, 305, 372, 375
Van Rensselaer, Kilian, 134
Van Rensselaer, Peter, 212, 273
Van Rensselaer, Robert, 18, 44, 51,
    91, 99, 131, 241, 254, 305,
    331, 362, 364, 367, 373,
    378, 387
Van Schaick, Goose, 61, 68, 81
Van Sickler, Rebecca, 333
Van Veghten, Cornelius, 227, 276
Van Waggoner, Andrew, 404
Veeder, John, 148, 343
Veeder, Volkert, 350, 359
Verchères, QC, **63**, 64, **301**
Vermont, Negotiations/Talks, 17,
    37–39, 43, 50, 51, 66, 77,
    101, 122, 125, 142, 144, 168,
    201, 239, 248, 250, 291, 301,
    313, 363, 379, 385, 402
Villefranche, Jean-Louis, 161,
    165, 208, 210, 242, 272,
    273, 294, 312, 361
Visscher, Frederick, 133, 231, 332
Von Franken, 392
Von Horn, 376, 392
Von Kreutzbourg, Carl, 17, 164,
    298, 369, 375, 379–81, 384,
    389, 392, 397, 398, 401
Von Speth, Ernst, 169
Von Stosch, 376
Vrooman, Adam, 157
Vrooman, Henry B., 90
Vrooman, Henry H., 90
Vrooman, Peter, 18, 134, 149, 203,
    229, 230, 275, 373

Wabakinine (Mis), 124
Waggoner, Peter, 153
Wagner, Joseph, 339, 346
Wait, Jane, 156
Wait, John, 156
Walbridge, Eben, 372, 384, 399
Walker, George, 406
Wallace, William, 330, 340–42
Ward, John, 247
Warner, Seth, 39, 40, 51
Warrensborough/bush, **148**, **172**,
    325, 327–29, 358, 395
Warwarsink, NY, **253**–57, 267
Washington, General George, 18,
    28, 51, 61, 81, 83, 96, 100,
    107, 108, 111, 120, 126–29,

135, 141, 142, 152, 153,
    163–67, 171, 182, 186, 199,
    209, 210, 221, 228, 232,
    236, 237, 240, 241, 244,
    247, 254, 260, 265–67, 288,
    295, 375, 377, 391, 399
Weissenfels, Frederick, 18, 69, 107,
    242, 261, 267, 294, 312, 373
Wemple, Abraham, 71, 134, 178,
    231, 232, 320, 331, 365, 388
Wemple, Andrew, 89
Wemple, Myndert, 387, 388
Western Union, **41**, **79**, 100, 128,
    151, 215, 216, 270, 272, 311,
    312, 371, 373, 393
Whelp, Anthony, 132, 134, 279, 406
Whipple's Farm, 222, 223
Whitcomb, Benjamin, 152
White, Stephen, 133, 212, 248,
    340, 406
Whiting, William, 133, 142, 212,
    241, 244
Willett, Marinus, 18, 97, **98**, 99,
    107, 114, 129, 132, 135,
    138, 139, 151, 160, 162,
    165–68, 171, 172, 174,
    177, 178, 182–88, 190–99,
    203–16, 219, 224, 230,
    232, 236, 242, 248, 252,
    254, 258–60, 262, 265,
    267, 269, 271–73, 276,
    277, 285, 287, 288, 291–
    94, 299, 301, 306, 311, 313,
    315, 318–61, 364, 374,
    387, 395, 396, 400
Williams, John, 153
Wilson, Randolph, 242, 273,
    282, 283
Windecker, Dorothy, 179
Windmill Point, **41**, 314
Wing, Abraham Jr., 221
Wing, Mrs., 221
Wingrove, Anthony, 296
Winne, Jacob, 248
Winne, James, 343
Woodworth, Solomon, 18, 90,
    166, 190, 281, 333, 406
Woolaver, John, 216, 217
Wormwood, Matt's, 405
Wright, Job, 212
Wright, Zadock, 219, 250

Yan (Sch), 230
Yates, Peter, 133, 270, 383, 388
Yates, Robert A., 323
Yokum, Moses (One), 284
Yost, Peter, 349
"Young David" (Moh), 326

Young, Henry, 315
Young, Jacob A., 191,
Younglove, John, 18, 110, 161, 162,
    233, 234
Younglove, Mrs., 233

Zeilie, John, 341, 342
Zimmer, Catharin, 228
Zimmer, Jacob, 229
Zimmer, Peter, 229
Zimmer, William, 228
Zimmerman, Jacob, 243
Zimmerman, Jacob (2), 243, 244,
    252, 253
Zimmerman, John, 243